The Tattoo

Escape the Grind, Do What You Love and Launch Your Kick-Ass Tattoo Career!

Shelly Dax

"Your unique gift is gleaming magic that blankets the world in flurry and wonder. Let it shine!"
~ *Shelly Dax, Artist & Author*

Visit shellydax.com

Author/Illustrator
Shelly Dax

Publisher
Garden of Ink

Graphics & Cover Design
Gil T. Rodello

Proofreading and Editing
Susan Brown-Horner
Joseph Davey
Phillip Davey
Samantha Bennett

Photos
Shelly Dax
Gil T. Rodello
Destiny Duerst

Special thanks to all current and former tattoo students for your contribution, allowing us to photgraph you & your process of learning and for being awesome.

Published by Garden of Ink
21 South 6th Street, Cottage Grove, OR 97424
www.shellydax.com/thetattootextbook

First edition: November 2019 | ISBN 978-1-7341852-0-1
Printed in the United States of America

Disclaimer:
VERY serious health consequences can occur from a lack of understanding of sanitation, sterilization and infection control. If you are in a location that does not require licensing, SEEK OUT A QUALITY APPRENTICESHIP OR EXPERIENCED MENTOR! This textbook is intended as a supplement to your coaching or mentoring experience.

The Tattoo Textbook

TABLE OF CONTENTS

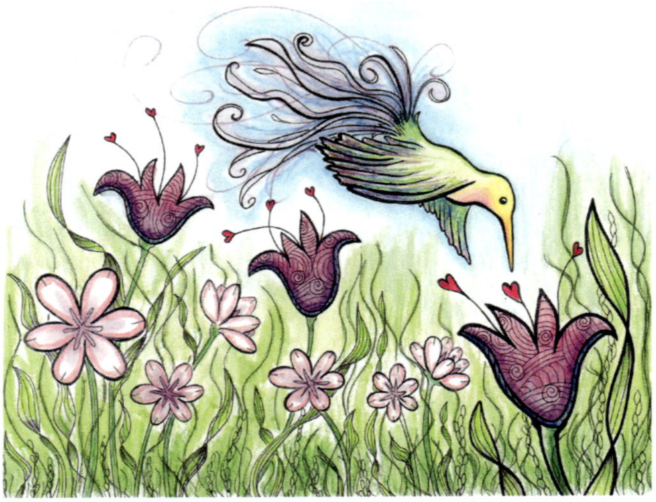

If you want to be part of an inspiring and high-vibe community, sign up for my e-mail list at shellydax.com

Dedication

This book is dedicated to all the students, past and current, who attended Garden of Ink Tattoo School and helped shape the curriculum through your struggles, questions, talents and quest for success. And many of you were extra supportive...you know who you are!

To the creative misfits, who wish to embrace tattooing as a unique artform, to share their vision of the world. And all the tattooers who have blazed the trail to inclusivity.

To the thousands of clients who have walked through the studio doors over the years, bringing your trust, enthusiasm and wonderful ideas.

To Ollie Nash for the incredible support as well as being welcoming and encouraging to our students.

To Shawn Winkler-Rios, the business coach, who helped me so much in the early days.

To my fantastic friends Susan & Denise, for your brilliant encouragement and adoration.

To my sweet buddy Marcie, who offered her skin as canvas for so many students to practice on! And my darling pal Tracy for placing your confidence in me from day one. And my sister goddess Cindy who let me tattoo her when I was a beginnner, and who sparks joy in this world.

To Shannon, Lia & Dustin for also offering your skin to a variety of students and supporting the effort with sweets, treats, laughs and songs.

To my three incredible children, Sami, Phil & Joe, for your never-ending love & loyalty, wacky humor and embracing your Mom's weird ideas. And their spouses, Daniel, Beck & Ruby for joining our crazy family and adding to the love quotient.

To my sweet grandies, Orin & Ezra, who light up my world with their giggles and warm my heart on the daily. They remind me that life is supposed to be fun!

And lastly, to my kindred spirit, Gil, for your belief in my dream, the tremendous amount of learning & work you put in, and the way you carry things. **Much appreciation Imzadi.**

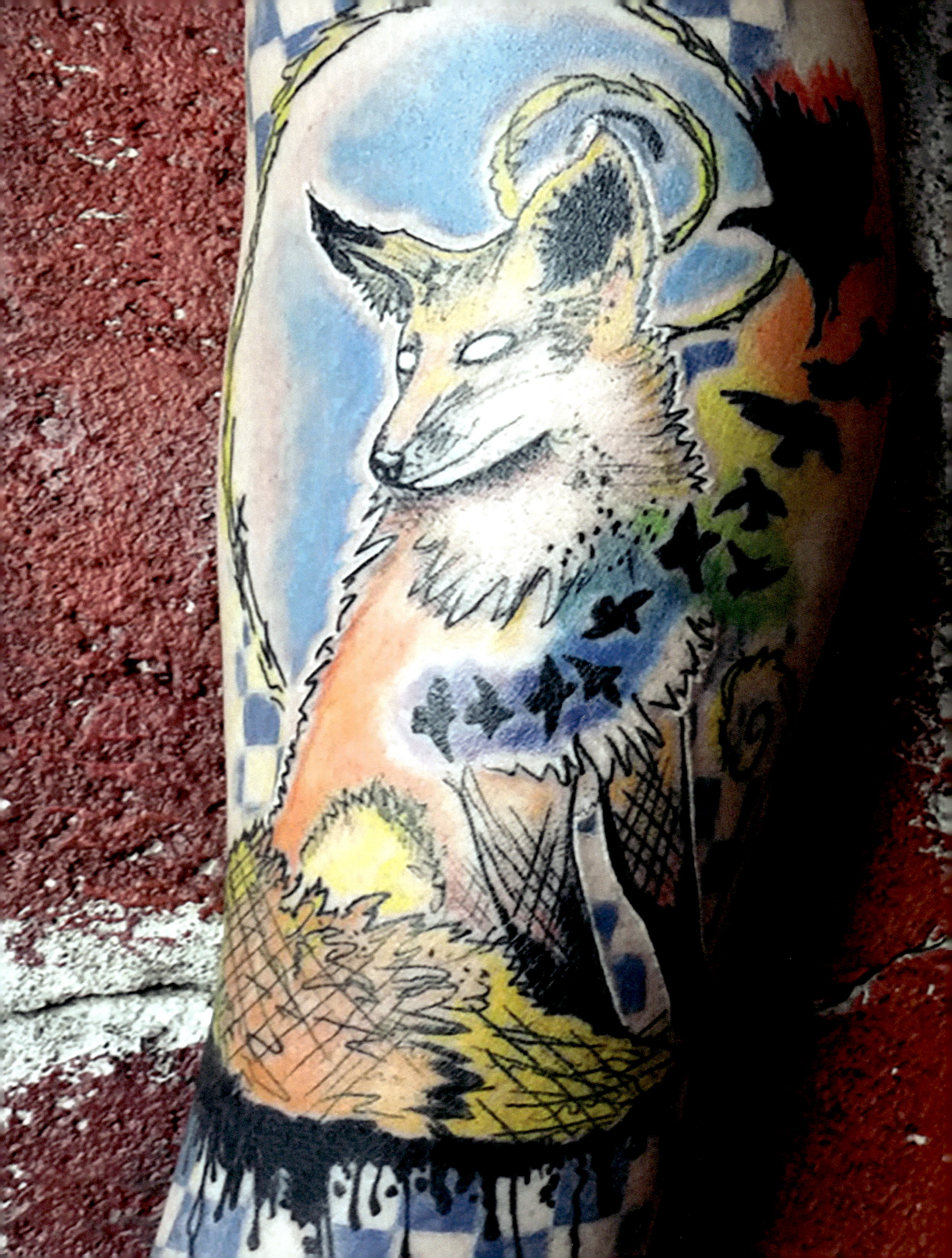

Introduction

So, you want to be a tattoo artist?

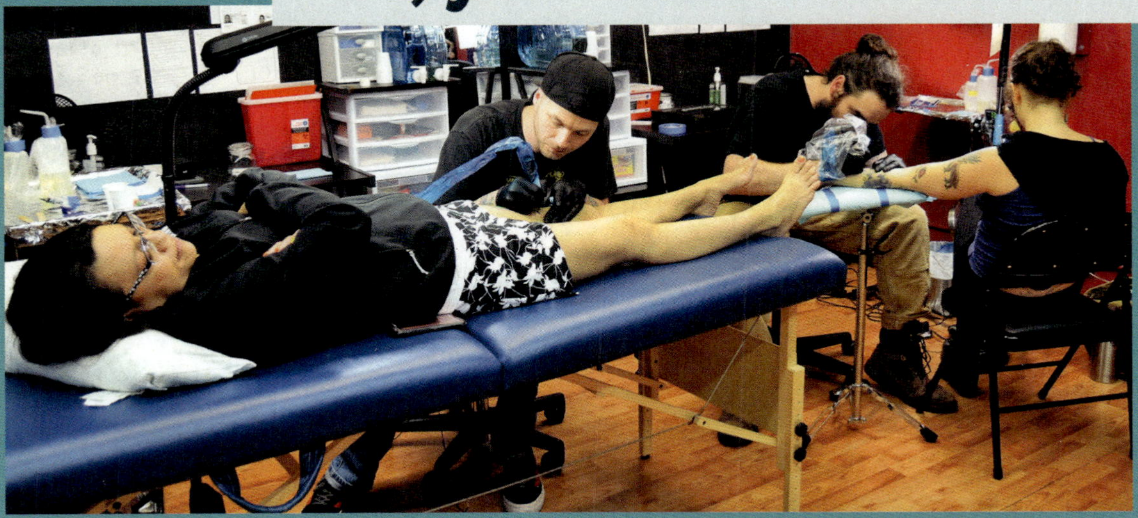

The glamour, the fame, the TV shows, the rock star attitude! THE BIG MONEY!!! If only it were that easy! First things first; forget everything you've seen on TV, forget those cheap tattoo machine kits online and forget the myriad of internet videos showing massively contradictory information. And finally, forget the small percentage of world renowned tattooers dominating the magazines and convention circuit.

Clear all of your preconceptions and prepare to take the baby steps you will need to venture on your own personal journey to becoming an amazing tattooer. Becoming a tattoo artist involves hard work, dedication, determination, devotion to your craft, and just like your mama said, "practice makes perfect."

Before you even set one needle to skin, there is an overabundance of crucial information to give you the solid footing you need to get your career off to a great start. It is our hope to provide that for you in this book.

> "Your life is short and rare and amazing and miraculous, and you want to do...and make, really interesting things while you're still here."
>
> *~ Elizabeth Gilbert, Author Eat, Pray, Love & Big Magic*

Before We Get Started:

This book is NOT advocating trying to learn to tattoo on your own. This book is the theory part of the tattoo equation only! Learning to tattoo requires

Shelly's Sidenote

WHO SHOULD READ THIS BOOK?

After teaching tattoo school for over eight years and refining our curriculum through the process of each individual program, I realized that there is no SINGLE book that gives you the basics of what you need to start a career as a professional tattoo artist. This book is great for students in tattoo schools, like Oregon, where attending school is a requirement before licensure and is a perfect companion to your apprenticeship. It frees your mentor to focus on the more technical and hands-on side of the training. In addition, it can be useful for licensed tattooers who perhaps did not receive an adequate initial tattoo education or simply need to brush up on the basics.

specialized hands-on training. We firmly believe you need a mentor, coach or instructor to guide you and assist you with the physical and technical aspects of this craft. DO NOT tattoo people in an unlicensed facility or at home. It doesn't matter how great of an artist you are, or if you "use new needles"—VERY serious health consequences can occur from a lack of understanding of sanitation, sterilization and infection control. If you are in a location that does not require licensing, SEEK OUT A QUALITY APPRENTICESHIP OR EXPERIENCED MENTOR! This textbook is intended as a supplement to your coaching or mentoring experience.

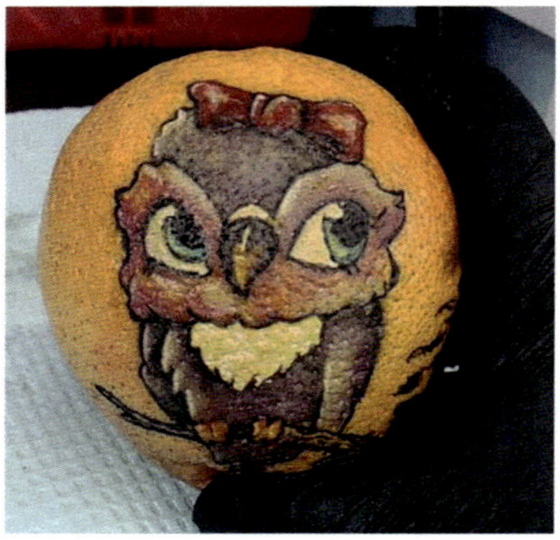

We've set this book up in a systematic way, as each chapter builds on the one previous. Learning all of the theory portion of tattooing is essential BEFORE you ever pick up a machine. Once you get through the chapter on machines and needles, tattooing on **grapefruits** and **fake skin** is highly encouraged.

Working on drawing, inking, painting, penciling, sculpting or other forms of art in conjunction with your endeavor to learn tattooing is extremely valuable. Our most successful tattoo school graduates are the ones who either had art experience or training before attending our program or were concurrently studying art. These students quickly grasped concepts, successfully designed compositions and rapidly advanced their tattoo skills. Fortunately, there are a myriad of online art courses and books easily accessible.

HOW DOES IT WORK?

Tattoos are created by injecting pigment in to a person's skin. Modern tattoo artists do this by using a mechanized needle which penetrates the skin approximately 1 to 1 ½ millimeters and deposits a drop of ink into the skin with each perforation. The needle is attached to an electrically powered tattoo machine that punctures the skin at a frequency of 50 to 3000 times per minute. Every time the needle punches through the skin it creates a tiny wound. This alerts the body to begin the inflammatory process to begin repairs. It is this process that makes tattoos permanent.

The insoluble ink is deposited into the skin through the epidermis (first layer) into the dermis (second layer). The epidermis is constantly shedding cells but the dermal layer is more stable. When done correctly, the tattoo will be visible for a person's entire life, with minor fading and slight blurring, dependent on age and sun exposure. Remember, when you look at a tattoo you are seeing it through the first layer (epidermis) of skin. How bright a tattoo appears is dependent on the color of a person's skin.

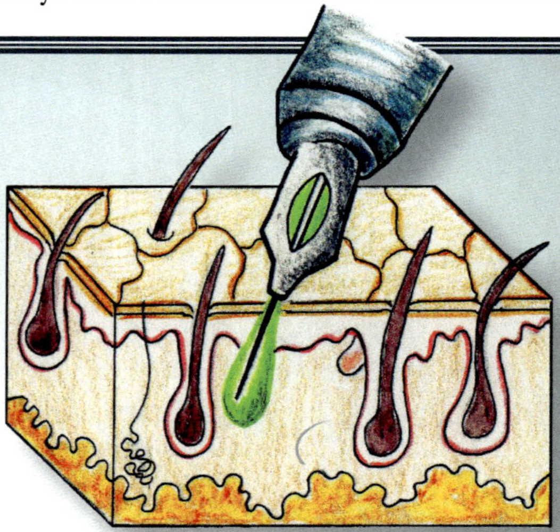

"When tattoo ink is deposited in the dermis with the little buzzing needles, the body mounts an immune response with macrophages [&] phagocytes...the rough equivalent of microbiological Pac-Men (or Ms. Pac-Men to be gender-equal), and literally eat and envelop the tattoo ink...to contain the invasion of foreign material. (If you put a stethoscope on your new tattoo, you just might hear a faint woc-ka-wocka-wocka.)...granulation tissue and specifically dermal fibroblasts interlock the ink-containing phagocytes in a collagen network just beneath the dermis/epidermis junction. That's how the ink stays put for years."

~Dawn Richardson, M.D. "Ask the Doctor", Velonews.com, 2006

Learning a new craft takes discipline and hard work. Everyone has a different way of learning. Open yourself to absorbing new material in a way that works for you. Your success is the main goal.

> "Every artist was first an amateur."
>
> -Ralph Waldo Emmerson, Author

A note about learning styles

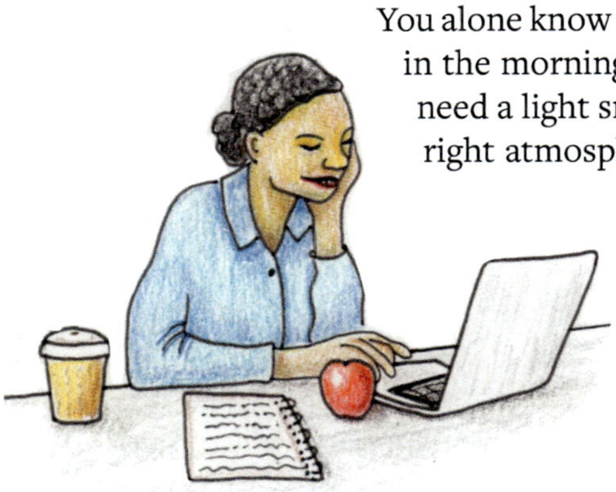

You alone know whether you will do your best studying early in the morning or in the middle of the afternoon. You may need a light snack or some background music to create the right atmosphere, and if you feel "trapped" in your room, get some fresh air and take a walk over to a coffee shop to do your work. Make sure that you have adequate desk space, good lighting, and a comfortable temperature as you study. Avoid being distracted by social media by putting your phone on silent.

Your journey begins now!

A Brief Overview of Tattoo

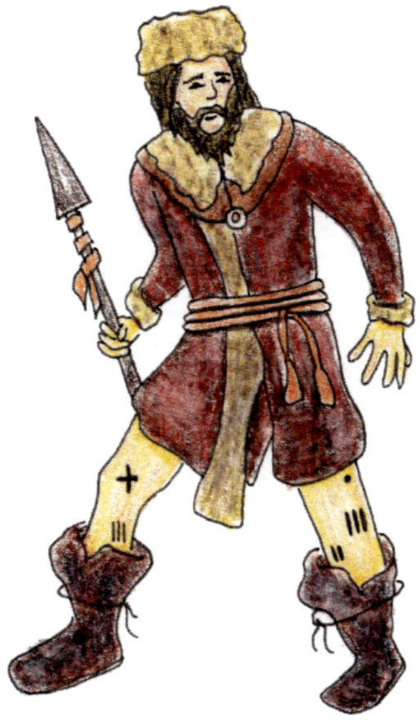

Otzi the Iceman

Tattoos have been around for over five millennia! Scientists identified over 50 tattoos on a 5,200-year-old mummy nicknamed "Ötzi the Iceman" discovered in 1991. These are believed to be the oldest tattoos ever discovered. Many cultures from India to Egypt to China and Japan have rich histories of tattooing for decorative, healing, identification and spiritual purposes.

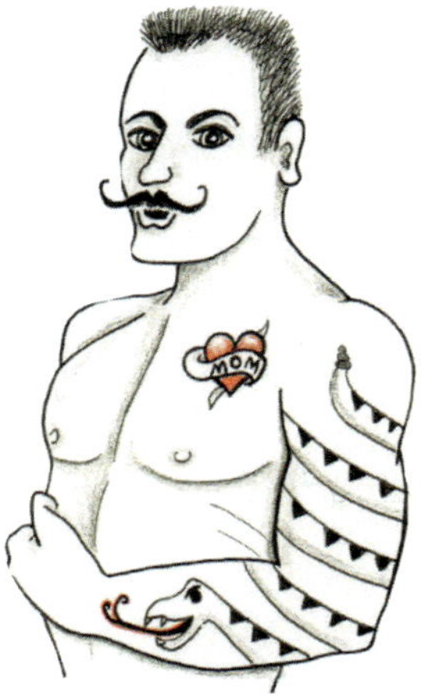

Despite their historical longevity, modern people have mixed feelings on tattoos. In the not too distant past, tattoos were associated with bikers, sailors, women of lesser moral standards and circus sideshows.

In the last 40 years or so, tattoos have become a mainstream part of our society, more common among all economic classes, all ages, and men as well as women. Tattoos have become even more popular in recent years, with tattoo reality shows giving us a peek into a once mysterious world. In the US, it seems that tattoos have shifted from a form of defiance to a form of expression. And the folks who now get them are as diverse as the styles and designs they choose. In addition, some people who would never think of tattooing their bodies use permanent makeup or cosmetic tattooing—to enhance their looks or correct skin issues.

The parts of a tattoo machine include:

- needle or needle cartridge
- grip
- tube and tip
- electric motor
- foot pedal
- power cord
- power supply

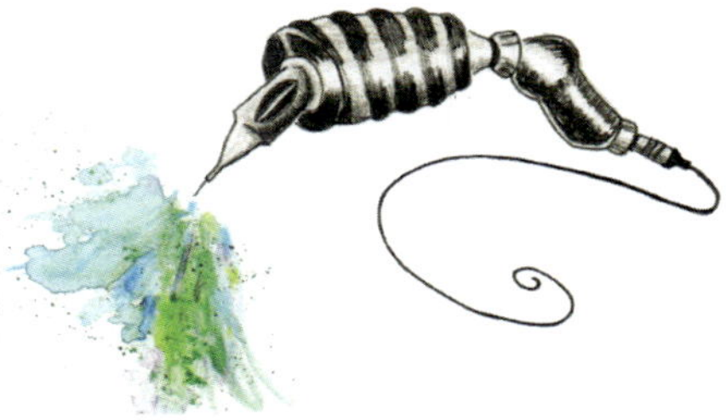

HISTORY NOTE:

In the late 1800s a tattoo artist named Samuel O'Reilly invented the tattoo machine and based his design on the electric pen, an engraving machine invented by Thomas Edison. Edison created the machine to engrave hard surfaces. O'Reilly modified Edison's machine by adding a tube and needle system and modifying its rotary-driven electromagnetic oscillating unit to enable the machine to drive the needle. He patented the machine in 1891.

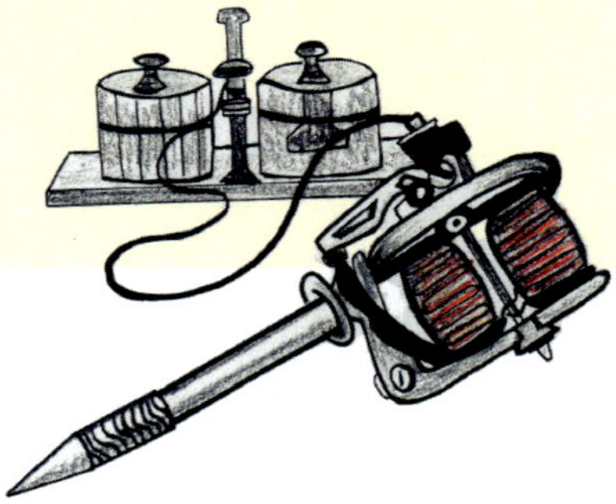

The Tattoo Process

Because getting a tattoo involves puncturing the skin, rigorous infection control practices must be followed. (Chapter two covers safety and infection control in depth.) A tattoo, like any wound, has the potential to become infected. In addition, the likelihood of transmitting diseases is increased when dealing with blood and bodily fluids. Being a safe and conscious tattoo artist is the most important part of the process.

To eliminate the possibility of contamination, most tattoo supplies such as needles, gloves, ink, ink cups and tongue depressors are disposable. Reusable materials, such as stainless-steel tubes must be scrubbed and sterilized between uses and the only acceptable sterilization method is an autoclave which provides a total kill of organisms.

In preparation to tattoo, an artist thoroughly washes their hands and dons a pair of gloves. Next, they prepare their sanitary work station by laying out sterilized & sanitized tools, machine and disposable products in a manner that prevents cross-contamination. The procedure area and all items the tattoo artist will come in contact with are covered with a barrier.

Next, if it is a new client, the artist will briefly explain the process. They will sanitize and shave the area to be tattooed. Lastly, the artist will place a stencil or hand draw the design on client's skin, which will be allowed to dry thoroughly. Then the tattooing begins!

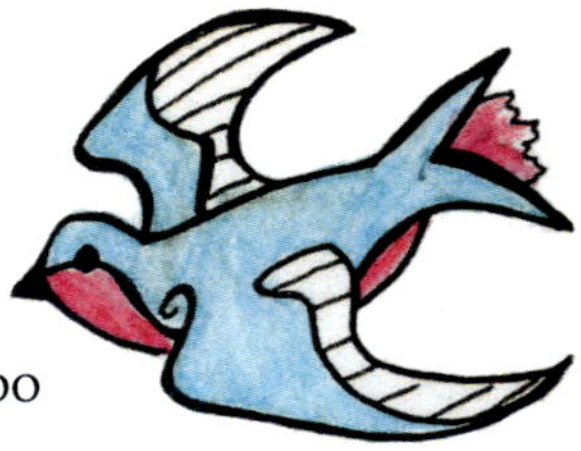

Creating the tattoo

Clients work with artists to create custom tattoo pieces or they choose images from "flash", which are pre-drawn tattoo designs displayed in the shop.

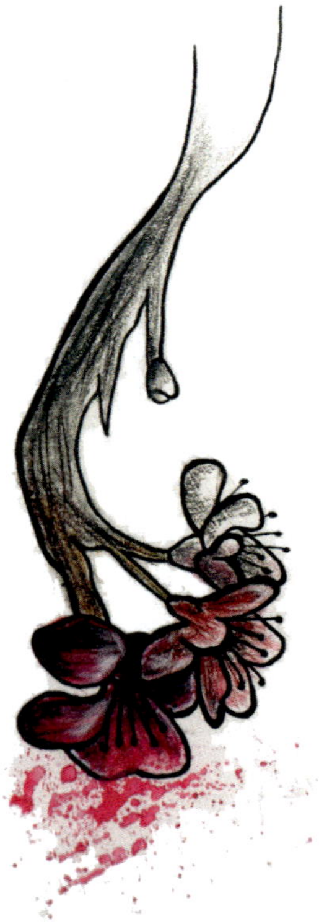

Because the skin can stretch out of shape based on the way the client is sitting or lying during the tattoo application process, the tattooer draws or stencils the design onto the person's skin before beginning. The artist must also know how deeply the needles need to pierce the skin throughout the process. Punctures that are too deep can cause excessive pain and bleeding, as ink inserted in the hypodermis (third layer of the skin) can cause blurred lines and scarring. Punctures that are too shallow can cause sketchy lines and/or a tattoo that quickly fades.

Tattooing itself involves several steps:

- **Outlining, or black work**: Using a lining needle, the artist creates a permanent line over the stencil. To avoid smearing or wiping away the stencil, most tattooers start at the bottom of the right side and work up (lefties generally start on the left side).
- **Shading**: After cleaning the area with green soap and water, the artist uses a thinner ink and a variety of needles to create a blend or gradation. Improper technique during this step can cause excessive pain and delayed healing.
- **Color**: The artist cleans the tattoo and then overlaps each line of color to ensure solid, even hues with no "holidays" or missed spots.

Final cleaning and bandaging: Some bleeding always occurs during tattooing, but most stops within a couple minutes. After using a disposable paper towel to remove any blood or plasma, the artist takes a photo of their work. And then covers the tattoo with some kind of ointment and absorbant paper towel/bandage or perhaps uses a dermal bandage, which adheres to the skin and is breathable.

HISTORY NOTE:

The use of **HOLIDAY** to mean "a missed spot" is of nautical origin. 18th century use of the word holiday, in the "missed a spot" sense, was in reference to crew members painting the decks of a ship or "paying" (sealing seams with tar or pitch) its hull. Paying in particular was an arduous, intensely unpleasant task, so even a small missed spot could be, sardonically, considered taking a "holiday".
Source: word-detective.com

After the tattoo

The client will need to take good care of their new piece of art by following the tattooer's advice on aftercare, to give the tattoo the absolute best chance to heal well and avoid infection. (More about this in chapter ten.) This involves somewhat of a committment to avoid certain things like swimming and sun exposure, as well as keeping the tattoo clean and moisturized when needed.

"Throughout the world, the rituals of transformation from infancy to manhood are attended with, and effected by, excruciating ordeals [like tattoos]. Ritual is mythology made alive, and it's effect is to convert men into angels".
-Joseph Campbell, Primitive Mythology: The Masks of God ©1959

It is advisable to have a written set of instructions, as well as the artist going over the highlights of aftercare verbally with the client at check-out.

Then the artist will clean up their contaminated station or work area. This involves gloving and carefully disposing of contaminated materials. (More on this in chapter two.)

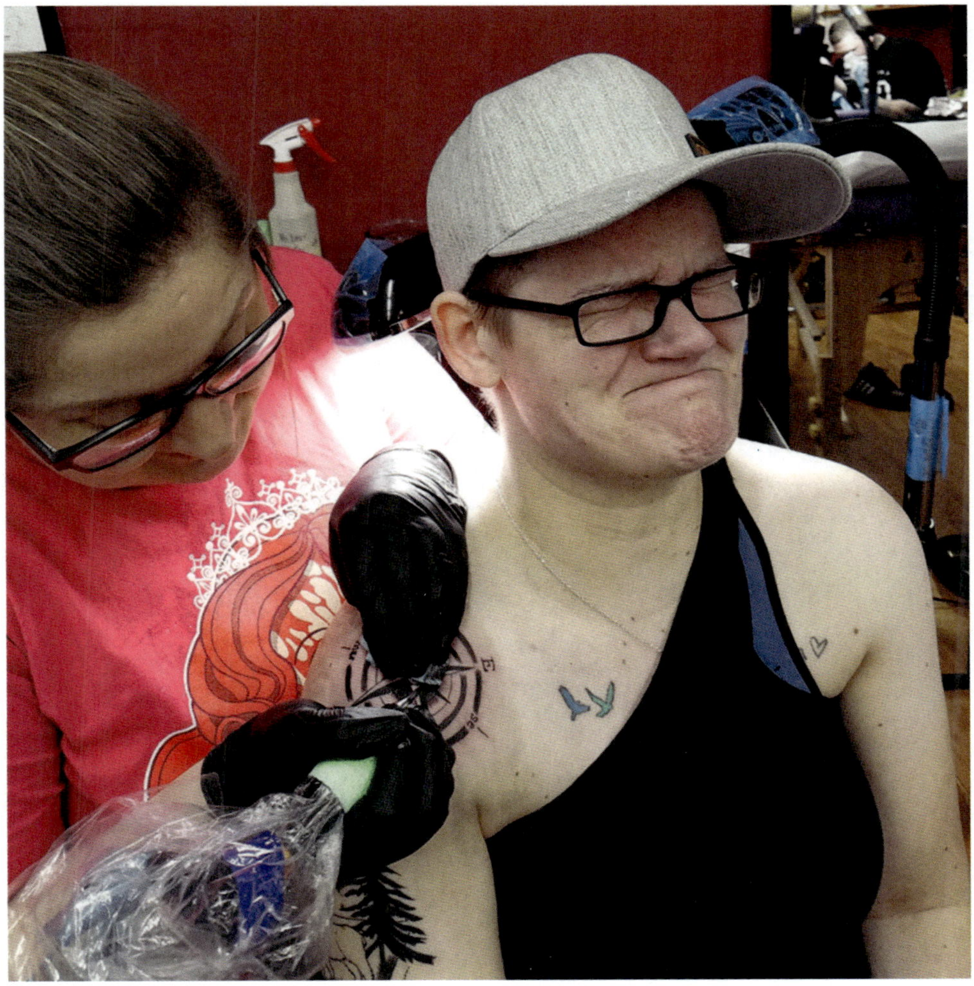

Pain

Most people describe the sensation of getting a tattoo as an intense, tedious scratching. Some say it's like an annoying sting. And still others say it feels more like getting scraped.

Throughout the process of getting tattooed a client may experience many different sensations and emotions, from "oh this isn't that bad" to "get me out of this chair right now!" The pain tends to come and go in waves, with the first few minutes being somewhat difficult and the last minutes of a longer session the most uncomfortable.

> "Humans have marked their bodies with tattoos for thousands of years. These permanent designs—sometimes plain, sometimes elaborate, always personal—have served as amulets, status symbols, declarations of love, signs of religious beliefs, adornments and even forms of punishment."
>
> *~Cate Lineberry, Jan.2007, Smithsonian.com*

Infrequently, you will get a client who has a very difficult time and this makes it much harder to relax and tattoo without worrying about the wiggling canvas under your needle. All aspects of dealing with a variety of clients, requires knowledge and skill on the artist's part, as well as patience and compassion. And occasionally, you will have to ask them to come back if you simply cannot get them to sit still.

Now let's go into depth regarding the many areas you'll need to understand for a solid tattoo education.

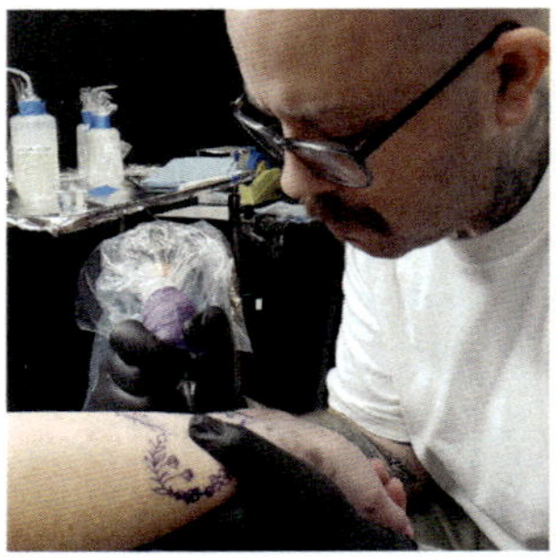

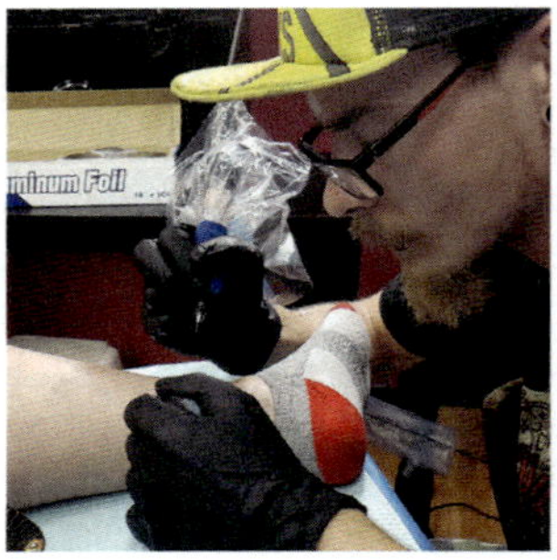

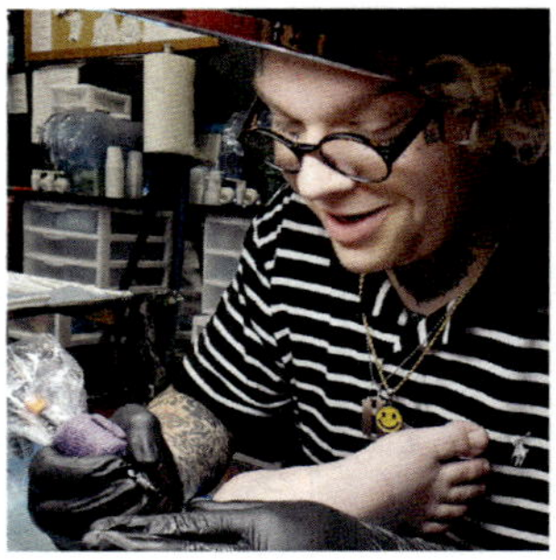

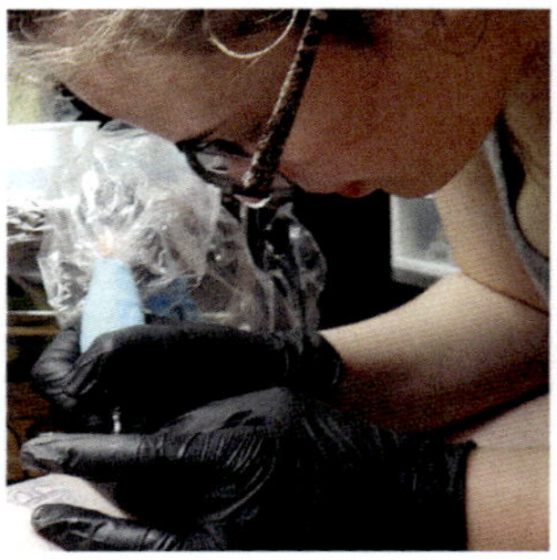

Shelly's Sidenote

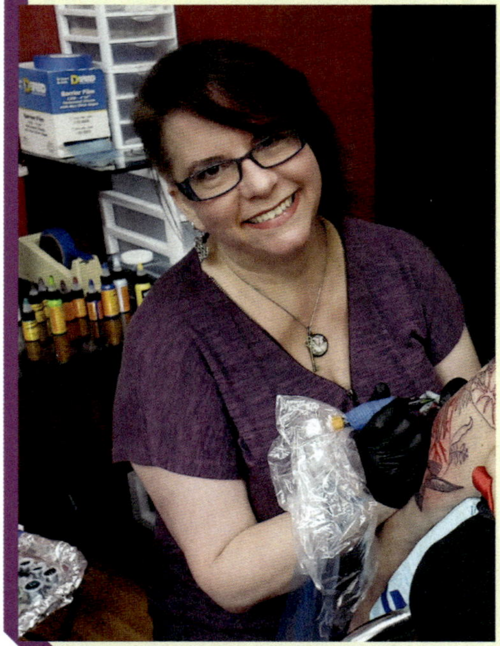

MY TATTOO JOURNEY

For me, becoming a tattoo artist was a difficult decision as I had little support from the people around me. I was on track to becoming an arts administrator, studying at the local university and I was in my late thirties! Almost everyone thought I was crazy. And yet I followed my intuition, left college and went to tattoo school. I questioned my being there many times. But I bit the bullet, paid the price and got through it.

And 13 years later it turned out to be the best decision of my life. I absolutely adore doing tattoos, meeting fascinating clients, teaching interesting students and being immersed in art of all kinds. I feel exceptionally fortunate. (If you'd like to know more--I wrote a blog about my beginnings as a tattooer. You can access that here: shellydax.com/tattoo-artist).

Though the beginning of my journey was rocky, and the middle years saw an economic downturn, I am beyond grateful that I stuck it out and eventually had the strong support of friends and family as well. Being a tattooer is an incredible vocation and I truly love what I get to do.

I hope you can use this book and my experience as a launching point for your tattoo journey.

Introduction Highlights

- Learning to tattoo requires specialized hands-on training.
- Tattoos have been around for over five millennia.
- Most tattoo supplies are disposable.
- A tattoo artist draws or stencils the design on the skin before beginning to tattoo.
- Some bleeding occurs during the tattoo procedure.
- "Holiday" means a missed spot in the tattoo.
- Getting a tattoo means making a commitment to great aftercare.
- Tattoo artist should have a written set of care instructions for clients.
- During a tattoo, pain tends to come and go in waves.
- The tattoo machine is based on an engraving machine invented by Thomas Edison.

I am thankful for the freedom to get the tattoos that express who I am.

And the ability to ignore those who judge me by them.

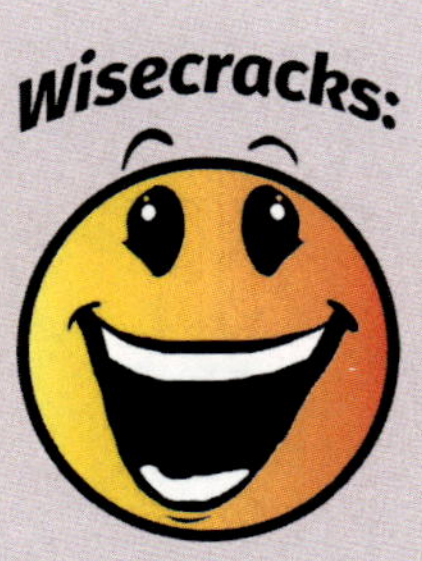

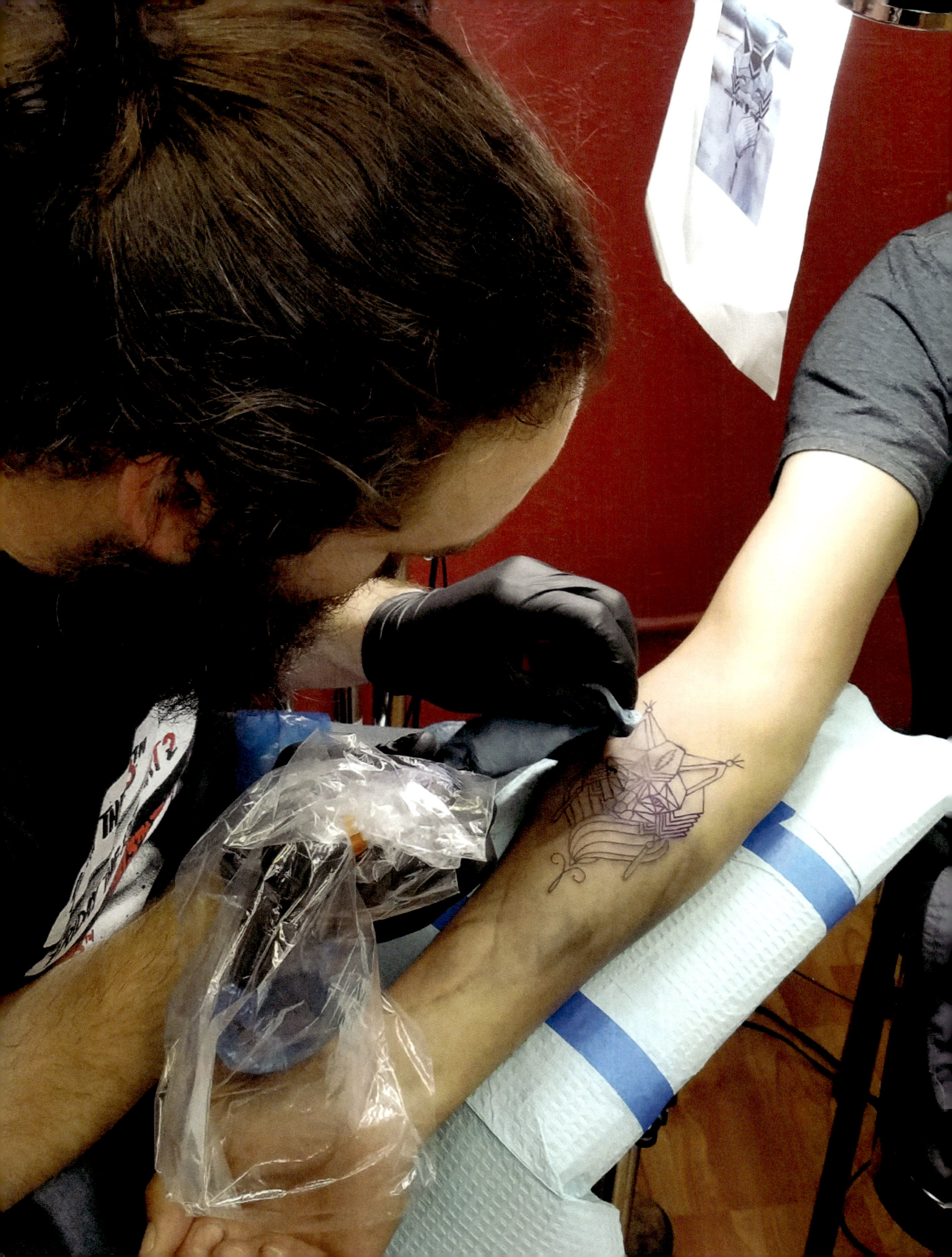

Chapter One

What's At Risk?

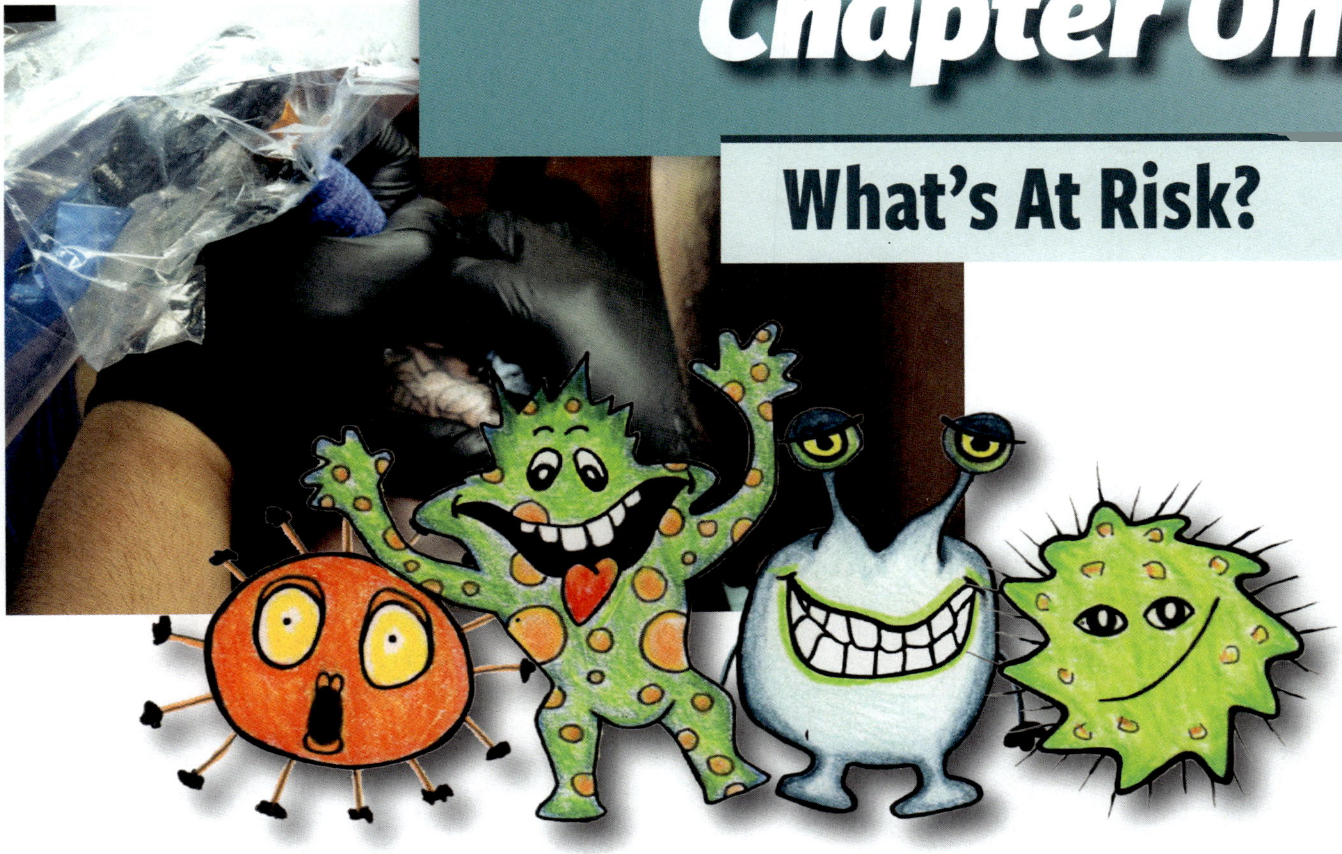

As you embark on your career as a tattoo artist you must FIRST consider the risks involved, both for you and for your clients. Transmission of disease and severe complications are potential hazards we MUST take seriously.

Risks

Needles, equipment, surfaces and even ink or rinse water can be contaminated with fluids that contain bacteria or viruses that may be passed into the blood stream. This may happen in places and situations where proper sterilization techniques or single-use equipment are not used or even in a licensed studio where the tattooer is uneducated, fatigued or careless.

> "True prevention is not waiting for bad things to happen, it's preventing bad things from happening in the first place."
> *~ Don McPherson, Athlete & Speaker*

If all standard precautions and proper procedures are observed during tattooing, then the process can be entirely safe for both the client and the tattoo artist. Unfortunately, not all states (or countries) have the strict legal requirements that offer the highest level of protection. Sadly, this leaves entirely too many tattoo artists simply uninformed.

Let's look at the potential danger clients face when receiving a tattoo and the risks for the artist when performing a procedure.

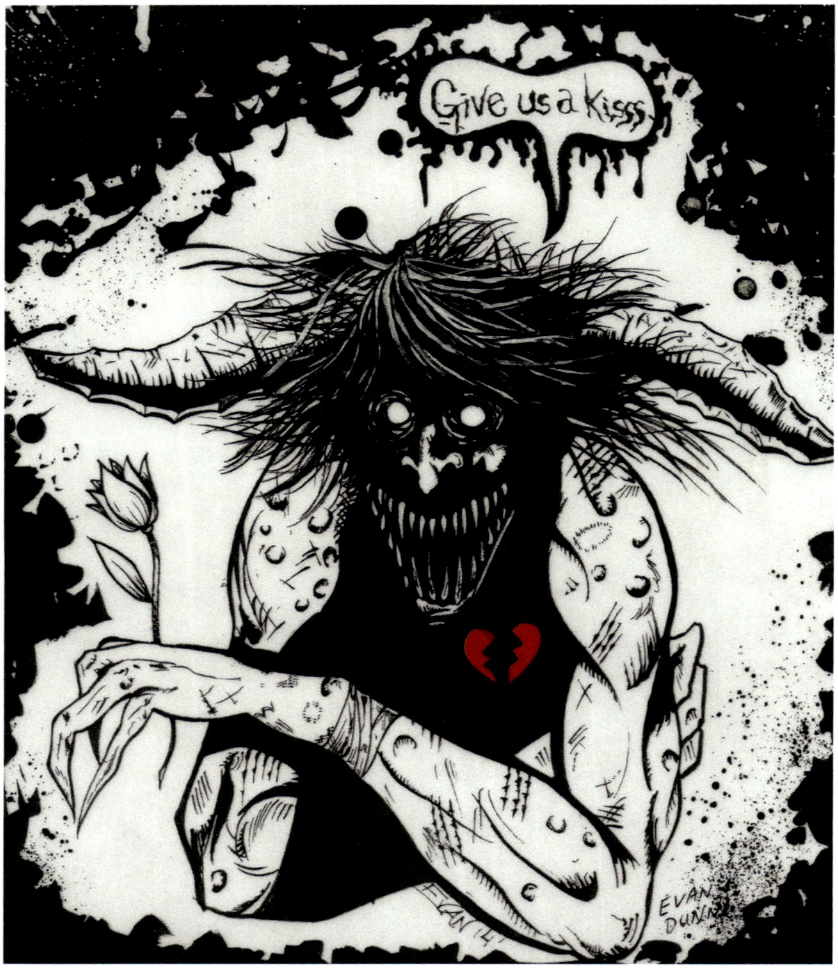

Artwork by
Evan Dunn

DISEASES

The following are illnesses (and organisms that cause them) that can be contracted through contact with infected body fluid. Many of these are permanent diseases!

- AIDS (H.I.V.)
- Aseptic Meningitis, Cold Sores (Herpes Simplex)
- Boils, Furuncles & Carbuncles (Staphylococcus Aureus)
- Encephalomyelitis (Herpes)
- Hepatitis (Hepatitis B & C most common)
- Infectious wounds (Escherichia Coli)
- Monilia (Candida Albicans)
- Pneumonia (Histoplasma Capsulatum)
- Respiro, Adeno, Syncytial (Influenza)
- Tetanus (Clostridium Tetani)
- Tuberculosis (Mycobacterium Tuberculosis)

Now we'll focus on a few that are of most concern in the tattoo industry:

Hepatitis

"Hepatitis" (hep-uh-tahy-tis) means inflammation of the liver and refers to a group of viral infections that affect the liver. The most common types are Hepatitis A, B and C. Viral hepatitis is the leading cause of liver cancer and the most common reason for liver transplantation. An estimated 4.4 million Americans are living with chronic hepatitis; most do not know they are.

What is Hepatitis B?

Hepatitis B is a liver disease caused by the Hepatitis B virus (HBV). It ranges in severity from a mild illness lasting a few weeks (acute), to a serious long-term (chronic) illness that can lead to liver disease or liver cancer. Hepatitis B is the most notable of concern to tattoo artists because people can become infected from direct or indirect contact for up to 7 days. The Hepatitis B virus is 50-100 times more infectious than HIV.

The incubation period for HBV from the time of exposure to onset of symptoms is 6 weeks to 6 months. The virus is found in highest concentrations in blood and the lowest concentrations in other body fluids (e.g., semen, vaginal secretions, and wound fluids).

How is Hepatitis B spread?

Hepatitis B is usually spread when blood, semen, or other body fluids from an infected person enter the body of someone who is not infected. This can happen through sexual contact with an infected person or sharing needles, syringes, or tattoo needles.
Hepatitis B can also be passed from an infected mother to her baby at birth.
The virus is very infectious and is easily passed through breaks in the skin or in soft tissue such as the eyes, nose, and mouth.

The virus can live on objects for up to 7 days and individuals can also become infected from contact with contaminated objects.

Hepatitis B is not spread by:

- Breastfeeding,
- Sharing eating utensils
- Hugging, kissing
- Holding hands
- Coughing, or sneezing
- Contaminated food or water.

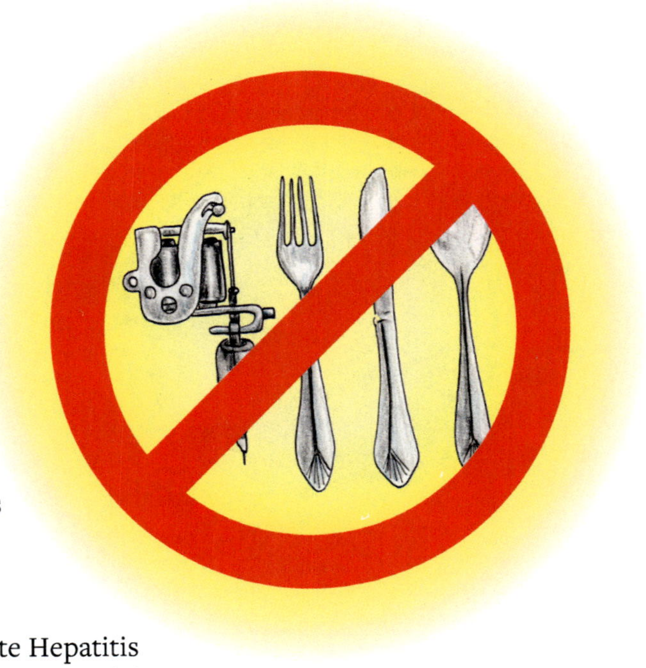

Can a person get Hepatitis B from a tattoo or piercing?

Yes, however there is little evidence that Hepatitis B is spread by getting tattoos in licensed, commercial facilities knowledgeable about infection control. Whenever tattoos or body piercings are given in an informal setting, such as a kitchen, or with non-sterile instruments, transmission of Hepatitis B and other infectious diseases are highly possible.

What are the symptoms of acute Hepatitis B?

It's important to know that not everyone has symptoms with acute Hepatitis B, especially young children. Even people without symptoms can still spread the virus to others. For those people who do have symptoms, they will typically appear within 3 months of exposure. Symptoms can last from a few weeks to several months and include:

- Fever
- Vomiting
- Joint pain
- Fatigue
- Abdominal pain
- Dark urine
- Yellowing of skin and whites of eyes
- Loss of appetite
- Grey-colored stools
- Nausea

Symptoms of chronic Hepatitis B can take up to 30 years to develop. Damage to the liver can silently occur during this time. When symptoms do appear, they are similar to those of acute Hepatitis B infection and can be a sign of advanced liver disease.

Is Hepatitis B common?

As of 2013, 240 million people worldwide live with chronic HBV infection.

In the United States, approximately 1.2 million people have chronic Hepatitis B. Unfortunately, many people do not know they are infected. An estimated 40,000 people now become infected each year.

Each year about 2,000 to 4,000 people die in the United States from cirrhosis or liver cancer caused by hepatitis B.

> "Health is not valued until sickness comes."
> -Thomas Fuller, Historian

How serious is Hepatitis B?

Over time, approximately 15%-25% of people with chronic Hepatitis B develop serious liver problems, including liver damage, cirrhosis, liver failure, and liver cancer. Every year, approximately 3,000 people in the United States and more than 600,000 people worldwide die from Hepatitis B related liver disease.

IMPORTANT NOTE:

Getting a tattoo in prison is extremely dangerous because it is done in secret with a limited amount of supplies and the inmates are often sharing contaminated materials. In a 2010 article, "Prison Tattoos", Lorry Schoenly, PhD, and RN stated "about 2 percent of the U.S. prison population is HIV positive and 30-40 percent have Hepatitis C. Although more people are infected with Hepatitis, allowing it to spread more frequently, inmates are at risk for both because they can be transmitted the same way."

How is Hepatitis B diagnosed?

Hepatitis B is diagnosed with specific blood tests that are not part of blood work typically done during regular physical exams. If the screening test is positive for Hepatitis B antibodies, different blood tests are needed to determine whether the infection has been cleared or has become a chronic infection.

What should I do if I think I've been infected?

If you think you have been exposed to the blood or body fluid of an infected individual, notify your primary care physician immediately.

HIV

H – Human – This virus can only infect human beings.

I – Immunodeficiency – HIV weakens your immune system by destroying important cells that fight disease and infection. A "deficient" immune system can't protect you.

V – Virus – A virus can only reproduce itself by taking over a cell in the body of its host.

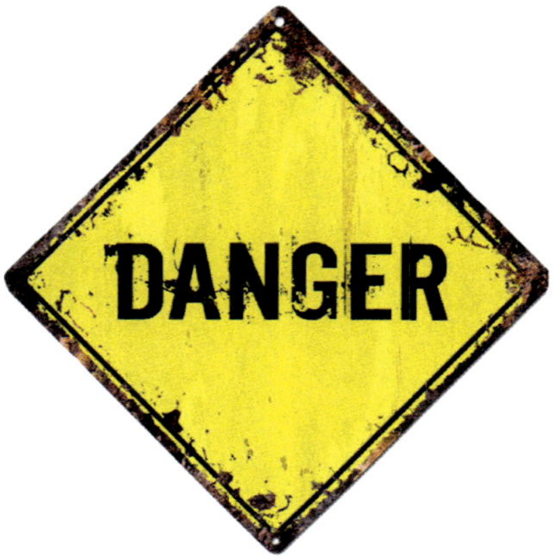

HIV is a lot like other viruses, including those that cause the "flu" or the common cold. But there is an important difference – over time, your immune system can clear most viruses out of your body. That isn't the case with HIV – the human immune system can't seem to get rid of it. Scientists are still trying to figure out why.

HIV can hide for long periods of time in the cells of your body. It attacks a key part of your immune system – your T-cells or CD4 cells. Your body must have these cells to fight infections and disease, but HIV invades them, uses them to make more copies of itself, and then destroys them.

Over time, HIV can destroy so many of your CD4 cells that your body can't fight infections and diseases anymore. When that happens, HIV infection can lead to AIDS.

AIDS

A – Acquired – AIDS is not something you inherit from your parents. You acquire AIDS after birth.

I – Immuno – Your body's immune system includes all the organs and cells that work to fight off infection or disease.

D – Deficiency – You get AIDS when your immune system is "deficient," or isn't working the way it should.

S – Syndrome – A syndrome is a collection of symptoms and signs of disease. AIDS is a syndrome, rather than a single disease, because it is a complex illness with a wide range of complications and symptoms.

AIDS is the final stage of HIV infection. People at this stage of HIV disease have badly damaged immune systems, which put them at risk for opportunistic infections (OIs). You will be diagnosed with AIDS if you have one or more specific OIs, certain cancers, or a very low number of CD4 cells. If you have AIDS, you will need medical intervention and treatment to prevent death.

There is very little chance of getting an infection from a tattoo studio using standard precautions and sanitary practices.

How Do You Get HIV?
HIV is found in specific human body fluids. If any of those fluids enter your body, you can become infected with HIV. HIV can live on surfaces for a few hours.

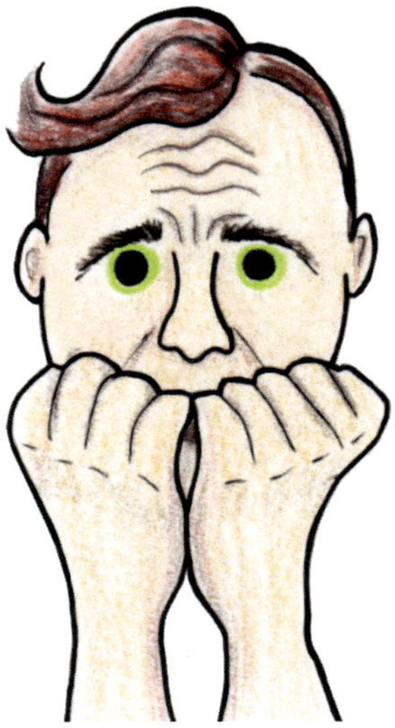

Which Body Fluids Contain HIV?
HIV lives and reproduces in blood and other body fluids. The following fluids can contain high levels of HIV:

- Blood
- Semen
- Pre-seminal fluid
- Breast milk
- Vaginal fluids
- Rectal mucous

Other body fluids and waste products—like feces, nasal fluid, saliva, sweat, tears, urine, or vomit—DON'T contain enough HIV to infect you, UNLESS they have blood mixed in them and you have significant and direct contact with them.

Can you get HIV/AIDS from tattoo needles?
The CDC says, though tattooing or body piercing presents a potential risk of HIV transmission, no cases of HIV transmission from these activities has been documented (as of 2015). While HIV transmission from body piercing or tattooing is highly unlikely in a LICENSED facility, it is possible for the blood of an infected person to be left on surfaces or a needle that is later used to pierce or tattoo another person.

To guard against this possibility, all needles and equipment used for tattooing should be new and protected from cross contamination OR should be sterilized between uses, and new ink should be used for tattooing. In addition, the person doing the procedure should be properly educated and licensed.

Tattoo Infections
There is very little chance of getting an infection from a tattoo studio using standard precautions and sanitary practices. The majority of the time an infection is caused by improper aftercare. Clients will touch the healing tattoo with dirty fingers or allow friends to do so. They might set their newly inked skin on used sheets or a dirty couch or counter. They may use wash cloth or towel several times or use bar soap, which both harbor bacteria. Some clients even sleep with their pets while the tattoo is healing—**a big no no.**

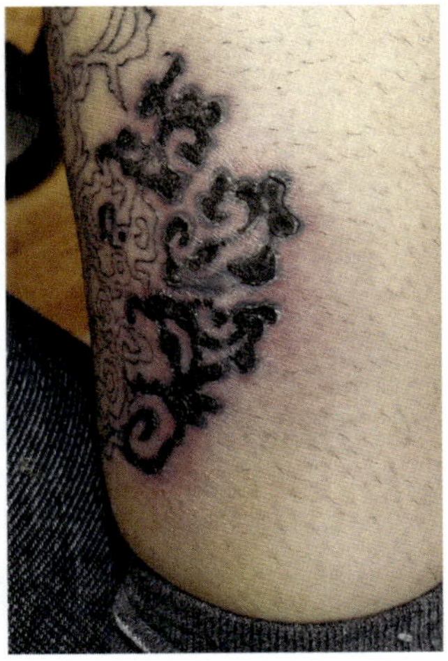

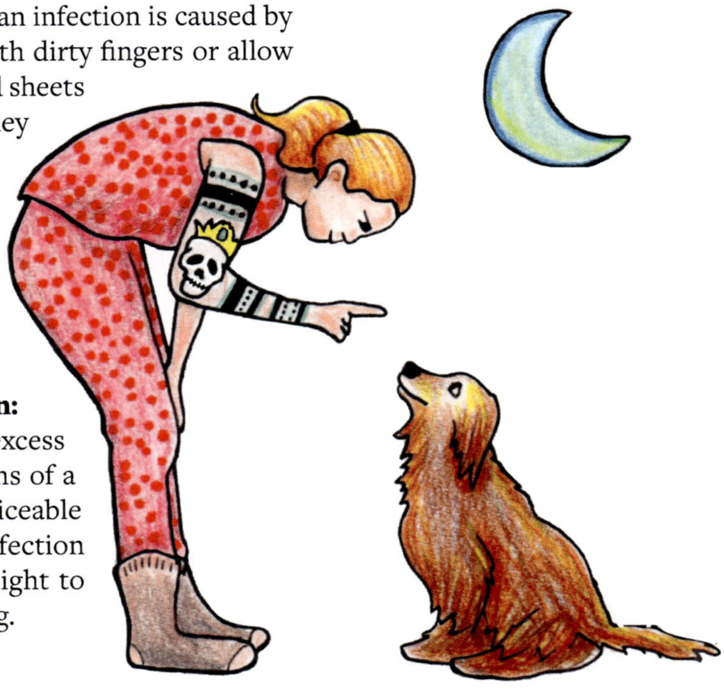

Symptoms of tattoo infection:
May include redness, pimples, excess bleeding and scabbing. The signs of a tattoo infection are mostly noticeable within the first few days. An infection usually begins with redness, slight to extreme tenderness and swelling.

> "It is very hard to say the percentage of people who may have been infected with the virus through tattooing. Most sources say there have been no documented cases of HIV transmission from this activity. Even so, the CDC still recognizes the possibility of becoming infected with HIV through tattooing....With the increasing popularity of tattoos, people are getting inked younger and younger. Teenagers seem to be unaware of the dangers and therefore make riskier decisions. It is good to talk about all the ways people can become infected with the virus because awareness brings about safety."
>
> *–Cambriae Bates, ActionAIDS Development Intern*

Additionally, if the tattoo begins to feel better then starts feeling worse, a client has likely contracted an infection.

Advanced stages of infection include redness traveling along the tattoo, red splotchy areas, blisters and fever. In severe cases, the infected area may ooze plasma or yellowish pus.

The two most common types of tattoo infections are caused by Staphylococci.

Staph Infections

There are more than 30 different types of bacteria that are classified as Staphylococcus; this bacteria lives on the skin, in the mouth, and in nasal passages and you can be a carrier without being sick. But for those with compromised immune systems, recent surgery or open wounds, such as during tattoo procedure, staph bacteria can cause an infection that ranges from a mild skin rash to potentially life-threatening blood poisoning.

Cellulitis

Cellulitis is a common bacterial infection usually affecting the surface of the skin. Cellulitis may first appear as a red, swollen area that feels hot and tender to the touch, is usually painful and can spread rapidly. In most cases, the skin on the lower legs is affected, although the infection can occur anywhere on your body or face. Untreated, the infection might spread to your lymph nodes or bloodstream and become life-threatening. Medical help is required for this condition.

OTHER COMPLICATIONS

Allergic reactions:

Reactions to tattoo ink are fairly common, with red ink having the highest risk for severe allergy. In addition, clients could be sensitive or allergic to petroleum jelly, green soap or even coconut oil; a common ingredient in aftercare products. Allergies generally appear as irritation, rash, itching and redness. These reactions can be seen even years after getting a tattoo. (More on allergies in chapter three.)

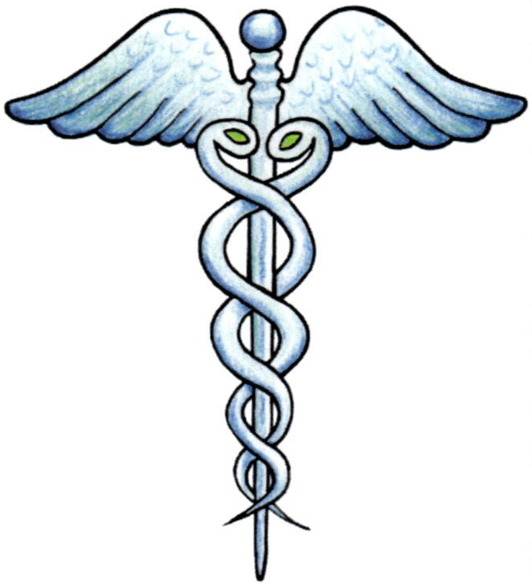

Ink Ingredients/Contamination:

It is possible to have microbial contaminants or other ingredients in tattoo ink that can cause problems for people. (More on tattoo ink in chapter eight.)

Possible MRI Interference:

In rare cases people who need an MRI (magnetic resonance imaging) for medical reasons, may experience stinging or burning in their tattoo areas. Some inks contain microscopic metallic fragments which may interfere with image quality.

DIABETES & TATTOOS:

Many clients with diabetes opt for tattooing a diabetic or "medical alert" symbol to replace their emergency ID bracelets.

Diabetes: A disease in which the body's ability to produce or respond to the hormone insulin is impaired, resulting in abnormal metabolism of carbohydrates and elevated levels of glucose in the blood.

- Type I Diabetes means the body has stopped making insulin. The onset of this is usually at birth.

- Type II Diabetes means the body does not produce enough insulin, or it cannot use the insulin that it makes. This usually develops in adulthood.

Having diabetes doesn't mean a person can't get a tattoo, but they should be aware of risk factors and have their diabetes under control. Because a tattoo procedure may take hours to complete, it is important for the client to have good blood sugar level and blood pressure before starting. In addition, blood sugar levels can rise during a procedure, but will typically return to normal shortly thereafter. Clients should also be aware that high blood sugar levels can extend the healing process and increase the risk of infection by having an open wound longer than normal.

> "The person who earns a million but destroys their health in the process is not really a sucess.
> *~Zig Ziglar, Author*

People with diabetes should consider placement of the design as well. Limbs, hands and feet may need to be avoided due to poor circulation and/or neuropathy (peripheral

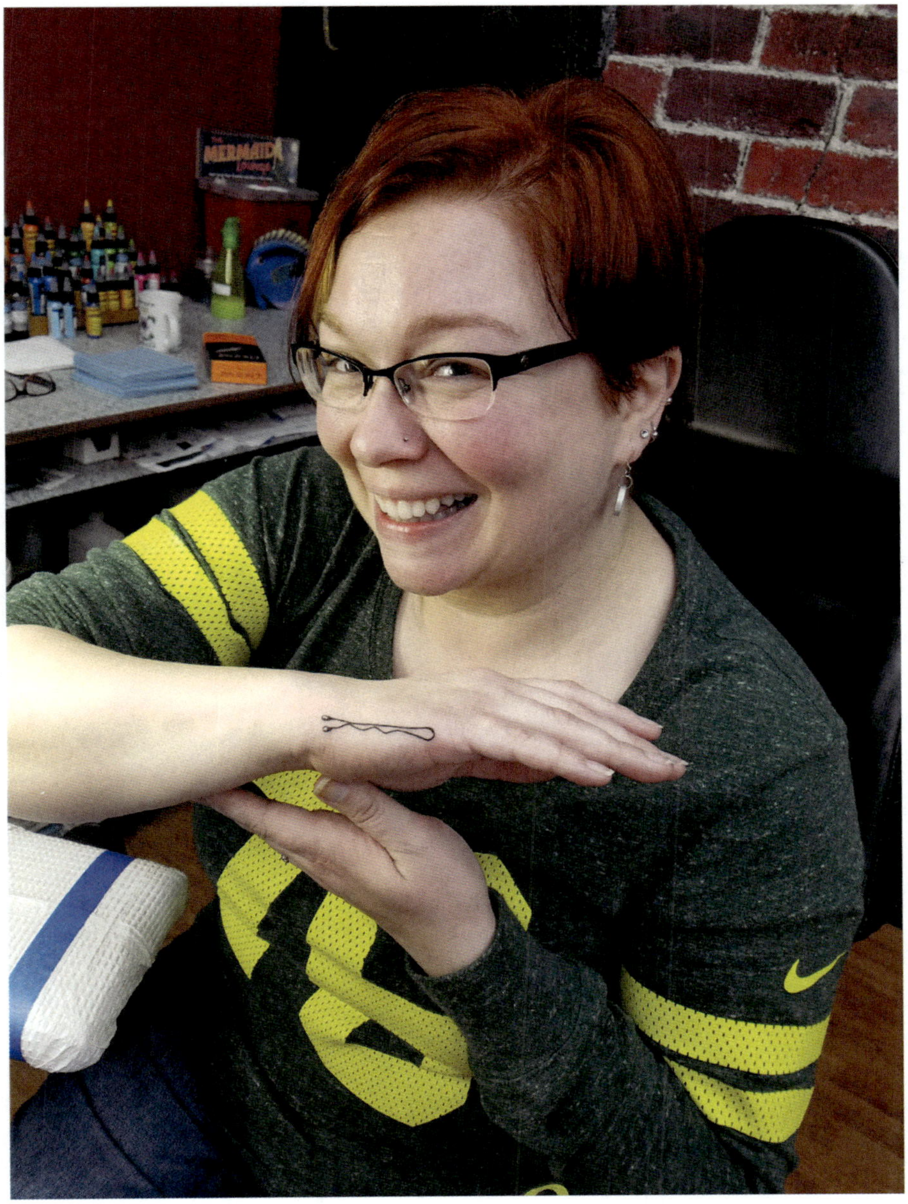

> The biggest investment in your future career is HAPPY HEALTHY clients! Do your part by being a mindful tattooer.

neuropathy, the most common type of diabetic neuropathy, causes pain or loss of feeling in the toes, feet, legs, hands, and arms). Tattoos in these places usually take longer to heal, which can lead to infection or complications. Awareness is key.

Consider asking client to get cleared by their physician in the following cases

HIV/AIDS: Client has altered immune system and very susceptible to infections.

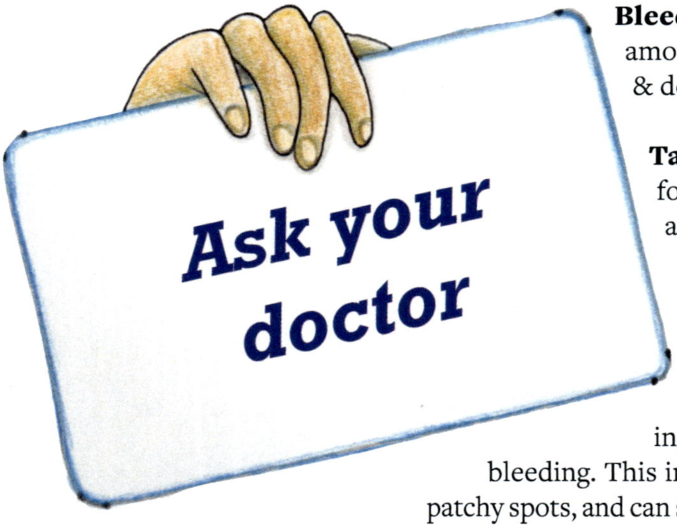

Bleeding disorders: Client will not stop bleeding in a reasonable amount of time [10 or 15 mins]. Extensive blood loss can lead to shock & death. Profuse bleeding requires medical attention.

Taking blood thinners: such as Coumadin or aspirin or even healthy foods in great amounts such as turmeric, ginger, curry, garlic, licorice, as well as supplements such as dong quai, feverfew and white willow.

Pregnancy: Slight risk of infection to mother and possible rare toxic effects to fetus.

Alcohol: If the client is a heavy drinker or even a client drinking within 24 hours before a tattoo procedure this can cause profuse bleeding. This interferes with artist's visibility, it dilutes the ink which can cause patchy spots, and can slow the healing process leaving client more susceptible to infection.

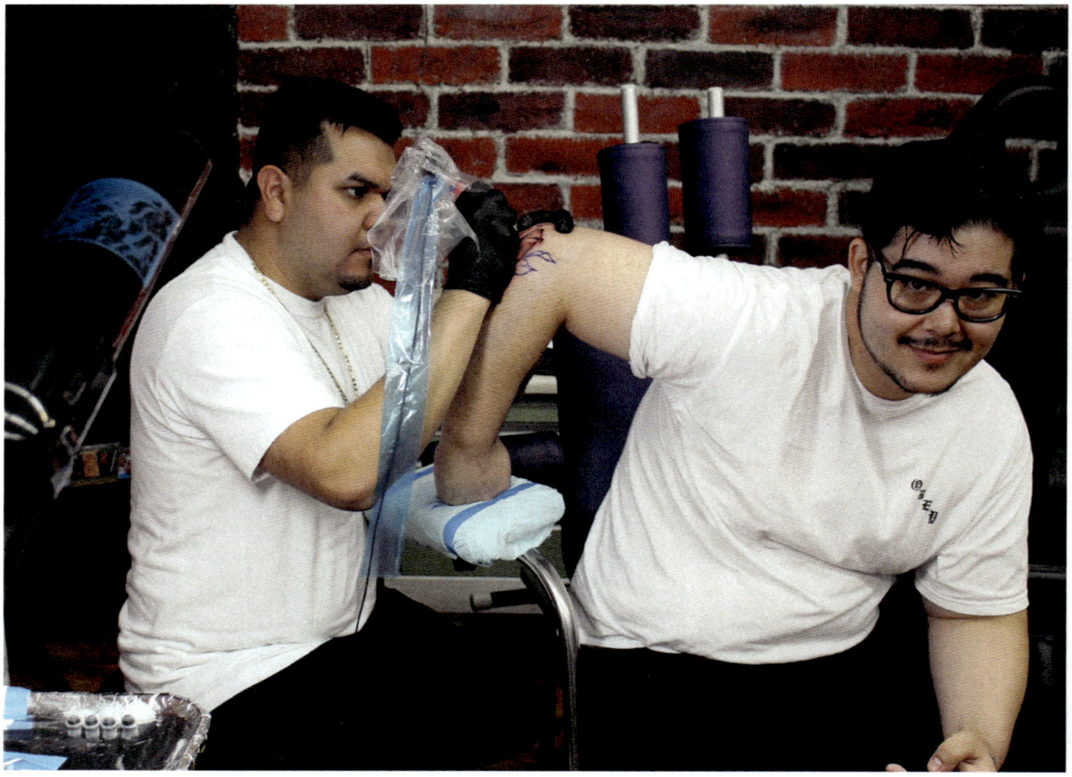

"My tattoo is of a cannon in Vancouver that I got in a fleeting moment of stupidity maybe 14 years ago. A lot of people have really beautiful tattoos, and I get real tattoo envy. But then other people basically just treat them like bumper stickers for their bodies."

~Ryan Reynolds, Actor

Sources:
HIV/Aids, The National Center for HIV/AIDS, Viral Hepatitis, STD, and TB Prevention (NCHHSTP), cdc.org, August 2018
Tattoo Health & Safety Tips, Orly Avitzur, M.D., Medical Adviser, Consumer Reports, September 2012
HIV/Aids, US ARMY Public Health Command, August 2018
Staph Infections, Anne L. Fritz, Medically Reviewed by Sanjai Sinha, MD, Everydayhealth.com 2017
Think Before You Ink: Are Tattoos Safe?, Federal Drug Administration: fda.gov, May 2017
Cellulitis, Bree Normandin, Medically Reviewed by Steve Kim, M.D. 2017
Diabetes Basics, American Diabetes Association, www.diabetes.org, August 2018

Chapter One Highlights

- If all standard precautions and proper procedures are observed during tattooing, then the process can be entirely safe.
- Serious diseases can be contracted through contact with bodily fluids.
- Hepatitis means inflammation of the liver.
- Hepatitis B is of most concern to the tattoo artist because people can become infected through direct AND indirect contact.
- Symptoms of chronic Hepatitis B can take up to 30 years to develop.
- Medical help is required to address cellulitis.
- There is very little chance of getting a tattoo infection from a studio using standard precautions.
- All needles and equipment should be new or protected from cross contamination.
- Reactions to tattoo ink are fairly common, with red pigment having the highest chance for severe allergy.
- Sleeping with pets, while a tattoo is healing, is a big no no.
- Advanced stages of infection include redness, splotchy areas, blisters and fever.
- People who have diabetes should have their blood sugar under control before getting a tattoo.
- In some cases, such as a client with bleeding disorders, it is advisable to have them clear it first with their doctor.

Wisecracks:

You don't like my tattoos? At least I can cover them up.

Your face on the other hand...

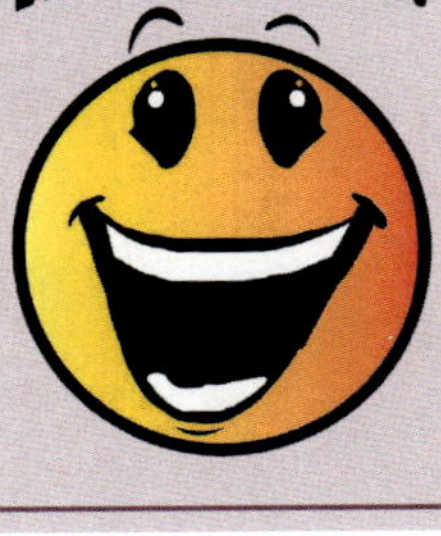

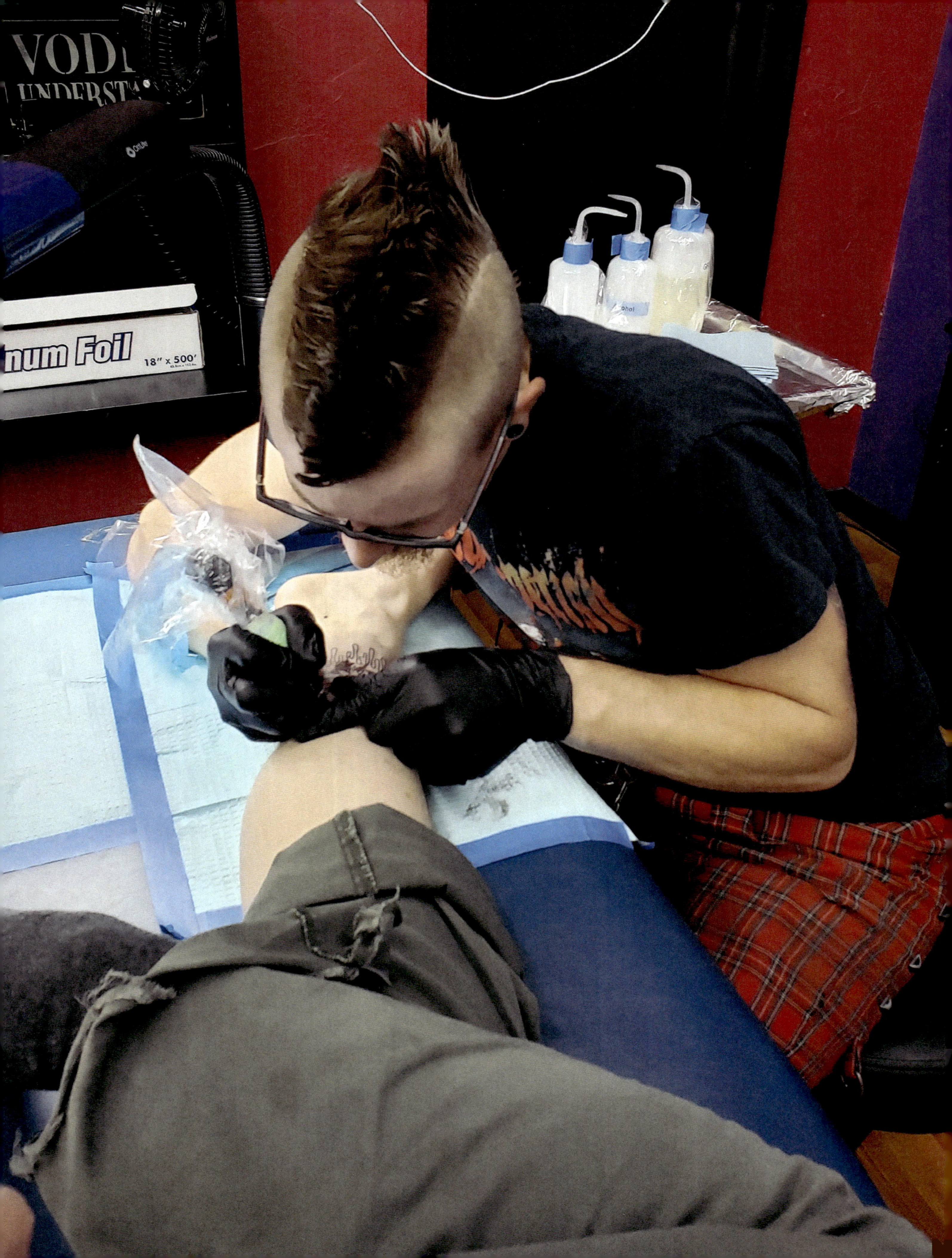
num Foil
18″ x 500′

Chapter Two

Safety & Infection Control

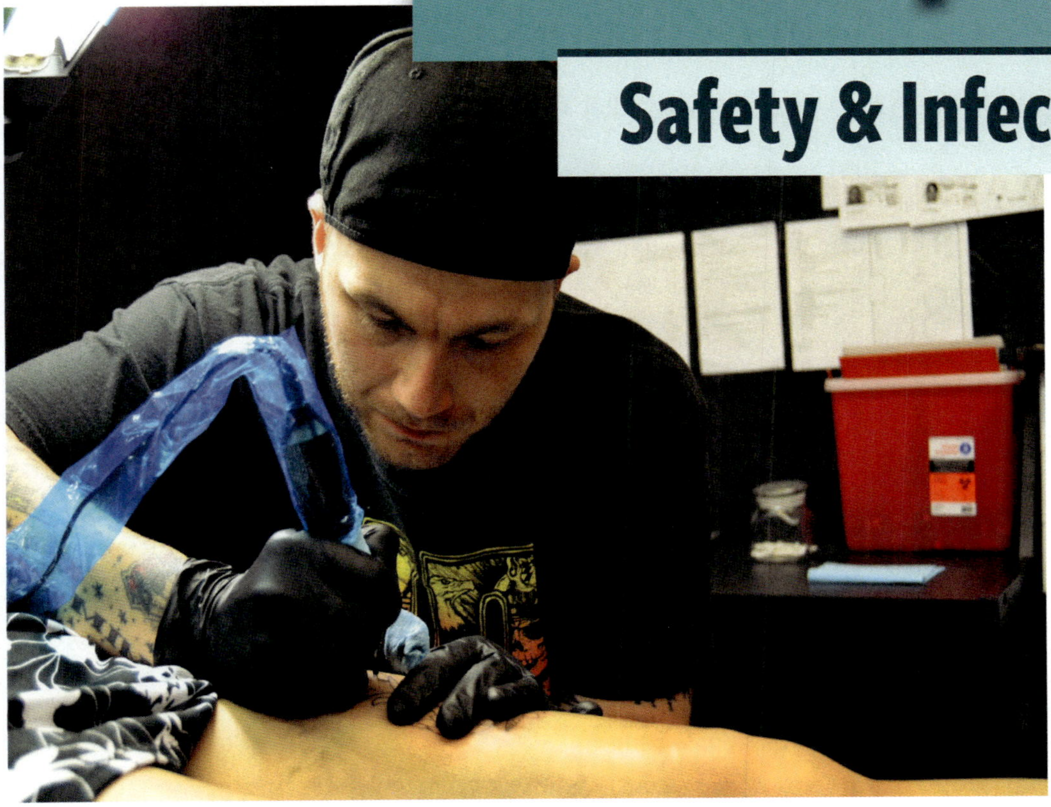

Despite being around for thousands of years, tattooing has always faced the challenge of being a health risk to artist and client—from the use of the same tools and needles on multiple clients, to the overall lack of sanitation. Beginning early in the twentieth century, regulations were applied to the profession of tattooing to minimize and even eliminate many health concerns.

With the advanced information available today, there is no excuse for poor sanitation practices. Tattoo artists have an ethical and, in some areas, a legal responsibility to educate themselves, and be highly literate on the latest procedures and practices to ensure minimal risk to self and client.

> "Cleanliness and order are not matters of instinct; they are matters of education. And like most great things you must cultivate a taste for them
>
> *~ Benjamin Disraeli, British Prime Minister*

Sanitation

Sanitation is the application of measures to promote public health and prevent the spread of infectious diseases. The importance of sanitation cannot be overemphasized. Tattooing brings the tattoo artist in direct contact with the client's skin. Skin is a host or carrier of many harmless bacteria yet opening this barrier with needles invites great risk. Once fluids and blood are present, these micro-organisms (bacteria & viruses) may begin to grow out of control and infection sets in. Understanding sanitary measures contributes to the protection of yours

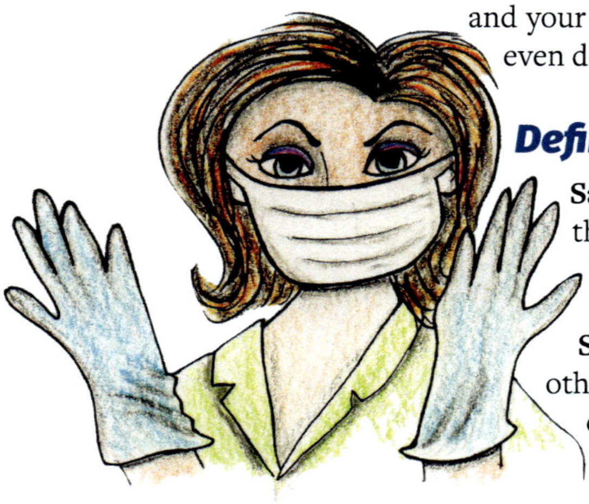

and your client's health. Overlooking these measures can result in serious illness or even death.

Definitions:

Sanitize: to render sanitary, or free from elements, such as filth or pathogens, that endanger health. This does not mean ALL possible microorganisms, etc. but MOST. Sanitizing does not remove ALL bacteria, microorganisms, etc.

Sterilize: to render sterile, or to make free from ALL live bacteria/germs or other microorganisms. A "total kill" of everything. Something that is sterilized can also be considered sanitary, but something that is sanitized is not considered sterile.

Antiseptic: substances that prevent the growth of disease-causing microorganisms that are applied to living tissue/skin to reduce the possibility of infection. (example: green soap & rubbing alcohol) This term is mainly used in reference to substances used on the body.

Disinfect: to destroy bacteria on any object.

Disinfectant: substances having the power to destroy bacteria (germs or microbes). The term "disinfectant" (also called germicide) is generally distinguished from "antiseptic" in that disinfectants are used to destroy microorganisms found on non-living objects.

High-level disinfectants: destroy all microorganisms, most viruses, most fungi, with the exception of high numbers of bacterial spores. Must have ability to kill tubercle bacilli (TB) & HIV.

Low-level disinfectants: kill most bacteria, some viruses, and some fungi, but cannot be relied on to kill resistant microorganisms such as tubercle bacilli (TB) or bacterial spores.

Sharps: A medical term for devices with sharp points or edges that can puncture or cut skin. (needles)

MSDS: A Material Safety Data Sheet is a document that contains information on the potential health effects of exposure to chemicals, or other potentially dangerous substances, and on safe working procedures when handling chemical products.

HISTORY NOTE:

"At the turn of the twentieth century many people began receiving tattoos. The common practice of mixing dry pigment with saliva contributed to diseases such as lockjaw, gangrene and syphilis, as did the nearly total lack of sterilization for the needles. In the 1920's and 30's New York and London authorities began regulating the trade, insisting on sanitary practices." David Morton, "Tattooing" -Invention & Technology Magazine, Winter 2002.

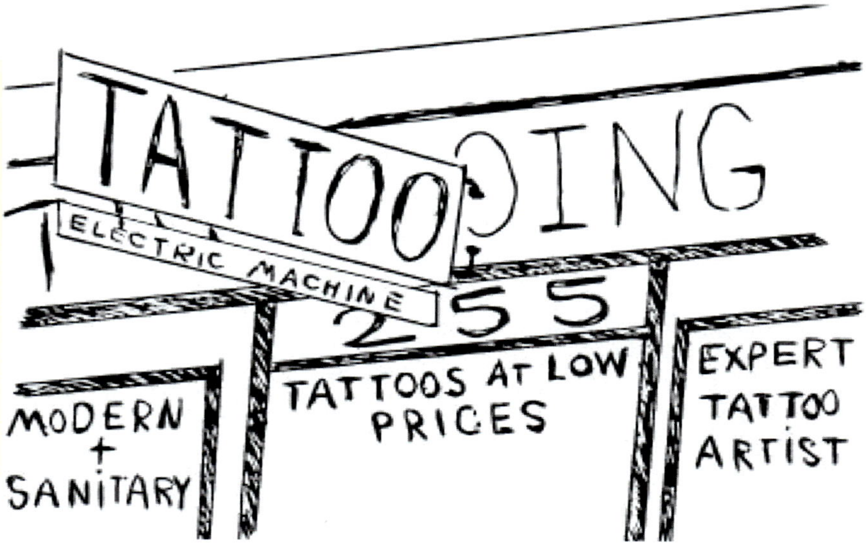

SAFETY PRECAUTIONS WHEN WORKING WITH CHEMICALS

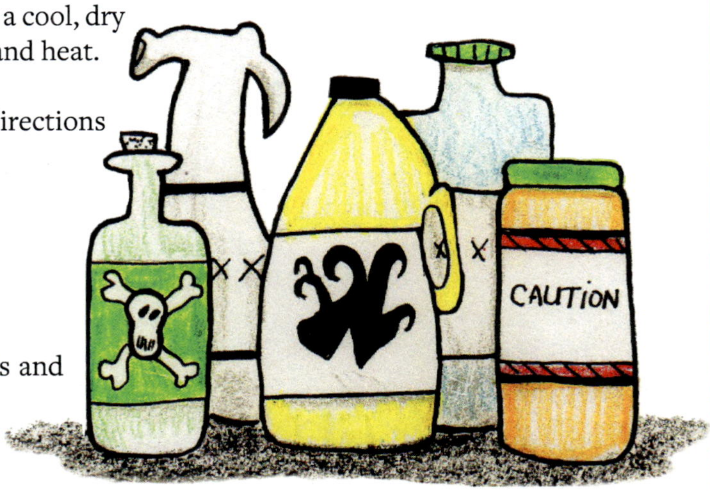

- Purchase chemicals in small quantities and store them in a cool, dry place; they can deteriorate due to contact with air, light and heat.
- Keep all containers labeled. Read all labels and follow directions carefully.
- Do not breathe fumes from chemicals or solutions.
- Avoid spilling when diluting chemicals.
- Keep all products organized to prevent accidental spills and breakage.
- Always keep antiseptics and disinfectants sealed and in a safe place. They should always be clearly labeled and never transferred to unlabeled containers where they may be mistaken for some other product.
- Have a Material Data Safety Sheet (MSDS) for all potentially toxic products available on site.

Even better, use environmentally friendly and toxin free products in the studio, such as ***Benefect*** a botanical high-level disinfectant. (www.benefect.com) →

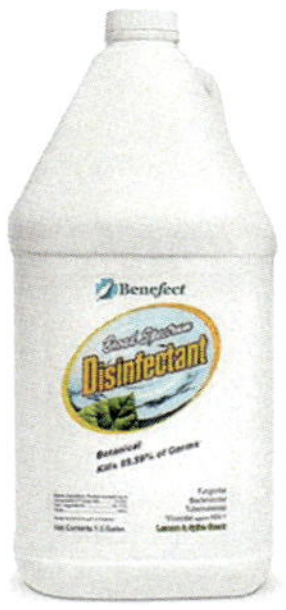

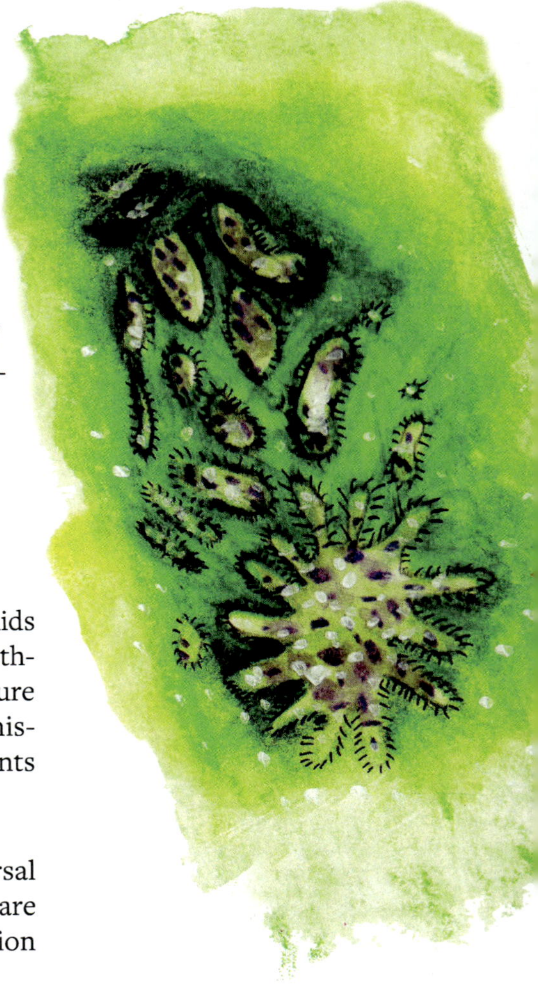

The air and everything we touch contains thousands of microscopic organisms and many of these are infectious. As discussed in the last chapter, breaking the skin exposes you and your client to numerous potential complications and possible hazards.

Just a few simple and inexpensive procedures, turned into habits, can virtually eliminate these risks.

Following carefully established procedures for break-down of station and cleaning of equipment is **MANDATORY**. Pay close attention. This is a critical time cross contamination can occur. (More detailed instructions in chapter four)

IT'S UP TO YOU TO PREVENT CROSS-CONTAMINATION!!

Infection Control

Bloodborne pathogens, such as bacteria and viruses are present in blood and bodily fluids and can cause disease in humans. Many individuals carry blood borne infections, without displaying recognizable symptoms of illness. A tattoo studio is open to exposure with such infections through direct contact, in-direct contact and airborne transmission. To prevent the spread of infectious diseases and protect ourselves and our clients we implement preventive procedures.

Tattoo professionals use rules known as standard precautions (formerly, universal precautions) to prevent the spread of illnesses during tattooing. These precautions are part of the Bloodborne Pathogens Rule issued by the U.S. Environmental Protection Agency (EPA). The same rules apply to hospitals and doctor's offices.

GENERAL SANITATION PRACTICES

In the studio:

- Always clean and properly ventilated.
- Non-porous, washable walls, floor and floor coverings.
- Work stations should stay clean, including floor. (Stools are often rolled around in dripped ink spots and cause build up on wheels and messy marks on floor.)
- All plumbing fixtures should be properly installed.
- Continuous hot and cold running water, easily accessible to artist.
- The tattoo area should never be used for cooking, sleeping or living quarters.
- The studio should be kept free of rodents and insects.
- Restrooms should be kept in a sanitary condition and provided with hot and cold running water, liquid soap, paper towels and toilet paper.
- Contaminated waste material, such as paper towels, dropped on the floor should be removed from the floor without delay, deposited in trash and gloves immediately changed.
- Studio should have good lighting. Bacteria have a more difficult time living in continuous light.

General Sanitation PRACTICES for the artist

- DO NOT tattoo when you are sick!
- Wear clean clothes and have good hygiene. Keep nails clean.
- Wash or sanitize hands before and after treating each client, after removing gloves, after eating, after using the restroom and as required by your health licensing agency.
- Take care NOT TO TOUCH eyes, nose, mouth, hair, glasses or clothes with gloved hands!!
- Keep your hair, sleeves and jewelry away from contaminated area.
- Wash or sanitize hands thoroughly and often.
- Remove rings, bracelets and watches before donning gloves.
- Inspect hands for cuts or sores and cover them with bandages.
- Remove hang-nails and keep nails short to prevent punctures to gloves.
- Check gloves frequently for tears during tattooing.
- Refrain from tattooing if you have lesions, dermatitis or allergic reactions.
- Remove contaminated gloves and re-glove to dispense additional ink during middle of procedure.
- Wash or sanitize hands after handling financial transactions. Money and credit/debit cards can harbor bacteria.

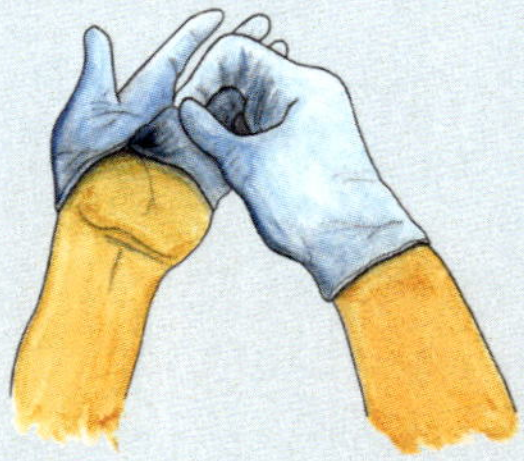

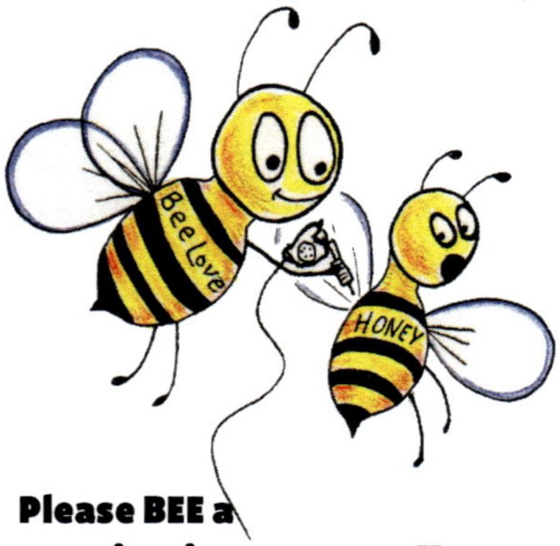

Please BEE a conscientious tattooer!!

Standard Precautions

Standard precautions are a set of basic infection prevention practices, adopted by the Centers for Disease Control (CDC) intended to prevent transmission of infectious diseases from one person to another. Because we do not always know if a person has an infectious disease, standard precautions are applied to every person, every time to assure that transmission of disease does not occur.

Standard precautions are based on the premise that all blood, bodily fluids, secretions, excretions, mucous membranes, non-intact skin or soiled items are potentially infectious. These practices, while mainly adopted by healthcare providers, apply to all professions in which workers may become exposed to infectious microorganisms through contact with blood and bodily fluids. Examples of these professions includes police officers,

General Sanitation for the Tattoo Station:

- Assure everything is functioning correctly before you begin procedure.
- Confine work area (tray or table that will become contaminated) to isolate biohazards.
- Easy access to all working tools and sharps container.
- Keep decorative items on a shelf or wall away from actual working area.
- Tattoo area MUST be separated from lobby.
- Minimize visitors allowed in work area to only what you and client are comfortable with.
- Tattoo station MUST be thoroughly cleaned between each client with an acceptable high-level disinfectant.
- No eating, (other than candy, if client needs a boost) no smoking and no handling contact lenses in the work area. Beverages are ok, but only water is preferred to minimize spills.
- Tattoo station should be set up according to standard precautions and your health licensing agency.
- Anytime a machine needs adjusting during a tattoo which requires you to touch a non-protected part of tattoo machine, TAKE OFF YOUR GLOVES, sanitize hands, make adjustment, sanitize hands again, then replace with new gloves.
- Everything that cannot be protected from contamination or autoclaved must be single use or disposable.
- ALWAYS dispense products in the most sanitary way. For example, use a tongue depressor to scoop petroleum jelly out of the jar.

General Sanitation Practices for the Tattoo procedure:

- Be aware of everything you touch during a tattoo.
- Gloves MUST be removed when leaving work area.
- Needles are disposable, and one time use ALWAYS.
- All trays and other items must be disinfected with high-level disinfectant before and after each client.
- Wipe needle tube tips with paper towel between rinsing-- never blow excess water from them.
- Refrain from using spray bottles during tattoo procedures as blood and contaminates can become airborne. Dispense liquids onto a paper towel then use to wipe the skin.
- Prevent tips of bottles used during procedure from touching contaminated towels and/or rinse water. Hold tip of bottle back from paper towel at least 6".
- If plastic barriers become torn or removed during tattooing-STOP-and replace with new plastic.
- After procedure, remove gloves, sanitize hands, take picture of tattoo, then apply a clean bandage or paper towels and adhere to skin using medical tape or self-stick bandage wrap.
- Verbally restate aftercare instructions with client.
- Wash or sanitize hands again.

trauma/crime scene clean-up crews, zookeepers, laboratory technicians, and body art professionals.

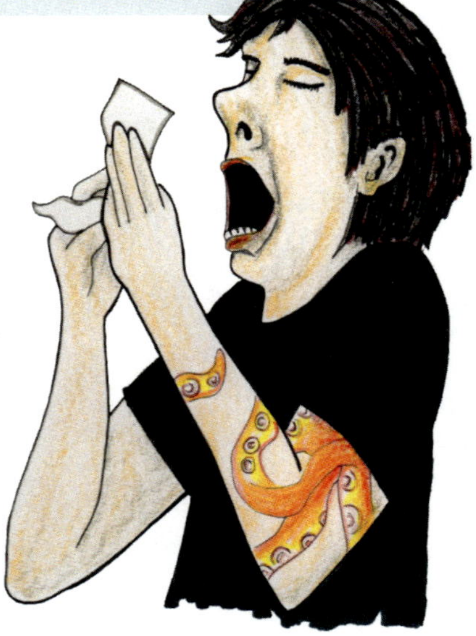

Standard precautions include:

- **Hand hygiene**: hand hygiene is the act of removing or destroying microorganisms on the hands while maintaining good hand integrity (keeping the skin healthy). Hand hygiene can be performed with an alcohol-based hand sanitizer or with soap and water. (Use soap and water instead of sanitizer at the start of a tattoo procedure and after station tear down. Also, when hands are visibly dirty, contaminated, or soiled)

- **Personal protective equipment** [**PPE**]: PPE helps create a barrier between the exposed worker and the source of microorganisms. PPE includes things like gloves, gowns, shoe covers and masks. PPE is particularly needed when disease transmission may occur through touching, spraying or splashing of blood, bodily fluids, mucous

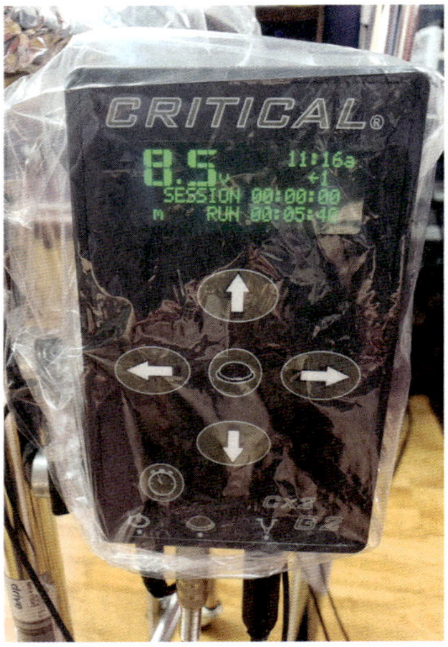

membranes and contaminated equipment and surfaces. Gloves, and occasionally, masks and sleeves will be used by the tattoo artist.

- **Equipment**: Equipment is handled in a manner that prevents transfer of germs to others and to the environment.

- **Environmental cleaning/disinfection**: Develop procedures for routine care, cleaning, and disinfection of environmental surfaces. In a tattoo studio there will be daily, weekly and monthly sanitation tasks.

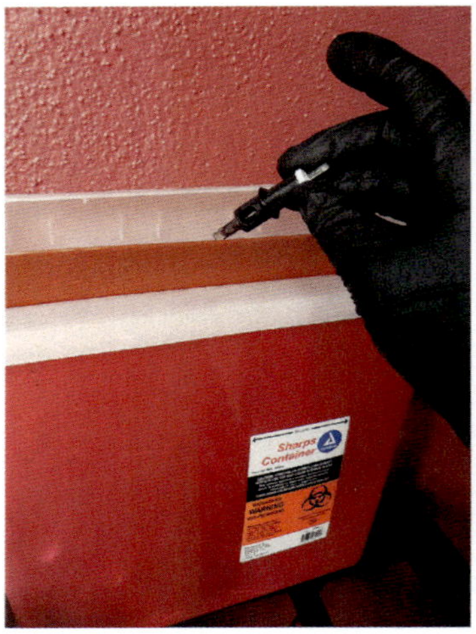

- **Safe needle practices**: Do not recap, bend, break, or hand-manipulate used needles. Use safety features when available. Place used sharps in a puncture-resistant container.

- **Spills**: All spills (blood or bodily fluids, contaminated ink or rinse water) must be wiped up immediately while wearing gloves. Absorb the spill with disposable towels then wipe down with disposable towels using a disinfectant.

- **Respiratory hygiene/cough etiquette**: Cover mouth/nose when coughing/sneezing or wear a surgical mask when necessary. Cough or sneeze into tissue first, or, during a tattoo procedure, your upper arm or sleeve—NEVER HANDS! Use tissues and promptly dispose of them in trash. Perform hand hygiene after soiling hands with respiratory secretions.

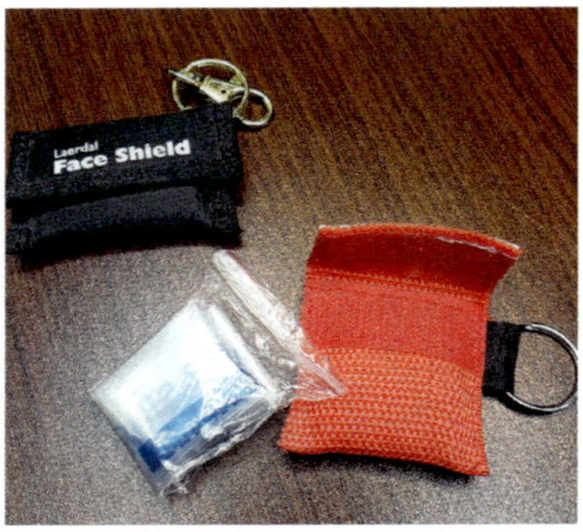

- **Client resuscitation practices**: Use a mouthpiece, resuscitation bag, or other ventilation devices to prevent contact with mouth and oral secretions.

- **Body substance isolation** (**BSI**): BSI aims to protect against the transmission of all microorganisms through contact with all bodily fluids, excretions, mucous membranes, non-intact skin and soiled items. This applies to urine, tears, nasal secretions, vomitus and saliva which you could possibly come in contact with during a procedure. These would be handled in the same way as spills, or in the case of skin contact, immediate cleansing.

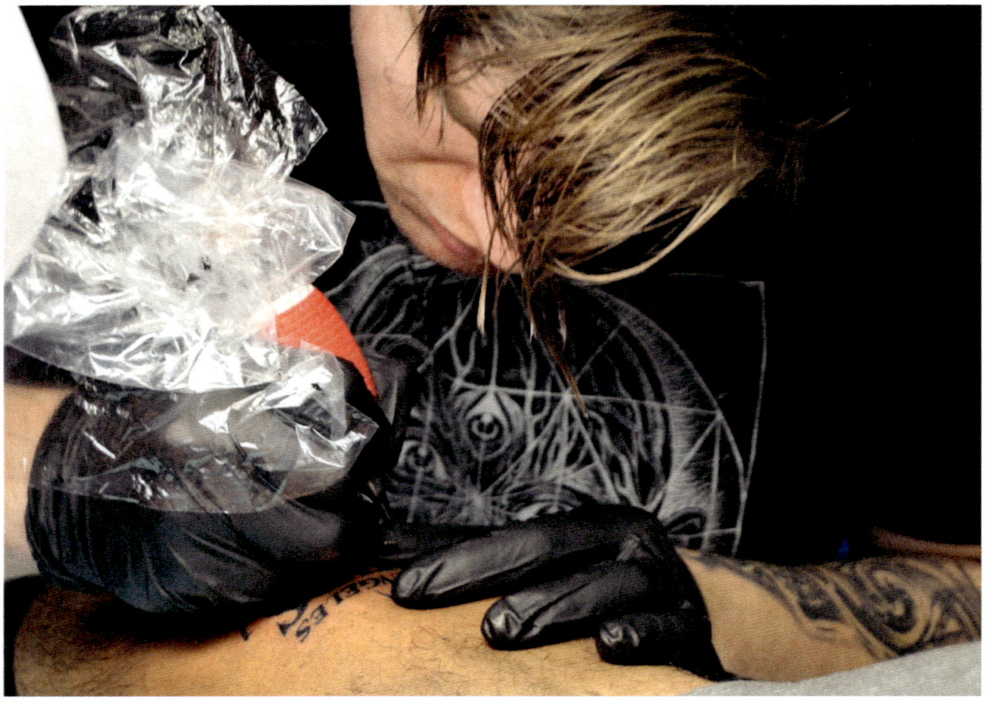

Appropriate strategies, such as the use of personal protective equipment and environmental disinfection, are practiced by tattoo professionals to reduce the risk of exposure and disease transmission. The number one most important precaution for tattooers is **hand hygiene**. Read through the handwashing technique on the following page:

Handwashing Technique

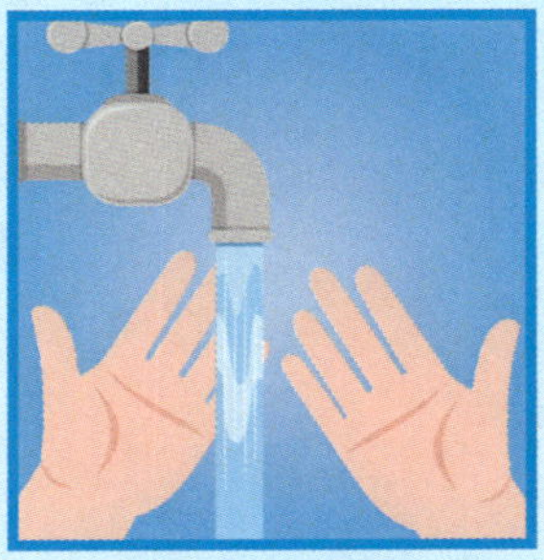

Wet hands and apply enough soap to cover hands

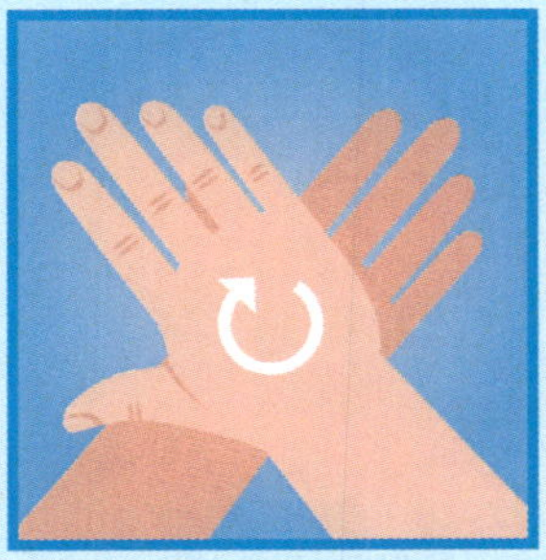

Rub palm to palm

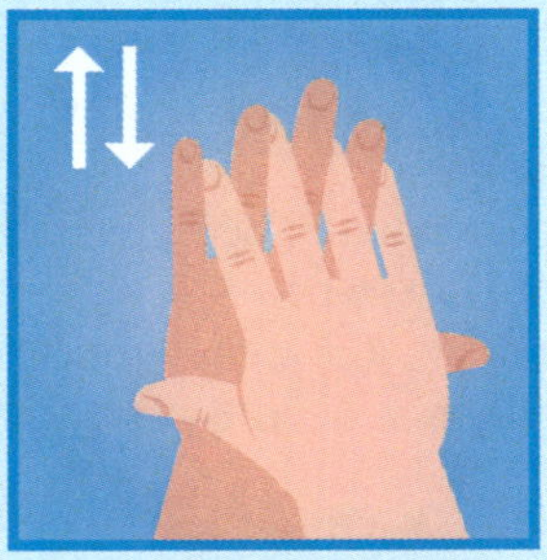

Right palm over left dorsum with interlaced fingers and vice versa

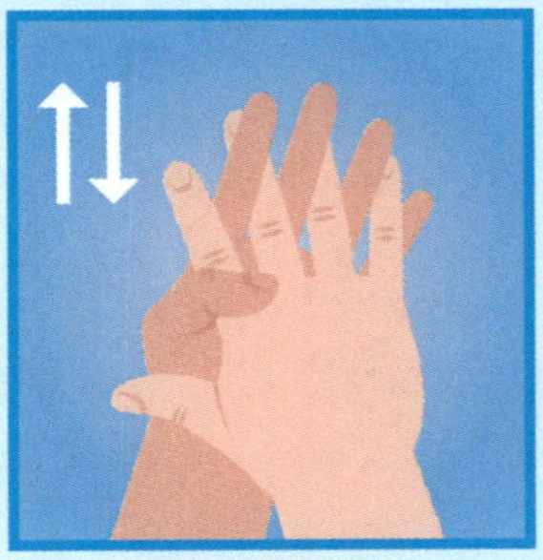

Palm to palm with fingers interlaced

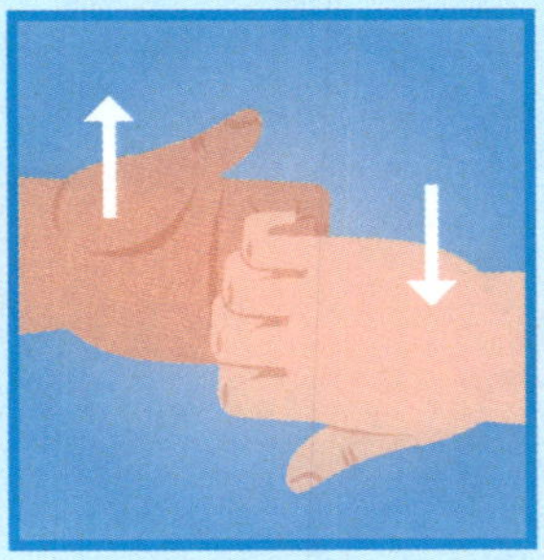

Backs of fingers to opposing palms with fingers interlocked

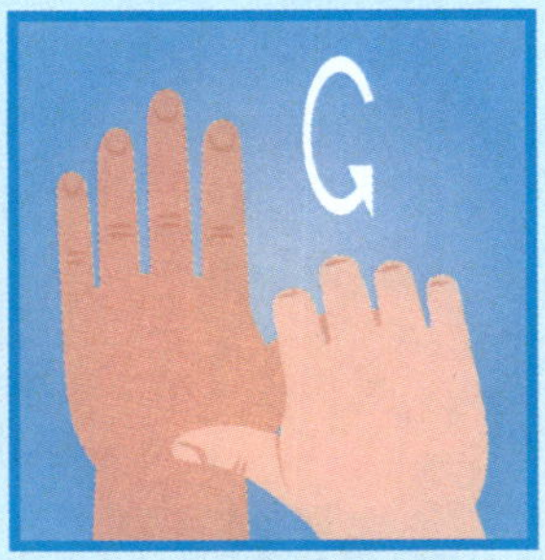

Rotational rubbing of left thumb clasped in right palm and vice versa

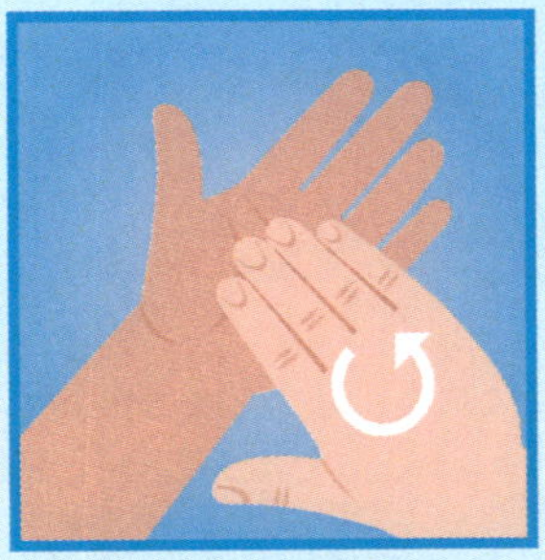

Rotational rubbing, backwards and forwards with clasped fingers

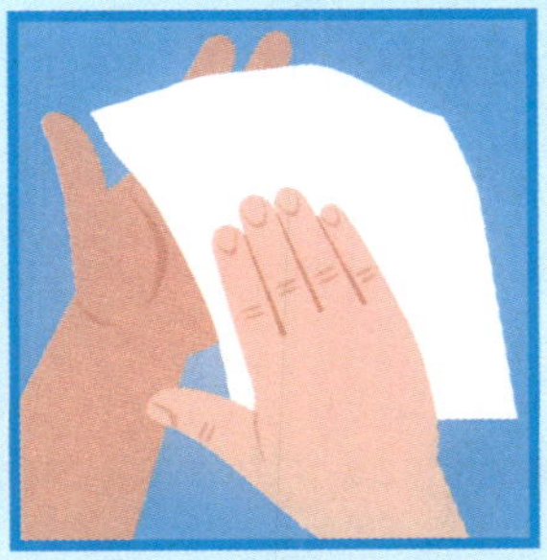

Rinse hands with water and dry well with a single use towel

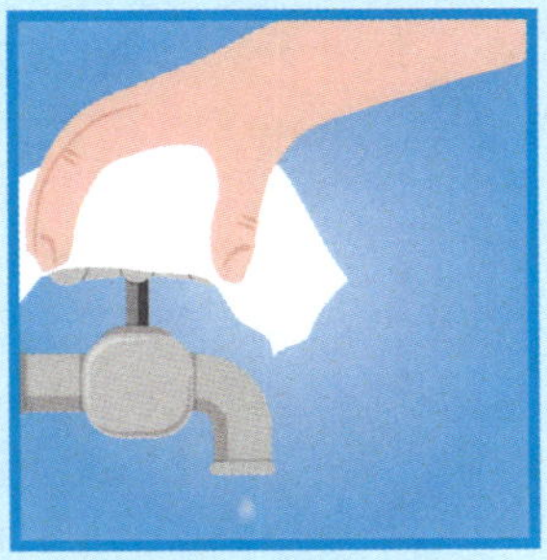

Use towel to turn off tap.

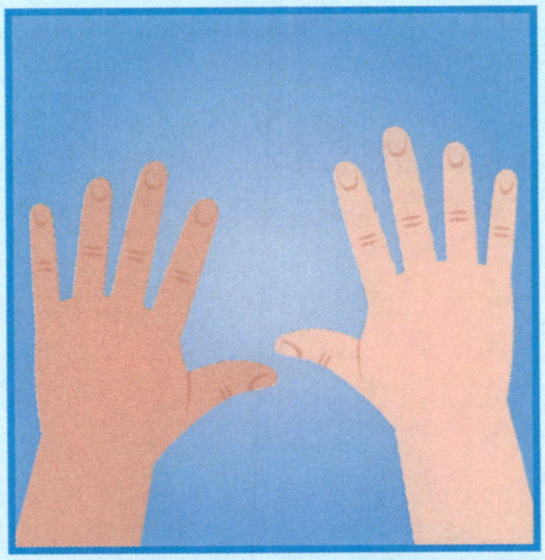

Your hands are now safe.

The CDC suggests the following questions for professionals to ask while assessing their risk:

1. What task am I going to perform?
2. What is the risk of exposure to:
   - Blood and bodily fluids & secretions, including respiratory secretions?
   - Non-intact skin?
   - Mucous membranes or body tissues?
   - Contaminated equipment?
3. How competent/experienced am I in performing this task?
4. Will the client be cooperative while I perform the task?

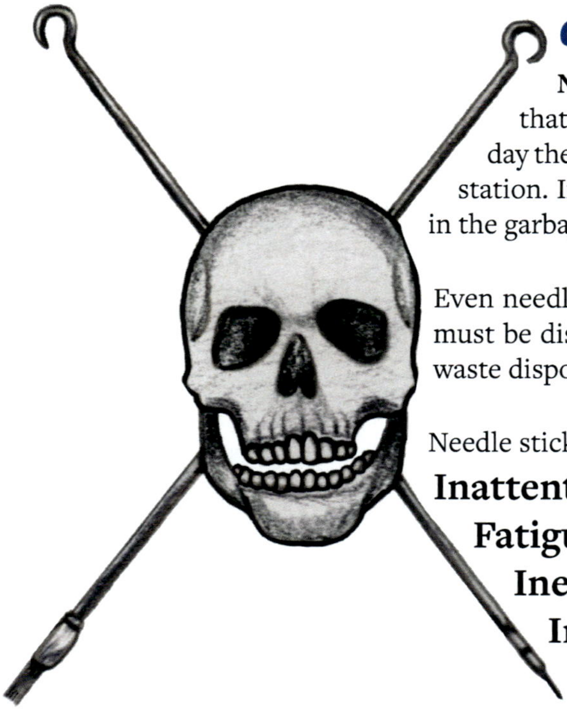

One precaution specific to tattoo profession

Needle Stick Injuries: Needle stick injuries are wounds caused by needles that accidentally puncture the skin. As tattoo artists work with needles every day these injuries can occur at any time during a tattoo or while cleaning up a work station. In addition, when not disposed of properly, needles can become concealed in the garbage and injure those who encounter them unexpectedly.

Even needle cartridges, which retract the needle fully into the plastic covering, still must be disposed of in a sharps container, as they could accidently protrude during waste disposal.

Needle stick injuries are caused mainly by these four reasons:

Inattention

Fatigue

Inexperience

Improper disposal

Source: National Center for Biotechnology Information, Needle Stick Injuries, 2004

The greatest potential risk to the tattoo artist for transmission of HBV, HIV and other bloodborne pathogens is the skin exposure to a needle contaminated with the blood of an infected person.

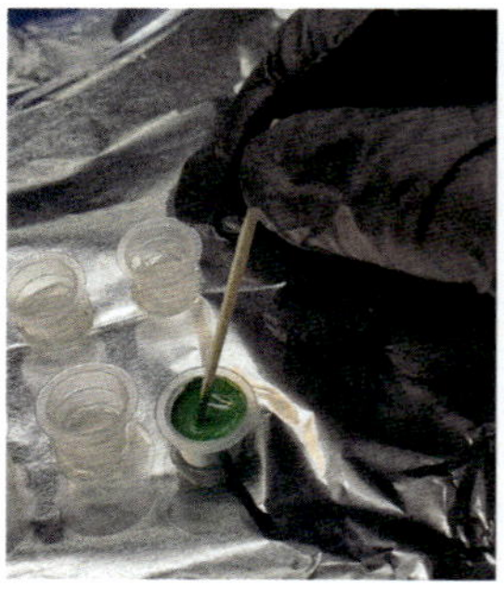

Sharps Disposal

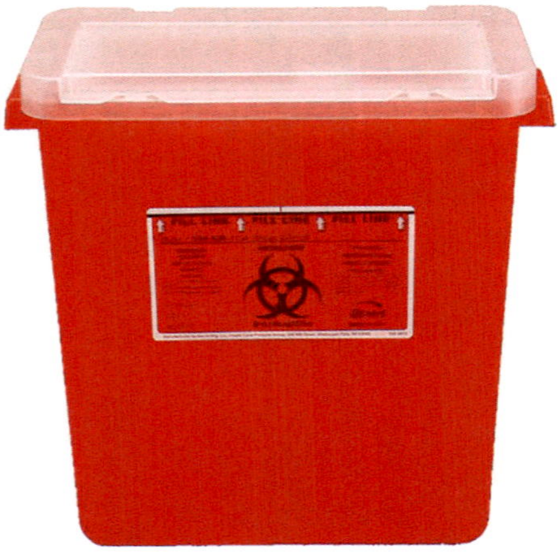

Tattoo shops generate sharps in the form of needles, razors and toothpicks. (Some health agencies state that razors can be recapped and placed in trash. Check your own area's regulations for more information.) Rigid plastic red or orange sharps containers are available from pharmacies, medical supply stores or can be ordered from tattoo supply companies online.

In most places, sharps placed in containers can be taken to a landfill without being treated (by incineration or autoclaving) if the containers are:

- Able to be tightly closed and sealed
- leak proof
- puncture resistant
- clearly identified as infectious waste
- red or orange in color

Source: OSHA's Bloodborne Pathogens Fact Sheet: "Protecting Yourself When Handling Contaminated Sharps", 2011

In addition to disposing at a landfill site that handles hazardous waste, tattoo studios may contact a licensed medical waste management company for information about pickup and disposal of sharps.

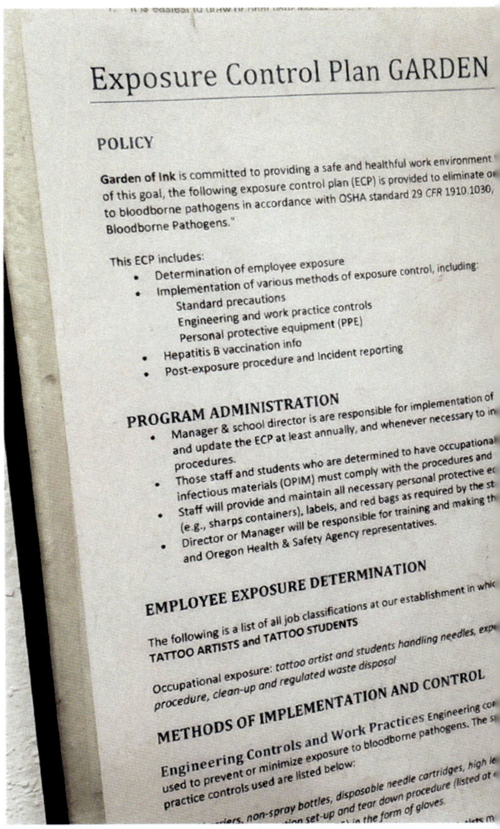

Exposure Control Plan GARDEN

POLICY

Garden of Ink is committed to providing a safe and healthful work environment
of this goal, the following exposure control plan (ECP) is provided to eliminate o
to bloodborne pathogens in accordance with OSHA standard 29 *CFR* 1910.1030,
Bloodborne Pathogens."

This ECP includes:

- Determination of employee exposure
- Implementation of various methods of exposure control, including:
  - Standard precautions
  - Engineering and work practice controls
  - Personal protective equipment (PPE)
- Hepatitis B vaccination info
- Post-exposure procedure and Incident reporting

PROGRAM ADMINISTRATION

- Manager & school director is are responsible for implementation of and update the ECP at least annually, and whenever necessary to in procedures.
- Those staff and students who are determined to have occupational infectious materials (OPIM) must comply with the procedures and
- Staff will provide and maintain all necessary personal protective e (e.g., sharps containers), labels, and red bags as required by the st
- Director or Manager will be responsible for training and making th and Oregon Health & Safety Agency representatives.

EMPLOYEE EXPOSURE DETERMINATION

The following is a list of all job classifications at our establishment in whi
TATTOO ARTISTS and TATTOO STUDENTS

Occupational exposure: *tattoo artist and students handling needles, exp procedure, clean-up and regulated waste disposal*

METHODS OF IMPLEMENTATION AND CONTROL

Engineering Controls and Work Practices Engineering co used to prevent or minimize exposure to bloodborne pathogens. The s practice controls used are listed below:

non-spray bottles, disposable needle cartridges, high le set-up and tear down procedure (listed at in the form of gloves.

You, as a generator of infectious waste, are responsible for seeing that your waste is collected, handled, stored, treated, and disposed of in accordance with all federal, state and local regulations.

Exposure Control Plan

As required by OSHA, an Exposure Control Plan is written by a studio owner and must be made and kept at each shop. This document describes the steps that will be taken to minimize exposure to blood and bodily fluids. The details included in an exposure control plan should be specific to each studio.

If you plan on starting your own shop, you can get a template to use as a model for your own plan by doing an online search: *CDC exposure control plan.* Their example is more complex than you will need as a tattoo studio but it provides a great starting point.

Underage Tattoos

Most places either forbid anyone under 18 to get a tattoo or require minors to have a parent's permission. Some adolescents will get tattoos from friends or amateurs, who use makeshift tools like pens and paper clips with little, if any, sanitary precautions. This is extremely dangerous, since proper equipment and sanitary measures protect people from disease and infection. It is our recommendation that you **NEVER** tattoo anyone under 18, unless it is with a physician's written request for medical reasons.

Cross Contamination

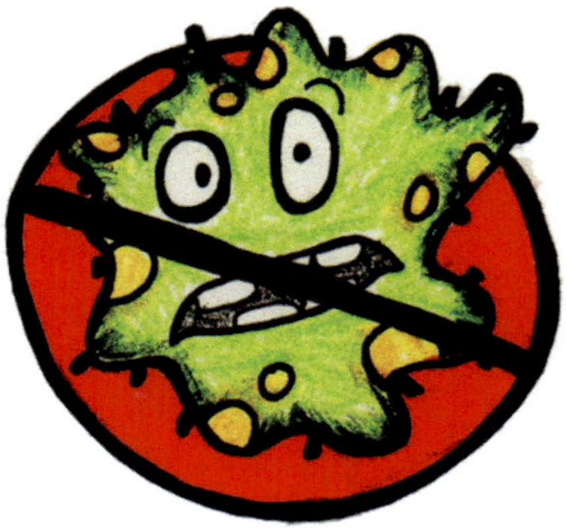

Cross-contamination is the act of inadvertently spreading bacteria and viruses from one surface to another. According to the CDC, bloodborne viruses can live on objects and surfaces for up to a week and spread when surfaces are not disinfected correctly or if equipment is not cleaned and sterilized between clients.

An example of cross-contamination:

A tattooist, while in the middle of a tattoo session, touches their unprotected lamp's surface with gloved hands. This can potentially leave bacteria and viruses on the surface of lamp. The artist later touches the lamp with ungloved hands and then transfers microorganisms to any other surface they touch. Other people can perhaps be exposed to disease by then opening a doorknob the artist has touched.

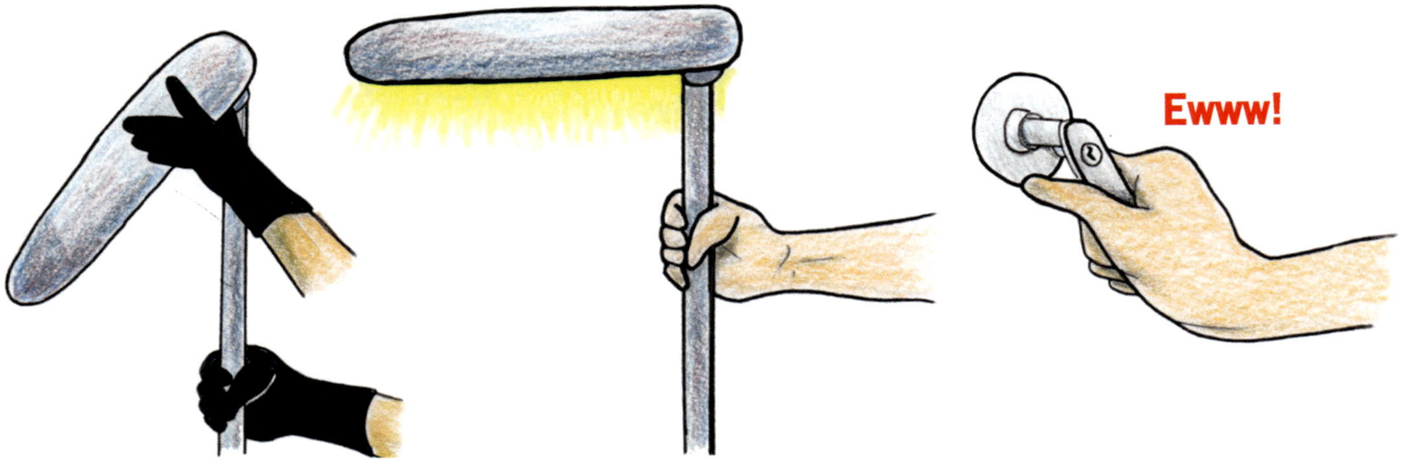

> "If you ask me what I came to do in this world, I, an artist, will answer you: I am here to live out loud."
>
> *-Émile Zola, Artist*

Hands/Gloves

Hand washing and/or sanitizing can get rid of most of the disease-causing organisms on a person's hands. When wearing gloves, heat and moisture build up. This creates the right conditions to allow bacteria to reproduce. To lessen the spread of viruses and bacteria, tattooists should wash their hands or sanitize before and after wearing gloves.

Zones

Infection control requires that a tattoo studio be considered in terms of separate areas or "zones". The zones are established by usage - reception area, tattoo work area, cleaning area, lobby and restroom. These zones should be designated as clean or contaminated.

The area in which tattoo work stations are located or sterilization of tools takes place would be considered "contaminated" zones. People entering these areas should be aware of potential cross contamination challenges.

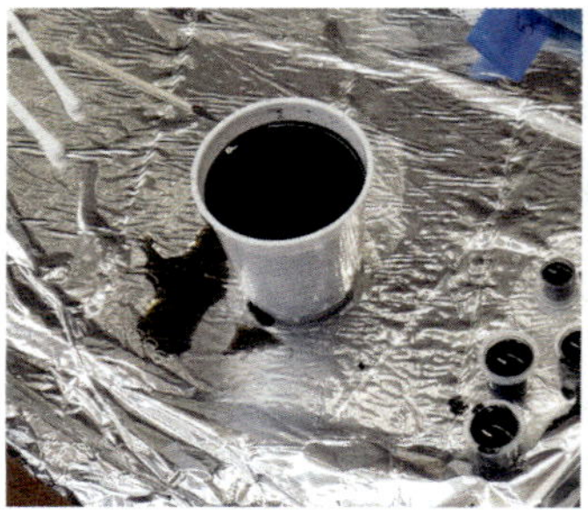

During a tattoo procedure, microorganisms can be transmitted to surfaces and survive until disinfected. Artists must be aware of bodily fluids, blood, ink and even rinse water produced during a tattoo procedure.

The tattoo work area is considered contaminated as soon as the tattoo procedure begins. The tattoo station must be returned to a sanitary condition before working on the next client.

Even while cleaning tools and equipment, such as scrubbing stainless steel grips, you are exposed to possible contaminates and must take precautions. This zone should be kept separate from the rest of the studio and only accessed by educated staff.

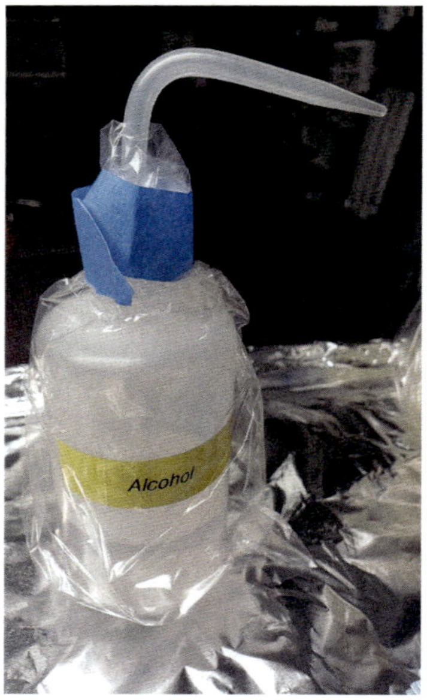

An area of the studio that has no possible exposure of contaminants would be considered a "clean" zone, such as restroom, reception area or lobby, and these areas should be kept orderly, uncluttered and sanitary. Never dispose of contaminated waste in a trash-can that is in a clean zone.

Reusable vs Disposable

Items that will be re-used, such as grips, tubes or needle bars, should be made of stainless steel and be cleaned and sterilized after each use. Disposable items should be used whenever possible. For example: disposable ink cups, razors, cord covers, paper towels and furniture barriers. Equipment or tools that are not disposable and cannot be sterilized must be covered with adequate barriers to prevent contamination.

Surfaces and Objects

Surfaces, such as work tray and tattoo furniture, that may not have been adequately covered, MUST be cleansed of ink or dirt and then disinfected after use and allowed to dry between clients. Follow the directions on your chosen disinfectant and allow adequate time for the solution to do its job.

After the Session

Following tattoo procedure, instruments that are to be sterilized should be stored in an appropriate container until sterilization can be done. Other items should be disposed of safely in trash, double bagged, and work station brought back up to clean and sanitary condition. Hands should be washed with soap and water or sanitized as soon as gloves are removed.

As tattooers we are responsible for ensuring our clients are safe from potential contamination by observing proper methods of infection control. In doing so, we also protect ourselves from disease and illness.

Note:
Double Bagged means the procedure trash will be placed in a second garbage can, with a trash bag, that is designated for contaminated waste.

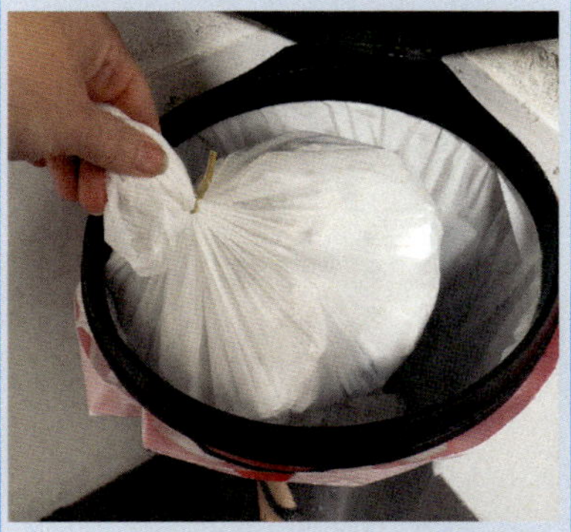

FOR THE LOVE OF GLOVE!

Besides handwashing, gloves are the single most effective tool in preventing cross contamination for a tattoo artist. These little thin skin coverings will become a part of your daily life and you may consider purchasing stock in a glove manufacturing company!

Gloves used in tattooing should be disposable, comfortable, well-fitting and single use only. You may need to change your gloves several times during a session if gloves become torn or heavily soiled. Wearing gloves does not replace the need to wash or sanitize hands as the inside of gloves can become warm and sweaty and this can invite bacterial growth. Gloves should be removed in such a way as to prevent contamination, and hands should be immediately sanitized between glove changes.

You will also need to put on fresh gloves if it becomes necessary to dispense more ink, adjust your machine or if a new needle is required.

Appropriate Glove Removing

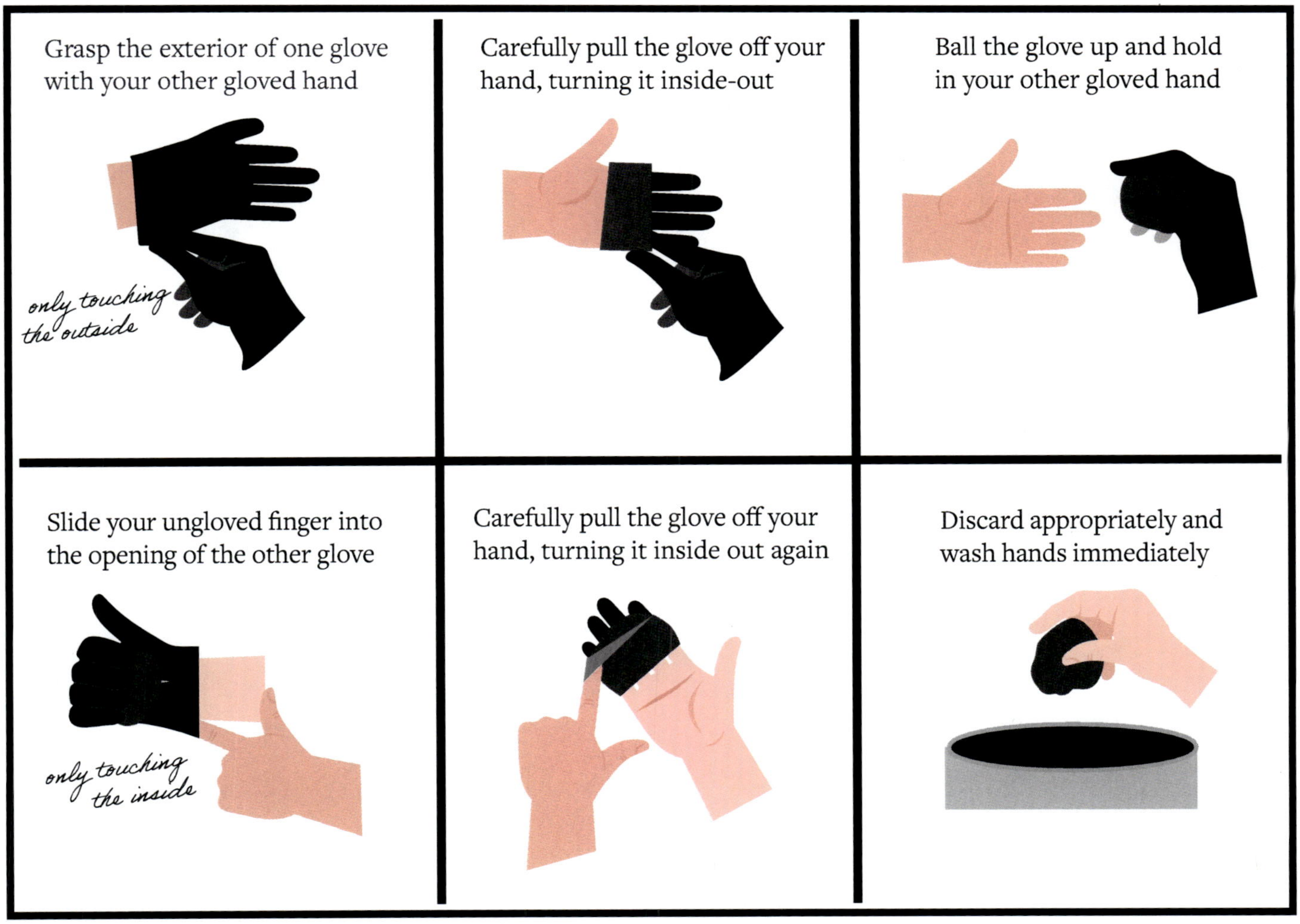

Three types of disposable gloves:

Vinyl: limited tactile sensation, more resistant to oils, solvents and chemicals. A poor choice for tattooing but a great choice for sanitation of the clean (or uncontaminated) zones of the studio.

Latex: inexpensive, variety of sizes/brands, good stretch, great sensitivity, thin. Major drawback: many people are allergic to latex.

Nitrile: made of synthetic latex, resistant to punctures, great sensitivity, allergy extremely rare. More expensive than latex, but well worth it.

Sterilization

Sterilization is the process of making an object germ-free. It involves destroying all pathogenic (infectious) bacteria, as well as all nonpathogenic bacteria, which are not harmful.

Sterilization is required if the tattoo artist will be using equipment or tools that will be multi-use items, such as a stainless-steel grip, tube or tip that hold the needle. Microorganisms left on instruments and tools are responsible for transmitting infectious diseases and must be eliminated before use. Steaming or chemical cleaning using an autoclave is one of the most effective methods of sterilization in the practice of tattooing.

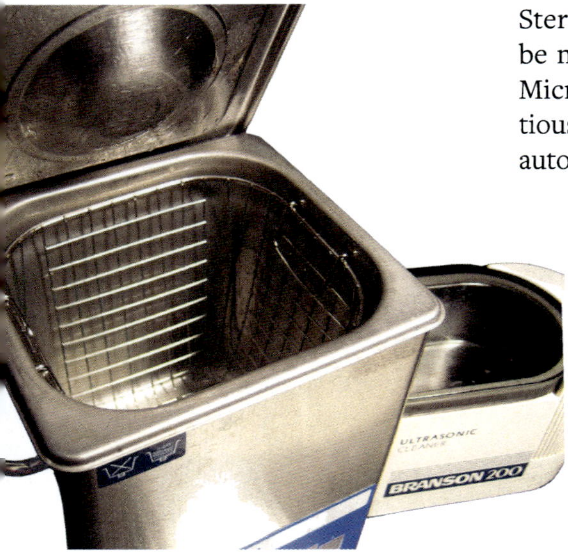

Ultrasonic Cleaner

Ultrasonic cleaning is a technology that uses high frequency sound waves to agitate water and detergent or special cleaning enzymes that act on soiled surfaces.

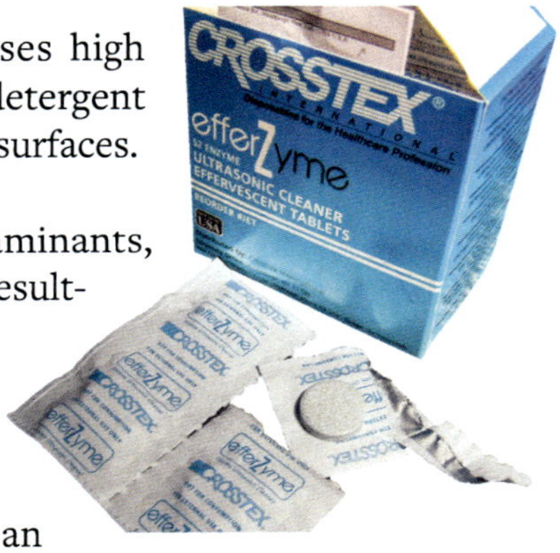

High pressure and gas bubbles agitate contaminants, effectively dislodging them from the surface resulting in a superior micro cleansing.

Tattoo equipment, such as tubes, often get clogged with ink and blood and are hard to clean. After a manual scrubbing, with a variety of brushes, using an ultrasonic cleaner is extremely helpful in getting a deeper clean with less effort.

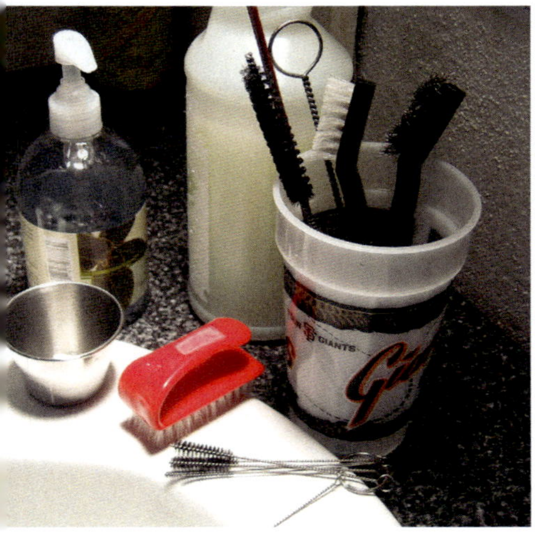

The Autoclave

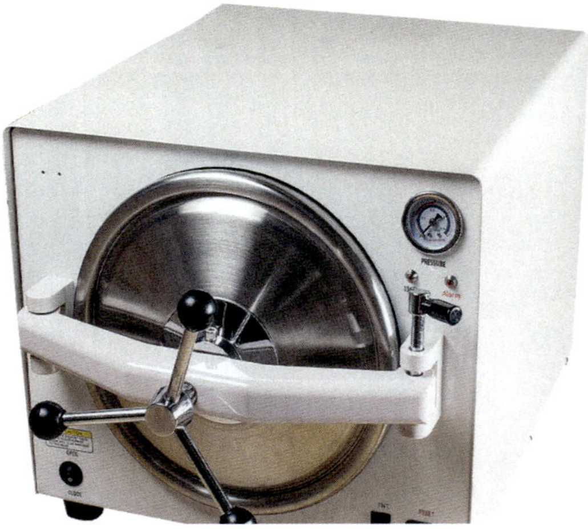

There are several types of sterilization equipment: steam sterilizers (autoclaves), dry heat sterilizers, chemical vapor sterilizers, and glass bead sterilizers. We will discuss the steam autoclave, which is the one typically used in tattoo studios.

The steam autoclave is an airtight chamber, filled with distilled water, which creates pressurized steam at a temperature of 250 + degrees F. The steam effectively sterilizes instruments left in the chamber at temperature

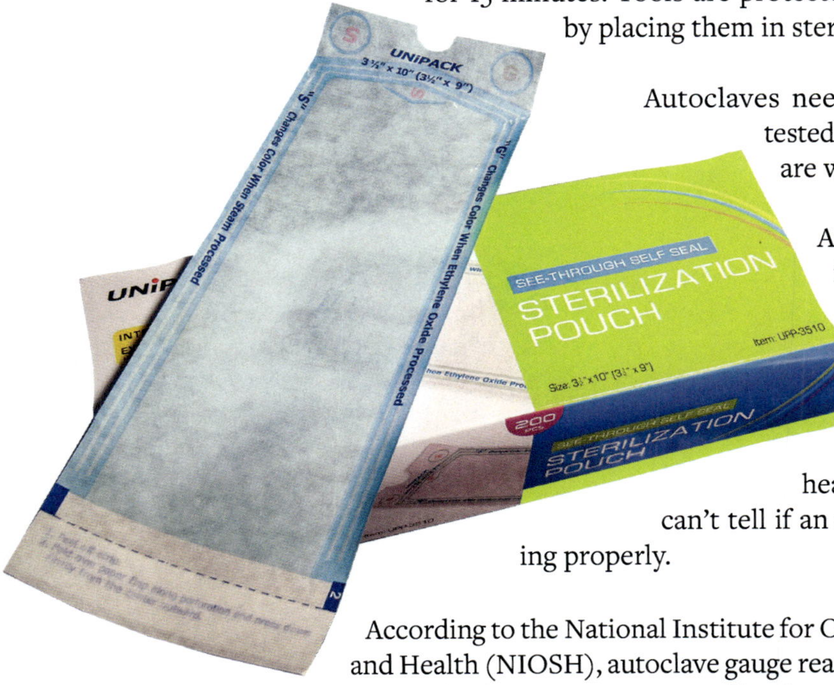

for 15 minutes. Tools are protected from corrosion by placing them in sterilization pouches.

Autoclaves need to be regularly tested to ensure that they are working properly.

An indicator strip is typically built in to the sterilization pouch and it changes color to show that the pouch has been heat processed. But it can't tell if an autoclave is working properly.

According to the National Institute for Occupational Safety and Health (NIOSH), autoclave gauge readings and the color change of indicator strips on sterilization packaging are NOT reliable ways of ensuring an autoclave is sterilizing correctly. Using an integrator strip with each batch will further detect if the autoclave is running properly.

An integrator strip is placed in an autoclave during a sterilization cycle. It confirms that all the sterilization conditions (time, temperature and steam quality) within each load were sufficient to inactivate (kill) a biological indicator.

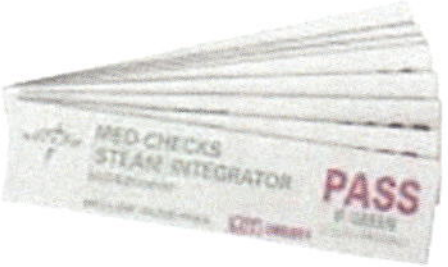

In addition, if the machine is not well cared for, it may not reach the conditions needed to sterilize reusable equipment adequately. Facility owners should ensure that the autoclave is regularly tested and serviced. Some health agencies require a special autoclave cleaning solution and regular maintenance.

Spore Testing

The CDC recognizes the risk associated with reusable equipment and recommends the use of spore strip testing. Each health agency has its own regulations regarding the use of sterilization equipment. Whether a tattoo studio is REQUIRED by law to perform routine spore testing or not, it should be a part of their standard operating procedure if they use an autoclave.

A spore strip is a small piece of filter paper that is impregnated with thousands of bacterial spores. The strip is sealed in a permeable glassine envelope and is used to monitor the effectiveness of an autoclave sterilizer. When run through a sterilization cycle, if the spores are destroyed, any potential pathogens on the items being sterilized have also been destroyed.

After the sterilization cycle has been completed, the test is mailed off to an independent testing company to check if the autoclave is functioning properly. If the spores are not alive, the test is NEGATIVE. In this case, negative is the desired result. If the test result is positive growth, indicating a sterilization failure, the business is contacted immediately and informed of a problem with the sterilizer.

History Note:
The autoclave was invented by Charles Chamberland in 1884. The term autoclave is French, and is derived from the Greek word auto, or automatic, and the Latin word clavis, which means key - hence the term "automatic lock," an important feature of an autoclave. As the cycle begins, the sterilizer automatically locks shut to prevent the door from opening accidentally when the pressure rises.

Source:
Vivian Tieu, "History of the Autoclave", Prezi.com, September 2013

Note:
Although an AUTOCLAVE is essentially like a large pressure cooker, kitchen pressure cookers do not reach the temperature or pressure required to effectively kill all blood borne pathogens. Professional sterilizers are designed specifically for killing bacteria, fungi and viruses.

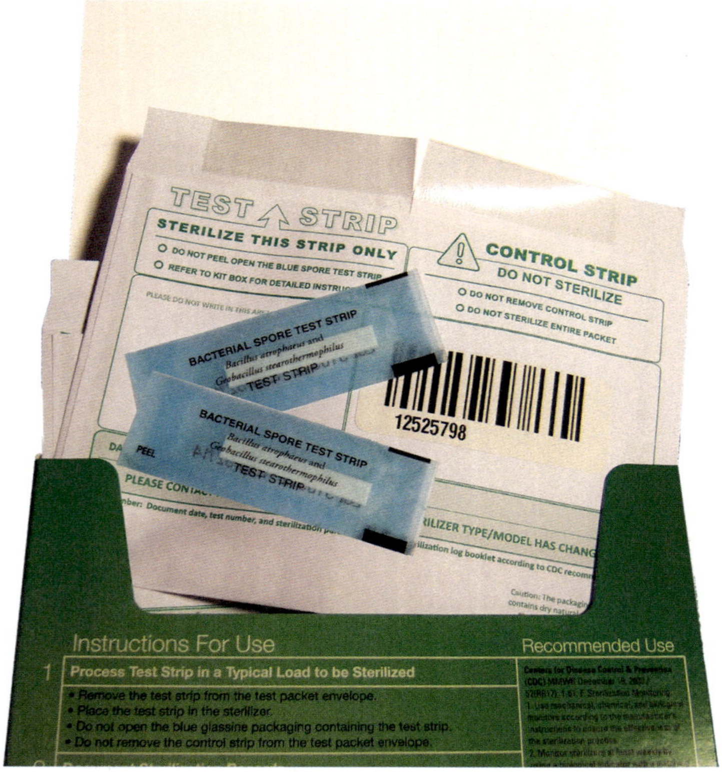

The autoclave should not be used until the problem is corrected. The testing should be done on a routine basis, usually monthly or even weekly in a busy shop. If your studio schedules routine testing, the lab usually provides a certificate for you to display indicating your current participation.

Expect that potential clients may ask to see documentation that sterilization equipment has successfully passed a spore strip test. The tattoo studio should willingly provide these records for review.

Make some clear decisions about how you will handle these safety issues. Many artists choose to use all disposable products simply because it is easier, more efficient and less risky.

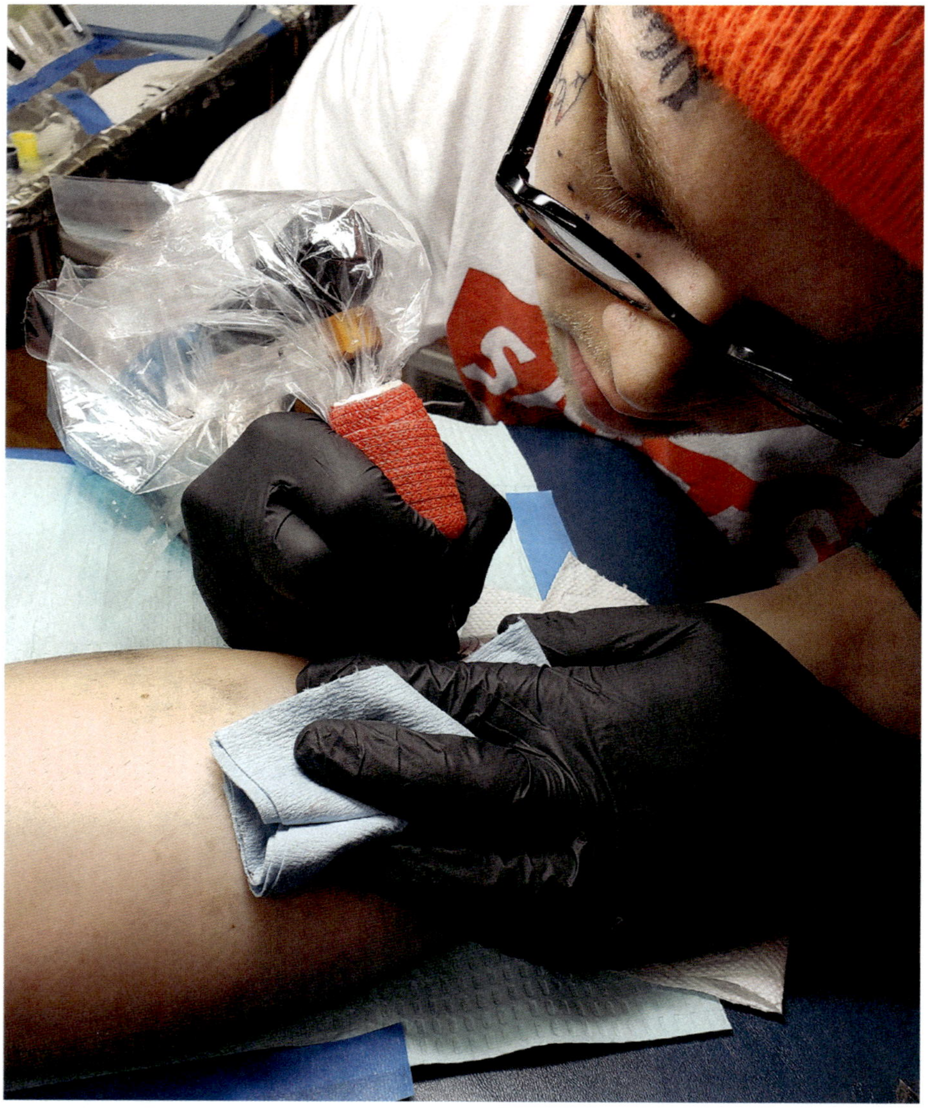

Sources:
Infection Control,cdc.gov/infectioncontrol/basics/standard-precautions.html, 2017
Bloodborne Pathogens, https://www.osha.gov/SLTC/bloodbornepathogens, 2017
Glove Use Information PDF, World Health Organization, (c) 2019
Zones in a Tattoo Shop, Eikon Device Magazine, May 1997
Living Canvas: Your Total Guide to Tattoos, Piercings, and Body Modification, by Karen Hudson, (c) 2009

Chapter Two Highlights

- **Sanitation is the application of measures to promote public health and prevent the spread of infectious diseases.**
- **A disinfectant is a substance having the power to destory bacteria.**
- **Sharps is a medical term for devices with sharp points or edges that can puncture or cut skin.**
- **Consider using an environmentally friendly high-level disinfectant.**
- **Following carefully established procedures for break-down of a tattoo station and cleaning equipment is MANDATORY.**
- **Tattoo profesionals use rules known as standard precautions to prevent the spread of illness during tattooing.**
- **Hand hygiene is the act of removing or destroying microorganisms on the hands while maintaining good hand integrity.**
- **Refrain from using spray bottles during tattoo procedures as blood and contaminates can become airborne.**
- **Needle stick injuries are caused mainly by inattention, fatigue, inexperience, and improper disposal.**
- **Sharps containers are red or orange in color.**
- **Bloodborner viruses can live on objects and surfaces for up to a week.**
- **Besides handwashing, gloves are the single most effective tool in preventing cross contamination for a tattoo artist.**
- **Sterilization is required if the tattooer will be using equipment or tools that will be multi-use items, such as stainless steel grips.**
- **If a spore test strip is positive, that indicates growth of bacteria and sterilization failure.**

Wisecracks:

Rule #1: the tattoo artist is always right.

Rule #2: If there is any doubt, please refer to rule #1

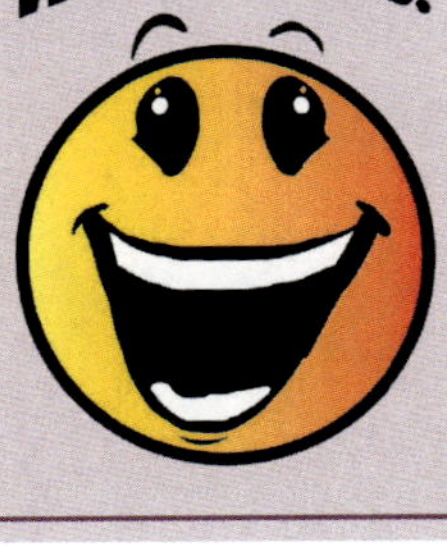

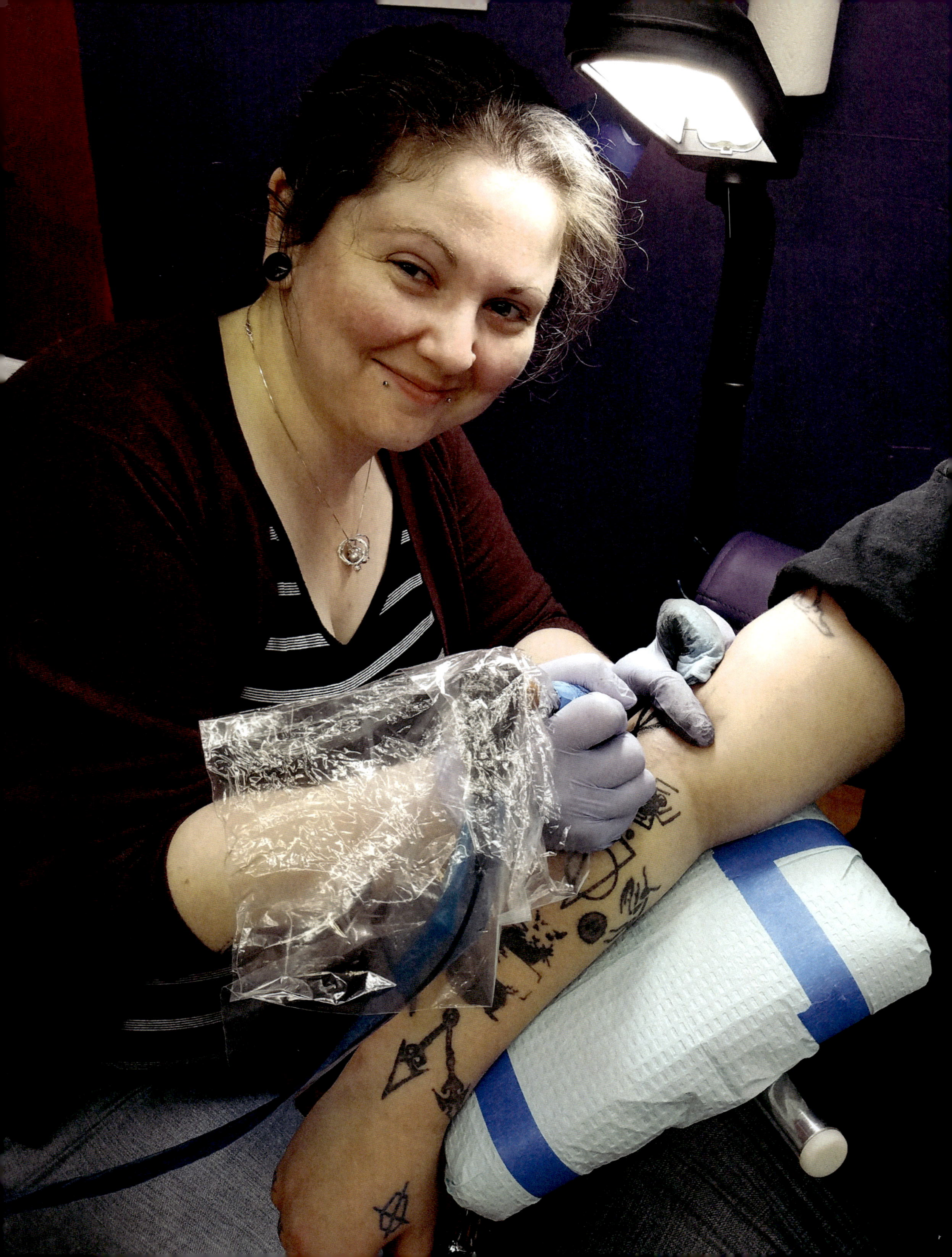

Chapter Three

Skin

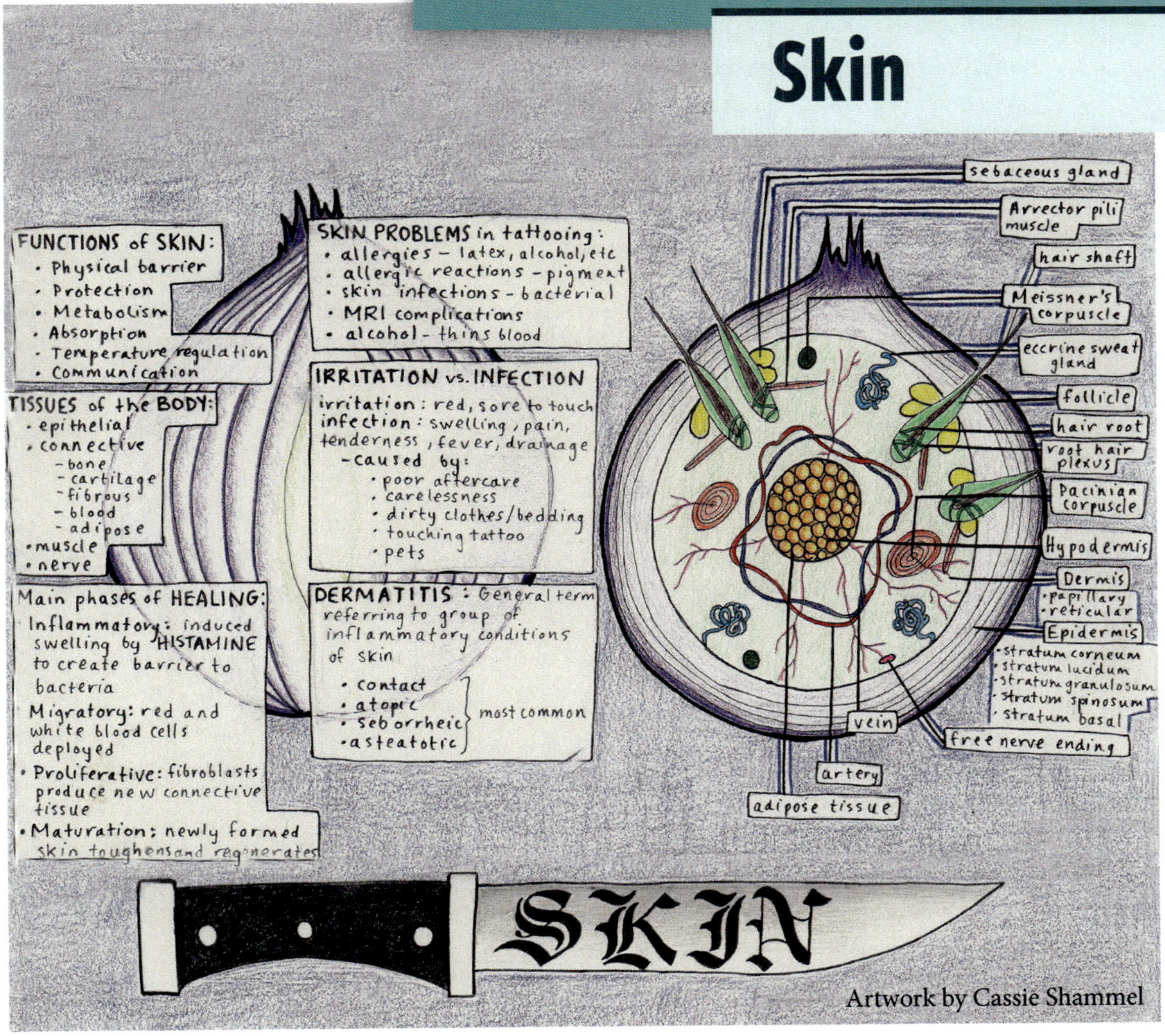

Artwork by Cassie Shammel

Skin is the protective covering of the body and is a very complicated organ that serves many functions. It is the largest organ of the body and weighs about 6 1/2 pounds. An adult is covered with almost 16 square feet of skin. Skin also makes a wonderful canvas for tattooing!

Skin's Myriad Functions

Barrier: Skin holds the other organs and tissues in place, keeping the body together.
Protection: Skin keeps bacteria, fungi, and viruses from entering the body.
Sensation: Skin helps us sense the world around us.

> "All the beauty of the world, 'tis but skin deep."
>
> *~Ralph Venning, Author*

> "Have no fear of perfection, you'll never reach it."
> *-Salvador Dali, Artist*

Regeneration: Skin repairs injury.
Regulate Temperature: Skin assists in keeping the body at a normal temperature range.
UV Protection: Skin keeps sunlight from damaging the body.
Attraction: Skin serves as a biological symbol of health.

There are three main layers of the skin:

The top layer of the skin that you can see is the epidermis, the second layer is the dermis and the third layer is the hypodermis (or subcutaneous fat layer). The thickness of these skin layers varies considerably, depending on the location. The eyelid, for example, has the thinnest epidermal layer, whereas the palms and soles of the feet have the thickest. The dermis is thickest on the back, where it is 30-40 times as thick as the overlying epidermis.

EPIDERMIS (outer layer of skin)
The epidermis is a continually renewing structure composed of different cells in five layers. As the cells move into the higher layers, they flatten and eventually die. The top layer of the epidermis, the stratum corneum, is made of dead, flat skin cells that shed about every two weeks.

DERMIS (second layer)
The dermis contains many specialized cells and structures such as collagen, hair follicles and sweat glands. Blood vessels and nerves also run through this layer. Nerves transmit sensation of itching, pain and temperature. The dermis is the layer in which the tattoo pigment is deposited.

HYPODERMIS (Lowermost layer)
The Hypodermis is the third layer of the skin and it contains fat and the larger blood vessels. This layer is responsible for regulating the temperature of the skin and body. The size of this layer varies throughout the body and from person to person.

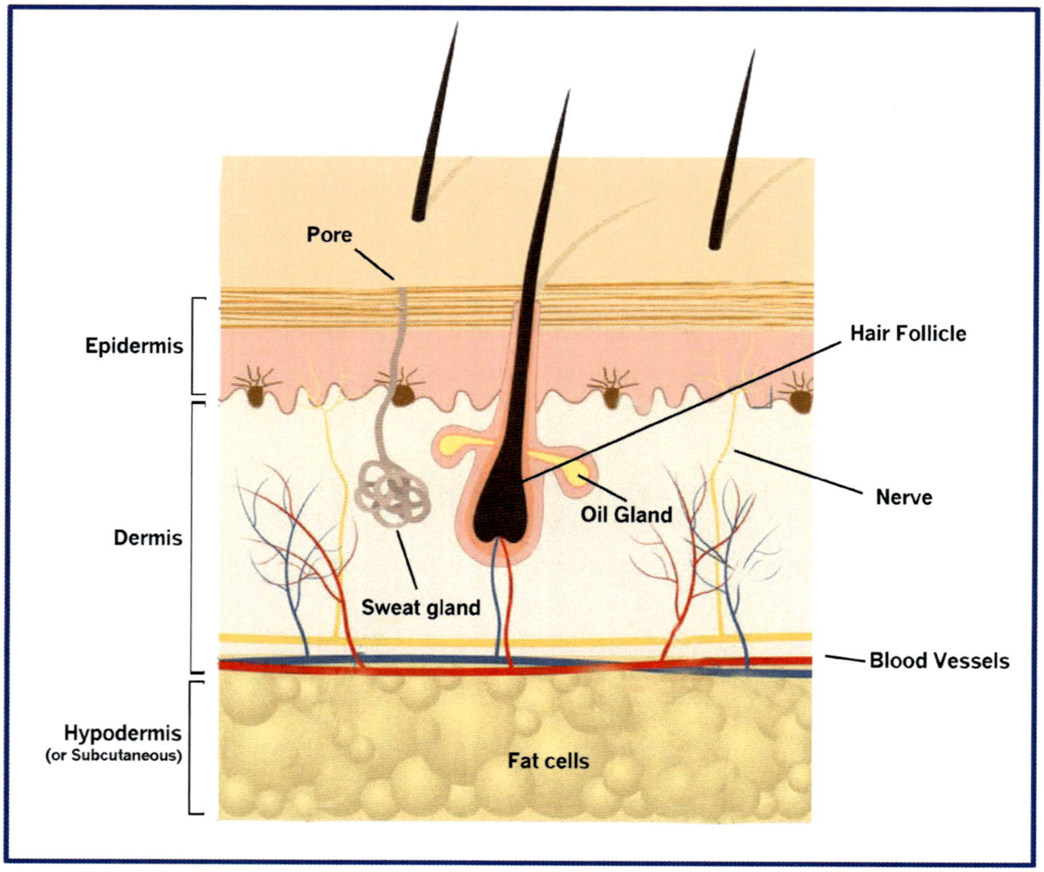

Skin and Ink

Tattoos are considered permanent, yet in reality they are affected by the mechanics of tattooing, aftercare, environmental effects, sun and aging.

The ink is inserted into the second layer of the skin, through the top portion of the dermis, just below the epidermal layer. If the ink is not inserted deep enough, it stays in the epidermis and disappears with cellular turnover. If the ink is inserted too deeply, it can blur, scar and cause "blow outs", where the ink travels along unpredictable patterns in the tissue, causing line shadowing or a bruised look.

When ink is properly inserted into the correct layer, the pigment (comparable to tiny grains of sand) is encapsulated and held in place. In normal healing, the pigment will stay in the skin permanently. Occasionally an individual may have a hyper active immune response which makes it more difficult to produce stable color. In addition, over time the pigment grains can migrate deeper into the dermal layer causing detailed tattoos to look fuzzy and diffused decades after they are completed.

In addition to placing the ink in the proper layer of skin, caring for the tattoo post-procedure is highly important to healing properly. Quality artwork is partially dependent upon proper repair of the newly damaged skin. Incorrect aftercare can result in infection that can not only damage the tattoo but overwhelm the immune system and cause more serious issues if left untreated. Furthermore, diseases such as diabetes, certain medications and even smoking can affect the skin's ability to regenerate.

American Skin Association Statement on Tattoos:

"Tattooing has been performed as a decorative art form since ancient times. Today, it is growing in popularity and is also being used as a form of permanent make-up.

Tattooing involves injecting dyes into the skin with multiple injections from one or more needles. It can take several hours to complete a tattoo and the procedure may be painful. It may also cause some bleeding. It takes about 7 to 10 days for the tattoo to heal.

Tattooing received a bad reputation in the past due to tattoo artists who neglected health and safety concerns. This resulted in outbreaks of infectious diseases and banning of the practice in some states and localities.

The two biggest risks in getting a tattoo are allergic responses to the dyes, and exposure to blood borne pathogens. The dyes are made from chemical compounds ranging from metal oxides to synthetic organic dyes. The most common illness associated with tattoos is hepatitis B, although hepatitis C and HIV are also possible. Proper disinfection and sterilization procedures must be followed. Someone thinking of getting a tattoo should check with the state or local health department to see what regulations exist in the area, such as a requirement that only new sterile needles be used."

americanskin.org/resource, 2012

Skin Healing Process

The immune response is key to the skin healing normally. The skin is designed to protect the body when there is an injury, such as a new tattoo, and the cells go to work to repair the trauma immediately. Even as the tattoo is being performed, the skin has already begun the healing process.

There are four main stages of skin's regenerative process:

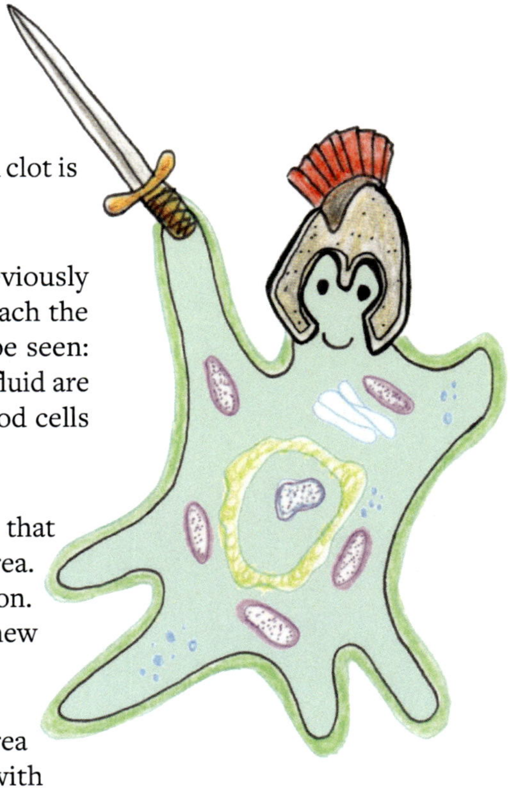

1. Hemostasis: The skin swells and vessels contract to stop the loss of blood. A clot is formed temporarily sealing the skin from invading microbes or bacteria.

2. Inflammation: With bleeding under control and the barrier secured, previously constricted blood vessels now expand or dilate allowing essential cells to reach the wounded area. During this stage, characteristic signs of inflammation can be seen: redness, heat, pain and possible edema (collection of fluids). Cells and lymph fluid are called upon to fight infection, protect the body and aid in healing. White blood cells remove dead tissue and bacteria.

3. Proliferation: The wound is rebuilt and closed by cells such as fibroblasts that knit together the skin. The cells and lymph fluid form a scab that protects the area. Other cells migrate under the scab to begin forming new tissue, called granulation. When the skin is mostly healed, the scab will fall off, revealing a pinkish white new skin layer that is slightly uneven in texture.

4. Maturation (or remodeling): Collagen fibers crosslink to make the skin area stronger. Newly formed skin cells toughen, mature and regenerate. Even with

> **NOTE**: It is important to learn about your client and consider any health or lifestyle challenges that may prevent them from receiving a tattoo or which may cause complications during or after tattoo services. Therefore, having good client records is recommended, and in some places, required. More on client records in chapter ten.

cross-linking, healed wound areas continue to be weaker than uninjured skin, generally taking at least a year to fully heal.

Irritation versus Infection

If the skin is injured it will react, whether from a foreign object, infection, scratching, rubbing or sensitivity to certain products or items. How can you tell the difference between irritation and infection in your tattoo? Clients can usually be asked a few questions and the culprit will be discovered, such as a client over cleaning or scrubbing their tattoo.

Irritation: soreness, redness and some swelling, typically caused by over cleaning, skin rubbing on skin, scratching or picking, or allergy/sensitivity to aftercare product.

Infection: redness, extending away from tattoo area, warmth, swelling, pain, tenderness, possible fever, drainage of fluid from area-- typically caused by not following aftercare instructions, being careless with tattoo, dirty clothes, client touching or allowing other people to touch tattoo, pets or children contaminating tattoo area. If infection is more than mild, advise client to seek medical treatment.

Allergies

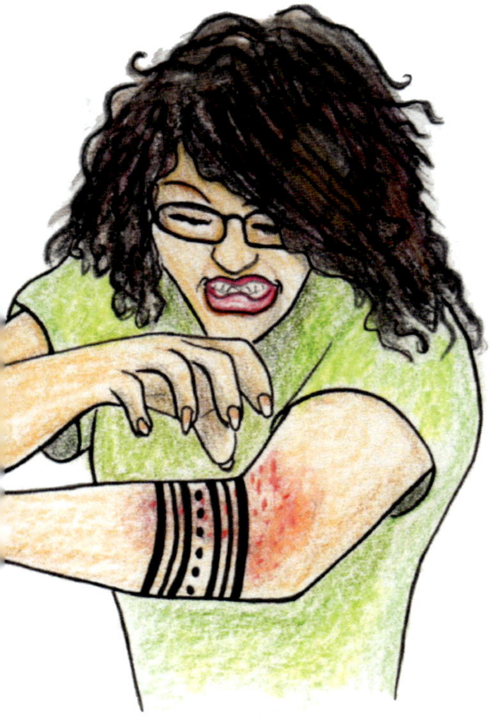

Allergy: a hypersensitivity disorder of the immune system.
Allergen: a substance that can cause an allergic reaction.
Allergic Reaction: a hypersensitive immune response to a normally harmless substance.
Histamine: chemical produced by the body that puts the body on lockdown to keep out foreign invaders.

Skin irritations are caused by a variety of factors. These include heat, immune system disorders, medications and infections. When an allergen is responsible for triggering an immune system response, the irritation is an **allergic skin condition**.

Contact dermatitis occurs when your skin comes in direct contact with an allergen.

Atopic dermatitis (**eczema**) is a chronic skin condition related to immune dysfunction in the layers of the skin. It is often associated with asthma, allergic rhinitis (hay fever) or food allergy.

Urticaria (**hives**) are an inflammation of the skin triggered when the immune system releases histamine, causing small blood vessels to leak, leading to swelling in the skin. Hives can result from non-allergic causes such as heat or exercise. Hives can also be an allergic reaction to medications, foods or insect bites. Although often uncomfortable and sometimes painful, hives and eczema are not contagious.

Allergies specific to Tattoos

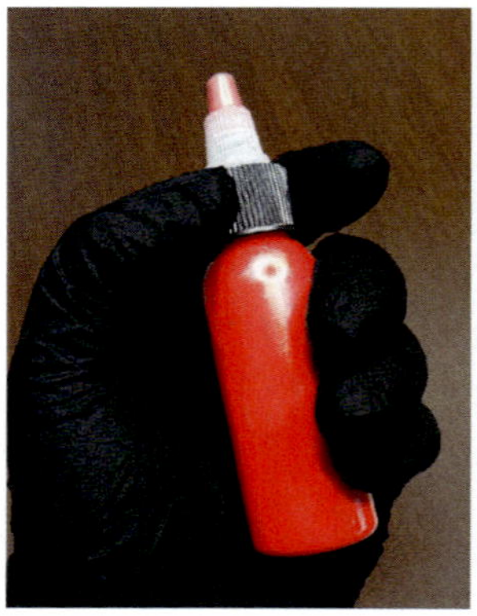

While most people have no ongoing side effects after a tattoo procedure, a small percentage of people will experience some type of allergic reaction. Often it is due to the pigments used.

Pigments

Few people are allergic to pigments, but if a client is prone to allergies, it is likely the client will react most to red ink, called a "red reaction". These people are often allergic to other things containing red dyes. Some red inks use a mercury derivative called cinnabar, known to cause hypersensitivity challenges in people.

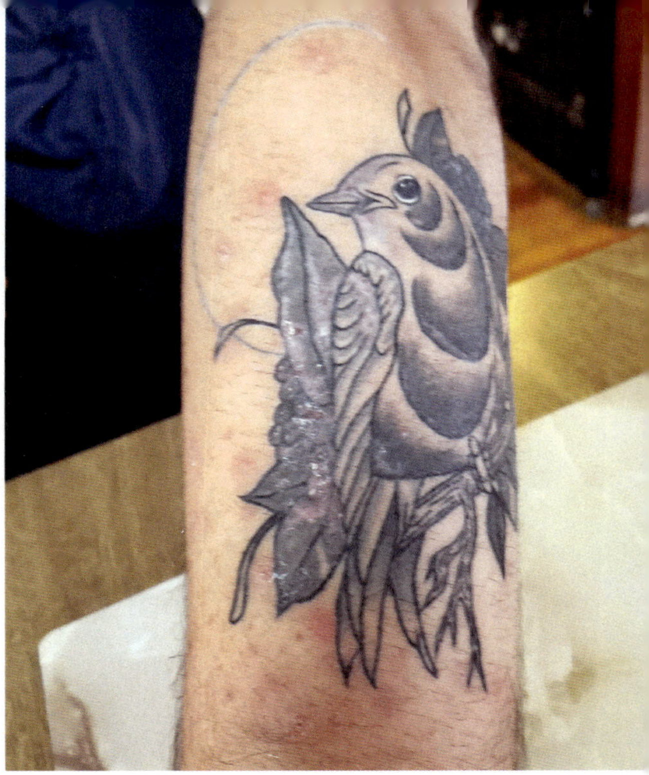

Tattoo ink is **not** regulated by the FDA and thus it is difficult to pinpoint the components which cause the allergic reactions. The practice of using mercury in ink has greatly declined because of its harmful effects. However, inks today can still cause reactions from elements such as nickel, cadmium and chromium contained in any color and/or color additives. (More on inks in chapter eight.)

Symptoms of allergic reaction

The three most common allergic reactions to pigment are:

- a red rash
- scaly and flaking skin
- inflammation

Most people have a mild reaction which can cause itchy bumps and redness. Other people have a more serious reaction such as severe scabbing and blisters. Occasionally a hyper immune response continues to push the ink out over the healing process.

Even years later some people report itchy, raised bumps in certain parts of their tattoo. Hot weather, sweating and high body temperature can cause swelling and discomfort even years later.

Treatment

Over the counter rash cream, anti-itch cream and cold compresses can be used in mild cases. If the reaction becomes more severe or doesn't clear up in a few weeks, client should seek medical advice. In extreme cases, tattoo removal may be recommended. (In addition to allergic reactions to pigment some people are allergic to soaps and ointments that are used during tattooing and during aftercare. More about this in chapter four.)

Latex Reactions

Latex gloves are much less commonly used in the tattoo industry due to the following reasons:

- Latex is a known allergen and can cause dermatitis and occasional severe and life-threatening allergic reaction in some people.
- Petroleum jelly can react with latex and compromise the barrier between artist and client.
- Tattoos heal quickly and can trap latex particles under the skin, creating complications for the client even after the tattoo is healed.

Nitrile is a synthetic rubber. Nitrile gloves provide a barrier protection equal, if not superior, to that of latex.

Skin Diseases & Disorders

There are many skin diseases and disorders that affect a client's skin and their ability to get tattooed.

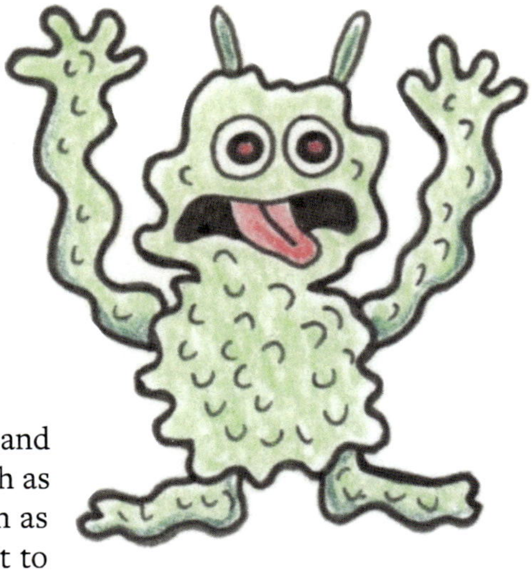

Here is a partial list of diseases and disorders:

- **Inflammatory skin diseases** such as dermatitis or eczema
- **Fungal skin infections** such as athlete's foot or ringworm
- **Yeast infections of the skin** such as candida
- **Viral infections of the skin** such as warts or shingles
- **Parasitic infections of the skin** such as scabies or lice
- **Disorders of hair, glands and vessels of the skin** such as alopecia or acne
- **Disorders of skin pigmentation** such as vitiligo or skin tags

In general, stay away from tattooing anyone that displays rashes, lesions, redness, and scaly or bumpy skin, unless they are cleared by a physician. Other conditions, such as alopecia, where the body is absent of hair, can benefit from creation of hair such as cosmetic tattooing for brows or micropigmentation of the scalp, but it is still best to have the client get cleared by a physician.

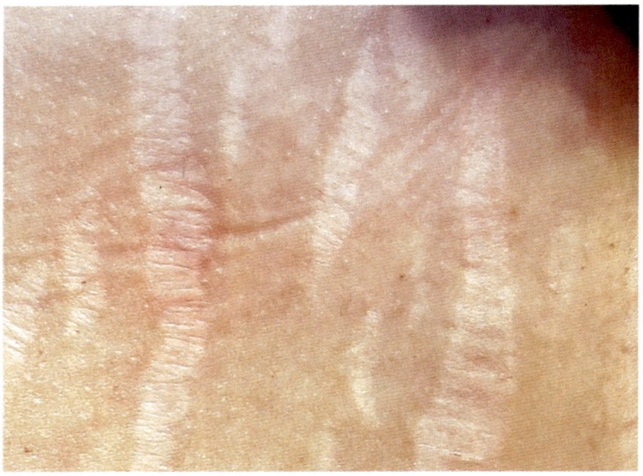

Stretchmarks & Tattoos

Stretch marks are linear scars that form below the dermis due to excessive stretching of the skin, such as in pregnancy, weight gain or rapid growth during puberty. They can also appear in individuals who do not produce enough collagen. These marks typically first appear as a red or purple line that gradually fades to a light silver or pinkish white color. Stretch marks are permanent, though they can be faded somewhat with laser surgery, chemical peels, or cosmetic surgery. They typically cannot be removed. Recently, more people have considered using tattoos to conceal or partially hide their stretch marks.

Before making this decision, artist and client should discuss the realities of tattooing over stretch marks.

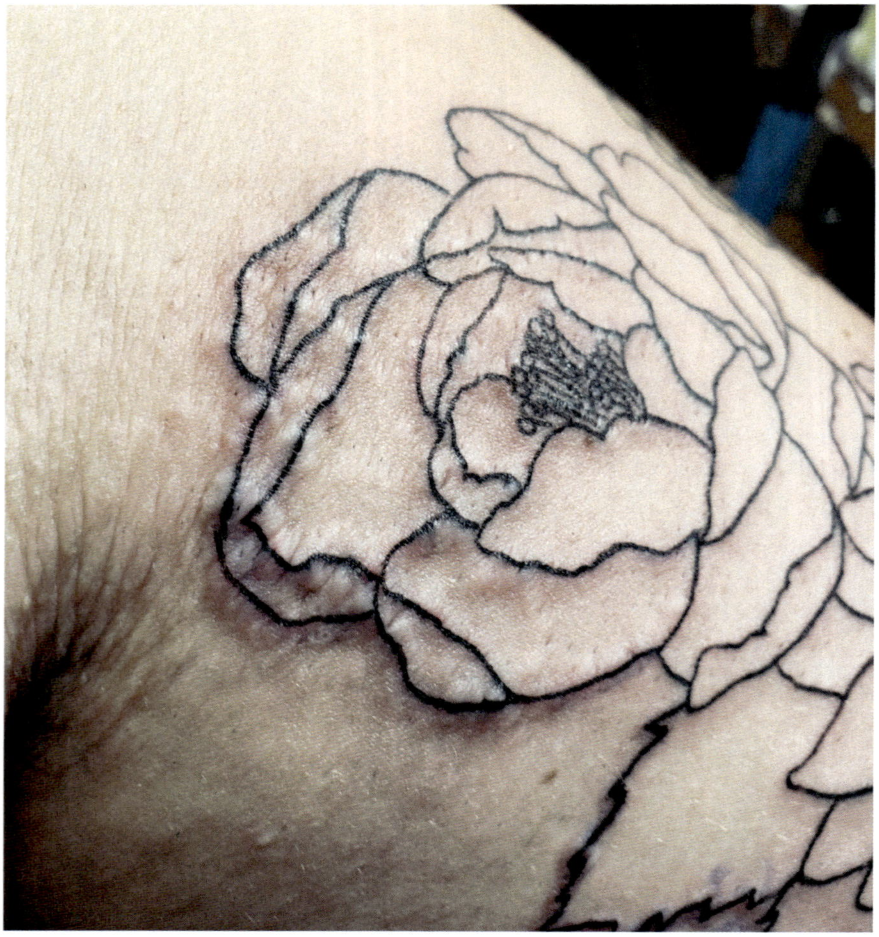

- Be prepared for it to take longer than a normal tattoo session, depending on the individual skin tone and how old the scar is. Most artists agree the scars should be at least a year old to help the skin retain the ink. In addition, the smoother the stretch mark (not raised), the easier it is to tattoo.
- Most stretched scar tissue is more sensitive than normal skin, since nerve endings are closer to the surface in the damaged skin, which can make it more painful.
- Stretch marks have an uneven, unpredictable surface, thus tattooing over them can be uneven and unpredictable as well. The more stretch marks in the area the more difficult it will be to conceal rather than draw attention to them.
- Raised stretch marks will not be hidden by a tattoo and likely will still be noticeable.
- Try tattooing a small design in the area to gauge whether it will be acceptable to the client. If the client is happy with the result, the small tattoo can easily be incorporated into a larger composition.
- Colored tattoos over stretch marks are more likely to fade or have a blotchy appearance. Black or dark ink can tend to shoot beneath the tissue and cause unwanted lines, stains or shadowing.
- It is much more challenging for an artist to tattoo over stretch marks and have it turn out successful--Think in terms of organic, flowy designs with texture versus linear, geometric, text or excessive linework.
- If your client is a woman and plans to have children, it is worth considering waiting till after childbirth to get stomach, love handles or hip tattoos.

> "If people knew how hard I worked to get my mastery, it wouldn't seem so wonderful at all."
>
> *-Michelangelo. Artist*

Sensitive Skin

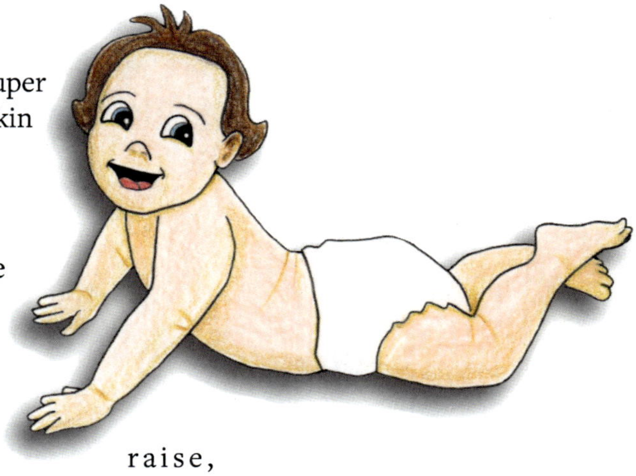

There are many different types of skin--from leathery to those with super tight pores--that can be difficult to work on, but tattooing sensitive skin is typically the most problematic.

Sensitive skin is characterized by very dry, tight skin, prone to redness, and is more permeable than normal skin. It is also more reactive to chemicals and allergies and can become inflamed and irritated. These people can bruise, rash and chap more easily than most and tend to be rather fragile when getting tattooed.

During a tattoo procedure, sensitive skin tends to turn red, swell and raise, making it more difficult to get the ink in. In addition, the use of alcohol or green soap can cause more sensitivity, and the act of wiping the skin multiple times can make it become more irritated. It is important to adjust your tattooing technique, perhaps slowing down, wiping less or more gently, using witch hazel to calm the skin, or giving the client more breaks.

In addition, people with very pale skin and freckles, and/or with reddish hair color, tend to have delicate skin and are prone to bruising and bleeding more.

Skin Tones:

When you are looking at a tattoo you are actually seeing it through the top layer of skin. Think of a color printer, printing on white paper versus color paper. The images printed will be affected by the color of the paper. The same is true for skin tone in tattoos.

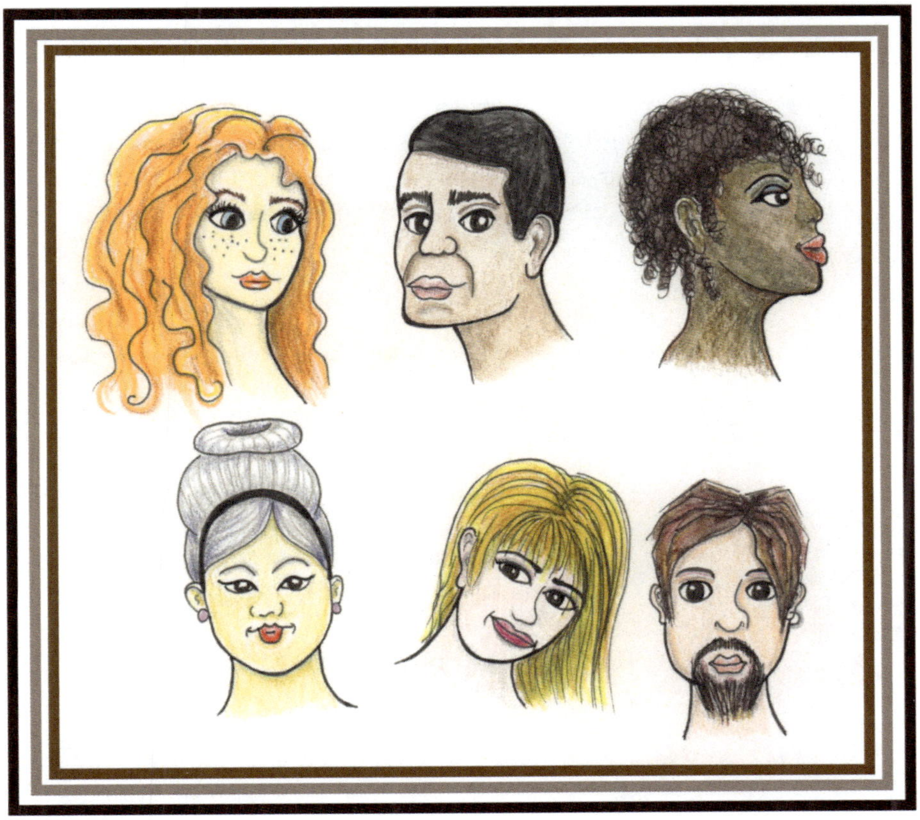

Color ink can be used on any skin tone, but just bear in mind that colors will tend to be proportionately more muted the darker the skin tone. On very dark skin the tendency is to mainly use gray shading and solid black as black work will usually show on any tone. In addition, using bolder, larger designs can help the tattoo look cleaner and clearer. Ethnic background should also be considered because even if skin appears light, people with mixed racial history may react differently to pigments as well.

Darker skin tones tend to be softer and more pliable and require a lighter touch when tattooing because scarring can be a problem. Scars on people with pale skin appear similar to their normal skin tone but in people with darker skin, scars tend to be several shades darker or several shades lighter.

In addition, darker skin tones are more prone toward producing keloids--rubbery scar tissue made up of fibrous nodules--which can become quite large, due to an overgrowth of collagen. These are not harmful but can be annoying to the client and can interfere with the overall look of the tattoo.

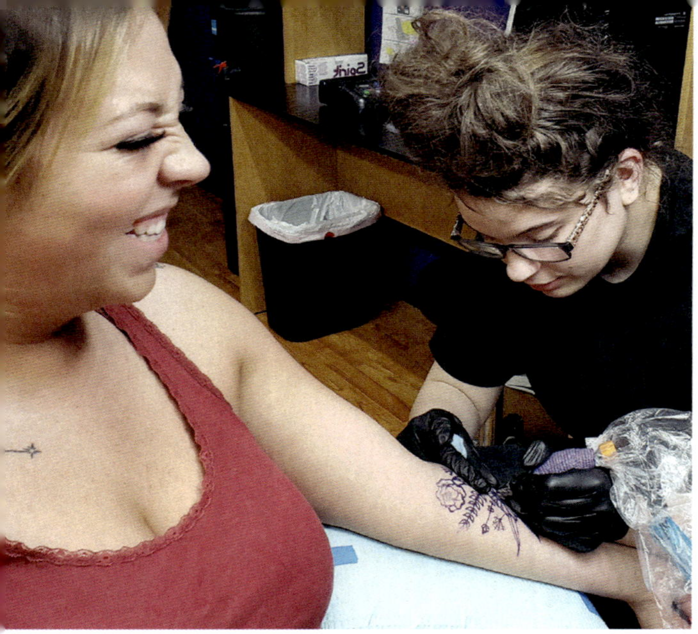

Is It Going To Hurt?

This is one of the MOST frequent questions people will ask. And the answer is yes. But the level of pain depends on the individual's threshold. If a client has a high tolerance for pain it may feel simply like being scraped or scratched. If a client has a low tolerance for pain it may feel more like stinging and cutting. The level of discomfort varies from person to person.

Some of the pain that clients experience is likely from not knowing what to expect. They approach their appointment with tension and nervousness, and they tend to hold their breath when they first get started. As soon as a client relaxes and breathes normally, the tattoo pain becomes minimal.

People getting their first tattoo go into it thinking it might be intolerable, and then quickly report it "wasn't that bad". This is mainly because our bodies release "feel-good" chemicals called endorphins, (a neurochemical) during a tattoo to help lessen the impact of the pain. In fact, according to Dr. Josh Axe, DMN, endorphins have a lot in common with prescription anti-anxiety drugs and opiate painkillers, without all the undesirable side effects, and they are a natural mood booster. This can explain why some people enjoy getting tattooed and why many people claim that tattoos are addicting.

It is agreed that certain parts of the body hurt more when getting tattooed such as ribs, underarms and over the sternum. Because the experience of pain is vastly subjective, even these general guidelines are not always accurate.

> **"When it comes to dealing with pain, two main factors are taken into account: pain threshold and pain tolerance. Pain threshold refers to the point at which a person first starts to sense pain after being exposed to a stimulus, such as the stab of a needle. Even though stimuli can be measured, the experience of pain remains entirely subjective. Meanwhile, pain tolerance refers to the amount of pain one can take without collapsing in agony. Thus the experience of pain is vastly subjective. The type of ailment, a person's mood, and stress can all contribute to the experience."**
>
> *Do women really tolerate Pain Better than Men?*
> *Signe Cane, Science Journalist August 28th, 2015*

Bleeding

Minor bleeding is perfectly normal in a tattoo, but excessive bleeding and leaking of bodily fluids can obscure the artist's view of the tattoo and can also cause the ink to thin. The machine sucks up some of the body fluid mixing it with the ink, which dilutes it and will cause faded pigment in the healed tattoo.

Causes of excessive bleeding during a tattoo:

- Alcohol before tattoo, or those who drink a lot on a regular basis
- Large amounts of caffeine
- Low vitamin K or potassium levels
- Very high or very low blood pressure
- Aspirin or blood thinners
- Drinking a lot of fluids

- Bleeding disorders
- Steroids and medications such as Accutane
- Certain foods in excessive amounts such as turmeric, ginger, curry, garlic, licorice

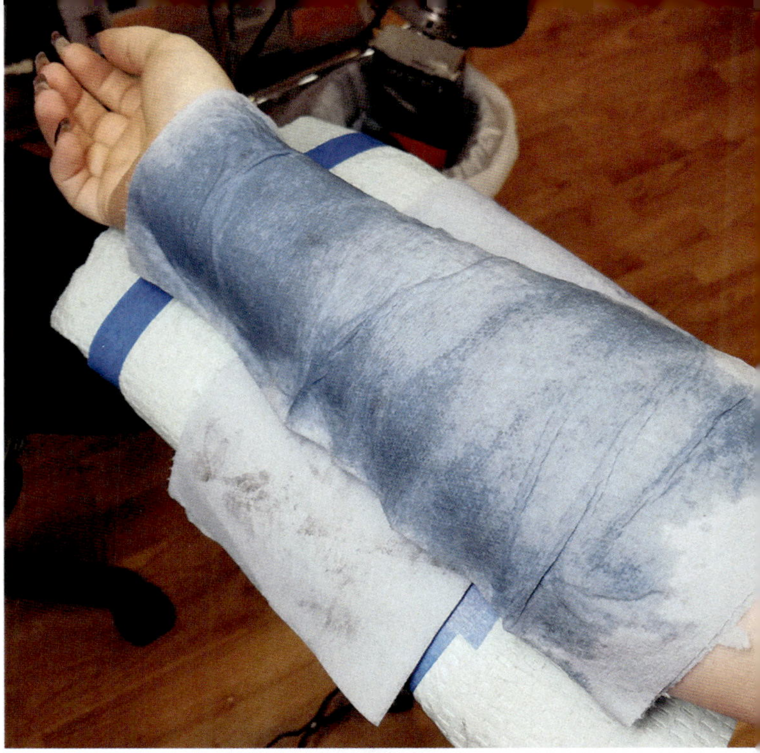

During the tattoo process you can use witch hazel, which is an astringent, to help stop the flow of blood as well as help with the pain and stinging. Soak a paper towel and set it on the tattoo for 3-5 minutes.

This also helps with calming the tattoo right before taking a photograph. In a pinch, if you have no witch hazel, soak a paper towel with very cold water and it should help slow the bleeding.

Tattooing Scars

Many people choose to get tattooed over scars to help distract the eye from what they consider unsightly marks. You may get asked to tattoo over surgery scars, childhood scars or even burn scars. As with stretch marks, this skin is uneven and unpredictable. Scar tissue takes time to heal, sometimes as much as two years, depending on the severity and the body's healing response.

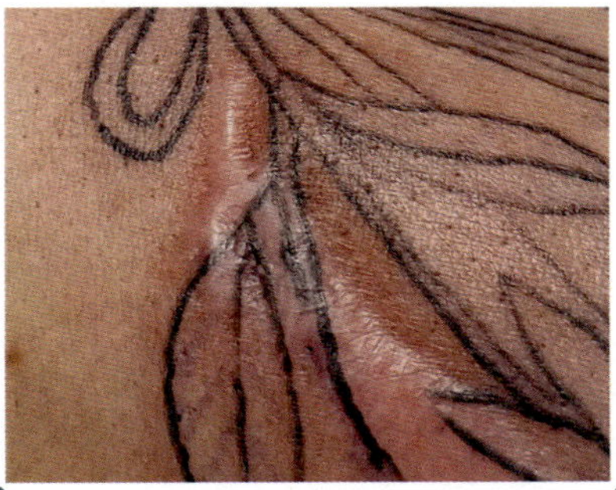

It's difficult to tattoo straight lines over scar tissue--better to choose organic shapes and a design that flows with the damaged tissue.

Scar tissue can also be very sensitive and may have nerve damage as well, so clients should be aware it will likely hurt more than normal.

In addition, scar tissue can be difficult to work with and the ink can easily blur under the damaged skin structure. The design should be carefully considered to work with the scars and not just smother them. The anatomy of the body under the scar tissue and the color, shape and size of the scars will help make the decision regarding what design will suit the client best.

Again, organic shapes with texture usually work better than geometric shapes, text and precision-lined designs.

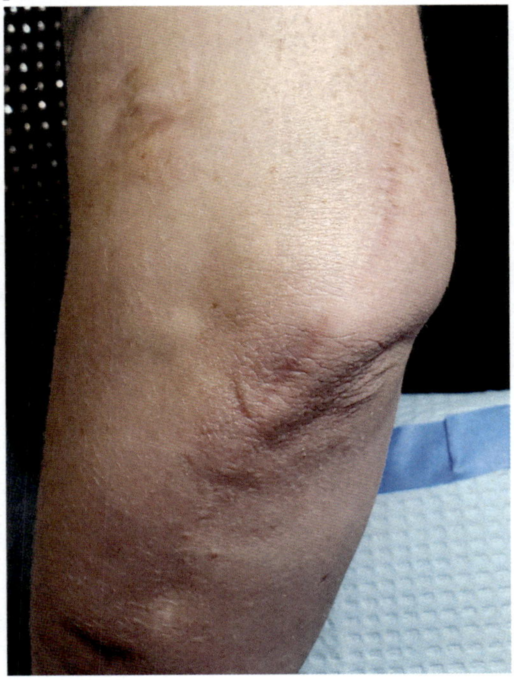

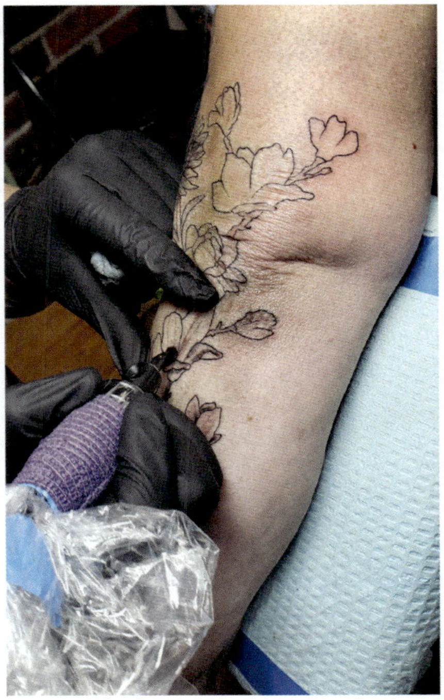

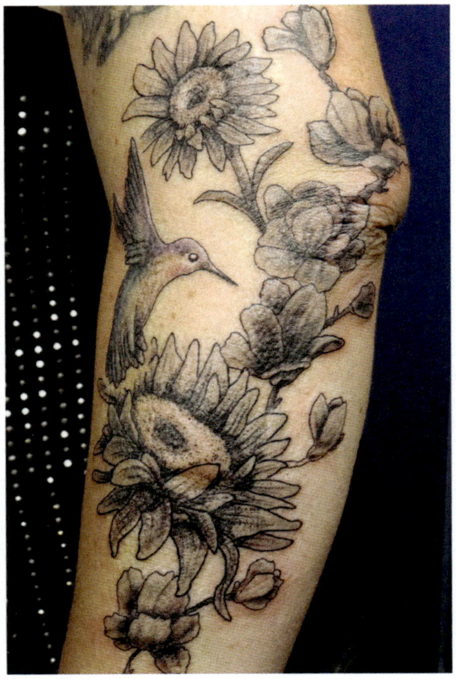

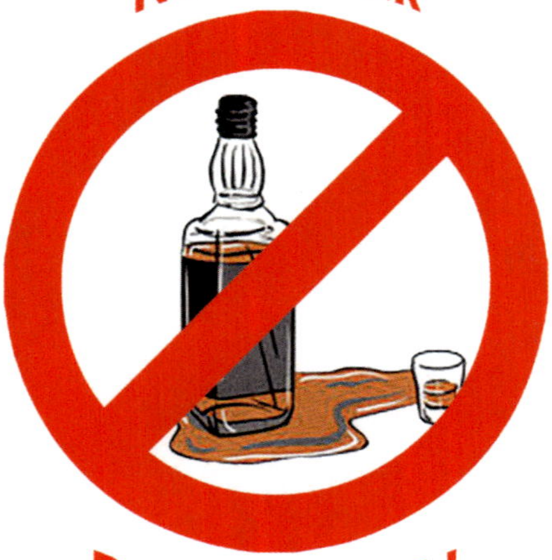

Drugs, Alcohol & Tattoos

The laughingly familiar scenario of someone getting a new tattoo while they are blacked out makes for a hilarious scene in the movies. In reality, receiving a tattoo under the influence of drugs or alcohol comes with numerous issues, the least of which is HATING the tattoo the next day.

If a client is inebriated or under the influence of drugs, their judgement is impaired and thus they are not able to make a decision that will affect the rest of their life. In many areas, it is illegal to tattoo a person under the influence, and even if it is not, an artist has an ethical responsibility to be sure the client is of sound mind, particularly when filling out intake paperwork and disclosing medical conditions.

Alcohol increases the chance that the client will bleed profusely, thus affecting the healed design. And tattoo artists can't tell what effect certain drugs will have on the client, such as potential vomiting, breathing problems, swelling or incontinence. Furthermore, drugs and alcohol do not necessarily lessen the discomfort of a tattoo and in many cases, will heighten the sensation of pain.

To save yourself and the client from potential risks, steer clear of tattooing anyone who is visibly intoxicated or under the influence of drugs (other than their prescribed medications).

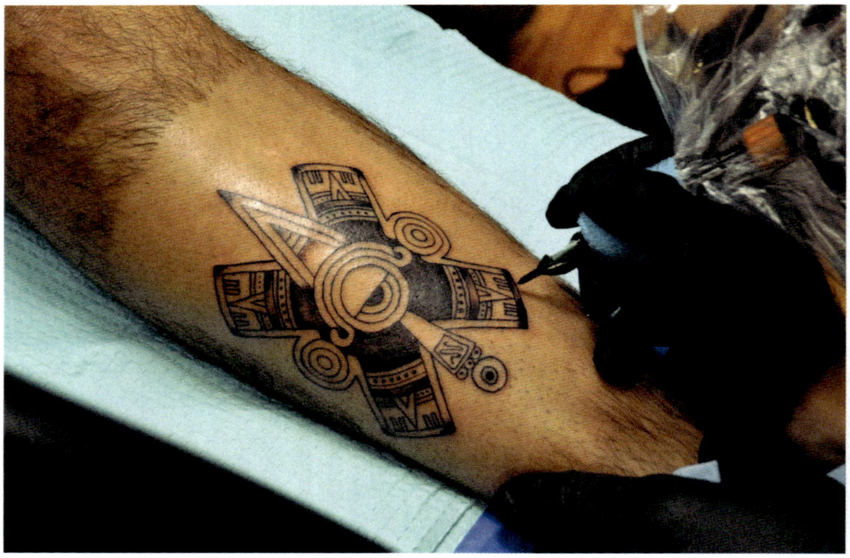

> "Show me a man with a tattoo and I'll show you a man with an interesting past."
>
> -*Jack London, Author*

Sources:
Andrews Diseases of the Skin, James, Berger & Elston, (c)2011
Skin Deep, Turkington & Dover, (c)2007
Diseases of the Skin, article by Jane Roberts, MD (c) 1993
Barron's EZ Skin Anatomy & Physiology, Krumhardt & Alcamo, (c)2010
For Tattoo Artists, Race is in the Mix, NPR, Dec. 1, 2016
Roberts Skin Type Classification System, Wendy E Roberts, MD, Journal of Drugs in Dermatology, (c)2016
Thinking of Tattooing Over Stretchmarks?, Judy Auli, Gotstretchmarks.net, 2013

Chapter Three Highlights

- Tattooing has been performed as a decorative art since ancient times.
- Skin is the largest organ of the body.
- The dermis is where tattoo ink resides.
- The four stages of skin's regeneration process are: hemostasis, inflammation, proliferation and maturation.
- The two biggest risks in getting a tattoo are allergic reaction and exposure to blood borne pathogens.
- Clients overwashing or scrubbing their tattoo can cause irritation.
- Allergy is a hypersensitivty disorder of the immune system.
- If a client is prone to frequent allergic reactions, it is likely the client will react to red ink.
- Common symptoms of allergic reaction include: red rash, scaly or flaky skin, and inflammation.
- Latex can cause dermatitis and occasionally, life-threatenting reactions in some people.
- Tattooing over stretch marks will take longer than normal.
- During a tattoo, people with senstive skin tend to turn red, swell and possibly bleed and ooze fluids more.
- Colors will tend to be proportionally more muted with darker skin tones.
- Very high or very low blood pressure can cause excessive bleeding during a tattoo.
- Scar tissue can be very senstive and may have nerve damage as well.
- The tattooer has an ethical responsibility to be sure the client is of sound mind when deciding to get a tattoo.

Wisecracks:

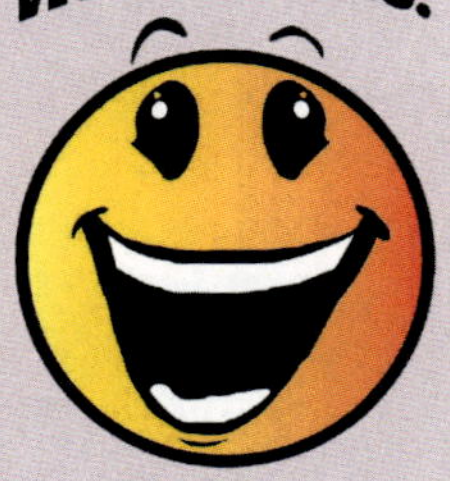

My mother said to find a guy with an embarassing tattoo and marry him.

Cause he knows how to make bad decisions and stick to them.

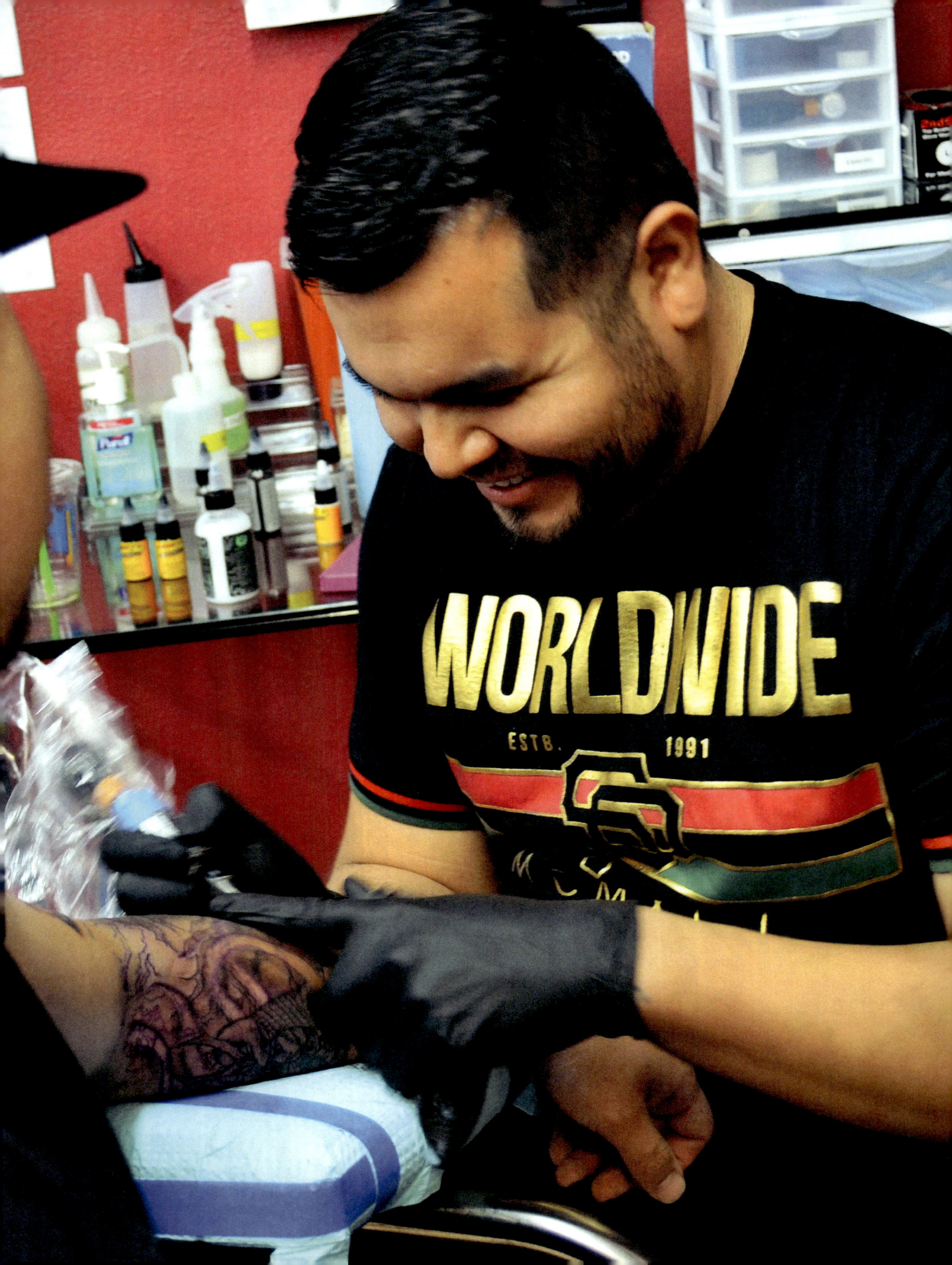
WORLDWIDE
ESTB. 1991

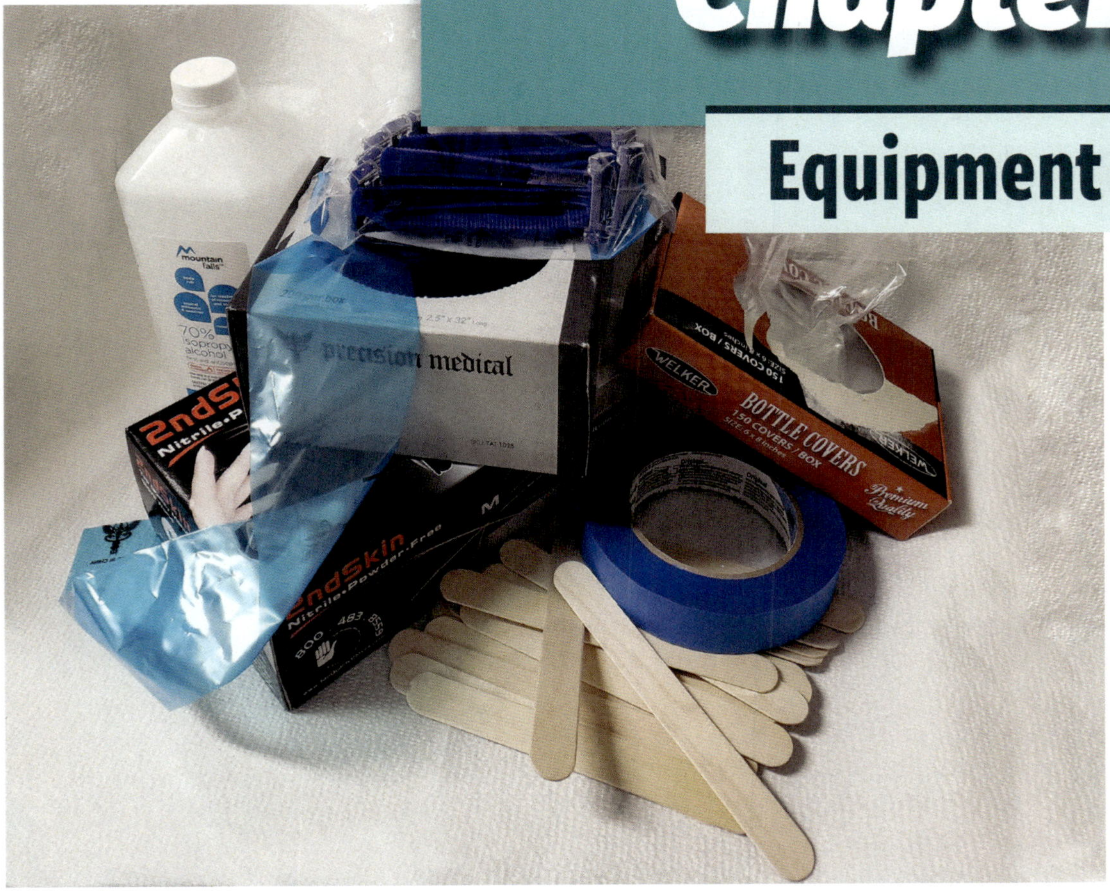

Chapter Four

Equipment & Supplies

Besides machines, needles and ink, which will be discussed in later chapters, there is a variety of equipment and supplies used in the process of tattooing:

- **Tattoo furniture such as stools, chairs and massage tables**
- **Lighting**
- **Design supplies, stencil printer and stencil paper**
- **Soaps, ointments and solutions**
- **Disposable/reusable supplies**

> "Man is a tool using animal. Without tools he is nothing, with tools he is all."
> *~Thomas Carlyle, Philosopher & Historian*

Tattoo Furniture

Tattoo Chairs & Tables

Choosing tattoo furniture is a consideration of both function, comfort and expense. While a simple chair and stool can be fine for starting out as a tattooer, it is advisable to progress to a chair or bed with more functionality as well as one that is resistant to stains from bodily fluids and ink—vinyl or treated leather are great choices.

The basic tattoo chair or table will allow for varying positions such as sitting backwards,

Shelly's Sidenote

STEADY SURFACE

Some long-time tattooers prefer a massage table or physical therapy table for their clients. I personally like having both the tattoo specific chair for upper body, neck and arm tattoos and an electric-lift table for legs, stomach and any work that requires a very steady surface (fine details or cosmetic, for example) as the chairs tend to have a bit more wiggle. Using a freestanding arm or leg rest is also fine, but takes a some getting used to, as they tend to be a bit wobbly.

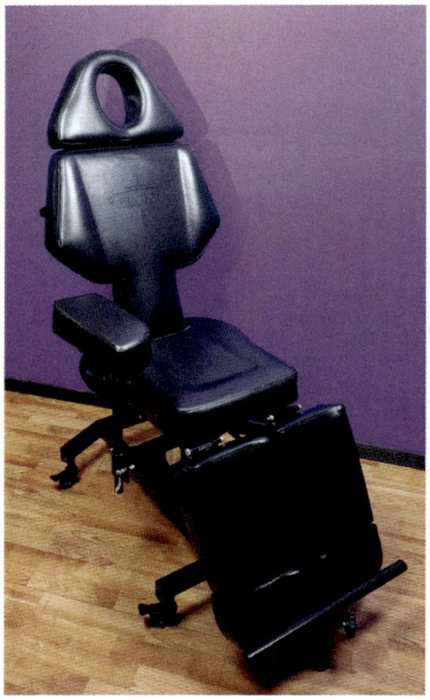

lying down or adding an arm rest or leg extension. Some also include a removable head rest. These features will allow you to access the area of the body you are working on with ease.

Other optional features include hydraulic or electric lift, which will raise and lower the chair or table with either a foot lever, pedal or button. In addition, cushions or bolsters to prop under the client's knees or joints can be helpful. Just make sure items are covered with barrier protection in the area of tattooing.

Note:
Please be aware you will need to clean the wheels of your stool quite often, as they can collect dirt and hair as well as roll over spilled drops of ink. Also, be aware of not rolling your wheels over your power cords!

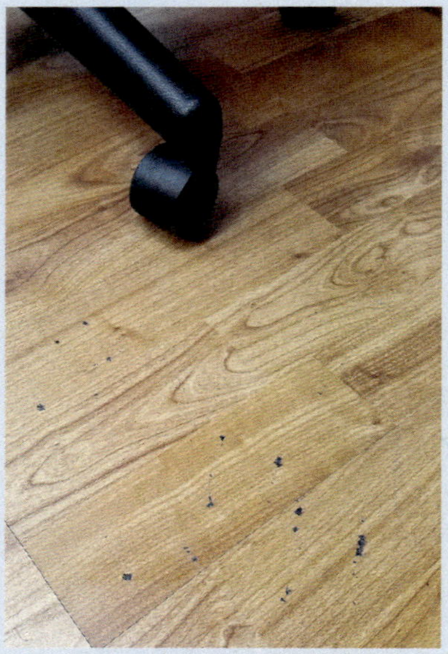

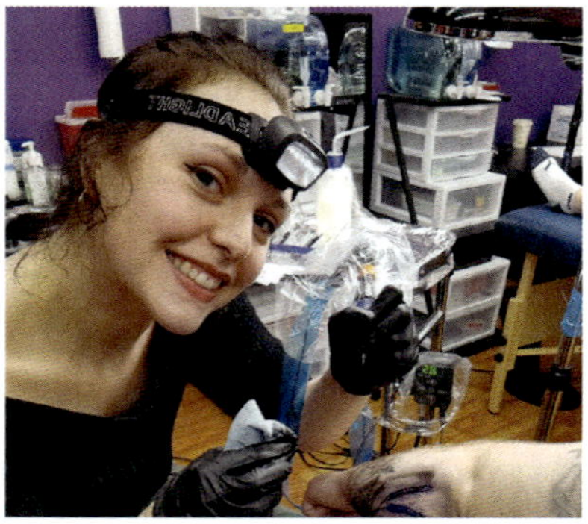

Stools

Tattooers will be sitting for most of the tattoo and having a stool with wheels allows the artist to maneuver around the client. In addition, tattoo artists need to reach continually for ink and to rinse or change needles, so having a stool that turns is essential. Having a stain resistant material is also important.

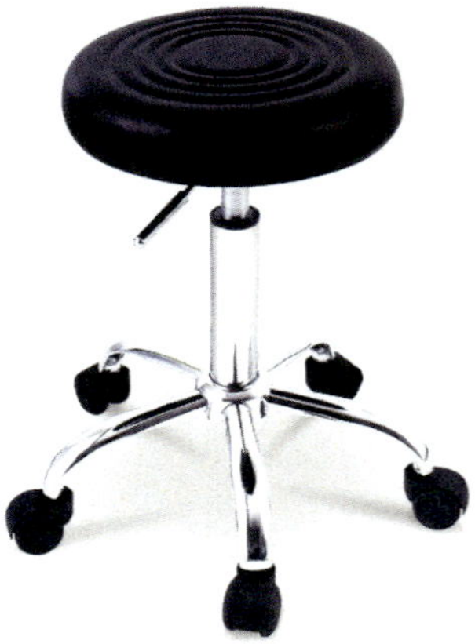

Many artists prefer a saddle style seat with a small amount of back-rest, while others prefer a bicycle shaped seat. Typically, the stool will be round and preferably well cushioned.

Occasional standing during a tattoo is also beneficial, both to access certain parts of the client's skin and to stretch your own body. This is where an electric or hydraulic lift can be helpful to move the client higher, instead of you bending over and putting extra strain on your back. Some tables can be easily raised to a comfortable height.

Lighting

Excellent light is crucial in producing quality tattoos. Because your hands tend to frequently block the area you are working on during the tattoo, the light should have the ability to be directed easily. Most tattooers prefer a standing lamp with daylight illumination that is adjustable in height, as well as bendable, to be projected directly on the tattoo work area to eliminate shadows.

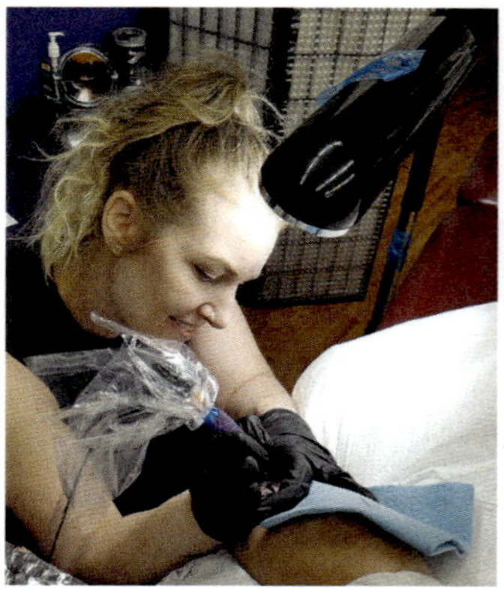

More expensive but a nice bonus would be a light that attaches to the ceiling and can be adjusted in all directions, such as a dentist's lamp. This would eliminate the hassle of the standing lamp pole and base being in your way.

One other option is a head lamp style light that would direct the beam exactly where you are looking.

Design Supplies & Stencils

Most tattoo artists begin the design process with a sketch, finalize the design, use black pens to create an outline, and then do a final rendering in color or black and grey. The outline is used to create a stencil which is applied to the skin and used as a map to determine where the ink goes. The final rendering is used to show the client what the tattoo will look like and for the artist to use while tattooing, to guide shading and color choices. In addition, many tattooers will use permanent markers or special tattoo pens to hand draw either parts of, or more infrequently, the entire design on the skin before proceeding.

> "The aim of art is to represent not the outward appearance of things, but their inward significance."
> *-Aristotle, Philosopher*

The most compelling reason to use a stencil before starting to tattoo, is the fact that the skin is stretched during a tattoo and the design could easily be distorted, affecting the final picture. Stencils tend to stay on the skin better and assist the artist in getting the linework done easily, so they can move on to the more creative parts of shading and coloring.

There are two basic ways to create a stencil for tattoo work:

1. hand drawn on transfer (spirit) paper (several brands available in classic purple, green and red)
2. printed by a machine: thermal or transfer machine

Tattoo Stencil by HAND using Transfer Paper

- Start with a hand-drawn or printed copy of your outline.
- Remove the protective tissue (off white or tan colored) from the transfer paper set.
- You will be drawing on top of the set which will transfer your outline to the back of the white piece which will pick up the ink from the blue piece.
- Place the transfer paper on a smooth, flat surface with the white sheet facing up.
- Place your outline on top of the white sheet.
- Tape your outline paper to the white sheet so that it doesn't shift.
- Using a sharp hard pencil or ball-point pen trace over the outline by pressing firmly.
- Check to see that all lines came through, without removing the outline.
- Once your lines are transferred, remove the tape, and gently tear the white piece off. Discard the yellow and blue piece. (be careful not to touch the blue as it will stain your fingers)

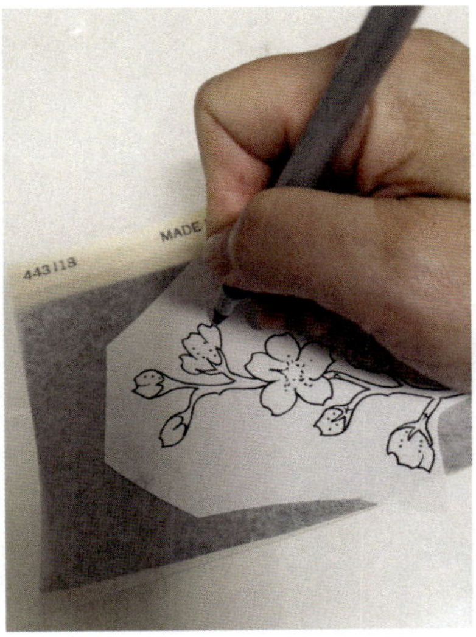

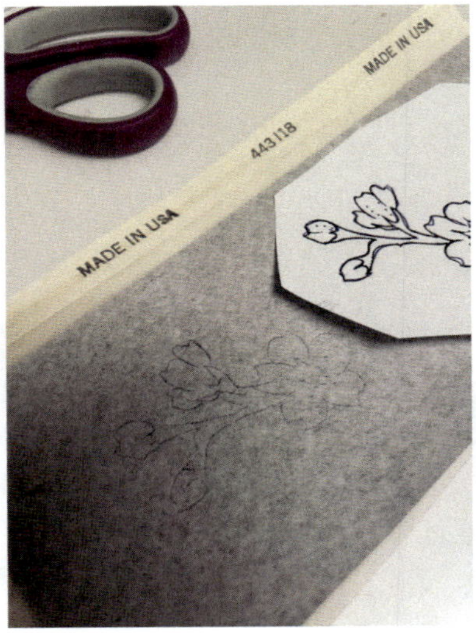

> "When I attempt anything, I have a passionate determination to overcome every obstacle."
> -Cecilia Beaux, Artist

Tattoo Stencil by MACHINE using Transfer Paper

Stencil Transfer Machines

Newer and more compact tattoo SPECIFIC stencil printers have dominated the market for the last several years. The price ranges from about $200 - $700 depending on whether you can use it with a digital device. This is particularly convenient because you can scan (or create) your tattoo piece using design software, such as *Procreate* or *Adobe Illustrator* and print it directly to the stencil transfer machine. Some are even capable of wireless print from a tablet or phone and many models even use a battery to allow the machine to travel easily.

If you are using the stencil transfer machine **without** a digital device:

- Print or copy your outline in black ink.
- Remove the protective tissue (off white or tan color) from the transfer paper set.
- Insert the transfer paper into the machine according to directions, usually from the back.
- Place your outline, usually face down, into the machine. (Follow your machine's instructions.)
- The transfer set will feed through at the same time as your original and your outline will be imprinted on the white sheet. Discard the yellow and blue pieces and trim your outline.

NOTE:
When you are wrapping a stencil around a body part, such as an arm, it can be helpful to put little snips all around the edge, to assist in smoothing the stencil.

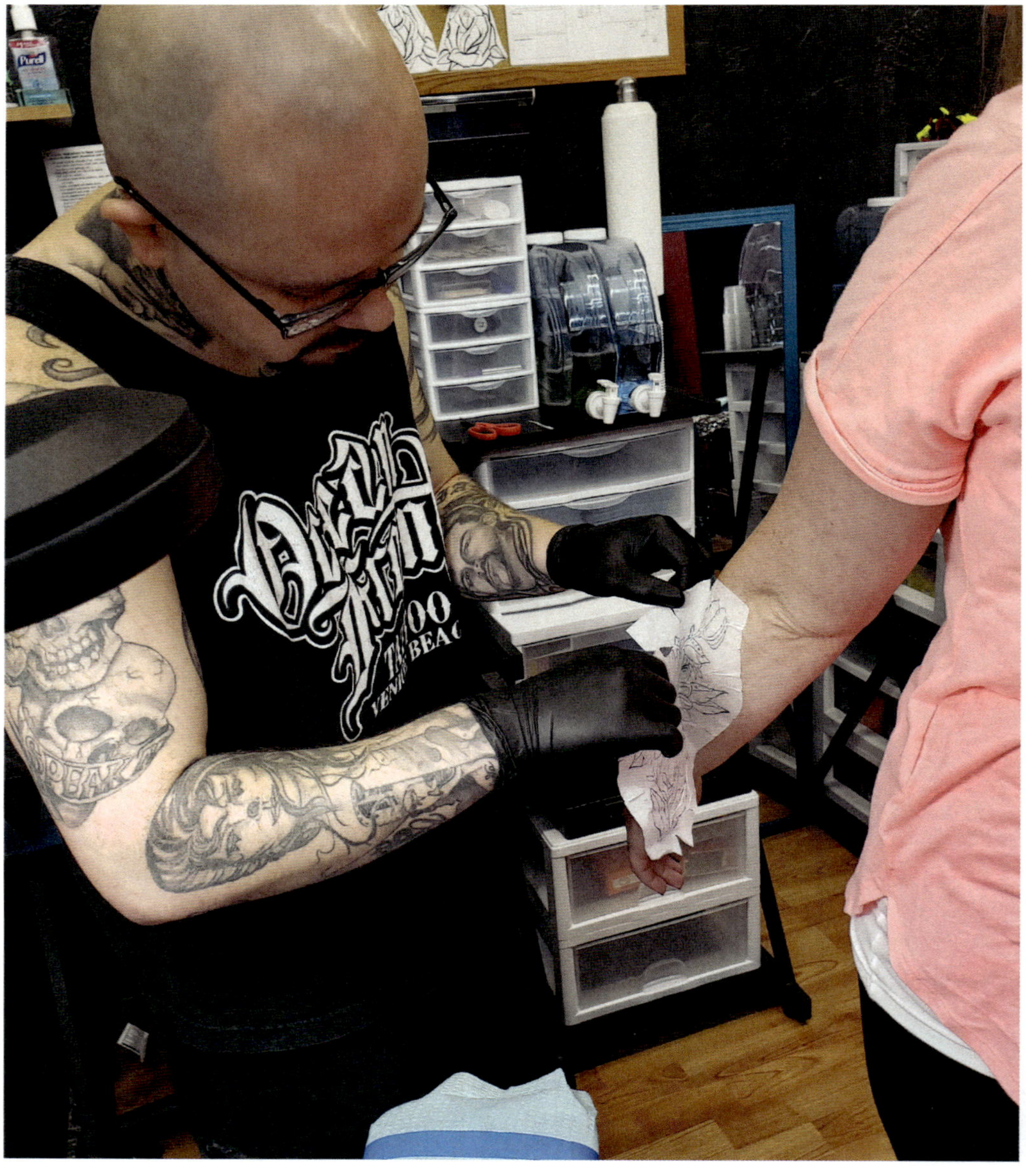

STENCIL:

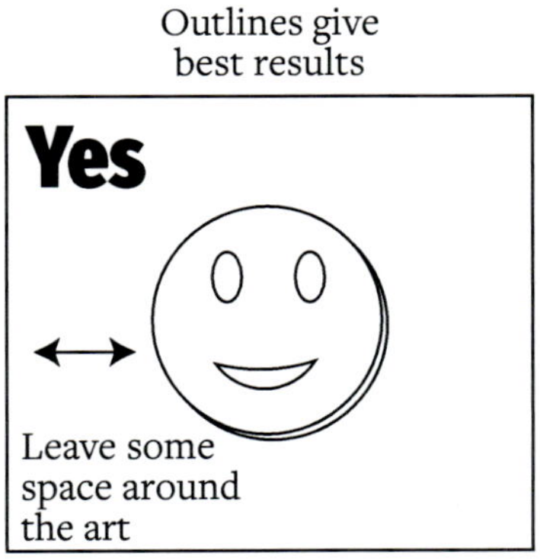

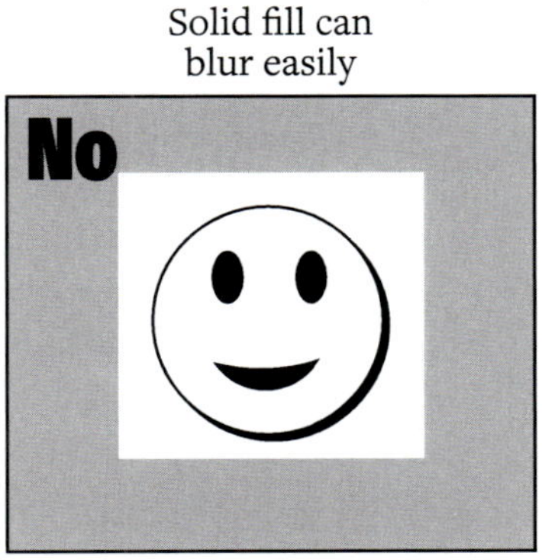

SETTINGS:

This is how the panel should look. MIRROR is always on unless you want to flip your artwork. If you do turn MIRROR off, make sure that you turn it back on. Otherwise the mirror should be toggled on at all times.

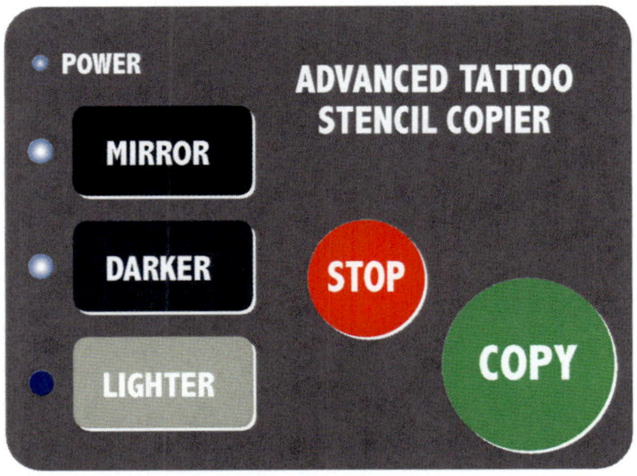

LOAD PAPER LIKE THIS:

Make sure you've removed the onion skin.
Load the paper centered in the machine.

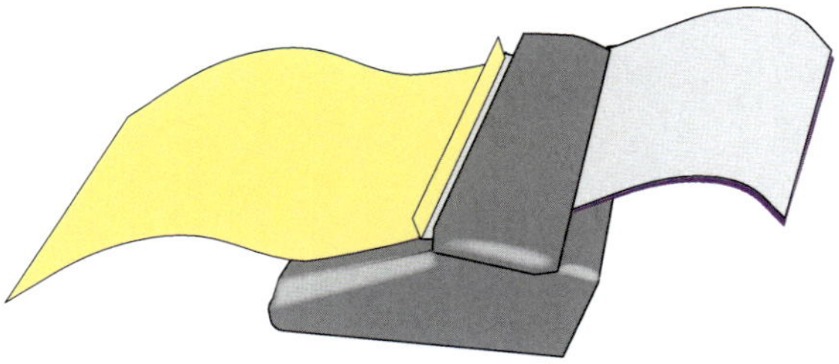

FOR SMALLER STENCILS YOU CAN PULL THE PAPER THROUGH FURTHER

Save the remaining piece in a box for remnants.

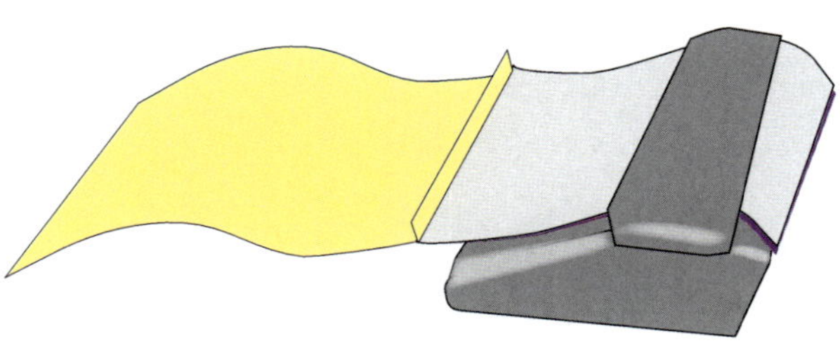

FOLD YELLOW SHEET BACK:

Place outline face down.
Press GO.
You may keep some.
tension on the yellow sheet.

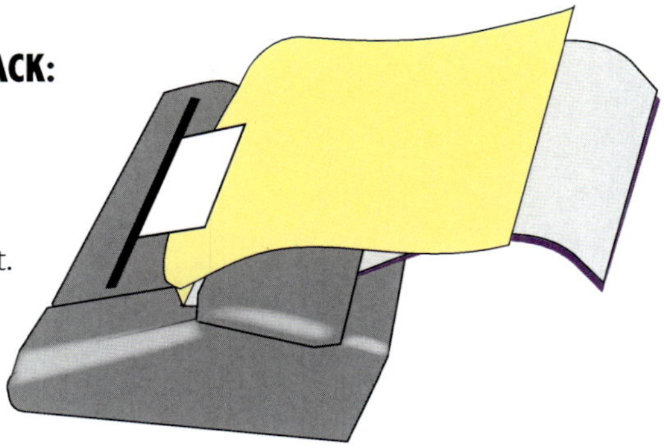

> "You can't use up creativity. The more you use, the more you have."
> *-Maya Angelou, Author*

How to Apply a Tattoo Stencil

- Cut your stencil out, approximately 1 – 2" from the edge.
- Wash your hands and put on gloves.
- Use alcohol on a paper towel to cleanse the client's skin of dirt, bacteria, oil or residual lotions and soaps.
- Use green soap (diluted with water) to moisten the skin and shave the area to make a smooth working surface. Shave beyond the size of the tattoo approximately 2" around to leave room for bandage later.
- Usually client should stand in a natural, relaxed position, looking straight ahead, with hands at their sides. This depends on where the tattoo will go.
- Apply a thin layer of either diluted green soap or if the design is more complex and will take longer, a stencil application fluid (many brands on the market).
- Allow the area to get slightly tacky (about one minute).
- Apply the tattoo stencil (dark purple side towards skin) by gently pressing it, center first, smoothing to the edges and making sure it is as flat as possible without wrinkles. Try not to rub or tear the stencil.
- Moisten paper towel lightly with diluted green soap (don't soak it) and dab gently on top of the stencil until the stencil is lightly damp and becomes translucent and the purple ink has a slightly darker look.
- Slowly peel the paper away. Use a surgical marker or stencil pen to correct any smeared or missing lines.
- If your design is complex such as a geometric or portrait design leave the stencil to dry at least 15 or 20 minutes, Otherwise, about 5 or 10 minutes is fine.

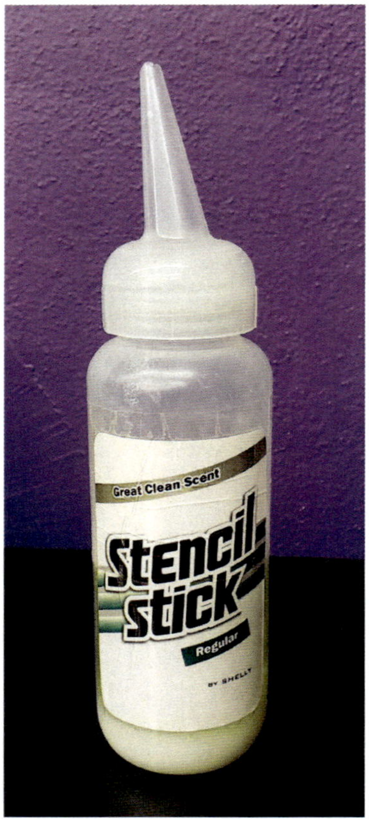

A DIY stencil application alternative from artist Nikko Hurtado, a master of portrait tattoos:

Ingredients:
- One stick of "Speed Stick" brand unscented deodorant
- Distilled water
- Alcohol
- Green soap

Directions:
- Empty deodorant into glass jar or microwave safe container (12 -16 oz).
- Melt deodorant in microwave in 15 second increments, just until liquid.
- Mix in ¼ cup green soap, ¼ cup distilled water & 2 caps alcohol.
- Stir thoroughly—let it sit one hour.
- Once cool you can transfer to a squeeze bottle.

To use:
- Dispense onto a paper towel and apply a thorough layer to skin, using gloved fingers to spread if necessary, over the entire tattoo area.
- Leave it until it becomes tacky, about 1 minute.
- Apply stencil as usual.
- Wait 15 – 20 minutes. Works great for portraits and intricate designs to keep stencil on skin much longer.

Applying a Stencil

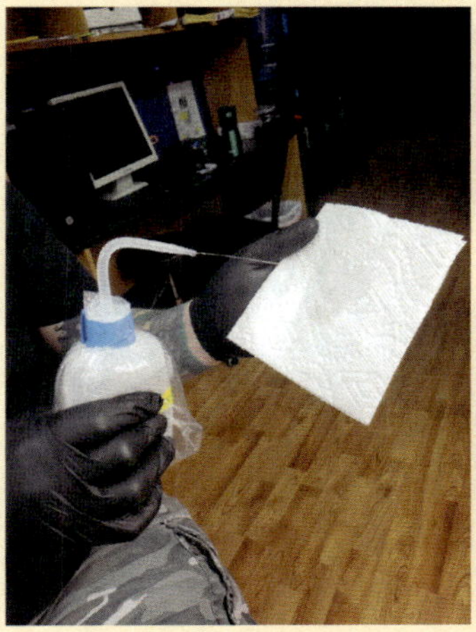

Spray alcohol onto a single-use disposable towel

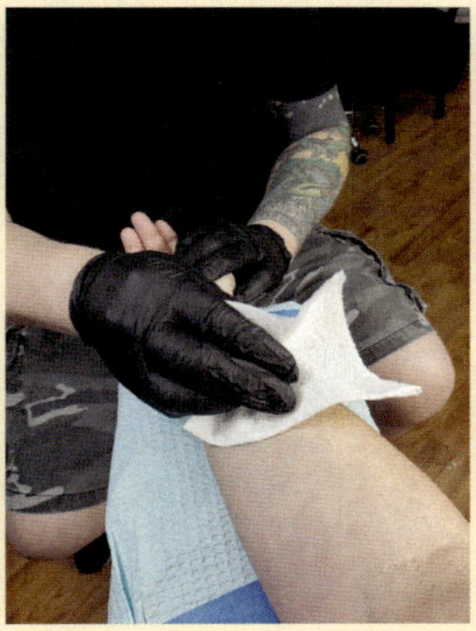

Wash the skin thoroughly with alcohol

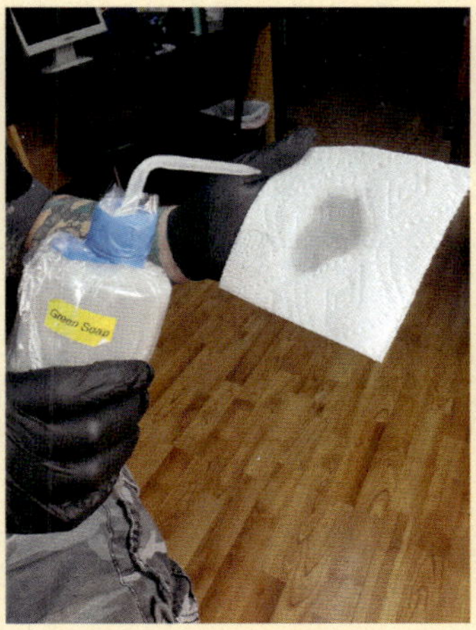

Moisten the skin thoroughly with green soap

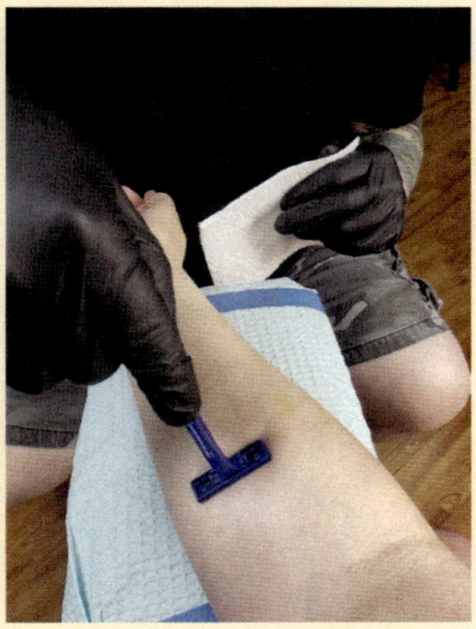

Shave the skin by moving razor up and down rapidly on the skin.

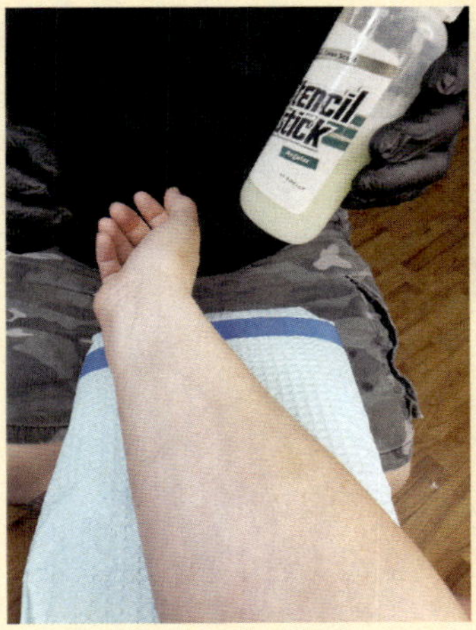

Shake stencil sticking solution well.

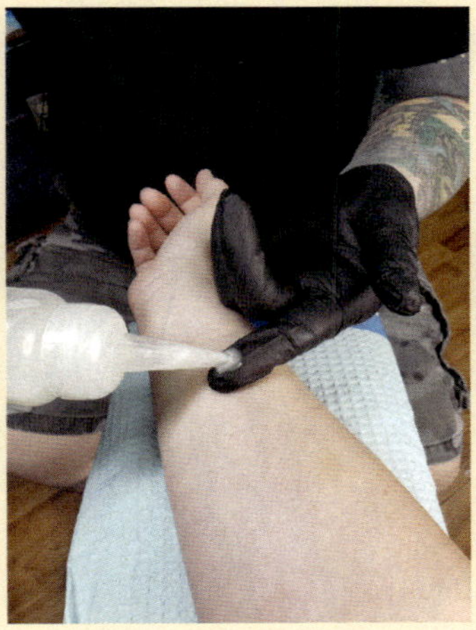

Apply a generous amount to your finger

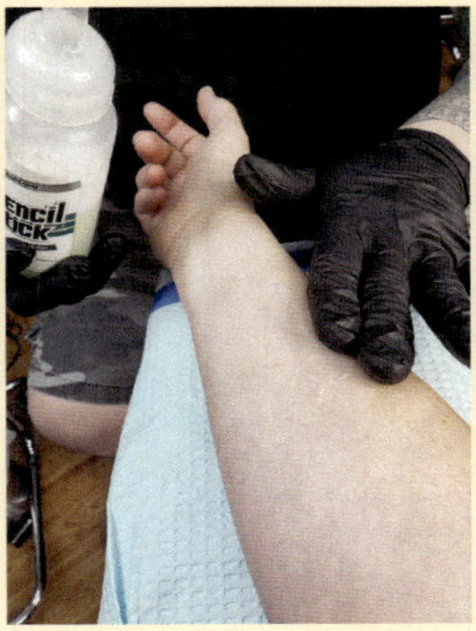

and rub it around the whole area where the stencil will be placed.

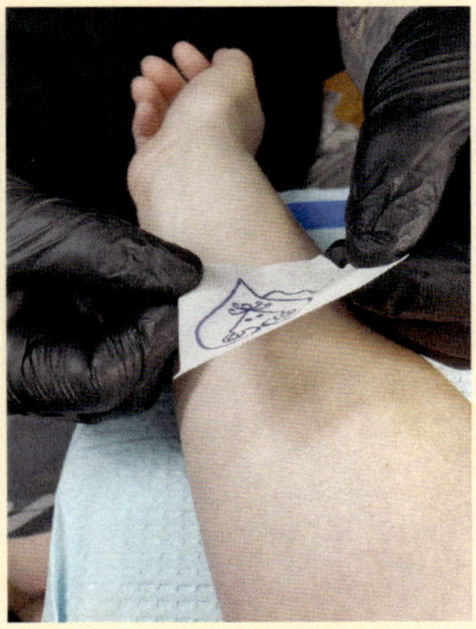

Once the solution is tacky, gauge where tattoo will go...

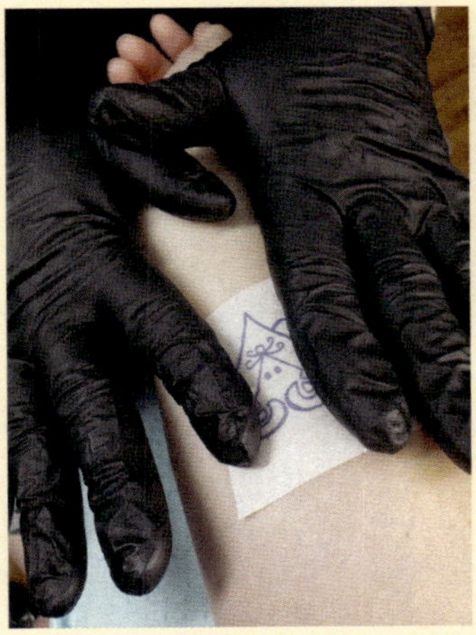

and place it firmly without moving it around.

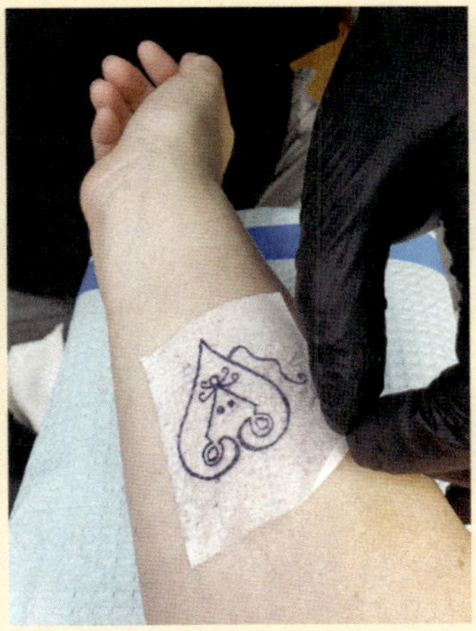

grab by the corner...

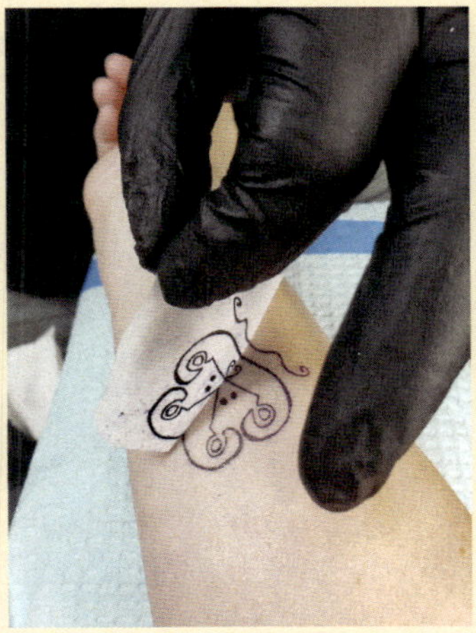

and peel... (save it for now, in case you need to reuse it.)

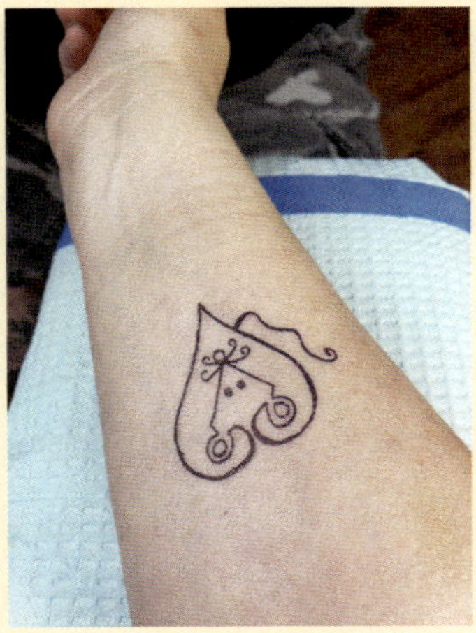

Tada! Let dry very well, minimally 5 minutes.

Soaps, Ointments and Solutions

There are many different products typically used in a tattoo shop from green soap to alcohol and there are disadvantages and benefits to every choice. In addition, there are countless opinions on what consists of good aftercare of a tattoo. (The aftercare steps we recommend are in chapter ten.)

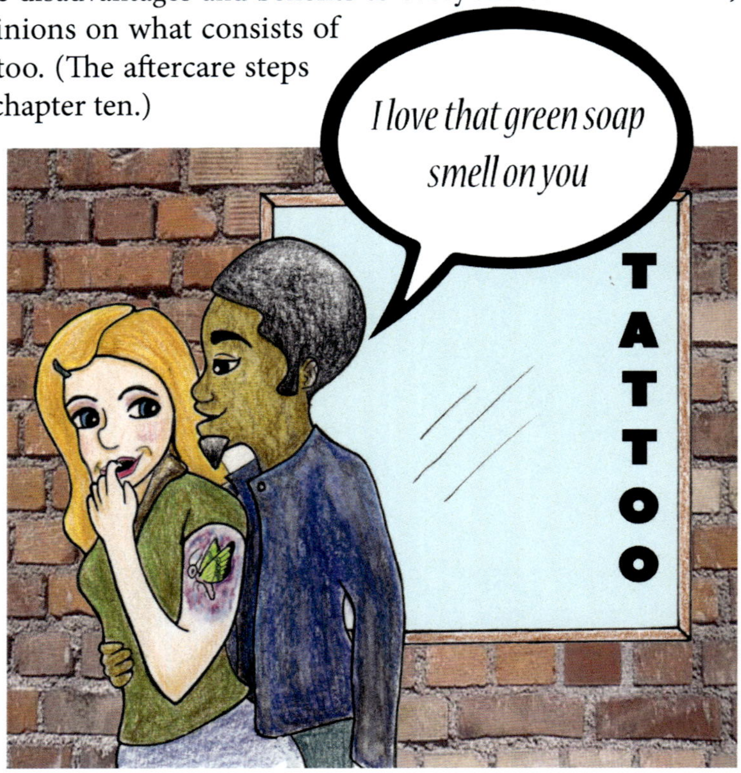

The best way to navigate the endless opinions and choices is to become well-informed. Read labels, ask other artists what works well for them and eventually get feedback from your own clients.

PROS & CONS of some of the most common products you may use or hear about in the field of body art:

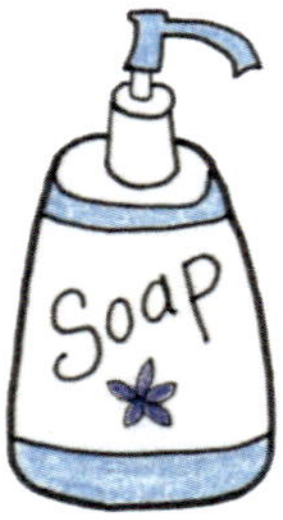

Soap

We use soap to wash our hands before and after a tattoo procedure. According to the U.S. Food and Drug Administration (FDA), there isn't enough science to show that over-the-counter antibacterial soaps are better at preventing illness than washing with plain soap and water.

To date, the benefits of using antibacterial hand soap haven't been proven. In addition, the wide use of these products over a long time has raised the concern of potential negative effects on health, such as developing antibiotic resistance or triggering allergies.

Furthermore, germs can grow on bar soap and spread from person to person thus **liquid soap** is preferred over bar soap for both the studio and for client's aftercare. It is easy to use, easy to keep sanitary and inexpensive.

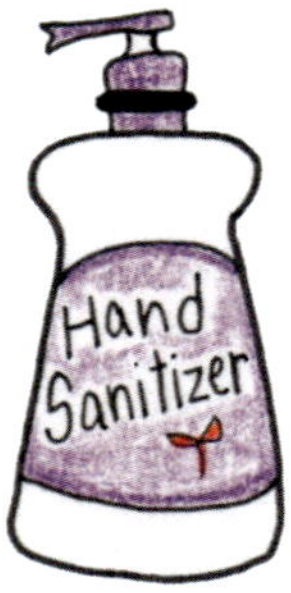

Hand Sanitizer

Alcohol-based hand sanitizers — which don't require water — are an excellent alternative to soap and water. Formula must contain at least 60% alcohol, which is necessary to kill germs effectively and safely. If your hands are visibly dirty, however, wash with soap and water.

In some areas, rules for tattooing include specifics on when to use soap and water and when you can use sanitizer, so be sure to consult your local laws!

Green Soap

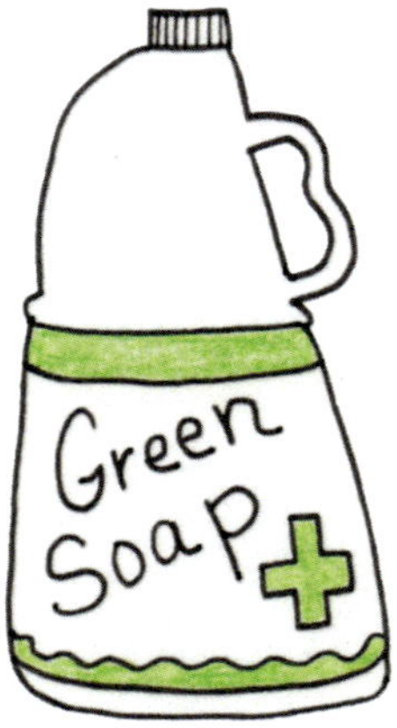

Green soap is commonly used in tattoo studios to prep and shave skin, adhere stencils, as well as cleanse and remove ink and bodily fluids during the procedure. Green soap is a medical grade, biodegradable soft soap made from vegetable oils and glycerin and gets its name from its natural yellowish green color. Because of its oil content it doesn't dry out the skin like other soaps and can be soothing during a difficult tattoo procedure.

Occasionally people are allergic to green soap. In that case, a good alternative would be baby shampoo diluted with water. Alternatively, some shops use castile liquid soap in place of green soap.

Rubbing (Isopropyl) Alcohol

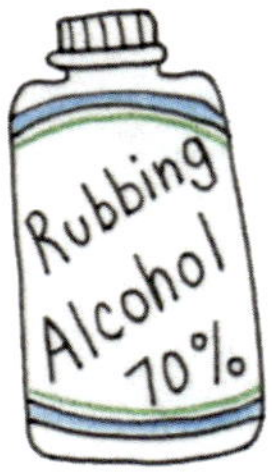

Rubbing alcohol is used as an antiseptic for the disinfection of skin to remove oils and impurities on the surface prior to penetration by needles. It is made up of two ingredients: isopropanol (70% or 91%) and water. In addition, it is more effective than green soap in removing a tattoo stencil, should that become necessary.

Heavy use of rubbing alcohol (higher percentage in particular) over a large portion of the body can become toxic. There is also a slight risk of inhalation poison if excessive amounts are used in a poorly ventilated area. It is also drying to the skin, so it should be minimized or avoided in aftercare products.

Witch Hazel

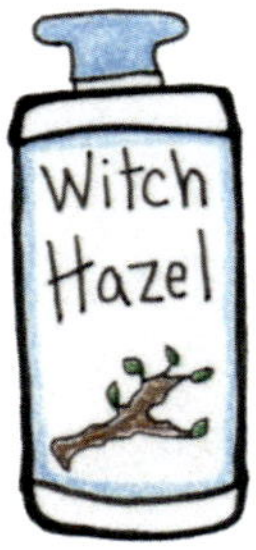

Witch hazel is an astringent produced from the leaves and bark of the North American witch hazel shrub (hamamelis) and possesses antioxidant properties. Many people refer to witch hazel as "nature's answer to *Neosporin*".
The many uses of witch hazel:

- During a tattoo, witch hazel reduces irritation and inflammation, as well as helps slow bleeding and reduce swelling.
- Artists can soak a paper towel at the end of a tattoo and let it sit on the client's skin for a few minutes, to reduce redness and bleeding and soothe the newly tattooed area, before taking a photo and prior to bandaging.
- Client can spritz with witch hazel often while tattoo is healing to protect against infection, soothe pain and itching, as well as encourage quicker healing.
- Mixing green soap, witch hazel and water works great for wiping and soothing skin during a tattoo procedure.

> "It's no wonder that Native Americans prized witch hazel so highly. I too regard it as indispensable. This time-honored topical agent can help alleviate many skin conditions. Whenever the skin is cut, abraded, irritated, itchy or burned or simply in need of refreshment, a witch hazel solution can usually provide relief."
>
> ~*Dr. Andrew Weil, M.D., author of "Why Our Health Matters".*

Note: Witch hazel is extremely safe but can have an exceptionally **rare** potential contact allergy.

Petrolatum

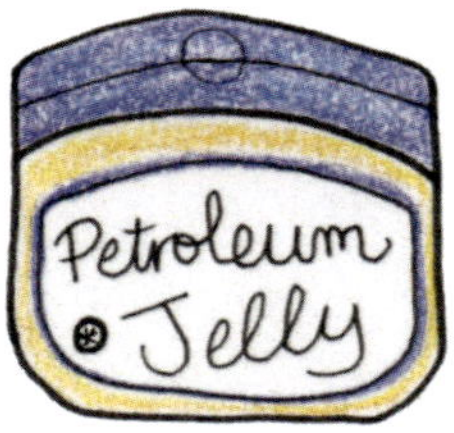

Petroleum jelly (commonly known by brand name *Vaseline*) is a semi-solid topical ointment traditionally used in the tattoo industry as an aftercare product, as well as to keep skin moist during tattoo and make skin smoother to wipe. It is also used to adhere ink cups and rinse cups onto the work area.

However, it is not recommended for aftercare anymore as a tattoo needs air to heal properly and pure petroleum jelly tends to smother skin, hold in toxins and clog pores. In addition, some types of processing can leave contaminants in the product and some people are allergic to petroleum.

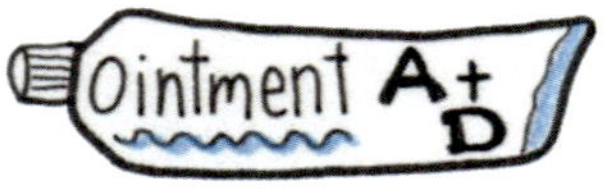

Vitamin A&D

A&D ointments are also used during a tattoo and as aftercare by many tattooers. They work by moisturizing, sealing the skin and aiding in skin healing. In addition to cod liver oil, which supplies a high content of vitamins A & D, these ointments also contain petrolatum (see above for those concerns) as well as lanolin, a fatty, wax-like substance derived as a byproduct from sheep's wool. Lanolin can be very soothing but can also cause allergic reactions. People already prone to eczema may be especially sensitive to lanolin.

In some people, A & D ointment can prolong the plasma cycle, or "oozing" process, of a new tattoo. When this process is lengthened there can be a greater chance for scabbing, infection and ink loss.

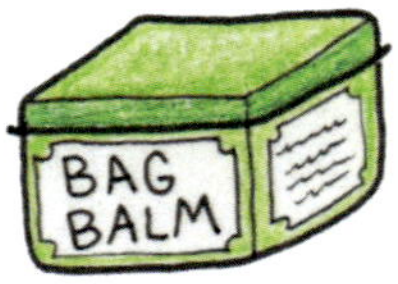

Bag Balm

Another soothing and moisturizing ointment frequently used in aftercare, *Bag Balm*, was first released in the late 1800s to help treat a cow's sore udders but has since grown in popularity as an all-purpose salve for humans, too. It also includes hydroxyquinoline sulphate, which is an antiseptic.

Like A & D ointments, Bag Balm contains petrolatum and lanolin with the aforementioned concerns.

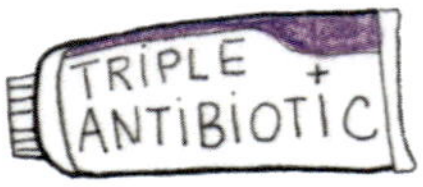

Triple Antibiotic

Triple antibiotics are over-the-counter topicals used in the prevention and fighting of infection. They also speed the healing of wounds--though the use of antibiotics has raised common concerns. Several brands contain three different antibiotics: bacitracin, neomycin, and polymyxin B, as well as cocoa butter, cottonseed oil, and petrolatum.

Some people have allergic reactions to neomycin and, as stated above, petrolatum tends to clog wounds. In addition, the "pulling" effect in speedy healing tends to also pull pigment out as well, thus triple anti-biotics should only be used on a tattoo if absolutely necessary. (Best to try witch hazel first to fight infection.)

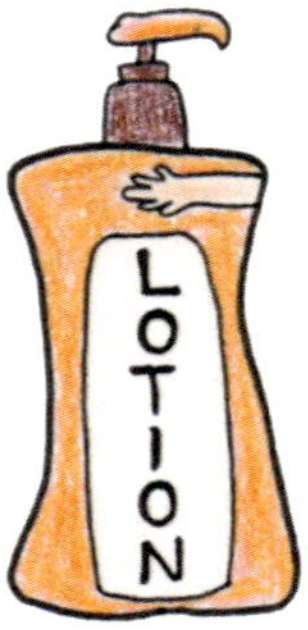

Moisturizing lotion

A complex mixture of chemical agents specially designed to make the external layers of the skin (epidermis) softer and more pliable. They increase the skin's hydration (water content) by reducing evaporation. Lotions can be useful when a tattoo is at the dry healing phase to ease itching and tightness.

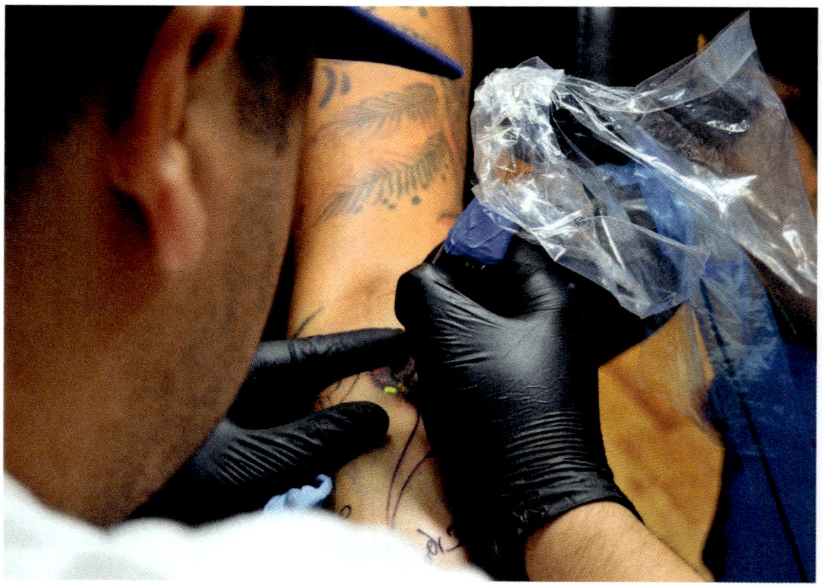

Problems with lotions usually come in the form of sensitivity, or allergy to, a specific ingredient.

Antiseptic/Anesthetic liquids:

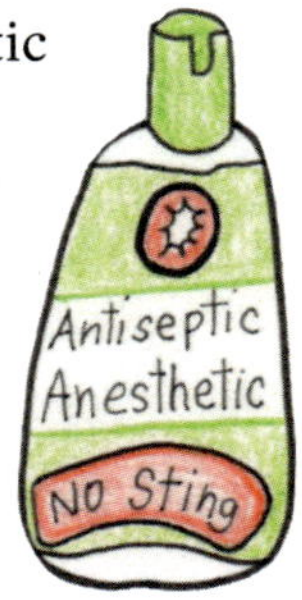

Topical first-aid cleansing & anesthetic liquids, such as *Band-Aid* or *Bactine* include active ingredients Benzalkonium chloride, an antiseptic, and lidocaine, a local anesthetic. These topical solutions can be used to numb the surface of the skin and help relieve the pain as well as prevent infection.

These solutions work best when the skin has been broken, as well as during long or painful sessions to help assist the client in sitting longer. Be aware that the skin gets a little sticky after use and you can simply wipe the first aid cleanser off after 10 or 15 minutes with your usual green soap mix.

> "Bactine is great, especially when it gets to that point with the client possibly not being able to sit there anymore...pour a good amount on a paper towel (really saturate the towel) then wipe down... you will need to reapply after about twenty minutes because it wears off...don't use the spray directly on the open tattoo area because of possible air-borne contamination and be careful if you still have stencil to worry about, as it will wipe it off easily. I usually will never use it until my stencil is gone and I'm fully mapped in...And keep in mind it only works when the skin is broken, it won't work to use it before you start. I have never heard of having any issues with healing from using Bactine, it's good stuff--also takes redness down for a better picture at the end."
>
> *~Mike Devries, Artist & tattooer*
> *mdtattoos.com, forum, Dec. 2009*

Topical Anesthetic

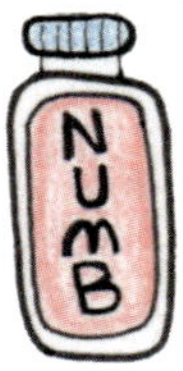

Though many tattooers and tattoo collectors believe that pain is an important part of the tattoo process, others disagree and would like a little assistance in that area. Tattoo artists have the option of using inexpensive mild topical anesthetic liquid, such as the antiseptic/anesthetic cleansers mentioned above. In addition, there are several other more expensive brands on the market, in the form of creams or gels, that are potentially more powerful. Most of these contain lidocaine, benzocaine, tetrocaine or prilocaine to numb skin surface. Other brands also contain vasoconstrictors, such as epinephrine, to help minimize bleeding and swelling.

> **NOTE**: Individual pain levels vary widely, and these products don't always work on everyone.
>
> Perhaps some of the benefit of these products comes from psychology or the "placebo effect" --just knowing it is supposed to help with pain. The more enthusiastic you are about the pain-relieving attributes the higher the possibility the client will feel it is effective.

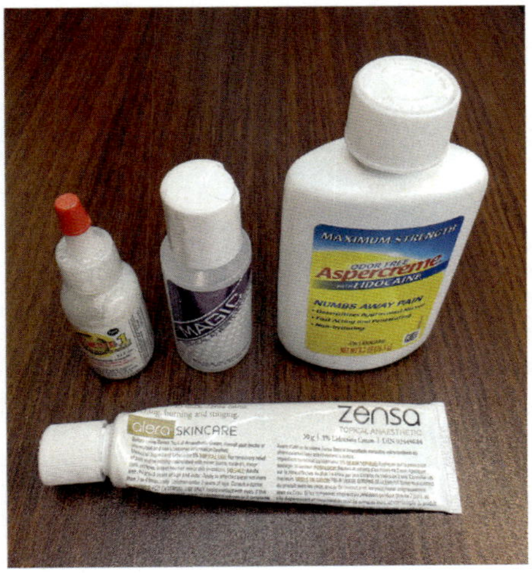

The creams and gels are designed to be on the skin for 30 minutes to an hour before the procedure, and then reapplied once the skin is broken to help with comfort during procedure. These are always used in cosmetic tattooing but can also be of benefit for long artistic tattoo sessions. Clients can be encouraged to buy their own numb cream and apply it, to the area they will be getting tattooed, one hour before they come to the studio. Directions should be followed on each individual product. Be aware that some people are also **allergic** to anesthetics.

Shelly's Sidenote

TATTOO BALM

My favorite product for use during tattooing and for aftercare is "Ink Balm" by Wild Rose Herbs, made in Oregon, using organic ingredients such as coconut, lavender and peppermint oil. This delightful smelling balm helps with moisturizing the skin,when needed, during tattoo procedures and soothes and protects the client's skin during healing.

And no, I am not paid to say this...I just love this product! Note: be aware some people are allergic to coconut oil, so always ask in advance.

www.wildroseherbs.com

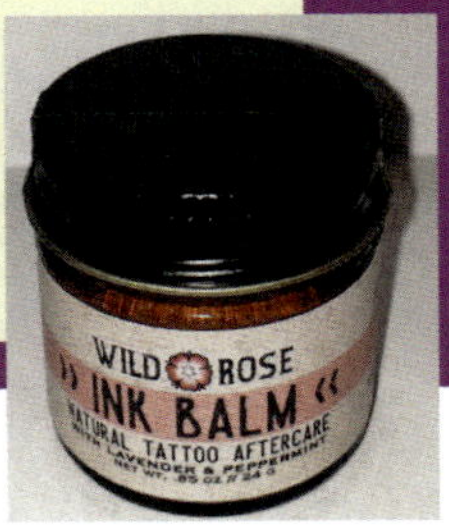

In addition to the previous well-known, readily available, and more commonly used products, there are numerous brand name tattoo balms, soaps, numbing agents and other aftercare products. Whether or not they work "better" than the inexpensive, readily available products, is a matter of some debate.

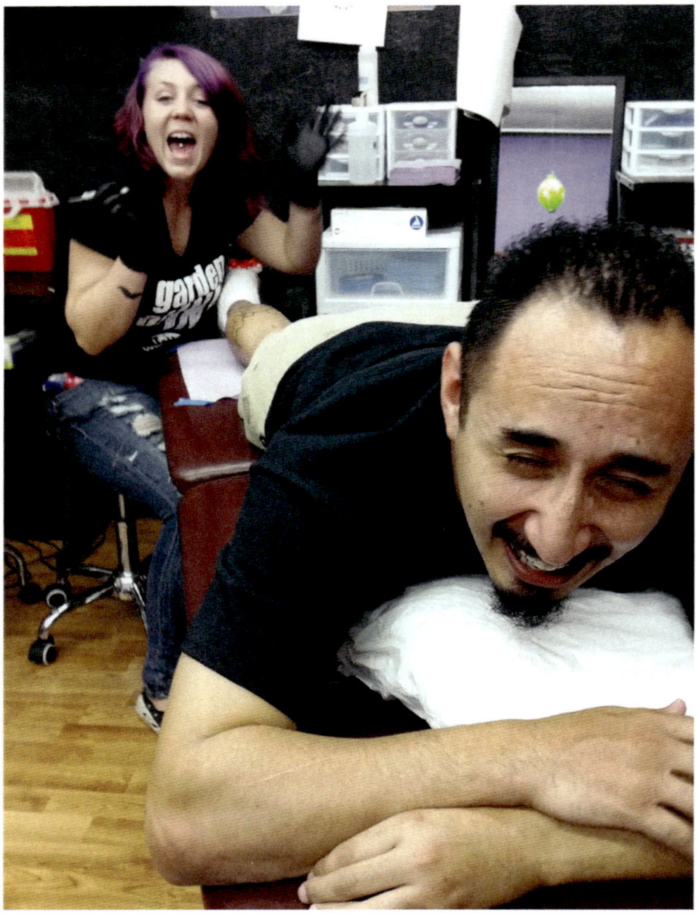

Disposable/Reusable supplies

Here is a list of the basic supplies you will need for tattoo procedures, in addition to machine, power supply, needles and inks:

Disposable
(never reuse these items)
Papertowels, rinse cups, barrier film, plastic or foil, cord covers, ink cups, tape, medical tape and/or stretch bandages, baggies or bottle covers, trash bags, razors, wooden applicators (tongue depressor), toothpicks, polyacrylate (water absorbent), petroleum jelly (for sticking ink cups and rinse cups to the surface)

Reusable
(must be covered and/or sanitized with high-level disinfectant solution)
Tray, squeeze bottles, flexible ruler, tattoo pens, plastic or acetate stencils, ruler

TATTOO STATION SET-UP INSTRUCTIONS

Photos to follow

Things You'll Need

***Sanitary work area** (**tray, table, tool box top, etc**)*
Antiseptics
Disinfected, cling-wrapped/foil-wrapped work area or tray
Disposable gloves
***Tattoo machine** (**rotary or coil**)*
Tattoo power supply & foot pedal
Power cord covered
Power supply covered
Sealed, sterilized or disposable needles & tubes
Baggies or plastic covers
Ink cups
Ink
Tongue depressor
***Petroleum jelly** (**to stick down ink cups and rinse cup**)*
Rinse cup
***Squeeze bottles** (**no spray bottles in tattoo procedure due to possible contamination from airborne particulates**)*
Disposable razor
Stencil & stencil application fluid or stencil pens
Green soap mix
Paper towels

- Wash your hands with soap, dry and put on disposable nitrile gloves.

- Place bag in trash can.

- Use barrier film, foil or cling wrap, where appropriate, to cover areas in your workstation. Anywhere the tattoo procedure will take place should be covered. This includes lamp, stool handle and tattoo furniture, especially arm or foot rests that will be utilized during the procedure, and the area where you'll be setting your tattoo machines, inks and other supplies.

- Cover squeeze bottles. Tattoo artists generally use a squeeze bottle to dispense green soap, alcohol, witch hazel or other products (such as stencil applicator fluid). These bottles should be covered to keep contaminated fluids from getting directly on the bottles. And the tips should never be touched to client's skin, needle reservoir, paper towel (used for wiping skin) or contaminated rinse water.

- Get disposables ready. You'll need items such as a disposable, one-time use razor for shaving the tattoo area, paper towels for wiping away excess ink, and a disposable plastic cup with water for rinsing between color changes. These should all be within easy reach on your disinfected, foil or cling-wrapped work surface. Secure ink cups with a dab of petroleum jelly. Place stencil and/or tattoo pens in work area.

- Set up tattoo machines with power supply, foot switch, power or clip cords. If using coil machine: place your rubber bands and grommets on machine and load your needle and tube. If using rotary machine with needle cartridges, open cartridge packages, cut them almost in half, tape them to your work surface and place your needle choices accordingly. (Grabbing cartridges from the top each time will prevent the bottom part from becoming contaminated).

- Cover these items as appropriate: clip cord, power supply and machines.

- At this point you remove and dispose of gloves, sanitize hands and welcome client and have them fill out paperwork. Then, bring client back to your station, wash or sanitize hands and don a new set of nitrile gloves.

- After sanitizing and shaving skin--apply a stencil and/or hand draw your design. Allow it to dry. Remove gloves, sanitize hands, don a new set of gloves.

- Dispense ink. Put the various colors of ink required in individual cups. The number of cups will vary depending on how many different colors will be used.

- Dispensing ink at this point allows client's stencil the needed drying time to ensure that it stays in place throughout tattoo.

- **Begin tattoo.**

> "The artist's world is limitless. It can be found anywhere, far from where he lives or a few feet away. It is always on his doorstep."
>
> *-Paul Strand, Artist*

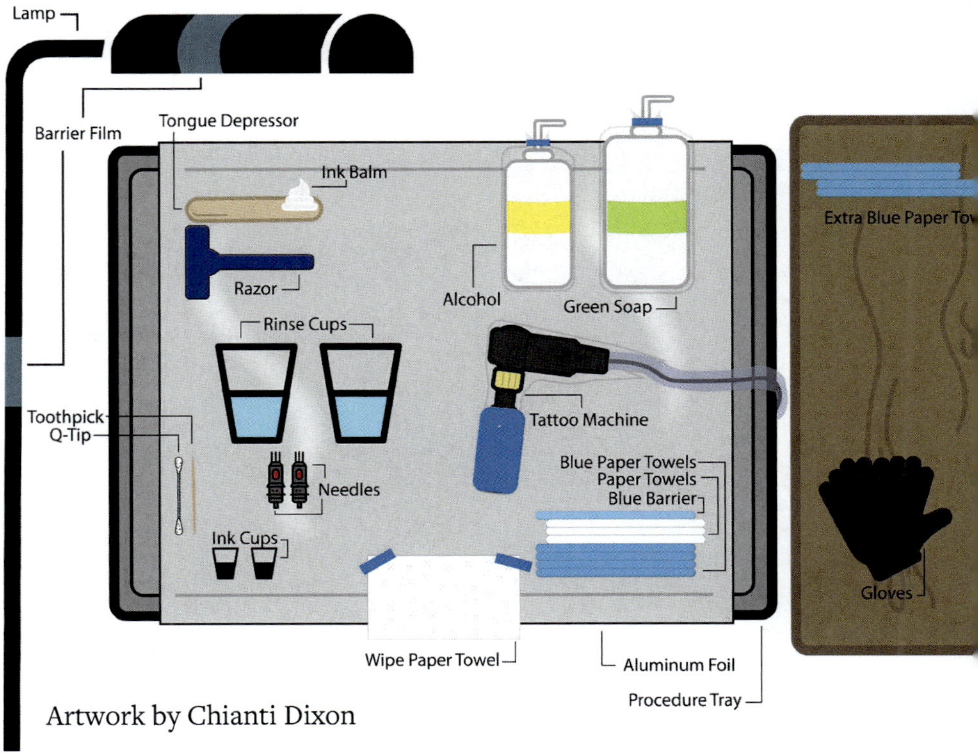

Artwork by Chianti Dixon

Basic Setup *Start with properly washed and gloved hands.*

Place Liner in Trash

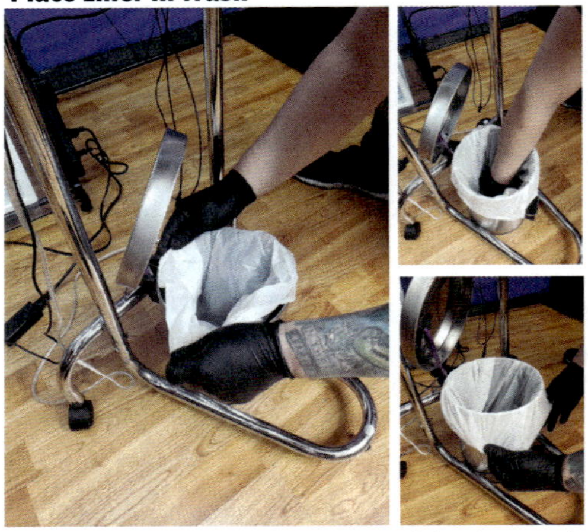

Push the liner to the bottom of the bin and pull the edges over the sides. This will help keep things tidy as the bag is filled with waste.

Cover Work Surface

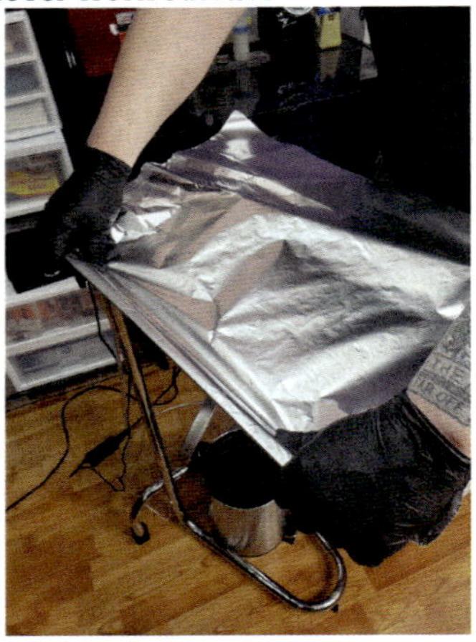

Use foil or plastic to cover your procedure area. This is where all contaminated items are isolated.

Use Tongue Depressor

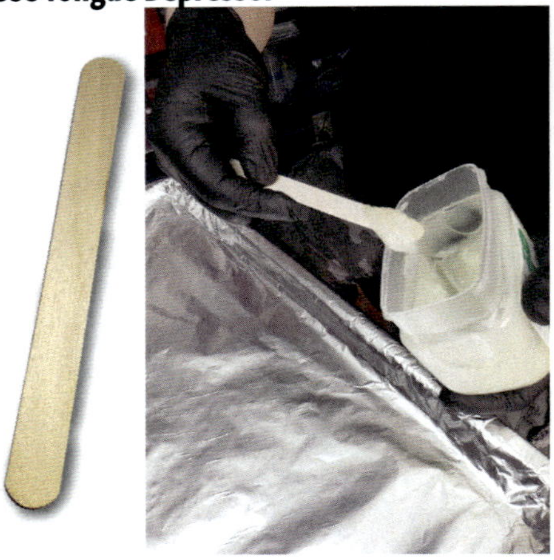

A tongue depressor will enable you to dispense product without contaminating it's source.

Get out paper towels and dental bib

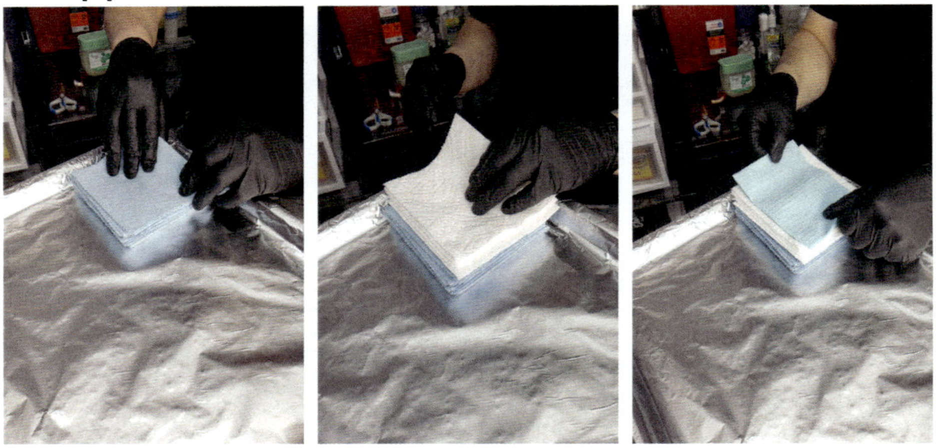

Get enough paper towels for the procedure and the dental bib you'll need for the next steps.

Place bottles in to plastic bags

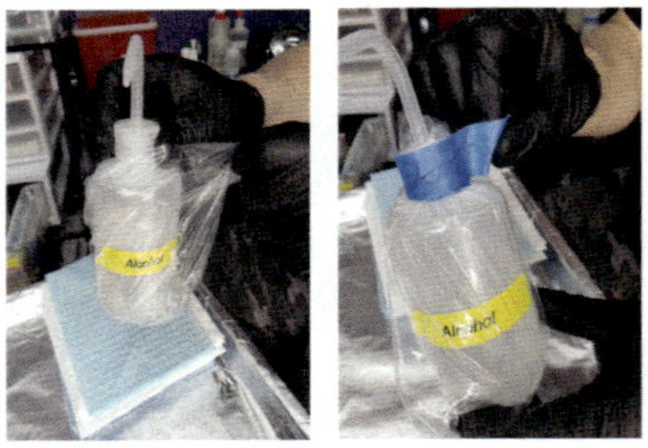

Cover squeeze bottles. Tattoo artists generally use a squeeze bottle to dispense green soap, alcohol, witch hazel or other products (such as stencil applicator fluid). These bottles should be covered to keep contaminated fluids from getting directly on the bottles. And the tips should never be touched to client's skin, needle reservoir, paper towel (used for wiping skin) or contaminated rinse water.

To cover everything...

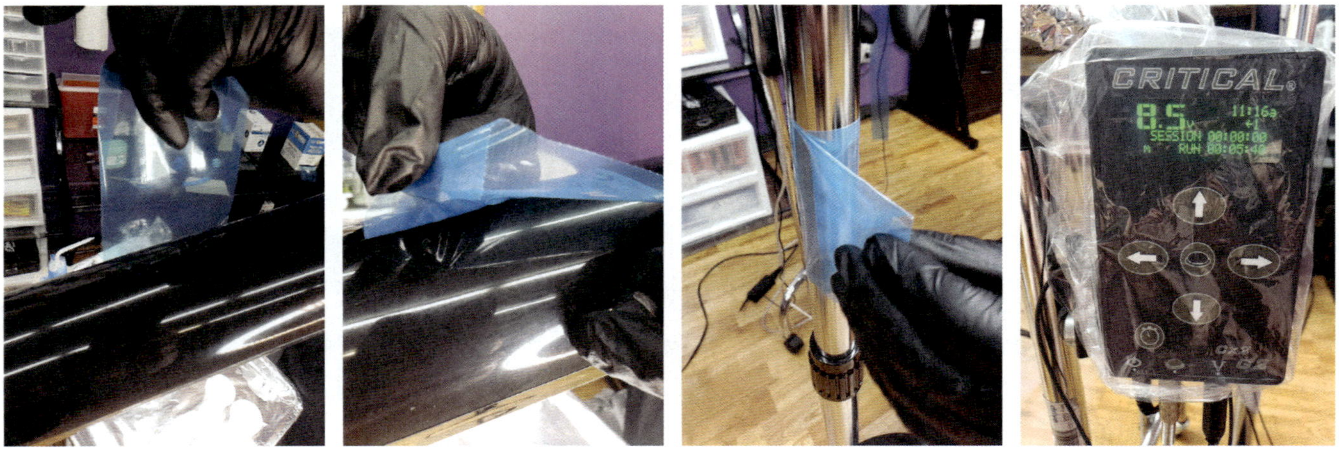

Lamps

Power Supply

Use Tongue Depressor

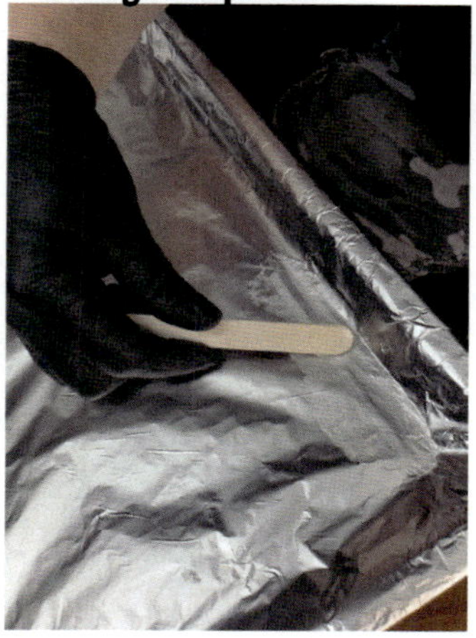

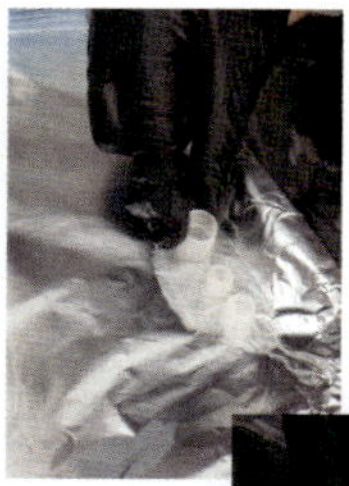

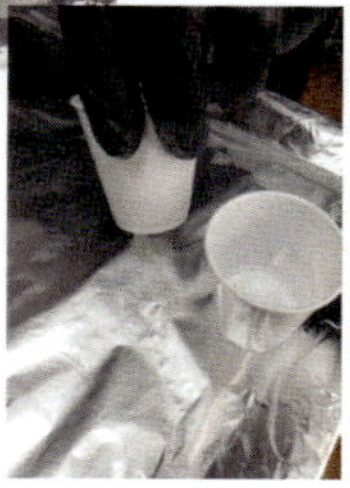

A thin smear of petrtoleum will keep things in place. Use it for securing ink cups and rinse cups.

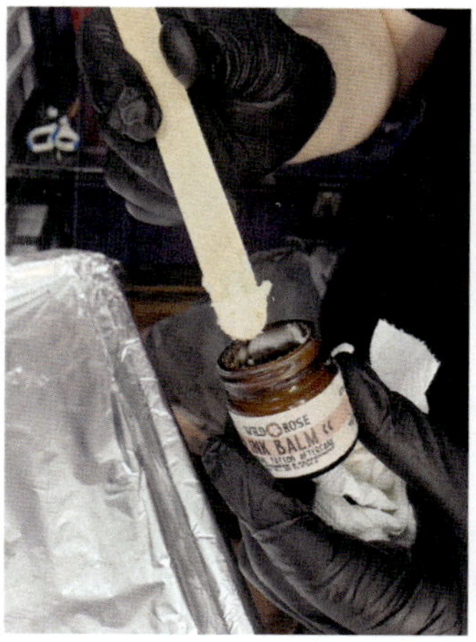

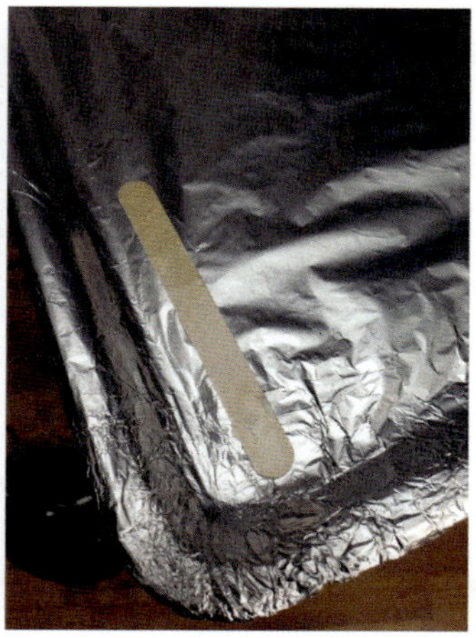

And some ink balm for use during and after the procedure. Just set it in the corner out of the way until needed.

Use these barriers

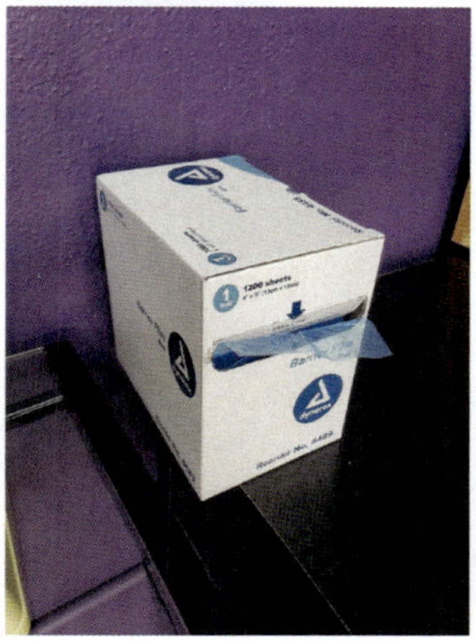

Barrier Film

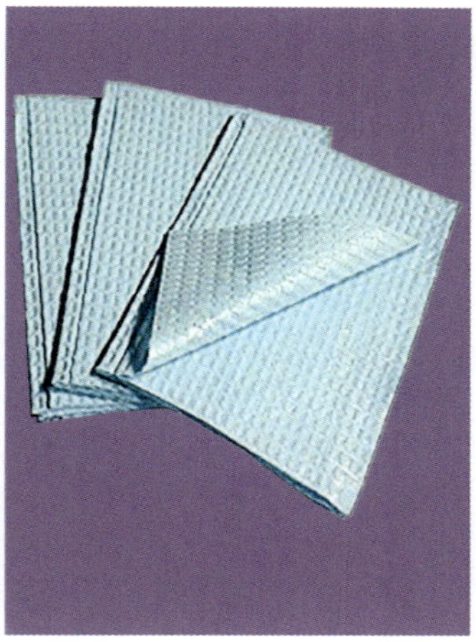

Dental Bibs

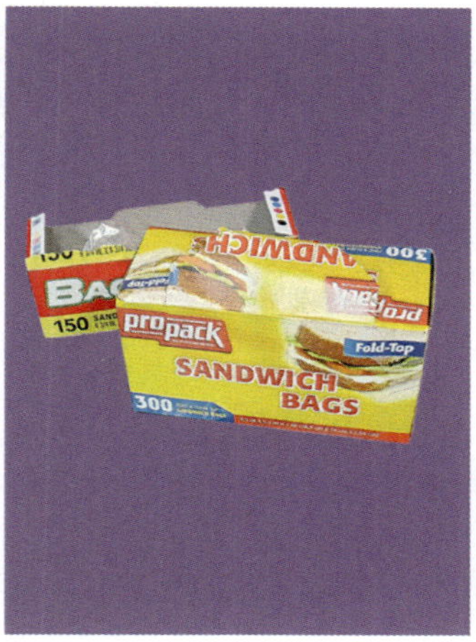

Plastic Bags

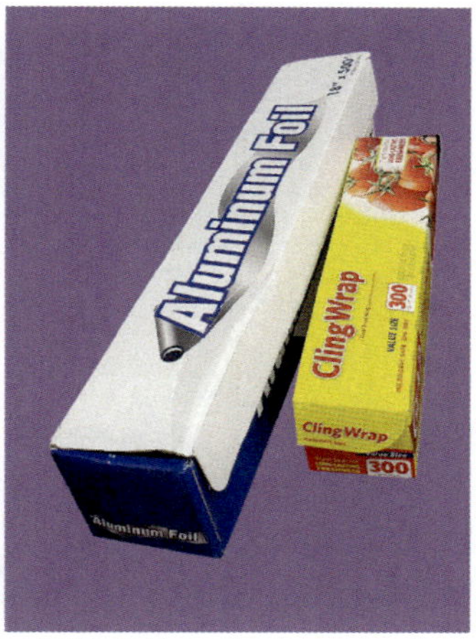

Foil/Plastic Wrap

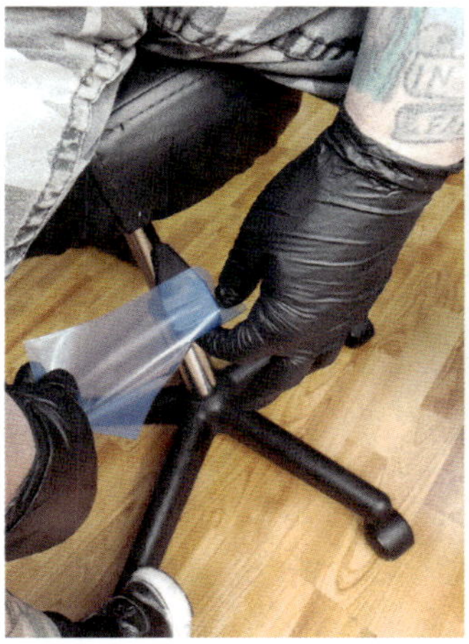

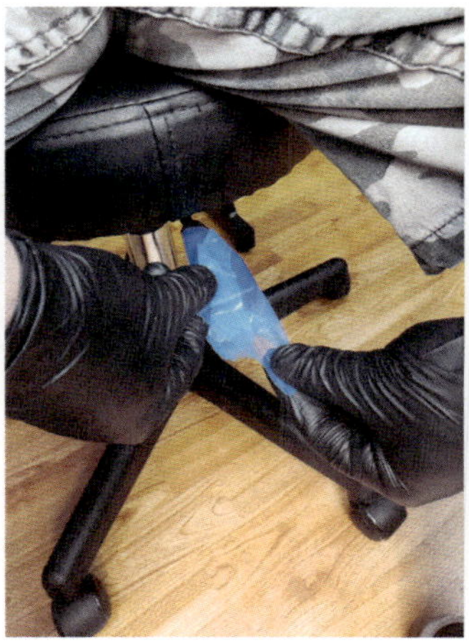

Stool Handle

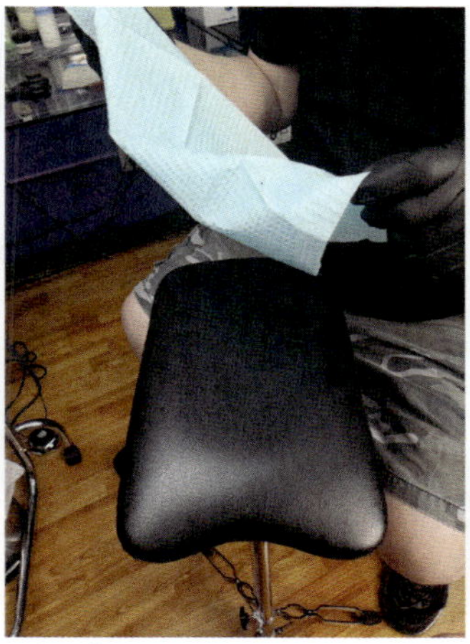

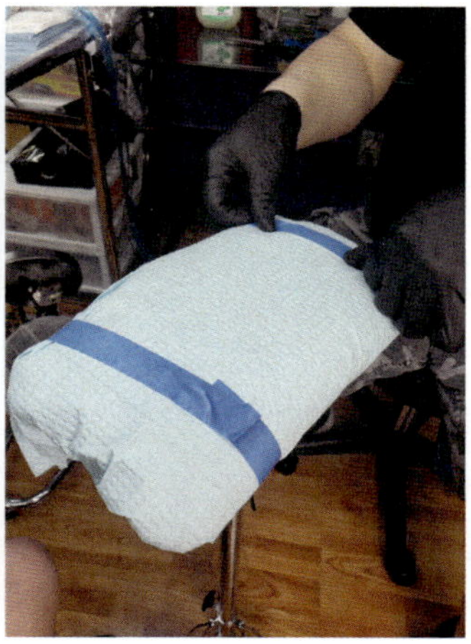

Arm Rest

Example of tattoo machine set-up

Your machine set-up will vary according to the type and brand

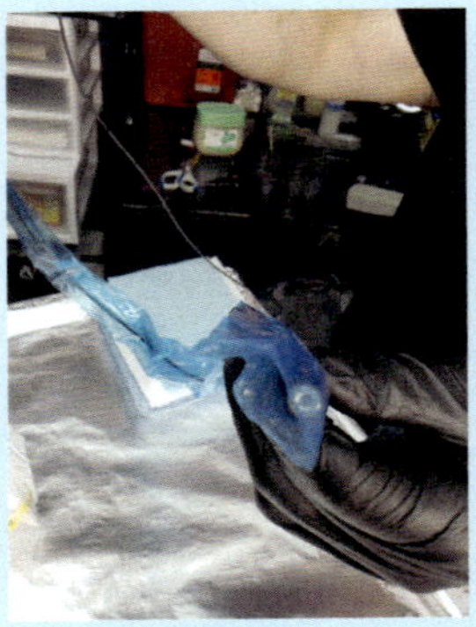

Put the power cord into a cord-cover sleeve...

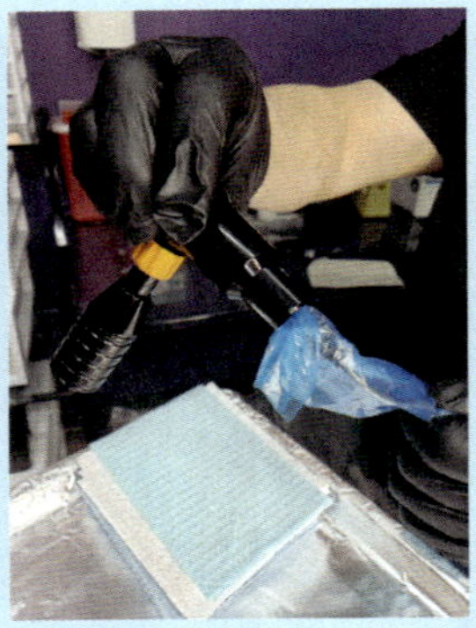

and pierce the cord cover with the pin from the machine and secure it between machine and cord.

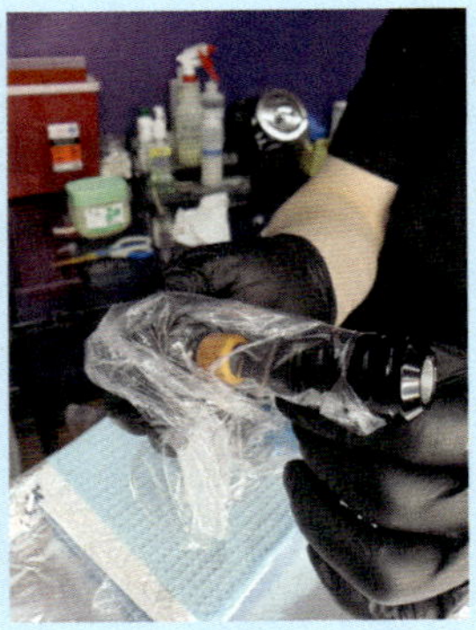

Cut or tear a small slit in the corner of a plastic sandwich bag and place the grip through.

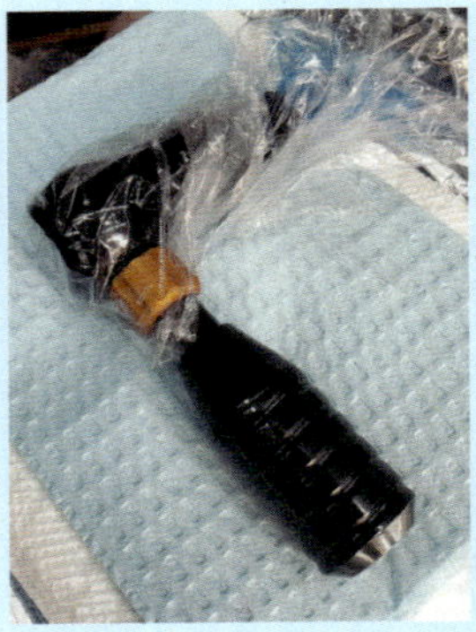

Make sure the hole in the bag isn't so big that the bag falls down the back of the machine.

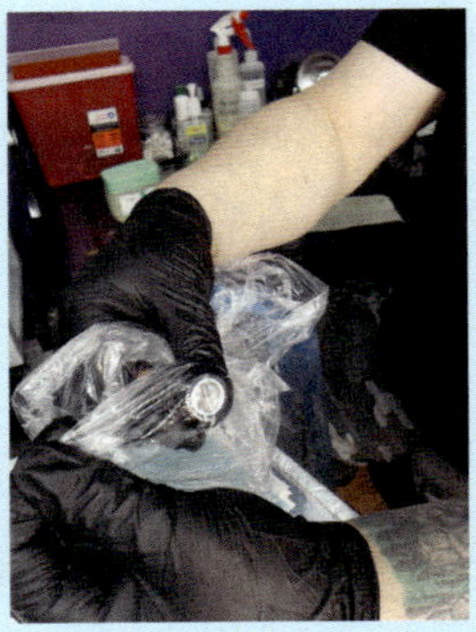

Place a second bag over the grip. The grip should be in the center of the bottom of the bag.

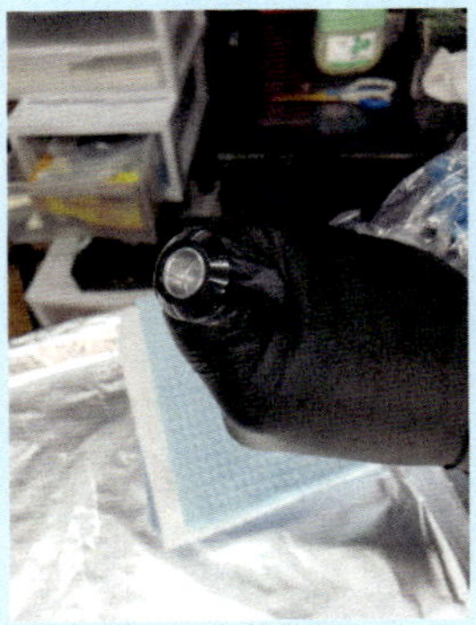

Pull it over the tip of the grip tightly...

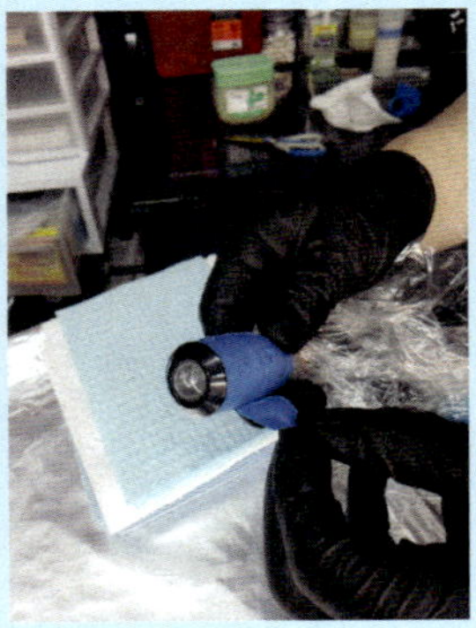

and tape it in place, using blue masking tape, at the slightly narrower area of the grip, so it will stay on tightly.

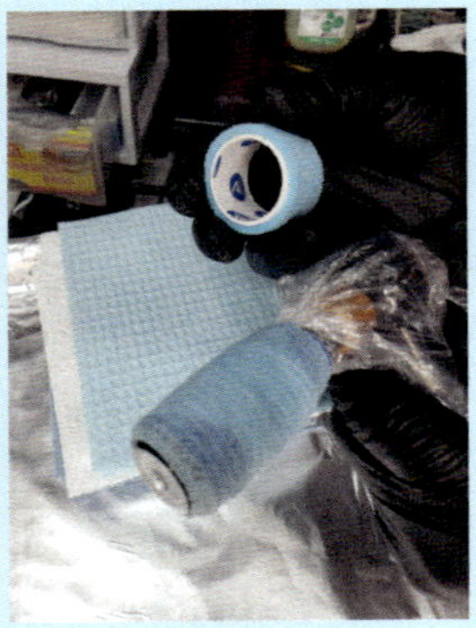

You could add paper towel or self-adherent bandage, for additional padding and gripping power.

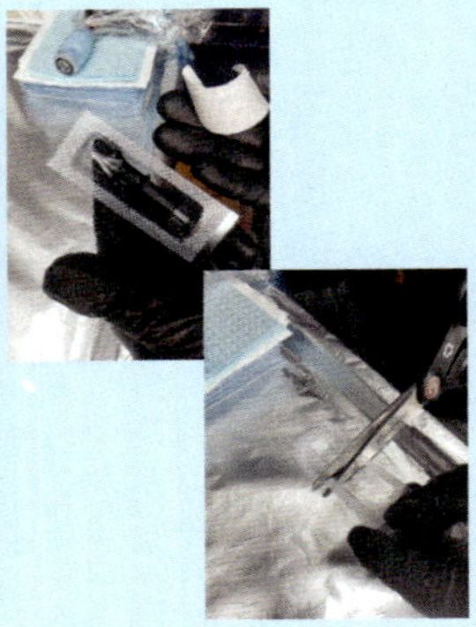

Remove needle cartridge from the package and cut the plastic holder just above half.

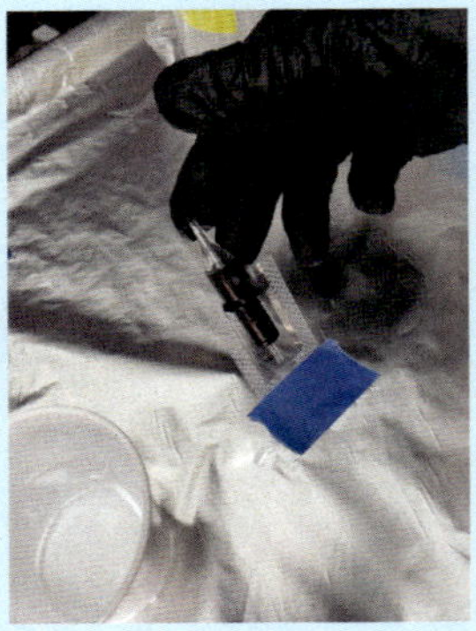

Tape it down so that you can grab the tip of the needle. Never touch the bottom of the cartridge as to avoid contamination.

TATTOO STATION BREAK DOWN INSTRUCTIONS

Photos to follow

- Sanitize hands and put on nitrile gloves. Designate one hand as **clean** & one hand as **dirty** & touch things accordingly.
- With clean hand pour approximately 1/2 tsp. of polyaccrylate in rinse cup.
- Pick up bottle by stem with clean hand, with dirty hand remove the plastic bag and place the plastic bag on the tray. Fold back a corner of foil (or plastic wrap) and put the bottle directly on tray. Repeat with all bottles.
- Using dirty hand, place all needles in sharps container, and include toothpicks if you used them to stir your ink. (they are considered sharps as well).

> "I want to touch people with my art. I want them to say 'he feels deeply, he feels tenderly.'"
>
> *~Vincent Van Gogh, Artist*

- Dirty hand picks up machine by the grip, place clean hand under the plastic bag on the machine. With dirty hand remove tape from grip and remove plastic bags and set them on tray. Dirty hand removes covered power cord from machine, clean hand takes clean portion of cord, slides it out of cord cover, and places it on the corner of tray where the foil has been folded back. Put cord cover on tray.

- With dirty hand, remove barrier protection from power supply, lamp, stool and place on tray.

- With dirty hand pull up paper towels, plastic, or barrier AND tape from tattoo furniture and place in trash.

- Wipe down any ink splatters or visibly soiled areas with green soap and cheapie paper towels. (clean hand grabs green soap bottle, dirty hand uses paper towel to wipe). Place paper towel on tray.

- At this point, consider both gloves as **dirty**.

- Carefully recap razor and place on tray.

- Gather foil (or plastic wrap) from edges & wrap up everything (like a "biohazard burrito") & carefully discard in trash.

- Carefully use gloved hands to pull up inside edge of trash bag (contaminated), to straighten it upwards, then remove dirty gloves and place in trash. Using both bare (clean) hands, grab outside of trash bag (uncontaminated), and pull the bag gently from container (avoid tearing). Use twist tie to seal the trash bag and dispose of it in your designated biohazard garbage can.

- Wash hands w/ soap and water, dry hands and then spray high level disinfectant on the areas touched (water faucet, soap top, counter, inside sink).

- Spray station surfaces thoroughly with high level disinfectant, and leave for appropriate santizing time. Check for any ink drops and clean if necessary.

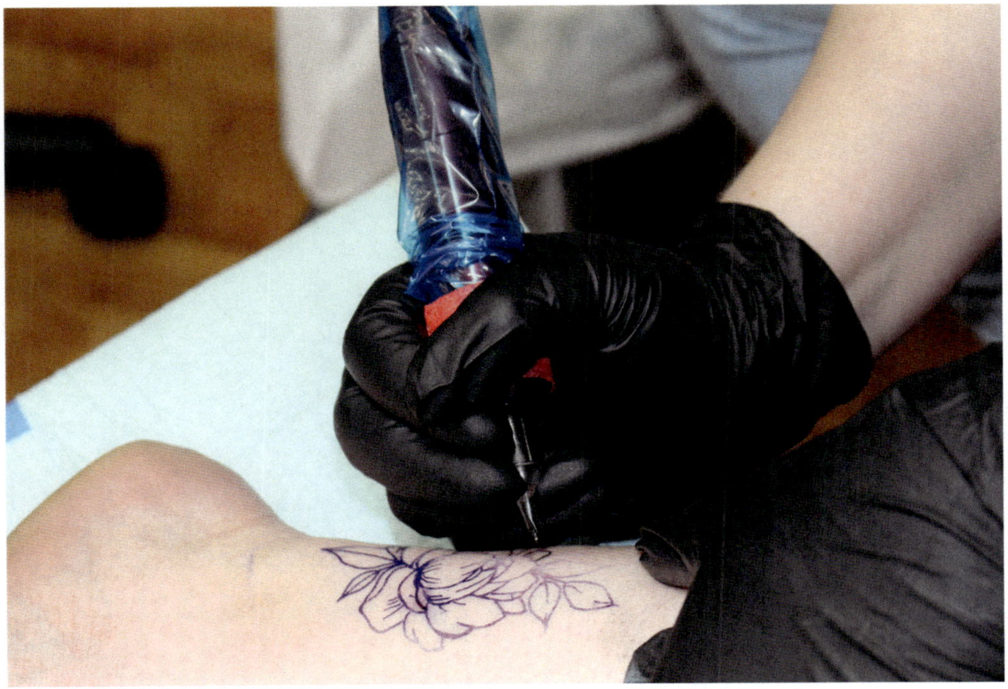

POLYACRYLATE

Sodium polyacrylate, also known as water-lock, is used in a variety of common products such as diapers, instant snow and plant beads. Polyacrylate can absorb as much as 200 to 300 times its mass in liquid and transforms it into a gel, making clean up of rinse water and ink at your station easy. Approximately ½ teaspoon can absorb about 10 oz. of liquid. This product can be purchased on amazon (just search for polyacrylate) or from tattoo suppliers under brands such as 'Solidify', 'Aquasorb", "Newsorb" or "Petrify'. It is also biodegradable and non-toxic, but it can irritate the lungs if inhaled. Obviously avoid getting it in eyes and mouth. and it can cause serious clogging if washed down the sink.

Tear Down

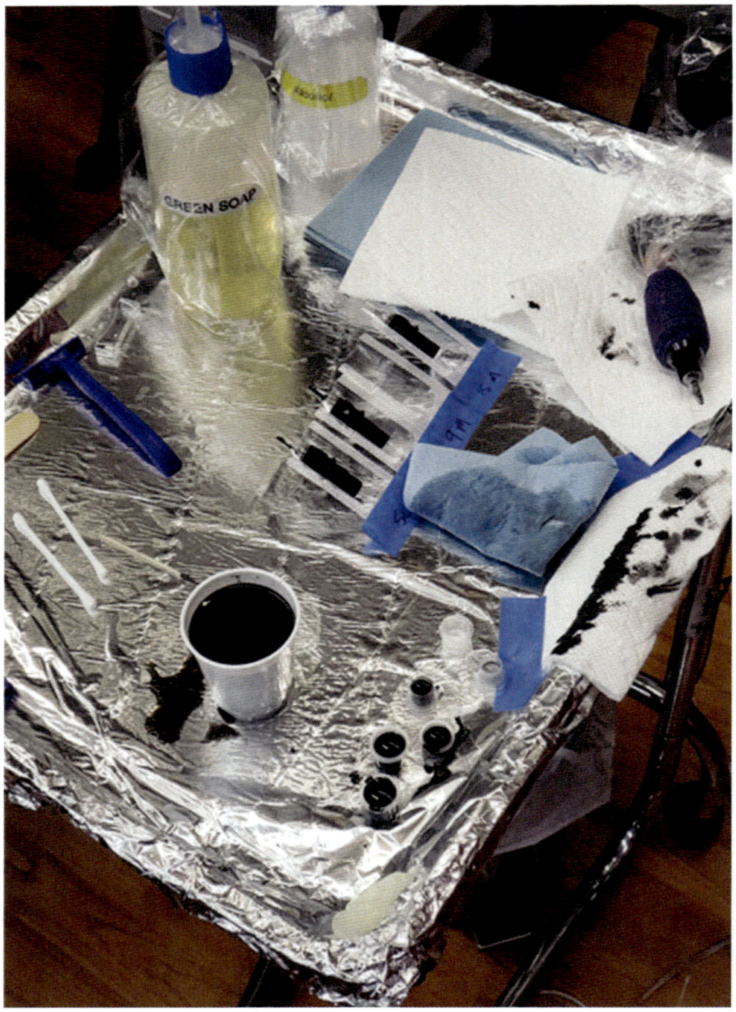

1 - Assign a "clean" hand and "dirty" hand

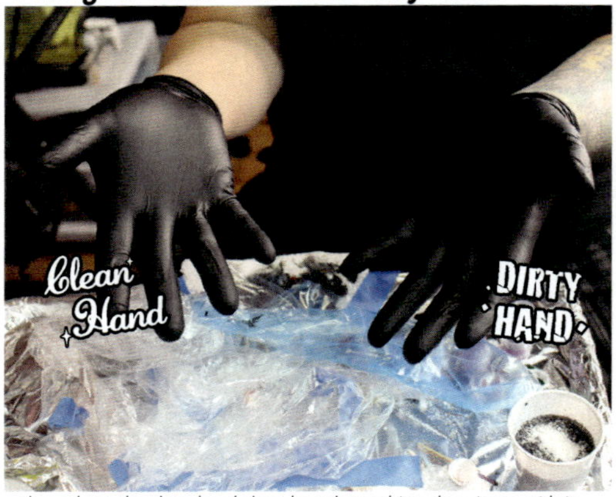

Always keep the clean hand clean by only touching clean items with it. The dirty hand only touches dirty items. Never mix up the two!

4 - Break down machine

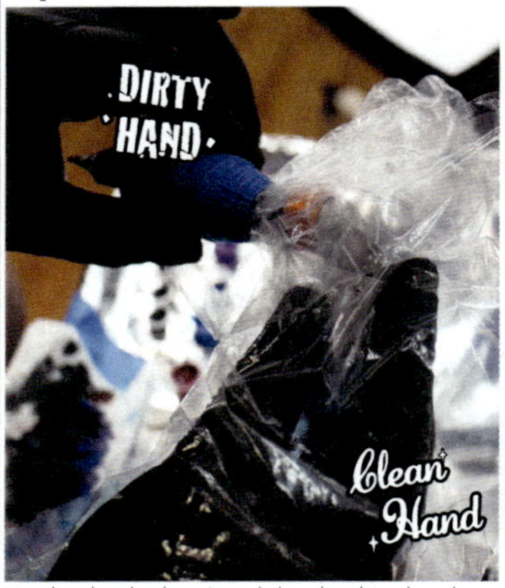

Dirty hand grabs the grip and clean hand reach under the plastic bag to grab the handle of the machine.

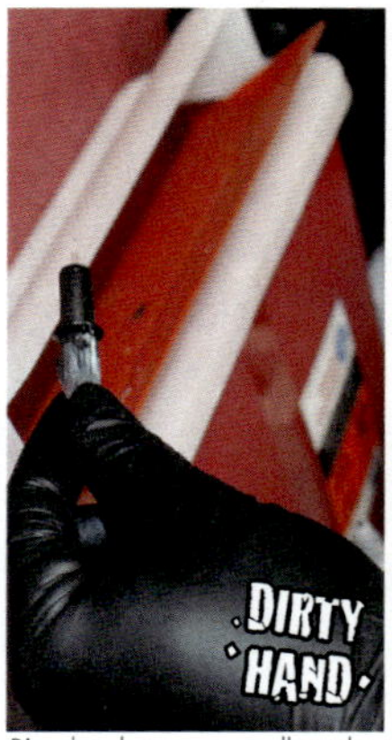

Dirty hand removes needle and places it in sharp's container

6 - Remove remaining barriers

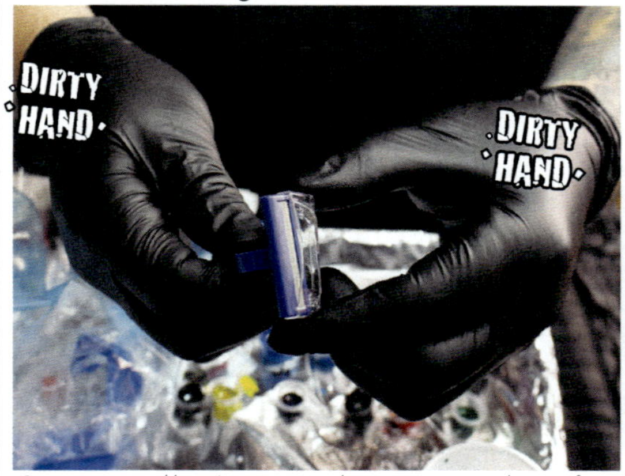

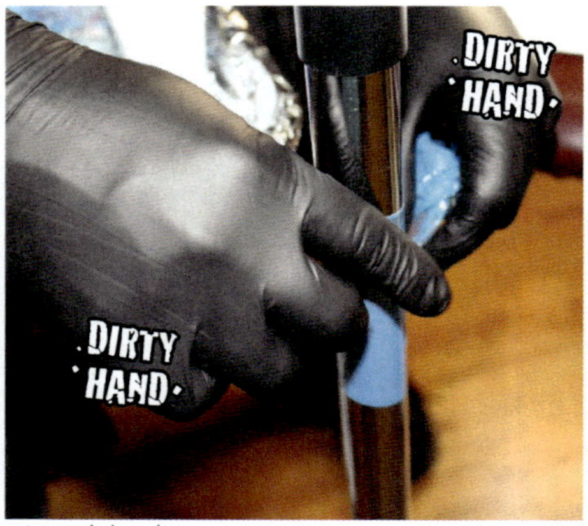

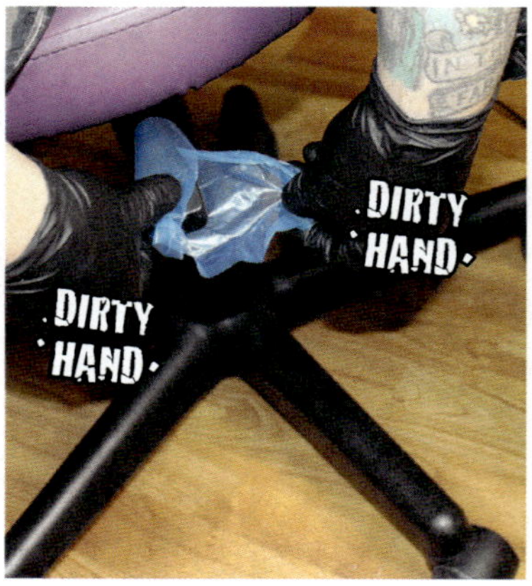

Cap your razor and leave it on your tray, then you can remove the rest of your barriers and place those o n your tray.

2 - Pour polyacrylate into rinse water

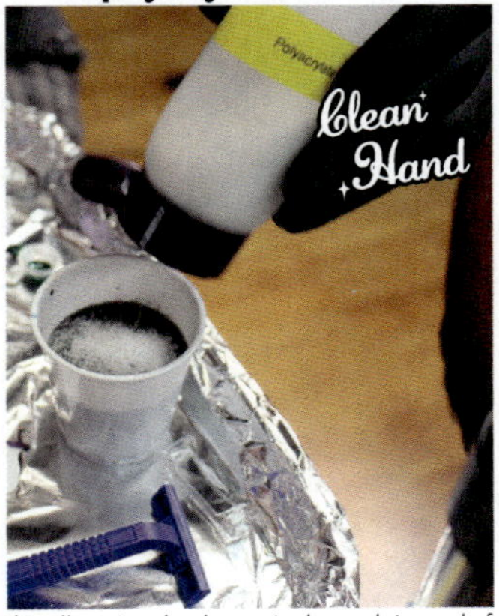

This allows it to be thrown in the trash instead of down the sink. Let sit until fully absorbed.

3 - Tear down bottles

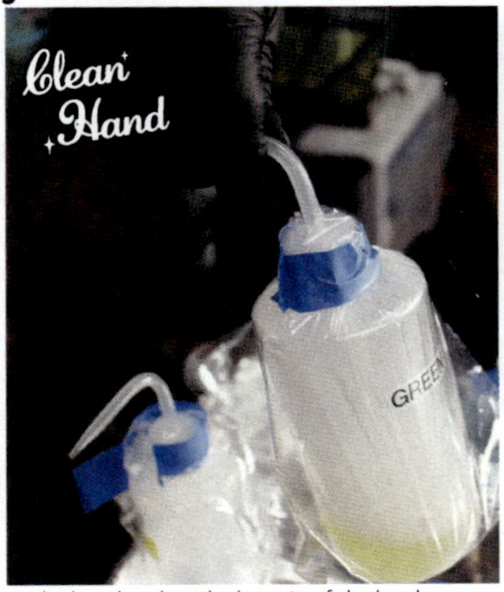

With clean hand, grab clean tip of the bottle...

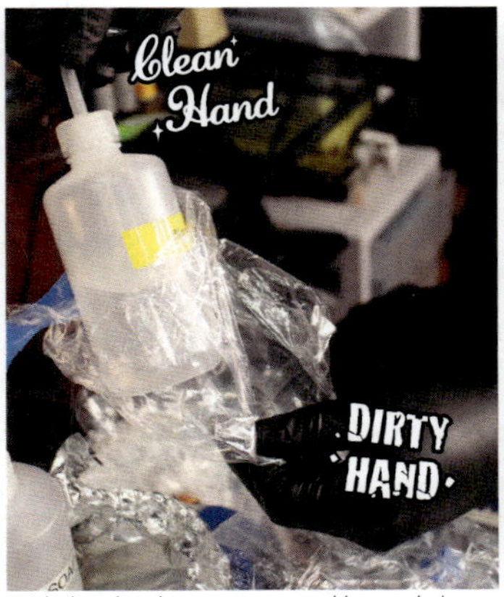

with dirty hand, remove tape and bag and place them on the tray.

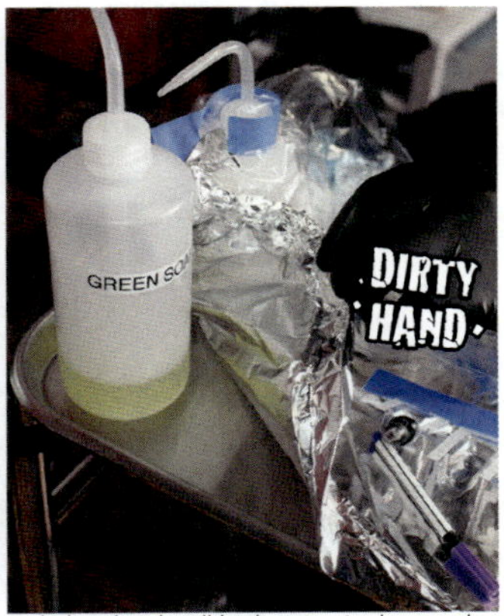

with dirty hand, pull back protective layer and place bottle directly on tray for later disinfecting

5 - Break down machine

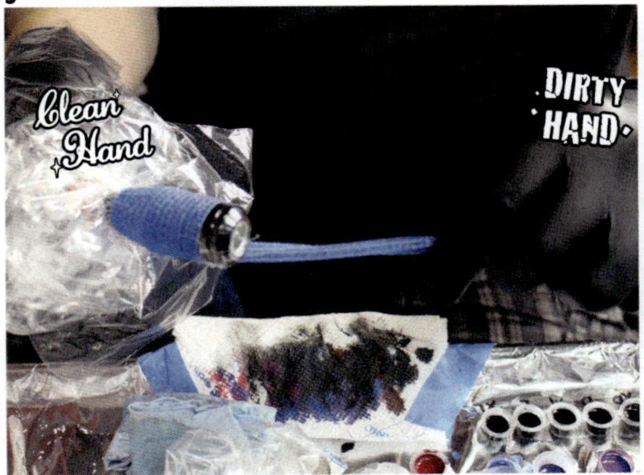

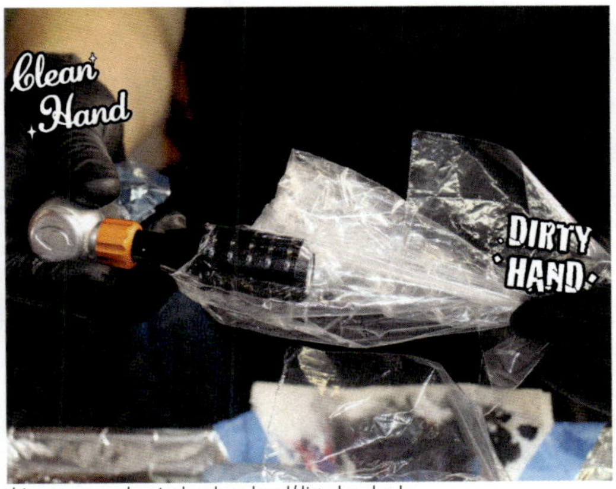

Each type of machine will be broken down in a slightly different manner. But the key thing to remember is the clean hand/dirty hand rule.

Both hands can be dirty now.

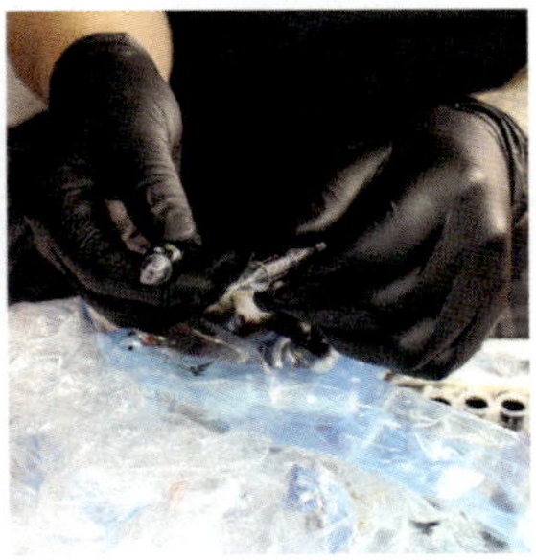

You've already touched everything that needs to be clean, so now can can use both hands for to remove all your contaminated barriers.

7 - Remove remaining barriers

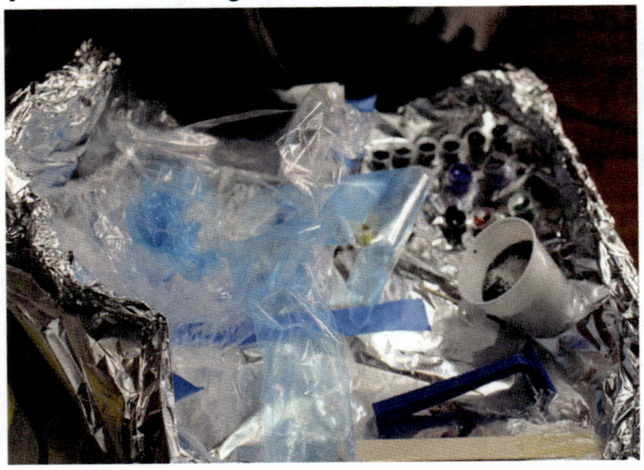

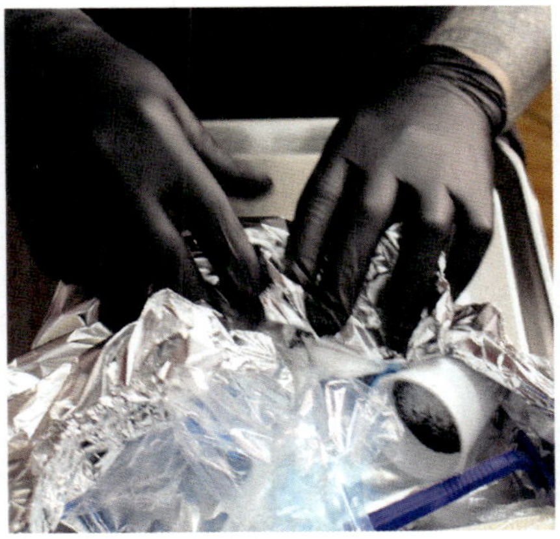

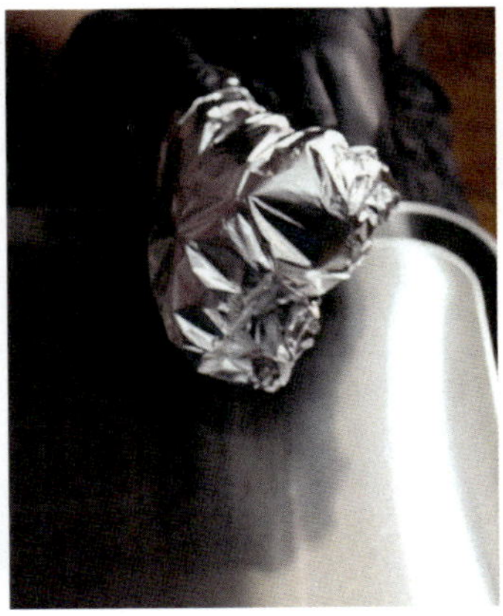

With all your barriers on your tray, roll everything up into what we affectionately call a "biohazard burrito" Thanks to Vaune Rush

> "Successful and unsuccessful people do not vary greatly in their abilities. They vary in their desires to reach their potential."
> – *John Maxwell, Author & Speaker*

Temporary Tattoo with Permanent Markers

You can create fake tattoo designs on skin by using permanent markers. This will give you the chance to practice shaving and stencil placement. You can also begin to see how images flow with the body and explore value & color harmony. In addition, this gives you the chance to practice different compositions before you actually tattoo them.

What you will need:

Stencil
Stencil application fluid (***diluted green soap or other***)
Disposable razor
Medium and/or fine-point permanent markers (***sharpies brand is great***)
Rubbing alcohol
Swabs and/or cotton balls
White out or white acrylic paint
Translucent loose powder
Cosmetic or paint brush

- Shave the area where stencil will be applied.
- Rub small amount of green soap or stencil application fluid over the area of skin where the stencil will be applied. Allow it to get slightly tacky.
- Press the stencil onto the skin, ink side down. Dab the back of stencil with paper towel moistened with diluted green soap. Peel up a small corner to check if it transferred and apply more pressure, if necessary, before removing completely. Allow to dry for about 10 minutes.
- Trace over the lines from the stencil transfer with a black permanent marker, experimenting with different thicknesses.
- Color in the design with permanent markers. Avoid crossing the black lines or colored ink will be muddied.
- Use different colored markers to produce a gradation of color, leaving skin space in some areas.
- Blend the color into skin spaces with swab or cotton ball, moistened with a bit of rubbing alcohol, to fade color out in some areas.
- Touch up any areas with more color as needed. Allow the "tattoo" to dry completely.
- Use white-out or white acrylic paint to add "highlights" (remember; white tattoo pigment would **never** be as bright).
- Load the powder puff or brush with translucent powder and gently dab it over the tattoo. Brush off excess.
- This fake tattoo will last several days if not scrubbed. You can remove it with rubbing alcohol and soap & water.

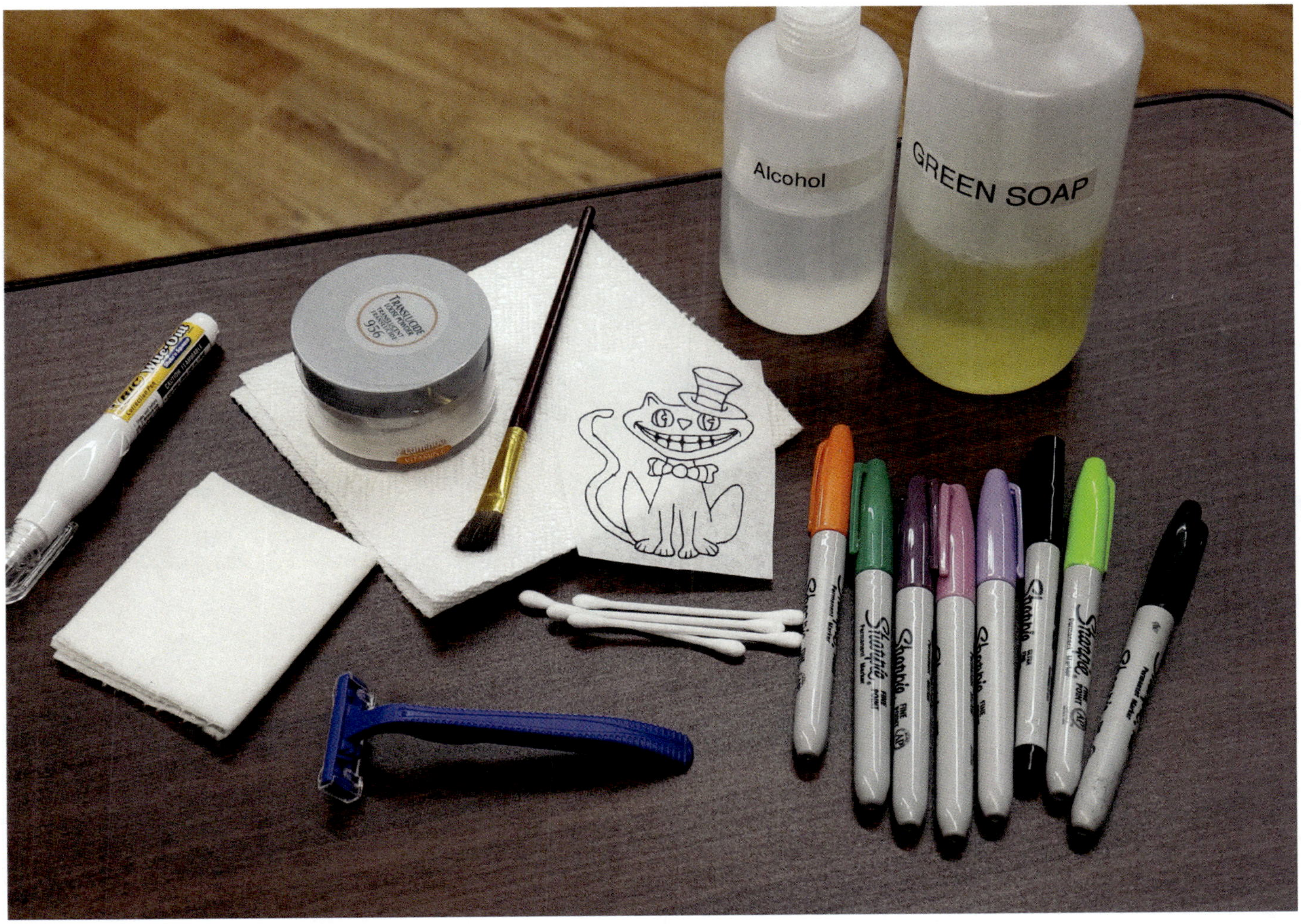
Alcohol
GREEN SOAP

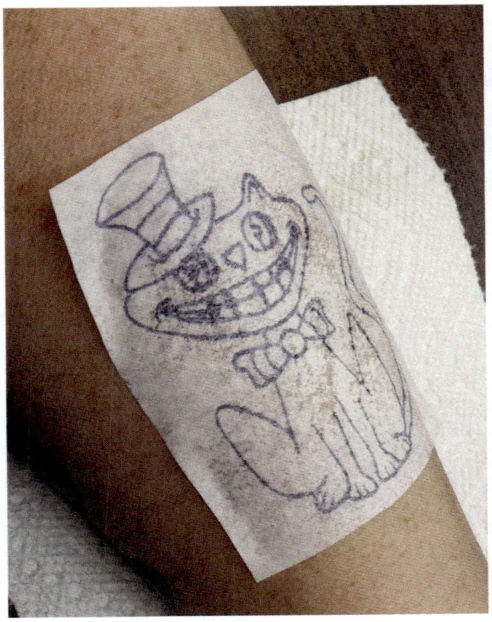

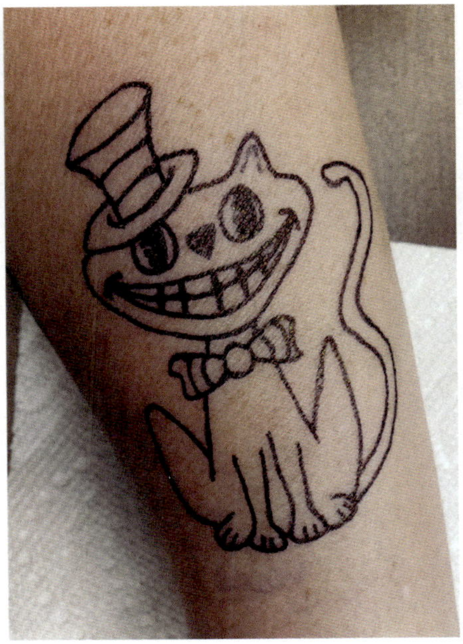

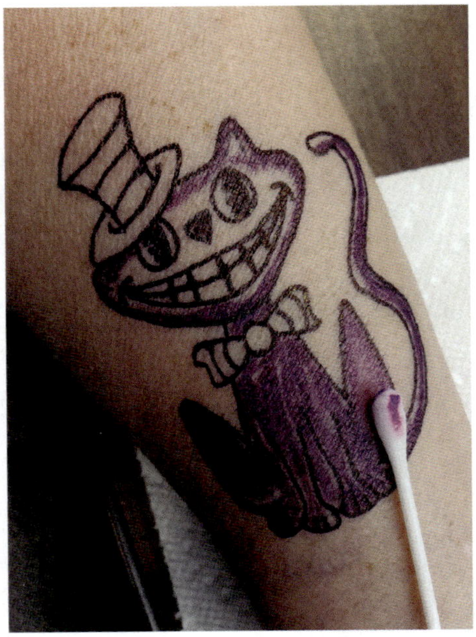

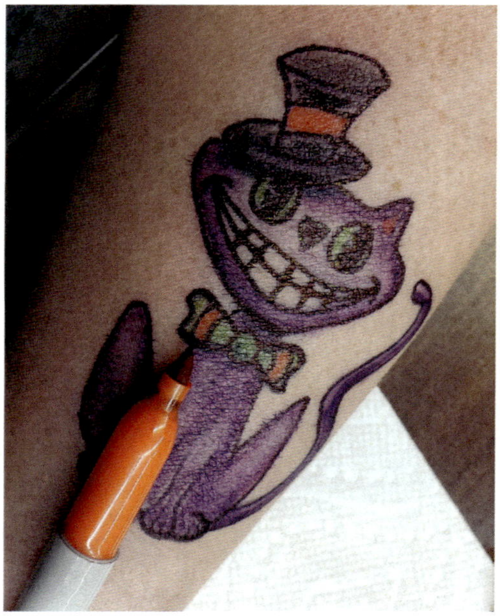

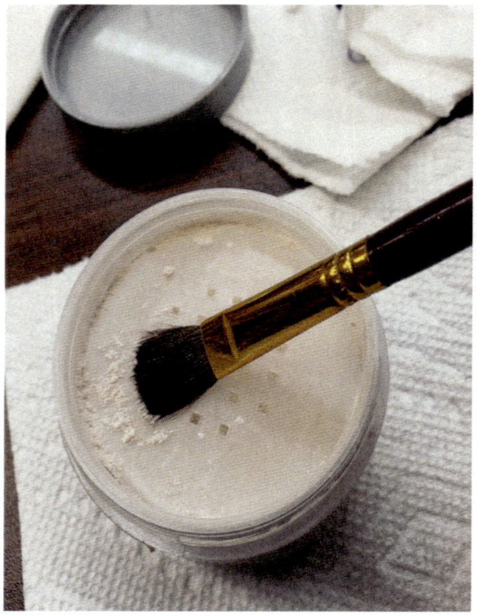

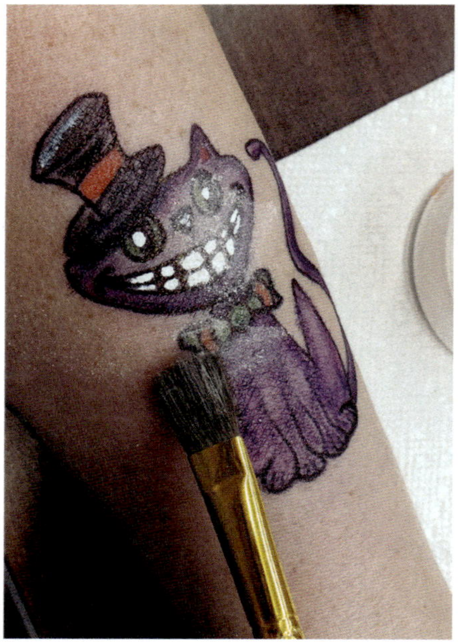

Creating fake tattoos is an excellent way to practice your skills. You could even add photos of your fake tattoos to your portfolio until you can fill it with real tattoos!

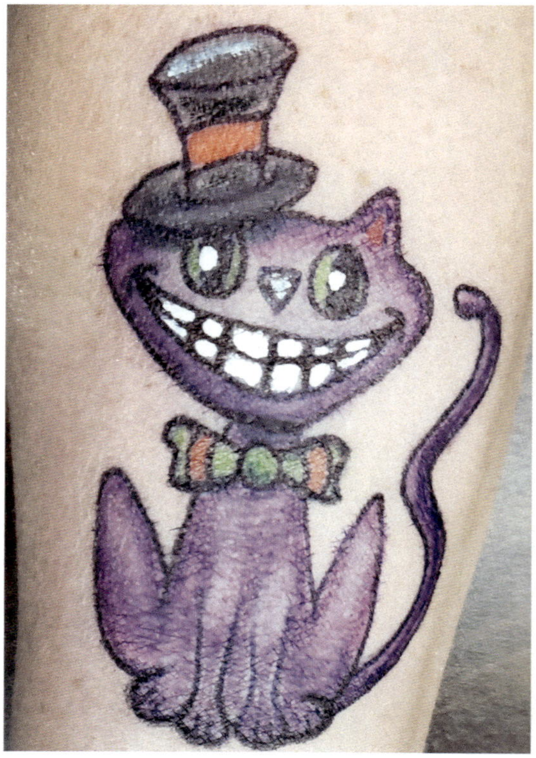

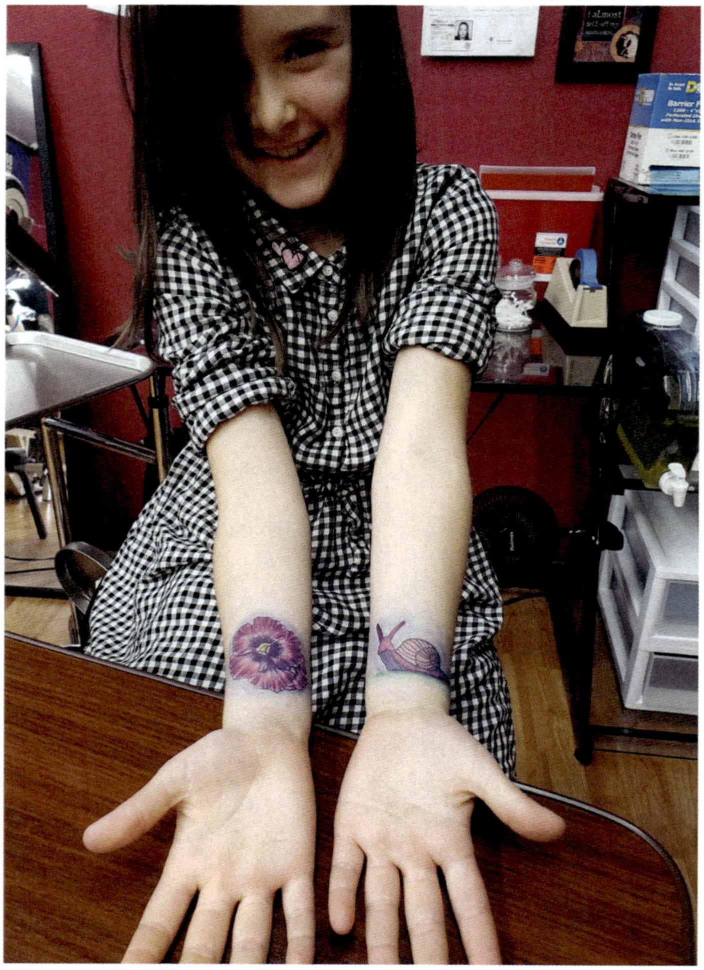

"Working hard for something we don't care about is called stress. Working hard for something we love is called passion."

~unknown

Chapter Four Highlights

- Choosing tattoo furniture is a consideration of both function, comfort and expense.
- Shave the skin before applying a stencil. Razors are one-time use and must be recapped before disposal.
- Green soap is commonly used to prep and shave the skin, adhere the stencil, and cleanse & remove ink and bodily fluids from the skin during the tattoo procedure.
- Witch hazel reduces irritation and inflammation.
- Individual pain levels vary widely.
- Single-use items must be disposed after every procedure.
- Ink cups can be secured to tray or work surface with a dab of petroleum jelly.
- Use barrier film, foil, or plastic wrap, where appropriate, to cover your work station.
- Machine set-up will vary according to the different types and brands.
- Always designate one hand as clean and one hand as dirty when you are breaking down a contaminated station.
- Use "dirty" hand to remove barriers from lamp, power supply, stool and furniture.
- Polyacrylate or "water lock" makes clean up of rinse water and ink easy.
- After breaking the station down, spray surfaces with high-level disinfectant and leave for the appropriate amount of time.
- Creating fake tattoos with permanent markers is an excellent way to practice composition and flow.

Wisecracks:

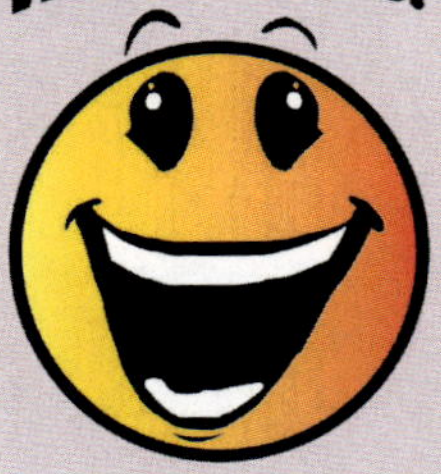

College students just received their financial aid and have some tough decisions to make.

Buy textbooks, buy groceries, pay bills or get that new tattoo.

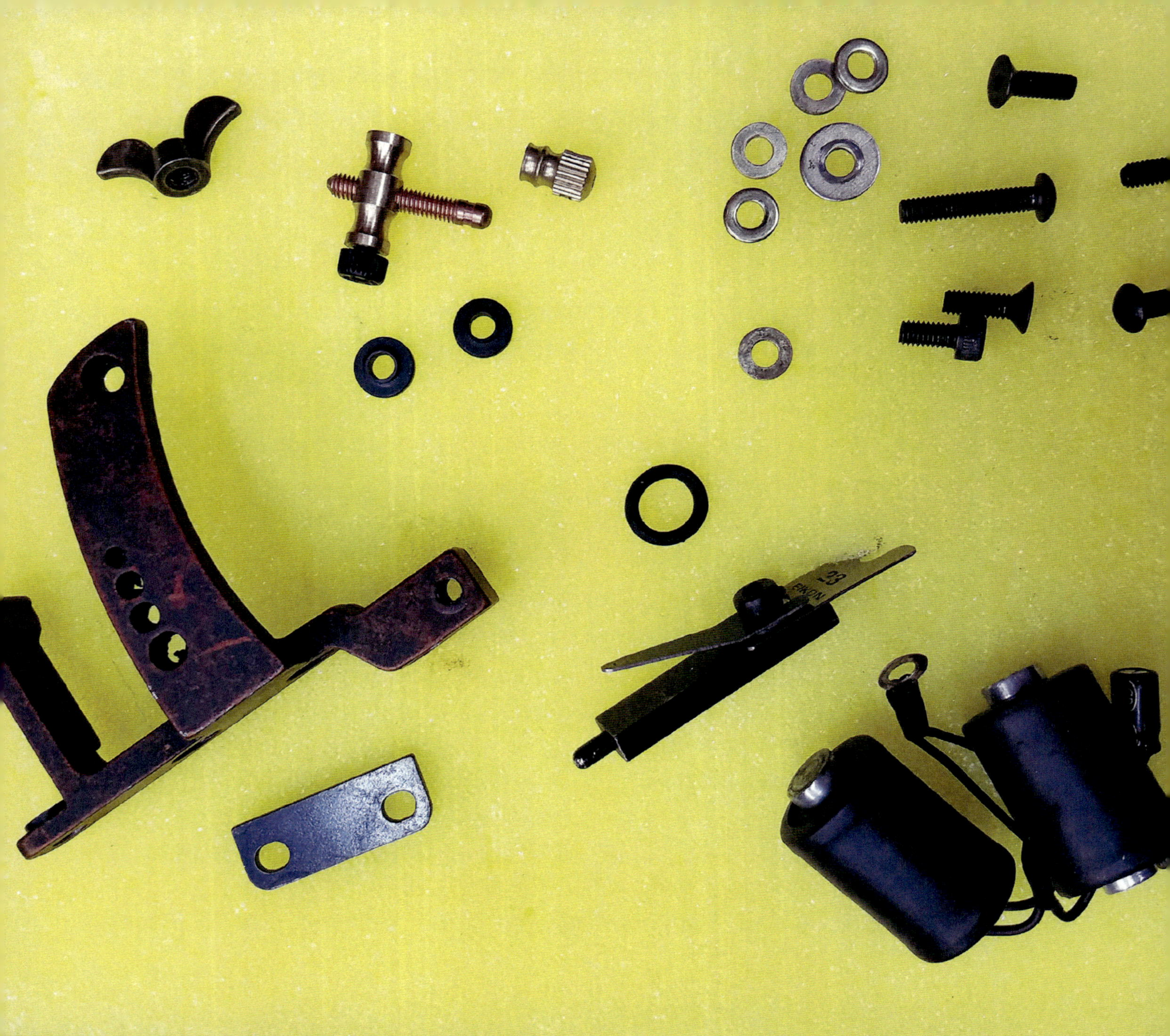
23
EIKON

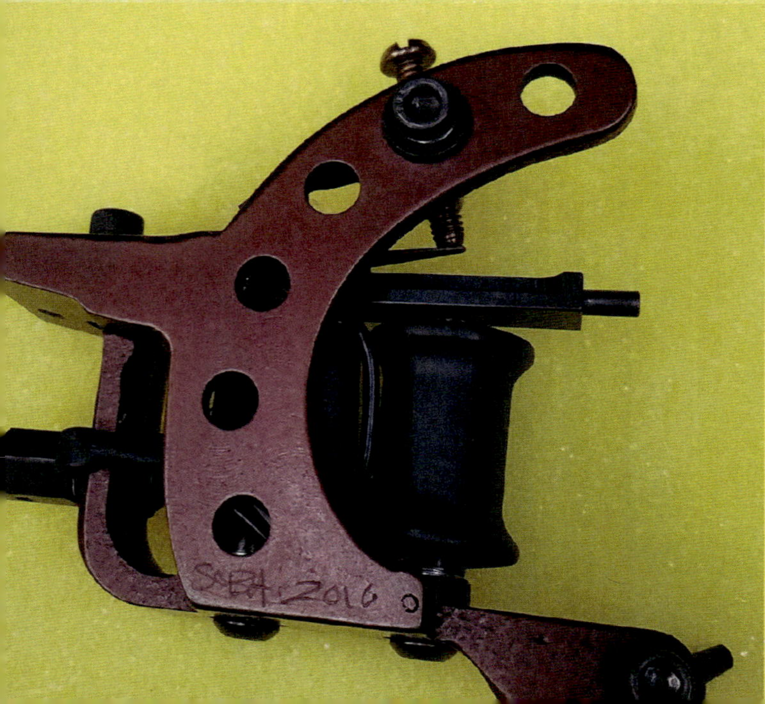
2016

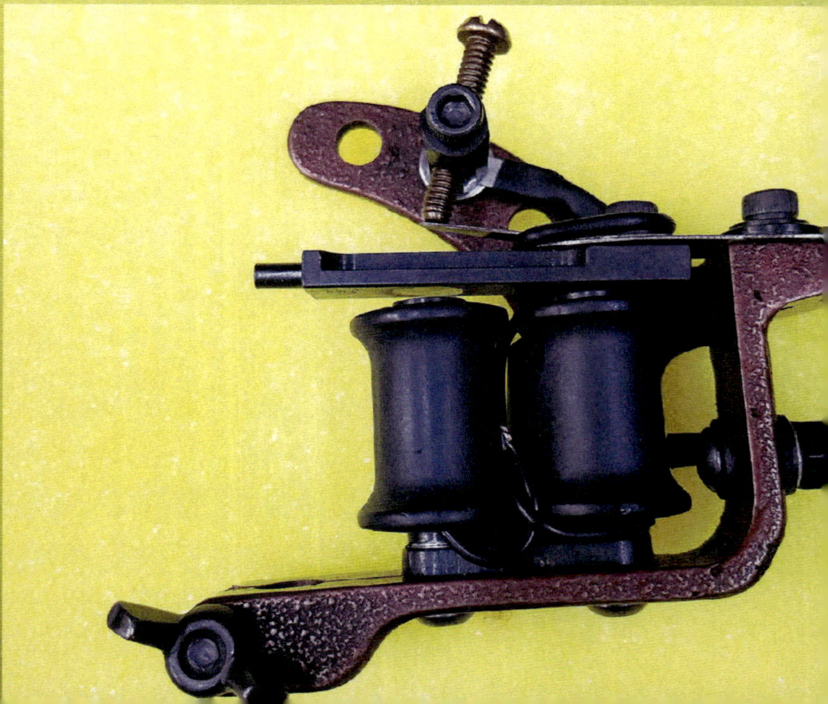

Chapter Five

Machines & Needles

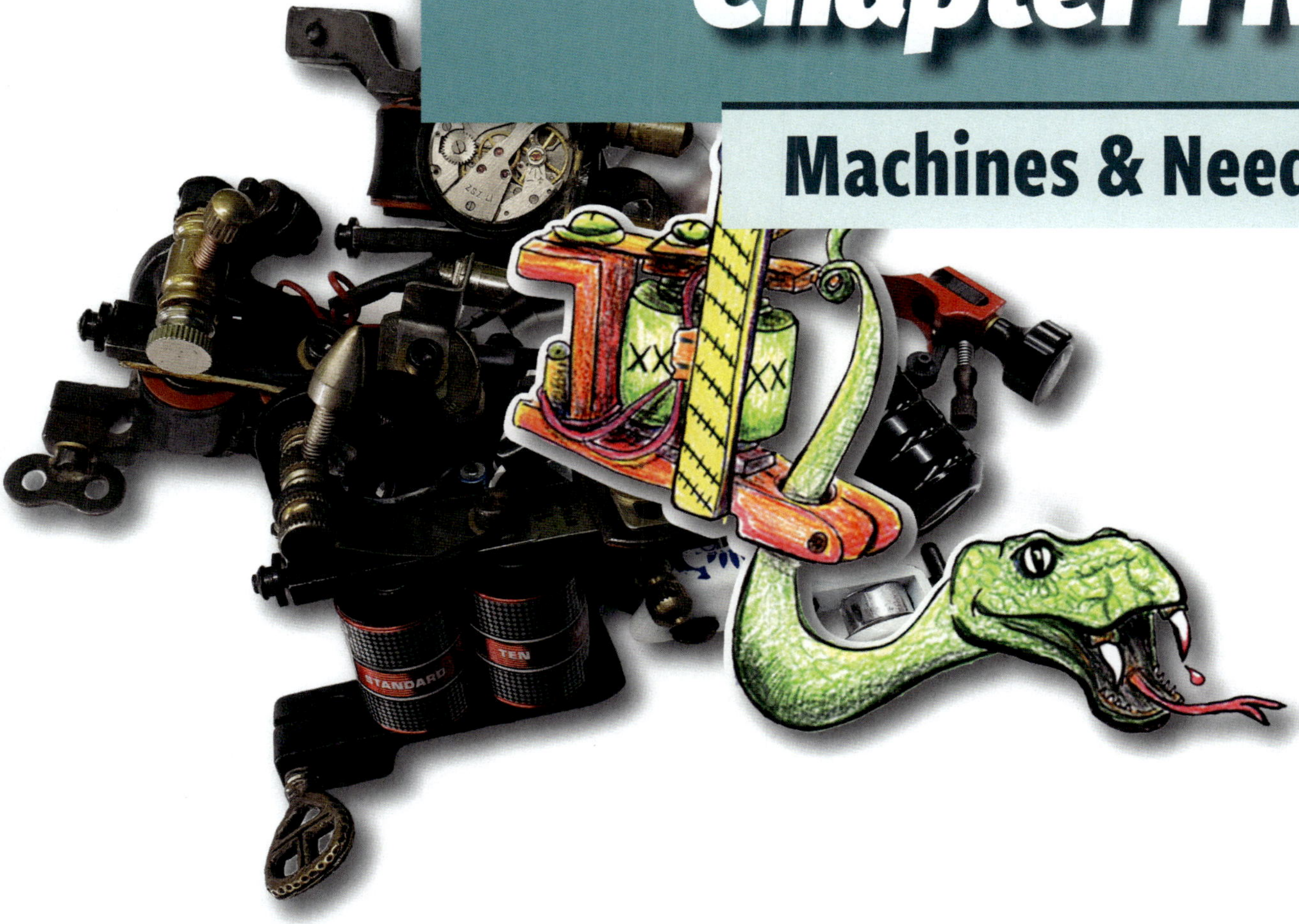

Years ago, tattoos were applied using items such as sharpened bones, picks, sticks and needle and thread. We are fortunate enough to have the tattoo machine to do our heavy lifting for us—a tool that makes tattooing much easier, less painful for the client and much faster than the old "stick and poke" of bygone days.

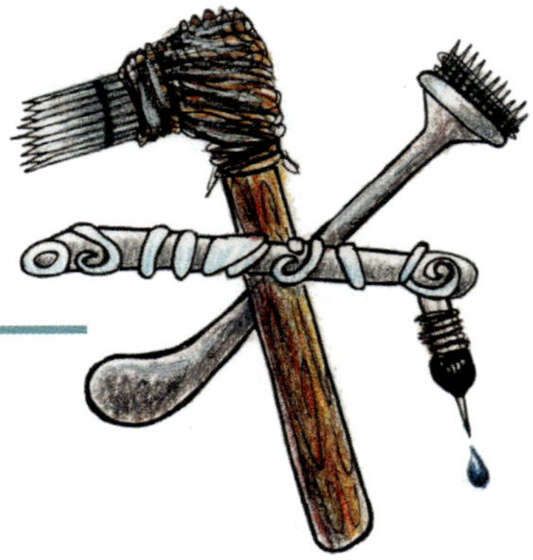

Tattoo Machines

Modern tattoo machines use several basic components:

- A sterilized needle
- A tube system, which draws the ink up into a reservoir
- A grip
- An electric motor
- A power supply
- A foot pedal, which controls the vertical movement of the needle.

> "For someone who likes tattoos, the most precious thing is bare skin."
>
> *~Cher, Singer & Actor*

How Does the Tattoo Machine Work?

The tattoo machine simply operates like a tiny sewing machine: the tattoo needle which is attached to a needle bar or embedded in a needle cartridge moves up and down rapidly as it penetrates the epidermis to deposit the ink into the dermal layer of the skin, while the artist steers the machine. The depth of penetration of the needle is only about 1.5 to 2 mm. The tube tip is dipped into the ink, which is then drawn up into the reservoir. This delivers enough ink to move a distance of about 1 ½" before needing to dip again.

> **Note:**
> "Early Tinkerers of Electric Tattooing", October 2015, by Carmen Forquer Nyssen, is a thorough and well-researched article about the early use of electric tattoo machines. This article can be found at:
> http://www.buzz-worthytattoo.com/tattoo-history-research-articles/early-tinkerers-of-electric-tattooing/

The Coil Machine and the Rotary Machine

Coil machines have been around since the late 1800s and are based on an original design for an engraving machine invented by Thomas Edison in 1876. It was later adapted by Samuel O'Reilly in 1891 to use as a tattoo machine and was actually a sort of coil-rotary hybrid.

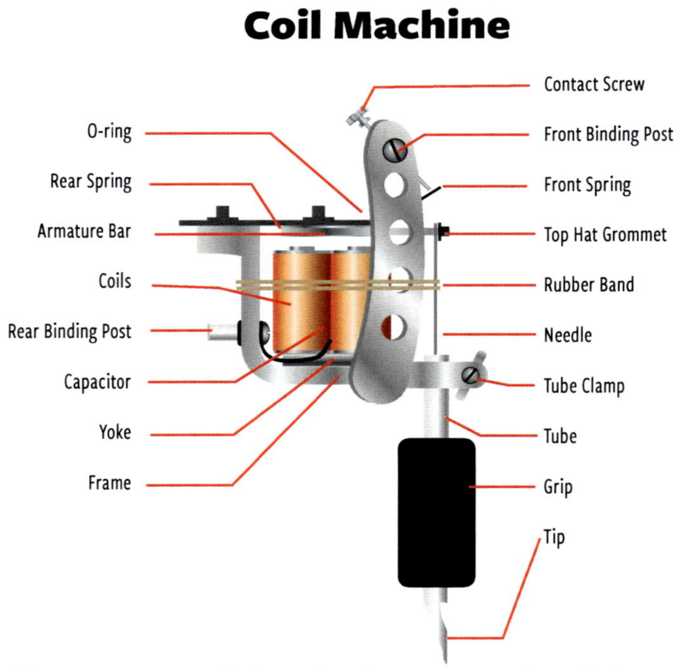

Coil tattoo machines are powered when the electromagnetic coils become magnetized. A magnetic circuit moves the armature bar up and down and the needle is attached to the armature bar. When the armature bar is in the down position this punctures the skin and deposits ink. When the armature bar is drawn down, it is separated from the contact point for a fraction of a second and loses power. This forces it to recoil back into the original position where the current is stabilized again. The buzzing sound that is typically heard

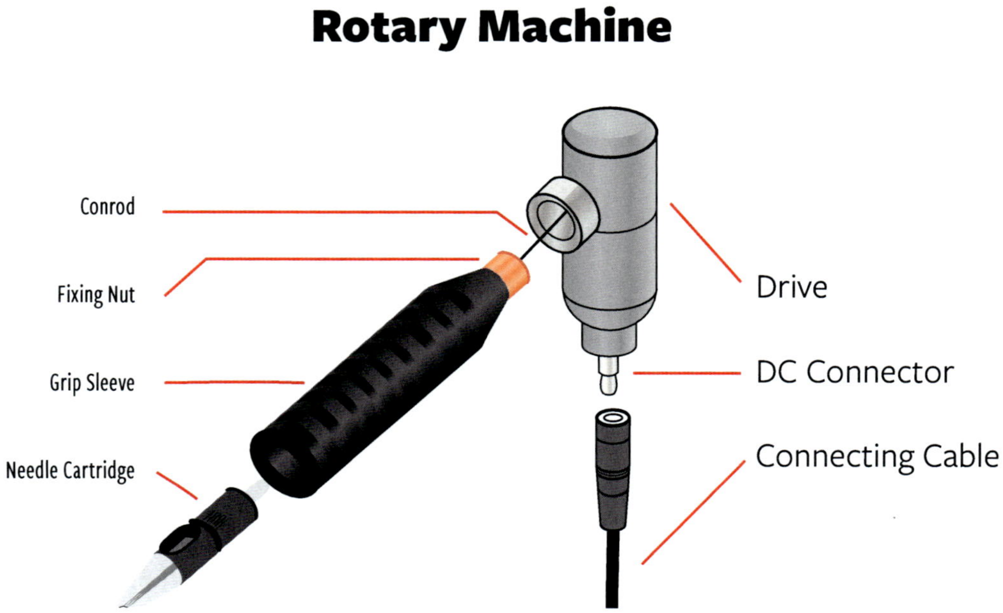

is the electrical current starting and stopping thousands of times as the machine is in use. Coil machines are fairly inexpensive to build and are a very popular type of tattoo machine on the market.

Rotary machines, which are driven by an electric motor instead of magnetic coils, were streamlined in 1978 by German tattooer Manfred Kohrs. Still based on the design of early tattoo machines, these machines mechanically deliver the ink into the skin. For many years the rotary machine was seen as the tool of permanent makeup artists and viewed as too limited for artistic tattoos. Recently, since around 2012, rotary machines have gained a much bigger audience and have exploded in popularity.

Coil Machine	Rotary Machine
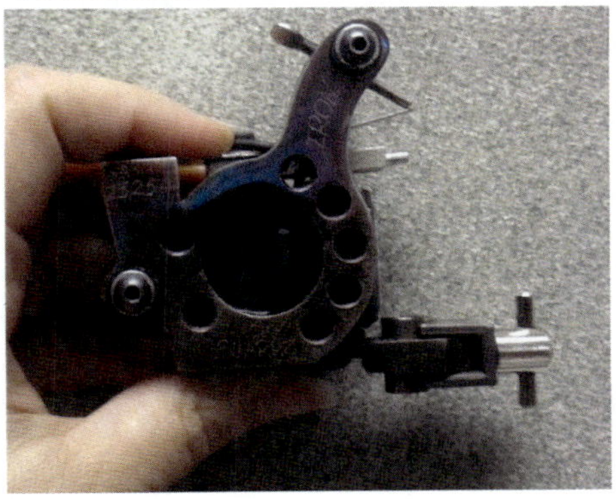	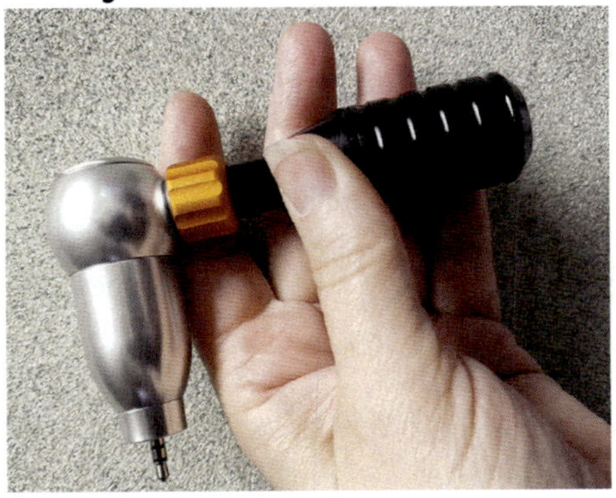
Heavy vibration and loud buzzing	Very little vibration and very quiet
Softer hitting, more give	Harder hitting, more consistent power
Exposed coils and wires	Motor encased in frame
Constant tuning and maintenance	Rarely requires tuning or maintenance
Adjustable and easy to customize, parts changeable	Not as adjustable, but newer models are being manufactured with more customizations
Coils are perceived to hurt more due to the loud buzzing sound and possibly the weight	Rotaries are perceived to hurt less, possibly because they are lighter and quieter

NOTE: Check out this video by French tattooer Lil B, a fantastic black and grey artist, on the subject of "Coil vs. Rotary": https://www.youtube.com/watch?v=UyV1TtEY2uw

Some general considerations:

The choice of purchasing a coil or rotary machine is an individual decision, likely based on what you've been exposed to the most. Many successful artists choose to stick with the tried and time-tested coil as they prefer the variation in "hit" and the adjustability. Yet, with new artists being trained on rotary machines, and new models being

Note: Building up lines or "sculpting" is not going over the same skin you just lined but rather coming right up next to the single pass line you created to vary the "weight" or variety of line size. You can also use multiple sizes of needles to accomplish the same idea.

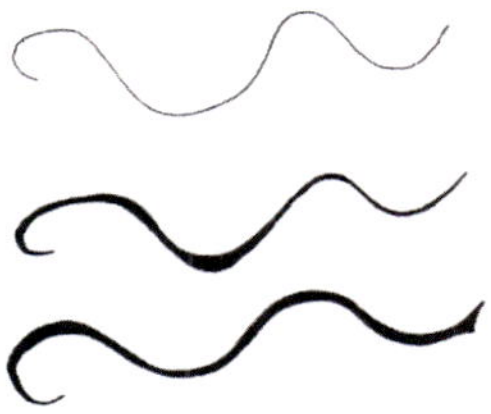

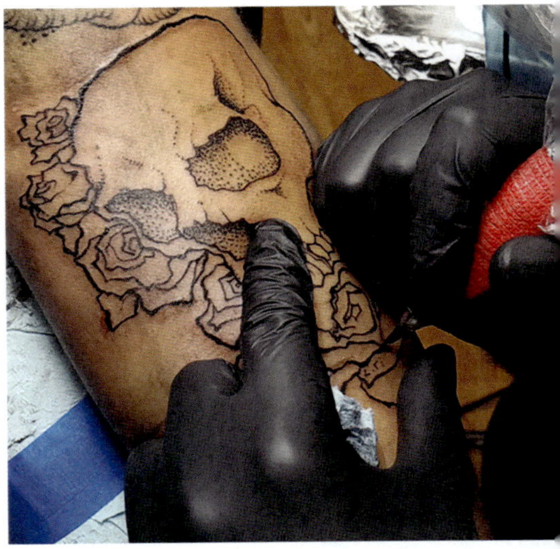

Sculpting lines

> **Note:**
> Painful Pleasures, an online tattoo supply company, has provided a great article, with photos, that explains the differences between many types and brands of tattoo machines. https://info.painfulpleasures.com/help-center/information-center/coil-vs-rotary-tattoo-machines

created with even more flexibility, (i.e. rotary machines with interchangeable components), the gap is quickly closing. Whether you choose a coil machine or a rotary machine, using the best tool possible for the job is ultimately the most important consideration.

We won't be getting into machine building or maintenance in this book. See chapter twelve for recommendations on tattoo machine specific books.

What's the Difference Between Lining and Shading?

Typically, when using coil machines, an artist would have at least two different machines, each set up according to whether they are lining or shading. One machine can be set up to create the outlines of a tattoo design, whereas another machine might be set up as a shader and used to shade or color in the tattoo. The primary difference is the speed at which the needle bar moves up and down while penetrating the skin. The secondary difference pertains to needle depth. On the other hand, one rotary machine can do all three jobs by simply adjusting the power level, hand speed and depth.

Lining:
To line a tattoo, typically the machine runs faster and is harder hitting. The faster speed compensates for the speed at which the artist moves the hand along a tattoo. To produce a nice straight and solid line, you want a machine that runs quick and smooth as you move your hand at a steady rate along the skin. The needles should puncture the

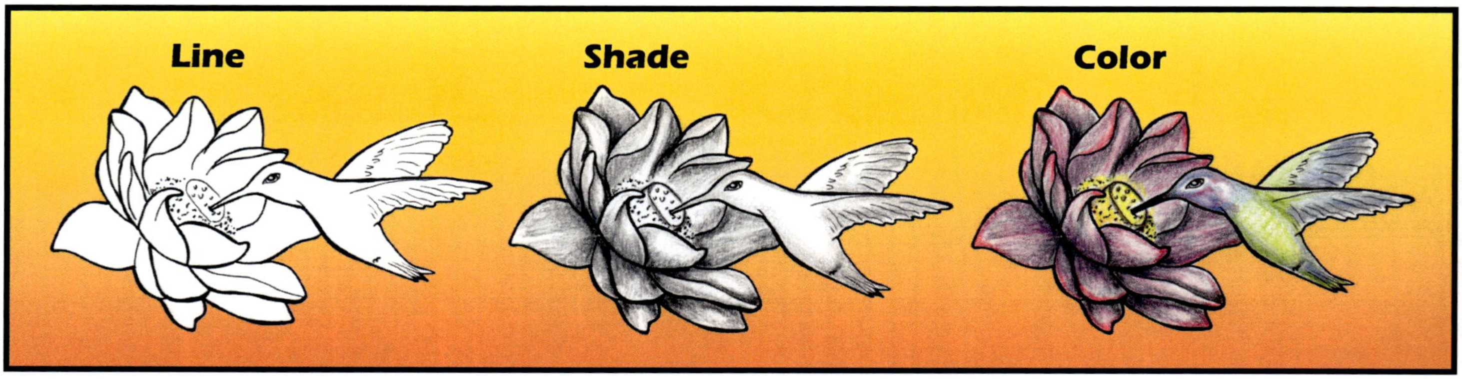

skin almost straight down, quickly delivering maximum pigment, through the epidermis and into the dermis and then pulling back out as smooth as possible. Lining should be done in one or two passes, so as not to overwork the skin.

> **NOTE**: In the beginning, it may be difficult to get used to the weight and/or vibration of the machine. Using it for several hours may cause pain and cramping in your hands, so strengthening your hands is crucial. Drawing with a variety of pen sizes (which you SHOULD be doing constantly) will assist you to not only build muscle but become proficient at tattooing even and consistent lines.
>
> You can also wrap the pencils or pens with paper towels and/or tape to simulate the size of a tattoo grip. Using an exerciser or squeeze balls several times a day, perhaps while watching TV, is terrific for speeding-up the muscle building process.
>
> 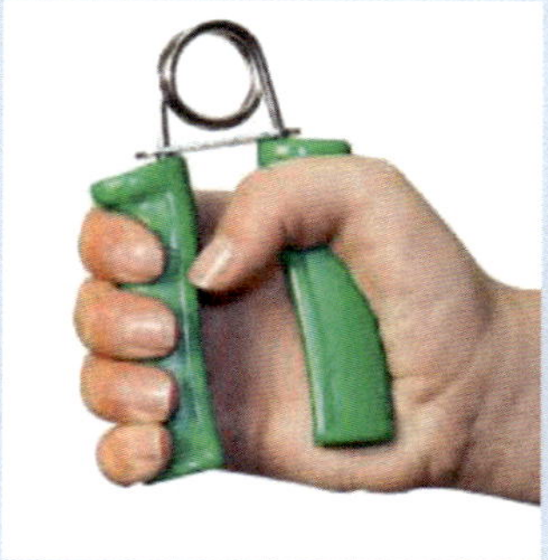
>
> In addition, purchasing rubber or cushioned covers for your grip can ease the stress to your hand.

Shading and coloring:
Shading in a tattoo design creates an elegant play of light, adds desired contrast and can create a three-dimensional feel that brings more life into the piece. Artists spend years developing their skills and much of the time when a tattoo lacks that "certain something" it is due to the fact that there is little or no shading, or the shading has been done improperly.

In the past, the term "shading" or "shader" has been used interchangeably to mean either coloring in or creating shadows in a tattoo. But to be more exact we'll separate these terms. When shading in a tattoo, you are creating different "value" levels within the design to add dimension and depth. This is generally done with a variety of thinned black ink, creating a grey value scale from extra light to extra dark. Shading can also refer to color washes which also create a value scale of whatever hue is being used. Coloring in, or "solid packing" can mean a solid black or a solid color.

> "Art is not what you see, but what you make others see."
> ~*Edgar Degas, Artist*

When you need a fully filled in black or color, the machine can be adjusted to hit the skin a bit slower with a longer needle depth, to minimize the amount of passes you need to get the color very solid. A slow and steady rhythm works best to avoid having to go over the skin too many times and risk overworking it.

When you want a softer, wispy or "washed out" shade of grey or gradation of color, you can adjust the machine to run as fast or faster than a liner so that it hits the skin faster and doesn't penetrate as deeply, allowing you to go over the same area of skin more times without overworking. You use hand speed and technique to adjust the way the ink is getting in the skin. In other words, you don't "push" into the skin as much as with lining and solid coloring. You are almost "brushing" the ink in and your hand can be moving quite a bit faster. (Though there are still some artists who prefer a "slow hand" shading style.)

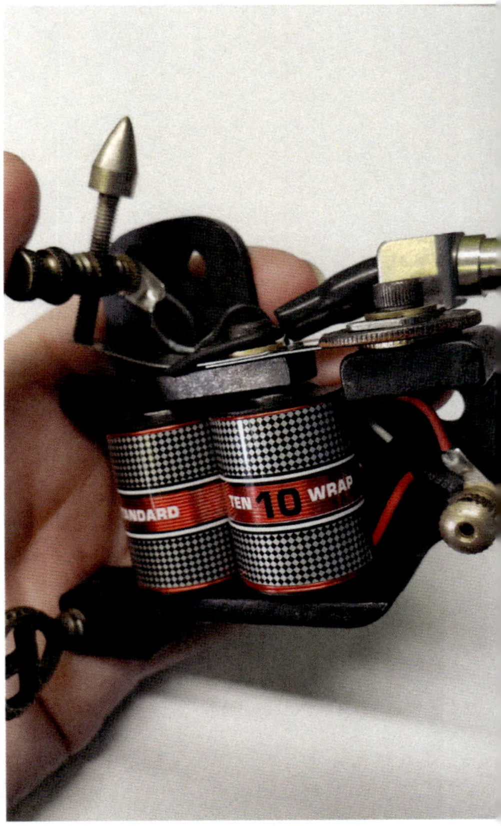

In addition to these considerations, the size of the needle grouping will affect the way you run the machine. For example, a 5-liner needle may tattoo great at a voltage of 7.5, but a 17-mag configuration will need a bit more "punch" to penetrate the skin and get good solid color. Furthermore, the voltage setting will differ between a coil machine and a rotary. Consult the machine manufacturer to determine the power supply's setting.

As with so many things, it's all about experimentation and preference. Just like a painter uses many different types of brushes, paints, pens and mediums, a tattoo artist will play with different machines, needles, hand movement and power supply settings until their designs look the way they intend them to be.

Using the Tattoo Machine

Mastering the use of a tattoo machine can take years, but it is very important if you want to become a truly competent artist. In addition to becoming artistically proficient, you need to limit the risk of damage to the client's skin by being as knowledgeable as possible regarding your most important tool.

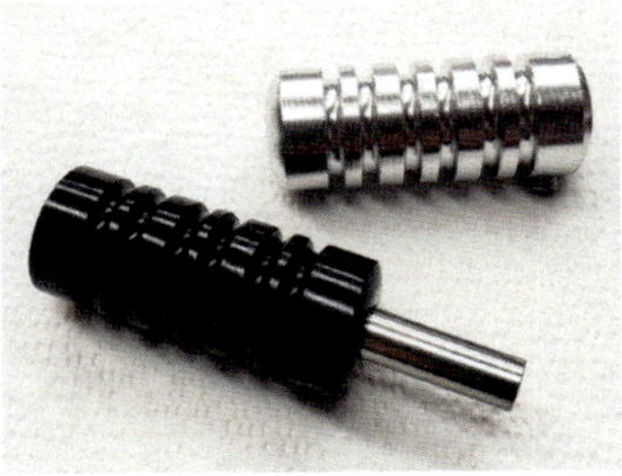

Every machine has a grip attached to the machine that the needle cartridge fits into or that the needle bar goes through. This is where you hold onto the machine, in much the same way you hold a pen or pencil. You will essentially be guiding the needle along the skin in the same way you'd use a drawing instrument. (Newer rotary machines are even being designed to look and handle more like a pen.)

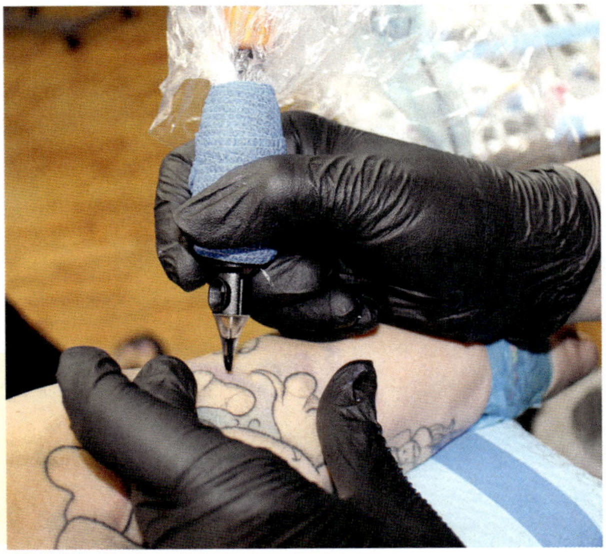

The general position for tattooing: Rest the side palm of your tattooing hand against the surface of the skin. Use the thumb and middle finger of opposite hand to form 3 touch points. You use the non-tattooing hand to stretch the skin. The tattooing hand rests and pivots on the surface of the skin to accomplish the most effective and stable reach. The machine is generally leaning at about a 50 – 85-degree angle (depending on whether you are shading or lining), with the ink reservoir facing up.

Other essential parts your machine needs to run:

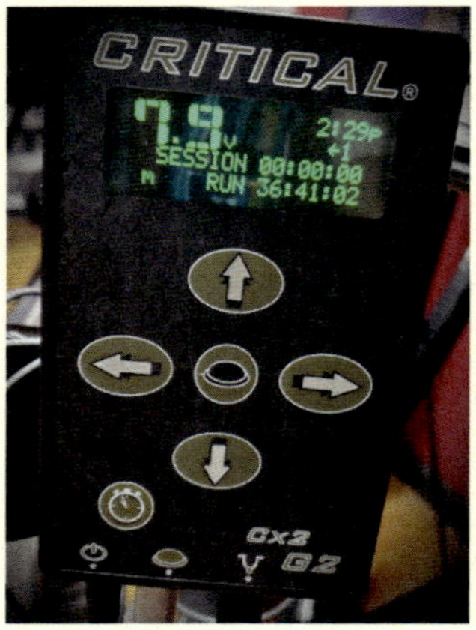

The power supply: to get electricity to the tattoo machine we need a power source. There are a variety of supplies available in a range of prices. Some are very simple, some have digital displays, and some have settings for keeping power engaged continually, without having to depress the foot pedal after every dip of ink. Some models even have a setting for tracking the time you are tattooing. Some of the newer rotary machines will only work with specific power supplies capable of handling higher voltage.

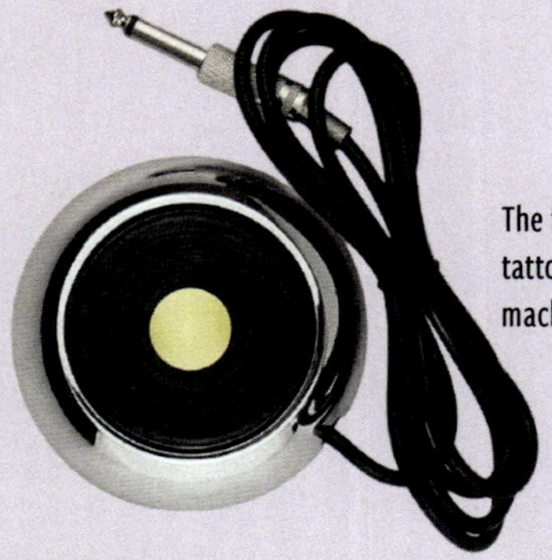

The foot switch: engages and disengages power to the tattoo machine--similar to a foot pedal on a sewing machine. (Some newer models come in the wireless variety.)

The clipcord (coil) or power cord (rotary): plugs into the power supply and into the tattoo machine.

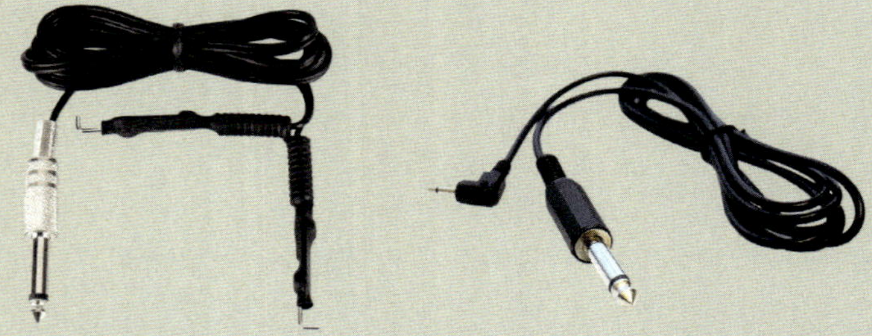

More on technique in chapter 9

Too straight up and down and the pigment may come right back out of the puncture. Angle the machine too steep and the needle could shoot ink outside of the outline or area you wish to tattoo, in addition to possibly causing a "blow out" in the line or "shadowing" next to the line.

The other main consideration in using the machine is needle depth and one of the more difficult things to learn as a beginner. Too shallow and skin will appear scratched and the ink won't stay. Too deep and you can cause excessive pain and/or scarring to the client. The ideal depth is approximately 1.5 to 2 mm but every person's skin is different. Learning what this means is accomplished by practice!

Shelly's Sidenote

GRAPEFRUITS

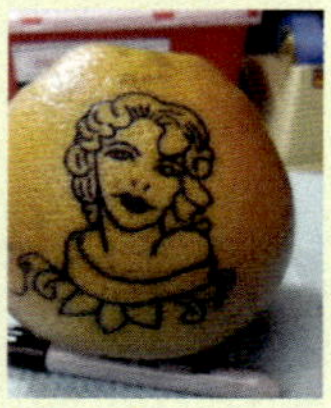

I highly recommend you practice tattooing on grapefruits before you even think about touching a client's skin. Grapefruits are inexpensive, readily available and have enough surface area to accomplish some nice designs. The skin of a grapefruit is easily punctured but tough enough to hold up to multiple needle passes. Tattooing grapefruits gives you valuable experience in the feel of the machine, strengthens your hand, aids in understanding needle depth and speed before you approach a real client.

Bonus! You have a snack when you are done! (I love Salty Dogs!)

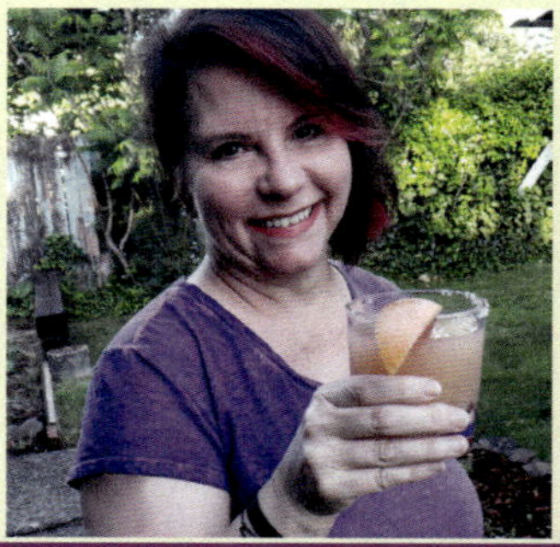

You can also purchase "fake skin" from a tattoo supply company, but most of these products are much harder than real skin and have no give. Push too hard on fake skin and your needle can go all the way through--push too lightly, the ink will come right out. There is a newer company called "Reelskin" (www.realskin.co.uk) which produces a unique practice skin that feels more like true skin and is somewhat flexible to allow for practice in stretching as well. It's more expensive than other brands, but is higher quality. Our students use this product after tattooing many grapefruits and before scheduling clients.

Practice on grapefruits and fake skin, strengthen your hands & arms and commit to drawing every single day. These three things will help you excel with your tattoo machine until you can begin training with an instructor or mentor.

Tattoo Grips

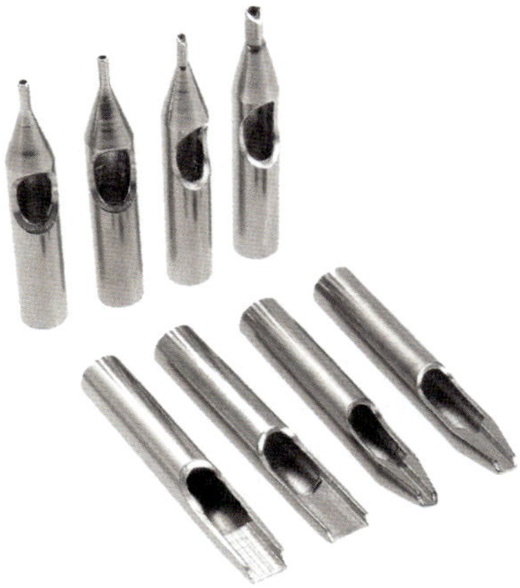

The grip is the part of a tattoo machine that holds the needle and becomes your handle. Your needle either slides through a tube in the grip, or, in the case of needle cartridges, self-locks into it. There are different choices in grips, depending on the type of machine and needles you will use.

For some grip and tube combos, the needle groupings typically correlate to a specific tip size. Liners and round shaders fit inside a small, medium or large tube tip. For example, a 3 or 5 liner fits into a small tube tip.

Flats and mags fit inside a tube tip numbered the same as each needle group. For example, a 7 mag grouping fits inside a 7-mag tip.

Reusable Grips

Reusable grips are divided into three categories:

- stainless steel grips, used with needles on a bar
- self-locking grips, designed for use with specific machines
- multi-use grips, used with needles on a bar, or cartridge style needles

Stainless Steel Grips

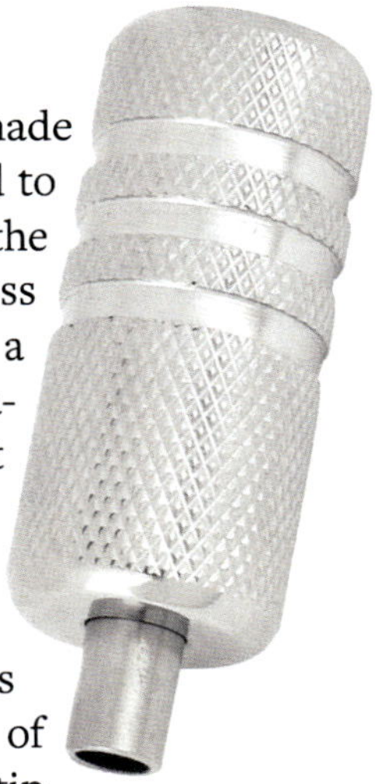

Stainless steel has been the main choice of tattooers for many years. Grips made from steel provide durability. They do experience some wear and tear and need to be replaced but can last for five to ten years. Many artists say that the weight of the grip balances the weight of a heavier machine. These grips are used with stainless steel tubes that slide through the middle, either prefabricated with a tip or with a separate tip. The tips come in a variety of sizes to fit a variety of needle configurations. Thus, tattooers using stainless steel must have a quantity of grips sufficient for the amount of tattooing they do.

On the other hand, the weight of stainless steel can be a detriment over time to the arm, wrist and hand of a tattooer. One challenge in using stainless steel grips is cleaning and sterilizing. Over time, it is more difficult to clean the germs out of every nook and cranny, particularly in a multi-piece set, (i.e. the grip, tube and tip are separate).

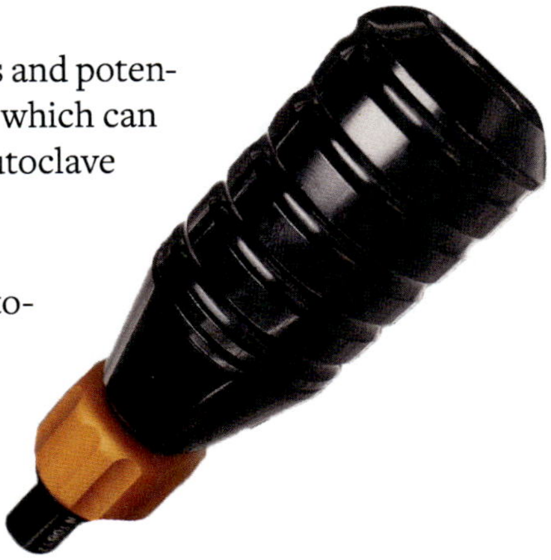

Additionally, the process of scrubbing can leave the artist vulnerable to cuts and potential infectious fluids. Occasionally bits of metal can rub off, due to friction, which can contaminate the ink. Furthermore, these grips **MUST** be processed in an autoclave after every use; no exceptions.

Newer grips are being made of lightweight aluminum that can also be autoclaved, so this is another potential choice.

Self-Locking Grips

With many rotary machines there is just one grip used exclusively, thus no need to have a large variety of grips to store or process. These grips are typically sleek, comfortable, lightweight and built to use the

MULTI-USE GRIPS

This type of grip is sold separately from the motor or machine and has more flexibility. There are many choices on brand, shape, color, size, material and these are designed to use needles on a bar or they can be adapted to use cartridge style needles by using a plunger bar. Therefore, these can be used with coil or rotary machines for the artist who likes to use both. These grips are built for comfort & durability and are covered with barrier film or designed to be autoclaved, depending on the brand.

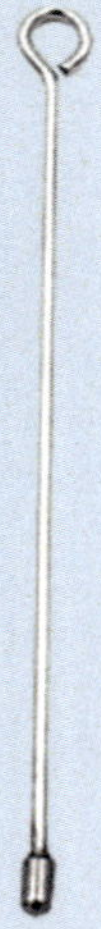

self-locking cartridge system in conjunction with a specific motor. These grips are covered with barrier film or designed to be autoclaved, depending on the brand.

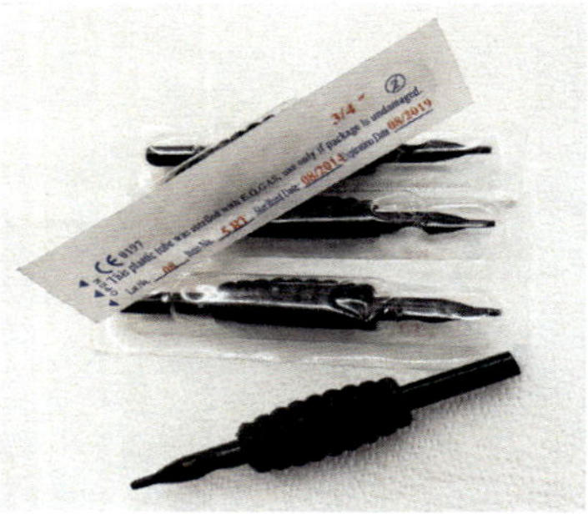

Disposable Grips

Disposable plastic or silicone grips, or grip & tube combos, assure that you're using safe tools with each procedure. They are inexpensive and easy to find in a variety of sizes and quality. Disposables are simple to store, easy to use and work great when traveling because there is no need for an autoclave. No metal means no contaminants in your ink. And when using disposables, you do not have to worry about sterilization or scrubbing grips and tubes; a time-consuming process. On the other hand, plastic is lighter and tends to be more fragile. Also, if an artist uses a heavy machine, the plastic grip will not help balance the machine over the hand.

Silicone or rubber grip covers can be used over disposable or metal grips to ease vibration in the tattooer's hand and make it more comfortable.

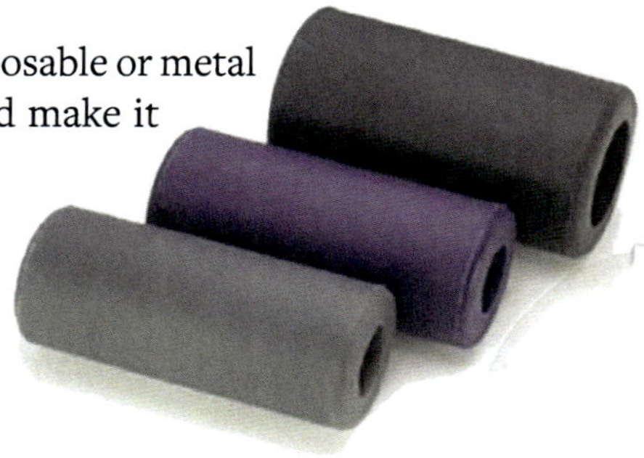

Bear in mind, if the grip cover is not the disposable kind, it MUST be autoclaved as well.

Needles

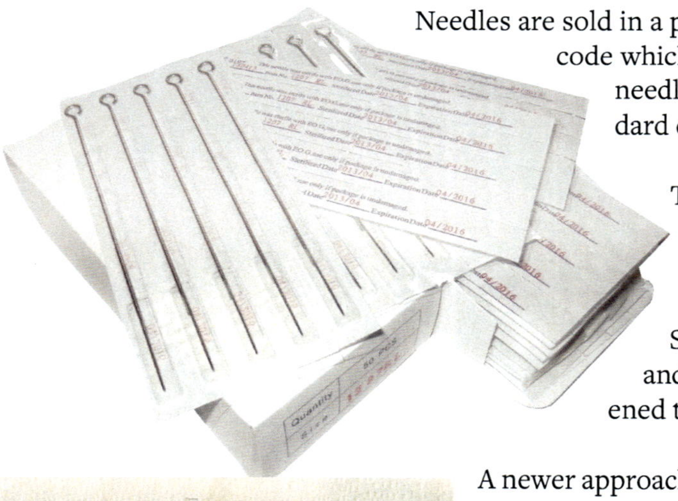

Needles are sold in a plethora of styles and sizes. Typically, the box is labeled with a code which describes the individual diameter of the needles, how many needles are grouped together and the style of the group. The standard diameter of the individual needles is #10.

Tattoo needles are generally pre-sterilized in individual blister packs, either sold as individual needles that require assembly, premade on a needle bar, or in a cartridge form.

Some needles are designed to fit inside of a tube/grip combo and the tube part is threaded through the tube clamp and tightened to the front of the tattoo machine, with a screw.

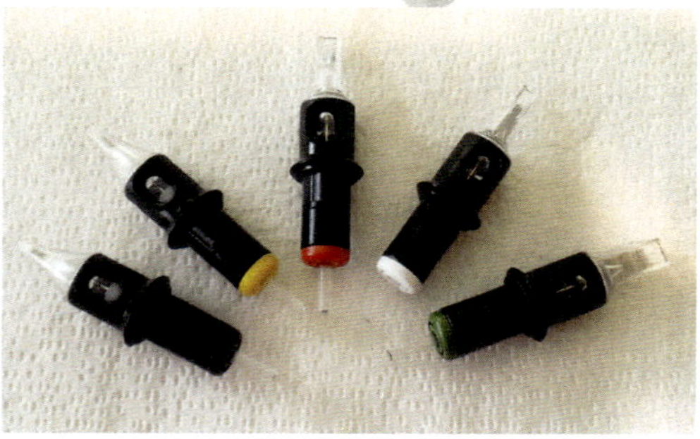

A newer approach to needles is the disposable cartridge, where the needles and tip are one assembly. The needles are molded into a plastic bar and the tip of the plastic is configured to hold a specific needle grouping. The back of the needle has a seal that prevents ink from flowing back up into the machine.

These are typically used with rotary tattoo machines such as the *Cheyenne*, *Inkjecta* or *Spektra* brand. These also come in the variety of needle configurations and types.

These cartridges can also be set up for use in a coil machine by using a plunger bar: a needle bar with a small ball at the end, which depresses the needle inside the cartridge. (*See note at top left of page.*)

Needle groupings: LINERS, ROUND SHADERS, FLATS, MAGNUMS.

Talking about the different types of needles that are available is a little like talking about paint brushes and tools.

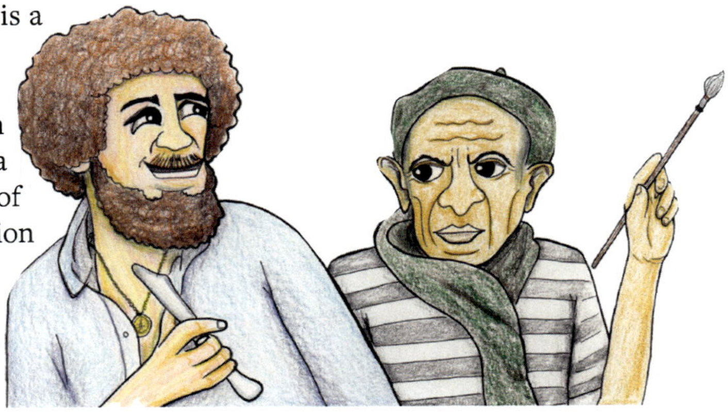

Picasso might prefer a sable pointed-round brush with a wooden handle and Bob Ross might use a #10 standard paint knife with a plastic handle to produce the same results. With the wide array of needle styles and groupings, as well as the lack of standardization in naming of sizes and shapes, it's easy to get confused.

Here are the basics:

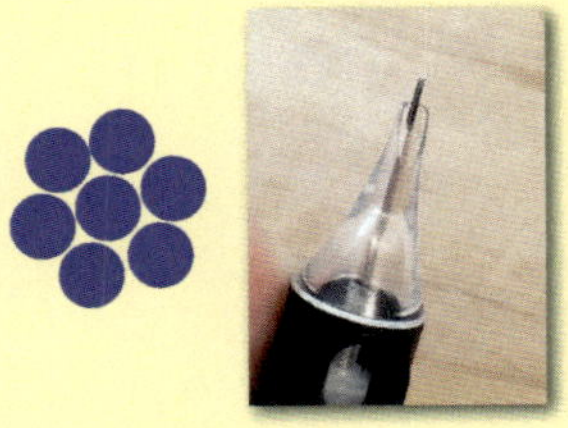

Liners (or tight rounds)
Used for outlining. It´s grouped like a circle, but the tips are clustered tightly together. Depending on how bold you want your outline to be, liner needles generally come in 1 to 14 needle groupings, but 5 and 7 are the most commonly used. Occasionally, liners are used to fill in very tight spaces, such as the points of a star design.

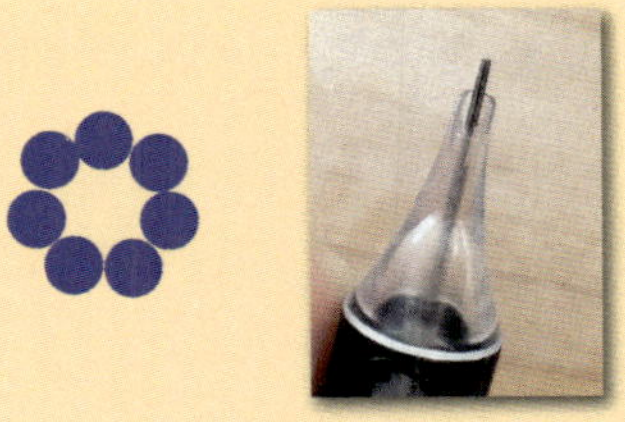

Round Shaders (or loose rounds)
Generally come in 5 to 18 rounds. A round needle is also grouped in a circle. Depending on the design being tattooed, they can also be used for thick outlines. Round shaders were used for many years in traditional tattoo shading and work great for shading in tattoos with color or black and gray work, particularly in smaller areas.

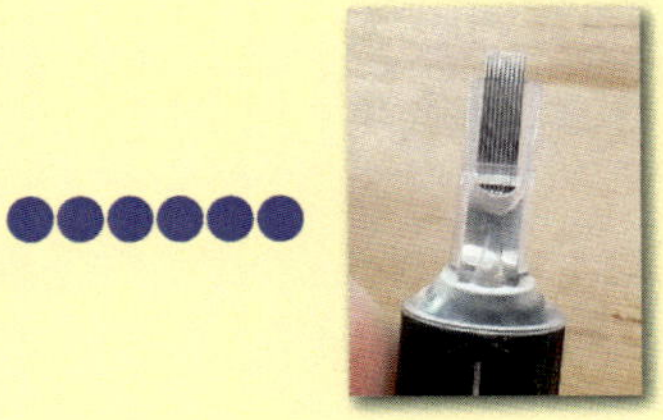

Flats
Groupings are all straight in a row and lie tightly together. They can be used for filling in solid color or shading. Flats range from 4 to 15 needle groupings. Nice for large dark, bold areas in a tattoo. Because the center needles "hit" the skin first, the edge needles can hit a little deeper, so trickier to use for soft shading.

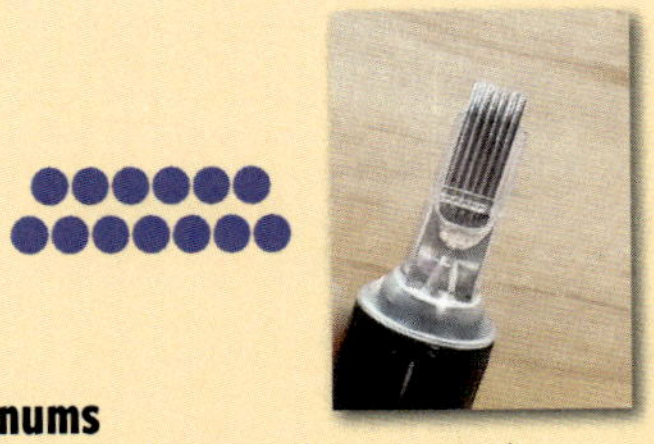

Magnums
The other shading needle option is the magnum or "mag". A mag has two zig-zag rows, and the needles are spread out. They have more needles on bottom then top. For example, a 7 mag has 4 needles on the bottom row and 3 on the top. Mags can be used to fill in solid color and blending or shading. They generally come in sizes 5 to 17, (some artists use even larger, up to 30 or more) The mag can cover a greater area fast, and give you a powdery, wispy look for shading. It's easier with a mag to miss spots if you are trying to do solid fill, but with experience, can easily be done.

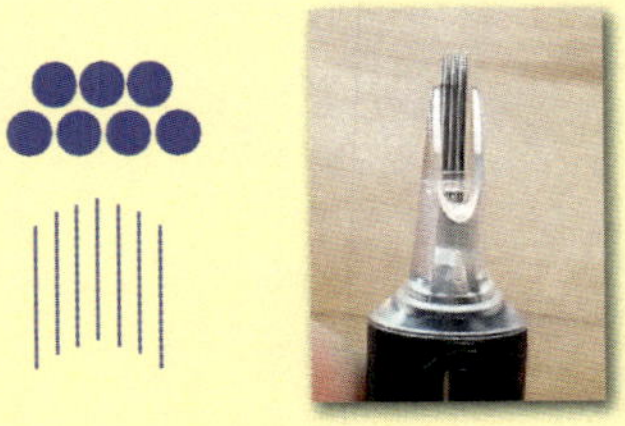

Curved (or soft edge) Magnums
Curved magnum tattoo needles are grouped the same as other magnums, but the needle tips have a slight arch to them on each side. This allows the center and edge needles to hit the deflecting skin at the same time. Very useful for softer shading.

ADDITIONALLY...
There are specialized needles that we won't go into detail about, but you may see these needles in various configurations such as:

Bug Pin

Carbon Tipped

Textured

Medium Taper (MT)

Long Taper

Power Liner

Micros and Nanos (cosmetic tattooing)

Which needles to use?

Other factors when choosing needles can get confusing: bug-pin, medium or long taper, carbon tipped, textured, etc. Our recommendation is to choose the more common needles in standard configurations, and then branch out once you have more experience, or a mentor who can teach you about their favorite needles directly.

It's really up to you which needle groups to choose. Most styles of tattooing can be accomplished with any of these groupings, as long as the artist has experience. Many artists will swear by one or the other variety as being "the best". Take some time to get to know the groupings and how you like to tattoo, or what the piece itself requires. **In general, sizes 5, 7, and 9 are the beginner's choice in liners, round shaders, flats and mags.**

Shelly's Sidenote

MACHINES AND GRIPS AND NEEDLES...OH MY!

The endless landscape of brands, configurations, styles and staunch opinions can make it utterly confusing. I personally used mostly *Micky Sharpz* brand coil machines for the first eight years of tattooing and Cheyenne brand rotaries for the last five. To simplify the beginner's journey, I recommend choosing the one you feel you can get the most help with directly from an instructor or mentor.

Outside of that, I will go out on a limb and say that the Cheyenne Hawk or Cheyenne Pen are great machines that can accomplish all manner of tattooing with ease. They are light-weight, quiet, compact and the cartridge system makes it extremely easy to quickly change needles.

If you are educated enough, or have an interest in doing your own maintenance, or even building your own machines, you may want to choose a coil machine or a coil with a multi-use tube. Once you've got experience and you are progressing nicely, research and experiment with other styles and brands of tattoo machines as well.

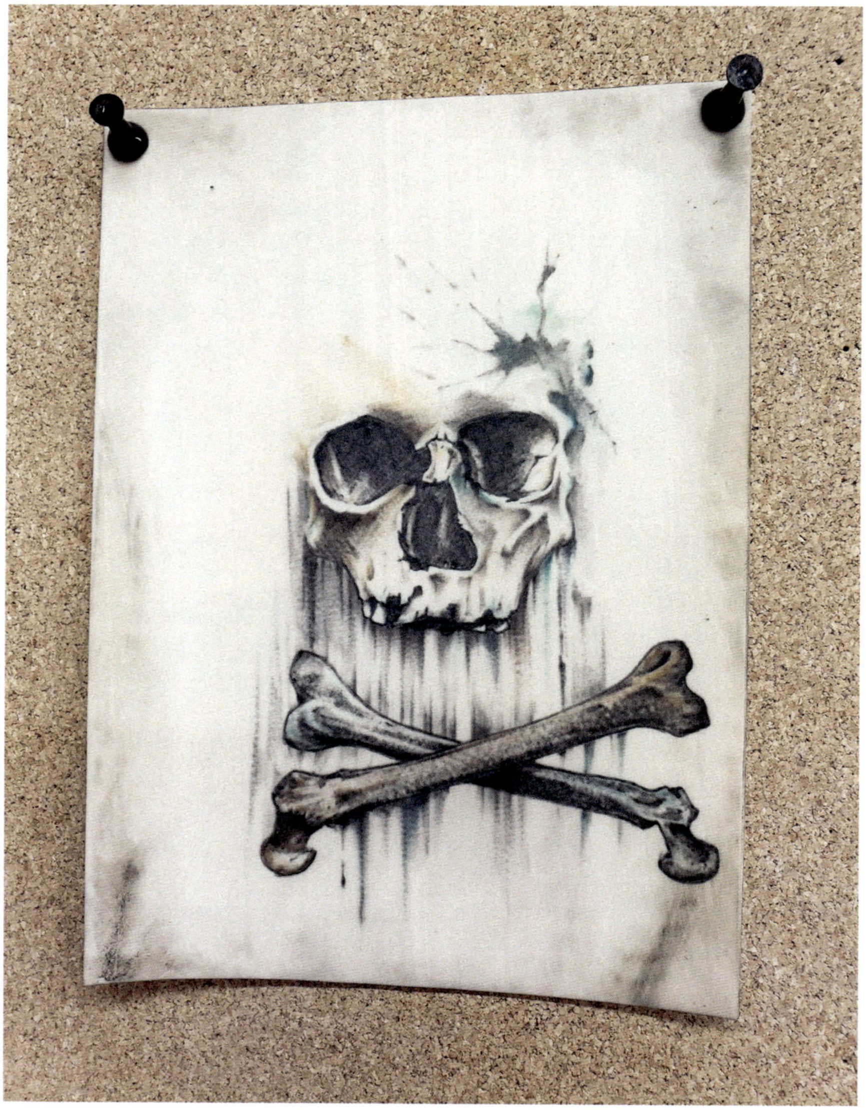

Fake skin tattoo by Rusty Hinshaw

> "Be who you are and say what you feel because those who mind don't matter and those who matter don't mind."
> *-Dr Seuss, Author & Illustrator*

Chapter Five Highlights

- The tattoo machine operates like a tiny sewing machine.
- Depth of penetration of the needle is approximately 1.5 to 2 millimeters.
- Coil machines are powered with electro-magnetic coils.
- Rotary machines are driven by an electric motor.
- Building up or "sculpting" is not going over the same skin, but rather coming right up next to the single pass line just tattooed to make lines thicker.
- The choice of purchasing a coil or rotary machine will likely be based on what you have been exposed to the most and can get help learning to use.
- When lining, typically the machine runs faster and hits harder.
- Adding dimension and depth to a tattoo is usually done with a variety of thinned black ink called gray washes.
- Mastering the use of a tattoo machines can take years.
- The grip is where you hold on to the machine and steer it.
- A foot switch engages and disengages the power to the tattoo machine.
- If you hold the tattoo machine too straight up and down pigment can come right back out of the puncture.
- Reusable stainless steel grips must be sterilized in an autoclave.
- Typical needle groups include" liners, round shaders, flats and magnums.
- Tattoo needles are generally pre-sterilized and sold in blister-packs.
- It is advisable to choose more common needle configurations and then branch out once you have more experience.

What do you call it when someone gets their whole face tattooed?

An ever-lasting job stopper.

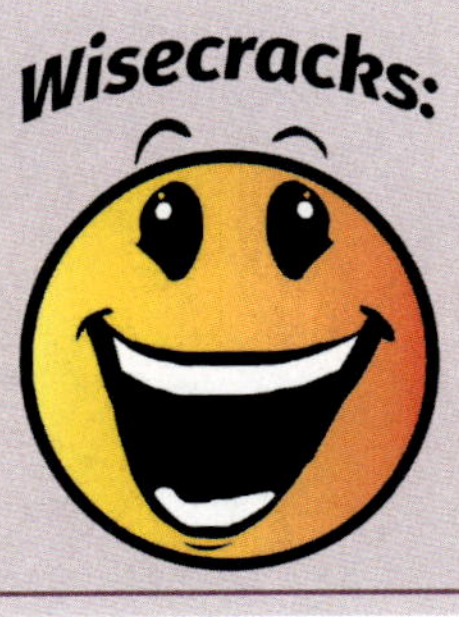

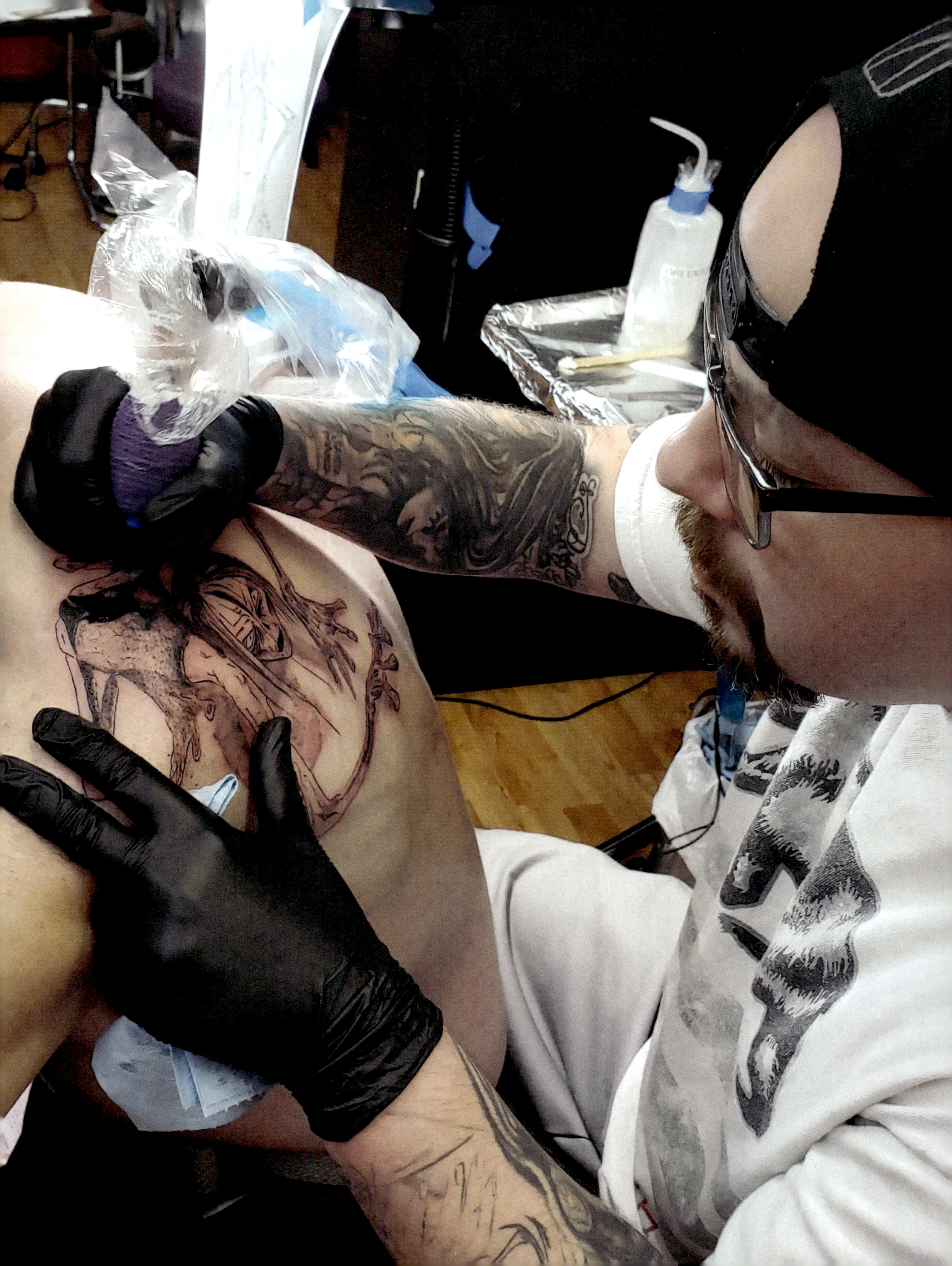

Chapter Six

Art & Design Fundamentals

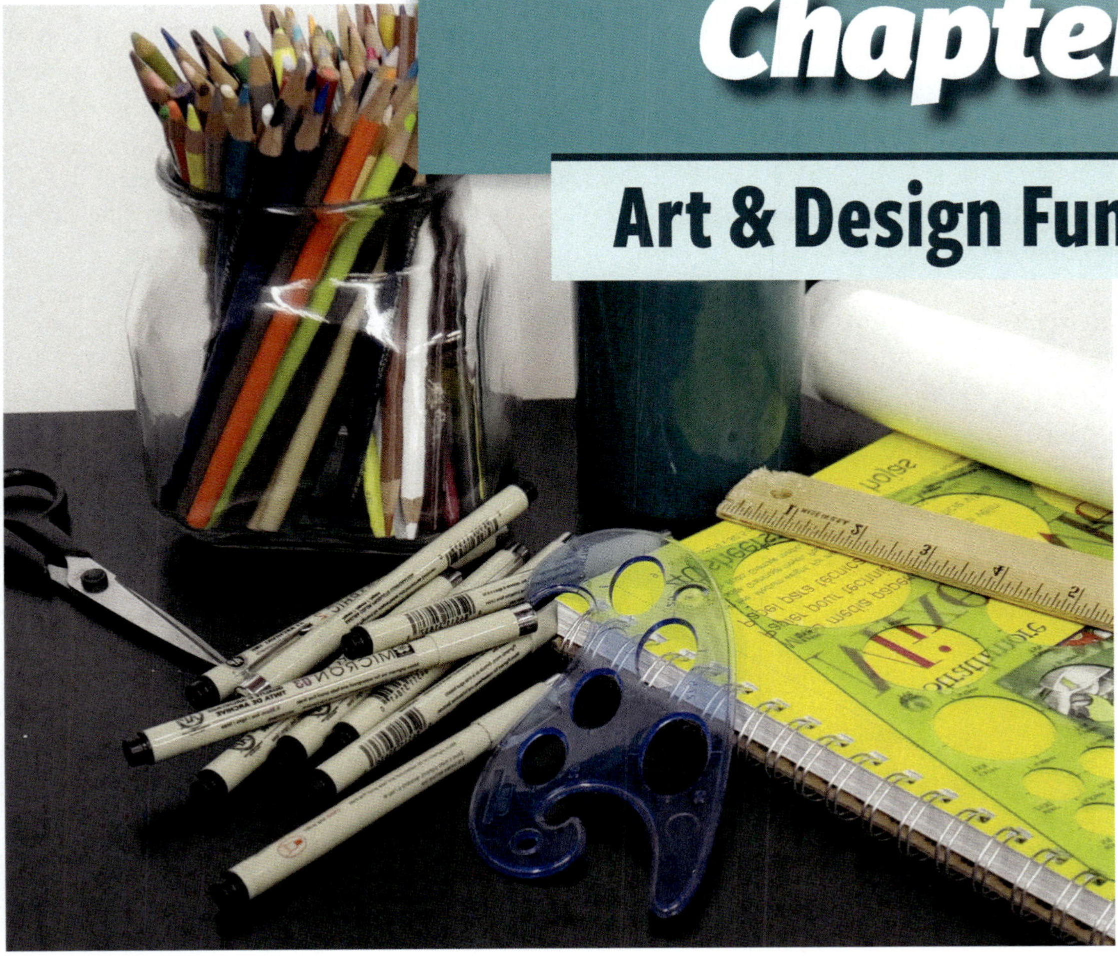

As an in-demand tattoo artist you will be expected to conceive skillful and appealing artwork, in the framework of a client's taste and ideas. If you wish to go beyond the basic flash style tattoos and create custom designs that showcase your skill and style, it will require an understanding of art and design. This chapter will introduce the basic elements that underlie effective composition and focuses on those that are most relevant to artwork placed on skin.

> "Don't think about making art, just get it done. Let everyone else decide if it's good or bad, whether they love it or hate it. While they are deciding, make even more art."
>
> *Andy Warhol, Artist*

The **elements of art** and **principles of design** are the language of the visual arts and if you want to make art, whether drawing, painting or tattooing, you'll need to understand these concepts.

But before we explore the elements and principles:

You Can Draw Right?

For a tattooer, drawing is the vital tool that brings your imaginative designs into reality, before you apply anything to the skin. You must be able to draw to become a highly successful tattoo artist. Of course, natural talent is wonderful, but really anyone can draw well if they take the time to develop the skill. Several factors are required to become adept at drawing: desire, time and practice. Here are some tips to help you improve:

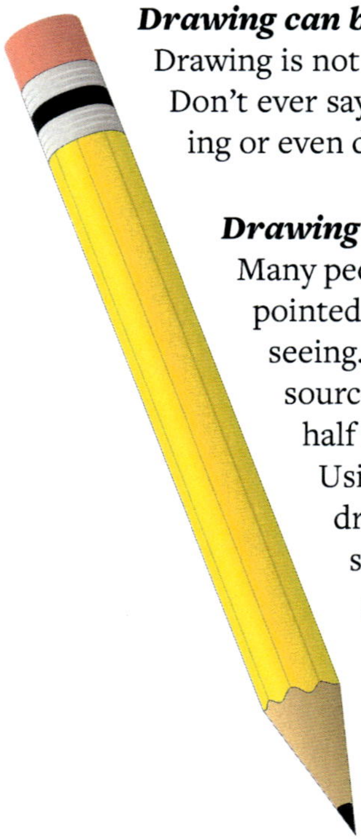

Drawing can be learned

Drawing is not magic. It is a skill that can be learned. You hear people say all the time "I can't draw". Don't ever say that! Anyone can become skilled if they have the desire to draw, improve their drawing or even draw at a professional level.

Drawing is observation

Many people expect themselves to be able to draw without looking at an object. They get disappointed when they can't get something correct, just from their memory. But drawing is about seeing. You must LOOK at objects in order to draw them. This requires having a reference or source of information. The amount of time you spend looking at your reference can be about half the time it takes to complete the drawing.

Using references in your art is basically like searching for information that will help you draw and tattoo better. If you were writing a book you would research information on the subject. Producing art is the same. You realize your current limitations and you need to gain new information from books, magazines, the internet, or real life. The more you use references the more you build your memory of shapes, movement, patterns and depth.

Using references means if you want to draw a rose, take the time to study it. Turn it upside down and look at all the contours, highlights, shadows and tones. All the answers are there. Take photos of the rose and trace them. Do this enough and eventually you will be able to draw a rose from memory. But remember, it is just not possible to draw everything from life. If you can't go to the rainforest and sketch that ring-tailed lemur, then find photos to work from.

"You can understand nothing about art... if you do not understand that imagination is a value in itself."

Milan Kundera, Author

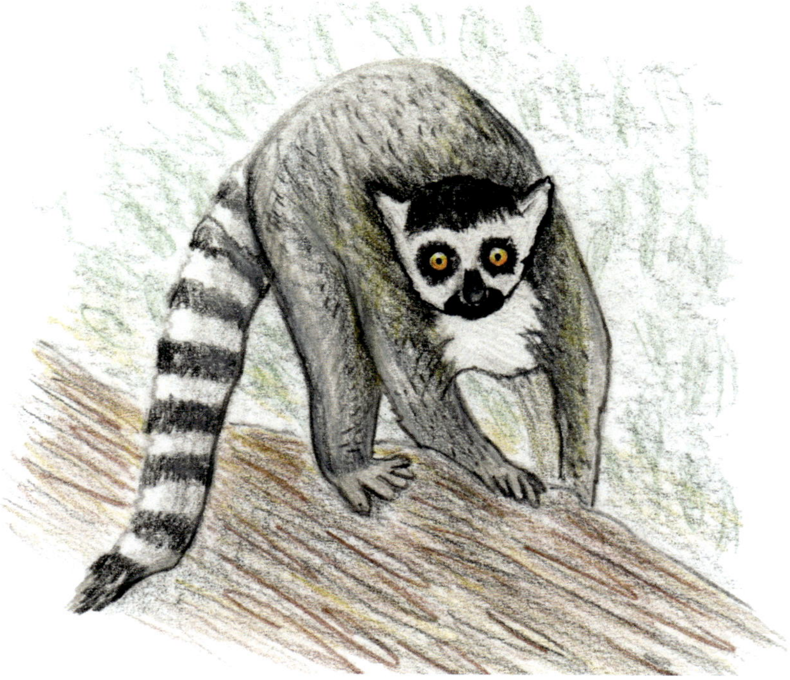

Pick out the shapes

All subjects, no matter how complex, can be simplified into basic shapes. Study the subject and look for the basic shapes that make up the overall shape. Shapes can be created by line, color or value changes that define edges. If you sketch shapes first it will help speed up your drawing. Draw shapes first then add the outlines. The process of finding shapes in your subject takes practice, but that is what sketchbooks are for!

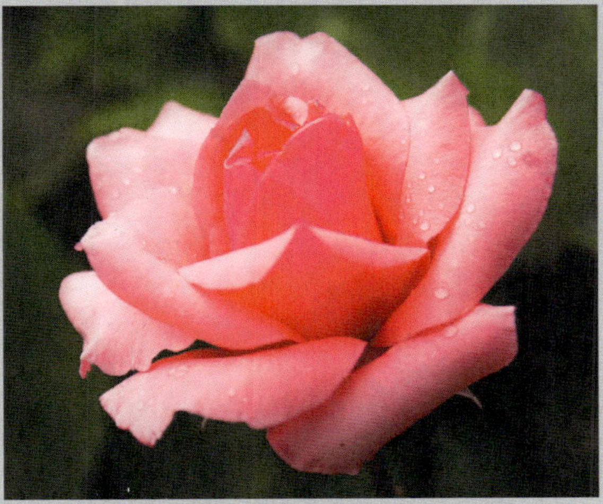

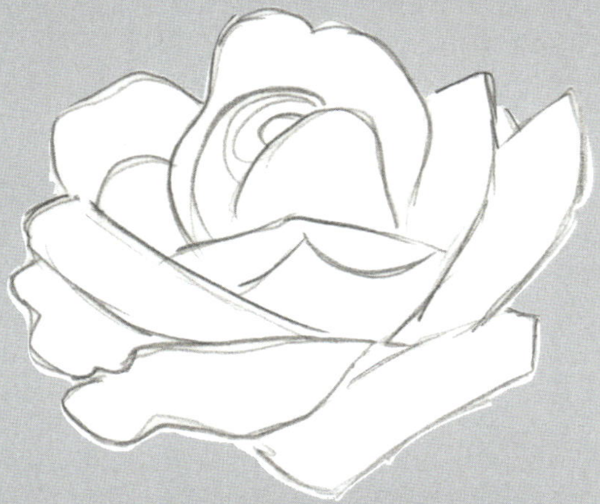

Value

Value means the darkness or lightness of tones. This can be black and grey or color. Drawings are most successful when a full range of value is used. Value helps us define the light source as well.

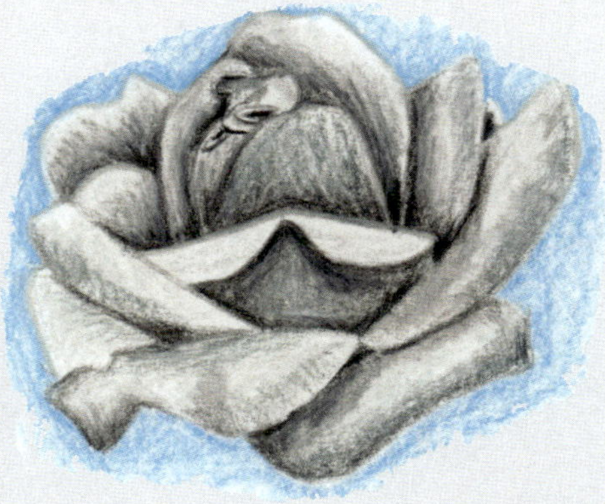

Line Variety

Line variety means the quality or thickness of a line. A drawing which has exactly the same thickness throughout is boring. Consider the quality of the lines you draw and how they will impress the viewer.

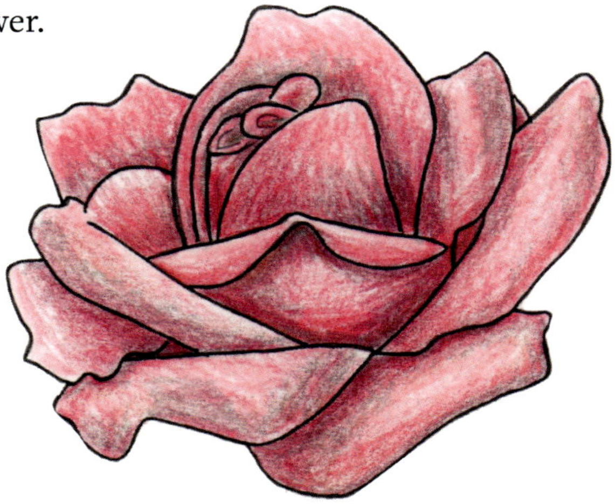

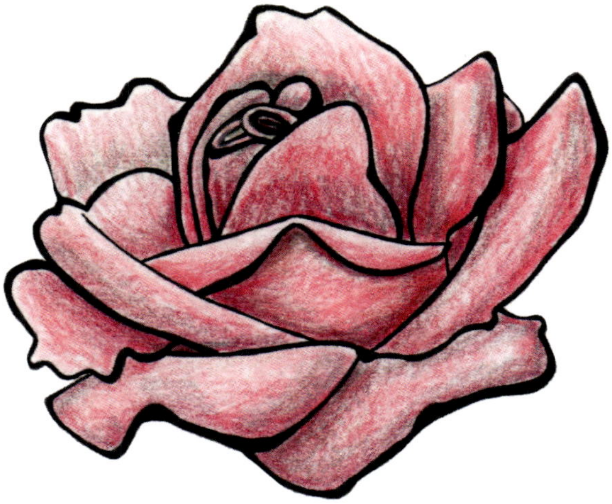

Loosen up

When you begin the first draft of a drawing it should be loose. When you start to sketch, you don't need to be stiff, but try each line a few times before you choose the ones you like. Sketching should flow from your fingertips and should move your whole arm, not just your wrist. Many artists begin their sketches in blue pencil and roughly pencil out what they imagine. Then they move to a red pencil to pick out the lines they like. Next, they use more precision to complete the finished drawing with lead or pen. And finally, the drawing is shaded and colored.

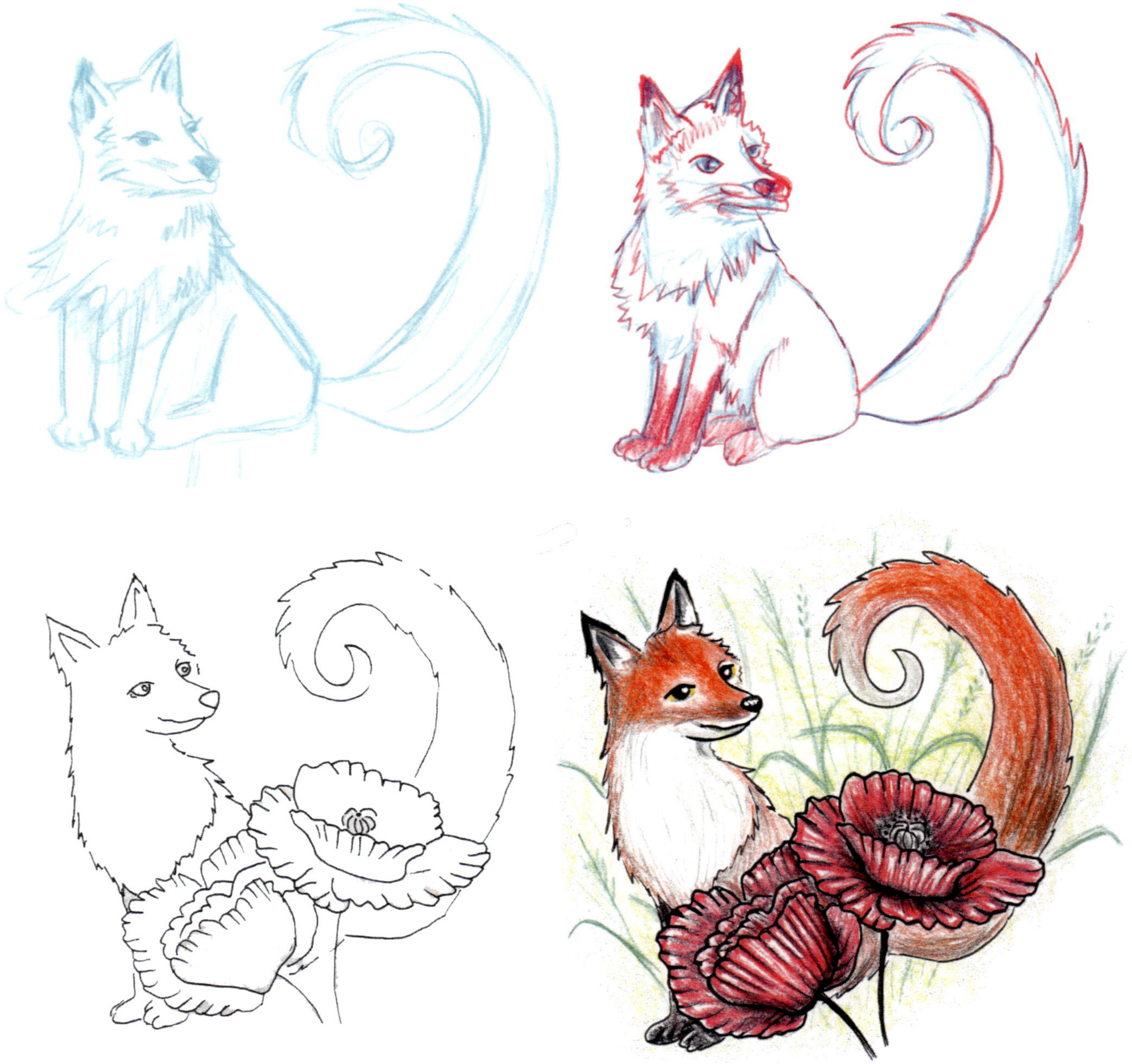

Practice

You MUST practice. Draw every day. Use a sketchbook and draw all the things around you. This is precisely how you get better. And when you can't draw, you can look at objects and imagine HOW you would draw them. Where are the contours? What are the values? What shapes are there? Train your eye to SEE because that's what drawing is all about.

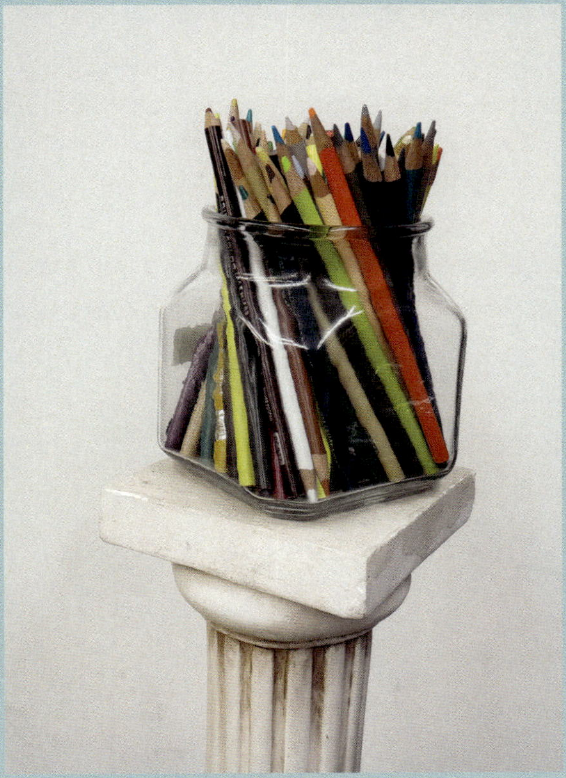

How do we define art?

The definition of art has changed through the centuries and there is no universally accepted definition. Ancient ideas emphasized **skill as a result of knowledge and practice, which produces an aesthetic result.** Over time the notions of beauty and taste were added.

Beauty is, of course, in the eye of the beholder so this raises more questions than answers. As far as taste goes, who is to say whether a carefully hand-crafted sculpture is more beautiful than a mass-produced flower print hanging above your couch? One person may think a random bunch of paint flung at a canvas is a sensation, while another may observe that it looks like a five-year old painted it.

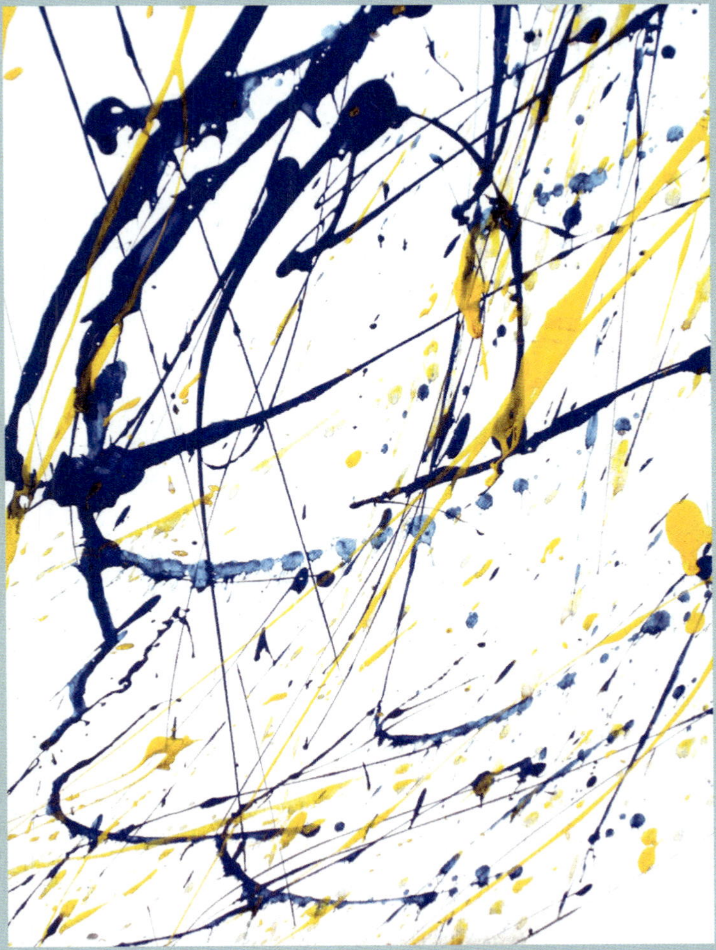

Anyone should feel free to love or hate a piece based on their personal preference.

However, Charlotte A. Jirousek, former Associate Professor of textiles at Cornell University says, "...Please note that there is a distinction between personal taste or preference and objective judgments of success or failure in a work of design or art. It is possible to recognize that a work is successful and significant, even though it does not suit our personal taste. It should be clear that unless one can lay claim to a high level of expertise it is rather immoderate to condemn a work as 'bad' just because one doesn't like it."

More recently in history, the additional concepts of **truth, talent** and **self-expression** have come to be accepted as part of the definition of art as well.

The Language of Visual Art

Elements of Art

The elements of art are the visual components which can be isolated and defined in any artwork. They are the structure of the work and carry a wide variety of messages.

Line: a variety of marks or strokes on a surface

Shape: external surface or outline of an enclosed form that has length, depth and width

Color: produced when light, striking an object, is reflected or emits light, back to the eye

Value: relative lightness or darkness

Form: objects having length, width and height

Texture: visual or tactile surface characteristic

Space: three-dimensional volume and expanse

> "A line is a dot out for a walk."
>
> *—Paul Klee, artist*

Line

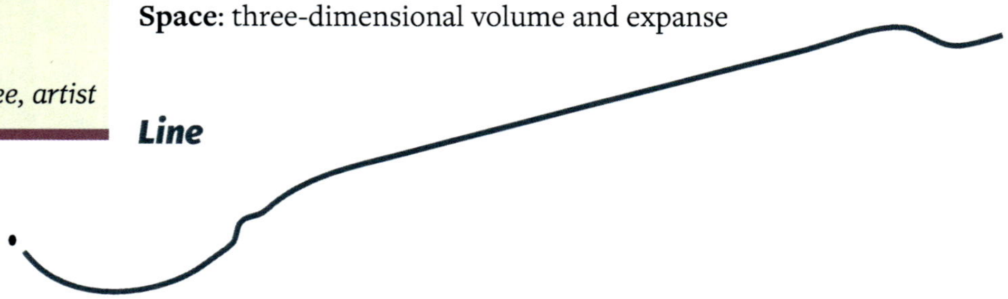

A line is a mark or stroke made by a moving point and impacts the viewer according to its character, direction and weight. People use lines to write words and create pictures. Nature possesses lines in many forms as well, such as a tiger's stripes, a seashell, cracks in the dirt or tall beach grass. Lines can act as symbolic language or communicate emotion. Line is the artist's most basic element and perhaps the tattooer's most important tool, so we'll spend a bit more time on this particular element.

Lines can function independently to suggest forms that can be recognized, even when the lines are limited.

History Note:
Human beings tend to see objects in groups and our brains will seek out relationships, order and meaning. If there are two points on a page, we will imagine a connecting line between them. If there are three points, our brain interprets it as a triangle. Our mind supplies the connections and attempts to organize visual elements. This compulsion to see things as connected, simple and orderly is described as grouping or 'gestalt'. This term means 'unified whole' and was developed by psychologists in the 1920s. Gestalt theories of visual perception help explain why certain principles in art and design work to create a coherent composition.

Contour lines define the edges of forms and shapes in the simplest ways.

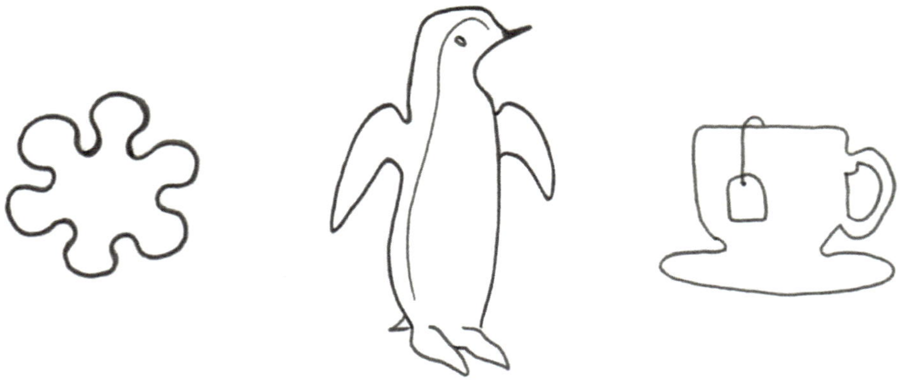

Lines can also be combined with other lines to develop form and value.

For example, hatching lines are drawn at an angle and parallel or close together and cross-hatching is when parallel lines cross each other.

Gestural lines indicate movement.

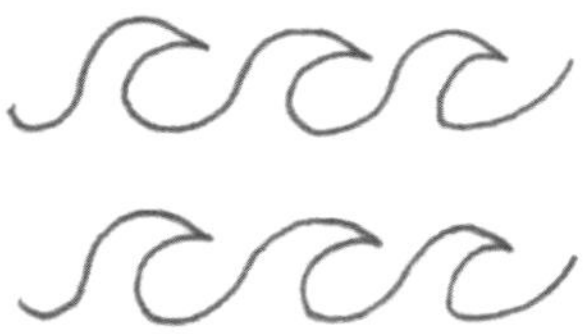

Implied lines can be dashes or dots that the brain interprets as an object.

We also imagine a line from one person's gaze to the other.
Your mind fills in the gap.

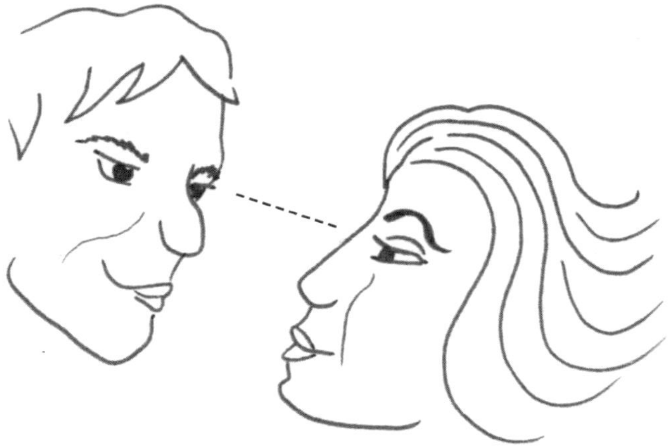

Expressive lines can be heavy or light in weight to give stronger or lighter meaning.

Thin lines can appear fragile or delicate, thick lines seem bold. This is called 'lineweight'.

Art is all about perception and the surroundings of a line will also affect the perceived lineweight.

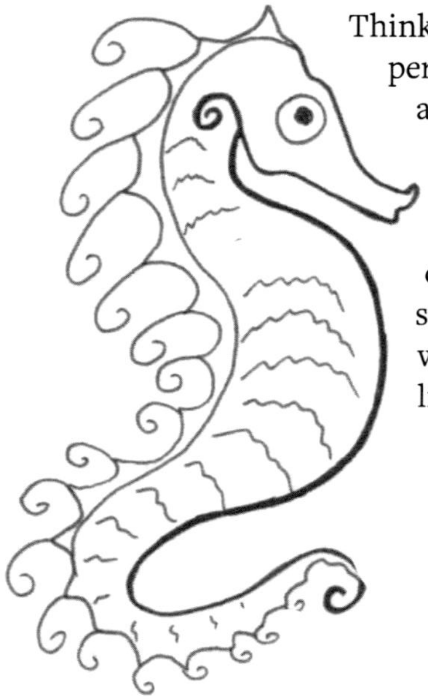

Think of how you perceive the volume of a person's voice when you are surrounded by a roomful of noise in a crowded night-club versus when you are talking with that person in a silent room. Similarly, a thick line can appear even heavier when surrounded by fine marks than it would when surrounded by strong, bold lines.

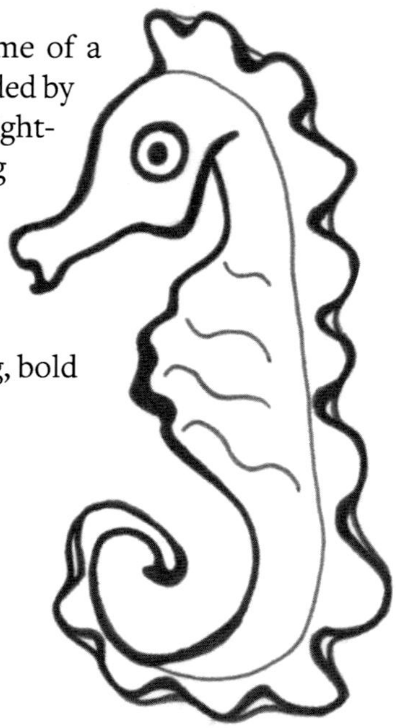

Long, perfectly even lines feel artificial. Nature is not perfectly straight. As variation is added to a line it becomes less artificial and more natural.

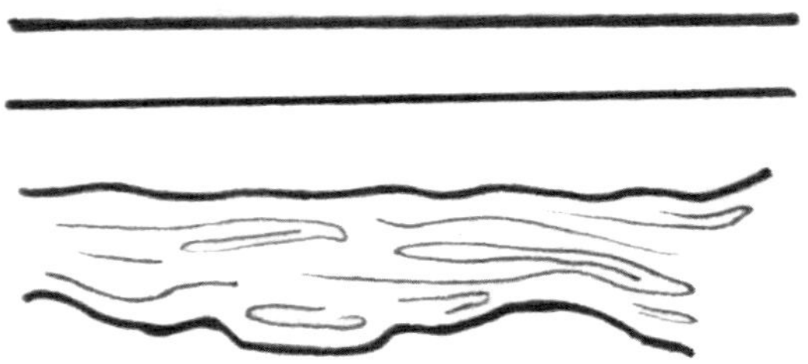

Line can also communicate certain emotions through its character and direction. **Horizontal lines** suggest a feeling of stability or repose. Compositions in which horizontal lines dominate tend to be quiet and restful in feeling.

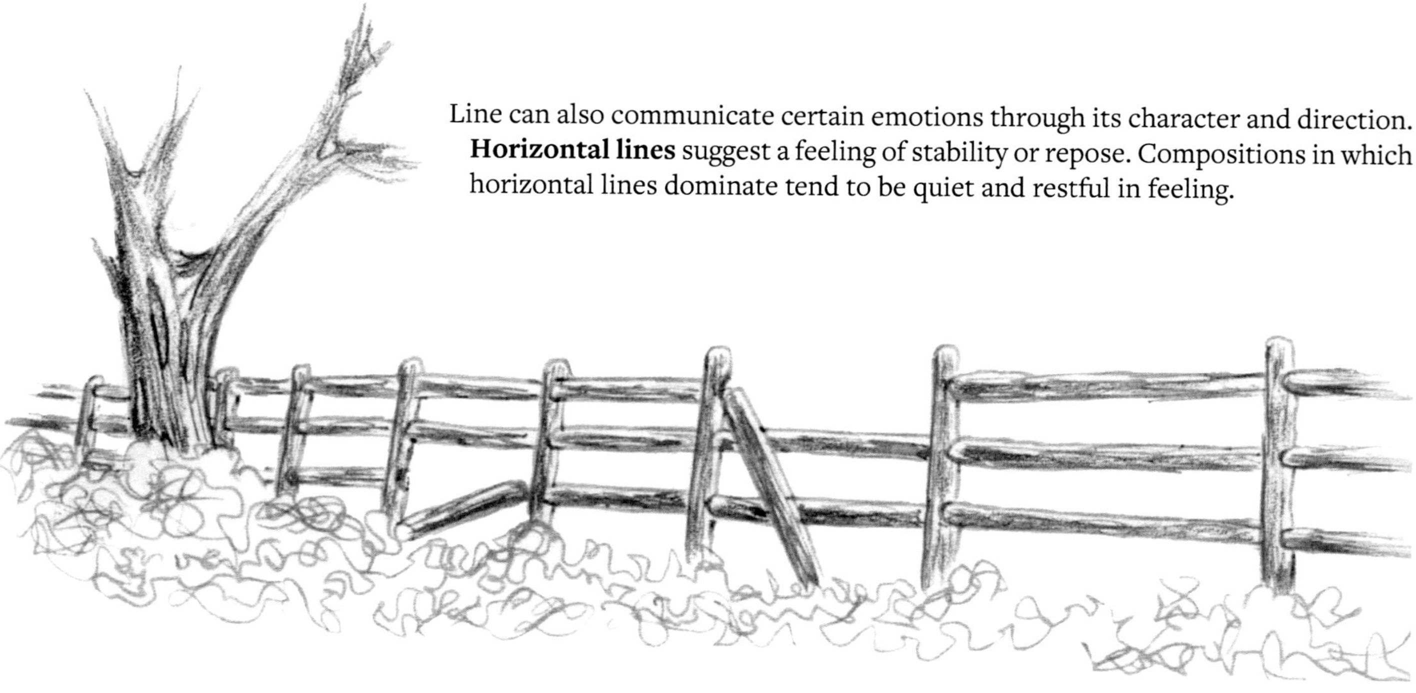

Vertical lines communicate a feeling of loftiness and spirituality. These lines imply an upward reach and movement toward the sky.

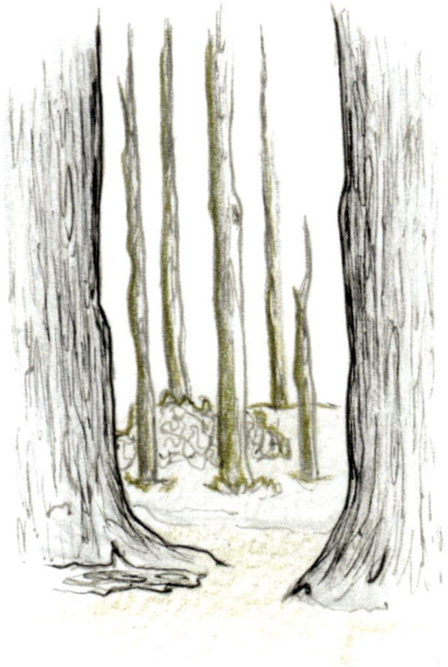

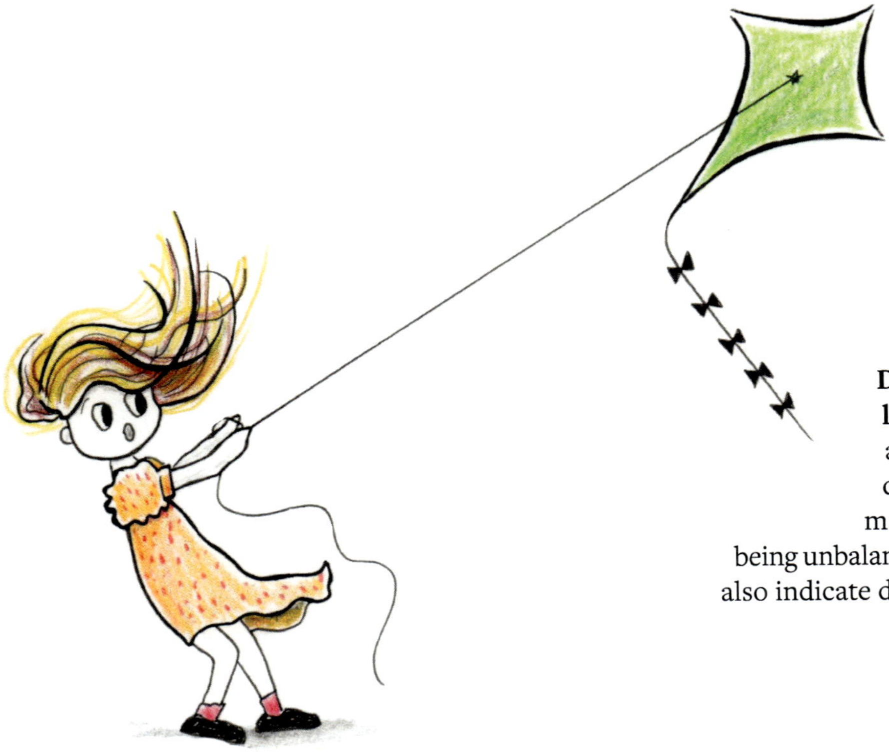

Diagonal lines give a feeling of direction and movement or being unbalanced. They can also indicate depth.

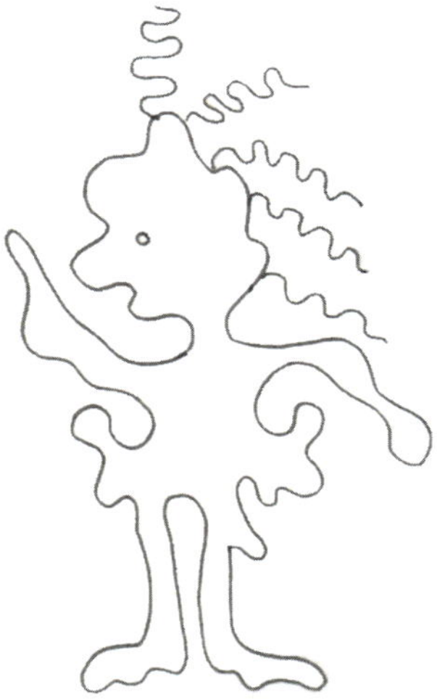

Curved lines vary in meaning. While shallow, soft curves imply familiarity, comfort, sensuality and relaxation, deep, acute curves can suggest turbulence, chaos and frenzy.

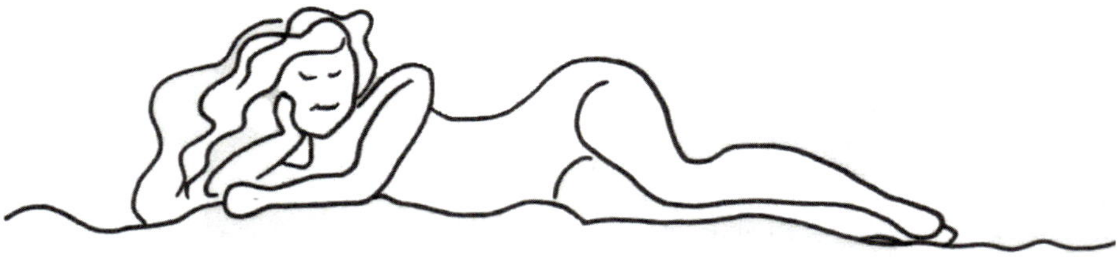

The language of line is so universal that we are all profoundly sensitive to it. People can attribute considerable meaning to the kinds of lines used, the mood of the work and the expression of an artist's style.

In tattooing, linework is arguably the most important element. Lines form the basis of our sketches and the stencils used to apply the artwork to the skin. Getting through the outline is a moment of relief for the tattooer, as the fear of wiping the stencil away disappears. It is also a moment of accomplishment for the client because they "made it through the outline" and technically could quit at that point if things got too uncomfortable.

In addition, due to the nature of tattoo pigment, most tattoos require an outline of some kind because colored ink tends to blur at the edges. Even on fully shaded pieces, some part of the tattoo will generally have a crisp line, such as the eyes, to help define the focal point. And last, a great number of requested tattoos consist of just linework alone such as text, script, geometric shapes, symbols and numbers.

Shape

Shape refers to an area enclosed in a line or seen because of an implied line, color or value change. Shape is two-dimensional, flat, or limited to height and width and can be organic, geometric or abstract.

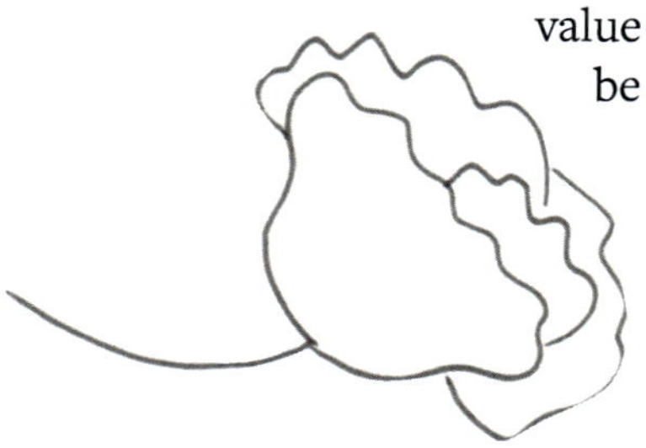

Organic shapes are most often thought of as naturally occurring and are freeform and curved.

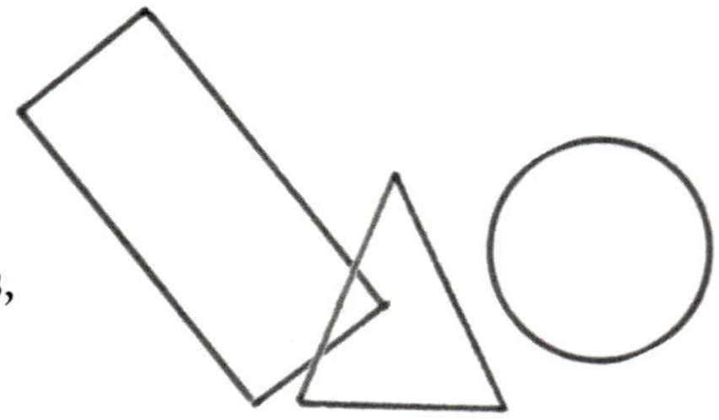

Geometric shapes are precise and regular and correspond to named shapes, such as circles, squares and triangles.

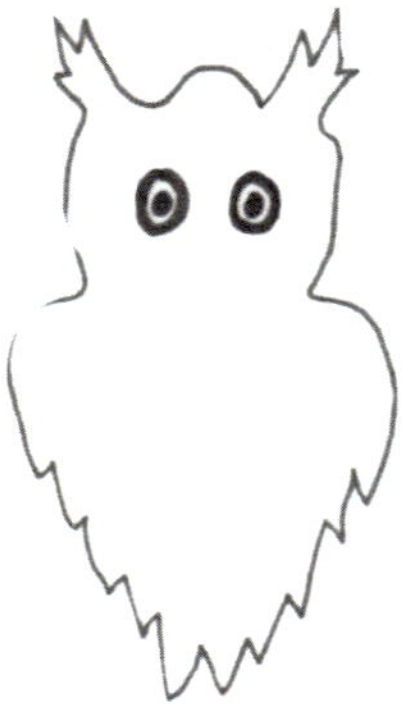

Abstract shapes are simplified, flat shapes of easily recognizable things.

Color

Color is a phenomenon of light reflected from an object to the eye. Color is an exciting element of art and can be defined by three properties: hue, saturation and value. The next chapter will go into more detail regarding color.

> "Art is something that makes you breathe with a different kind of happiness."
> *~ Anni Albers, Textile Artist*

Value

Value means relative lightness or darkness. Successful art has value contrast (also called tonal contrast), or a range of values, which creates drama and visual interest. Training yourself to see value is a skill that will serve you in making tattoos that are pleasing and can hold the viewer's gaze.

The following value scale, created by Denman Ross in 1907, is still used today. This helps artists understand and identify values more easily and emphasizes that value is independent of hue (color).

White, highlight, light, lowlight, mid-value, high dark, dark, low dark, black.

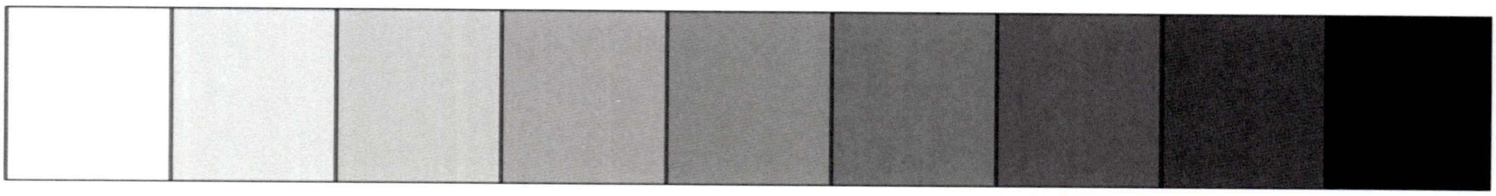

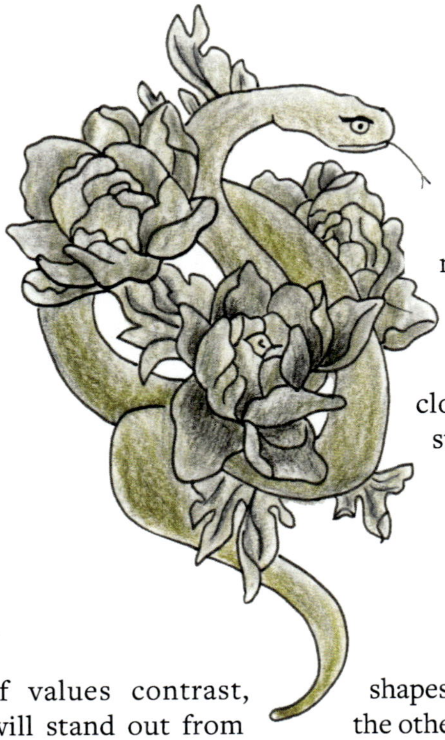

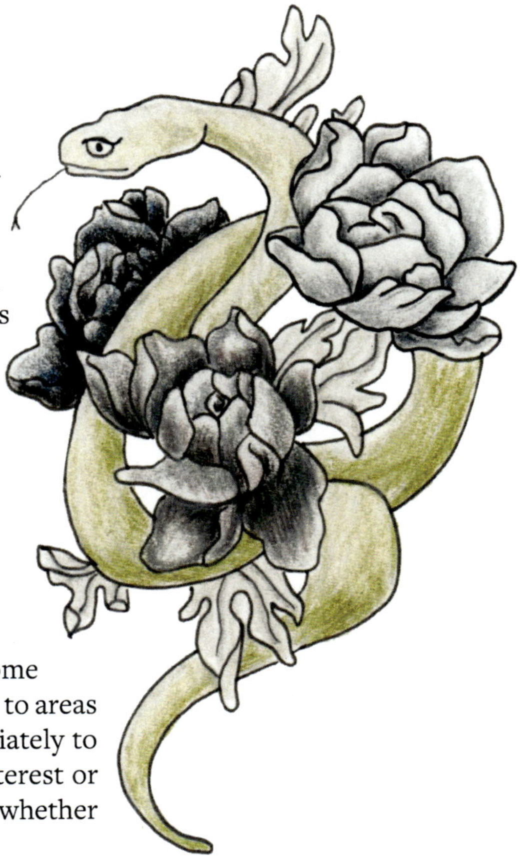

Getting the value right is very important. If your values are mostly in the mid-tone range, then the whole composition can be visually uninteresting and dull due to a lack of contrast. Shapes will seem to flatten out and seem too closely connected in space; none will stand out from the others.

If values contrast, shapes will appear to separate in space, and some will stand out from the others. Remember, the viewer will be drawn to areas of sharpest contrast. This is because the eye tends to be drawn immediately to a light element that is against a dark element. This helps create a point of interest or "focal point" in a design. This works whether you use just black and grey, or whether colors are involved.

> **"With the black and white films, one was concerned with tone (value)... You had to make sure that the tone of your dress was not the same tone as the curtains, for instance."**
>
> *~ Julie Harris, Actor*

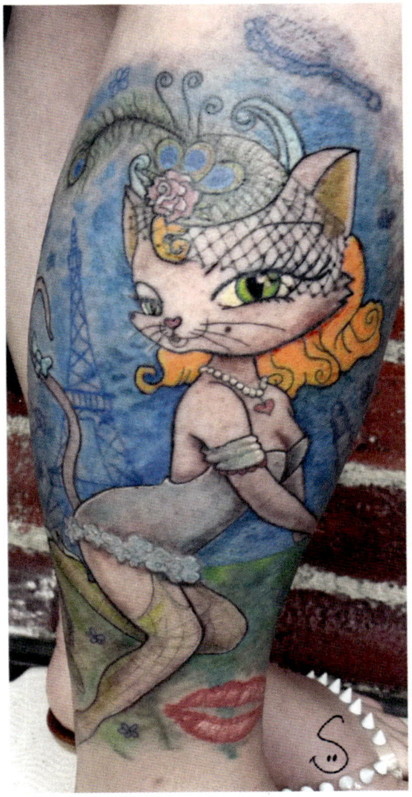

Similar value levels scattered throughout the design will help lead a viewer's eye around the piece.

Also, when working on a flat surface, like skin, we need illusion to help us make our design look like it has depth and space. A gradation of value creates shadows and light areas which give us the three-dimensional feel.

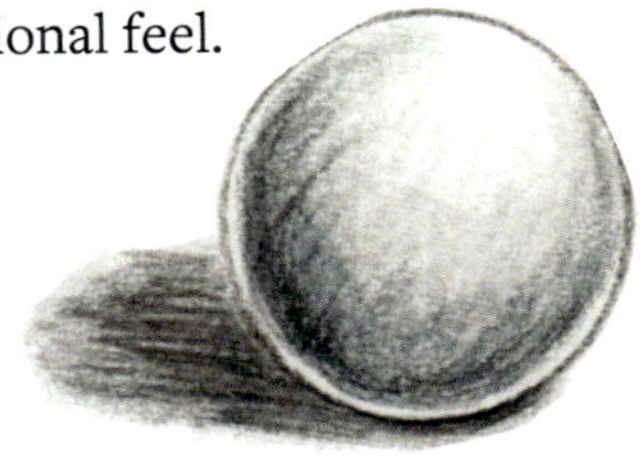

A flat circle can be made to look like a ball by incorporating a transitional value scale, smoothly blending from dark to light.

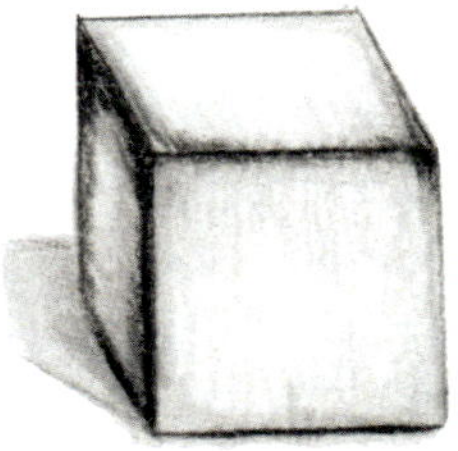

To change a square into a box, you need more abrupt value changes to give the illusion that the light is different on the corners, top and side.

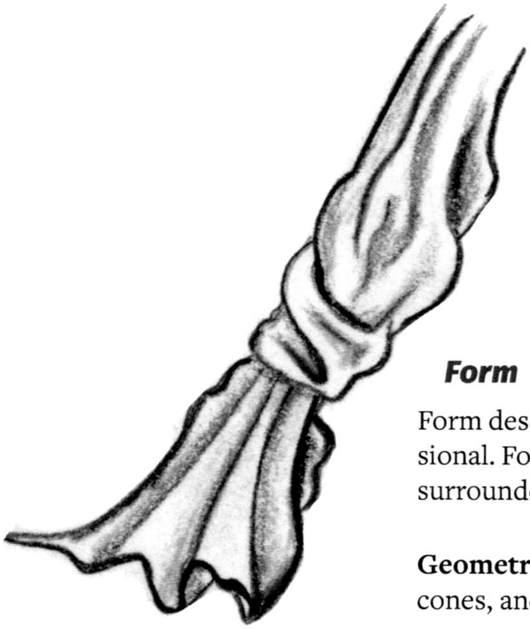

To make a piece of fabric look realistic, you would use broken values to represent the texture. There are many different value changes in the following sketch, but they blend together to create the illusion of fabric that is bunched and wrinkled.

Form

Form describes objects having length, width, depth and/or height and are three-dimensional. Forms take up space. You can see three-dimensional forms from all sides. We are surrounded by forms, either organic, geometric or abstract.

Geometric forms correspond to named shapes such as cubes, spheres, cones, and other regular forms.

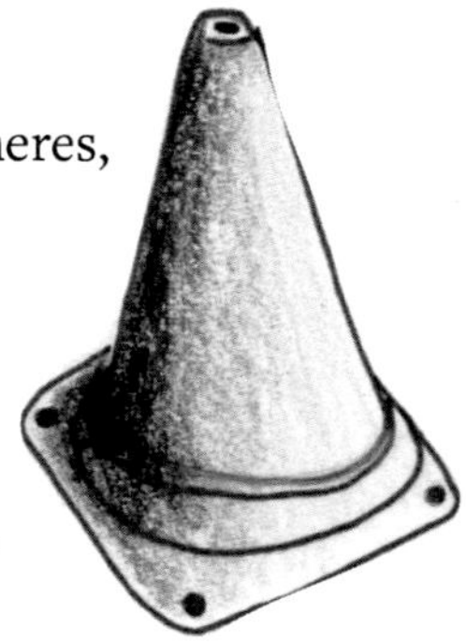

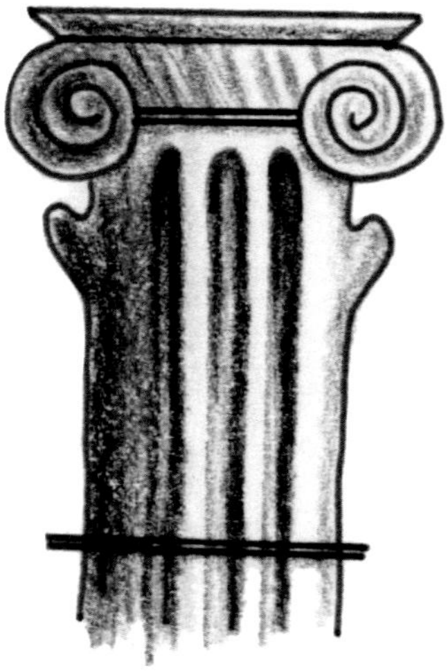

Architecture is usually composed of geometric forms.

Organic forms describe objects with a natural shape, such as rocks, sculptures, humans and mountains. Yet, not all naturally occurring objects are organic; snowflakes and soap bubbles are among many geometric forms found in nature.

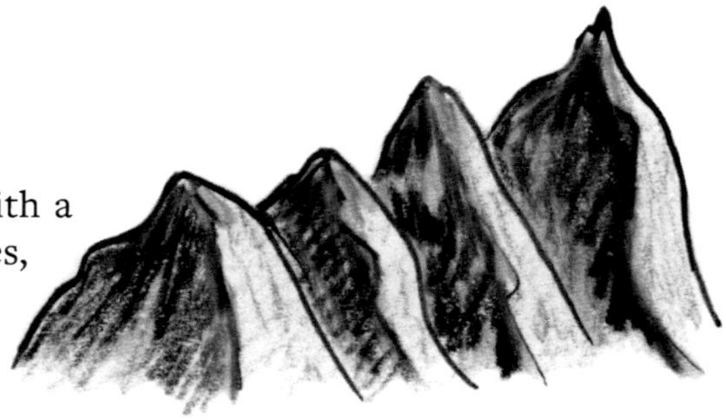

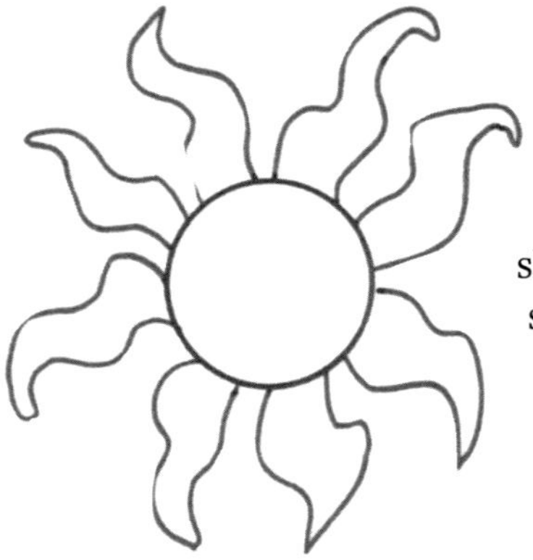

Abstract forms are stylized or simplified versions of organic shapes, with recognizable form. A stick figure is an abstract shape depicting a person. Icons are abstract shapes that represent ideas and concepts.

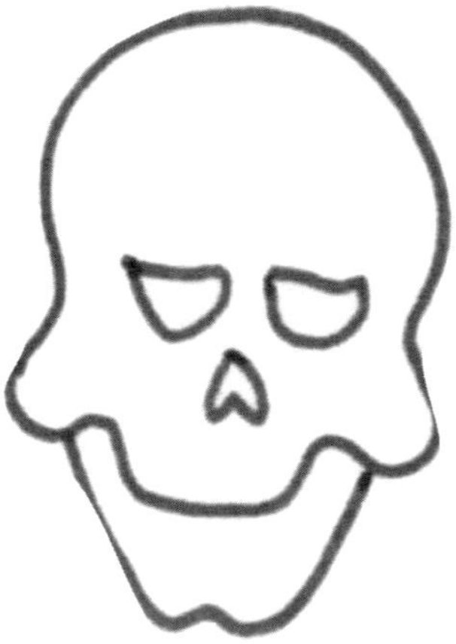

Texture

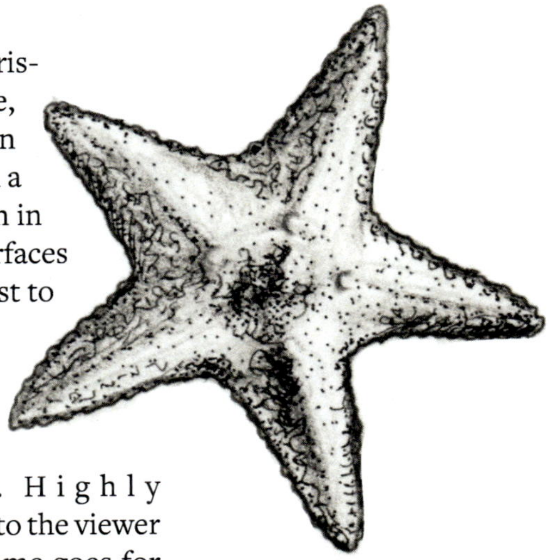

Texture describes visual or tactile surface characteristics such as smooth, bristly, rough or sharp. If your hand can actually feel textures in the surface, such as a collage with various papers or a clay pot with a design etched on the surface, it is called actual texture. If the texture is simulated, such as in a tattoo of rocks, plants, sand or animals, this is called implied texture. Even in two-dimensional works you can convey the sense of touching a variety of surfaces by using implied texture. You can use line, value, color, pattern and contrast to create simulated textures on flat surfaces.

Contrast between textured areas and smooth areas in a tattoo can help direct the viewer's eye to the most important elements. Highly textured areas will draw the eye and feel 'closer' to the viewer than areas with smooth or solid elements. Same goes for highly detailed areas vs. more blurred and soft areas.

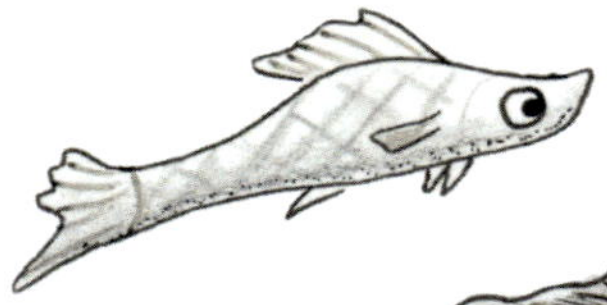

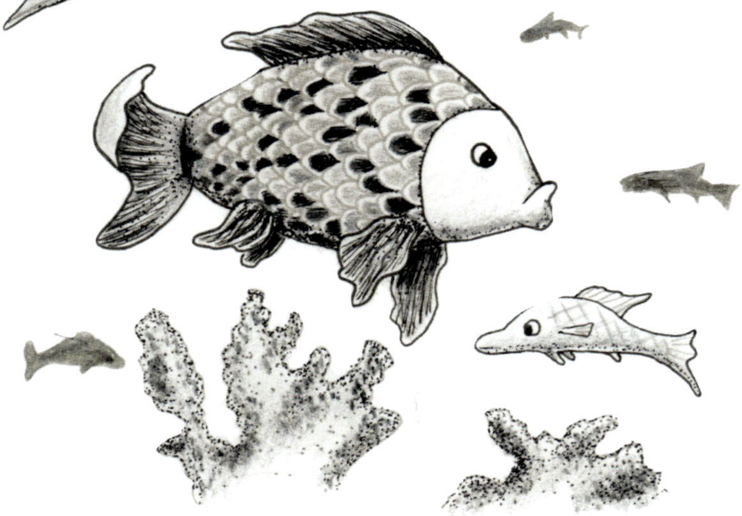

> "There is something magical in seeing what you can do, what texture and tone and color you can produce merely with a pen point and bottle of ink."
> *-Ida Rentoul Outwaite, Illustrator*

Space

Space, in art, refers to three-dimensional volume and expanse. Sculptors and architects work with actual space but tattooers work in two-dimensions—height and width—and must create an illusion to show depth in a design.

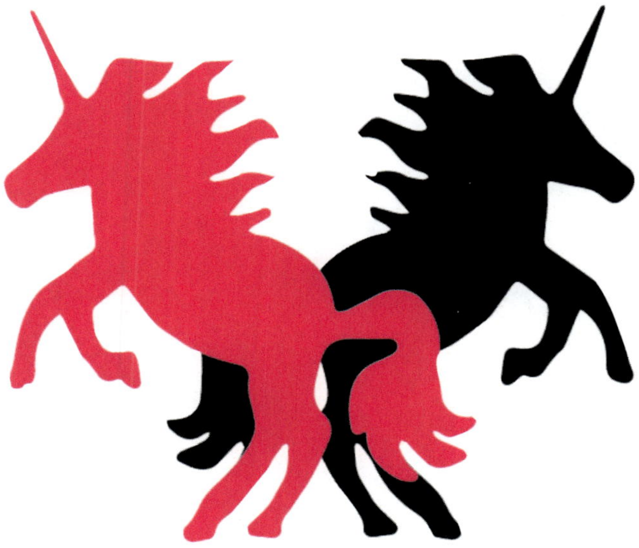

The easiest way to indicate three-dimension is by **overlapping**. This is where one object appears to be in front, or behind, another.

You can also convey depth by **changing size and changing placement**.

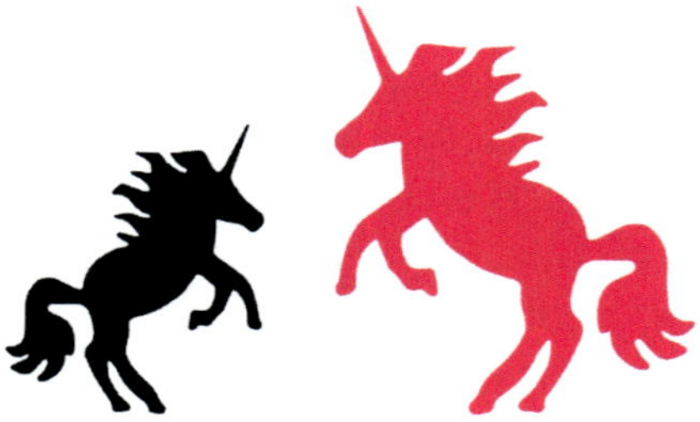

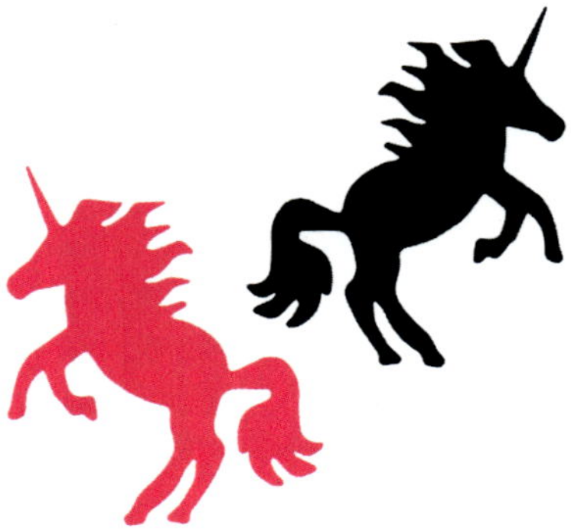

When straight lines and edges seem to come together at a distant point it is called **linear perspective**. This refers to the illusion that objects appear to grow smaller and converge toward a "vanishing point" at the horizon line.

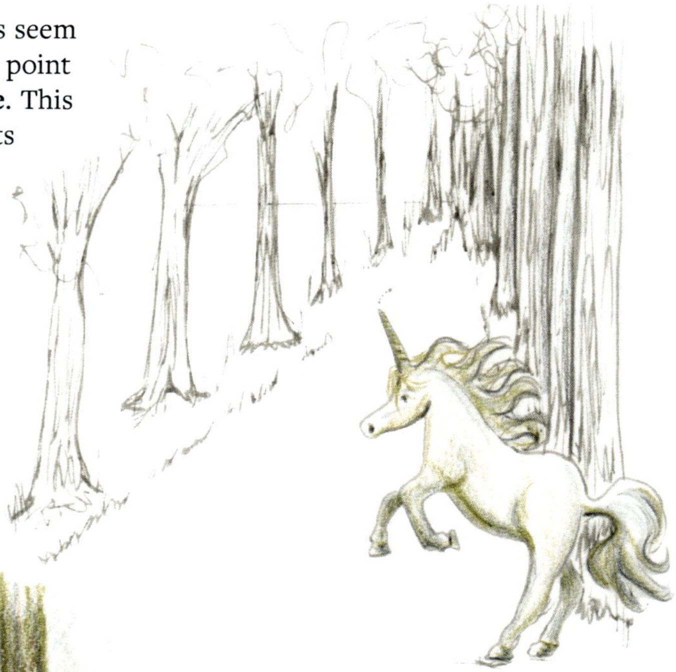

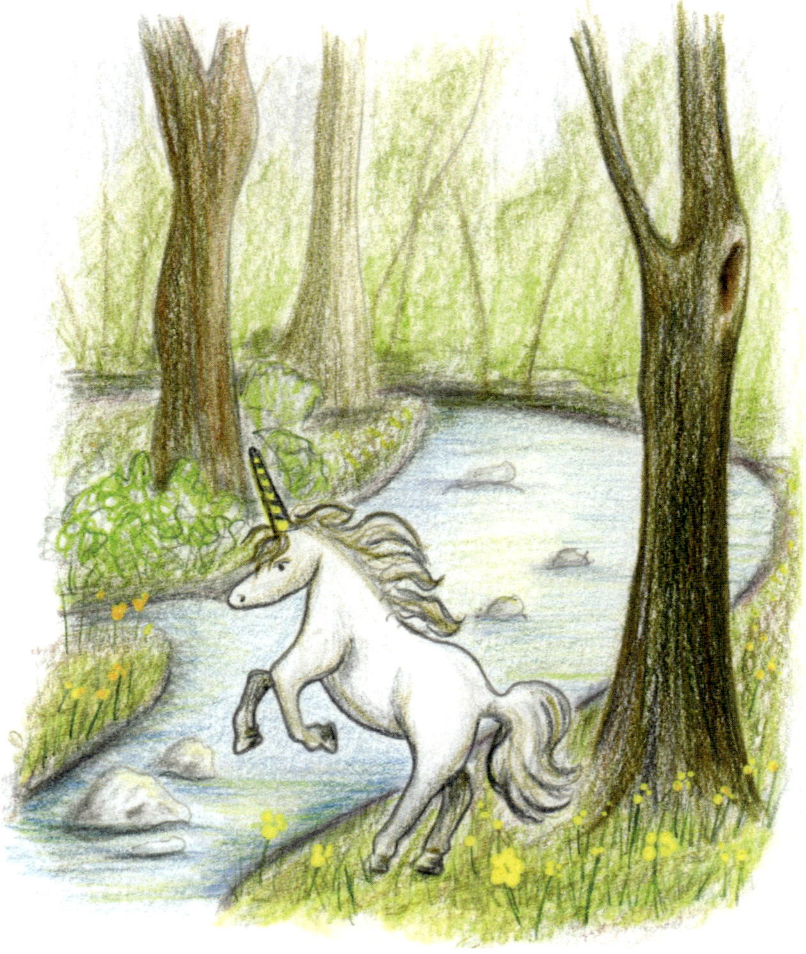

Atmospheric perspective is a way of using value and color to imply distance. Things further away appear lighter in value and things close-up appear darker. Objects also get less sharp in detail, and color becomes less saturated the further they are in the background; they lose their original color saturation and take on the atmosphere's saturation.

Objects, people and buildings take up

positive space and the area between the forms is called negative space.

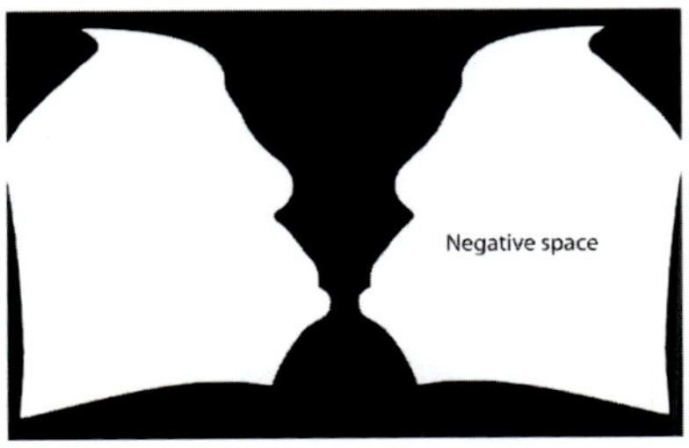

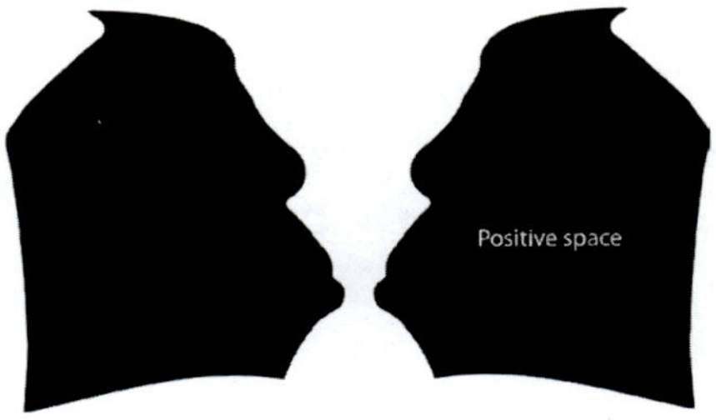

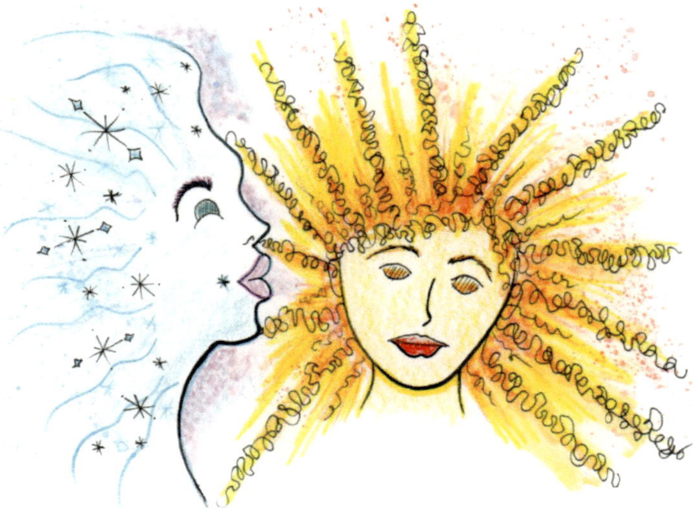

Temperature, value and hue are also in the bag of tricks that create the illusion of three-dimensions. Colors that appear warmer tend to seem closer and colors that are cooler tend to seem more distant.

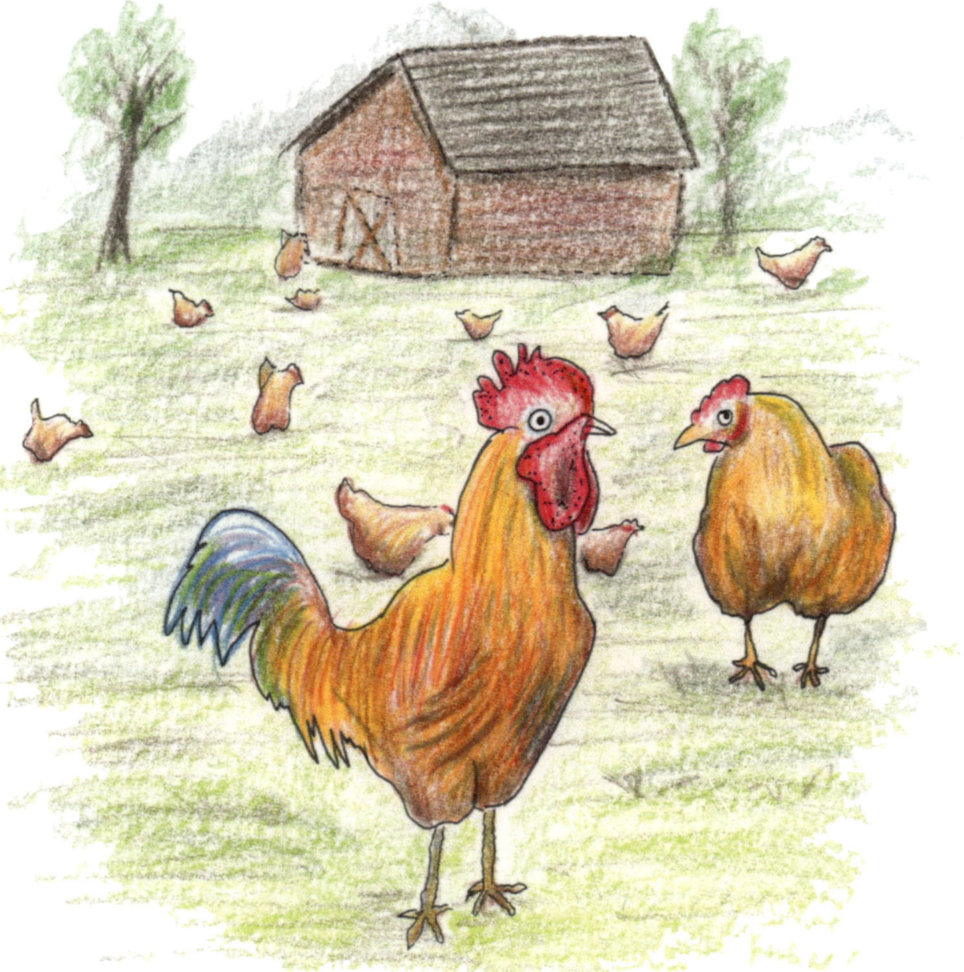

In addition, values that have a strong contrast appear separate in space and seem closer to the viewer while less contrast in value reads as more blended and further in the distance. Close objects tend to exhibit stronger, more saturated hues, while far objects are weaker and less saturated.

These tricks are used in combination to generate the appearance of depth and expanse in artwork. If any of these concepts is ignored, accidentally or purposefully, it interferes with the three-dimensional illusion.

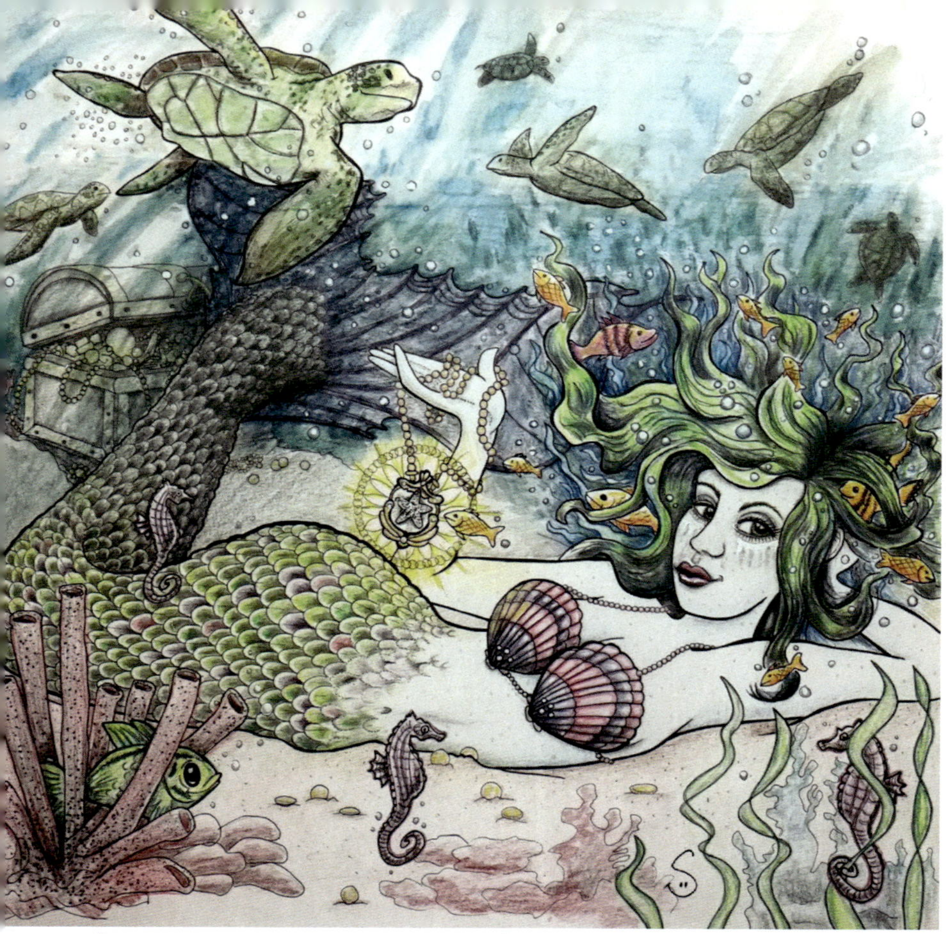

Look for the elements that make this composition inviting.

Principles of Design

Now that you have become familiar with the basic elements of art, the principles of design are the means by which we select and organize the elements to fulfill our purpose and make our artwork successful. Artists use these principles to create a design that feels satisfying and inviting to the viewer. Artists also break these rules to evoke emotion or perhaps disturb the viewer.

Balance: comfortable arrangement of things
Proportion: relative size and scale of various elements
Contrast: difference between elements
Emphasis: creation of a focal point
Movement: how we get around in a work of art
Pattern: decoration of surfaces, with planned, repeated units
Rhythm: repetition of art elements, such as shapes, lines and forms, to create continuity
Unity: consistent, orderly, or pleasing arrangement of parts

Balance

Balance, in art, refers to the pleasing arrangement of things or visual equilibrium. This refers to how we arrange the elements in the composition to "hold together" the design. Visual balance is essential as it provides a sense of order and helps your composition feel complete and harmonious. This doesn't mean everything should be perfectly symmetrical, but that the visual weight of objects, space and color should be equally distributed across the canvas. Without balance, a design feels off-kilter, inconsistent, and unsettling, which can also be used intentionally.

Symmetrical balance means things on either side of the "center" line are exactly or mostly alike. This can be very successful in some applications such as fabric patterns, clothing and ceramics, but can tend to be fairly boring in drawings, paintings and tattoos.

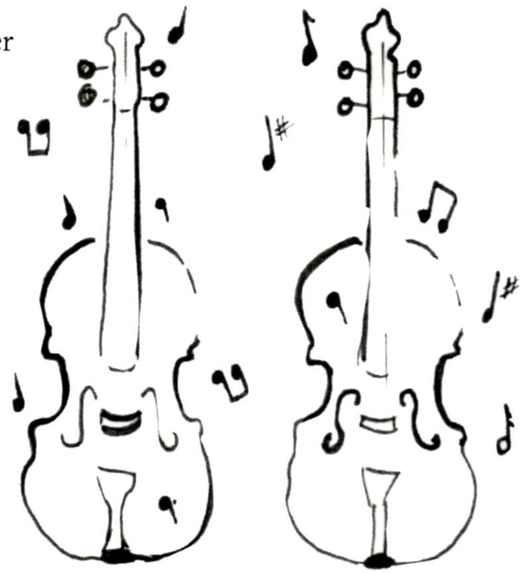

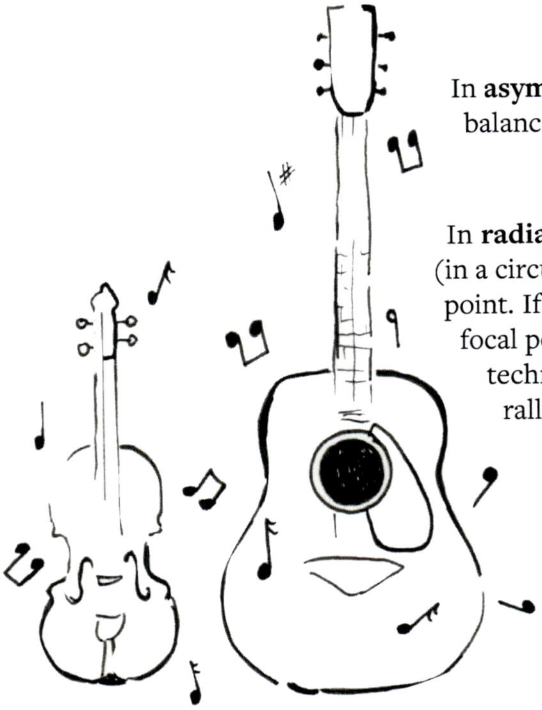

In **asymmetrical balance**, a larger shape is balanced by a smaller shape (or shapes).

In **radial balance**, elements radiate out (in a circular shape) from one main center point. If you're looking to create a strong focal point, radial balance is an effective technique because your eyes are naturally drawn inwards to the center.

You can also balance things like warm and cool colors, patterns, shapes or lineweight.

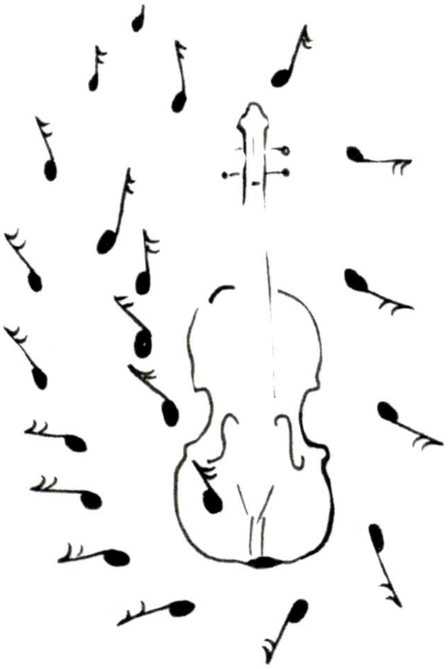

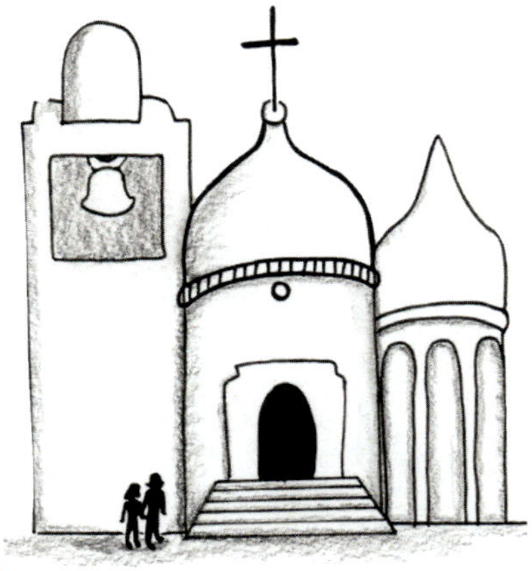

Proportion

Proportion describes the relative size and scale of various elements or the relationship between the objects or parts of a whole. People tend to judge the correctness of size by the measure of a human body. Consider large architectural spaces, such as a college, museum or church. These are intended to dwarf the human body and make an impression on the viewer. In contrast, a private home is more in scale with the human body, thus creating a space of friendly comfort and a less intimidating feel.

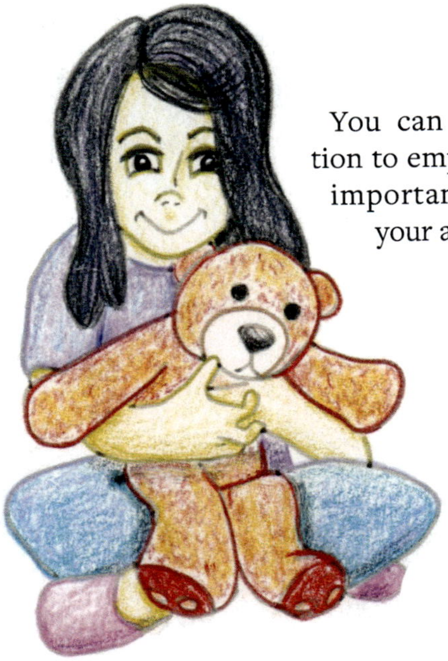

You can also use proportion to emphasize certain important aspects of your artwork.

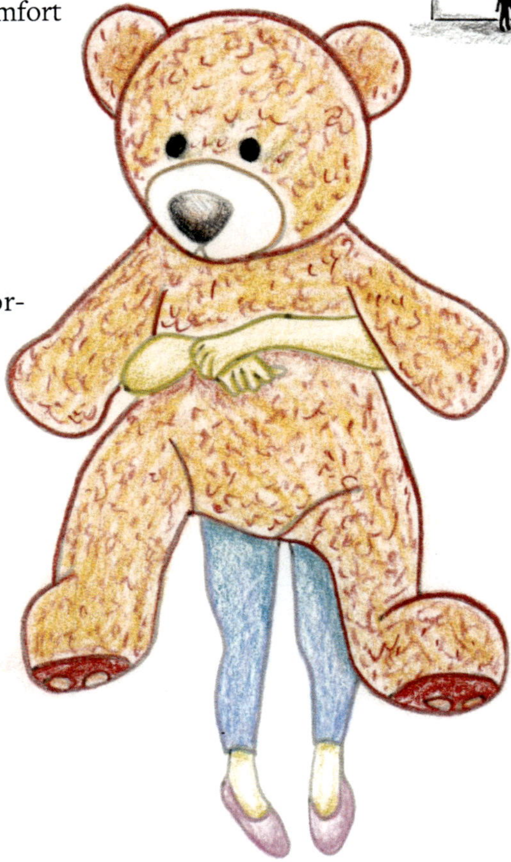

Contrast

Contrast describes the differences in art elements or the arrangement of opposite elements. Contrast makes art visually interesting.

Contrast of values can be either strong or soft to help convey the meaning in a piece. Strong value contrast is typically bold with easy to distinguish details, while soft value contrast (less distinct differences between values) can show softness, rain, fog, snow etc.

Contrast can be achieved by using a graphic element contrasted with realism.

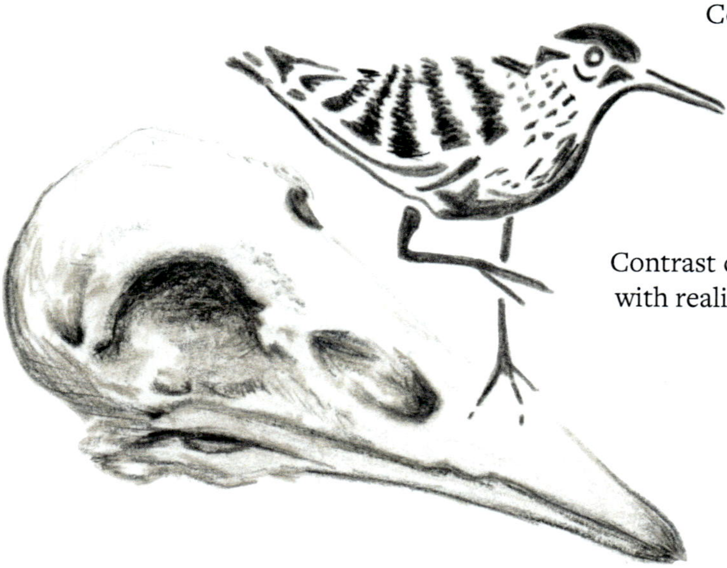

Contrast in proportion can provide drama. as mentioned previously.

Contrast of colors can provide excitement or inspire an emotional response.

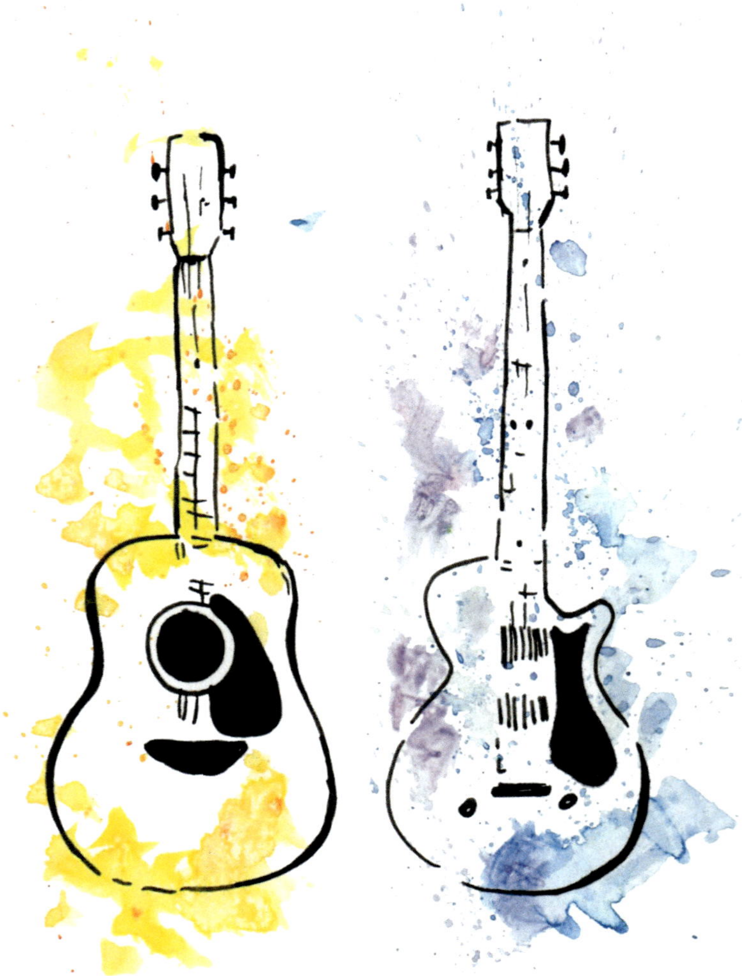

Emphasis

Emphasis is when we use art elements to accentuate a focal point or center of interest. This important principle helps us avoid things looking dull and muddled by giving the viewer a place to anchor their eyes temporarily. We emphasize the most important areas in our work by using elements, such as color, size or contrast to highlight a specific part.

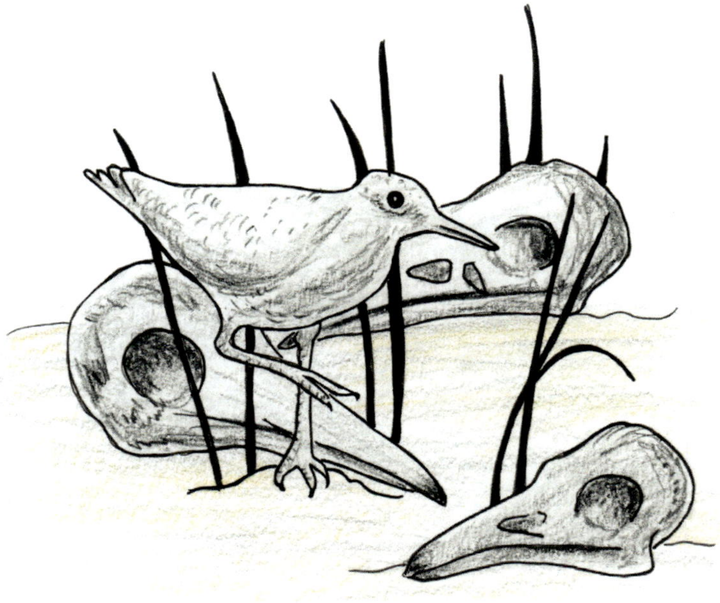

The emphasis in the scene at left is not quite right. Design appears flat and the eye tends to dart around with nothing to draw you in. The black grass steals the emphasis from the bird.

Emphasis can be created by using texture in your focal area and softer values in less important areas, to direct the eye where you want it to go first, as in the scene at right.

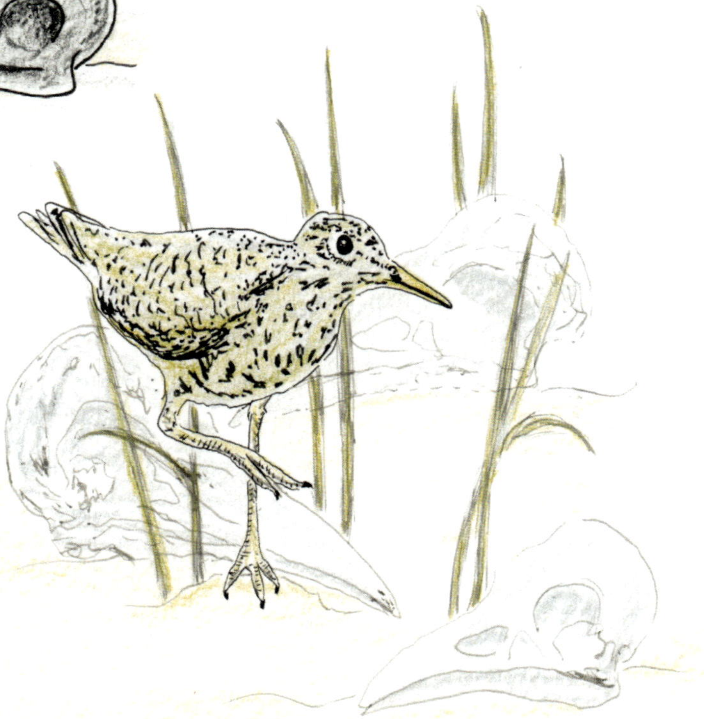

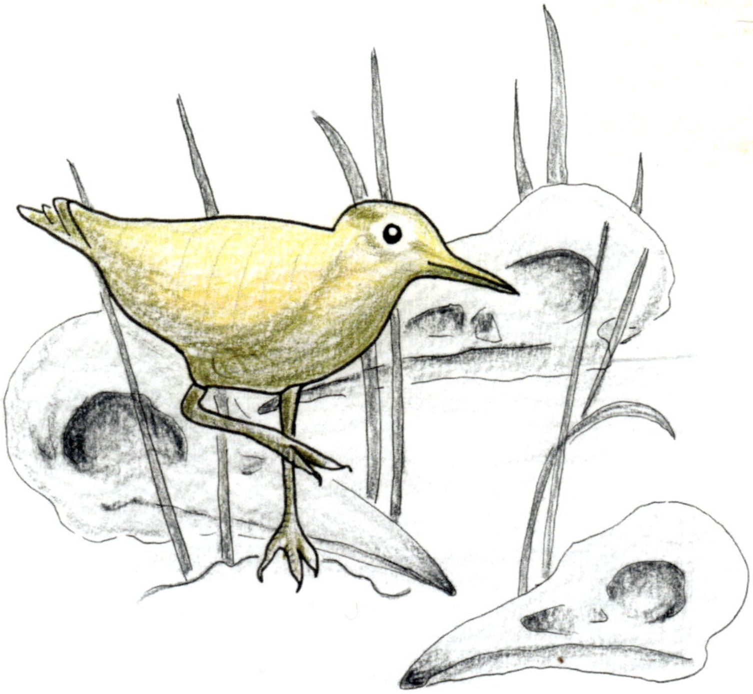

In the scene at left, emphasis is created by using thicker line weight and brighter color on the bird.

Emphasis is of particular importance in tattoo art because tattoos can tend to be jumbled along body parts, such as an arm sleeve, and thus difficult to "read". For example:

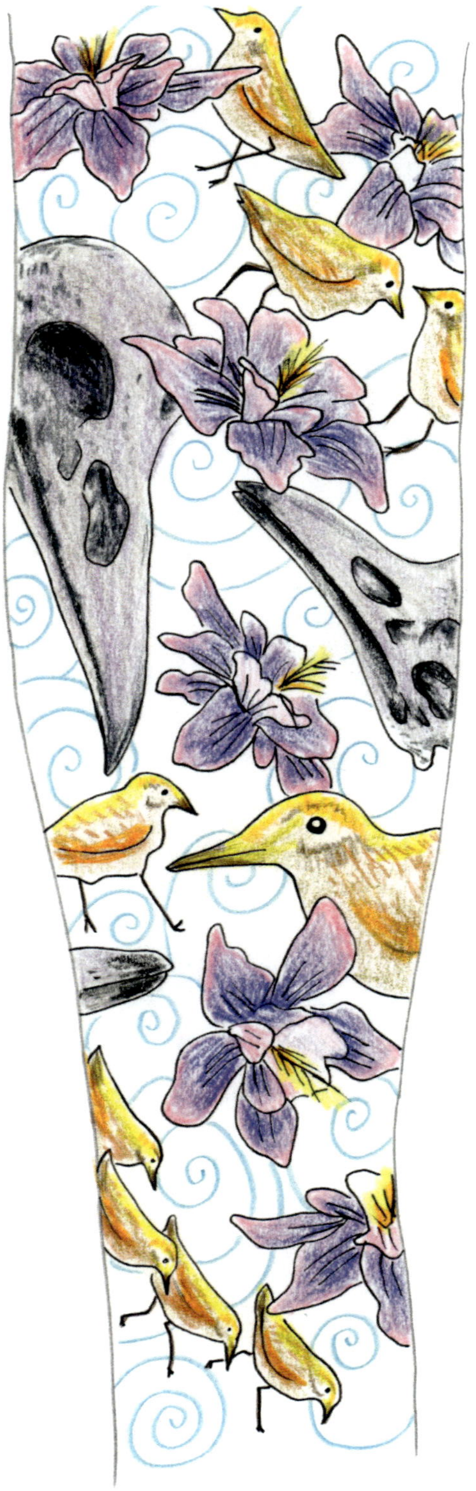

A Tale of Two Sleeves

Look carefully at these two designs for a tattoo sleeve. Think about what makes the one on the right a better composition and a more successful design. The two designs have the same overall elements and color scheme.

But the one on the left has no clear focal area. The two skulls are the darkest element and do pull your eye somewhat. Yet all the elements have the same line weight. The birds and flowers all have similar color value and saturation which doesn't create much separation. And the swirls in the background add unwanted texture and brightness that makes this design look cluttered.

The design on the right uses softer, less saturated colors on the background birds. The flowers at the top are desaturated and employ thinner lines. The flower near the main bird's beak leads your eye to the bird's face, both by how it is tilted up toward the bird and the use of a brighter violet color and yellow. The main bird has brighter yellow in feathers and has a heavier line on the outside and a white space around its body.

In addition, the top skulls have a medium grey value, thinner lines, with beaks pointing toward the main bird (leading lines) and the bottom skull is more contrasting in blacks and gray as well as having a heavier line.

And lastly, the background is soft and washed out, which allows the main focal point to pop forward.

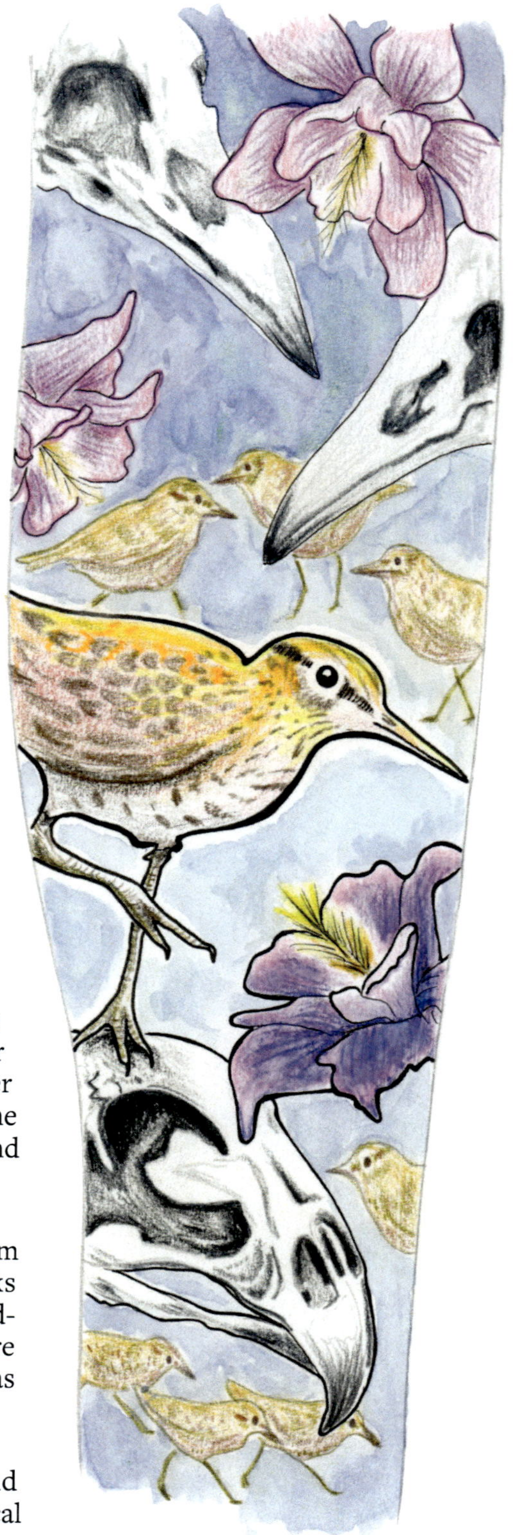

Movement

Movement is the process of the relocation of objects in space over time. But in this context, it describes how we assist the viewer in getting around in our work of art. The eye naturally moves from simple to complex areas. When we observe art, our eyes move around along edges and lines as well as to connecting shapes and paths of color. This helps the observer move from the outer edges to the central point of interest in our work, as well as create a sense of unity and organization.

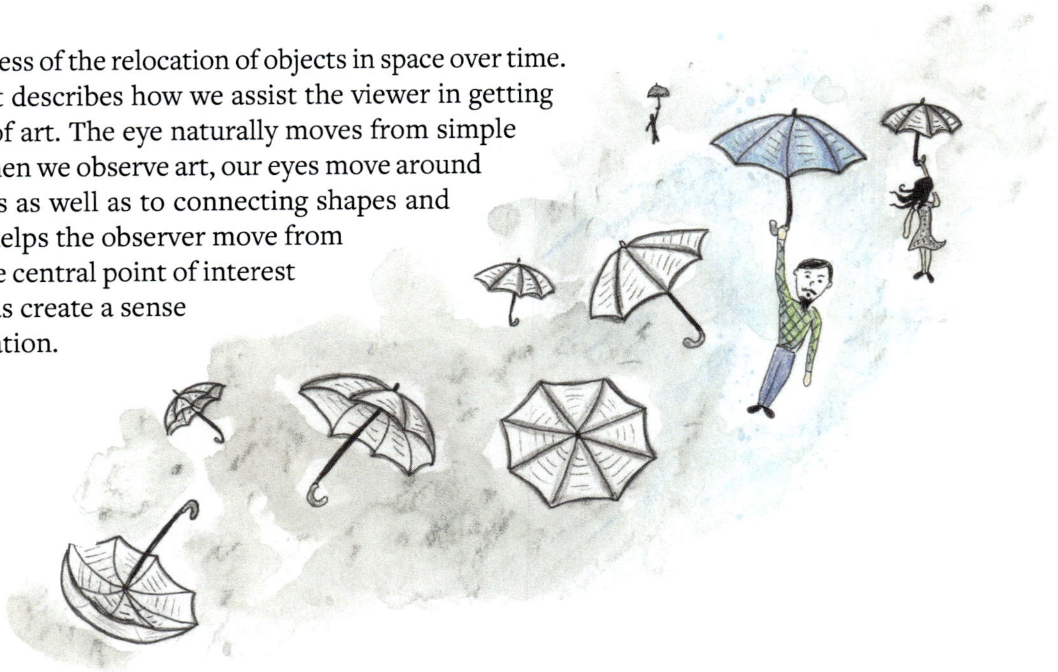

Pattern

Pattern decorates the surface with repeated units and provides an underlying structure. And pattern is everywhere—such as clothing, animals, flowers, buildings and home décor. Pattern makes art exciting by creating planned or random repetition to enhance surfaces. This could be repetition of shapes, colors, textures or lines.

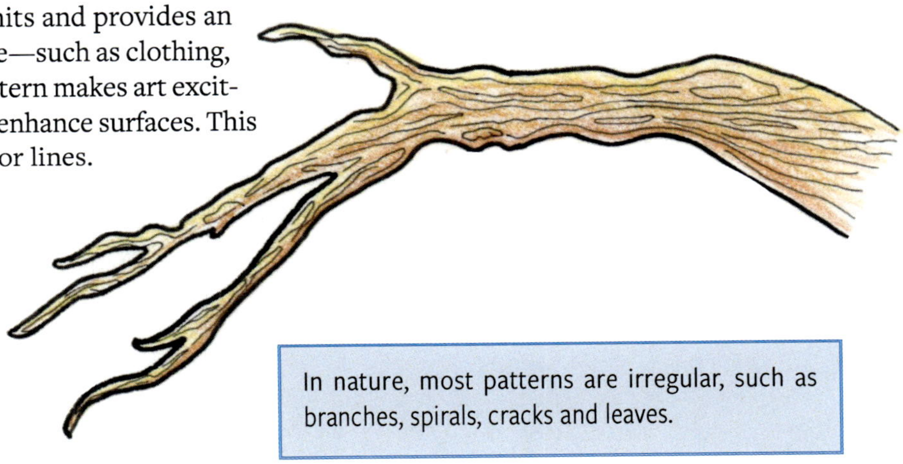

In nature, most patterns are irregular, such as branches, spirals, cracks and leaves.

> "Every child is an artist. The problem is how to remain an artist once we grow up."
>
> *-Pablo Picasso, Painter*

Regular patterns are made by using the same shapes or elements in an organized way.

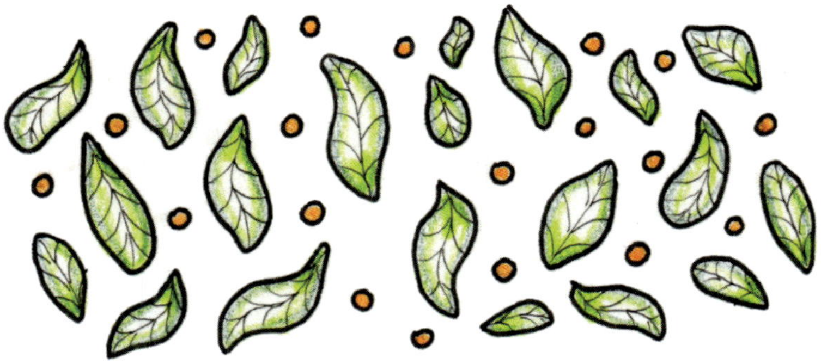

Rhythm

Rhythm refers to the repetition of art elements to help unify the surface and create a feeling of continuity.

Just as in music, when we plan the strong (loud) or weak (quiet) elements to flow together in a regular or irregular way, we control the feeling and interest in an artwork.

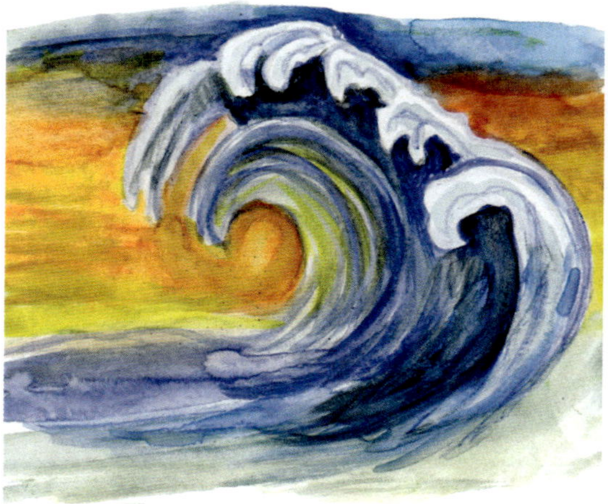

Irregular or unplanned rhythm, such as a sandstorm or wave is not repeated exactly throughout the piece but has a rhythmic flow.

Regular or planned rhythm mayhave variety and need not be repeated exactly to show continuity.

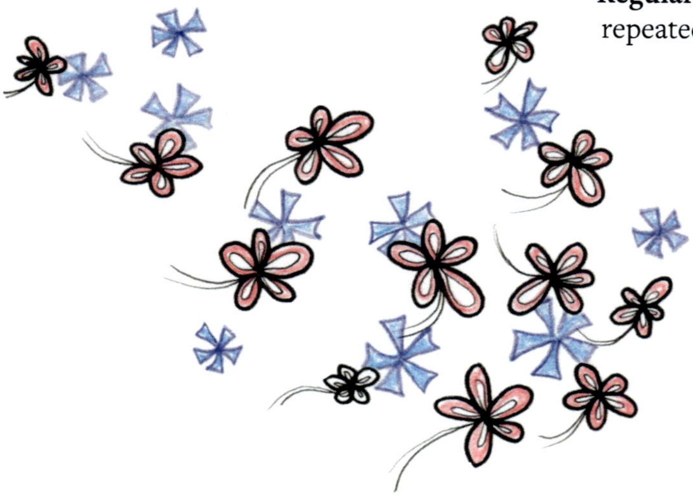

Unity (with variety)

Unity means a consistent, orderly, or pleasing arrangement of parts. Unity makes a work of art seem complete because everything works in harmony.

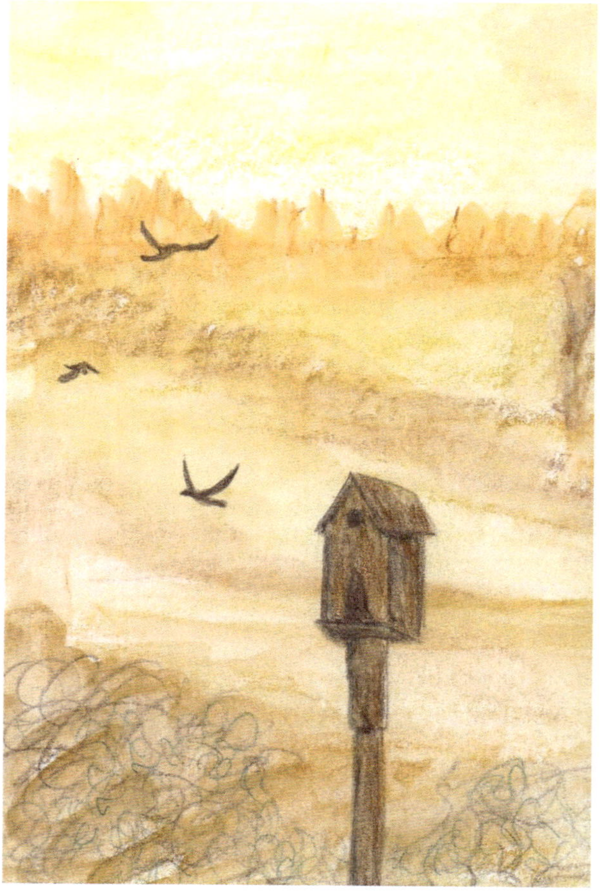

But variety creates visual adventure. If everything looks too much alike it becomes dull. Thus, unity with variety is much more pleasing.

There is unity in color as well as shapes in the image at right, but the variety of having a yellow banjo with sparkles makes the painting more compelling.

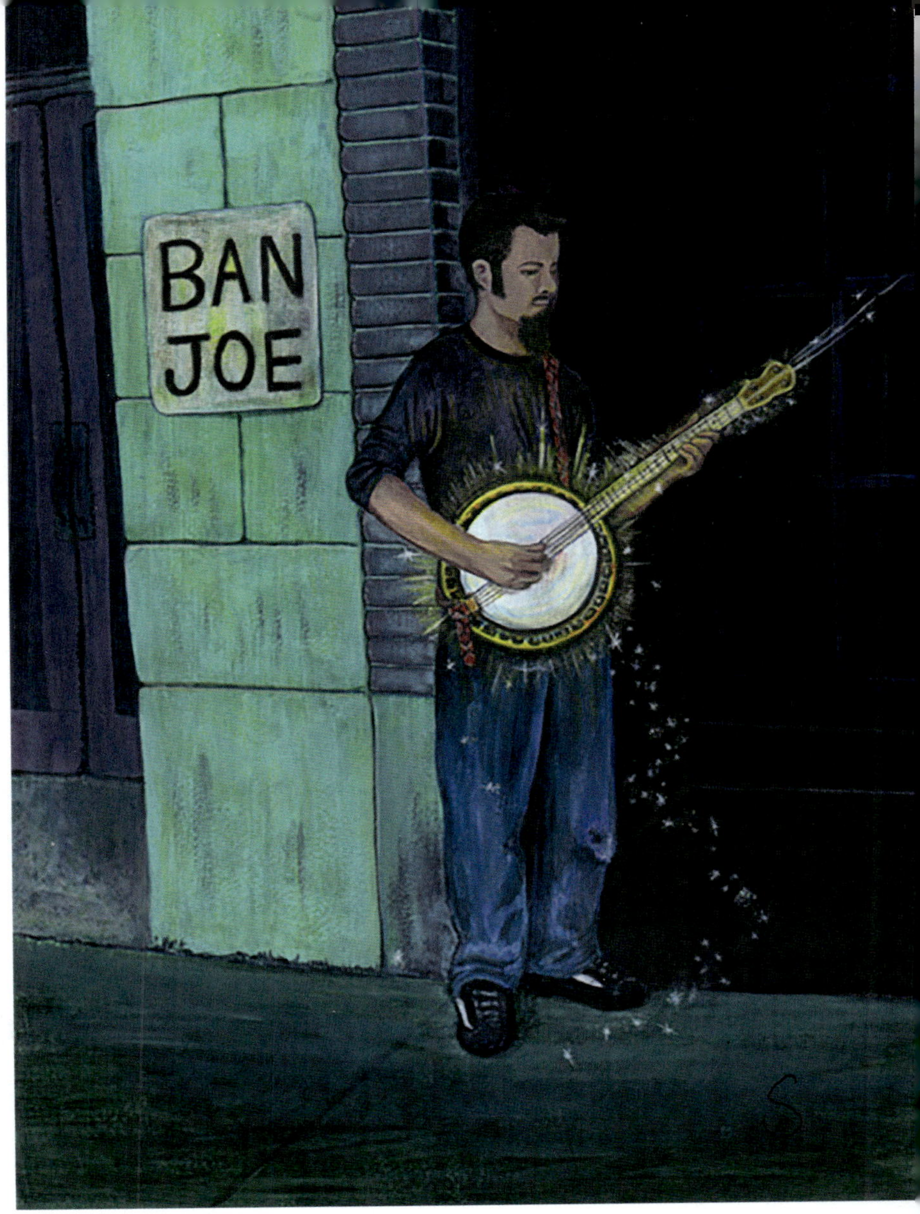

In your art you could use similar shapes, colors, patterns, movement, texture, temperature, and value throughout, and still have variety as well.

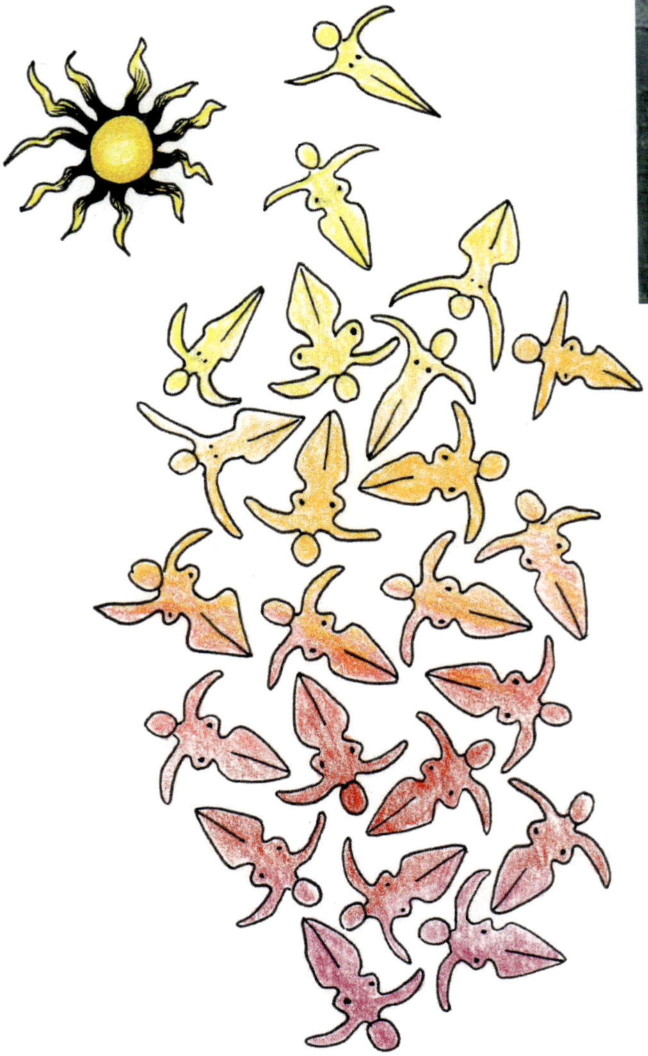

"As my artist's statement explains, my work is utterly incomprehensible and is therefore full of deep significance"
~Calvin, Calvin & Hobbes, Bill Waterson

Similar repeated shapes, such as the ladies at left, create unity, but the shapes are not exactly alike so visual interest is created.

CREATING A COMPOSITION

You've learned about the elements and principles of art and design, so how do you put these concepts together to create a successful tattoo? Composition is the arrangement or organization of the visual elements. The composition is your usage of the "ingredients" to form a whole design. You control how the viewer's eye moves through the piece to produce a beneficial result. When composition is good, you don't really notice it, but you definitely notice when compositional elements are ignored. An artwork will seem unsuccessful or 'wrong' to you, even if you don't know why.

> "And after drawing comes composition. A well-composed painting is half done."
>
> *~Pierre Bonnard, Painter and Printmaker*

Some basic composition rules provide a starting point for creating pleasing works of art, whether we are talking about painting, drawing or tattooing. Of course, these are more suggestions than rules, but successful composition can make or break your work. It's what holds the eye and encourages the viewer to keep looking. Pay attention to the following compositional guidelines:

Simplification
Rule of Thirds
Value in Threes
Rule of Odds
Leading Lines
Balancing the Elements
Focal Point

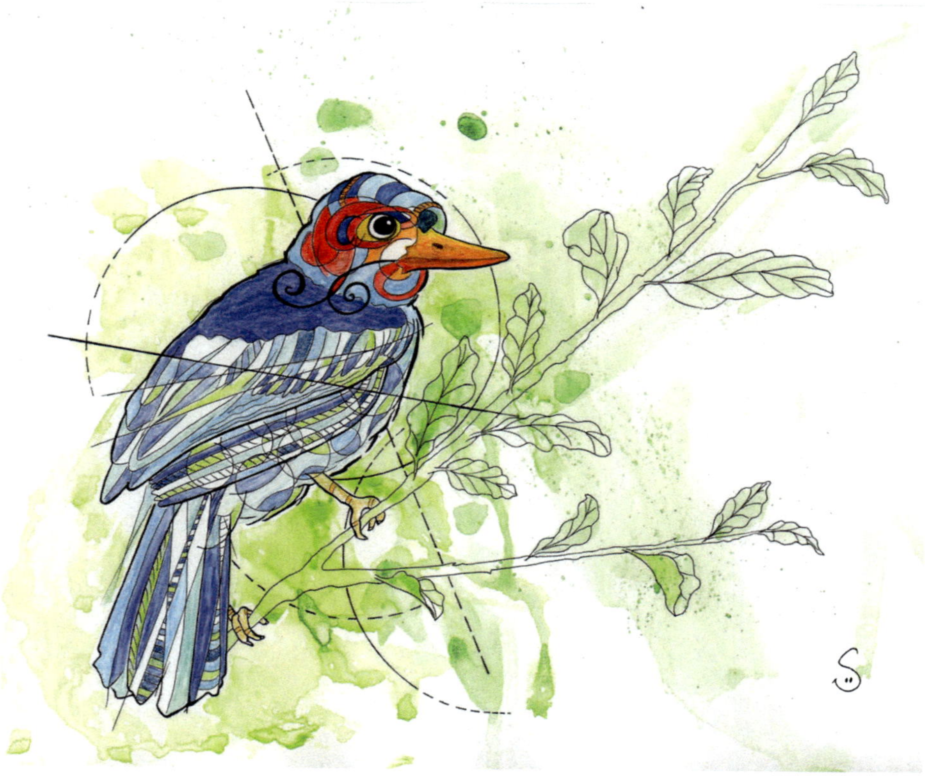

Simplification

Simplifying your artwork is an important skill and the painting masters of old used this concept to reduce clutter in their art and direct the viewer's eye.

To simplify your composition, you can try using a limited palette (color range), limited value range, limited detail of unimportant areas and/or remove unnecessary subjects or objects.

Simplification is best combined with targeted complexity. Best to use variety to make your artwork more interesting. You can try making it highly detailed or brightly colored in one area, so as to bring attention to the focal point, while having less detail in most of the other elements.

Rule of Thirds

This is the concept that if you divide any composition into thirds, vertically and horizontally, then place the key elements of your image either along these lines or where they intersect, you'll achieve a more pleasing arrangement. This will add tension and interest, as well as help guide the viewer's eye to wander around the piece.

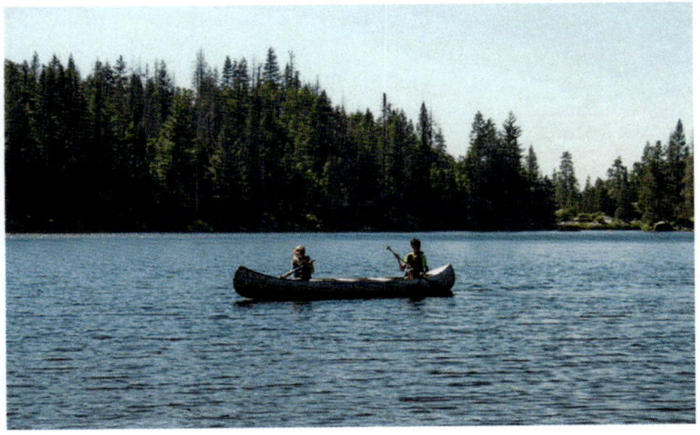

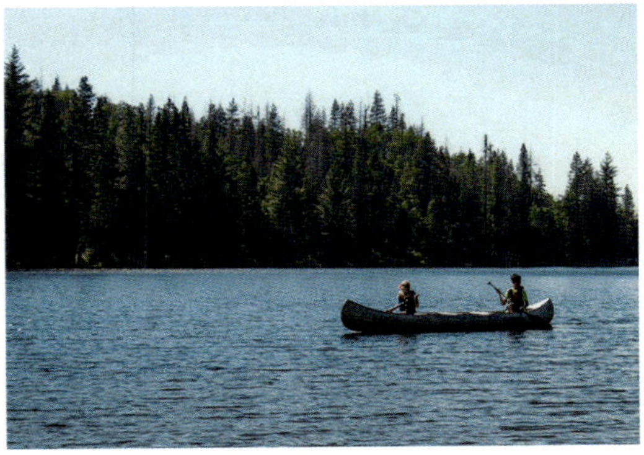

photo credit
Mike Bowman

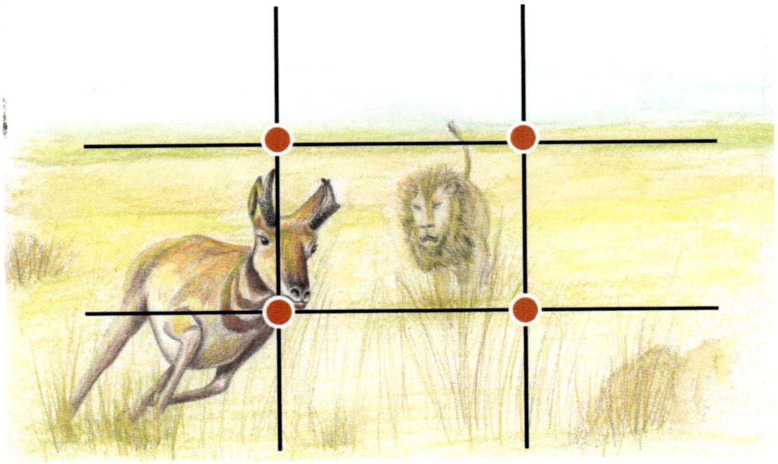

This works well because it forces the artist to make one element more dominant than another, creating imbalance. And imbalance will attract the viewer's eye.

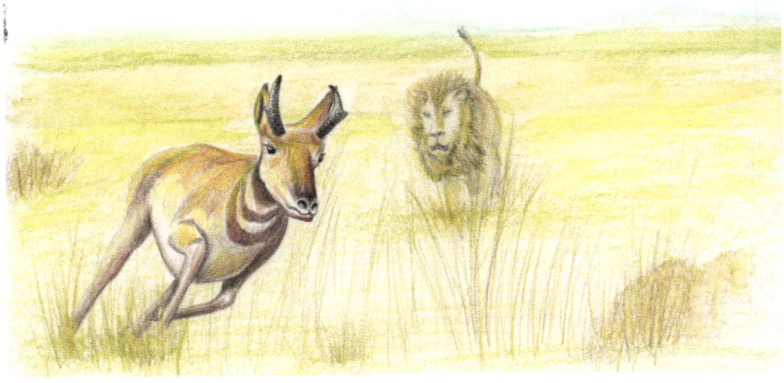

Generally speaking, creating a composition perfectly balanced on both sides of the imaginary center line is usually somewhat boring because it lacks visual interest.

Shelly's Sidenote

INSPIRATION FROM NATURE

I attended a tattoo seminar taught by German tattooer Markus Lenhard and he stressed the idea of exploring nature to find shapes, patterns and rhythm that we could emulate in our tattoos. He showed many slides with examples of beautiful and intricate designs found in plants, rocks, seeds, flowers and even organisms. This shifted my thinking regarding sourcing references in nature and I've tried to take more photos to inspire my drawings.

And if you can't realistically get out into the natural world to all the places you'd like to explore, I suggest acquiring full color photo books. "The Mandala Book" by Lori Bailey Cunningham, "Seeing Seeds" by Teri Dunn Chace & Robert Llewellyn or "Citizens of the Sea" by Nancy Knowlton are filled with stunning pictures of geometric shapes and patterns from natural sources, as well as brilliant close-ups of remarkable creatures.

Making one area of your composition more dominant creates interest and tension which forces the viewer's eye to move around the "canvas" searching for relationships.

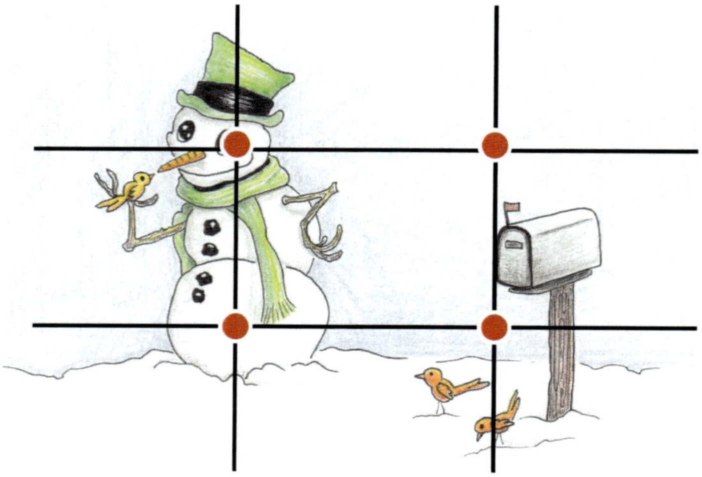

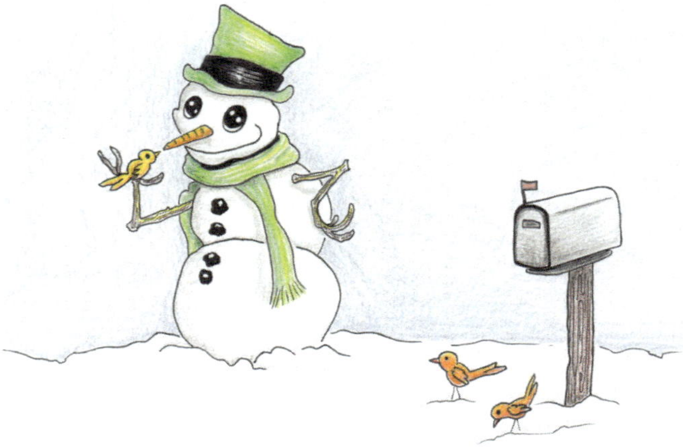

Value in 3's

Value can be thought of in threes as well. Break your composition into foreground, middle ground and background. Then, to emphasize the relationship between these three you can restrict each area to a range of value: light, medium and dark.

This will help reinforce the sense of depth in your design as well as make contours easier to read.

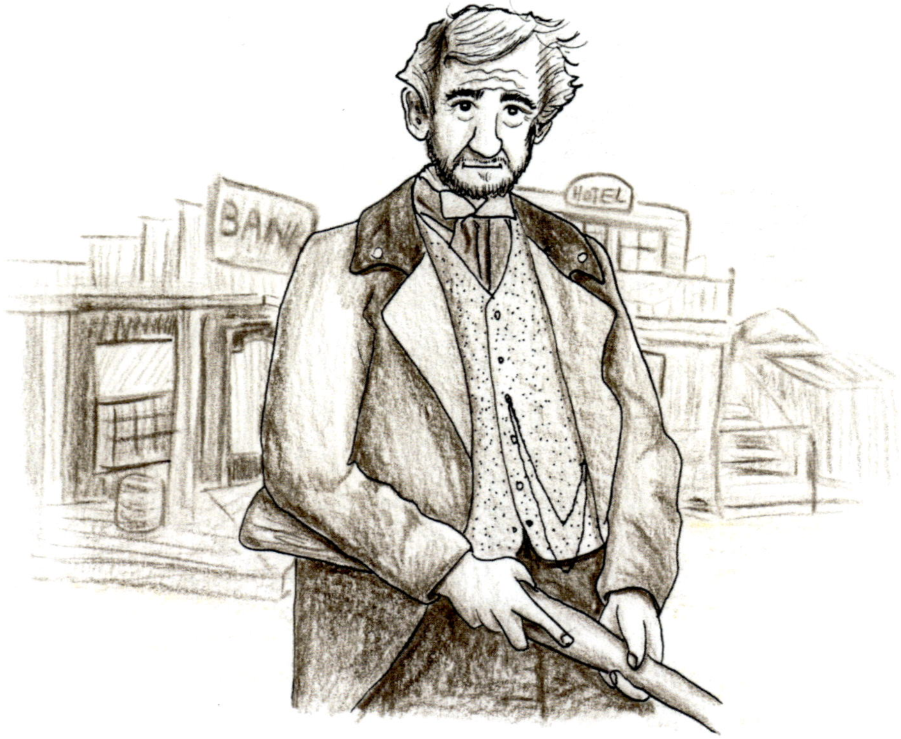

Rule of Odds

Having an odd number of elements in your composition will make it much more dynamic. Humans tend to naturally pair things up. Perhaps because our bodies are designed in pairs; two legs, two arms, two ears, two eyes and two nostrils! This idea even works in interior or landscaping design.

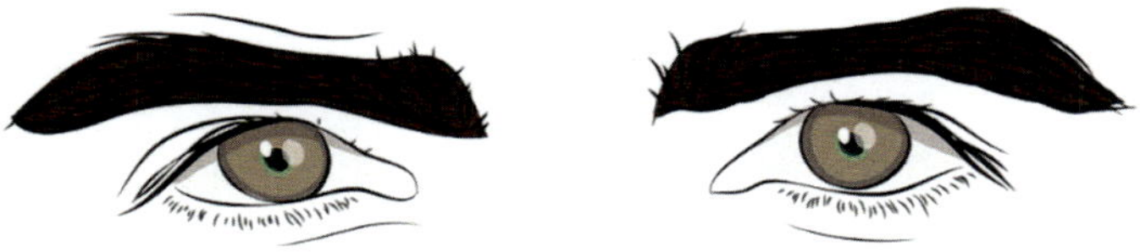

With an even number of elements, your eye instinctively pairs them up--whether it's two left and two right or 2 + 2 = 4.

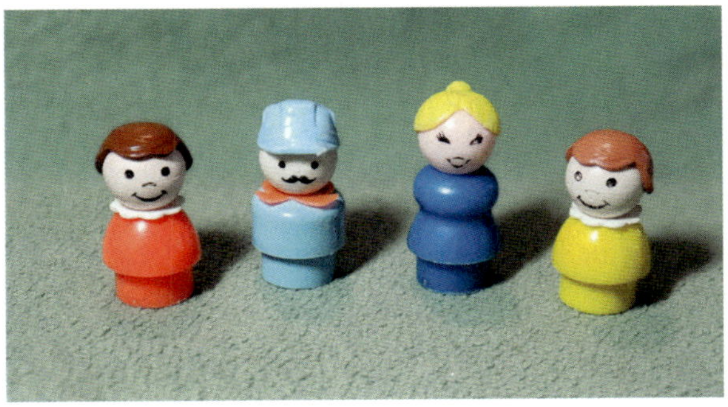

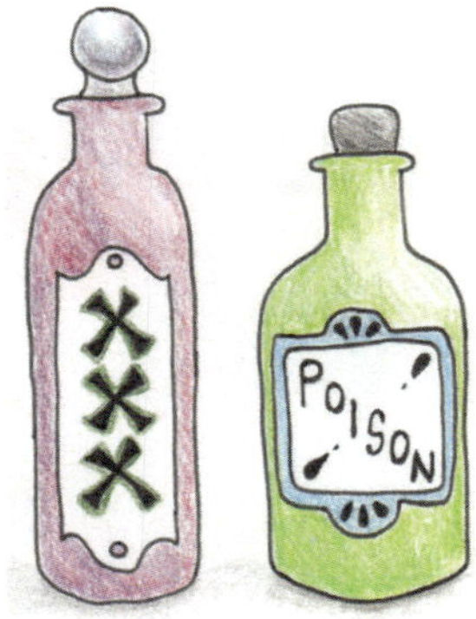

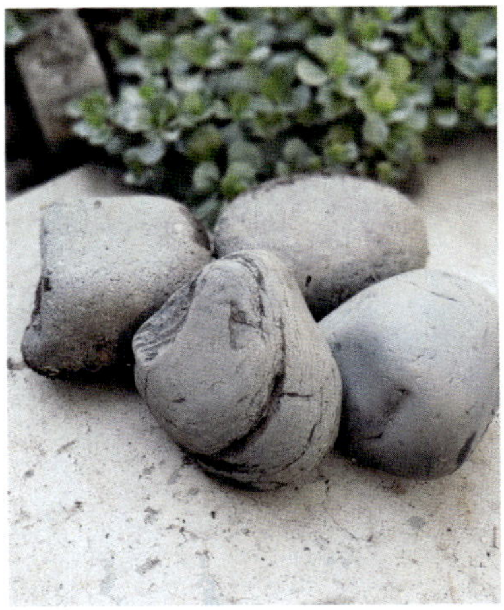

Having an odd number of elements in your composition means something is always left over and keeps the eye moving across the design.

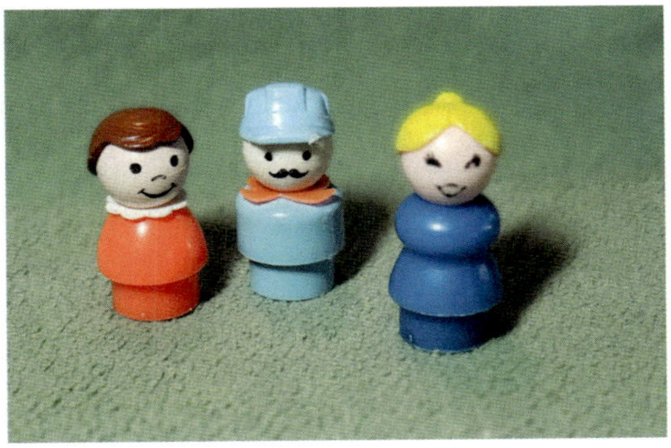

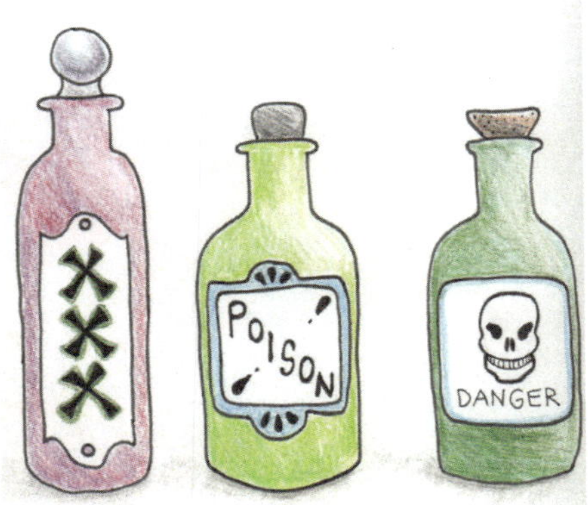

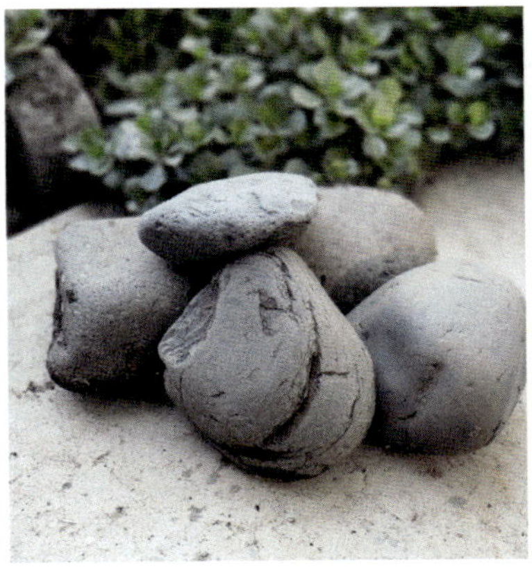

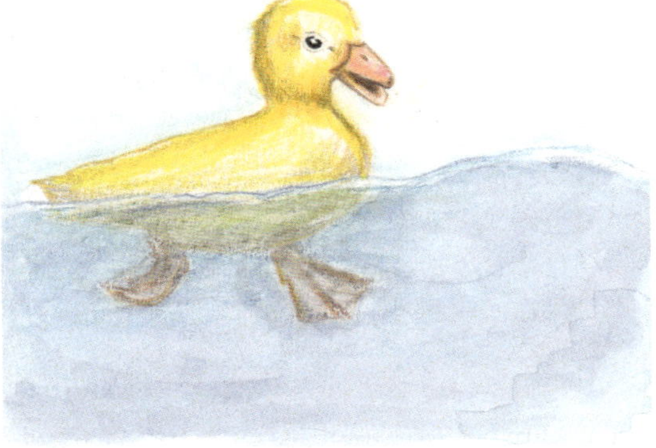

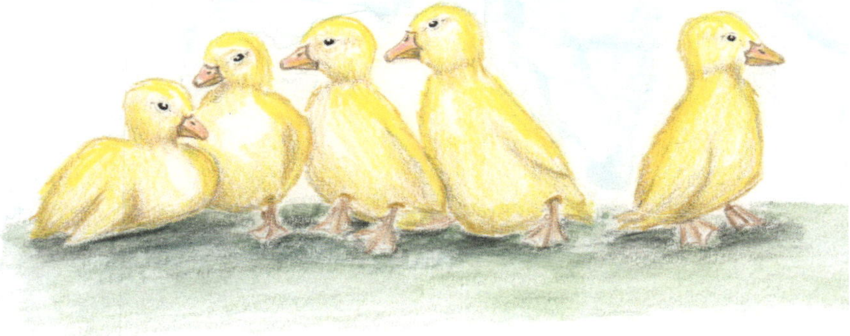

Shelly's Sidenote

TOO MANY ELEMENTS

You will occasionally have an enthusiastic client with an enormous list of the images, symbols, names of loved ones and pets to include in their tattoo design. They likely don't understand the principles of good composition and you will have to take charge and help make decisions about how to best convey the main concepts in their idea. Only so many "themes" will work in one tattoo, especially if they are insisting on a small piece. It may help to explain that tattoo lines spread over time and restrict your ability to put tons of detail in small spaces.

In addition, I believe tattoos "read" better with one main idea and too many elements can tend to muddle up a piece.

The rule of odds may be difficult to follow in tattooing clients because of their personal requests (i.e. "I want FOUR ducks...one for each of my kids."). If this is the case, you can still give the illusion of odds by making one element much larger or smaller than the others, or even positioning it differently -- like the fourth duck sitting and facing the opposite way of the other ducks--thus making it seem like a different element.

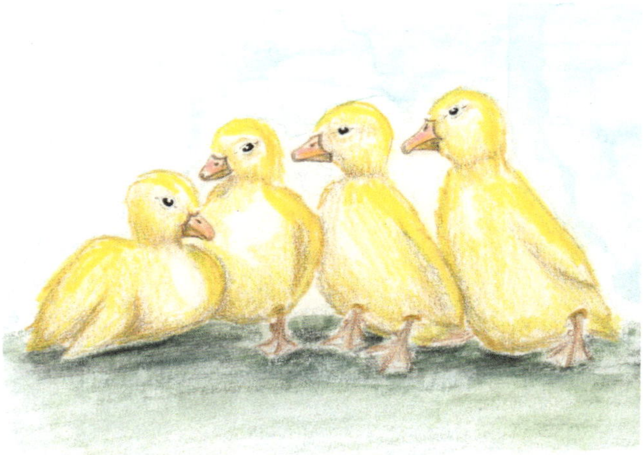

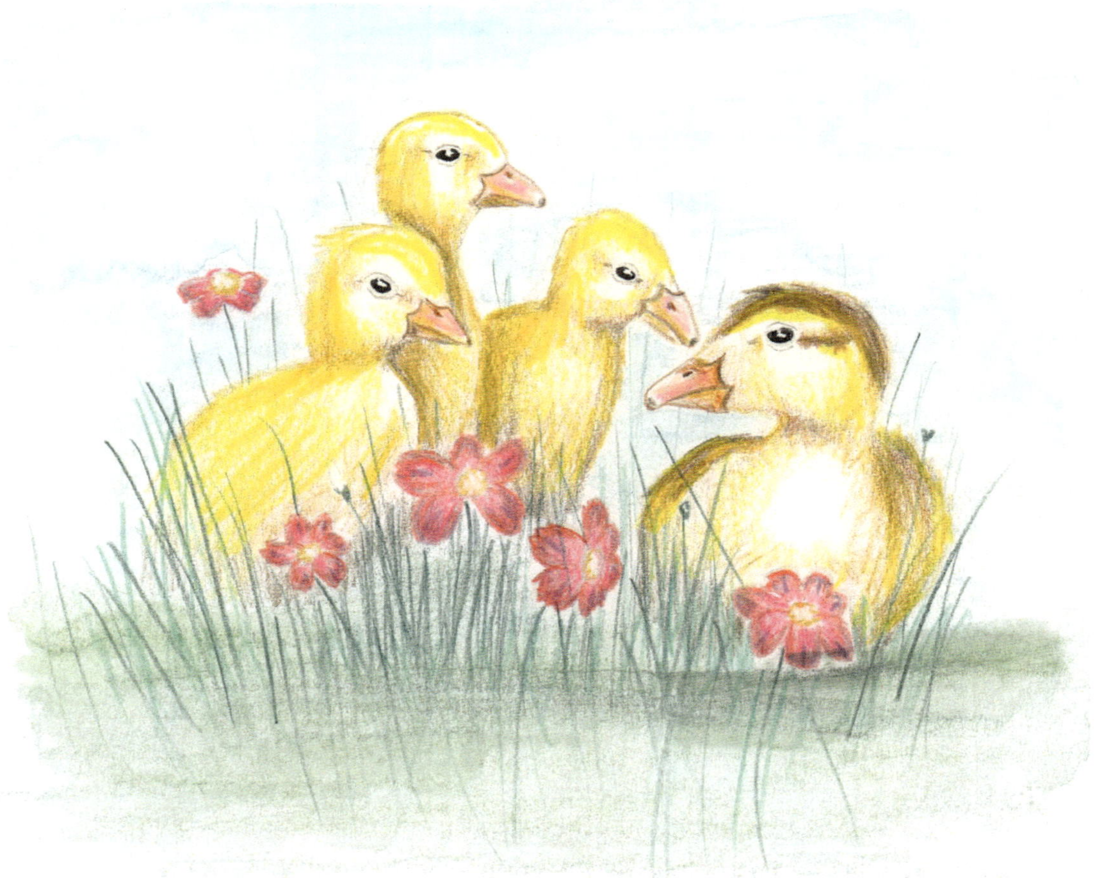

You can also try using differences in color, value, pattern, size and texture to make one element appear different.

Also, adding other elements, such as flowers, adds to the count... now there are nine objects in the design at left—very subtle but it helps create interest.

Leading Lines

The human eye is very sensitive to lines, real or imaginary, and the use of lines is a good way to lead the viewer's eye. When we look at a composition, our eye is naturally drawn along lines. By thinking about how you place lines, you can decide which path you want people to take when they "journey" through your scene.

The eye naturally will create lines even when they are not there, as we discussed earlier, such as with two people staring at each other. This is called implied line.

We can also use lines to make the viewer's eye move around the key elements and hold their attention.

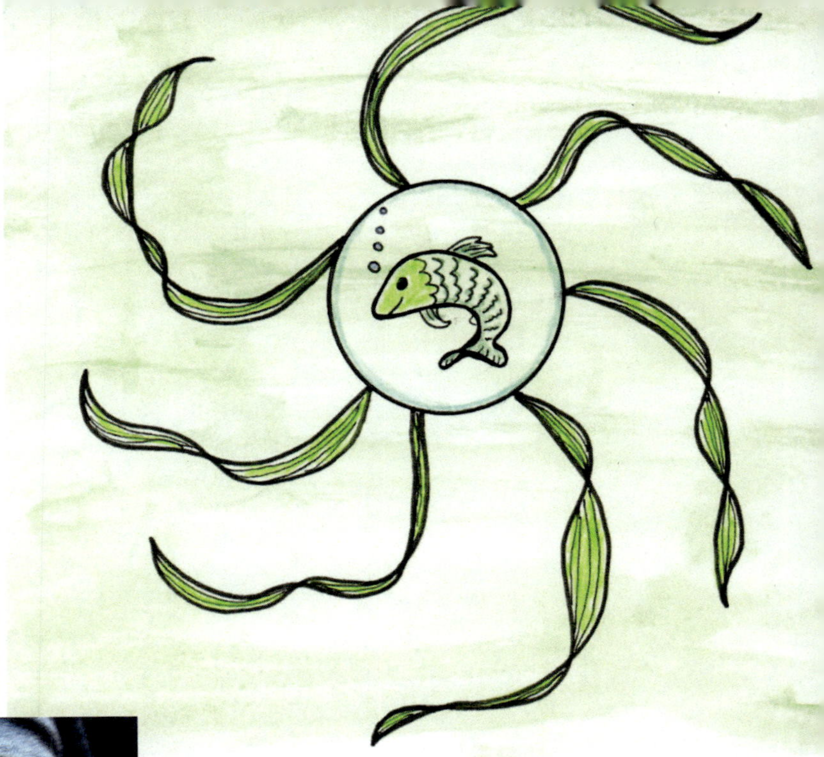

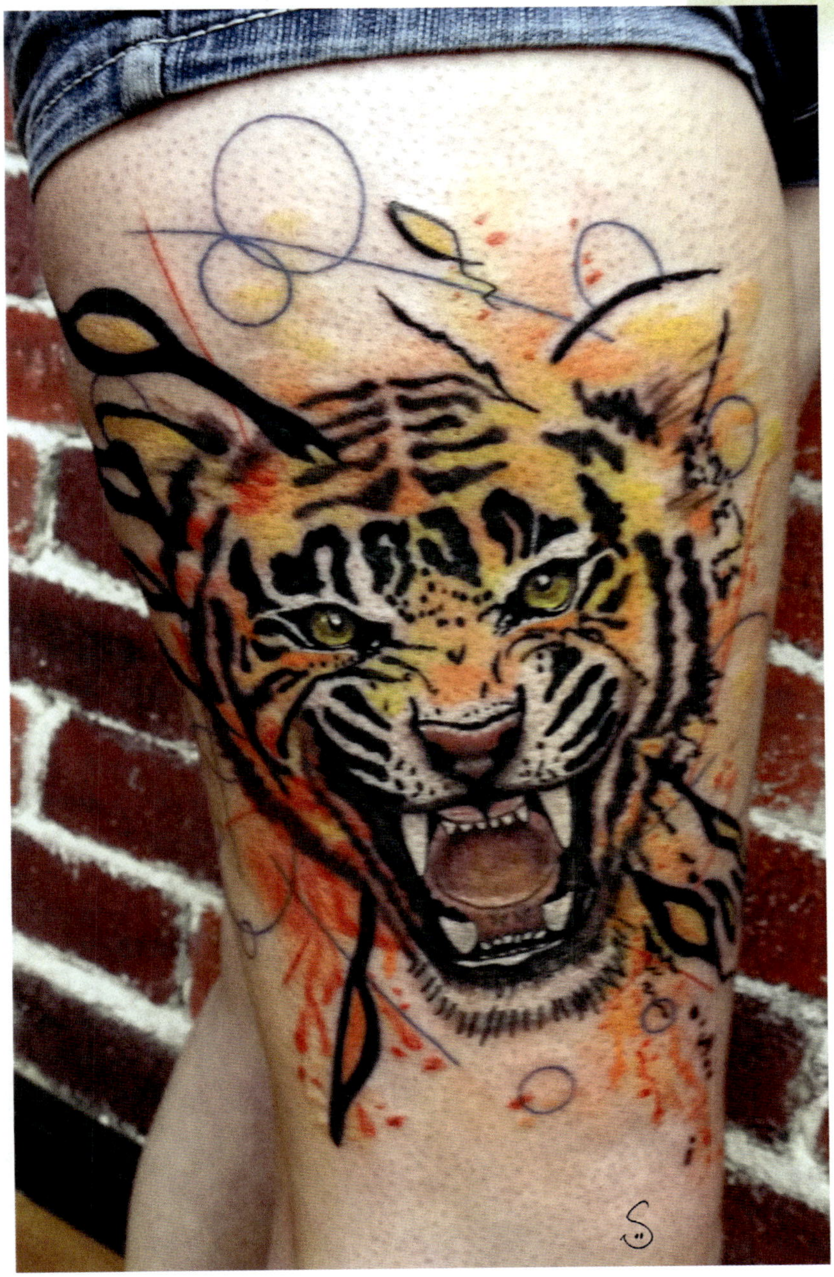

And don't forget that the borders of a tattoo can create an implied line, too. You can dispel this look by making tattoo edges fade into the skin.

> "If I could say it in words there would be no reason to paint."
> ~*Edward Hopper, Painter & Printer*

You can also use real or implied lines to make the viewer look directly at your focal point, thereby reinforcing it. This is particularly useful when your focal point is a face. To bring more attention to a specific subject, try to make surrounding objects point to your subject.

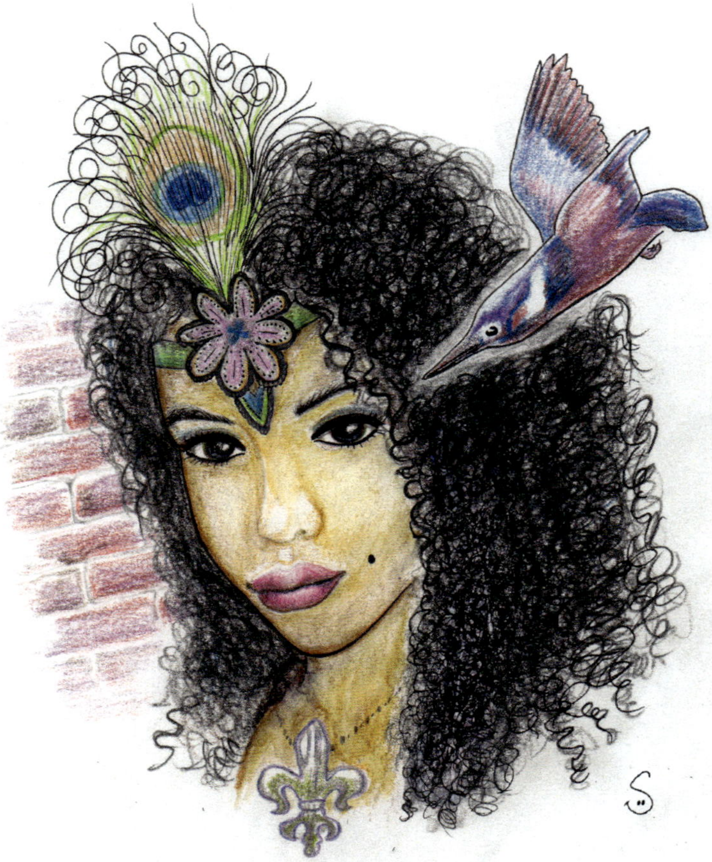

The bird's beak, the necklace, the bricks and the feather headdress all point in toward the subject's eyes.

Balancing the Elements

Placing your main subject off-center, as with the rule of thirds, creates a more interesting design, but it can leave a void in the composition, which can make it feel empty.

You could balance the "weight" of your subject by including another object of lesser importance to fill the space, or an element more out of focus in the background.

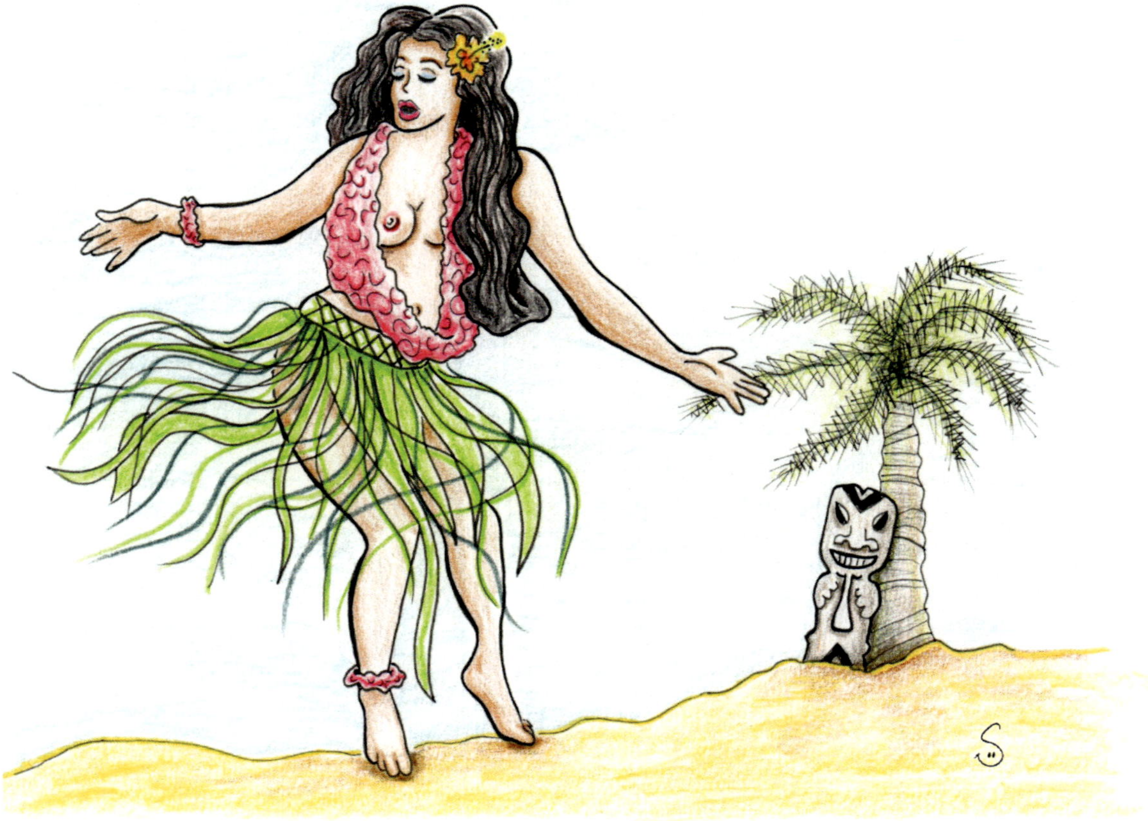

Focal Point

Focal point is an area of emphasis that is unique and will be your center of attention. Decide where you want the eye to go first and use the elements and principles to direct focus. It could be harder lines, placement, color or pattern that assists you in helping this area stand out.

Minimize, or tone down, other compositional elements in order to bring attention to the focal point. Backgrounds can be made lighter or darker in value, crisper or softer in focus, or textured or not textured, to lend support to where you want the eye to go.

Help WIth Composition

When you're working on a composition and it just seems displeasing or boring, consider whether the elements are working well together. An easy way to test this is to cut out the shapes and then try them out in various locations on the drawing, copying and resizing if necessary. Or using a light table, arranging the elements under or on top of each other until it looks "correct". You can also do this in a drawing program, such as Photoshop, or on an electronic pad or tablet, which allows for incredible flexibility in changing line-weight, color, value and size. This is a tremendous help in making the design flow.

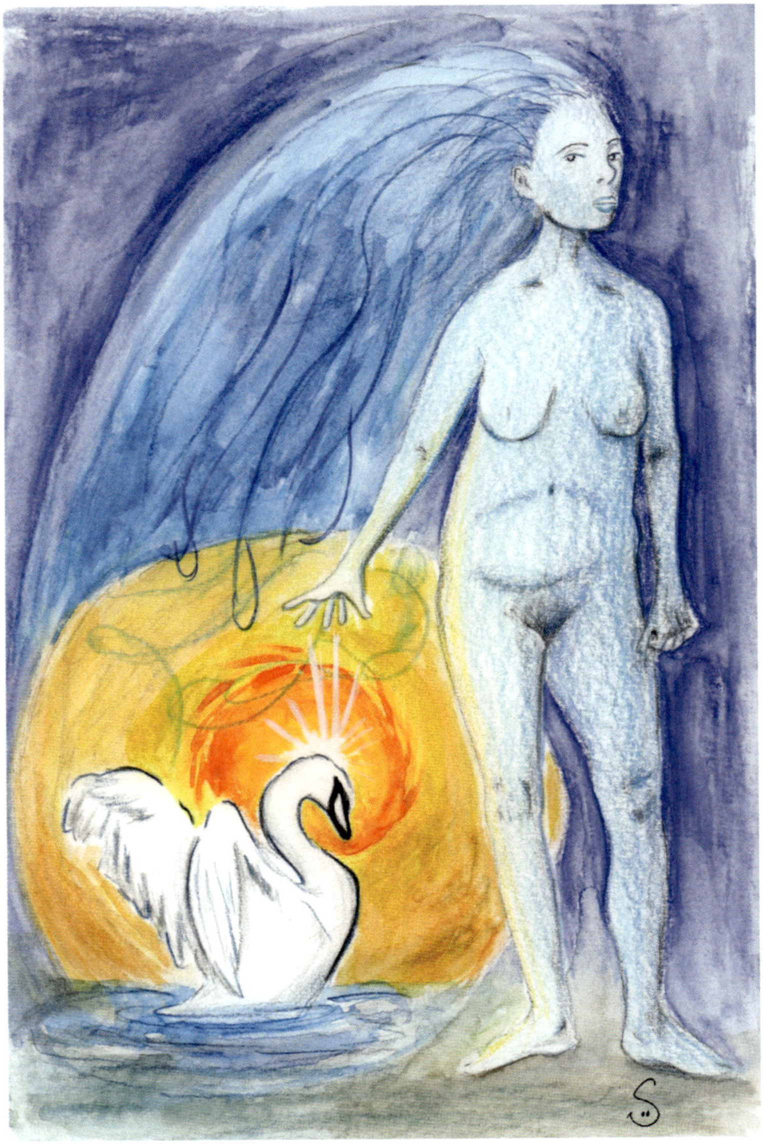

Finding Your Style

To distinguish yourself amongst a sea of artists and project a professional image, you should be able to define yourself and your talents. To do this, you must find your own style.

Style means a distinctive characteristic or group of traits that we identify as constant, recurring or coherent. It is what people recognize represents YOU in your artwork. Your style is a mix of the technique, mediums and subject matters you choose, and how you execute these. It's also about the unique extras you put into your work to distinguish it from others.
Here are a few ideas to help you discover your style:

Time Commitment

You'll need to set aside regular time to work on your art. Respect the promise to yourself and treat this time as non-negotiable. To get better, and find your unique style, you need to MAKE ART.

Shelly's Sidenote

FOCAL POINT

A tattoo can be ruined by a too busy background or too many elements all having emphasis. In fact, I would say this is a major problem in many larger tattoo pieces such as sleeves or backpieces—so much going on that the viewer can't focus on anything and you can't tell what it's "supposed to be". Use what you have learned in this section to create a distinct focus and your tattoos will immediately be more successful.

When I am creating a composition to place around a body part, there can be more than one focal point. Just think about what you can see all at once without them moving their body, then how much you can see if the limb is rotated or seen from the opposite side. The area you can take in with your eyes all at once should have one main center of attention.

Look at Art

Look at art; lots of it! Become inspired by the successes of others. Take the time to study artists you admire and yes, even practice drawing their works. Of course, you won't claim this as your own, but you can get better by emulating great artists. Fill your sketch books with drawings and tracings. All this will help you learn what influences you and help you find your own voice. You can also watch art documentaries or even take an art history class.

Mary Cassatt
Pablo Picasso
Vincent Van Gogh
Claude Monet
Frida Kahlo
Helen Frankenthaler
Jackson Pollock
Andy Warhol
VIGÉE LE BRUN
Suzanne Valadon

Draw and Journal

As mentioned previously you should be drawing all the time. Sketching people, scenes and animals. Wherever you are, there is something to draw. Also, write your brilliant ideas down as well as your impressions of other's art. If you see a tattoo or painting that isn't executed well, make note of why and what you would do different. Your doodles and scribbles lead to your self-discovery.

Experiment

Don't be afraid to try a variety of things. Step out of your comfort zone and draw in different styles, colors or mediums. Try painting, sculpting, markers, collage or watercolor. No one else needs to see any of this. You are just investigating different mediums and seeing what inspires you! This experiment will help you become a better tattooer as well!

Evaluate

Look at what you've created and try to figure out what works and what doesn't work. Ask other artists, friends, family or strangers to share what they like and don't like. This analysis will help your figure out your strengths and weaknesses.

Build a Body of Work

Once you find a groove, keep at it. Keep practicing. Eventually your distinctive style will shape into something recognizable, it will start getting people's attention and you can begin to build a body of work.

> "The object isn't to make art, it's to be in that wonderful state that makes art inevitable.
>
> *~Robert Henri, Painter*

An exercise to help discover your style

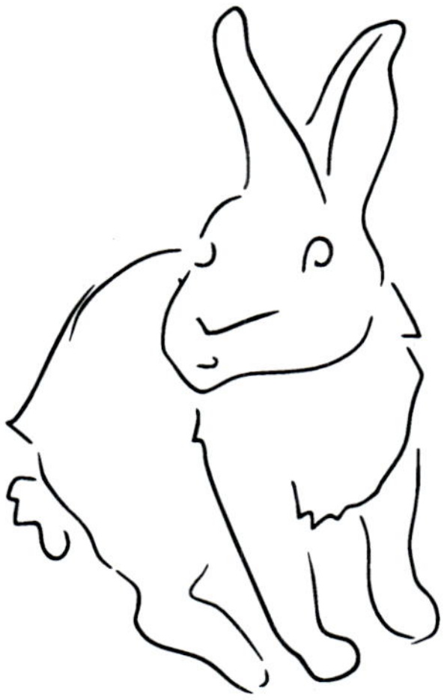

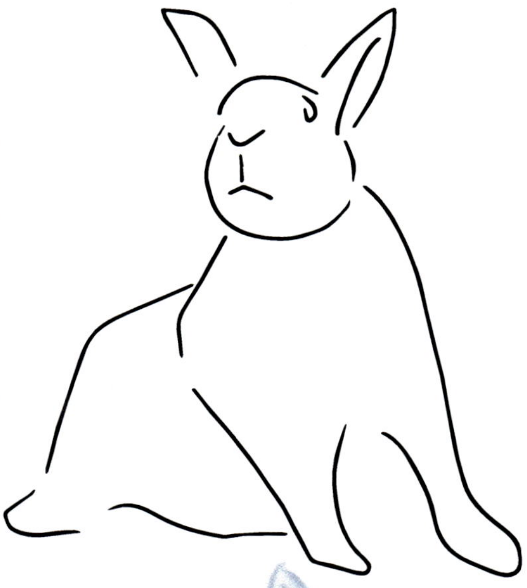

Decide on a medium, a subject matter, a style and a palette that you like to work with and then narrow it down. Like to draw mammals? That's too broad. Rabbits? Still too many to choose from. Choose one species, one specific breed of rabbit and that will narrow down your work.

Now draw or paint just that one rabbit over and over. Do that rabbit in the same narrow range of colors or values multiple times. From multiple angles. Hopping, eating, sleeping or standing on it's hind legs. Get to know that one rabbit. BE the rabbit! Do a series with the same medium, on the same size and type of canvas or paper. Focus on that rabbit and that rabbit's life and feelings until you understand that one rabbit.

The more you narrow it down the better. This process can be repeated with many different subjects, but to really discover your style, give yourself the time to fully explore one subject at a time.

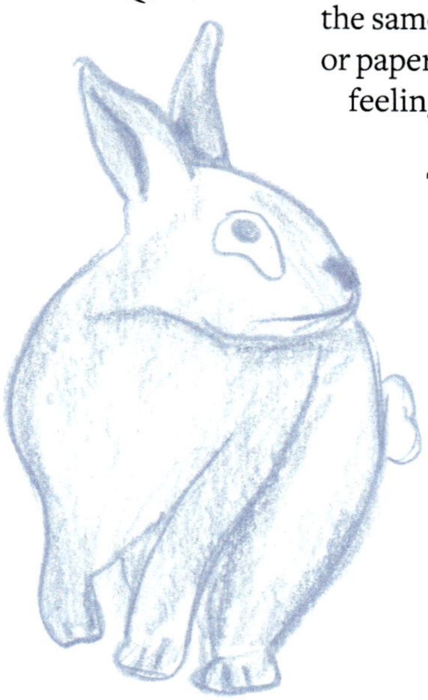

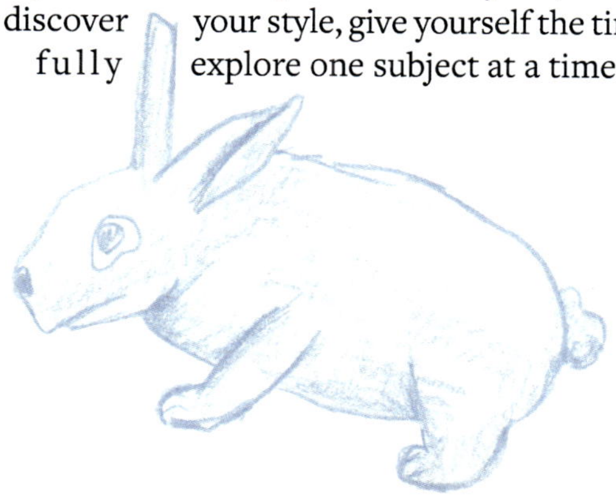

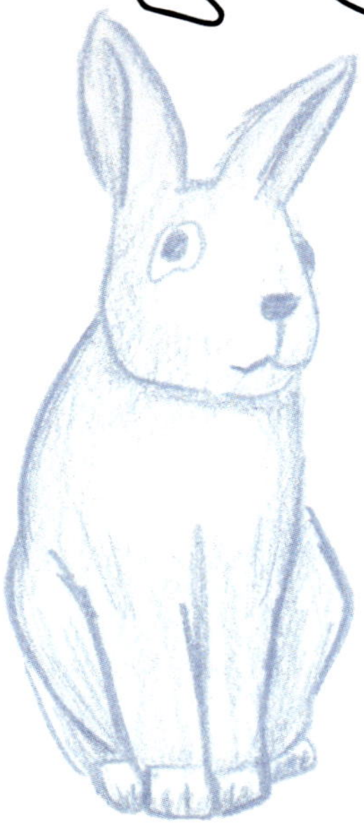

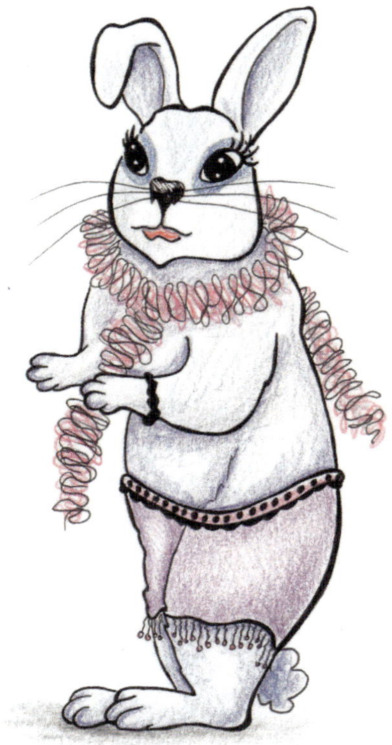

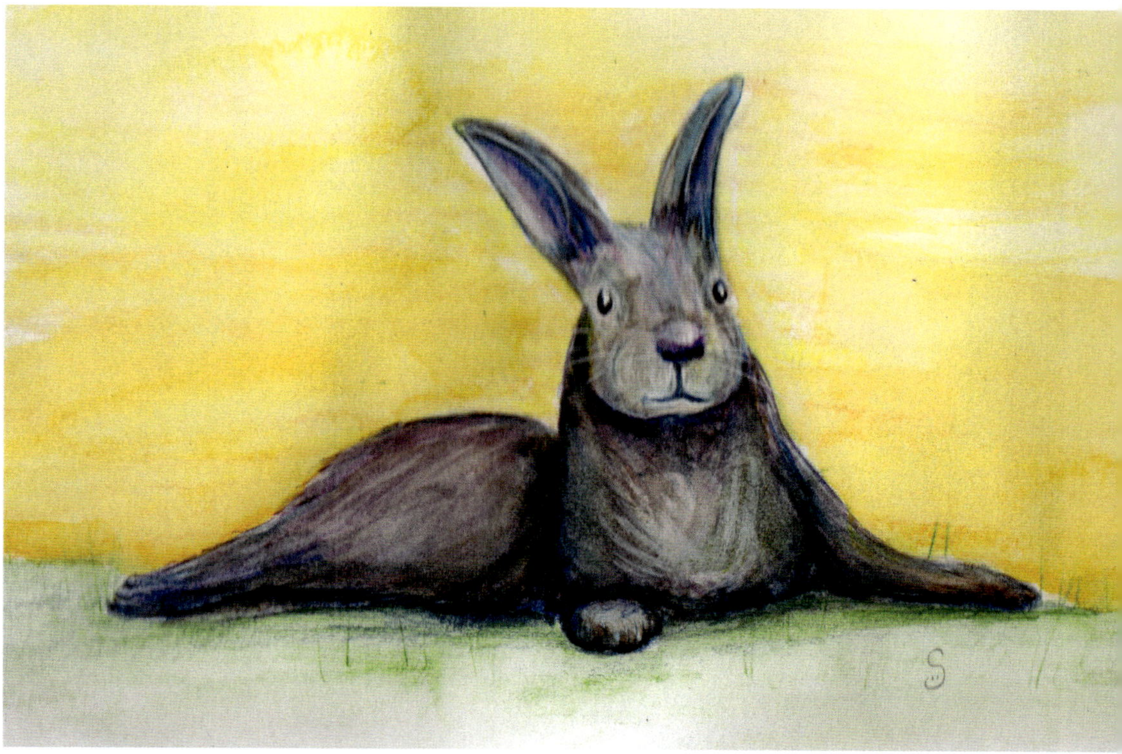

> "Just as you develop yourself and become more like "you" as you grow up, your artistic voice is doing the same thing. With every experience you have, your self changes and grows, and with every piece of art you make, your style changes and grows."
>
> *-Christine Nishiyama, Illustrator*

Finding your style is an on-going process, that evolves throughout your lifetime of making art. Habits develop, skills increase, mistakes are made and imagination expands. The secret to discovering your style is truly to MAKE ART. Then make more art.

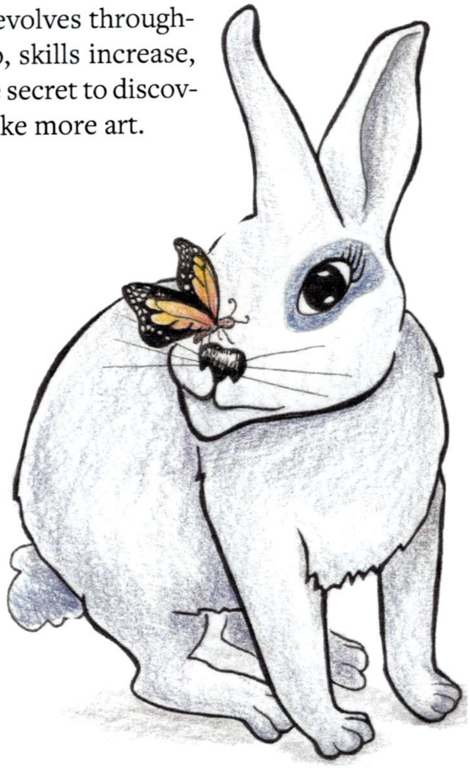

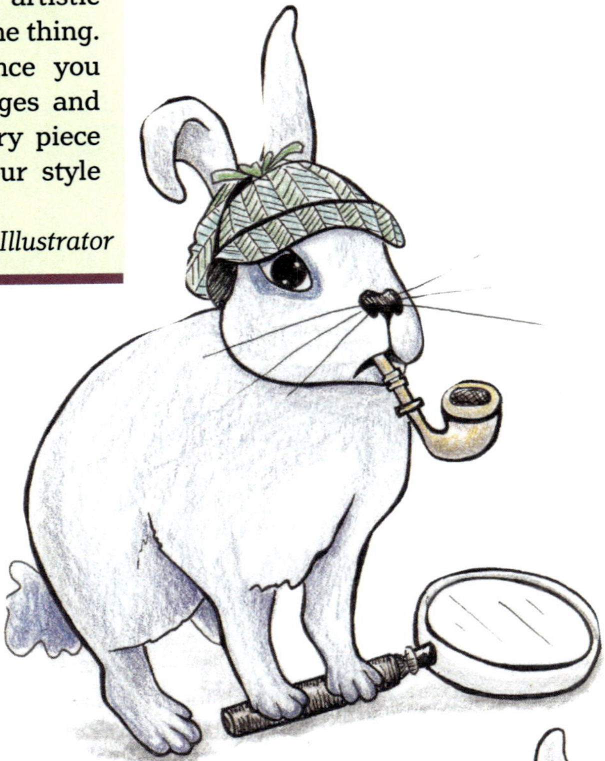

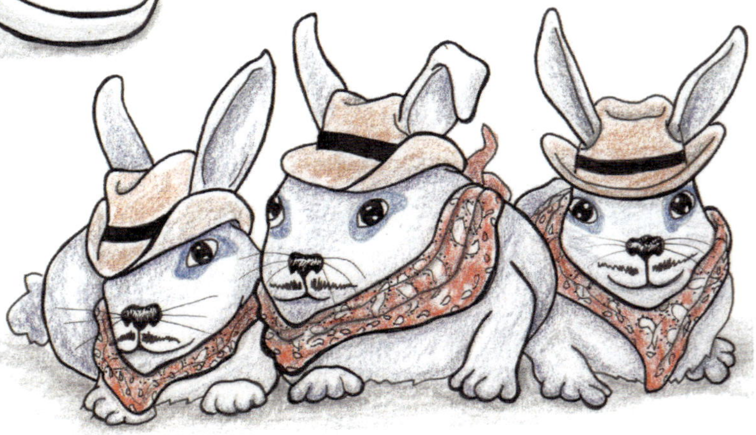

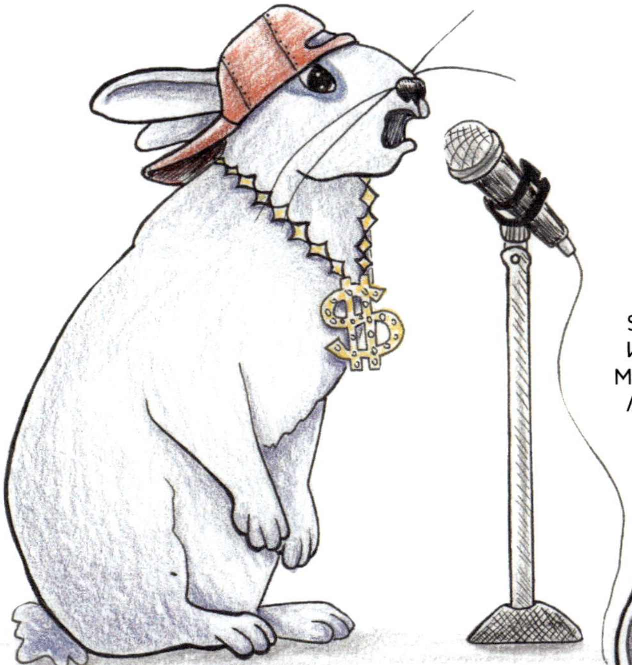

Sources:
Visual Perception and The Principles of Gestalt, Stephen Bradley, Smashing Magazine, March 29, 2014
*Illustrated Elements of Art & Principles of Design,*Gerald F. Brommer (c)2011
*Elements of Design*Poppy Evans and Mark Thomas (c)2004
Art, Design and Visual Thinking Website Course, Charlotte Jirousek, (c)1995

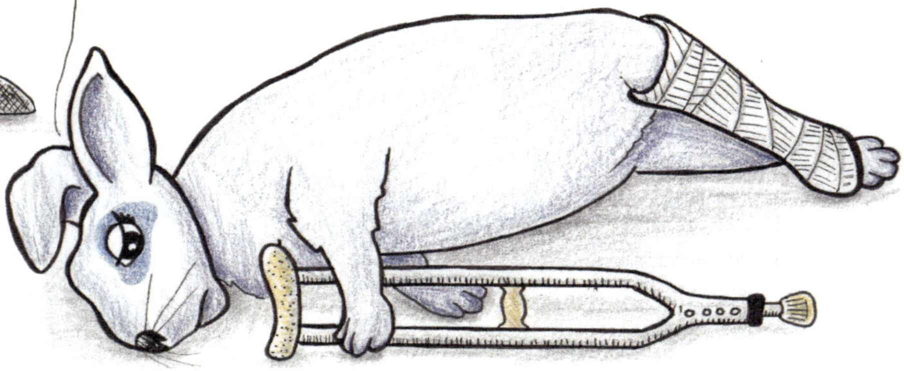

Chapter Six Highlights

- Elements of art and principles of design are the language of visual art.
- Drawing can be learned.
- Art is defined as "skill as a result of knowledge & practice, which produces an aesthetic result", in addition to truth, talent and self-expression.
- Human beings tend to see objects in groups. This concept is called "gestalt theory".
- Expressive lines can be heavy or light in weight to give stronger or lighter meaning.
- If values contrast then shapes will appear to separate in space and some will stand out from others.
- Organic shapes are most often thought of as naturally occurring and are free-form and curved.
- The easiest way to indicate three-dimension is by overlapping.
- Colors that appear warmer tend to seem closer and colors that are cooler tend to seem more distant.
- You can balance things like warm and cool, patterns, shapes and line-weight.
- You can use proportion emphasize certain aspects of your artwork.
- Contrast makes art visually interesting.
- Unity with variety is most pleasing.
- Simplification is best combined with targeted complexity.
- Having an odd number of elements in your composition makes it more dynamic.
- Focal point is an area of emphasis that is unique and will be your center of attention.

Wisecracks:

Crossed "get a tattoo" off my bucket list.

Then immediately wrote "get another tattoo".

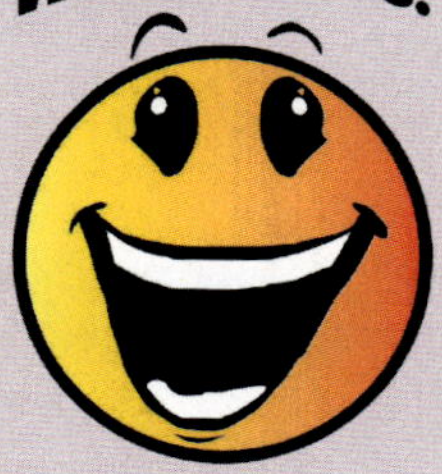

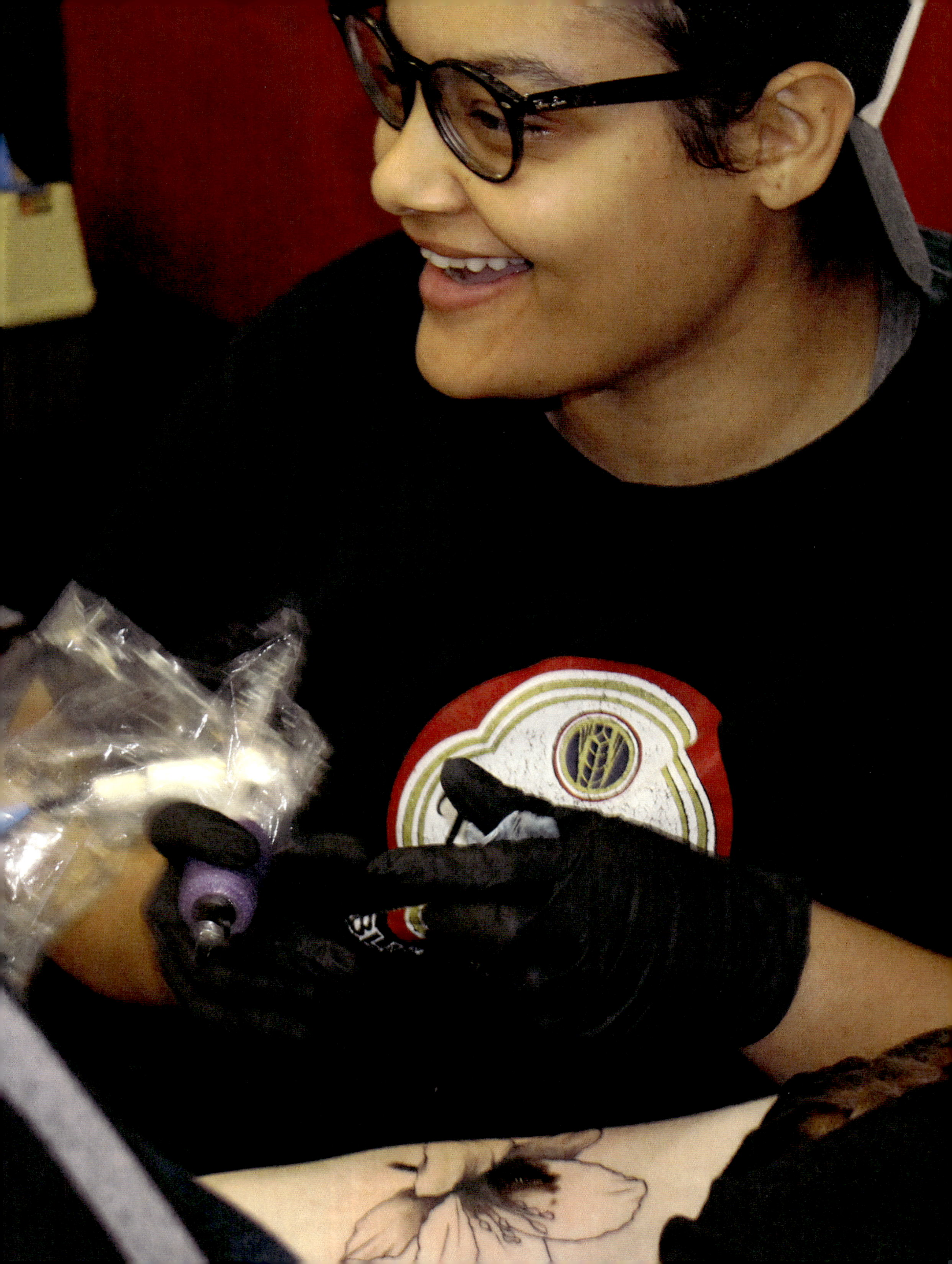

Chapter Seven

Color Theory

One key element of producing high quality and visually appealing tattoos is understanding basic color theory. In this chapter we will explore the minimal color knowledge you'll need to create captivating art pieces on skin.

COLOR THEORY 101

Color is a powerful mood changer and has tremendous expressive qualities. Understanding the use of color is crucial to effective composition in tattooing.

Definitions:

- **Color**: element of art that is produced when light, striking an object, is reflected or emits light, back to the eye.
- **Color Spectrum**: the distribution of colors produced when light waves are dispersed by a prism.
- **Hue**: pure spectrum color (hue and color are sometimes used interchangeably)
- **Color wheel**: color spectrum bent into a circle.
- **Primary colors**: the most basic hues on the color wheel: red, yellow and blue. These colors cannot be made by mixing.

> "Mere color can speak to the soul in a thousand different ways."
>
> *~ Oscar Wilde, playwright/poet*

History Note:
ROY G BIV
The 17th century physicist and astronomer Isaac Newton developed a sophisticated theory of color based on the observation that a prism separates white light into the colors of the visible spectrum. He recognized seven basic hues: red, orange, yellow, green, blue, indigo, violet (you may remember it as the acronym ROY G BIV). Newton's conception included a seventh color, indigo-- between blue and purple. (It is possible that what Newton referred to as blue is nearer to what today we call cyan—a greenish-blue color.)

- **Secondary colors**: colors that are made by mixing two primary colors together: Orange, green and violet (commonly called purple but this is not quite accurate according to color theory).
- **Tertiary colors**: colors that are made by mixing a primary color with a secondary color: red-orange, yellow-orange, yellow-green, blue-green, blue-violet and red-violet.
- **Saturation**: the brightness (vividness) or dullness of a color (also called intensity).
- **Value**: the darkness or lightness of a color (in some contexts, also called tone).

Having theories when it comes to color is very helpful, but the range of concepts, definitions and applications are not a simple matter, as there are numerous books and opinions regarding color theory.

But four basic categories of color theory are useful: **the color wheel**, **color properties**, **color relativity** and **color harmony.** In addition, the various **psychological effects** bear discussion as this will affect people's perception of color.

The Color Wheel

> "I found I could say things with color and shapes that I couldn't say anything other way."
>
> *~Georgia O'Keefe, Painter*

The old familiar color wheel most kids learned about in elementary school is the traditional tool for combining colors in the field of art. The first circular color diagram was designed by Isaac Newton in 1666. Over the years, many variations of the basic design have been made, but the most common version is a wheel of 12 colors (or pure spectral hues) based on the RED YELLOW BLUE (RYB) artistic color mode.

Any color concept which presents a logically arranged sequence of pure hues has merit, but we will discuss the traditional 12 color wheel here:
Generally speaking, dark and warm colors tend to advance toward the viewer and cool and light colors tend to recede into the background or distance.

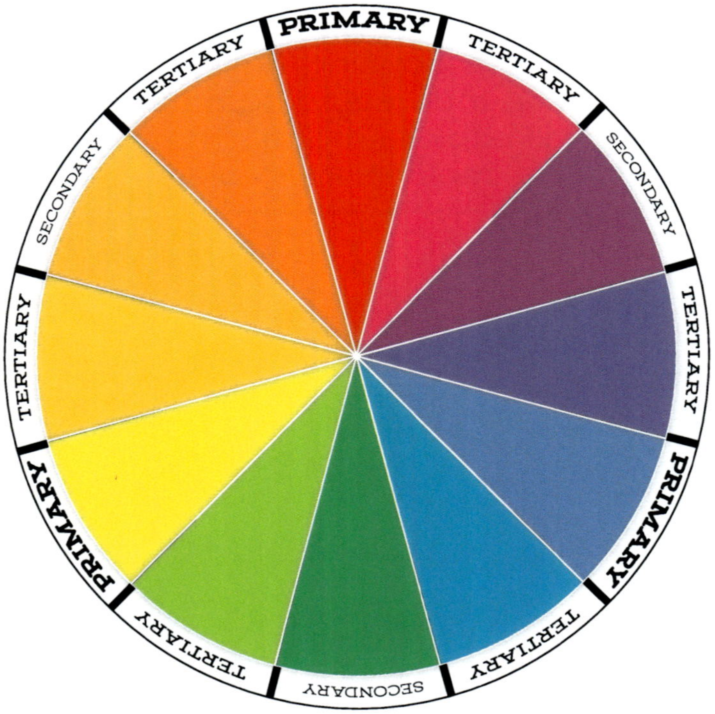

Note:
Differences of opinion about the validity of one color scheme format over another continue to be debated. A currently popular theory uses the CMY model as the primary color scheme: Cyan (a bluish green), Magenta (a reddish violet) and Y (yellow), which is used primarily in printing, also called "printer's primaries". You might also be familiar with RGB which stands for RED GREEN BLUE and is the format used on computer screens.

Categories of color based on the color wheel

PRIMARY COLORS
Red, blue and yellow

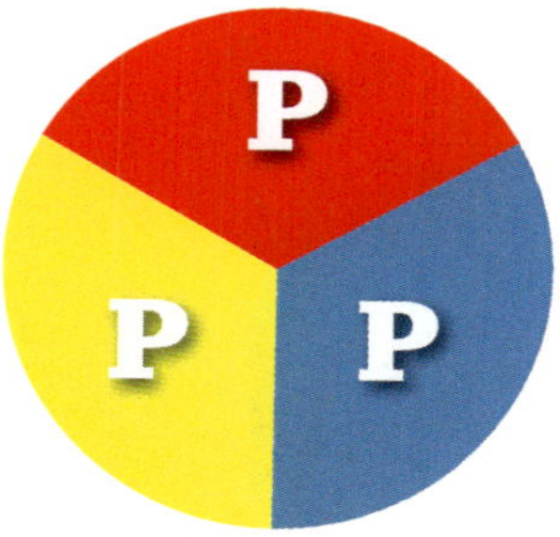

Can't be mixed or formed by any combination of other colors. All other colors are created from these THREE hues.

SECONDARY COLORS
Green, orange and violet

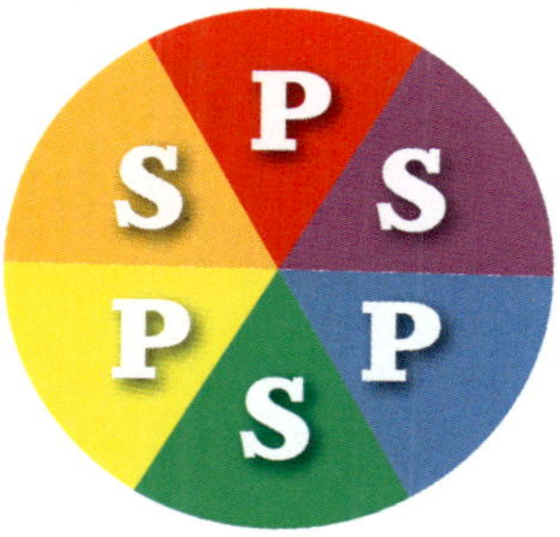

These colors are created by mixing the primary colors.

TERTIARY COLORS
Yellow-orange, red-orange, red-purple, blue-purple, blue-green & yellow-green

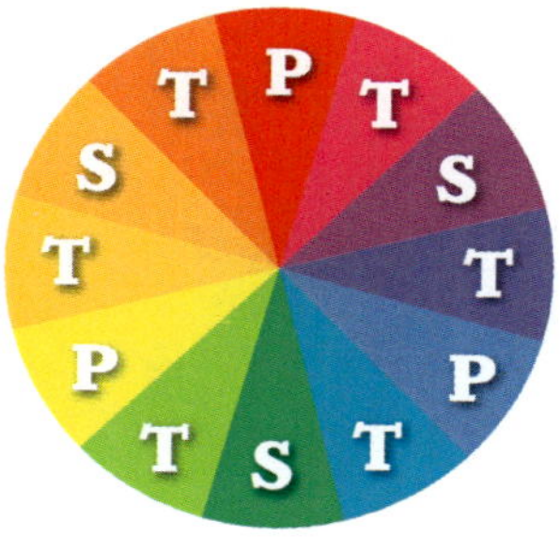

These colors are created by mixing a primary and a secondary color.

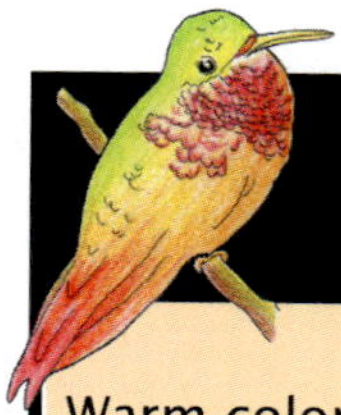

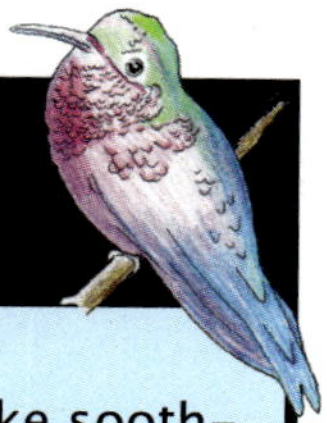

Warm and Cool colors:
The color circle can also be divided into warm and cool colors.

Warm colors evoke a sense of heat—for instance yellow and orange conjure images of the sun, or bright summer days and adding an orange filter to a photograph will give it a warmer appearance. Warm colors tend to feel as if they are advancing in space and particularly vivid warm colors can remind you of passion, blood, love and fire.

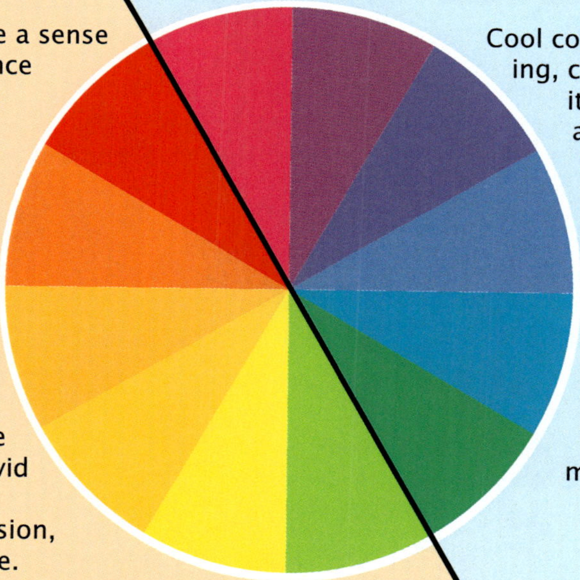

Cool colors evoke soothing, calm and tranquility. They can make an object or space seem larger. Cool colors are also associated with chilly wintery landscapes, ocean depth, sadness (the "blues"), darkness, growth, harmony, health, mystery, night and water.

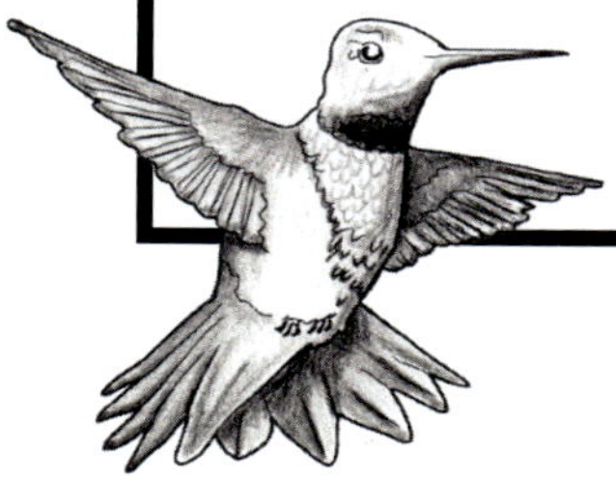

White, **black** and **gray** are considered to be neutral.

> "I think it pisses God off if you walk by the color purple in a field somewhere and don't notice it."
>
> *~Alice Walker, novelist/poet*

Note:
According to author Gunter Wyszecki experts estimate that we can distinguish perhaps as many as 10 million colors. Familiar colors are referred to by standard names such as red or blue. But there is enormous variation of each color. A blue color can be dark or light or may appear more colorful or "full of color" thus rich and vibrant. Blue can be greenish, steely, purplish or dusty. Thus, other creative names have been imagined describing the plethora of examples. Look in any paint store and you'll see an impressive list of descriptive colors; dandelion, sea foam, pumpkin, azure, snowfall, acorn--and the list goes on.

Color Properties

There are three properties to color:
HUE, SATURATION & VALUE.

For example, a light green color would be described as green (*hue*), dull (*saturation*) and light (*value*).

Hue

Hue refers to pure spectral colors, or colors that can be produced by a single wavelength. Simplified, this means the name we give to a color [green, yellow, blue, etc.]. In general color theory, a hue refers to a pure color—one without tint or shade. (Sometimes color and hue are used interchangeably.)

Saturation (also called intensity)

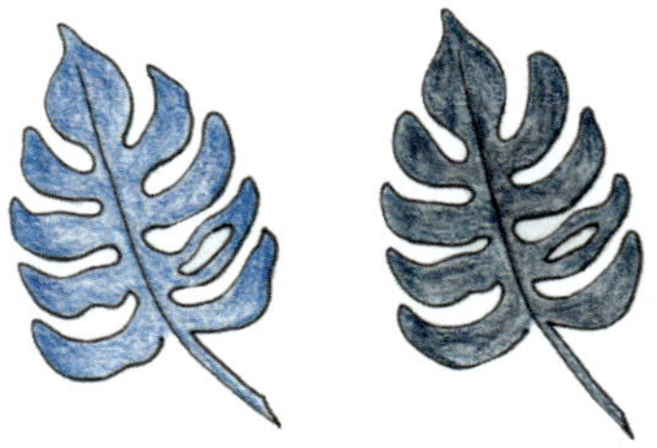

Saturation refers to the intensity or brightness/dullness of a color. For example, we may describe the color blue as "**royal**" (bright, rich, vibrant) or "**steel**" (desaturated or "greyed down").

Saturation is one of biggest culprits when it comes to unsuccessful color work. A lot of artists choose highly saturated colors because they think it will make their work pop. Yet highly saturated colors tend to look fake and using them everywhere in your artwork gives the eyes nowhere to rest. Being able to rest the eyes in a design is important as it gives the viewer a chance to anchor and then explore.

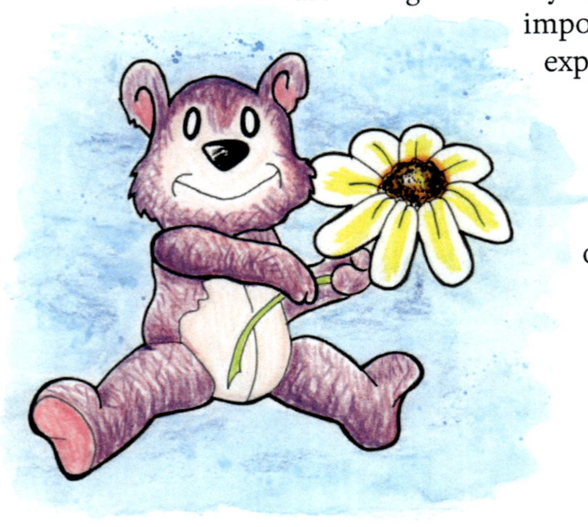

In some cases, such as cartoon images, bright colors help emphasize the unrealistic elements and can convey a sense of liveliness and joy, thus can work in your favor.

A deliberate use of high intensity colors can be used as a compositional element to help guide the eye to an important or powerful element in your design or draw attention to a specific element.

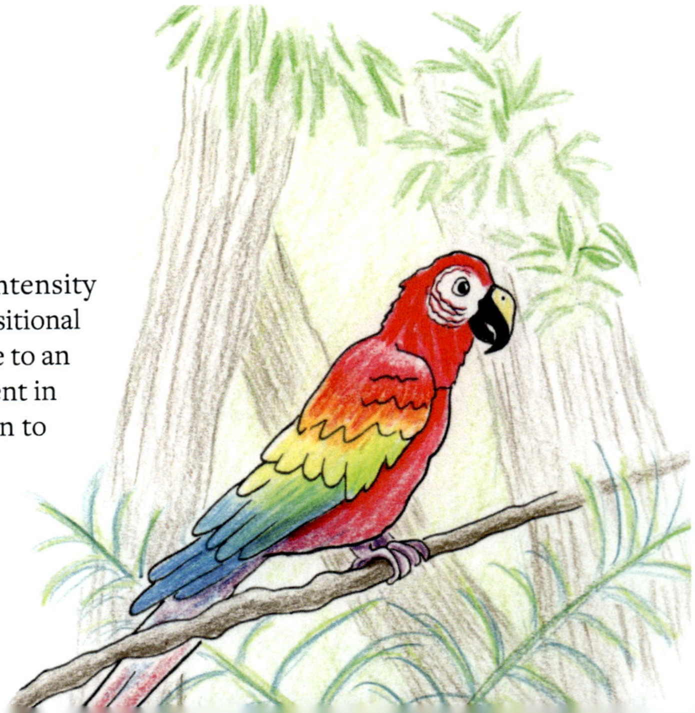

Saturation can also help tell a story. Saturated vibrant colors can express cheerful, optimistic feelings and desaturating the colors can help set a mood of sadness or convey darker emotions.

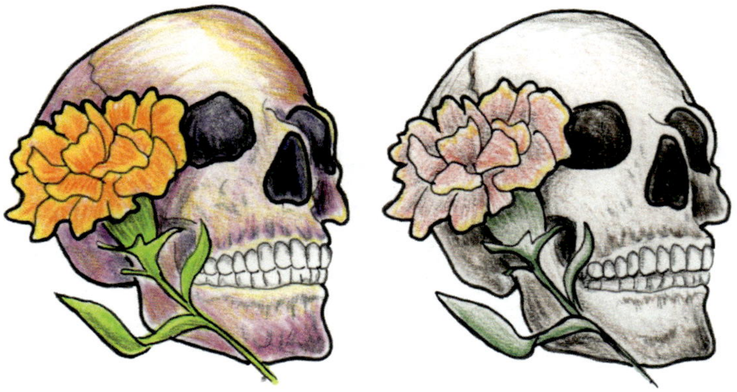

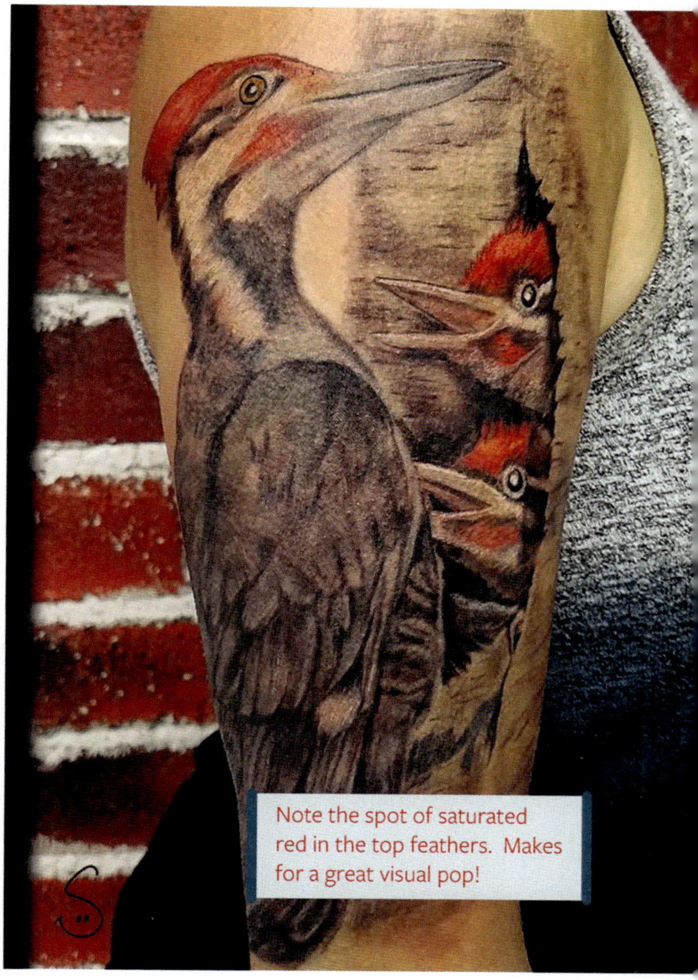

Note the spot of saturated red in the top feathers. Makes for a great visual pop!

Value

Value describes how dark or light a color is. As discussed in the previous chapter, successful art has value contrast, or a range of values, which creates excitement or visual interest. Recognizing the value of a color, rather than just the hue, helps you use colors to your advantage.

It can be challenging for artists to create successful values in their colored designs, as the strong allure of color can be distracting. The first step to doing this is to remove color from the equation; to revisit the range of values using only black. This helps artists understand and identify values more easily and emphasizes that value is independent of hue.

> "I've been 40 years discovering that the queen of all colors was black."
> ~*Pierre Auguste Renoir, painter*

Going back to the value scale:
Black, low dark, dark, high dark, mid-value, lowlight, light, highlight, white.

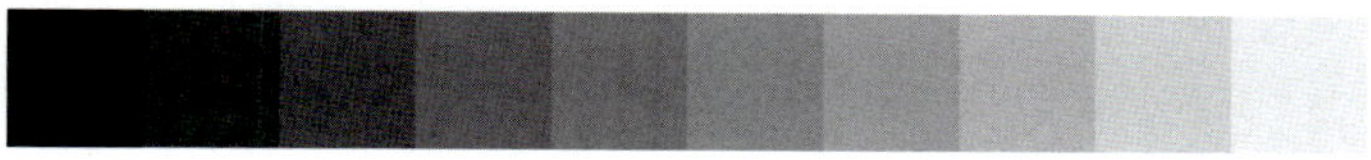

Now we can take a hue, such as blue, and create a range of values to work with based on the same scale.

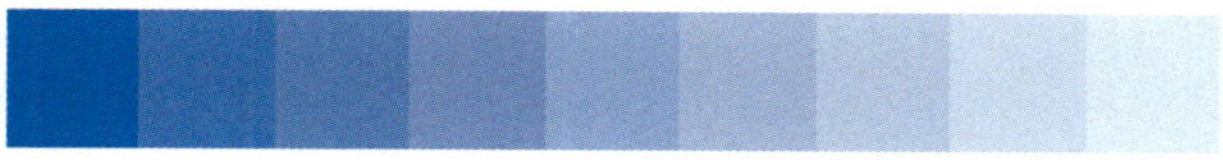

Every color will have a range of value and how light or dark these appear is dependent on the color you choose. In addition, the size of the value range also varies between colors. A lighter hue such as yellow will have a smaller range than darker hues such as blue.

And a color that's obviously light in one context may seem darker in another, if it's surrounded by even lighter values.

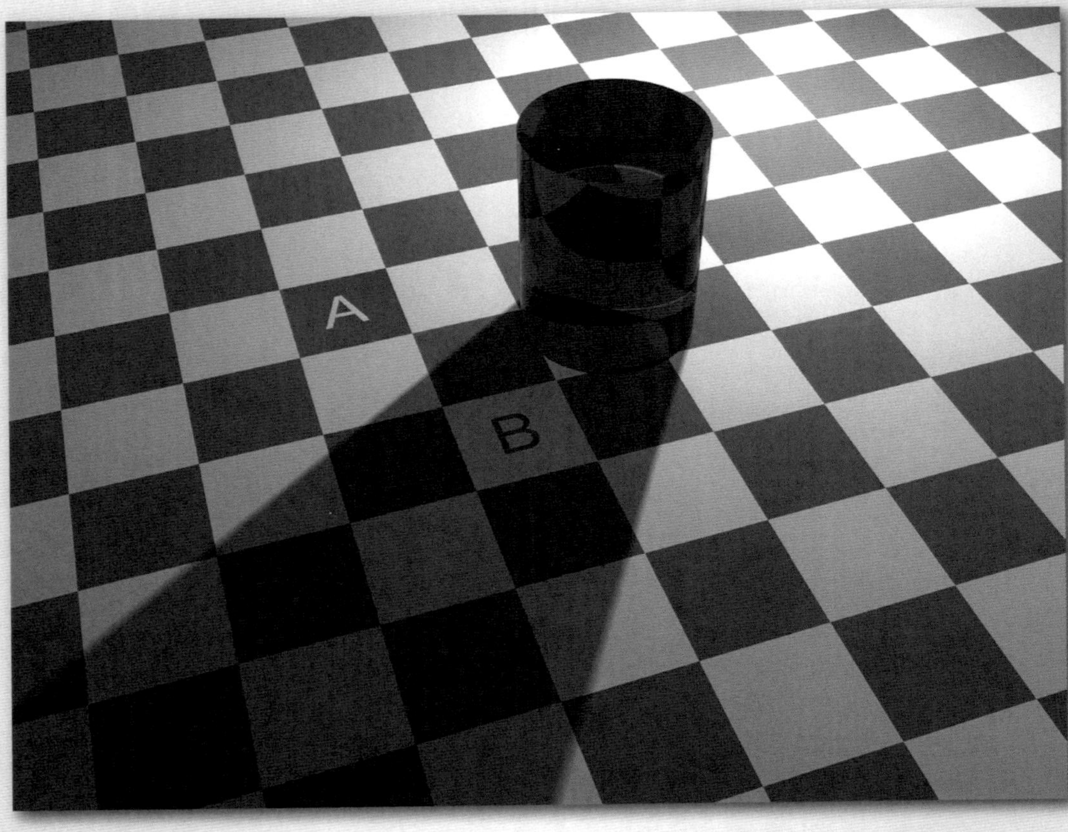

Here's a fun optical illusion that illustrates how the background affects the value of a color. Looking at the checkerboard, would you say that square A is darker than square B? Would you be surprised to find out that they're the same color? See the proof copy at the end of this chapter.

Getting your values correct in a color design is just as important as in a black and white design. If the values are too close there will be little contrast and the design will appear flat and lack interest.

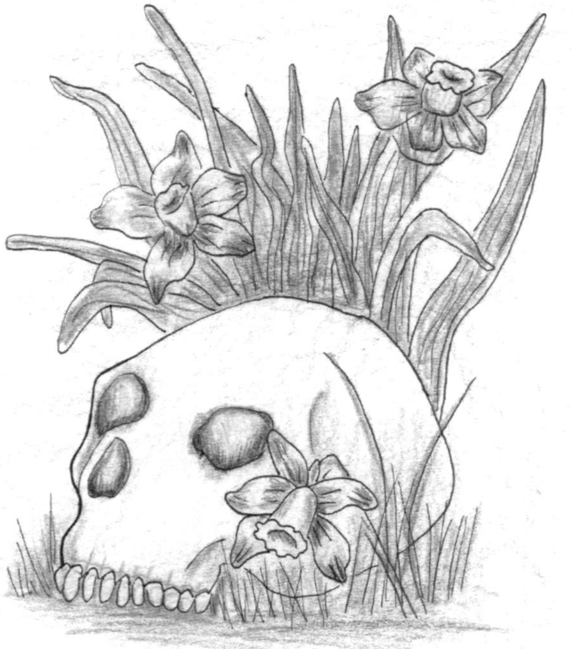

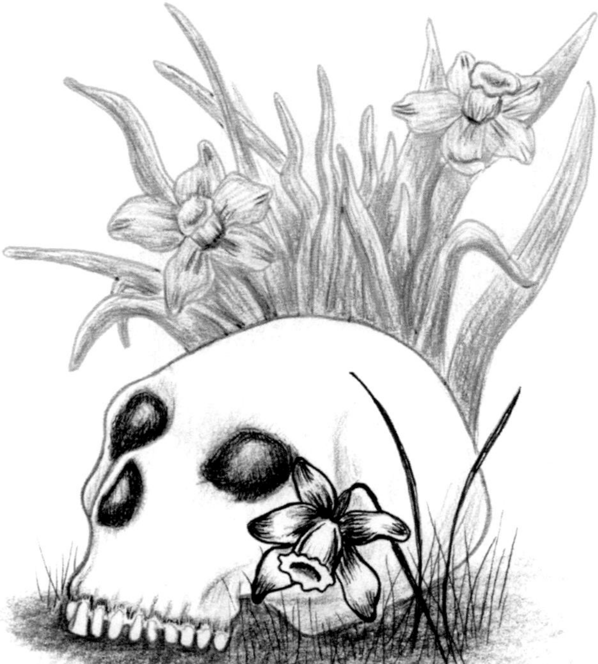

Creating Your Color Value Scale

Tints, Shades and Tones

The terms tint, shade and tone refer to value changes in colors.
Color can be desaturated (reduced in purity) in one of three ways:

Tints: are created by adding white to a color.
Example; pink is a tint of red

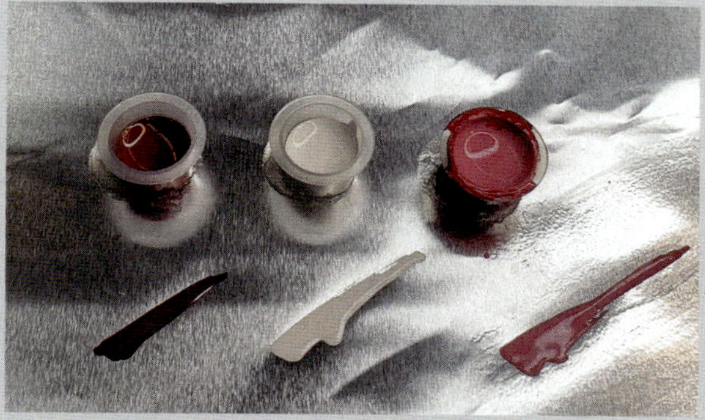

Shades: are created by adding black to a color.
Example; brown is a shade of red-orange

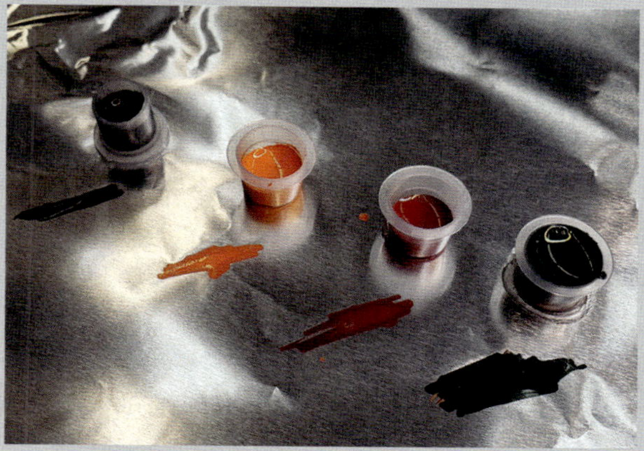

Tones: are created by adding grey to a color.
Example; steel grey is a tone of blue.

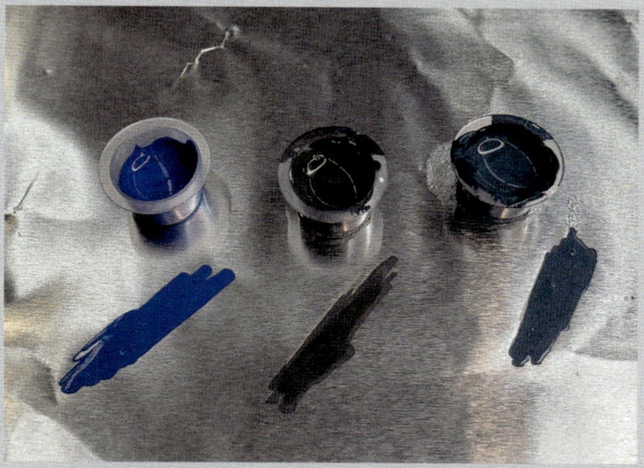

In addition, it is common in tattooing to simply add water or witch hazel to ink to "weaken" the color (or black) and that creates a scale of different values. This dilutes the color and reduces some vibrancy but makes an effective wash for blending gradations of color (or greys), watercolor style tattooing, creating soft backgrounds, and producing more of a "matte" finish on the skin.

You can also lighten a color by adding another color of a lighter value. For example, to lighten a dark red, you could add a little white or yellow. You can also darken a color by adding another color of a darker value.

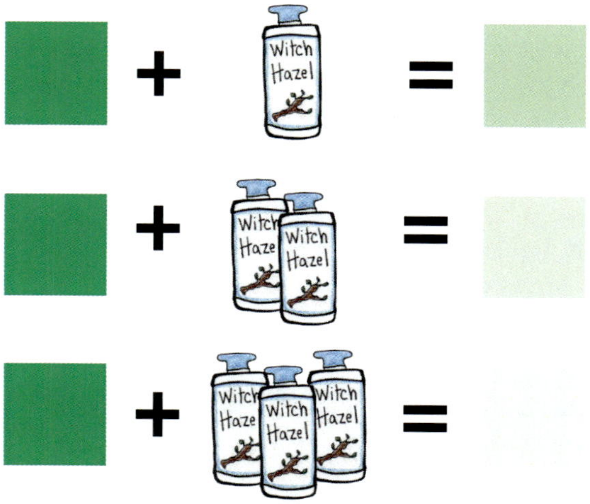

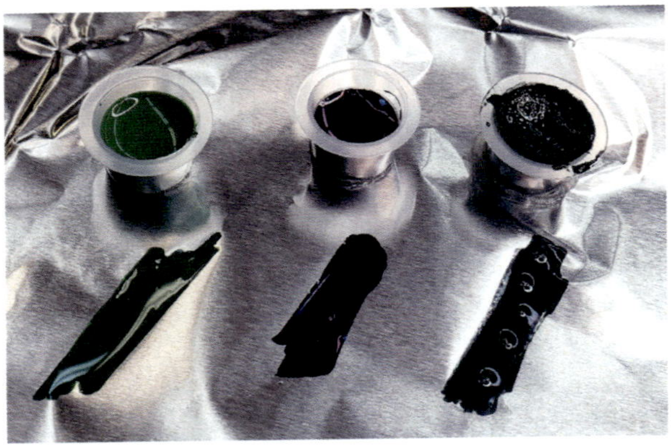

For example, to darken a medium green, you could add dark blue. This technique can also make your shading more interesting than if you just added black, which can lean toward looking flat on the skin.

Furthermore, adding tan or taupe inks at the lighter end of your value scale, in place of white, can help blend color into a client's skin tone, if they have moderate to light skin.

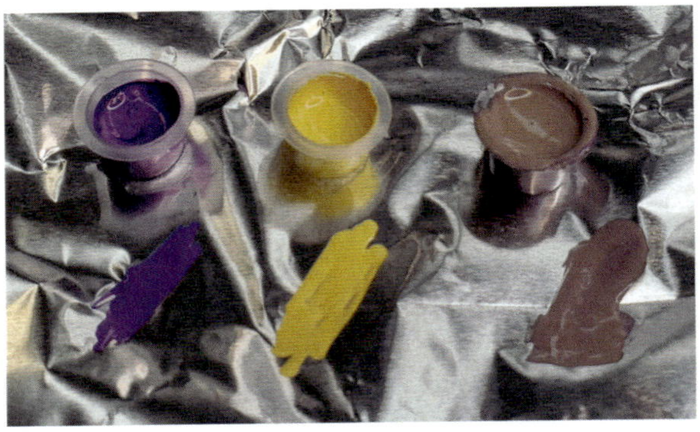

Color Relativity

The context surrounding a color affects how we perceive it. In other words, color is relative to the external conditions surrounding it. What color we see is influenced by things like; how many colors are used, intensity, value, shape, size and balance of warm and cool. All of these can affect how a color looks and what it means to us.

Compare the contrasting effect of assorted color backgrounds for the same image:

Red appears more brilliant against a black background and somewhat duller against the white background. In contrast with orange, the red appears lifeless; in contrast with blue-green, it exhibits brilliance. Notice that the red image appears larger on black than on other background colors.

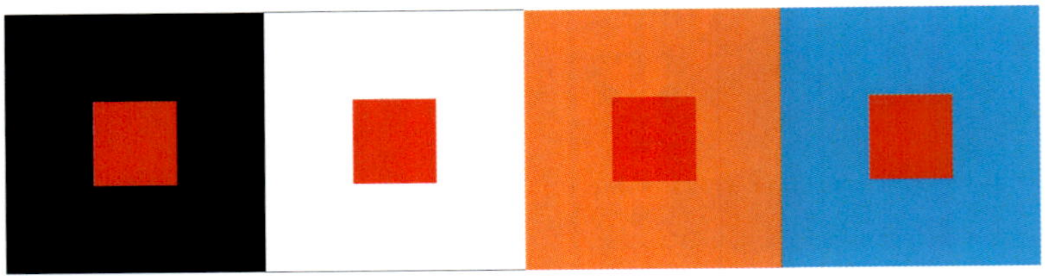

You can see that the small purple rectangle below, on the left, appears to have a red-purple tinge when compared to the small purple rectangle on the right. This demonstrates how three colors can be perceived as four colors.

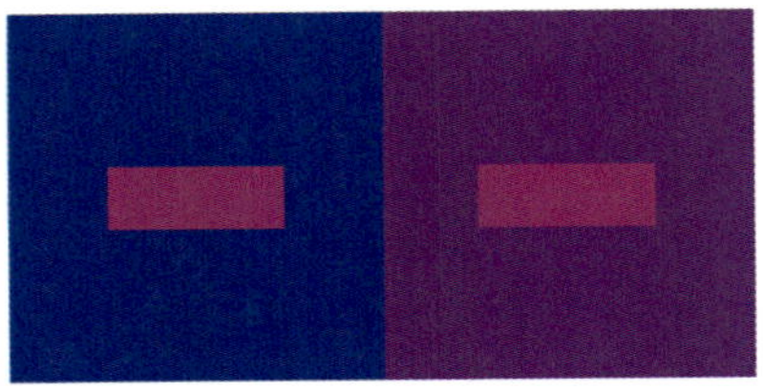

When a color is juxtaposed with other colors, we perceive it as a different color. For example, most people will say the small square below, on the left, is orange, whereas the one on the right is brown. Actually, the squares are the identical color. The surrounding context dictates the color you perceive.

> "To practice any art, no matter how well or badly, is a way to make your soul grow. So do it."
> *-Kurt Vonnegut, Author*

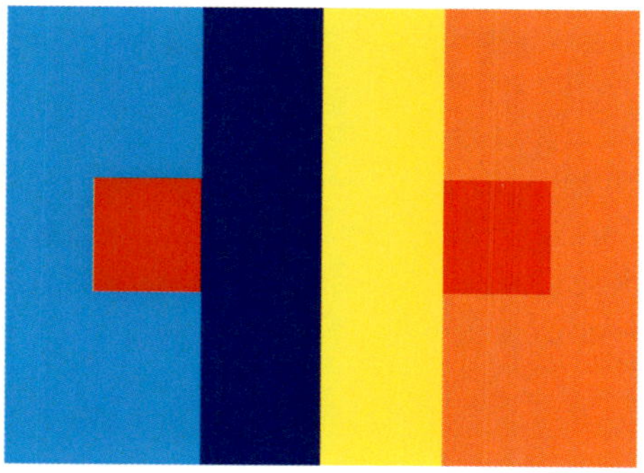

In addition, colors that have a blurred edge will appear to recede more than a color with a crisp edge. This is one reason so many tattoos are outlined in black, as colored ink tends to fade and blur the edges unintentionally. In general, outlining a tattoo in color will result in fuzzier, imprecise edges, that will fade over time.

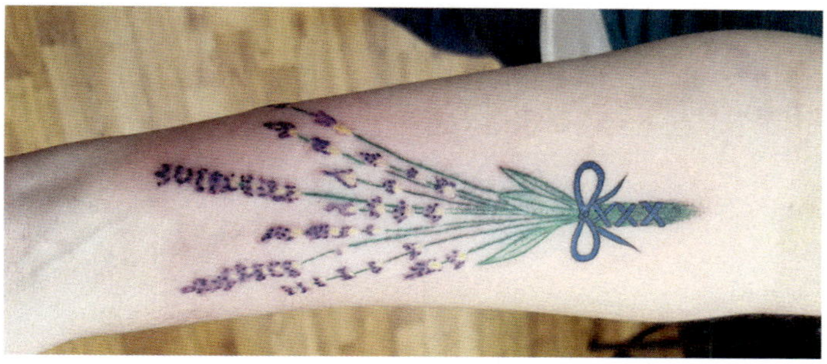

The value of the color will also affect how close or far away it seems to the viewer. Pale colors (lighter on the value scale) will appear to recede and a dark color will appear to advance. Place a pale green next to a dark green and the dark green appears to come forward.

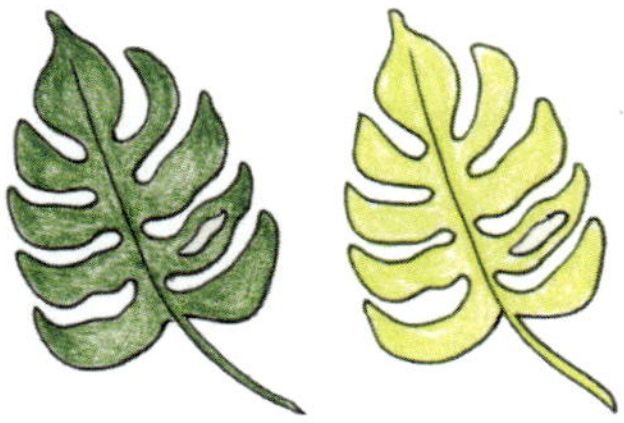

Even if there are two similar greens, the darker one will appear to advance somewhat.

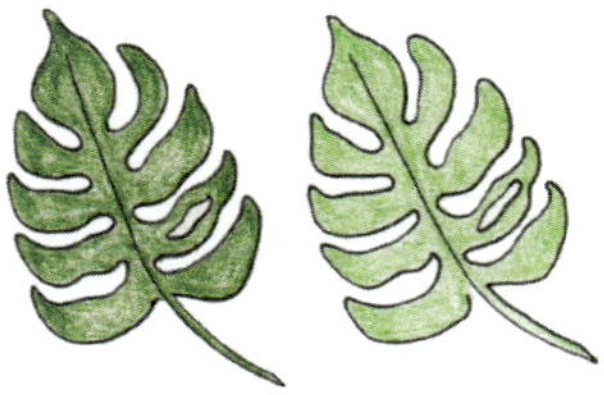

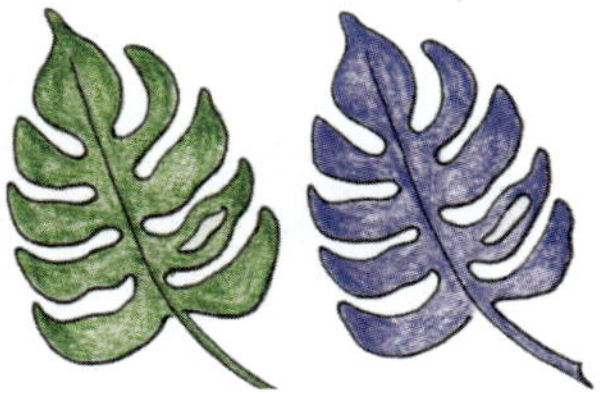

The saturation of a color also affects how distance is perceived. Pure brighter colors will pop out more and duller, more neutral colors will appear to recede. This green and blue are both around the same value (lightness or darkness) but notice the brighter blue comes forward a bit more.

If you mix a little grey, dark green or brown in to this royal blue, it will begin to retreat.

Muted colors will appear to recede; pure colors will appear to advance.

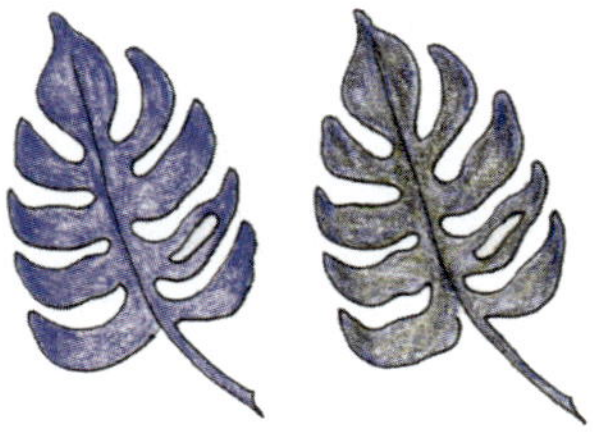

> "Inhale possibility, exhale creativity."
> *~Laura Jaworski, Author & Crochet artist*

Color Harmony

Being able to use colors consciously and harmoniously can help you set the right mood and create spectacular results in your tattoos. Understanding the principles of color combinations will help you choose schemes that work well together and create the right amount of contrast within your design.

Color harmony refers to the fact that some colors look better together than others. Harmony is defined as a "pleasing arrangement of parts", whether discussing food, music, architecture or color. Colors affect us in numerous ways, both mentally and physically and traditionally there are several basic color combinations that are especially gratifying. These pleasing combinations are made up of colors with a specific position on the color wheel.

COMPLIMENTARY

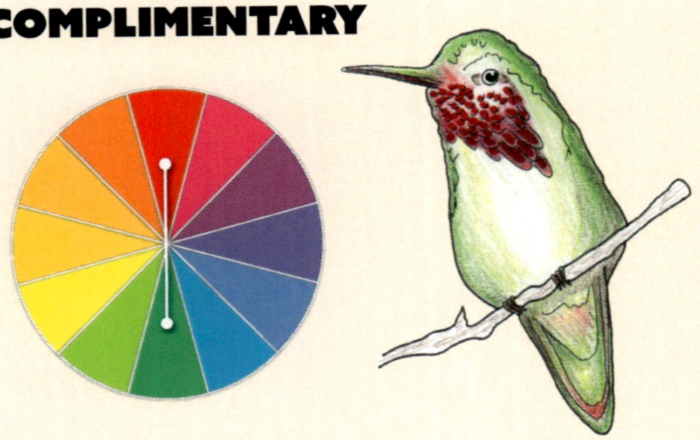

Complimentary colors are colors that are opposite each other on the color wheel and are a very popular color scheme. Main combinations are blue & orange, red & green and yellow & purple and these schemes are very pleasing together. This color scheme is vibrant and contrasting but can be jarring for the viewer, especially if colors are used at full saturation or if both colors are used equally. Complementary colors also make text difficult to read.

ANALOGOUS

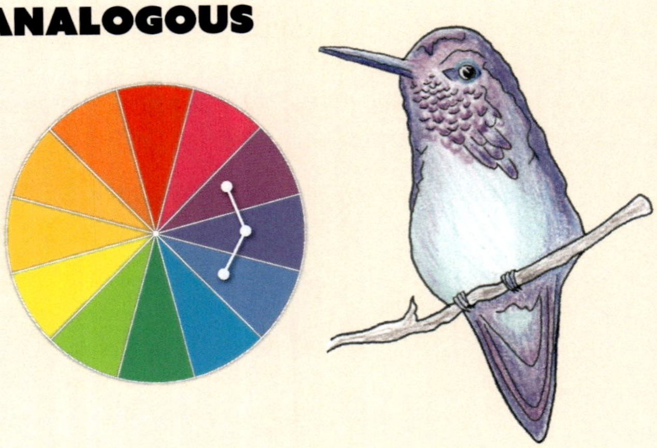

Analogous colors are those that are situated next to each other on the color wheel and generally create serene and comfortable designs, typically reflected in nature. This color model is easy on the eyes. Typically, you would choose one color to dominate, a second to support and the third as an accent.

MONOCHROMATIC

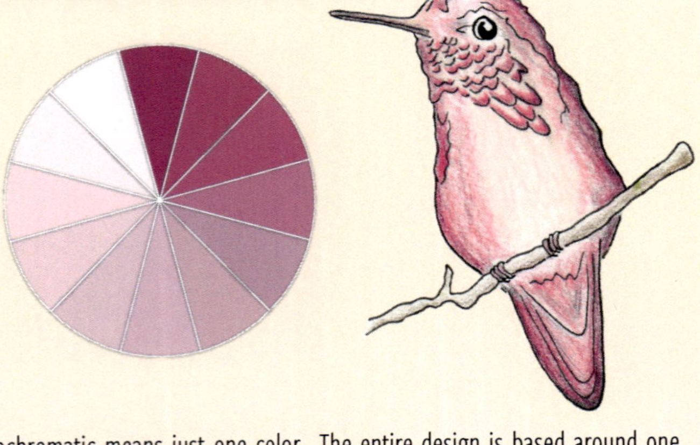

Monochromatic means just one color. The entire design is based around one color, plus white or black. Works best on single subjects because it forces the viewer to focus on the details of the image (not the color) and it can be used to produce a striking atmospheric effect (the effect you get when far away objects take on the colors of atmospheric haze).

SPLIT COMPLIMENTARY

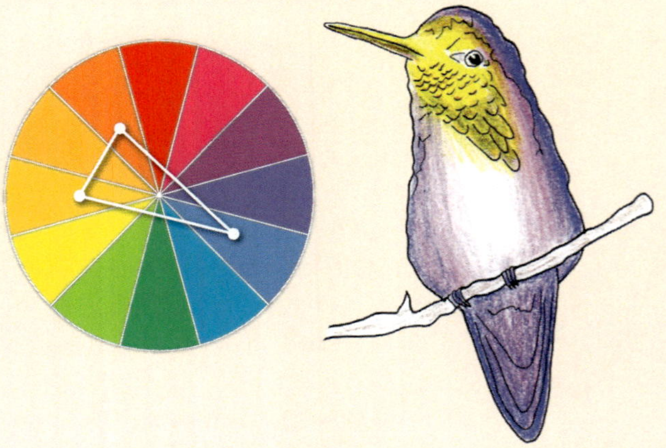

Split complimentary schemes take a color and, instead of choosing the color directly across from it on the color wheel, uses the two colors on either side. This creates coordinated, contrasting colors that are livelier and more joyous than the complimentary color scheme but can still make a dynamic statement.

SQUARE

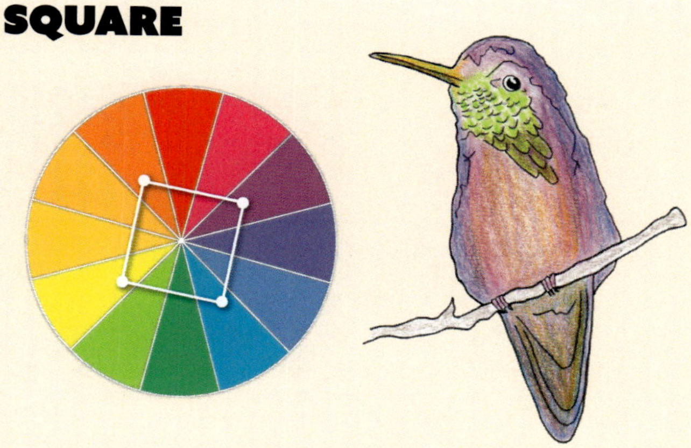

The square color model uses four colors evenly spaced around the color wheel. This color scheme is very pleasing and would work well with one strong (or saturated) color and muted (or desaturated) versions of the other colors. Pay attention to the balance between warm and cool.

TETRADIC

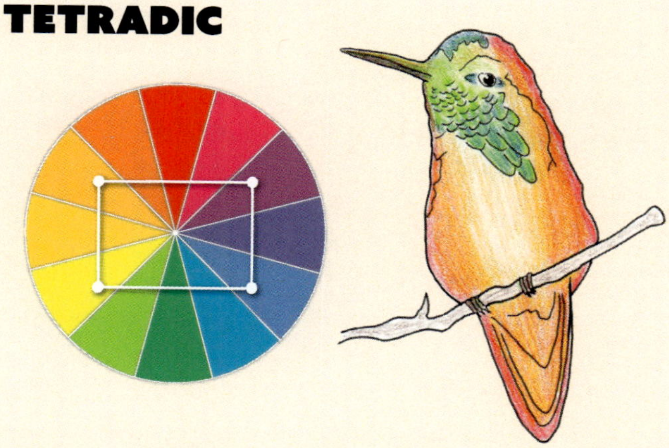

Tetradic (or rectangular) color scheme uses four colors arranged into two complementary pairs. Hard to pull off but can be gratifying when done well. A tetradic color scheme gives you a variety of possibilities that are rich and resonant and work best when you use the pairs in the background or foreground. Best not to use equal amounts of each color, as this can appear chaotic, but allow one color to dominate.

TRIADIC

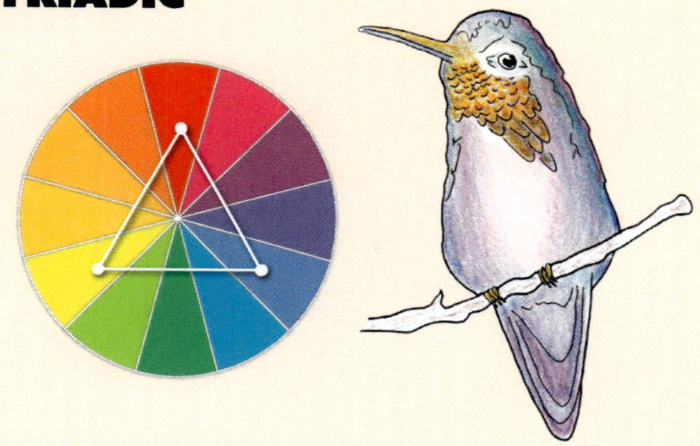

A triadic color scheme uses three colors evenly spaced around the color wheel and is one that is harder to pull off and best for cartoony or surreal scenes. Triadic color schemes tend to be quite vivid, even if you use pale (or unsaturated) versions of your hues. The three colors should be carefully balanced - let one color dominate and use the other two as supporting players.

Note:
Color schemes are most interesting when colors are used in unequal amounts. The greater the disparity, the greater the attention it receives. A color can appear intense simply by making the rest of the composition somewhat desaturated in comparison.

Check out the dragon lady tattoo at right. Can you guess what color scheme this represents? Three main colors; Yellow-orange, yellow-green and blue, with yellow-orange being the most dominant.

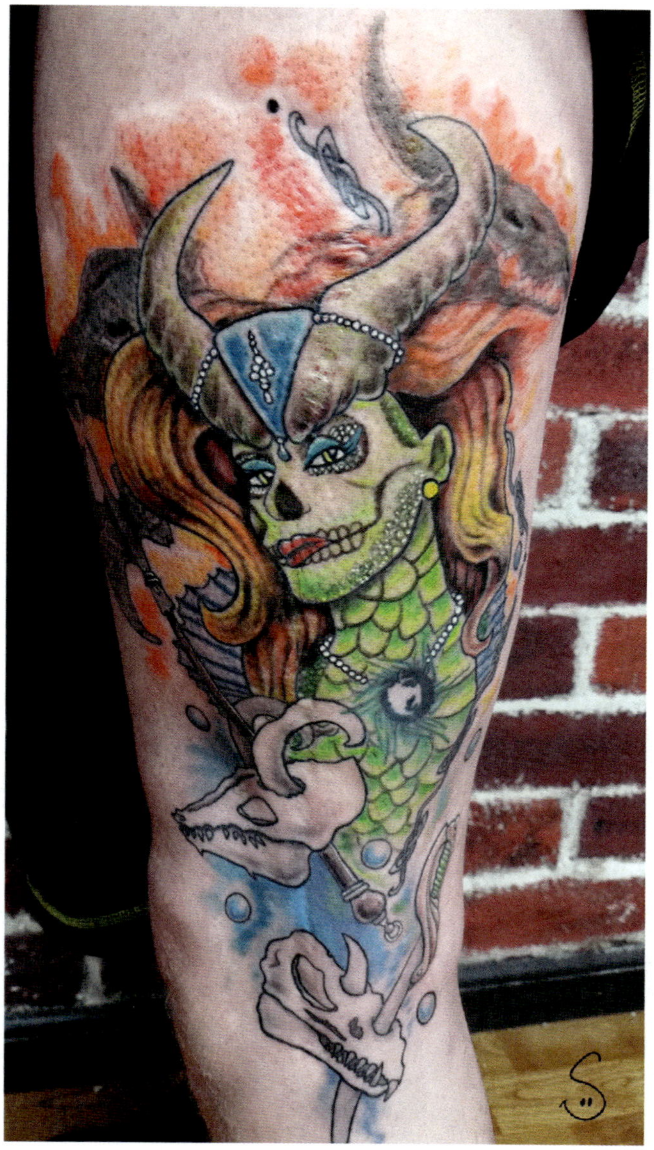

> **"If I create from the heart, nearly everything works; if from the head, almost nothing."**
> *~Marc Chagall, Artist*

If you guessed triadic, you were correct!

Use color properties (hue, saturation & value), color relativity and color harmony to guide the viewer, to help move their eye through the composition and to tell a story.

You can also emphasize what is most important or powerful in your scene or use color to bring attention to certain parts of your design, as well as to set the overall mood.

Even for experienced artists it can be difficult to choose the right colors for your designs. We tend to choose colors we are comfortable with over and over. Break this habit by exploring color on paper. Try different color schemes, even things you wouldn't normally put together, just to see what happens. Use colored pencils, markers, or paints to create grids of color you can use for reference when designing your tattoos.

Weird Fact:
Chromatophobia, refers to an irrational fear of, or aversion to, certain colors. In most cases, chromophobia stems from a conditioned response, or a past negative experience, but is fortunately an extremely rare diagnosis. --phobiasource.com

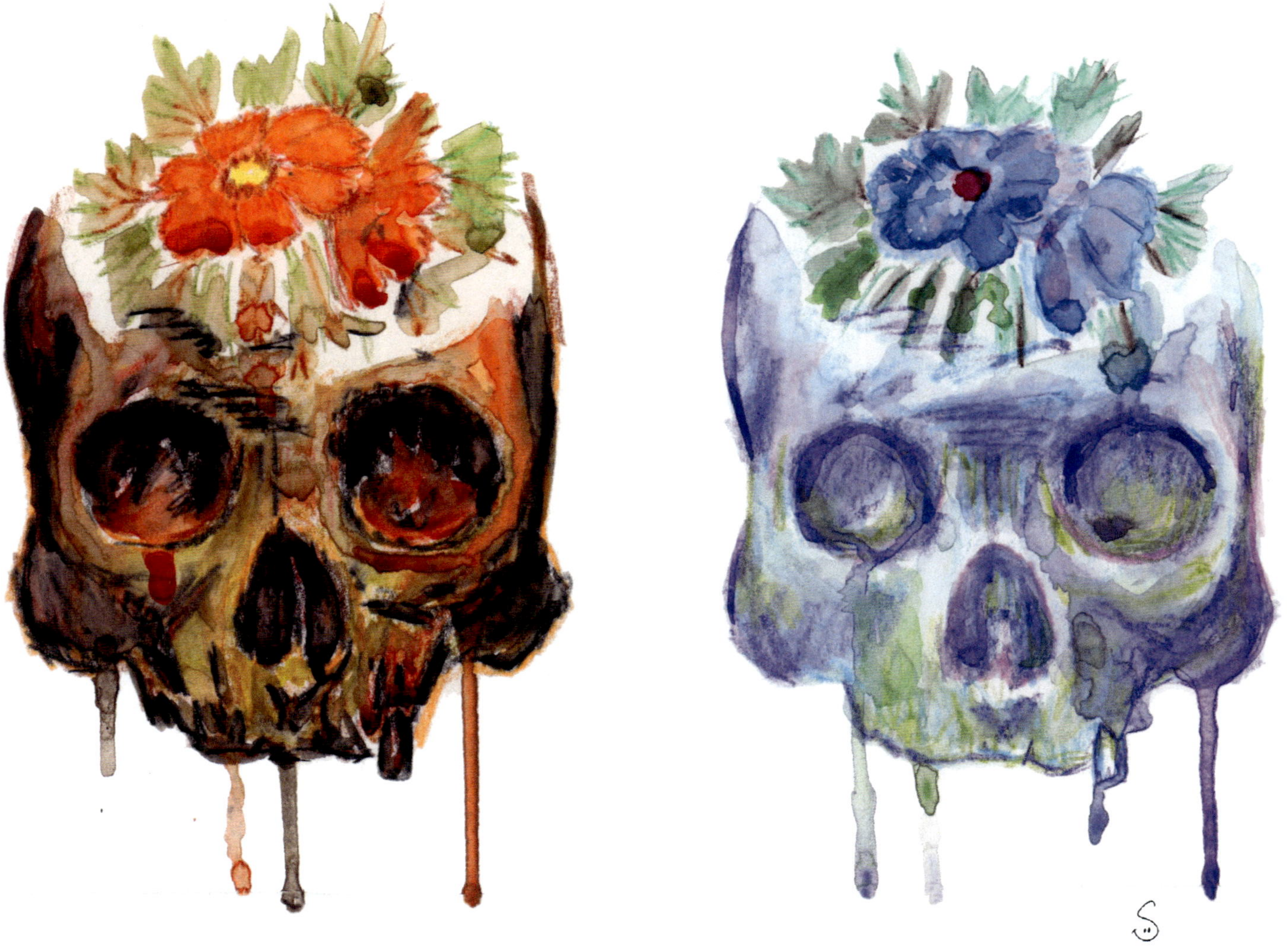

Psychological Implications of Color

Researchers have done many studies exploring the response of humans to color. Though much of a person's response can be culturally biased, many of these emotional reactions are powerful and universal.

Most colors also have a perceived positive and negative side, which again depends on the context they are used in. Using colors with a consciousness of the impact it will have on the viewer will make your tattoos more interesting, appealing and perhaps even more meaningful.

RED "Painters use red like spice." *— Derek Jarman, Artist/Film Director*	Recognized as inherently exciting (think red sports car), and evokes passion, stimulation, aggression and love. Red is associated with blood or the heart, anger (think "seeing red") and red draws attention (stop sign or "red alert"). A smart use of red in a composition can immediately draw focus, convey a strong confidence or simply accent an important message.
ORANGE "Orange is the happiest color." *— Frank Sinatra, singer/actor*	Fun, flamboyant, warm, rejuvenating and energetic. It's the color of flesh tone, sunsets or the warmth of a fire. Usually people feel strongly about pure orange, either loving it or hating it but conversely many values of orange such as rust, terra cotta or salmon are more widely appreciated. Orange is associated with Autumn (think fall leaves and pumpkins), appetite (peaches, papayas, apricots, oranges, sweet potato) and fierce tigers. On the other hand, orange can be a sign of danger (think traffic cones, prison jumpsuits and safety vests).
YELLOW "What a horrible thing yellow is." *— Edgar Degas, Artist/Sculptor*	The color of sunshine, seen as bright, optimistic and happy. Yellow tends to advance forward from surrounding colors. Yellow is associated with enlightenment, creativity and springtime (Easter eggs, daffodils and baby chicks). Energetic yellow can be overwhelming, if too excessive, and can represent caution (yellow light on traffic signal or yellow flag in racing). Yellow variations can be seen as sickly or sallow (yellow fever or jaundice) and can evoke thoughts of cowardice (yellowbellied).
GREEN "It's not easy being green." *~Kermit the Frog*	The most common color in the natural world. Green makes us think of vitality, freshness, growth, earth, rebirth, nature, money, calm and relaxation. It is associated with prosperity, eternal life and progress (think "giving the green light"). Even love can be "ageless and evergreen". On the downside, people can be "green with envy" and a grayish green tone can represent an unpleasant skin pallor or an institutional paint color. Green can also mean decay, alien, mold or poison (think "Mr. Yuck" or a witch's bubbling brew).
BLUE "Blue color is everlastingly appointed by the deity to be a source of delight." *— John Ruskin, Artist and Art Critic*	The overwhelming choice for favorite color. Some shade of blue is flattering to every person's wardrobe and the physical effects of blue are calming, relaxing and help reduce blood pressure. Blue is perceived as constant (think sky and ocean) and it can represent spirituality, rest, mysticism, loyalty (think "true blue"), high quality (think "blue ribbon" or "blueblood") water, serenity, wisdom and winter. It is also associated with sadness ("the blues"), being cold or unfeeling (icy), loneliness and depression. Some brilliant blues can be perceived as dynamic, elegant, dramatic and exhilarating.
PURPLE "When I am an old woman I shall wear purple." *~Jenny Joseph, Poet*	Calming, creative and uplifting. It represents royalty, prosperity, nobility (think "the purple heart") and spirituality. The color purple is often the favorite of creative or eccentric types as well as teenage girls. It embodies fantasy and playfulness but can also be the color of nightmares, impulsiveness, and trances. Yet in many cultures it is considered a sacred color.

> "I found I could say things with color and shapes that I couldn't say any other way!"
> ~Georgia O'Keefe, Artist

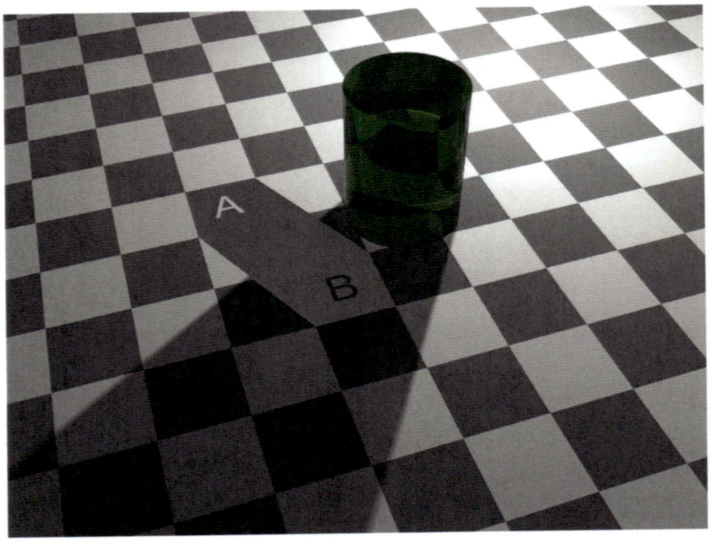

MORE FUN COLOR OPTICAL ILLUSIONS

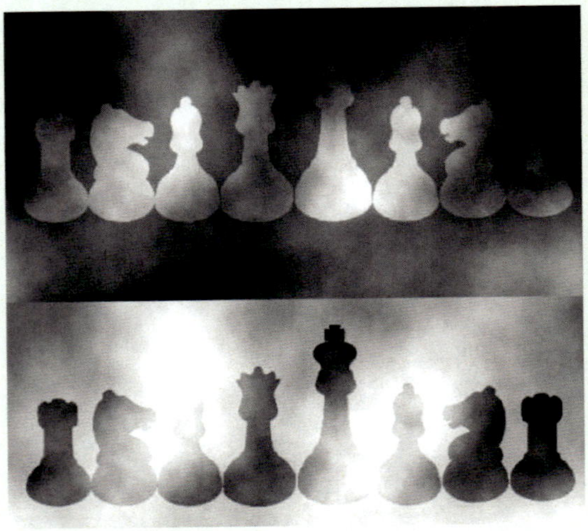

The white chess pieces are the same color as the black ones.

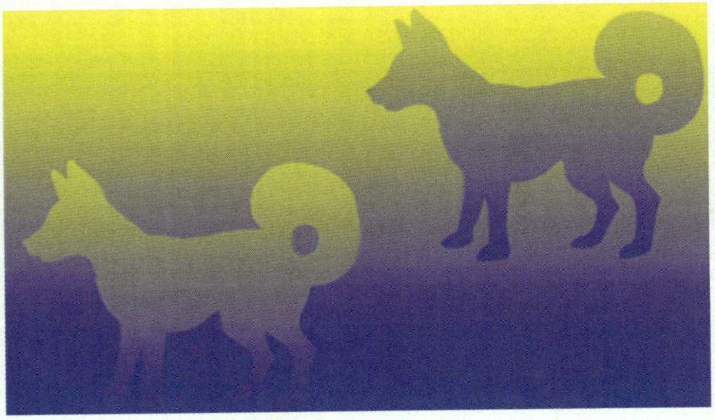

These dogs are the same color

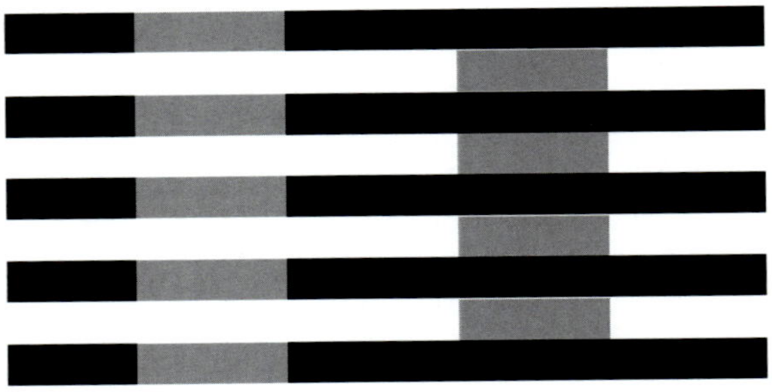

Both stacks of gray are the same.

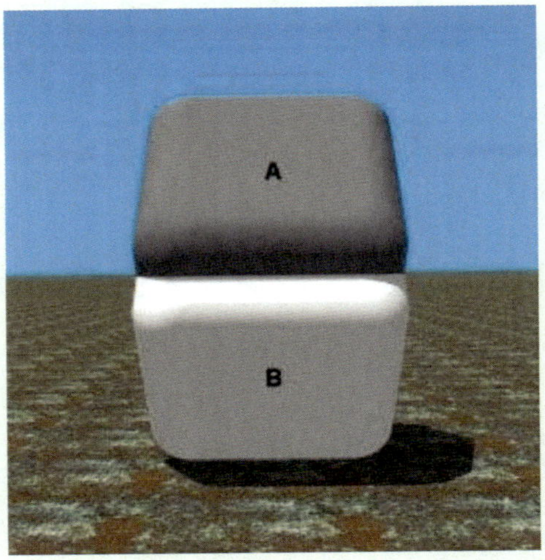

A and B panels are the same color. Don't believe it? Put your finger across the center.

Sources:
Color, Gunter Wyszecki, World Book Inc, (c)2006
Understanding Color, Andrew Price, blenderguru.com, 2014
Color, Betty Edwards, (c)2004
Color Theory, webinar, Chairi Adams, Udemy, 2018
Color Symbolism, Mabel Weaver, 2015
Color Illusions, brainden.com, 2019

Chapter Seven Highlights

- Hue is pure spectrum color without shade, tint, or tone.
- Saturation means the brightness or dullness of a color. Also called intensity.
- The categories of color include primary, secondary and tertiary.
- Warm colors evoke a sense of warmth and brightness. Cool colors evoke a sense of calm and tranquility.
- The three properties of color are: hue, saturation and value.
- Value describes how dark or light a color is.
- You can create a range of values from any color.
- You can change the value of a color by adding a tint, shade or tone.
- Tints are created by adding white to a color.
- Shades are created by adding black to a color.
- Tones are created by adding gray to a color.
- Colored tattoo ink tends to fade and blur on the edges.
- Muted colors will appear to recede; pure colors will appear to advance.
- Color harmony refers to the fact that some colors will look better together than others.
- Color schemes are most interesting when colors are used in unequal amounts.
- You can emphasize what is most important or powerful in your design by using color.
- Blue is the overwhelming choice for favorite color.
- Even for experienced artists it can be difficult to choose colors.

Wisecracks:

Do not keep calm and carry on.

Call in sick and go get a tattoo.

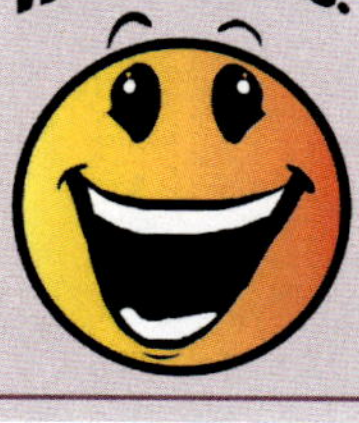

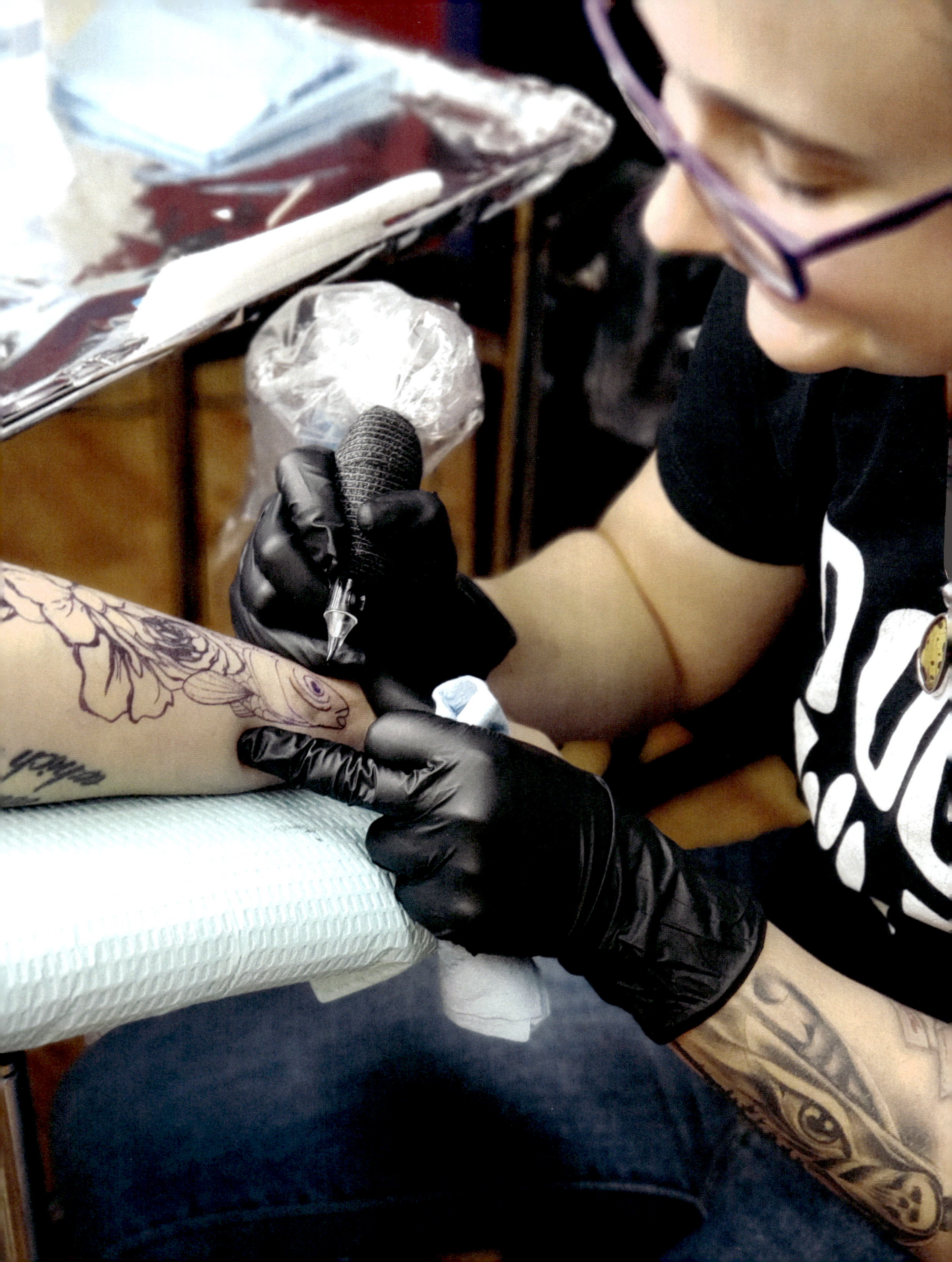

Chapter Eight

Tattoo Ink

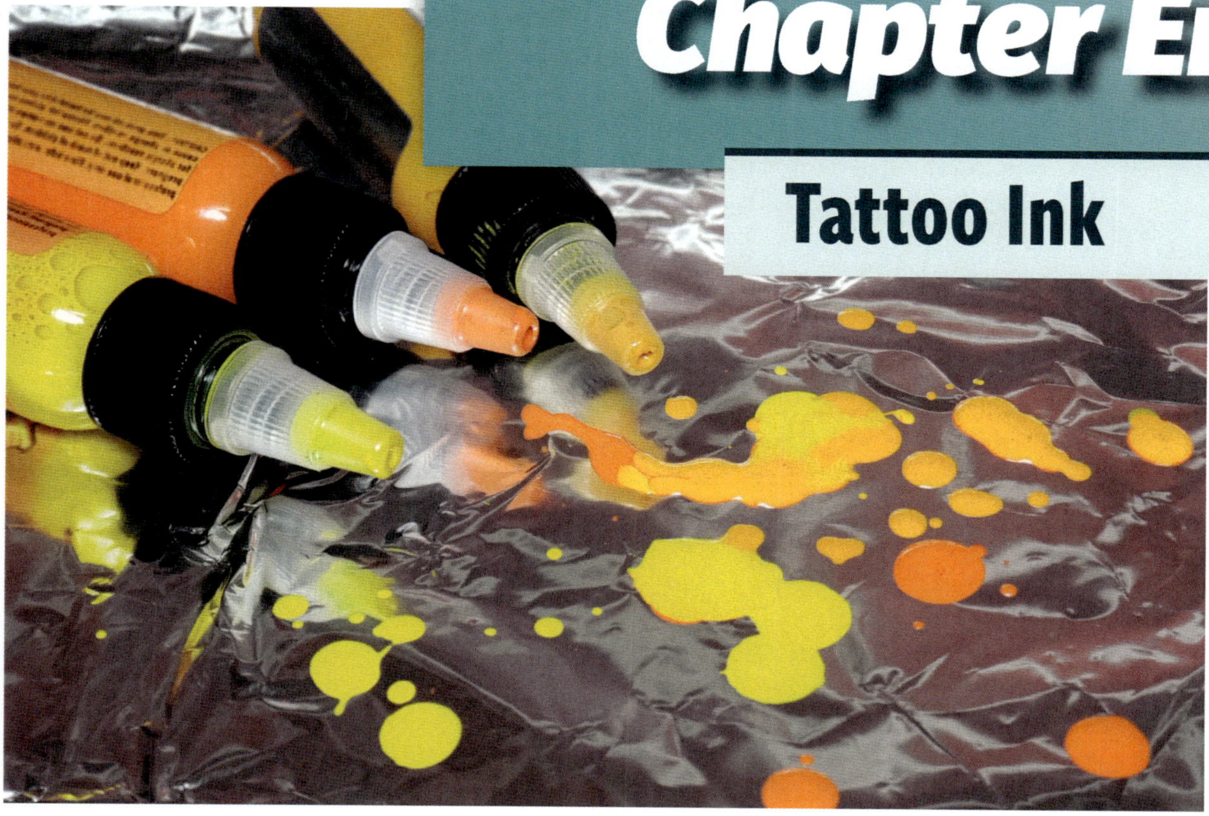

Tattooing is an art form dating back thousands of years, beginning with pigments created from dyes made of natural substances. The oldest pigments came from using ground-up minerals and carbon black.

What's in the Ink?

> "Colour is my day-long obsession, joy and torment."
> ~*Claude Monet, Artist*

Over the last 20 years, ink manufacturers have moved toward using more organic and vegetable-based dyes suspended in a carrier solution.

Very few countries have any regulations controlling the composition of tattoo inks. The actual practice of tattooing is regulated by local jurisdiction.

Inks are not regulated by the US Food & Drug Administration (FDA) but they're considered cosmetic and proprietary and therefore do not require ingredient disclosure. Because of a previous lack of evidence for safety concerns, the FDA has not regulated tattoo inks. So, we don't know exactly what is in the ink, unless a company chooses to disclose.

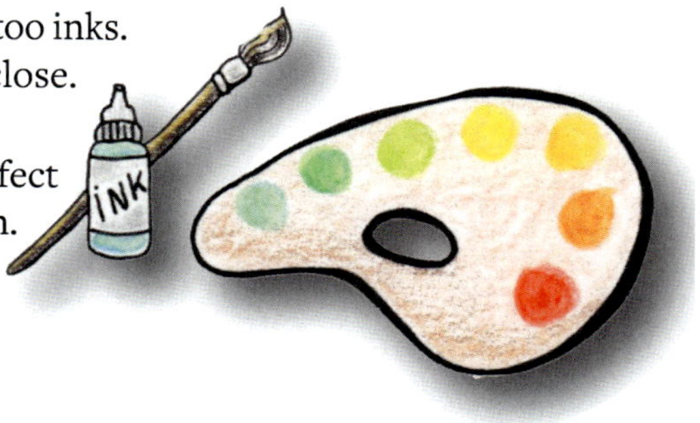

Tattoo ink is composed of a pigment or colorant and a carrier substance to disinfect the solution, keep it evenly mixed and assist with smooth insertion into the skin.

The safest and most common carrier ingredients include:
- ethyl alcohol (ethanol)
- purified water

- witch hazel
- propylene glycol
- glycerine (glycerol)

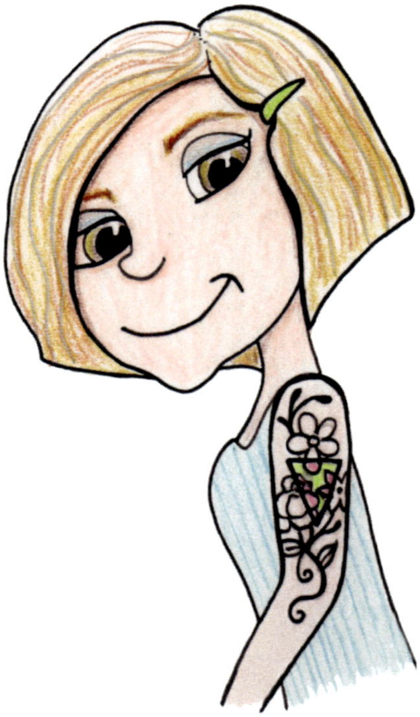

These ingredients are typically used in small amounts, not retained in the skin, and the body's normal waste processes would deal with them.

Though pigments are not regulated and there is no way to know positively which ingredients will cause problems, tattoo ink is what we use to create the art in skin. Ask more experienced tattooers about how the colors and brands have healed in their client's skin over the years. Do your own research and you can make the most informed choice when choosing which inks to invest in.

Ingredients in Common Pigments

Black: iron oxide, carbon, logwood, magnetite, wusite, bone black, soot or heartwood extract.
Brown: ochre, which is composed of iron/ferric oxide and mixed with clay.
Red: cinnabar, cadmium red, napthol, iron oxide known as common rust.
Orange: disazodiarylide and/or disazo pyrazolone cadmium seleno-sulfide.
Flesh: ochres or iron oxides mixed with clay.
Yellow: cadmium yellow, ochres and curcuma which is derived from plants of the ginger family (aka tumeric or curcurmin).
Green: chromium oxide, malachite, ferrocyanides, lead chromate and monoazo pigment.
Blue: azure blue, cobalt blue, copper, azurite, lapis lazuli, calcium copper silicate and chromium oxides.
Violet: manganese, various aluminum salts, quinacridone, dioxazine and carbazole.
White: lead carbonate, titanium dioxide, barium sulfate, zinc oxide, anatase or rutile.

The Ink Palette

Black is the oldest known tattoo pigment used, but the range of colors has exploded in the last twenty years, and has become even more varied in slight value differences due to the popularity of cosmetic tattooing and portrait tattoos.

Though many colors can be blended from a very simple palette, most artists prefer a range of premixed colors to work from. This can make it easier to remember the colors that were used with an individual client, particularly in a large tattoo, which requires multiple sessions.

The scope of colors available can be a bit overwhelming. In addition to the basic color names we all recognize: red, orange, yellow, green, blue, indigo, violet, pink, black, grey, and white, there are hundreds of descriptive names such as sage, espresso, sable, marine, sangria, ocean, chestnut, salmon, and even swamp! Likewise, black inks now have a variety of titles including: midnight, super, ultra, extra, stupid and dynamic.

The best way to navigate through this infinite territory of color choices is to pick a basic set of inks, choosing the brand based on your research, and add in new colors as you can afford to experiment and as needed based on the actual tattoos you will be completing.

Shelly's Sidenote

CHOOSING INK

Tattooers could decide to mix their own ink by using a carrier solution (or mix several) and dry pigment powder. However, I believe choosing tattoo ink from well-established companies who supply ink to the public, use safe handling practices, and regularly test their ink, is an excellent choice. These companies, such as Eternal Ink, Mom's, Intenze and Fusion Ink provide an ingredient list, safety seals, proper sterilization techniques and they understand chemical handling requirements. Furthermore, they readily answer any questions about their ink with candor.

There are many other reputable companies, so please do your research; check their ingredients and MSDS, ask other artists and call the company directly with your questions.

"Over the years, the FDA has received hundreds of adverse event reports involving tattoos. Published research has reported that some inks contain pigments used in printer toner or in car paint. FDA has not approved any pigments for injection into the skin for cosmetic purposes. Although research is ongoing at FDA and elsewhere, there are still a lot of questions about the long-term effects of the pigments, other ingredients, and possible contaminants in tattoo inks. FDA has received reports of bad reactions to tattoo inks right after tattooing and even years later."

- Dr. Linda Katz, M.D., FDA's "Think Before You Ink", May 2, 2017

"On the positive side, I couldn't find any evidence that tattoo pigments are responsible for serious harm. Certainly, there are problems, such as allergies, but there is no evidence of generalized toxic reactions. On the negative side, there is no evidence that the newer synthetic pigments are safe. Many of them have been used for only a short time, they are not produced specifically for tattooing, and their use is not regulated."

- Graham Coghill, "Are Tattoos Safe?", Science or Not? September 14, 2013

A good starting point for a beginning tattooer would include:

Lining black (**thinner for lining**), **extra black** (**thicker for solid fill**), **grey wash set, dark brown, light brown, dark red, light red, dark blue, light blue, dark green, light green, orange, gold-yellow, bright yellow, dark purple, light purple, turquoise or teal, magenta, light pink, flesh and white.**

From this simple palette a LARGE range of tattoos can be completed. Furthermore, artists can extend the range by mixing inks and tinting with white or pastels and darkening or creating shade colors with black, grey, dark blue, dark green or purple.

Variations of color can be created by mixing ink in the cup or blended in the skin. Colors that are next to each other on the seven-color spectrum are easiest to blend.

Think of a rainbow when choosing easy colors to blend: **green to blue to violet to red to orange to yellow to green.**

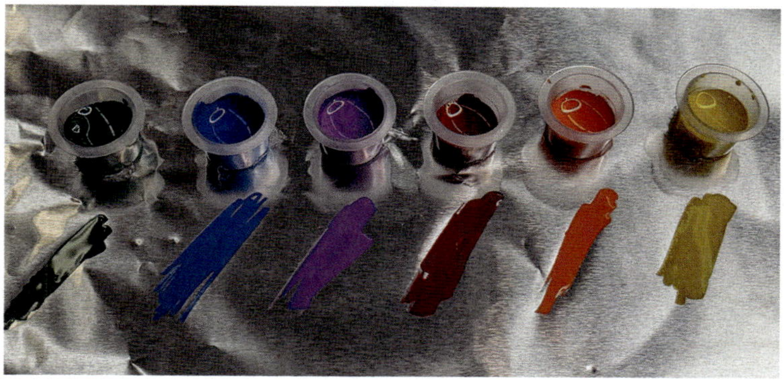

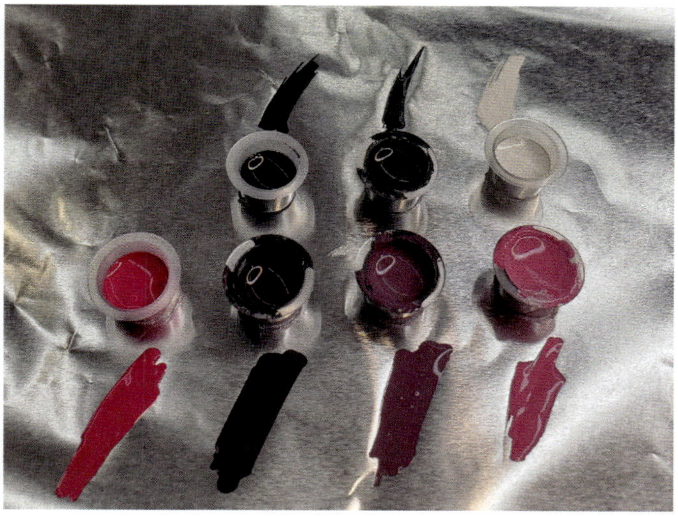

Also, different values of the same color make for easy gradation.

[think adding black (shade), grey (tone) or white (tint) to the same color)

> “In art, every ‘rule’ is merely a suggestion and is therefore meant to be broken. That said, I don’t advocate drinking the turpentine.
>
> *- Lupa O’Malley, Artist*

Remember: a tattoo doesn’t need to have tons of color in it to be successful. Many artists use a pared down palette to create spectacular works, including the prevalent black and grey style, monotone style, and even the tritone style called “trash polka” that uses just black, grey and red.

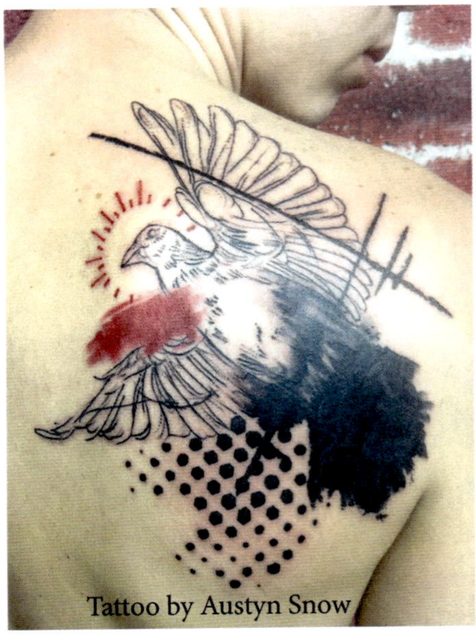

Tattoo by Austyn Snow

As you experiment with color, you can buy small bottles (typically 1/2 ounce) to add to your palette. Tattoo inks have a limited shelf life (generally two years) and if you overdo the purchase of additional colors you may find yourself stuck with infrequently used pigments that go bad; usually indicated by the pigment getting thicker and dry or crusty around the top, as well as a certain off-smell.

> **Note:**
> Shake ink bottles with paper towel over the tip (just in case they are not closed all the way). Open inks and take safety seals off with gloves (this can be a bit messy, as tattoo ink is very concentrated).

Ink Characteristics

All tattooers want their blacks to be solid, their greys smooth and their colors bright and beautiful. Yet there are many variables that affect how the ink goes in: different skin types, client’s ethnic background, condition of the skin, bleeding, experience of the tattooer, placement of design and quality of machine and needles.

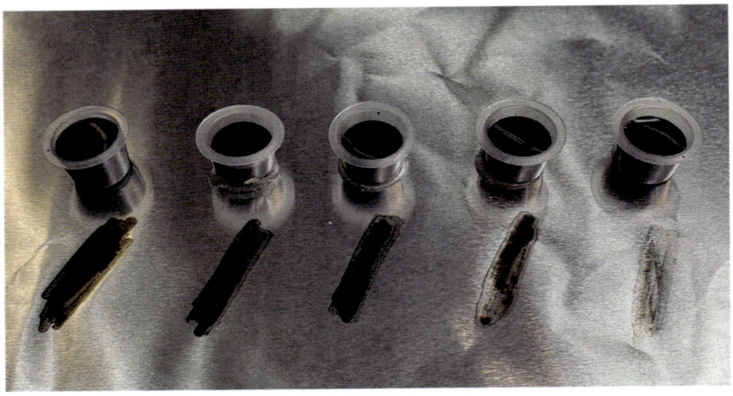

And to top all that off, several individual colors have some quirks and challenges as well:

Grey washes:
Basic grey tones ranging from extra light to extra dark (not quite black) gives the artist a full breadth of values to create dimensional work. Washes are more “watery” than standard inks, making them simple to blend. They are very easy to wipe (use less paper towels during procedure) and helpful to use for outlines to “map” in your tattoo stencil when you don’t want a hard line; though the lines produced from watery ink are more inconsistent. →

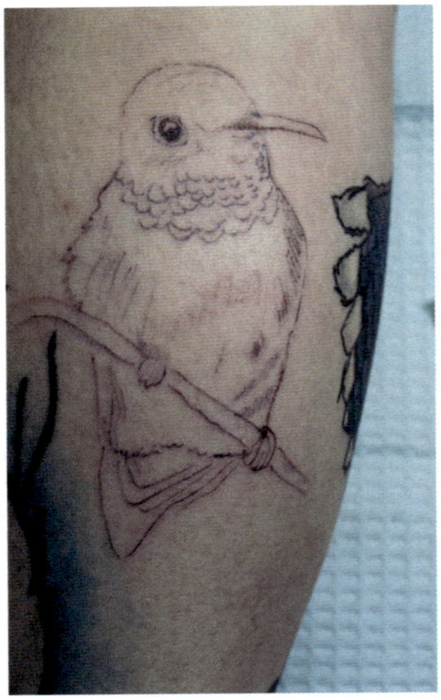

Though they are simple to blend with each other, getting a very smooth gradation of tone in the skin can take years to master. As mentioned in the chapter on color, many artists simply use a black ink and dilute it themselves with distilled water or witch hazel. Becoming proficient with this takes some practice.

> “Life isn’t black and white. It’s a million gray areas, don’t you find?”
>
> *- Ridley Scott, film director*

Green: greens are available in a variety of values and saturations, created from many different sources of pigment, and usually have yellow or white added, thus they can be touchy. The main mistake made with green is overworking, since you can't always tell it is in the skin. Beginners tend to overwork the area, thinking the green is not showing up. Paying careful attention and working slowly is important in recognizing when you have covered the area. Experience will help you learn to trust when green is in. A good way to remember; "green not seen; heal will reveal".

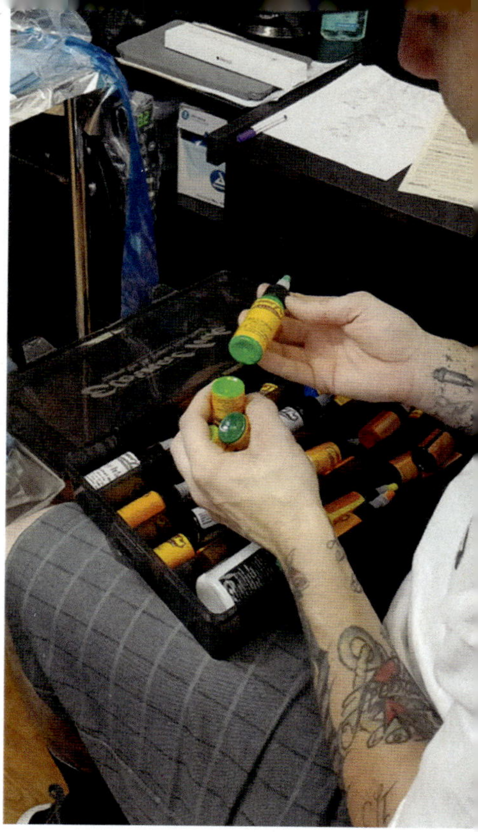

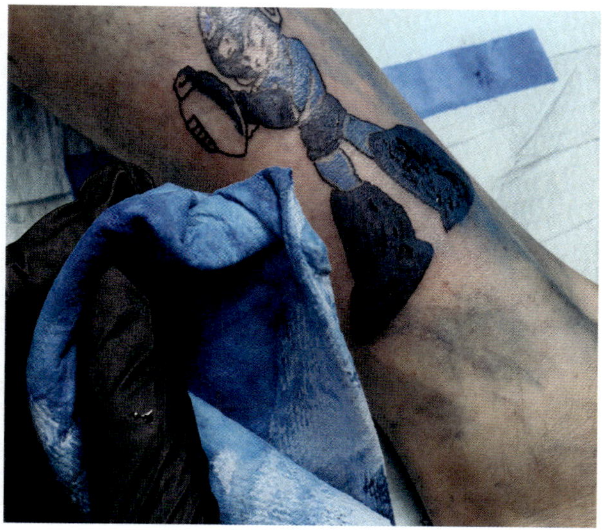

Blue: blues can have similar challenges as green, depending on their composition. Obviously the "greener" shades of blue will be more difficult to see in the skin too. Also, when tattooing blue, you typically use more paper towels to wipe away this pigment as it appears very concentrated and 'sticks' to the skin. Blues can be great as washes when thinned with distilled water or witch hazel, though their concentrated nature makes them a challenge to gradate smoothly. Washed out blues make a nice background to help pop a tattoo forward.

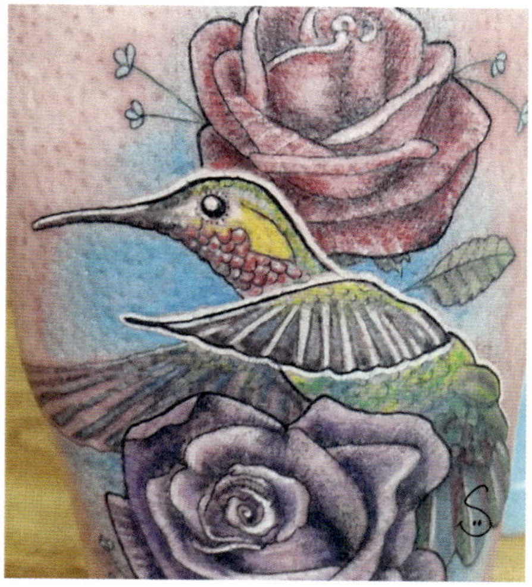

White: white is the trickiest pigment in the palette. It is lighter than any skin color and because it is inserted into the dermis, it will take on some of the skin tone of the epidermis that covers it. And it is sensitive to sun exposure. Thus, it can turn fleshy or yellow colored over time, perhaps even looking like scar tissue in some people. It is very pastel, making it hard to tell when it is fully in the skin; complicated by the blood coming to the surface and turning it slightly pink.

Despite its fickle nature, it is good for lightening other colors, creating highlights and getting a metallic or shiny look in a design. White is usually the last color tattooed during a session and artists must be careful not to wipe darker colors over it because it will stain the white, while the skin is still open, dulling the brightness. Though white is very subtle in some skin tones, it can create just enough of a contrast to make a nice effect.

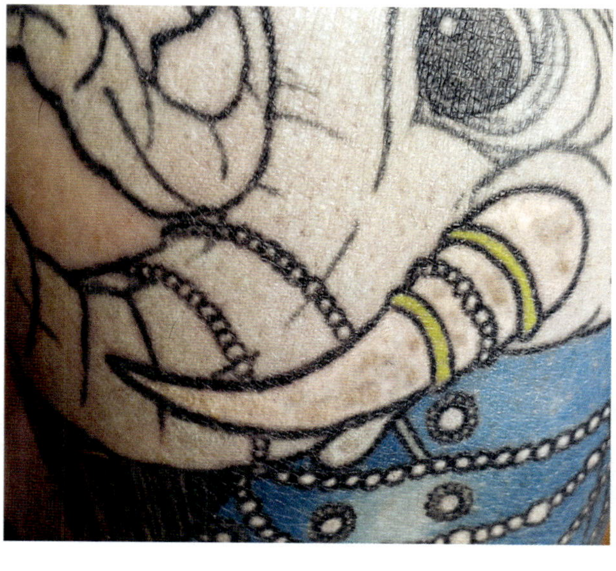

White ink in the elephant tusk at left, gone over twice--healed six months--but still a bit patchy.

Some people have experimented with tattooing an area entirely white, waiting for it to heal, and then tattooing color over the white area. This can result in much brighter colors but requires patience. In addition, many people like the idea of white-only tattoos, because the look heals very subtle and soft on the edges, even though it never stays truly white.

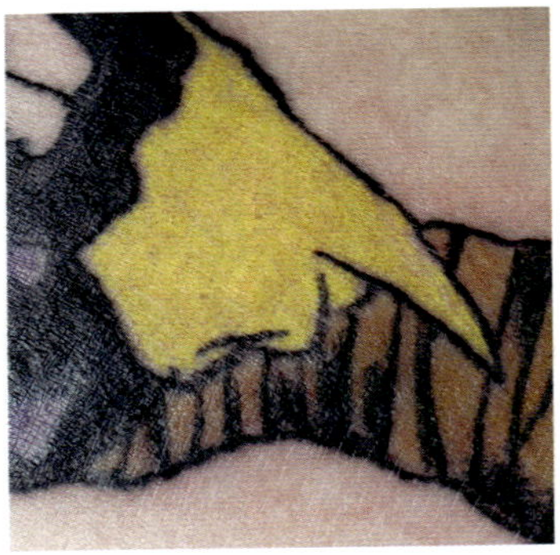

Yellow: like white, yellow is pastel and can be a fickle color in some people, occasionally needing to let it heal then go over it a second or even third time, (known as "building up the color"), before it really shows in the skin. When tattooing yellow ink, blood can come to the surface and make it look orangey-brown and spotty, which can worry beginning tattooers. Like green, it will require experience to know when you get it in correctly.

Consideration When Choosing Colors

In addition to some inks having touchy characteristics, pigment colors react differently depending on a person's unique skin tones and undertones. Generally, you will encounter people with warm or cool undertones. People with warm undertones will usually have a peach, yellow or golden complexion and likely have reddish tone in hair and brows, and greenish veins. People with cool undertones tend to have pinker skin with a bluish cast, black, brunette or dark blonde hair and brows, and bluer veins.

Note:
Remember, ink is deposited into the dermis (second layer of skin) where the pigment remains stable for a person's entire life, with minor fading and dispersion over time. When you look at a tattoo you are seeing the ink THROUGH the epidermis (outer layer of skin). Thus, the color you see in the bottle of pigment will not necessarily be the color that heals in the skin. The skin tone of the individual will affect the appearance of the healed colors.

Ink situates in the dermis layer, but the epidermis will cover the ink and influence the healed color, depending on how much melanin you have in your skin. Less melanin means more of a bluish tone in skin and more melanin will have more of a greenish yellow undertone. So, choosing colors that are on the warmer side for warm-toned people and on the cooler side for cool-toned people will result in a very pleasing tattoo.

For example, on a person with red hair and fair skin, you could choose a brownish black versus a cool dark black.

Consider too that the client's skin tone will be the lightest value in the tattoo (except when using white) and use that to your advantage. Leave the skin tone untattooed, or tattooed with just barely-tinted water, in areas you wish to keep light.

Remember, the closer your chosen shade is to the client's skin tone, the less contrast there will be. And the darker the person's skin the less likely pastel colors and white will show.

Ink Line-up

The typical sequence for use of colors in a tattoo procedure goes from darkest to lightest. The main concern is staining or dulling your light, bright colors. As you are tattooing, you are puncturing the skin thousands of times, and when you wipe, you are wiping across open holes. As the skin settles and the immune response starts, these holes will close up and then it becomes safer to use dark colors and wipe next to lighter.

Before the tattoo begins, it is helpful to line up the colors, on your work station, in the order they will be used, generally from darkest to lightest, to avoid mistakes, particularly with greys, as they all look identical.

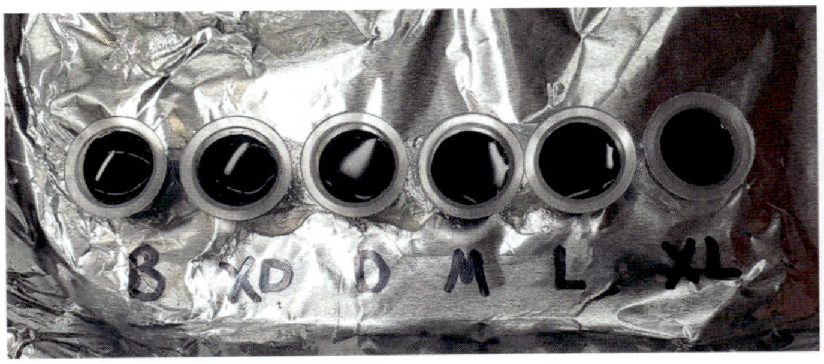

With experience, "rules" can be broken, and many artists jump all over the palette, simply being careful how they

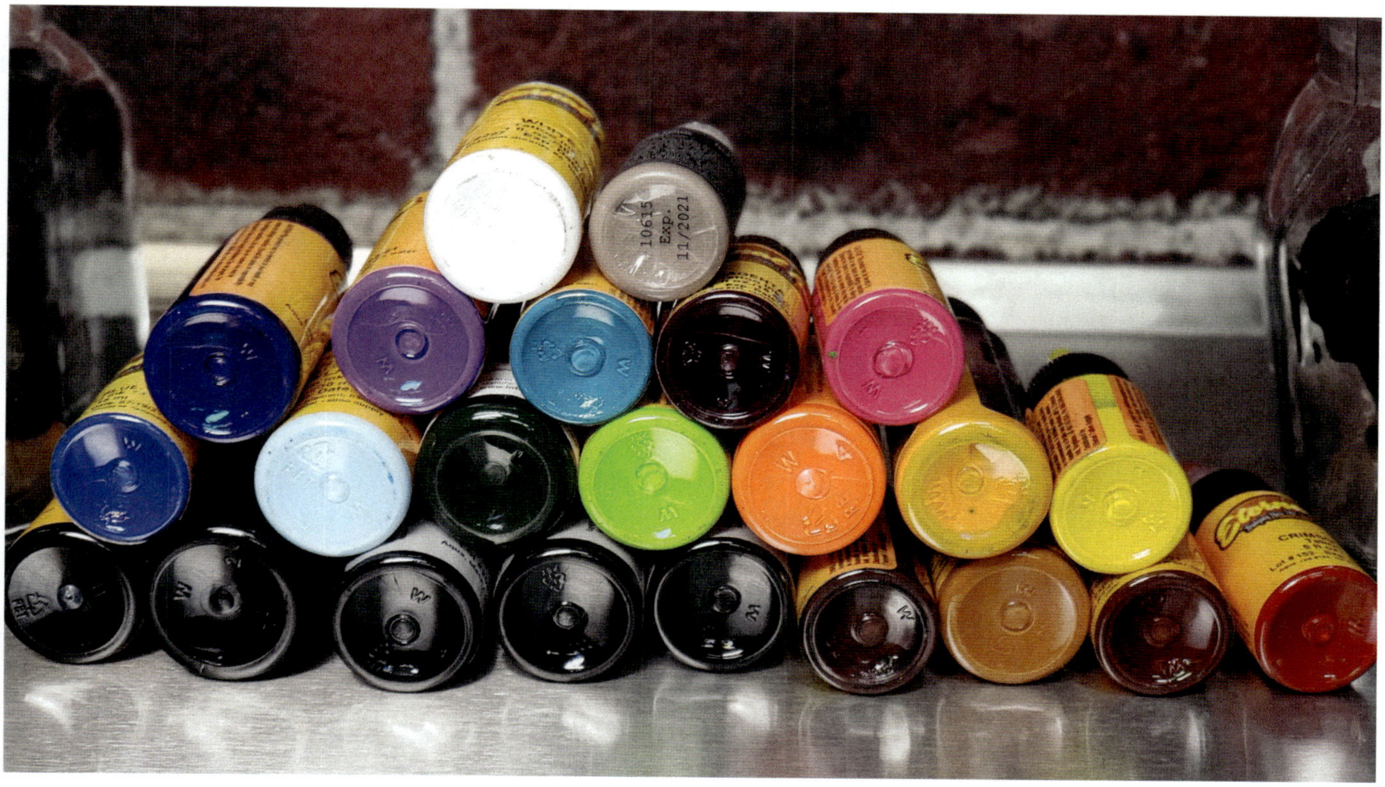

wipe, and aware of which skin areas are still open and receptive to ink.

Another consideration when tattooing dark colors: you can always go back after a tattoo has healed and add additional dark, but you can't take it away once in the skin (short of tattoo removal). Thus, it is helpful to err on the side of too light when you are new to tattooing and let your client know to come back for a follow-up visit to adjust levels and possibly build up color.

> "When I attempt anything, I have a passionate determination to overcome every obstacle."
> *~Cecilia Beaux, Artist*

Tattoo Ink Removal

There are a variety of reasons someone might choose to have a tattoo removed: poor tattoo, allergic reaction, ex's name, tattoo altered by surgery or weight gain, new employment, or they simply regret their decision.

It is also very useful to have a client do a few sessions of laser removal to lighten an existing tattoo and make it easier to place a new tattoo over an old one.

Despite advances in laser technology, removing a tattoo is a painstaking and painful process, usually involving several treatments and considerable expense. Complete removal without scarring may be impossible. Lasers selectively target the tattoo pigment without damaging surrounding skin by use of short pulses of light. This causes the pigment to break up into finer particles that are removed by the body's immune system.

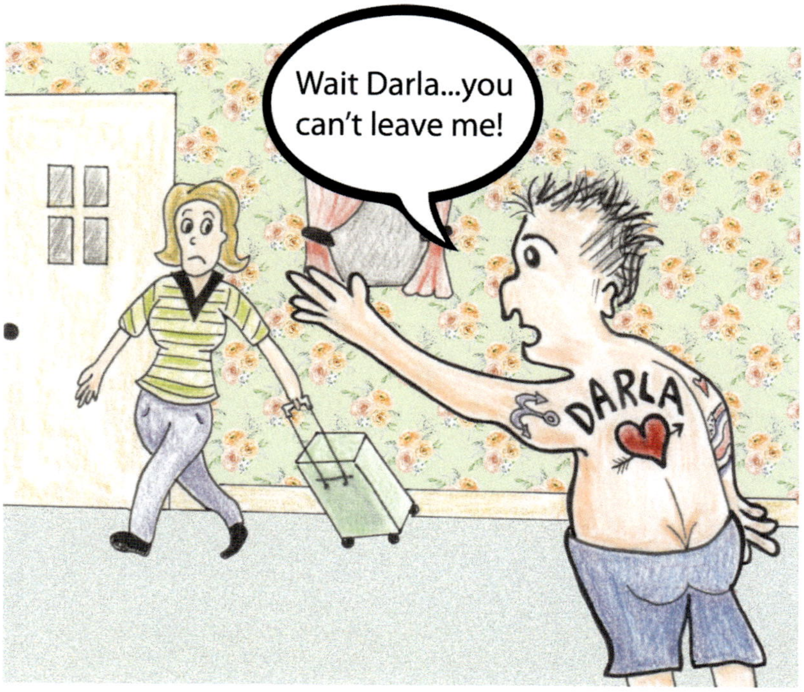

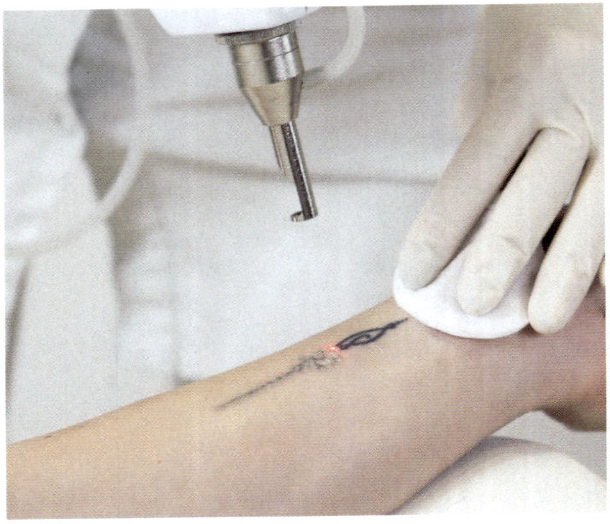

The basic laser removal procedure:
Client can prep for removal by applying a topical anesthetic up to two hours before and covering with plastic wrap. Some doctors recommend acetaminophen pre-procedure to also help counteract pain. (Aspirin or ibuprofen may cause bruising post-procedure). Some have described the pain of laser removal as being snapped by a rubber band over and over, but pain again depends on the individual's threshold. There is general agreement that it hurts worse than getting a tattoo but is over much quicker.

Pulses of light from the laser are directed onto the tattoo, fragmenting the pigment. Over several weeks, the body's cells eliminate the pigment. The treatment usually only takes a few minutes, though multiple sessions are typically necessary to remove tattoos depending on the depth, type of ink, and the size, as well as what colors were used. Usually a client is advised to wait at least 3 - 4 weeks between sessions.

After the treatment, practitioner will apply an antibacterial ointment and bandage over the area. Aftercare of treated area should be discussed with the treatment center staff, but likely will include avoiding soaking, picking or scratching the area. The skin will feel irritated and sting for a few days and may scab. After a week or so the area will begin to heal, and the existing tattoo will look slightly more faded. Side effects may include: hyperpigmentation, hypopigmentation, infection, lack of complete pigment removal and possible scarring.

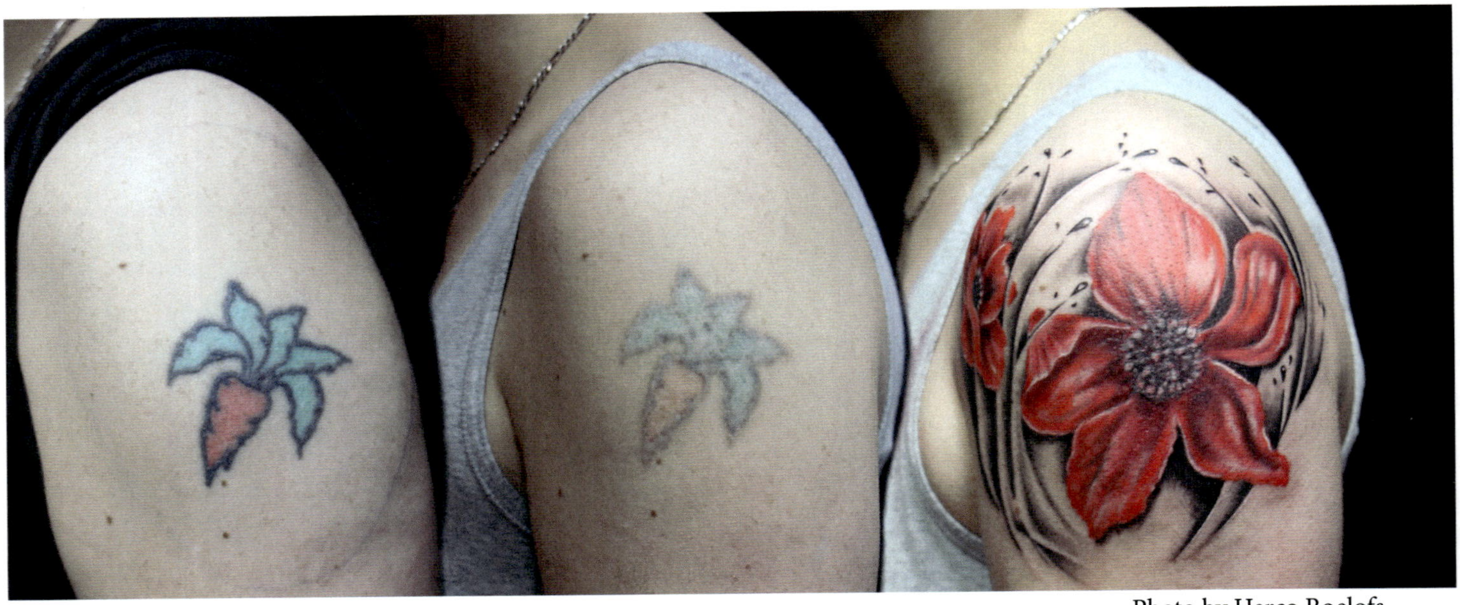

Photo by Herco Roelofs

It is generally agreed that home tattoos are easier to remove than professional tattoos. In addition, black is the easiest color to remove and green can be one of the hardest.

Sources:
Tattoos & Permanent Makeup, FDA consumer info, February 1, 2010
What Are Tattoo Inks?, Anne Marie Helmenstine, Ph.D. Thought Co, Oct. 30, 2017
The Chemistry of Tattoo Ink, Christine Dunn, Reactions Blog, July 11, 2013
Are Tattoos Safe?, Graham Coghill, Science or Not? September 14, 2013
Going Deep; The Culture & Chemistry of Tattoos, Frankie Wood Black, February 1, 2017
Tattoo Removal, FDA consumer info, June 22, 2017

Chapter Eight Highlights

- Very few countries have any regulations regarding the composition of tattoo inks.
- Inks are not regulated by the US Food & Drug Administration.
- The safest and most common ink carrier ingredients include; ethyl alcohol, purified water, witch hazel, propylene glycol and glycerin.
- Black is the oldest known tattoo pigment used.
- Choose ink brands based on your research and your tattoo mentor's recommendations.
- The FDA has received reports of bad reactions to tattoo ink even years after getting the tattoo.
- From a beginning palette a large range of colors can be created.
- Different values of the same color make for easy gradation.
- A tattoo doesn't need a ton of different colors to be successful.
- Washes are more watery than standard inks.
- White is the trickiest pigment in the palette.
- Ink situates in the dermis layer.
- As you are tattooing you are puncturing the skin thousands of times.
- It is helpful to err on the side of too light rather than too dark when you are a beginning tattooer.
- Laser removal selectively targets the tattoo pigment without damaging surrounding skin.

Wisecracks:

"Tax return refund?"

You mean "new tattoo fund".

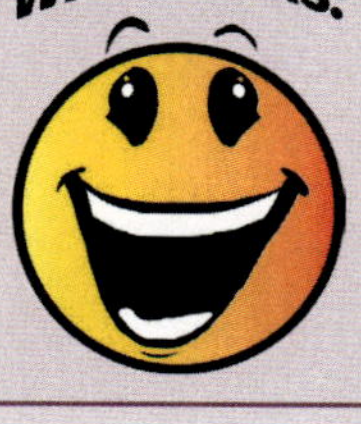

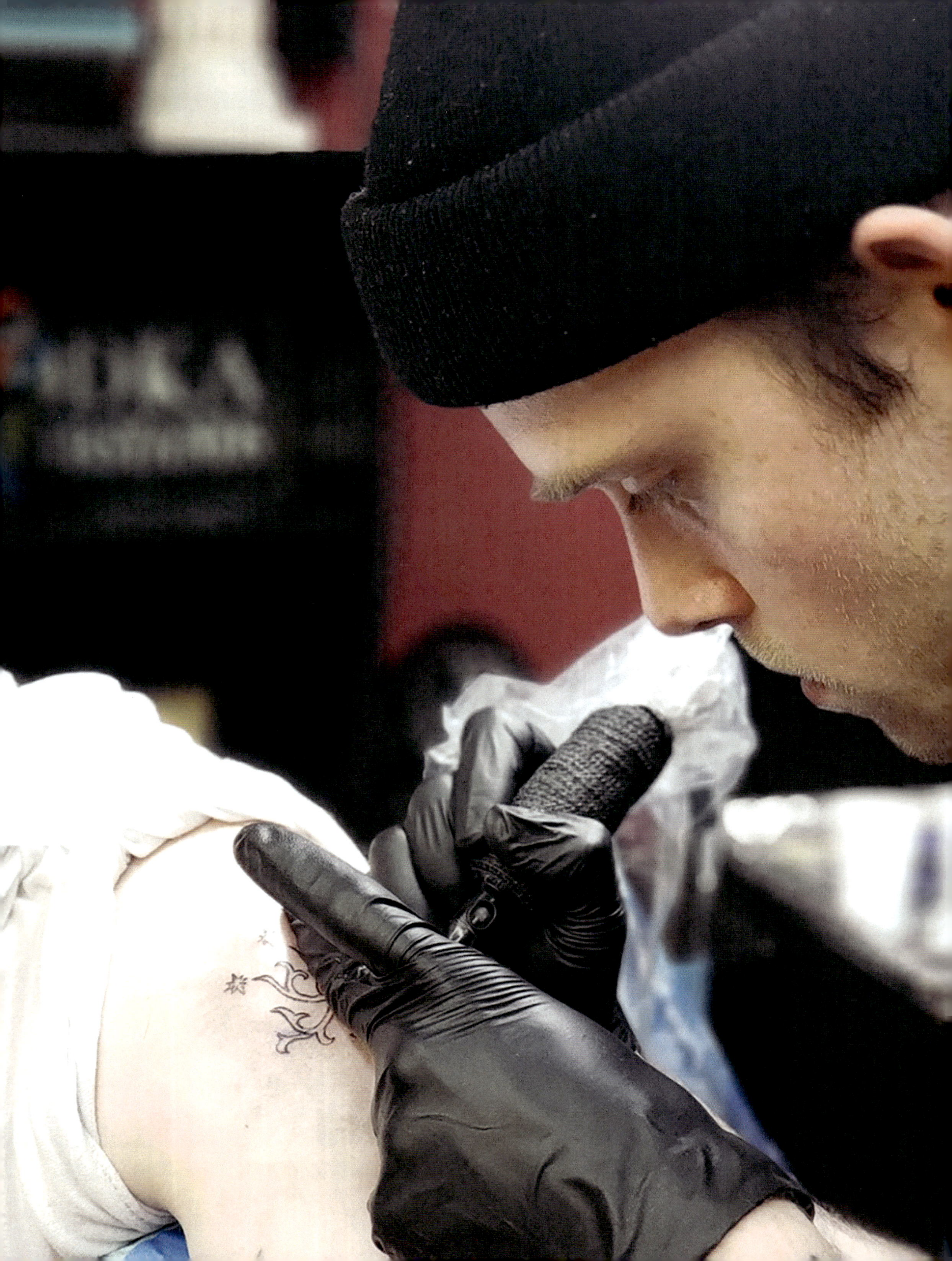

Chapter Nine

Tattoo Technique

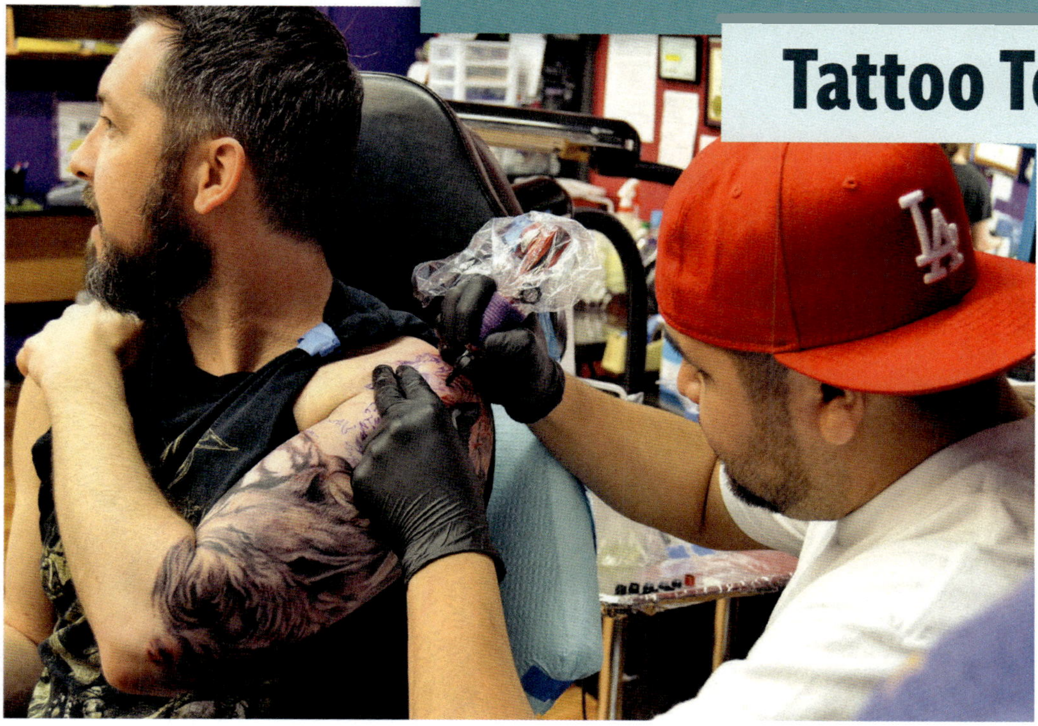

You've made it all the way here! You are now familiar with the risks, the sanitation, the equipment & tools, the art fundamentals and the inks. Let's get practical and apply this newfound knowledge to the actual process of tattooing.

At this point, you've been DRAWING meticulously with little erasing, strengthening your hands and have been experimenting with a variety of composition ideas. Also, you've tattooed at least 10 grapefruits and 10 fake skins. And you have a tattoo mentor or coach, right? You have the feel of the machine, power, hand movement and what you can accomplish with different needle groupings and pressure. But here is the truth: there is NOTHING like tattooing skin!

> "A good student learns from his teacher. A great student learns to teach himself."
> *-A.P. Sweet, Author*

Your Medium is Needles & Ink-- Your Canvas is Skin

There are major differences between traditional art tools and tattoo needles. Just because you can draw or paint well, doesn't necessarily mean you can tattoo. And producing lovely images on grapefruits and fake skin with a tattoo machine is just the beginning. Real skin has many unique characteristics that must be addressed:

Mistakes are NOT easy to fix

There is no erasing a tattoo (short of laser removal) so mistakes become a serious challenge. Mis-spelled words, going outside the lines, blowouts, too thick, wrong colors, too dark--many of these things cannot be easily corrected as in other art forms. Cover-ups are a difficult process and require advanced skills.

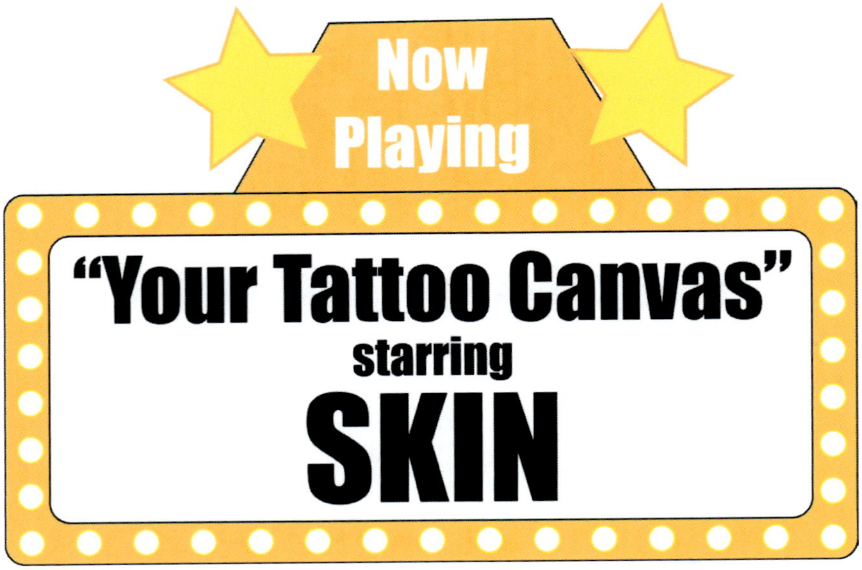

Your client feels pain, bleeds and moves

Your client is your canvas and this canvas will not sit there like a stone without moving for hours of tattooing. They bleed, they ooze plasma, they react to pain, they twitch, they wiggle, they squirm, they cough, and they need to get up to use the restroom!

Your client has opinions

Your client also has a say in what you will be putting on their skin permanently. They may not agree with the way you design their tattoo, they may want changes or tweaks, they may even change their mind at the last minute. The more experienced you get at tattooing, the more you can influence your client and hold fast to your artistic standards. But this takes time!

Before you Begin on People

Review the station set-up and tear down instructions in chapter four. Make sure you know how to set up your tray or work surface, so it is the most efficient and comfortable for you. And be absolutely certain you are aware of how to break the station down after it is contaminated. (Hint: clean hand/dirty hand, remember?)

Choose your first clients based on their understanding of your newness to tattooing and their lack of objection to needing a touch-up or even a cover-up later—family and friends are usually your biggest supporters!

Typically, when planning beginning tattoos, we encourage our students to stay away from precision lines and go for a very organic design. This makes it easy to make corrections later if your first attempts at lining are wiggly, too shallow or too thick.

The Process of Tattooing

Any time you learn a new skill set there are basic rules or guidelines to follow in the beginning. Of course, technical rules can and will be broken when you gain more experience, but learning the basics is essential to start you down the right path.

General guidelines:

- When placing stencils or drawing on skin have the client in a relaxed, natural position and don't stretch the skin out of shape or your tattoo will look crooked or off.

- Tattoo lines spread a bit over time, thus making them appear thicker than when originally tattooed. Use caution when tattooing small designs that must remain crisp and readable, such as lettering or symbols. The smaller the tattoo the less detail you can put into it.

Organic Designs

We ask that students choose ORGANIC designs for their first few tattoo procedures to give yourself a break when first learning to tattoo. This makes it so much easier to correct beginner mistakes.

When you first attempt to tattoo it is common to have unintended thick and thin lines, skips, blobs and line shadowing. Look at drawing #1 and all the potential challenges you could have:

#1

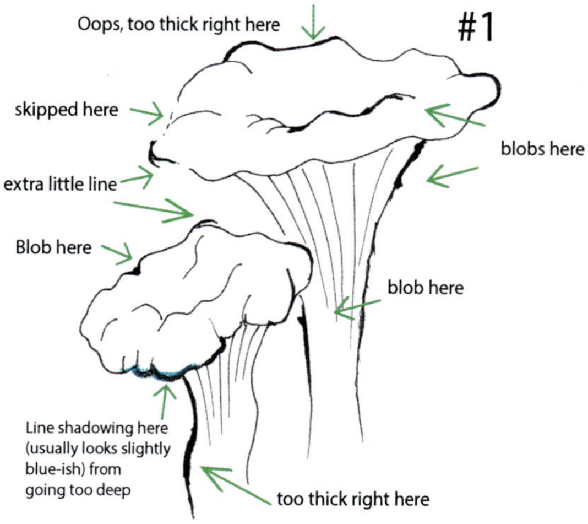

#2

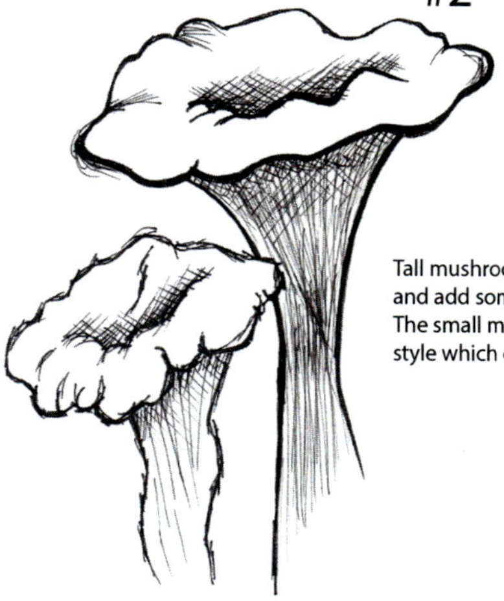

Tall mushroom in #2 shows you could thicken the lines and add some cross hatching.
The small mushroom shows an even more "sketchy" style which can readily hide any problem lines.

#3

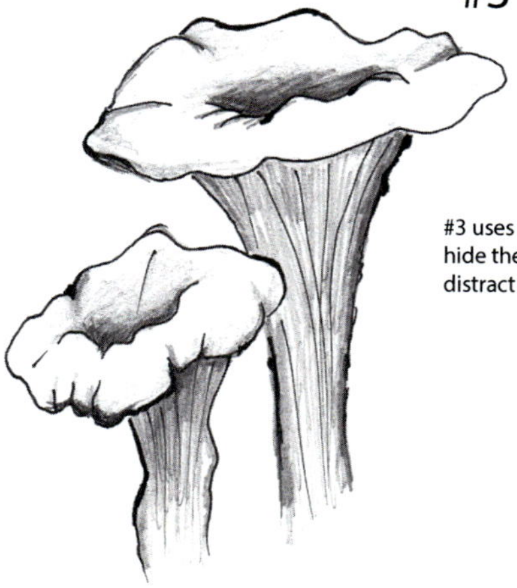

#3 uses shading to help hide the accidents and distract the eye.

#4

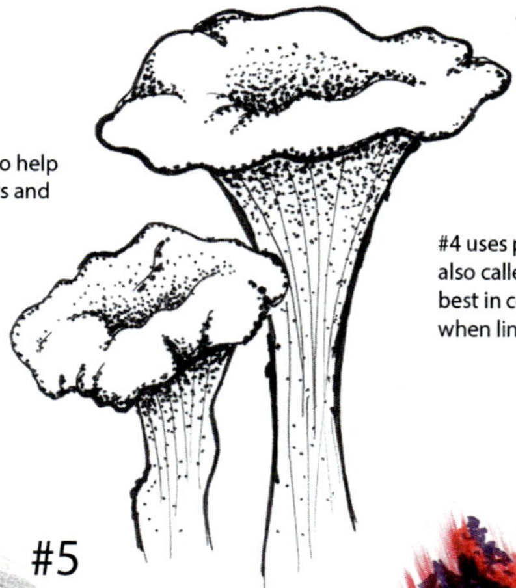

#4 uses pointillism to distract from messy lines; also called stippling or stipple shading. Works best in combo with shading and/or bolder lines when lines are very poor.

Sometimes you can add a background, as in #5, either black, grey or color, to help blend out the mistakes.

#5

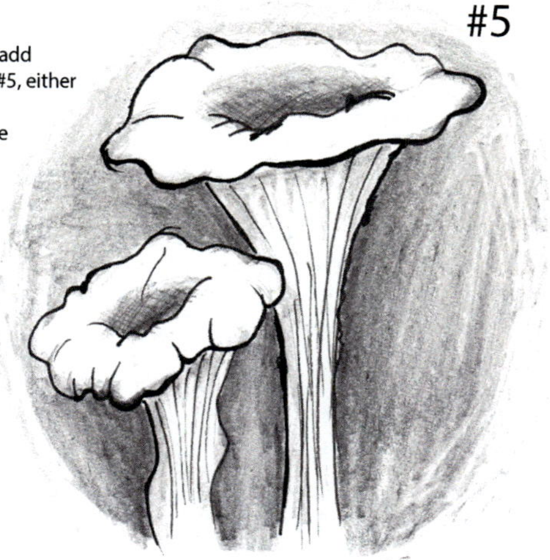

#6

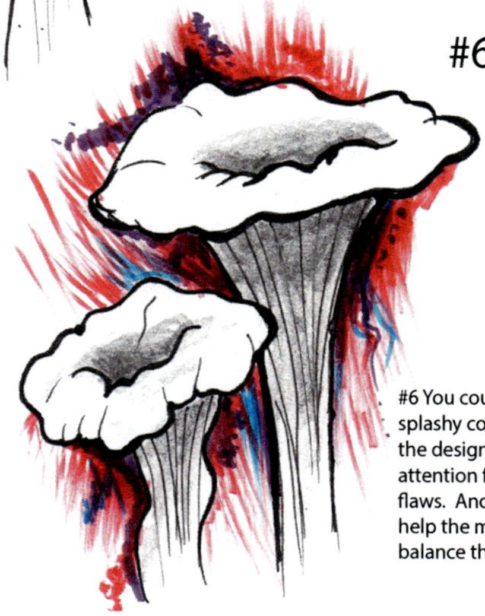

#6 You could try adding splashy colors around the design to divert attention from any obvious flaws. And bold lines help the mushrooms balance the bold colors.

REALIZING THAT NOT ALL REQUIREMENTS AND REGULATIONS ARE THE SAME IN DIFFERENT STATES AND COUNTRIES, SOME PEOPLE WILL HAVE ACCESS TO A SCHOOL OR APPRENTICE SITUATION, AND SOME WILL NOT. IF YOU DO NOT HAVE ACCESS TO AN OFFICIAL TEACHER OR MENTOR, WE HIGHLY ENCOURAGE YOU TO FIND AN ONLINE COACH OR EXPERIENCED TATTOOER TO AT LEAST REVIEW YOUR WORK, ANSWER QUESTIONS AND GUIDE YOU WHEN YOU GET STUCK. NO MATTER WHERE YOU FIND YOURSELF ON THE ROAD TO BECOMING A TATTOO ARTIST, ALWAYS USE STANDARD PRECAUTIONS AND FOLLOW STRICT SANITATION RULES. DO NOT TAKE CHANCES WITH YOUR HEALTH OR YOUR CLIENT'S HEALTH EVER!

- When you are tattooing, the skin MUST be stretched tight to provide a firm and taut canvas. Your non-tattooing hand does most of this work. The design will likely look stretched out of shape at times during the procedure, but you can trust that a properly placed stencil will result in a good tattoo once client resumes a natural position.

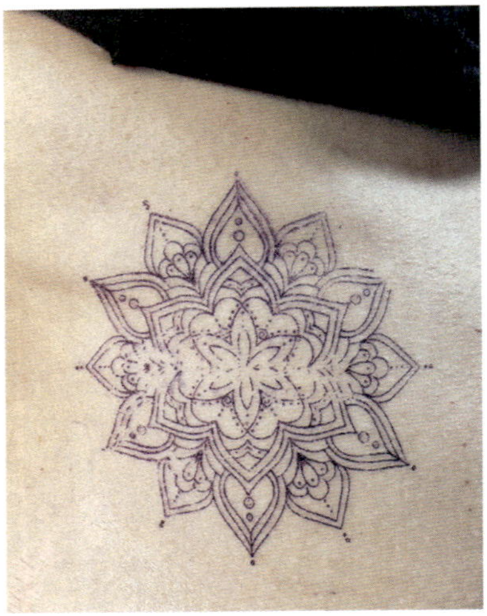

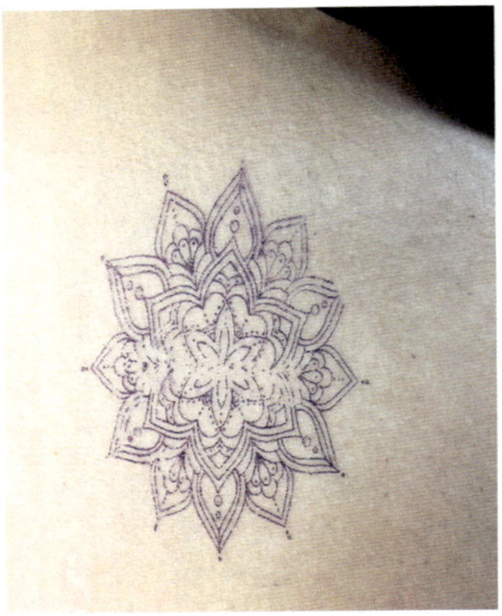

- Start tattooing at the bottom of your stencil and work your way up the design, so as not to wipe away your stencil or pen marks too soon. (Lefties generally start at bottom left, righties start at bottom right.) The longer you leave the stencil to dry the better the chance it will stay put--15 - 20 minutes for complicated designs!

- After dipping and touching needle to skin, the ink will naturally puddle a bit. You must learn to "see" through this to make straight lines.

- Once you touch the needle to the skin, the sound of the machine will muffle slightly.

- If you start to lose the stencil, you can put a dry paper towel under your stretching hand to avoid smearing.

Shelly's Sidenote

TINY TATTOOS?

I have a policy of never tattooing any lettering smaller than ¼" per letter, as words smaller than this tend to blur together and become unreadable over time. It is important to educate your clients who want tiny tattoos as to what they will look like in a few years.

Having experimented with super fine needles and 1-liners to do some cosmetic tattooing, I can safely say that even the tiny eyebrow "strokes" which look so excitingly hair-like at first, do not stay crisp over time. You can simply envision each needle grouping as healing a bit thicker than it looks when first tattooed. After a couple years, a fresh 5-line will end up more like a fresh 7-line, a fresh 7-line more like a fresh 9-line and so on. Always keep this in mind when choosing your needle size, particularly when designing smaller and/or highly detailed tattoos.

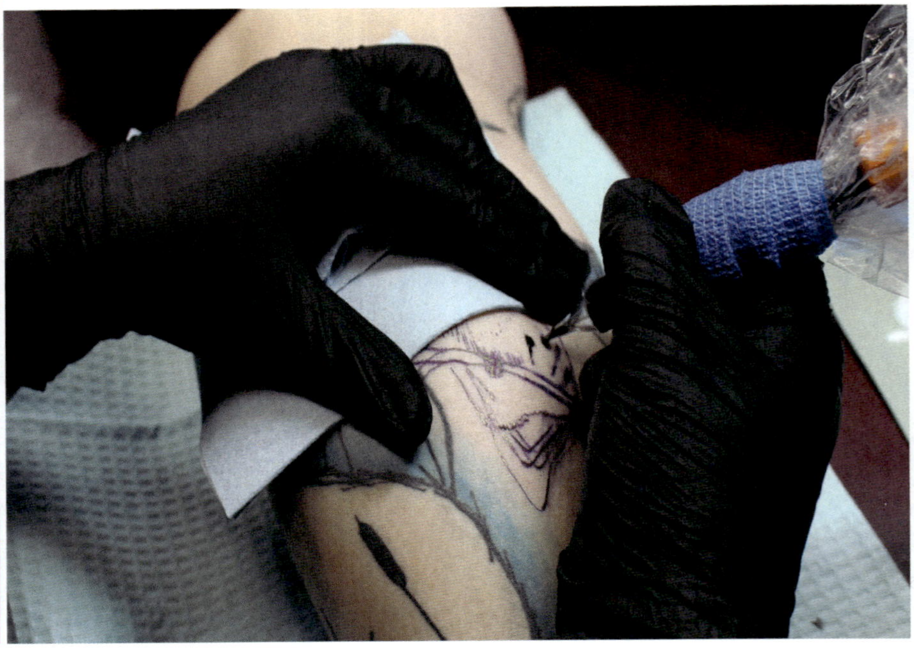

- Tattooing solid color or black, your hand speed slows down. Tattooing grey or color washes, hand speed increases.

- Pulling lines toward yourself is generally more stable than pushing lines away from you. →

- When you are penetrating at the correct depth, you can feel the even steady vibration in your non-tattooing hand, as it touches the skin.

- Start with the darkest colors first and work your way to the lightest. This helps avoid muddying up the lightest colors in a tattoo, by wiping darks over them while the skin is still open. (Once you have more experience, this guideline can be broken.)

- Holding a paper-towel moistened with green soap mixture in your non-tattooing hand makes quick wipes easier. This should become a habit. →

- Use white at the very end to keep it brightest.

- Rinse completely between color changes unless you are using similar tones and don't mind them mixing in the ink cup or skin.

- During the tattoo process, ink can easily get smeared all over the skin. Take time to carefully clean the area so you can see how well your lines and colors are going in and to avoid obscuring the outline. Also, keep ink off the perimeter of tattoo design. It shouldn't turn into a muddled mess.

- After dipping the needle(s) in ink, you can wipe the tip of the needle to dab the drop off the end. This will help minimize puddling. Tape a paper towel to your station where you can easily dab the tip, without hitting the needle on the tray. →

- Keep surface of the skin as clean as you can throughout the whole session, UNTIL you become very familiar with how well you are getting the ink in (probably several years).

- If you lose part of a stencil during the

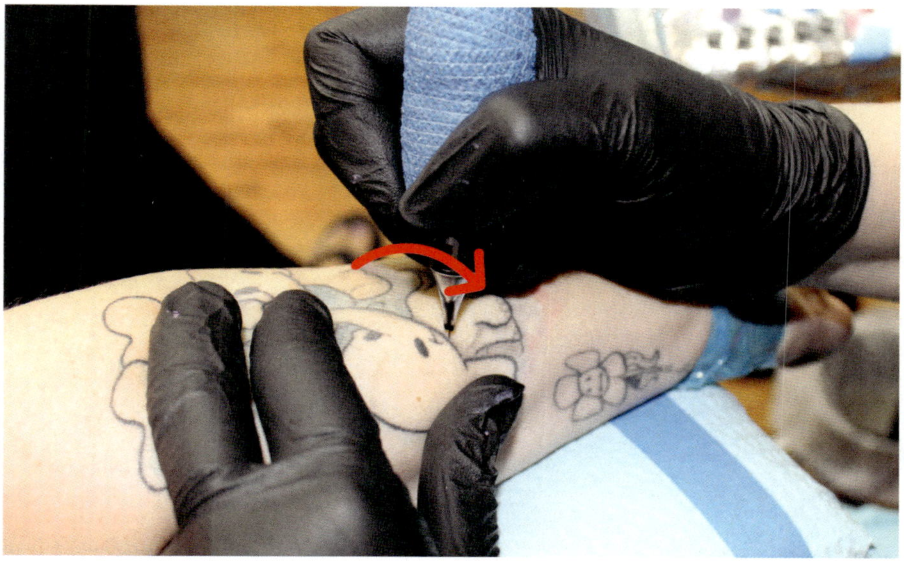

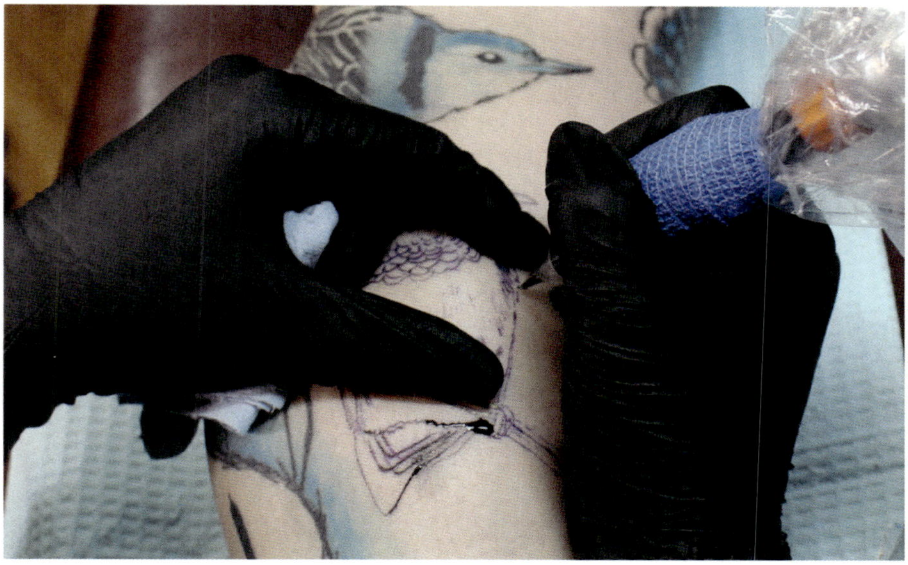

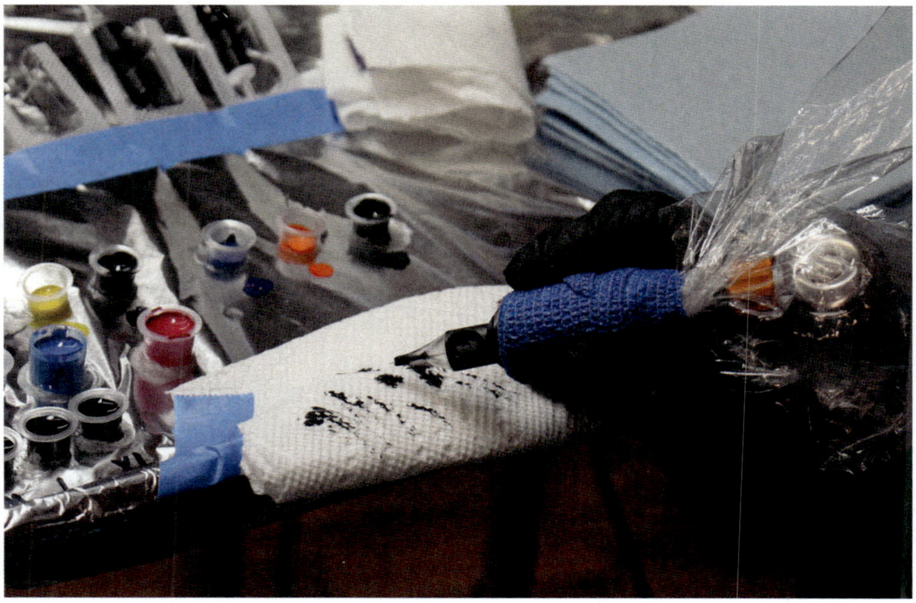

procedure, stop and draw it back on with a tattoo marker or sharpie, being sure client is in a natural relaxed position and skin is NOT stretched while drawing. (Sanitize marker after tattoo procedure with a high-level disinfectant or discard it.)

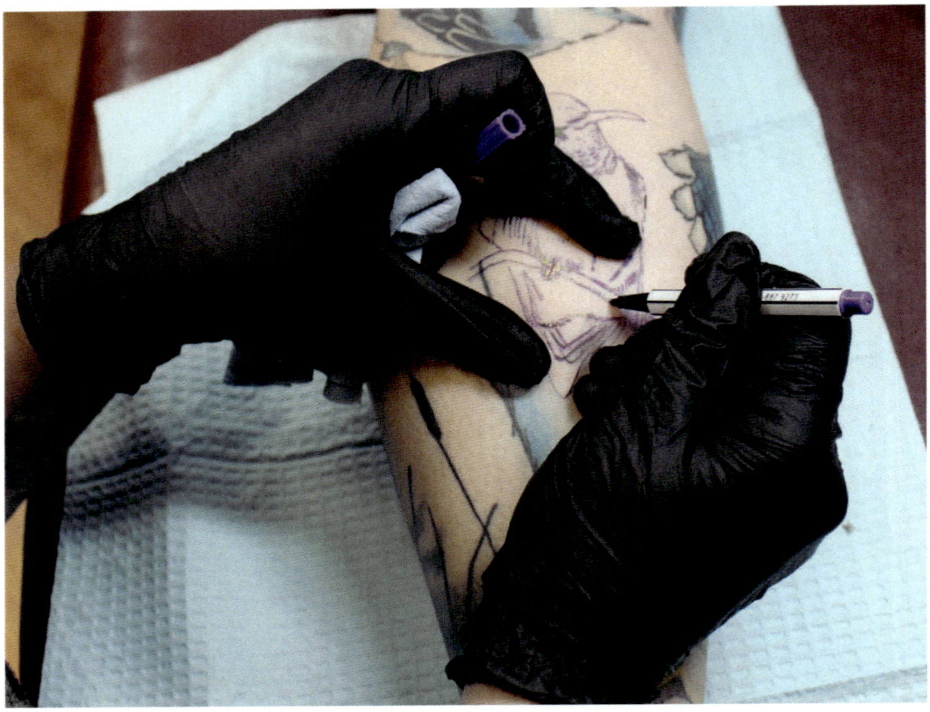

←

- Foot pedal controls on/off function for power supply and power supply is plugged into the back of the tattoo machine with the power cord or clip cord. On newer power supplies the foot pedal can be set to 'constant on' feature. This allows you to tap the pedal to turn power on and keep it running and tap again to turn power off. (More recently, wireless foot pedals have become available as well.)

- Average voltage is set between 6 – 10, depending on your brand of power supply.

- Needle tips should be set out of the tube approx. 1/16" or approximately 1.5 mm. Liners and round shaders can be out a little further, mag needles pulled back a bit.

~*On a coil machine*, just press down on the armature bar while the machine is off. Check how far the needle is set out. Turn the tube vise screw to adjust the grip up or down.

~*On a rotary machine*, or with disposable cartridges, you'll check how far the needle is out with the machine running. On most rotaries, have the needle facing away from you, adjust the length of needle set by turning the grip of the machine to the left to put it out and to the right to bring it in. (lefty loosey, righty tighty)

Approximate needle length when tattooing:

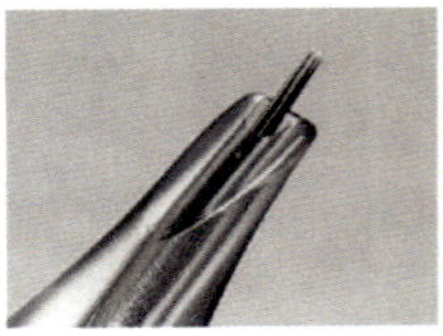

Liner

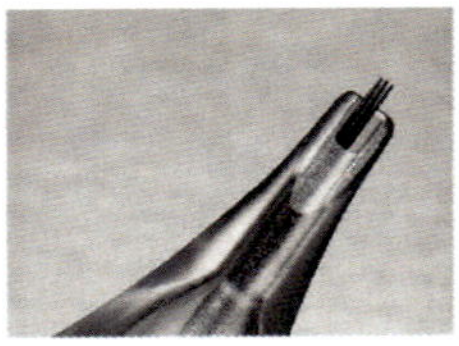

Round Shader

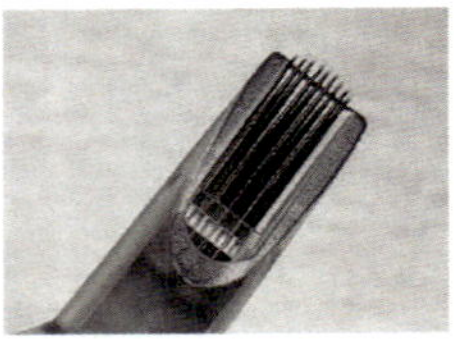

Magnum

Shelly's Sidenote

GREEN SOAP

In general, most tattooers wipe ink, blood and bodily fluids away during the procedure with some combo of green soap and water. I personally use a mixture of approximately one gallon of water, two cups green soap and two cups of witch hazel. This gives me the "soapiness" I need, slightly diluted with water, for getting the ink off the skin smoothly, and the witch hazel for soothing client's irritated, open skin.

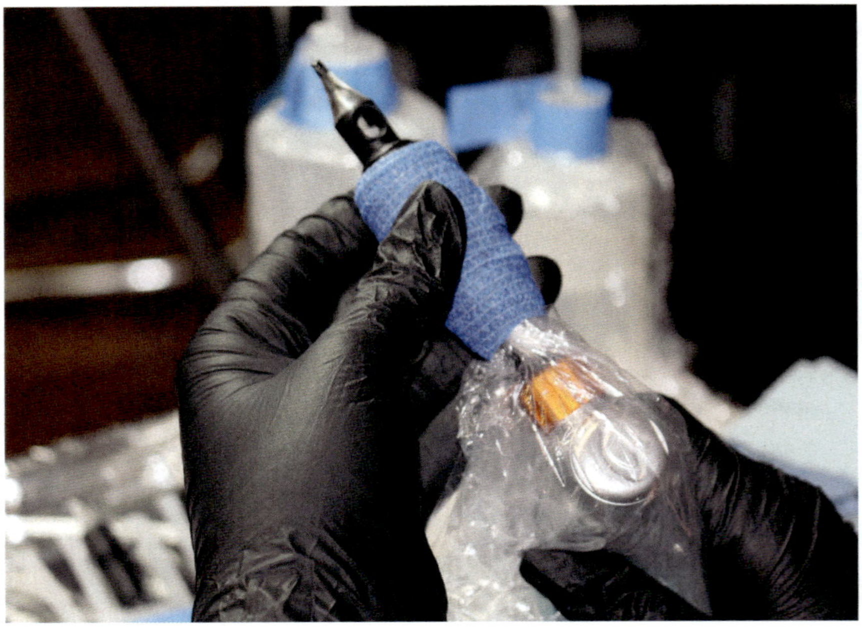

Stretching the Skin

When tattooing, the machine is held very much like a pencil or pen and the side of the hand--partly the heel of your hand and partly side palm--rests on the skin, forming what is known as "the bridge". This creates a solid foundation for swiveling the wrist while the hand and fingers do the work.

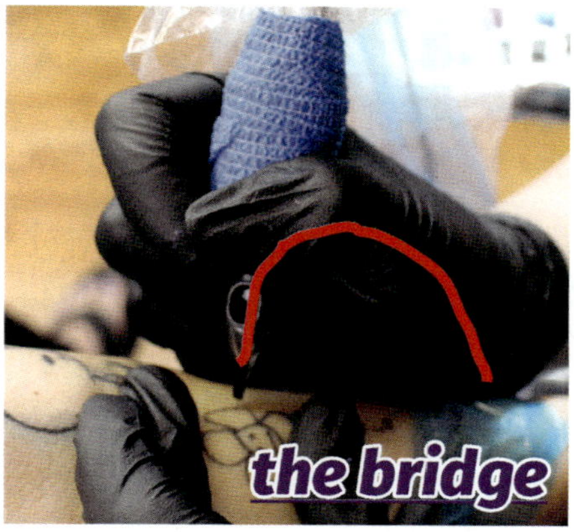

But, skin is very elastic and must be stretched to apply a tattoo and get the needles to penetrate the skin properly. The skin must be stretched tight enough to keep your needles from bouncing or getting stuck in the skin. When the skin is not stretched adequately the linework will not come out with precision and the shading and color work can look patchy and blotchy.

Think of creating a taut canvas in the area you will be tattooing. Your non-machine hand will provide most of the stretch, with the side palm of your tattooing hand assisting. This is commonly called the "3-point stretch". The heel and side palm of the tattooing hand forms one point and the thumb and middle finger of the non-machine hand make up points two and three.

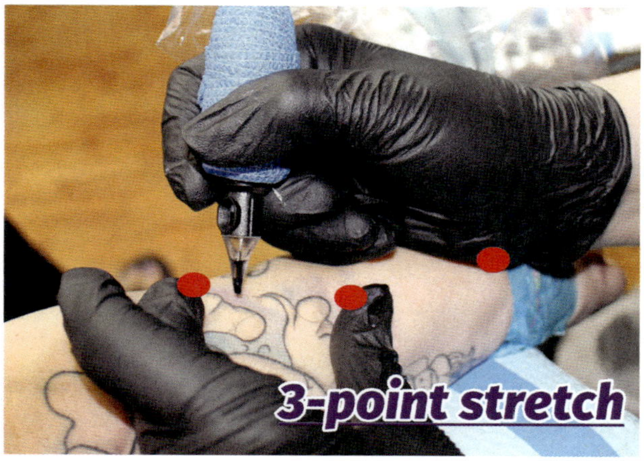

The thumb and middle finger of the stretching hand spread in opposite directions on the skin, and the side palm helps tighten the skin. The heel and side palm of machine hand will be stretching in the opposite direction.

The ring and pinkie fingers of both hands will usually be curled under and resting on the skin along with the side palm.

Typically, when there is solid bone backing the skin, such as the forearm, it is much easier to get the ink in with less stretch. But in some areas of the body, such as hips or stomach, this stretch can be more difficult. Your non-machine hand will be getting more of a work-out. If your non-machine hand has a tough time stretching in a particular area, use a dry paper towel as additional gripping power or ask a second person to wash hands, glove-up and help stretch.

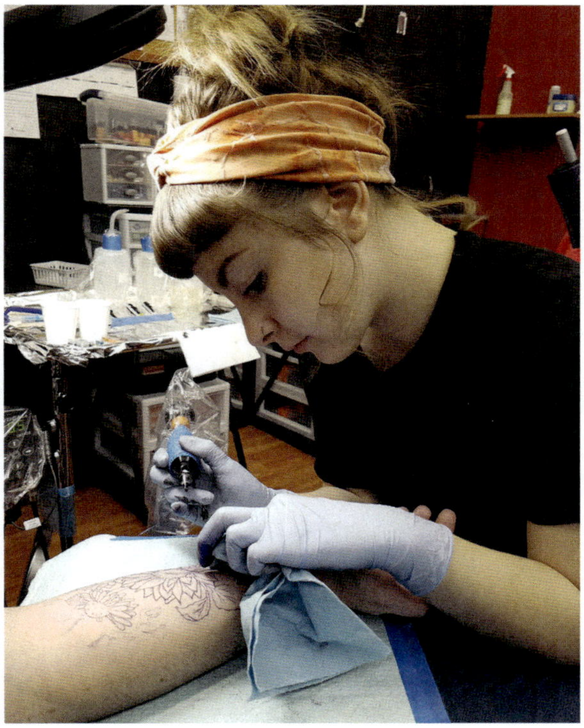

To improve your ability to stretch without tiring out, work on a flat surface, such as a massage table, where you can rest your arms to help you remain steady. In addition, client should have proper support so that when you push into their skin with the machine, they are not being pushed away from you.

Lining

Your lines are the foundation for building the rest of the tattoo design.

The first step in starting to line is adjusting your needle to stick out from the tube so you can clearly see the tip of the needle.

NOTE:
There is much discussion these days regarding tattoo work done with no hard lines or no black. The reason that most tattoos have black outlines is that black holds up in the skin better over time and keeps edges and values looking sharp as the tattoo ages. The debate over the longevity of "painterly" style tattoos rages on. Only time will tell.

The next step is dipping the needle into the ink, pulling it away from the ink cup, and then running the machine for a couple seconds to draw the pigment into the reservoir. (If you are using continuous "on" setting on your power supply, be careful not to hit your needle on the bottom of ink cup. This could dull the needle tip.) This reservoir of ink should provide you with enough pigment to get through about 1 ½ - 2" inches (or 3 – 5 cm) of tattooing before needing to dip again.

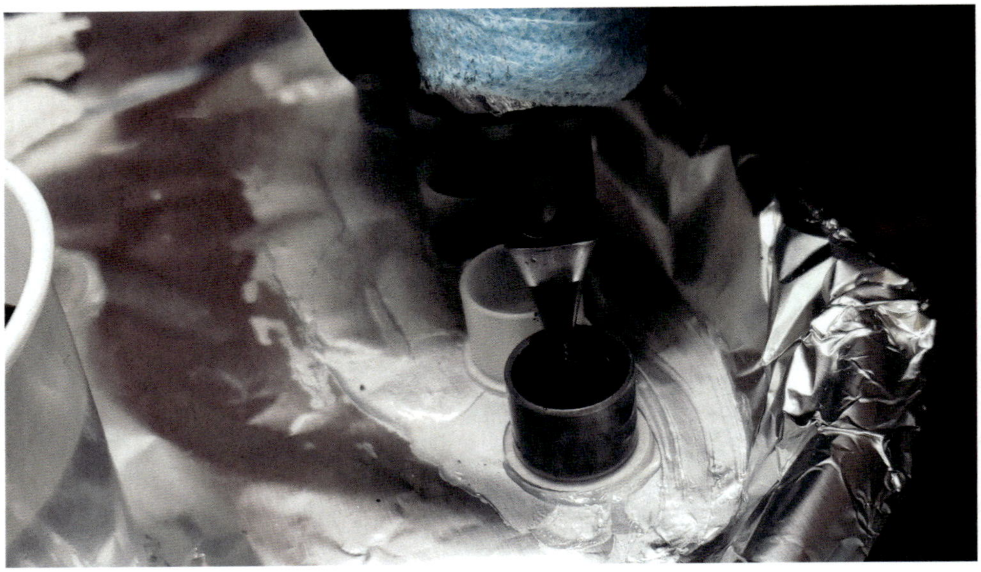

While tattooing a line, try to maintain one continuous long motion. Hesitation or inconsistent depth will cause you to have wobbly or sketchy lines. Some beginners tend to press too hard at the beginning of a line, then lighten up their hand as they move along the length. This will cause a blob or dot that is difficult to fix without the need to make the entire line thicker to cover the mistake.

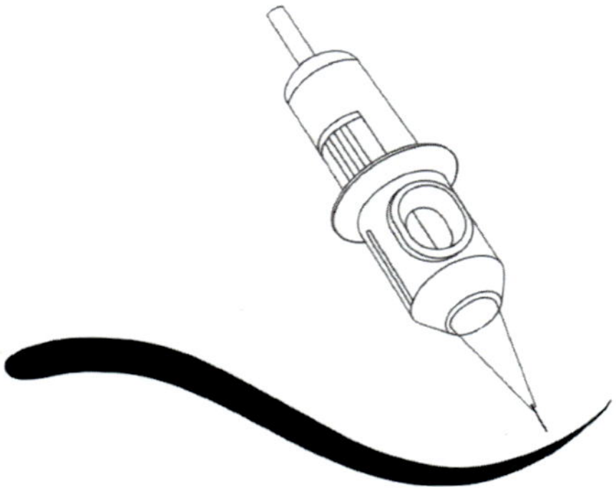

Remember: it is your job to **guide** the machine along the skin, as it does much of the work for you. Your goal is to maintain a steady hand, steady angle, steady pressure and steady focus.

The need to lift the machine and dip it in ink makes doing long lines and perfect circles or geometric shapes more difficult. If you think in terms of starting lightly back in the existing line, then press a bit harder as you come out of the existing line, it will make the continuous line look smoother and avoid blobs.

When finished with the whole outline, wipe the entire design with a clean, moist paper-towel and check your lines for any irregularities or missing parts then go back and touch them up carefully.

Indications that you are tattooing at the correct depth:

- You watch the needle tip carefully and can see it going into the skin at an even depth.
- Ink is not oozing back out of the puncture hole.
- You can feel a steady vibration in your non-tattooing hand.
- Bleeding and plasma seeping are minimal.
- Client is not in excessive pain.
- Needle moves smoothly through skin with no skipping or snagging.
- Color is solid, stable and smooth.

Remember that when lining a tattoo, the goal is a single pass so as not to overwork. If you need to touch up lines that are too light, two passes are okay, but use caution; if you go over a line too many times, the ink will likely fall out later or the skin could scar.

"Art washes away from the soul the dust of everyday life."
~Pablo Picasso, artist

Each time you go over the line you risk it getting thicker than you want. Using a smaller liner needle grouping than your original liner to "tighten" up, or smooth the wobbly parts, is a skill worth learning.

Shelly's Sidenote

I'VE GOT THE POWER!

When teaching beginning tattooers using the power supply that we provide, I've found a voltage of 8.5 covers generally all the basic lining, shading and filling. This average setting forces the student to learn their most effective hand speed and pressure without messing around with power much. Once they gain some confidence, I let them experiment with the power--generally faster for shading, larger needle groups, leathery skin and quick lining, and slower for solid fill, smaller needle groups, eyebrows/eyeliner, soft skin and stipple shading.

Knowing when to turn your power up or down comes with cautious experimentation. Remember, that when you adjust the power supply setting you must compensate by adapting hand speed, pressure and hand movement to avoid damage to the client's skin.

Tips on Great Linework:

- Breathe normally. Beginning tattooers tend to hold their breath, especially during line work. Try to relax and release your tension

- Take your time and move at a comfortable pace. If you line too fast the line will be thin and may not stay in the skin. The slower the pace, the thicker the line. Keep hand speed as consistent as possible to maintain line width. Adjust hand speed as you move along depending on what kind of lines you wish to produce.

- Focus closely on where the needle is going into the skin. Be sure you can see very well. Use good lighting, a head lamp, magnifying glasses or getting close in on the design. Whatever it takes.

- Firmly plant your hands. Lining is mostly in the fingers. The arm doesn't move much, and the wrist will pivot. If you can't reach an area, stop and move your hand. Be sure your tattoo hand is steady (the bridge) and skin firmly stretched BEFORE you set the needle down (3-point stretch).

- Use the middle finger of tattooing hand under the grip to steady the machine.

- In general, pull the needle towards you versus pushing the needle. This provides a steadier pass.

- Keep your machine at approximately a 75-80 degree angle to the skin--not quite straight up and down, but slightly off from straight. (If the needle penetrates the skin perfectly straight the ink tends to push back out of the puncture hole.) →

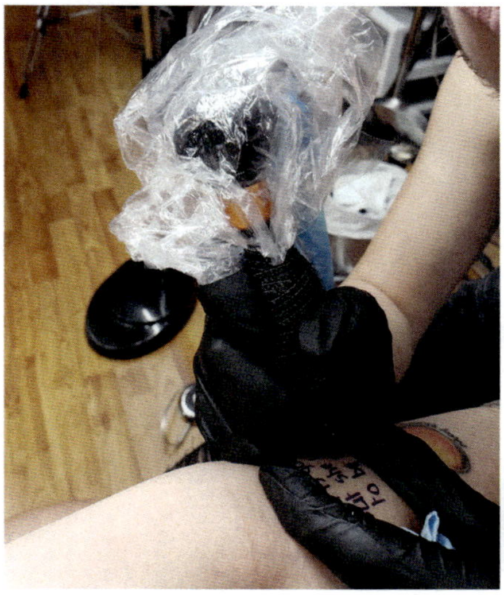

75 - 80 degree angle. for lining

- The bigger the lining needle size, the easier it is to make straight lines. Smaller needle groups tend to be tricky, as they take less pressure to pierce the skin, and tend to be harder to control. A 7-liner is a good solid starter needle.

- Wrap your grip (over your barrier plastic) with self-adherent bandage or medical tape so your gloved fingers don't slip. You can also use a disposable grip. →

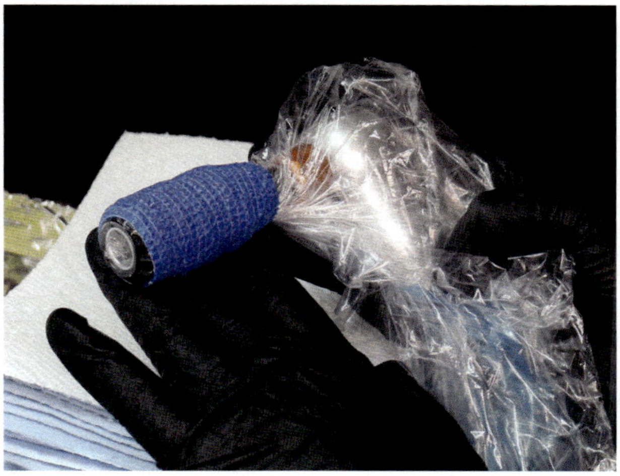

- Consider using a sketching or small circle motion on areas of loose skin or to thicken lines. This takes careful practice.

- Always keep your needle wet with ink.

- Make sure you are not running out of ink towards the end of a line.

- Practice drawing with a grip on your pen or pencil similar to the

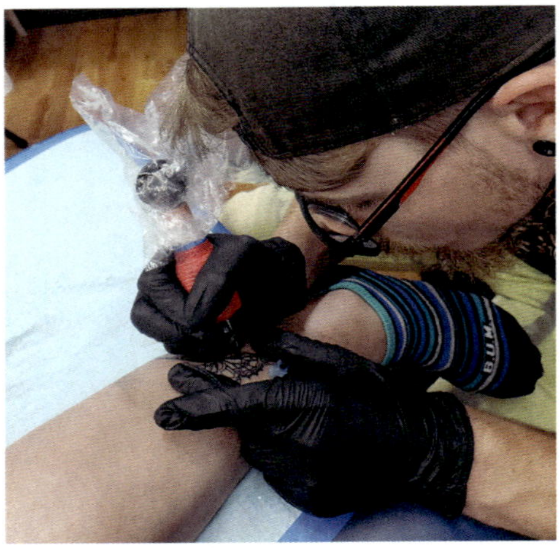

size of your machine grip.

- Check hand speed: too fast and the line won't go in, too slow and it might be too thick. Check depth: Do you need to push harder or lighten up? It also depends on the area you are tattooing on the body.

- Stretch the skin very firmly. If the skin looks bouncy, you need to stretch even more. The area between your fingers should be smooth, taut and firm, like a tiny canvas.

- The thumb and middle finger of stretching hand should not be too far apart, maybe a 2" – 3" spread. And stretch these two fingers in the direction you are tattooing.

- When the stretch and depth are correct you can feel the vibration in your non-tattooing hand.

- Keep your eye on the TIP of the needle, not the tube.

Note: Occasionally you may see a tattooer grip the underside of an arm or leg with the non-machine hand, pulling the skin tight in an attempt to stretch a challenging spot, but this tends to unevenly stretch the skin resulting in wobbly or weak lines.

Solid Fill

Solid black fill typically comes before shading and solid color fill typically comes after shading. For solid color or solid black, hand speed is much slower, circles or scrubby motions are smaller and a steady even pace is desired to avoid patchy spots.

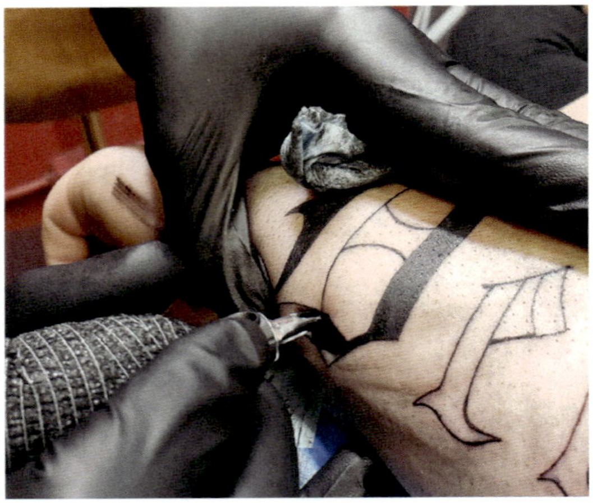

Tips on Solid fill:

- In general, tattoos that have a larger variety of colors will take longer as you will need to rinse between colors more often.

- Solid color will be accomplished with small overlapping circles, and slower hand speed. Some lighter colors may require more passes than darker colors.

- Be conscious of overworking. Some colors, such as yellow, may require more than one session to obtain the brightness you desire.

- If you continually get holidays in your solid black or color work, you can try slowing your hand speed down even more.

- Remember: slow overlapping small circles. Think of making rows of small circles and slightly overlapping the last row. Kind of like mowing a lawn, where you overlap the last row of grass slightly. Filling large areas of solid black or color can be tedious, but "slow and steady wins the race".

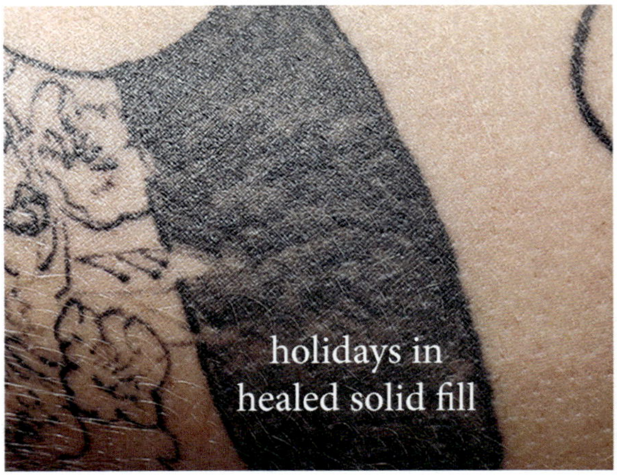
holidays in healed solid fill

Note: "Holidays" or patchy spots in solid fill, will be more obvious once the tattoo is healed.

Shading

When you see an object or creature in the real world, there is a play of shadow and light which makes them look three-dimensional and real to our eyes. Using a variety of grey washes (i.e. blacks that are watered down to different value levels) will help achieve the depth and contrast needed to convey this sense of reality.

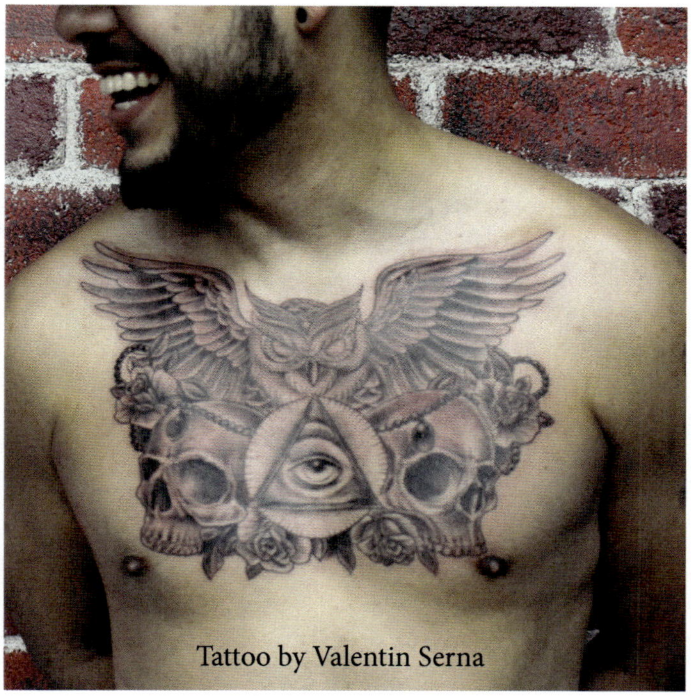

Tattoo by Valentin Serna

In addition, shading can be done with a combo of grey and color, or complimentary colors mixed together to create interesting grayish shadow effects.

Typically, after the outline and solid black fill comes shading. Even with a brightly colored tattoo, artists will do gray shading as the next step.

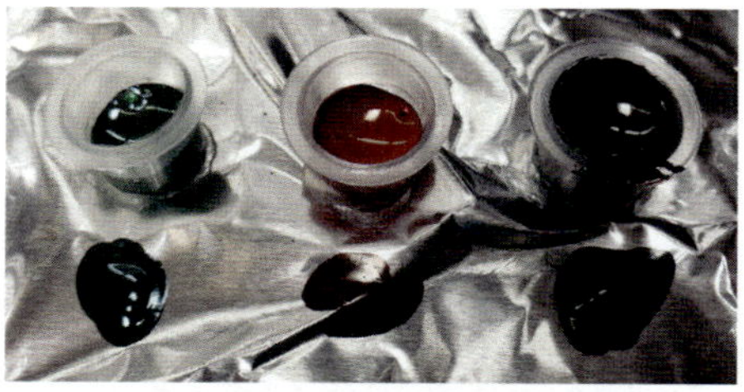

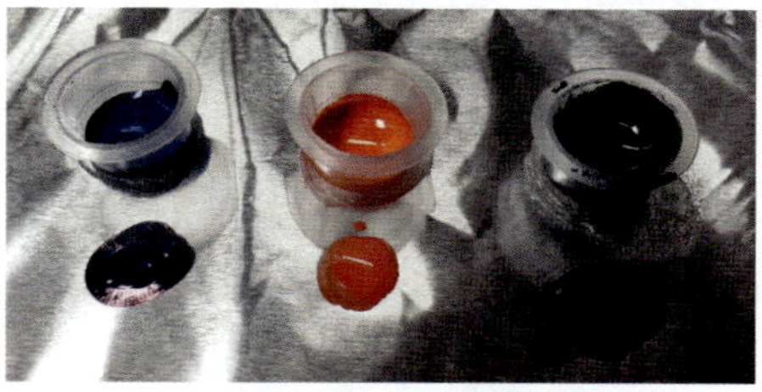

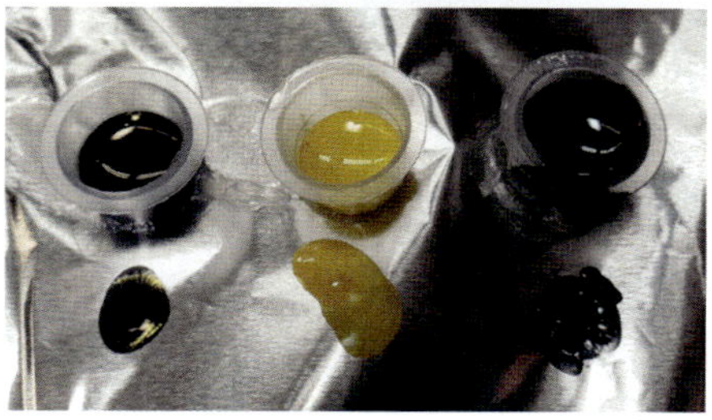

Try mixing complimentary colors green and red, blue and orange or purple and yellow together to make grays. This works especially well in areas of the tattoo that will be getting color over the shadows.

Also try varying the ratios to create the gray scale that will work best in your composition.

Lastly, you can add equal amounts of blue, red and yellow together to make a nice neutral gray.

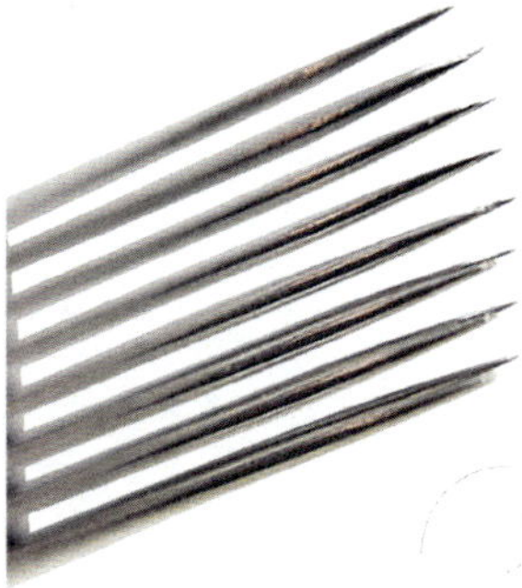

You can almost think of shading as using your needles like brushes, such as a painter choosing a variety of sizes and techniques to achieve the desired effect. Some shading needle configurations are round, some are flat, and some are curved. You'll need to try out each type to discover what works best for you.

Adjustment of tattooing technique, needle depth and hand speed will apply to individual needle groupings and understanding will come with practice. In general, needles will be set out around 1/16" or 1.5 mm but you'll need to experiment to get the right set for your desired outcome.

When shading a tattoo, you can go over the same area of skin multiple times to build up the saturation because you are not pushing into the skin as deeply as you do when lining and your hand is almost constantly in motion. Hand speed is quick, almost brushing the pigment into the skin.

In general, when grey shading, you may make three to six faster passes but please watch carefully until you figure this out for yourself. You must still be cautious of overworking, as too many deep passes can cause damage and create scarring. Overworked skin will take on an almost velvet looking texture.

Shelly's Sidenote

MAPPING IT IN

Even if you are planning on a design that is not "hard-lined" (i.e. done with a bright black outline), it is generally helpful to outline the tattoo in a light grey line to get your lines in before the stencil disappears—I call this "mapping it in". It is also helpful to outline different areas of the tattoo according to the value of coloring or shading it will receive, for instance, extra light grey for light areas or mid-tone grey, for areas that will be medium to dark green or blue, with no black outline.

This mapping is very effective if you are doing a large tattoo piece in multiple sessions but wish to get the line-work done in one sitting. After the lines heal, and the client comes back in, you can simply focus on shading and coloring. Just be sure if you use extra light greys, that they come back within two or so weeks, as these lines could fade completely if more time passes.

Start with the black or darkest areas of shadow first and work your way out to the lightest. Shading is accomplished with sweeping, brushing, "scrubby" or circle motions.

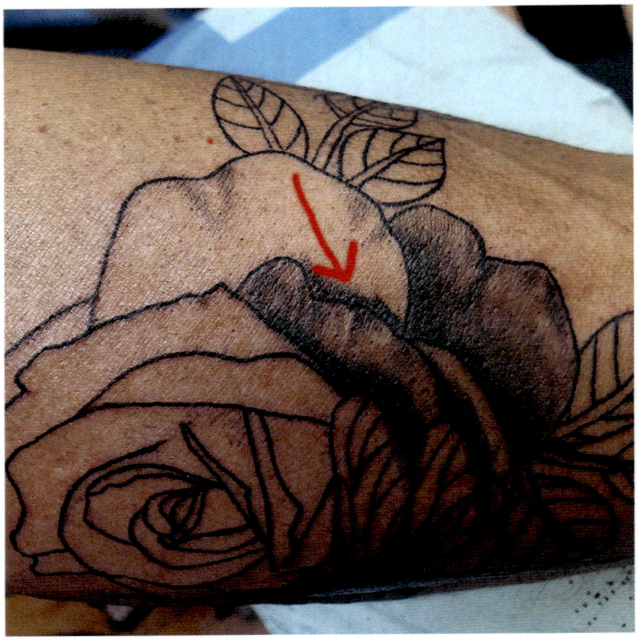

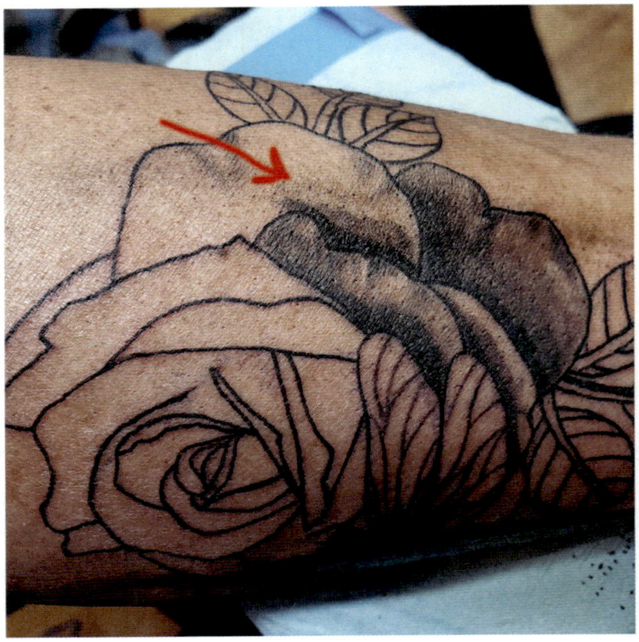

As you move toward the lighter area, you sweep the needles up off the skin to lighten the value. You will press a little harder where you want the value darker and reduce the pressure as you move to lighter areas. In addition, you will slow your hand speed

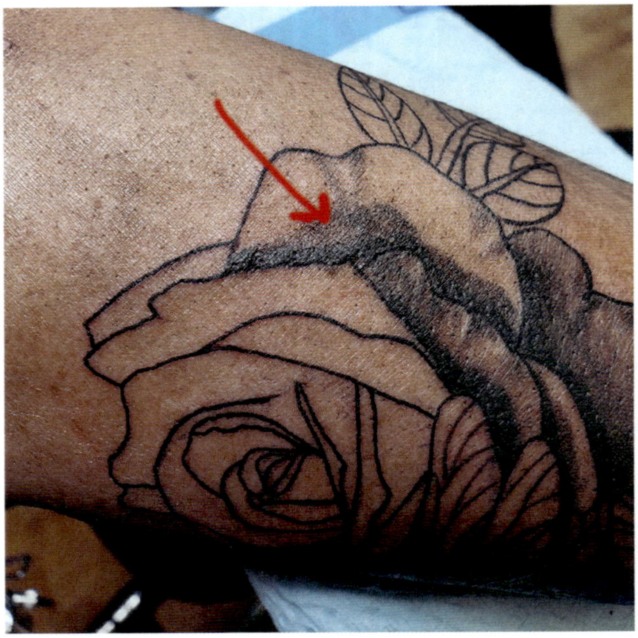

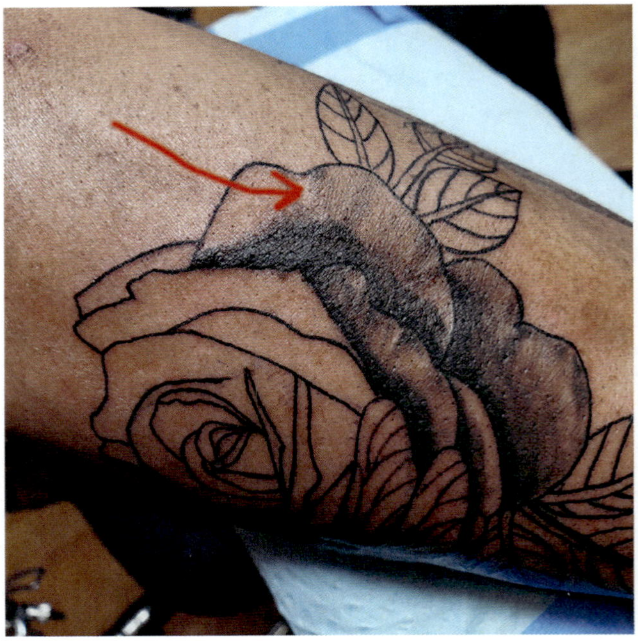

down to accomplish darker values and speed your hand up to accomplish shading that is wispy and light.

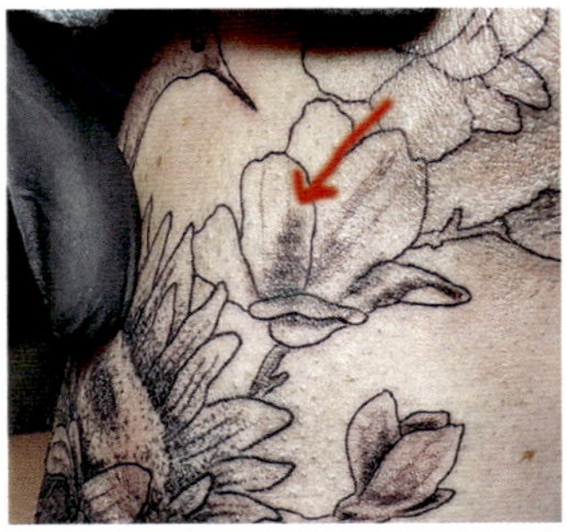

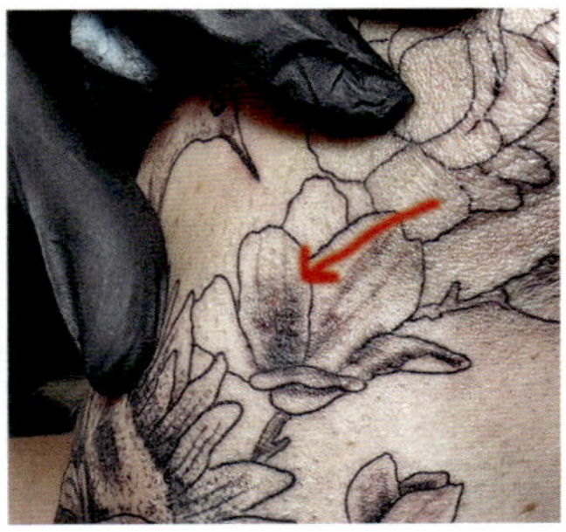

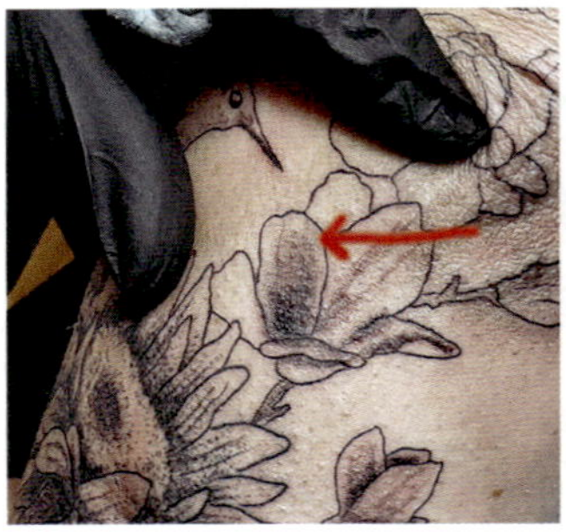

As you experiment with different types of shading, you should adjust hand speed up or down, adjust pressure harder or lighter, and change the depth of your needles slightly in or out to avoid overworking skin. As everyone's technique of using the machine is slightly different, you'll practice until you find what works best for you.

> "This world is but a canvas to our imagination."
> ~*Henry David Thoreau, Poet*

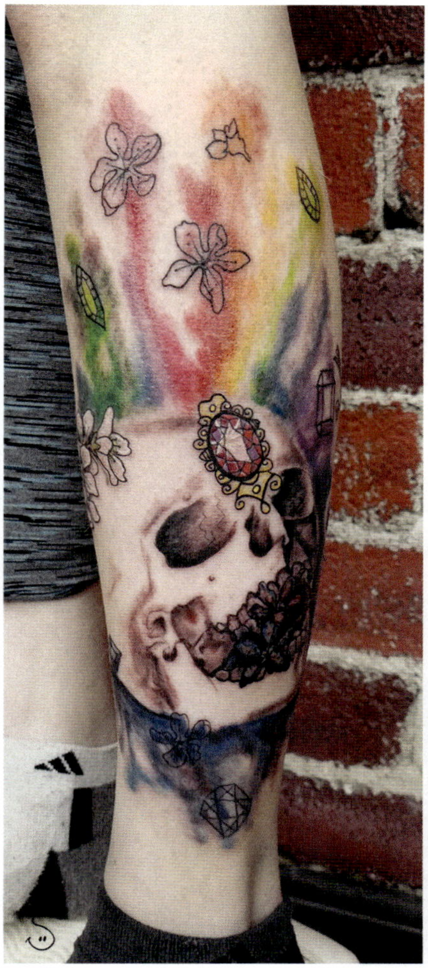

The tattoo at left uses gray mixed with dark blue, for the shading, which helps blend the blues through the bottom of the tattoo and inside the mouth of the skull. Also, adding darker colors to your grays can give you more variety of grays to choose from.

Think of gray shading under the color as darkening the value of the color, such as drawing on toned paper. This helps you use a full range of values.

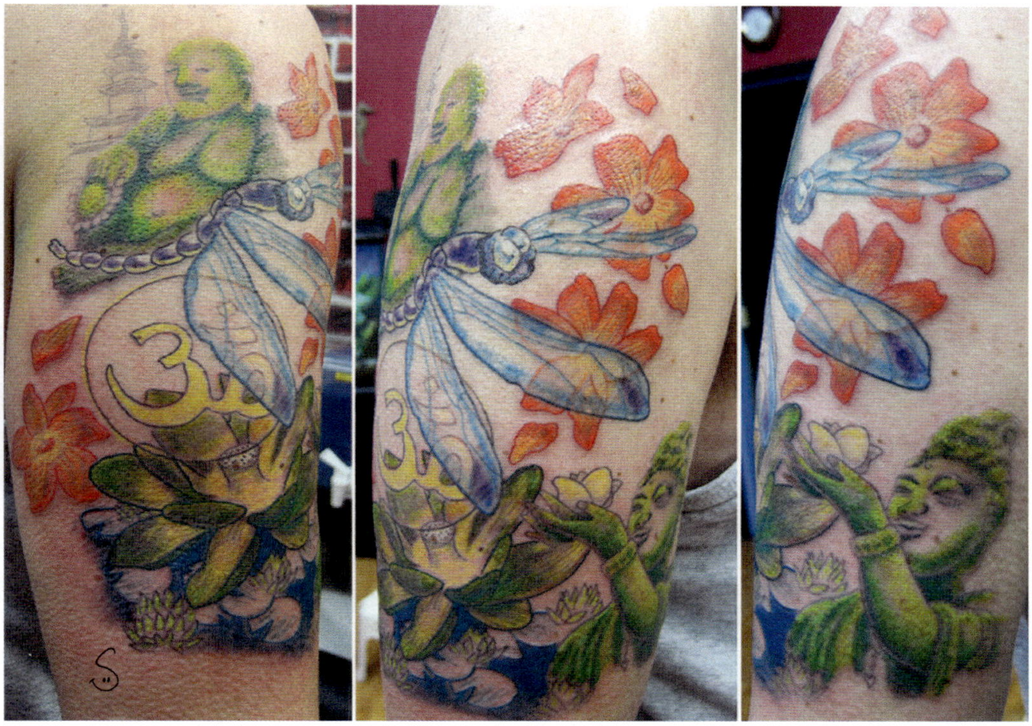

Also using a variety of darker colors to shade, instead of just grays, can create effects in a tattoo design such as skin tones, textures, muscle shapes and lowlights.

Be aware; if there is not enough contrast in your tattoo designs, they will not hold up as well. The dragonfly tattoo compostion above will likely end up with not enough contrast over time and will need more darks added later.

THOUGH TATTOOING STYLES, SKILLS OR ARTISTIC THEORY "RULES" CAN BE BROKEN, WHEN IT COMES TO SANITATION AND CLEANLINESS, THESE RULES ARE MEANT FOR THE SAFETY AND HEALTH OF YOU AND YOUR CLIENTS AND MUST BE FOLLOWED EVERY PROCEDURE, EVERY TIME!

The main difference between gray shading and color shading is that the color pigments each have their own unique properties, are generally opaquer and require faster hand motions to get them into the skin effectively without leaving blobs of color.

> "The artist's world is limitless. It can be found anywhere, far from where he lives or a few feet away. It is always on his doorstep."
> ~*Paul Strand, Artist*

Also, the needles are generally set out of the tube a slight bit further than for grey shading.

When working on gradations of gray or color (attempting to blend one tone or color smoothly into the next), your hand speed increases and you use sweeping motions to lighten the current color towards the edge where the color will change. This creates a slight speckled or mottled effect in the skin.

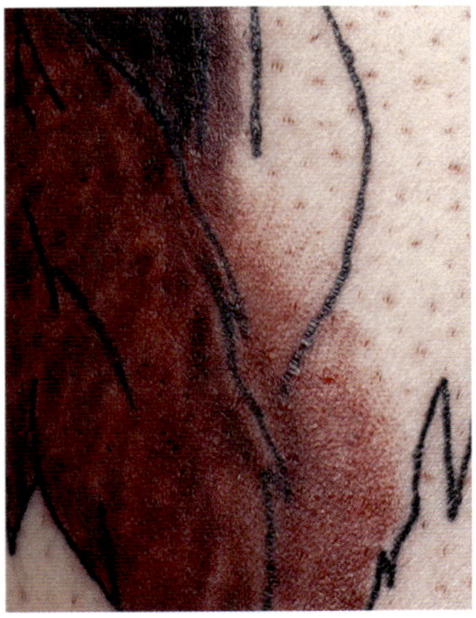

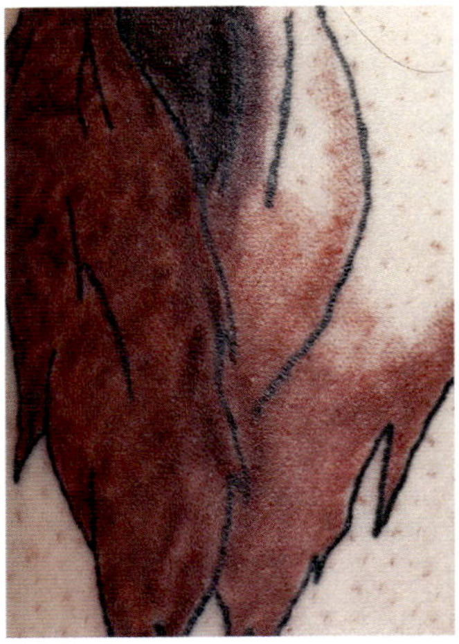

To blend the next color in, start back into the previous color right before the spot where your hand speed increased, and the mottling began.

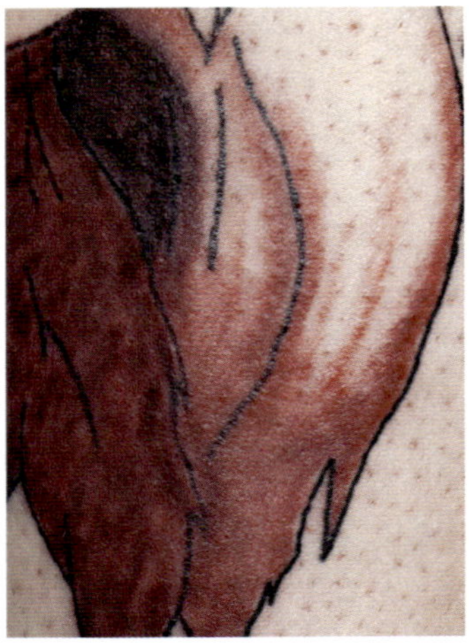

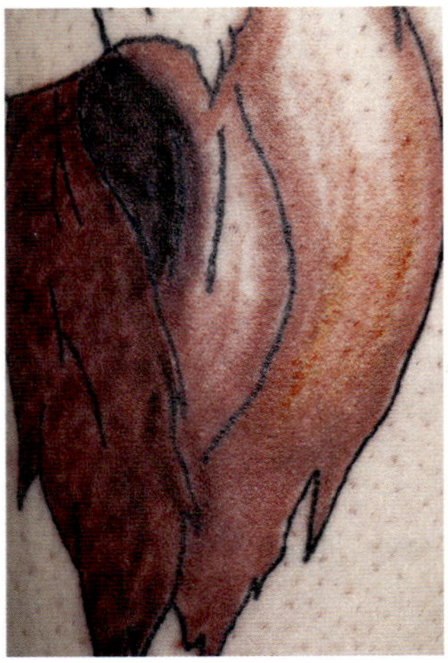

Tips on great shading:

- Use a premixed grey wash set to get the most dependable results. You will quickly learn how each shade of grey heals and you can easily choose the same tones to finish a multi-session tattoo.

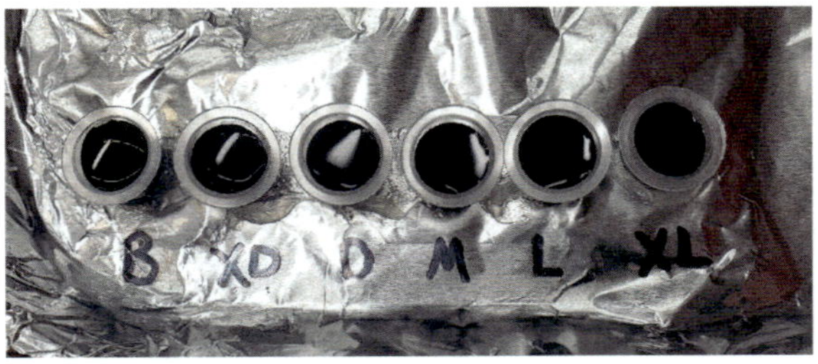

- When tattooing grays, you can think in terms of a black and white photograph. There are generally 5 – 6 main tones of gray that convey the image and you will use a similar palette.
- Lay out your ink cups from darkest to lightest. Label them on your station with a sharpie, if necessary, so you don't get confused, as they will all look like black.
- Choose slightly lighter shades of gray than you think you need when you are first starting out. You won't know how the values of grey are going to heal in the skin until

you've seen it in your own clients. You can always darken a grey later but lightening a too-dark gray is almost impossible.

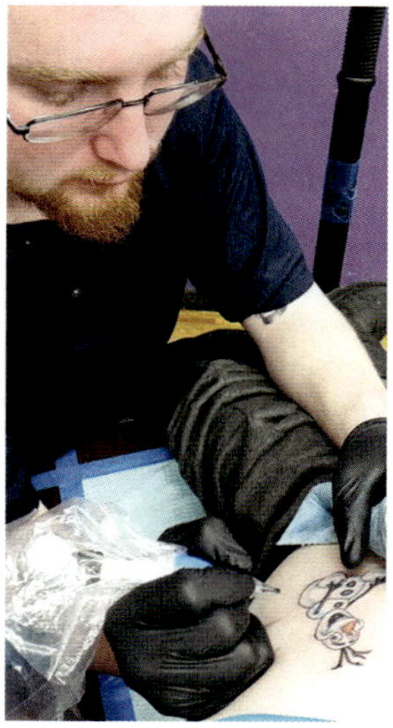

- You can dilute the ink by dipping the needle in your rinse water as you move through the shading. This helps get a smoother gradation, particularly at the edges of where you want the lightest tone--even using the tinted water as your extra light shade.

- Change the angle of your machine to graze the surface of the skin with the needles and make the shading softer. When shading, the machine is angled around 45 degrees. →

- Remember that the skin itself is the lightest value and areas for white highlight must be preserved. You can't go back and add highlights once an area has been tattooed. ↓

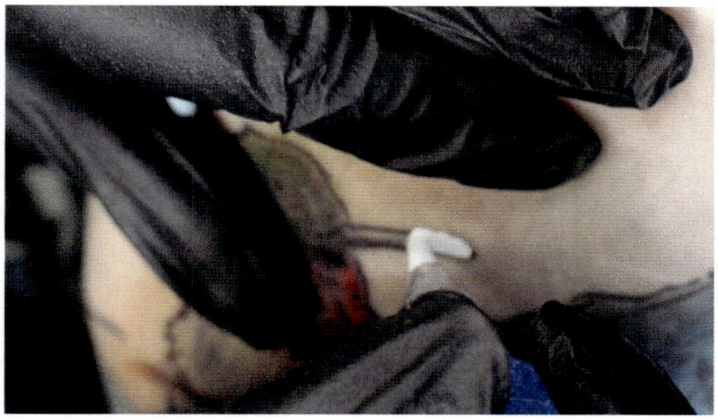

- If your mag needles are causing a choppy or "line-y" look in your shading, try pulling the needles back into the tube a bit more, which allows more ink to flow. You can also try sweeping in slightly different directions rather than the same pattern over and over--think of it like crosshatching.

> "Patience, persistence and perspiration make an unbeatable combination for success."
> *~Napoleon Hill, Author*

- Remember, each client has unique skin and you may need to adjust speed, needle set, voltage or even needle grouping to accommodate the variations in skin types.

- When a black and grey piece is freshly tattooed it will look somewhat reddish brown, or sepia toned. You won't see the actual greys until it is healed.

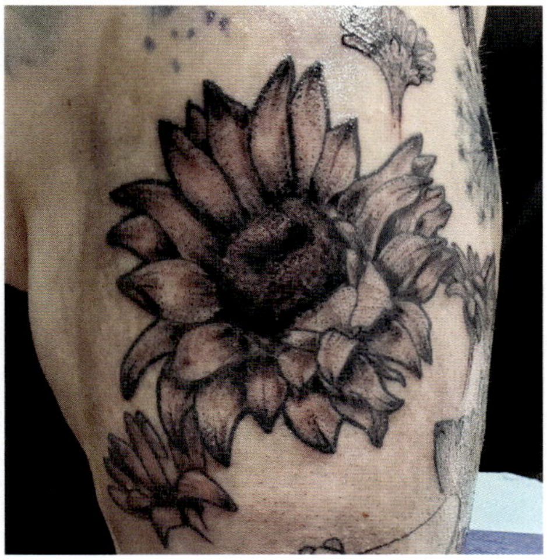

←

- Use high quality needles that give you dependable results. Don't be afraid to pay a little more to get the end results you want.

- Experiment with different stretches in the skin, depending on if you are using a coil machine or rotary. Coils tend to bog down a bit when the skin is loose, while a rotary machine's hit is more consistent. Thus, letting the skin be a bit looser can help give you a softer shade.

- Getting smooth gradations of greys or colors demands practice and patience. Coordinating hand speed, pressure, machine speed, needle groups and characteristics of different colors will require experimentation. →

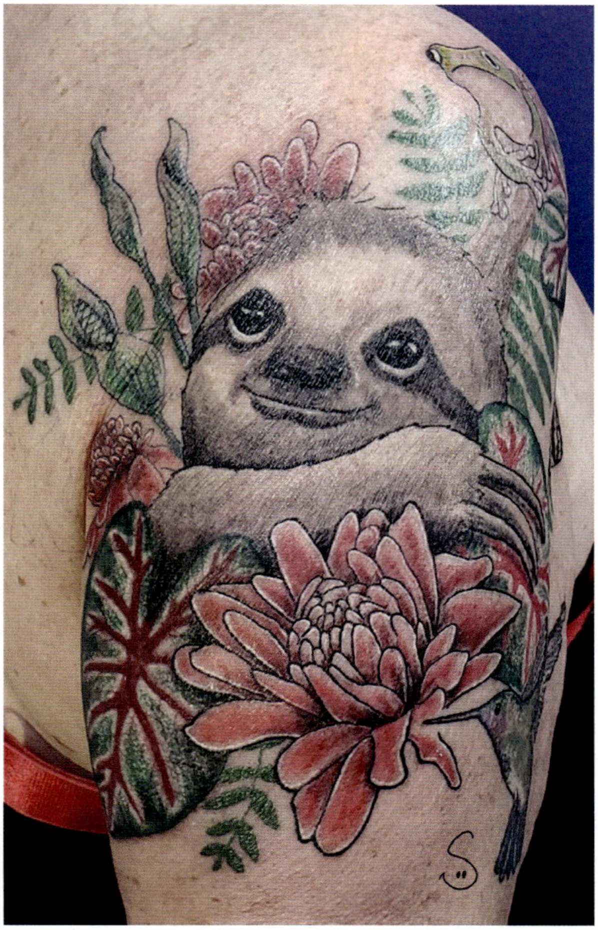

Working with Old Tattoos

One aspect of the tattoo business is cover-ups. But be careful. Cover-ups are much more challenging than tattooing fresh skin, and as a beginning tattooer you could easily get in over your head. The lighter the existing tattoo is the easier it will be to rework and reshape. In addition, some tattoos could just benefit from a "tattoo make-over", (i.e., just refreshing the lines and colors).

And remember that tattoo ink is deposited into the dermal layer of skin. Tattooing over old designs is actually mixing new ink in with ink that already resides in that layer. Thus, the term cover-up is somewhat misleading as its more of a camouflage than an actual covering.

As the newer ink heals, the older ink shows through to some degree, and this is hard to predict in advance. Using black, grey and dark colors will help hide the existing tattoo, but with careful planning you can design a new tattoo using the open spaces and lighter colors of the old tattoo to your advantage.

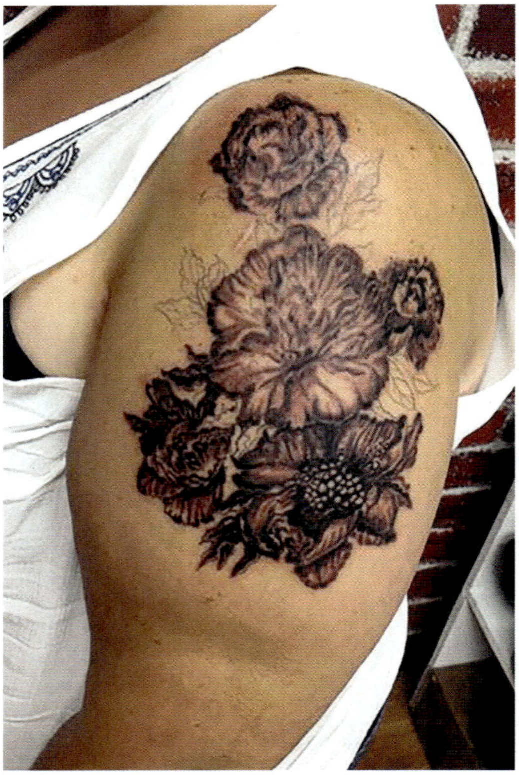

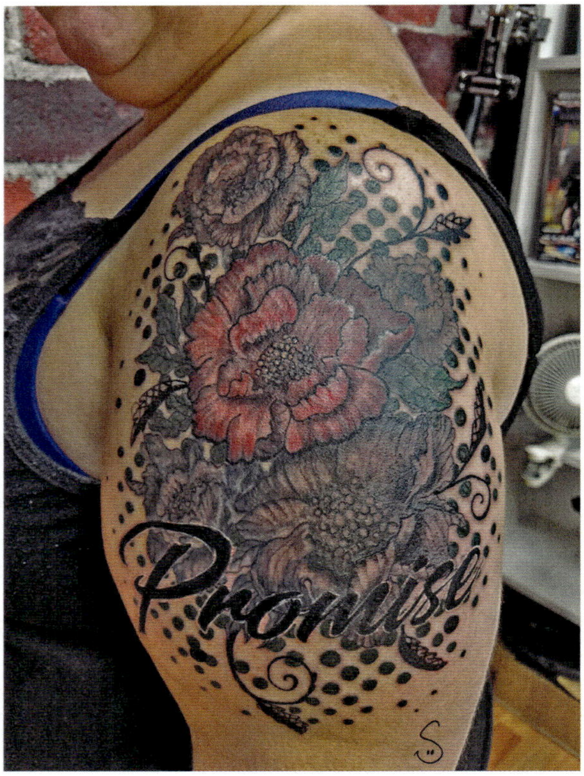

Use tracing paper to trace the old tattoo, put this on a light pad or table, and put a new sheet of paper over the top. Begin sketching new ideas for the design. You could also scan your tracing and put it in a drawing program to experiment with new designs.

Incorporate the existing tattoo shapes and flow in as much as you can. Use texture, contrast, focal point and a range of values to distract the eye from the old piece.

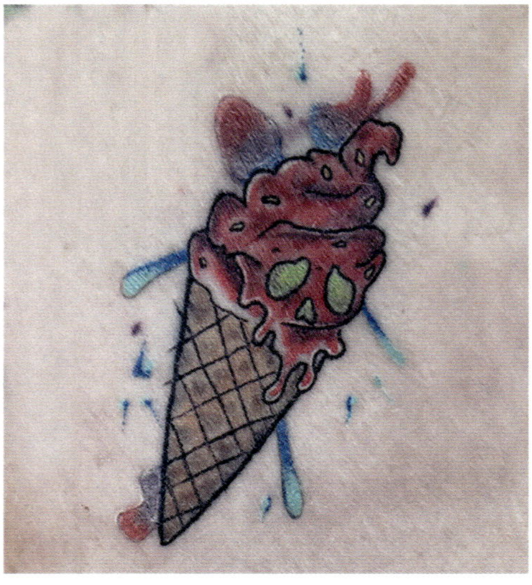

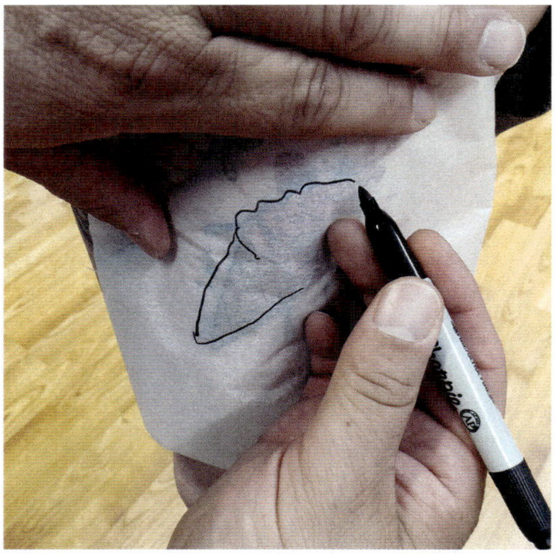

In addition, you could tattoo white over the old color to reduce it's value by about 10%. Sometimes this is just enough to help tone something down. And if it is a multiple appointment large cover piece, you could pack some white in each time, and reduce the value a bit with each session.

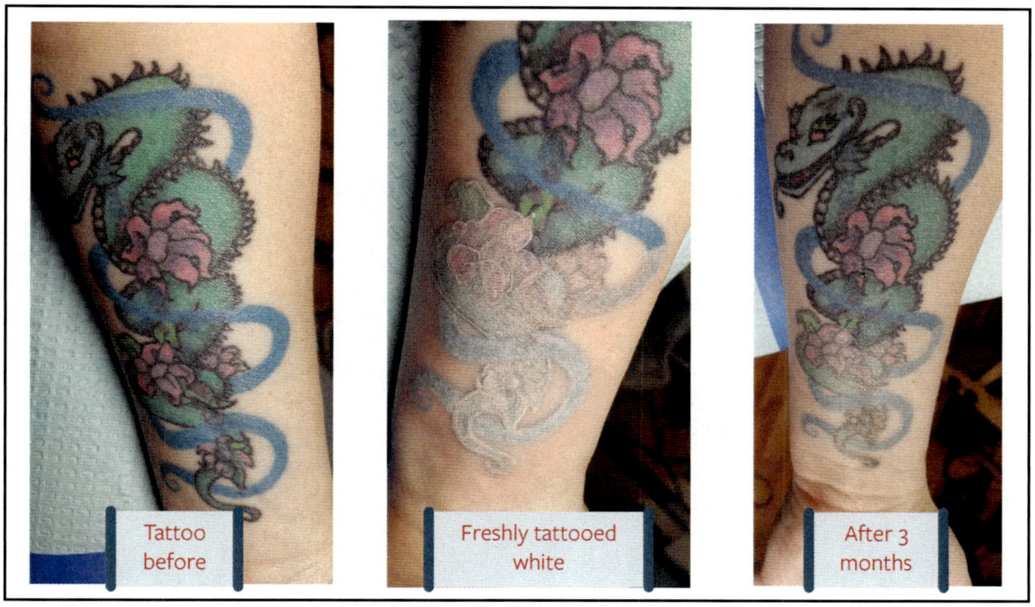

Getting Comfortable

After much experimentation and practice, you will find the pace, the depth, the power setting and the needles with which you feel successful. Most artists have their favorite go-to for each type of tattoo. Be patient. The feeling of being "in-the-groove" will happen over time. Beginners frequently get nervous, as well as upset that they aren't advancing as quickly as they had imagined. When students allow themselves to get tense and overly frustrated, this affects their ability to progress.

Do yourself the favor of making your situation as comfortable as possible and be patient with the time needed to succeed.

Shelly's Sidenote

OVERWHELMED?

I remember learning how to drive a manual car up-hill: push clutch pedal in with left foot, right foot is on the brake, adjust stick with right hand, check mirrors, slowly let up on clutch, don't roll backwards, watch your speed, ease on the gas or the car will stall! How did I ever do that?

Beginning to tattoo is kind of the same thing: hold a vibrating machine, stretch skin just so, fine-tune hand speed, depth & pressure, adjust lighting, watch needle tip, regulate power supply, push foot pedal, dip needle in ink and be nice to your client! I was overwhelmed at first, but with practice it became second nature.

Tips:

- Make your working conditions as ergonomic as possible. Keep your tray or work station as close as possible to your tattooing hand to minimize the reach needed to constantly dip your needles in ink. This eliminates the excessive stretch, which creates unnecessary strain on your shoulder and back.

- You should be well-rested, healthy and comfortable, as you will likely be working for hours at a time.

- The client's comfort is of concern, but YOU being comfortable and in no pain is more important, because you are producing the art they will live with for life. They will only have to be in discomfort for a short period of time. Therefore, allow them to move their limbs or body into positions that help you succeed, even if they are temporarily uncomfortable.

Shelly's Sidenote

PUSH HARDER

The most common thing I say to students when they first start tattooing skin is "push harder". I think it may be the natural reluctance we all have to cause pain to someone else.

Of course, how hard to push into the skin depends on needle size and power supply setting, but, in general, if your lines are weak and faint, this is the problem.

- You should try to get up at least once an hour, even if it is literally to stand-up, roll your shoulders and sit back down, which takes about 10 seconds. Also try and look far away occasionally, to give your eyes a chance to refocus. And every two or three hours you should get up and have a good stretch, walk around, get some water and allow your client to do the same. This doesn't have to take more than 5 minutes. (If your client is a smoker, you will probably notice them get fidgety every couple of hours! Better to let them have their nicotine break then try and work against this.)

- Get a comfortable stool and invest in adjustable tattoo furniture as soon as you can afford it. Having an adjustable table is great for being able to stand up for part of your tattoo. →

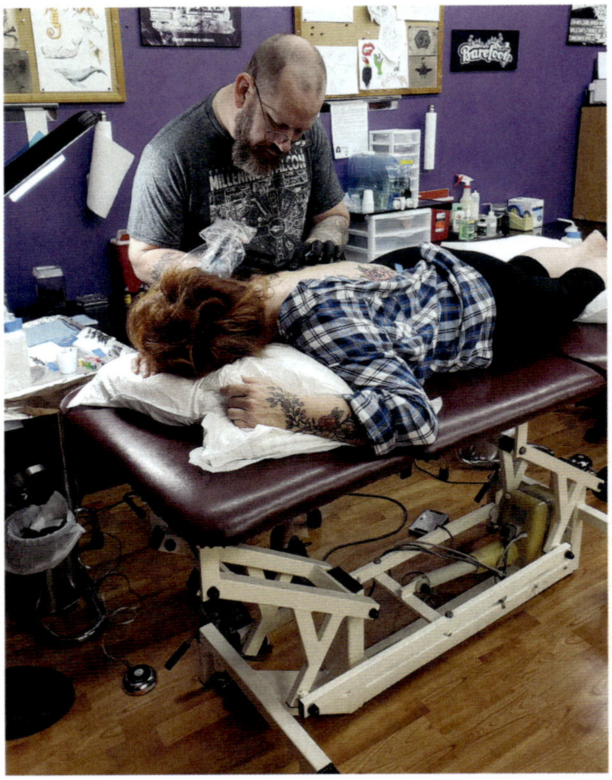

- Make sure you have a great light source. Since your light will be covered with barrier film, you should not be afraid to adjust it as much as needed during the procedure. It is important to see exactly where you are setting the needle down, and much of the time your hands will block the light. Many artists decide to use a headlamp.

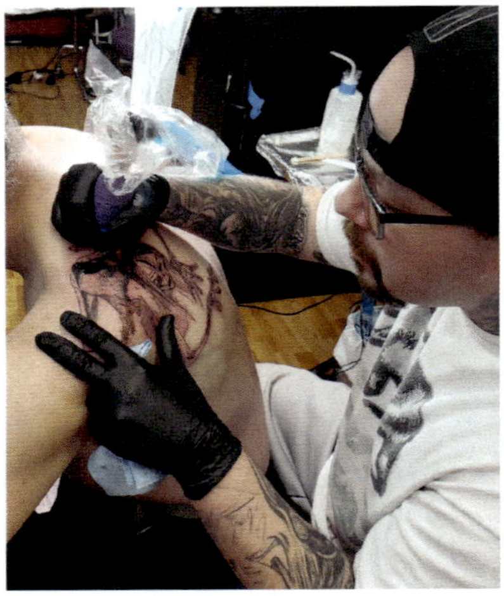

- ← Get in the habit of holding the moistened paper-towel in your non-tattooing hand so you don't have to reach for it

- Don't wait too long to wipe the tattoo. As a beginner, you absolutely NEED to see if your lines are going in correctly. Many students get fearful of wiping their stencil away and keep lining without wiping. This is fine when you have a lot more experience, but at the start of your learning journey, you need to get immediate feedback as to whether your depth and hand speed is correct.

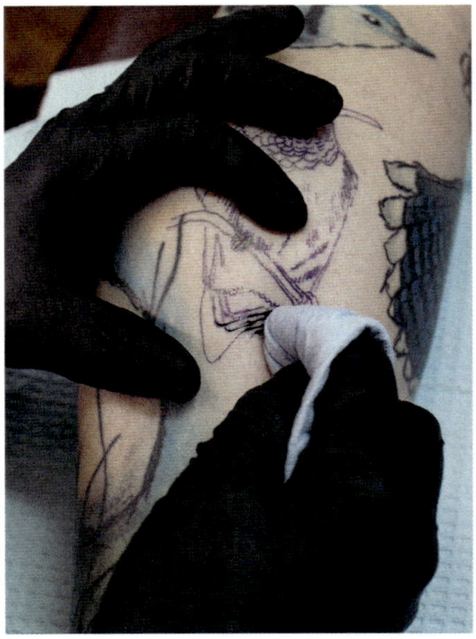

- Set the machine down when needed and wipe tattoo carefully. Tattoo newcomers tend to resist setting the machine down when they are in the groove. Better to set it down, use your dominate hand to wipe very carefully without wiping away the stencil, and then pick it back up. Be sure and face the needle away from you when you place it on your station or tray to avoid injury. →

- Be adamant about having a solid position for your hands BEFORE you set the needle down. Get your hands set, the needle ready and the stretch firm, before you try and tattoo. Beginners tend to start speeding up as they go. If you inadvertently let the skin loose, speed up your hand, lighten your pressure, or allow your hands to block the light where you are trying to tattoo, this will result in wobbly, sketchy or thin lines, and possibly misplaced lines.

- Don't allow your hands to get in an awkward or unstable position. This impedes your ability to press firmly into the skin, and again, results in low quality lines and shading. Move the client's limb or body, get solid with your hands, make sure you can see the tip of the needle and ← then proceed.

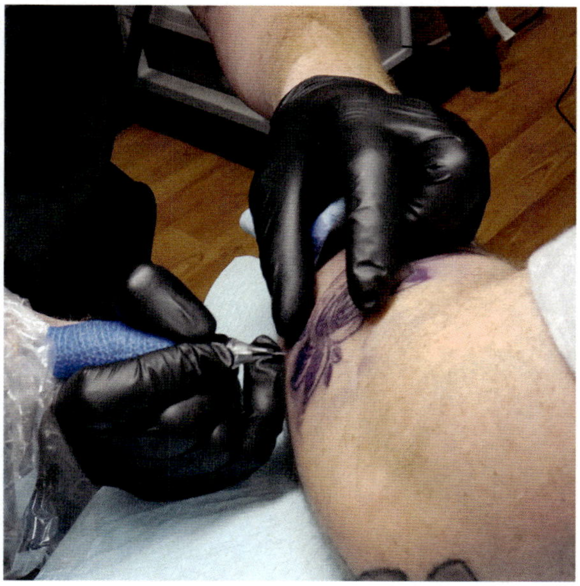

- Some types of skin will easily accept the ink and others will be more difficult. If your client's skin raises, turns red and seems to ooze more plasma than normal, these sensitive skinned folks can be a real challenge to tattoo. Try using witch hazel or cold water on a paper towel to calm parts of the tattoo down between passes. And using a dry paper towel under the side of your stretching hand helps to keep it from sliding too much. →

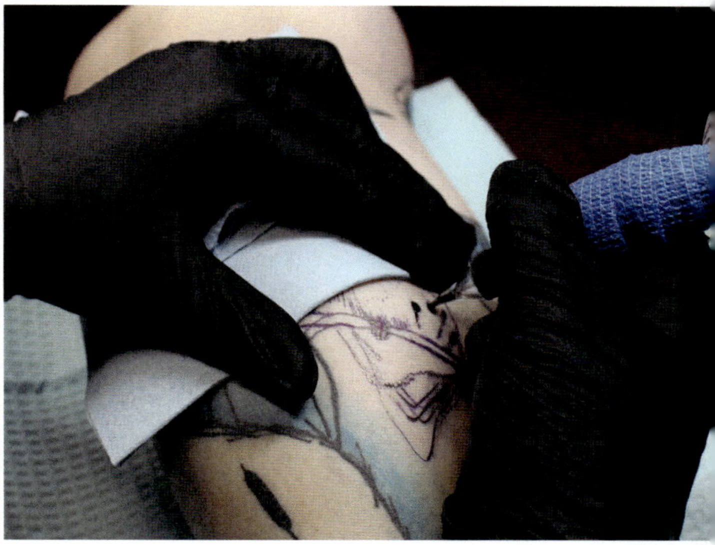

- If you are nervous about losing the stencil, wait a FULL 20 minutes for it to dry. This takes patience but will be worth it to eliminate that pesky worry. And if you do start to lose the stencil, STOP and use a surgical marker to draw your missing elements back in. Don't try to wing it until you have much more experience.

- To access the specific area you are tattooing, sometimes it's best to have a client sitting up, sometimes lying down. Don't be afraid to switch furniture in the middle of a tattoo if something is not working for you or you are having trouble stretching the skin. The more the client can help with the stretch, for example reaching both arms around the chair to make the mid-back taut, the less the strain on your arms and hands.

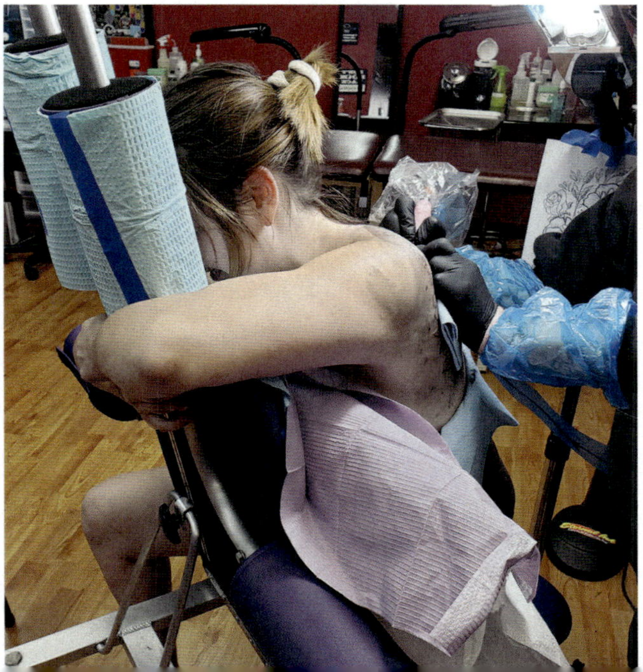

> "Airplanes are off course 99% of the time. The role of the pilot is to continually bring the plane back on course so that it arrives on schedule at its destination. Do as a pilot does. First, determine your destination. Second, you take off toward your destination with no guarantee of success. You must be willing to move out of your comfort zone and take risks continually, even though you know that most of them will not succeed, at least in the beginning. Lastly, be prepared to make continual course corrections. Just as an aircraft faces headwinds, downdrafts, storm fronts, wind shear, lightning and unexpected turbulence, you will experience the same in the pursuit of any worthwhile goal.
>
> *-Brian Tracy, Author & Speaker*

> "Go and make interesting mistakes, make amazing mistakes, make glorious and fantastic mistakes. Break rules. Leave the world more interesting for your being here. Make. Good. Art."
>
> *-Neil Gaiman, Artist*

- Have enormous patience with yourself! During your first months of tattooing you will make mistakes. But getting flustered will only make it worse. Accept that it will happen and make corrections as you go along. Take the time to breathe, relax and analyze what you are doing right! Every time you get a successful line, ask yourself questions such as: "What was my hand doing? What pressure was I using? What speed was I moving at? How was my machine angled? How far out is my needle? What was my stretch like? How was my lighting?" These questions will help you identify your challenges when something is not working well.

- Don't be afraid to STOP. If things are not going well, stop and figure out the problem before continuing, or even reschedule the client if necessary.

Developing your skills requires more than just reading about them in a textbook. It is essential that you have someone show you how to do it properly and professionally. It's crucial to correct mistakes immediately in the beginning of your career to discourage bad habits from becoming ingrained. Beginning to tattoo has a very steep learning curve and requires a multitude of skills, keen awareness of cross contamination, extensive observation, and practice, practice, practice.

Though tattooing is a beautiful artform, it also happens to be a trade where you put yourself and your clients at risk in multiple ways: from something as simple as a bad looking tattoo, to more moderate issues such as scarring, to very serious issues such as transferring a dangerous disease through exposure to bodily fluids.

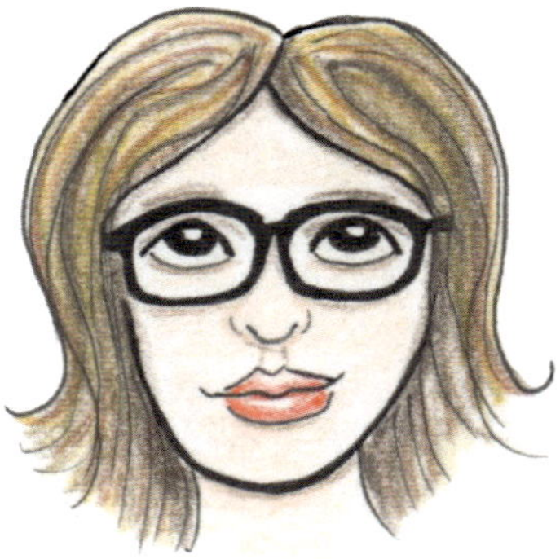

Please be a conscientious tattooer from DAY ONE!

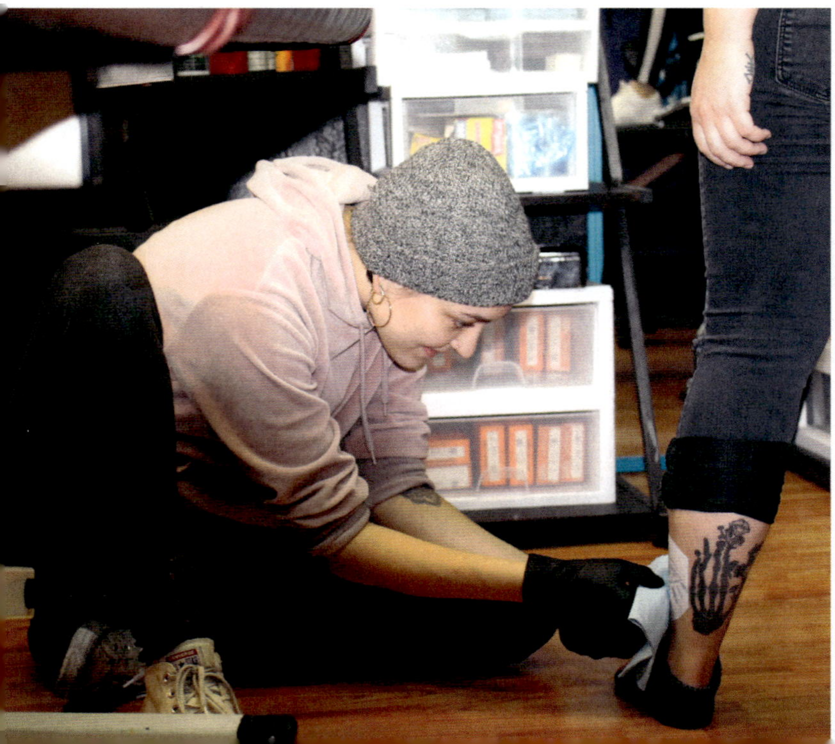

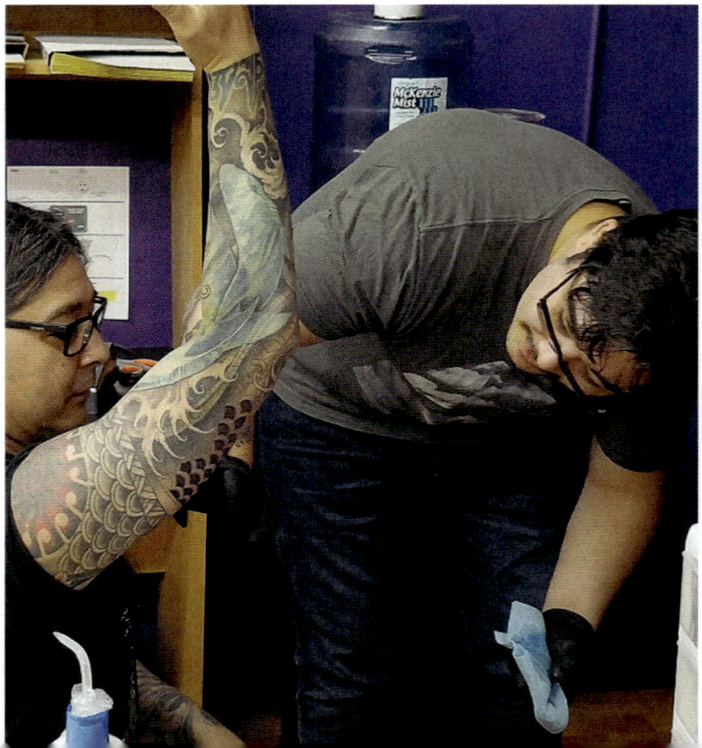

Chapter Nine Highlights

- There is nothing like tattooing real skin.
- Just because you can draw or paint does not necessarily mean you can tattoo.
- Choose your first clients based on their understanding that you are a student or apprentice.
- When placing stencils or drawing on the skin your client should be in a natural and relaxed position.
- It is recommended that beginners choose organic designs for their first few tattoos (meaning free-form and curvy lines) to make it easier.
- Once you touch the needle to the skin the sound of the machine will slightly muffle.
- Pulling lines toward you is generally more stable than pushing the needle away.
- Use white ink at the end to keep it brightest.
- The "bridge" creates a solid foundation for swiveling the wrist while the hand and fingers do the work.
- Think of creating a taut canvas in the area you will be tattooing. This is called the "three-point stretch".
- Your goal is to maintain a steady hand, steady angle, steady pressure and steady focus.
- The goal is a single pass line so as not to overwork the skin.
- The bigger the lining needle the easier it is to make straight lines.
- Tattoos that have a larger variety of colors will take longer to complete.
- You can almost think of shading as using your needles like a paint brush.
- When a black & gray tattoo is freshly tattooed it will appear reddish brown or sepia toned.

Don't worry.

My tattoos don't like you either.

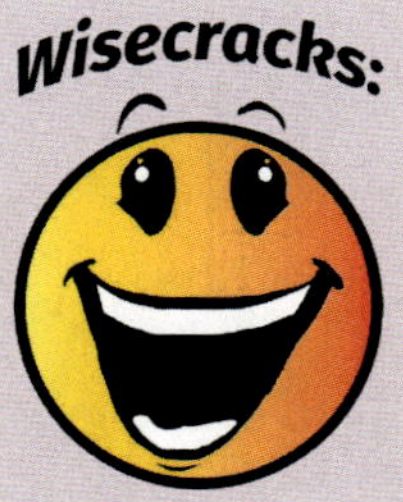

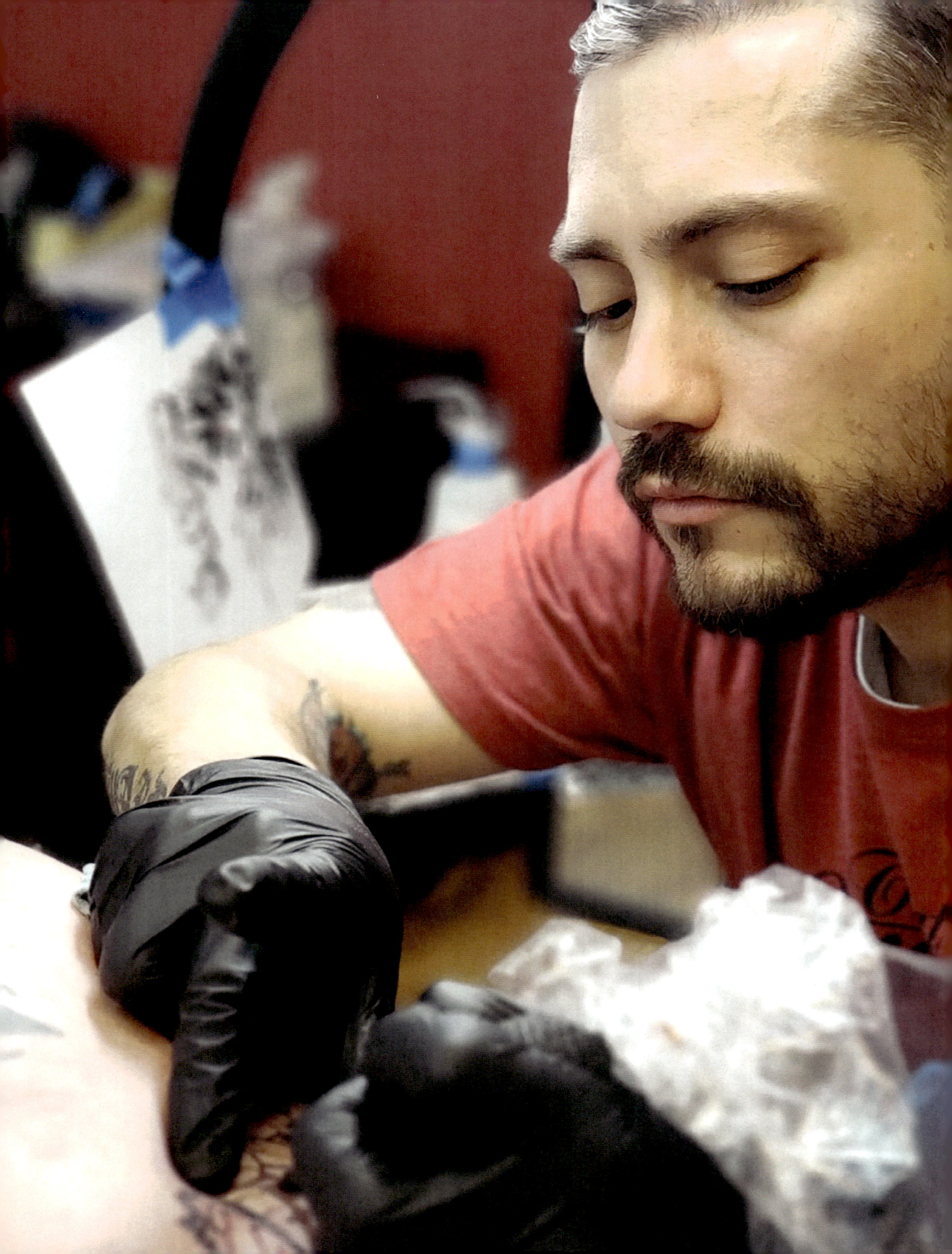

Chapter Ten

Client Services

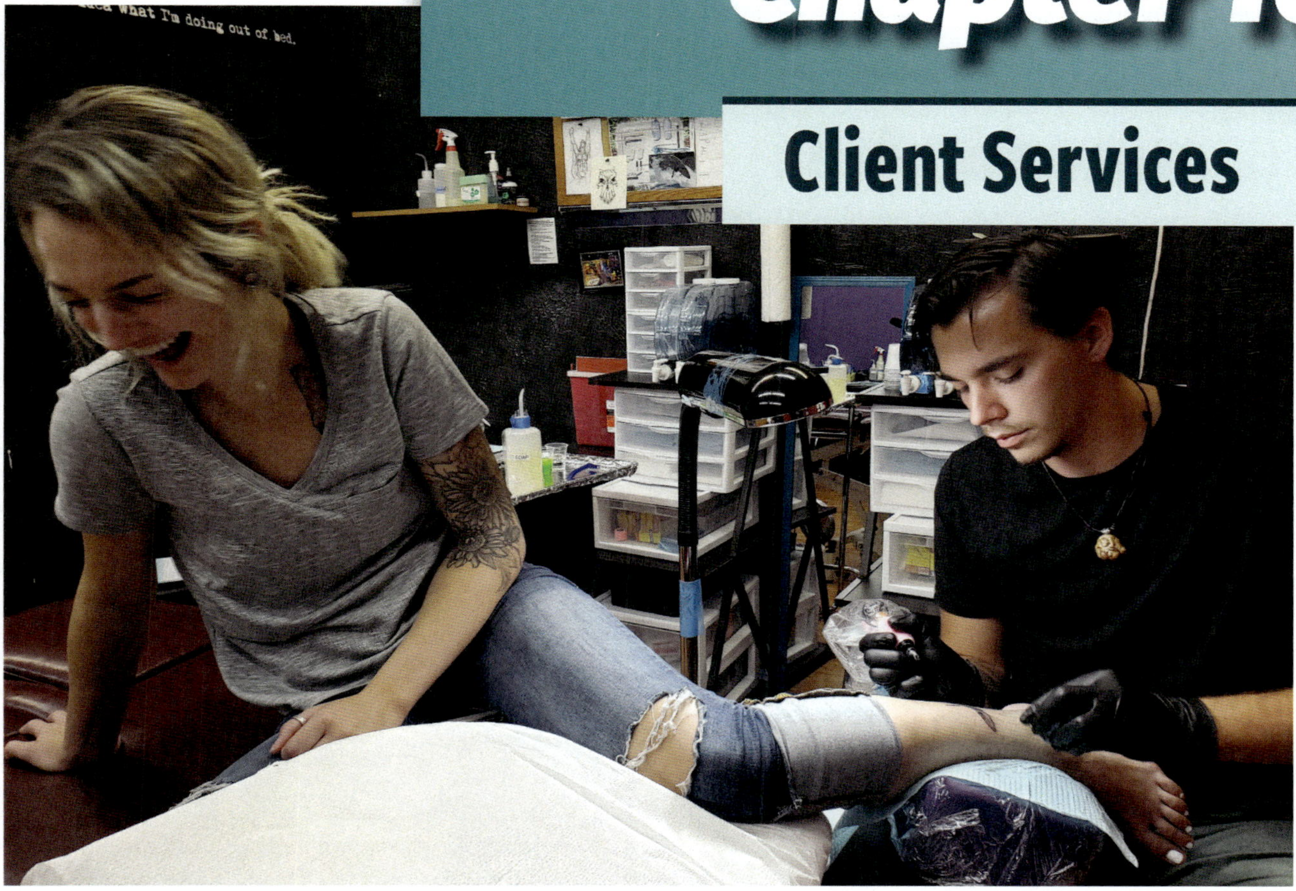

A tattoo studio's clientele is its most vital asset. Clients are essential for tattooing as we need their canvas to produce our artwork! Without customers choosing to spend time and money on your services, our business could not exist. And building a great clientele takes knowledge, experience, an excellent reputation, talent, customer service, marketing skills and incredible patience.

Excellent Client Service

When you satisfy your clients, do great work, treat them with respect and kindness, they will want to do business with you again. They will also recommend you to family and friends. Here are some ideas to increase your skills:

> "I've learned that people will forget what you said, people will forget what you did, but people will never forget how you made them feel."
> *~Maya Angelou, Author and Activist*

- **Be a great listener**: ask questions and focus on what your client is saying. Listen to their words, feelings, tone and watch their body language. Don't assume you know what they are thinking and do consider what is important to them.

- **Be open to their needs and wants**: the reason most people buy services or products is based on emotion, not logic; they want to buy good feelings and a good experience. Communicate with clients regularly.

> "If you don't appreciate your customers, someone else will."
> *~Jason Langella, Marketing Specialist*

- **Be aware**: they pay your bills: in the tattoo business you are there both to serve your client's needs/wants and to have an outlet for your creativity. This is a balance between feeling good about what you provide and fulfilling the client's desires. But always remember in the end, they pay your bills. Listen and lead them into solid decisions that will establish a good relationship between the two of you.

- **Be informative**: take the necessary time to explain how your business works. From making the deposit, to consultation and drawing of the design, all the way through to the end of the tattoo and aftercare. Don't let client's get confused or feel misled. Make it easy for clients to want to work with you.

- **Be sincere**: appreciate your clients, be honest, treat them as important individuals and use their name to address them. Think of ways to compliment and thank your clients often. Clients know when you are sincere and that creates trust. Look for ways to say "yes" to client's ideas, if their requests are reasonable. (This is good advice for your employees as well.)

- **Be open to feedback**: the old saying "the customer is always right" is not a hard and fast rule, particularly when it comes to the subjectivity of art. Yet, the client must be made to feel that they "win" in the end. Apologize if you are late for an appointment and deal with challenges immediately. Value the client's feedback and yes, even criticism. They like to be heard and their opinions valued. In addition, we can learn valuable things when we use their critique to improve. Even if you are having a bad day, take a deep breath, and work to make your client feel comfortable in your studio.

- **Be generous**: what can you do to stand out from the crowd? Make doing business with you easy. Always give a little more than expected to leave your clients feeling happy and satisfied by their visit to your studio. Elevate yourself as a generous and thoughtful artist. And don't forget to surprise and delight your loyal client's now and then.

Shelly's Sidenote

PLACEMENT

Many clients come into the studio saying, "this is the ONLY tattoo I will ever get," very certain of their stance. They will, for example, place a tattoo right in the middle of their bicep. And then, some time later, come back in wanting to add more. UGH! Now you've got to figure out a way to work around the existing tattoo when some of the prime "real estate" has been taken.

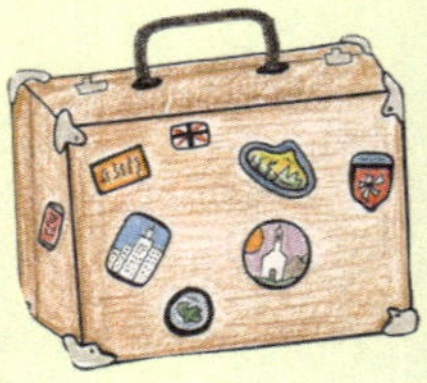

In addition, some people get multiple tattoos that have no flow, almost like "stickers" on a traveling suitcase, and these can be difficult to tie together once their arm or leg is filled up with random images.

I remember one time, at a tattoo workshop, tattoo artist Jeff Gogue commented, even if the client thinks he or she will NEVER get another tattoo, it is helpful to think in terms of the whole body. Such as when doing an arm or leg sleeve, imagine a Japanese body-suit style tattoo, and work backwards from there. This leaves room for connection and addition of new pieces, if they ever change their mind. This was great advice because they usually DO change their minds!!

Helping the Client Choose Placement & Size

In addition to providing a safe, sanitary and comfortable environment for the tattoo process, it is our responsibility as tattooers to guide our clients in making good decisions regarding tattoo design, placement and size. Most clients have an idea of where they would like to place their tattoo, but many don't. They will tend to look to you as the artist to help them decide. And occasionally, you may need to talk naïve or impetuous clients out of their chosen placement because of cost, stretch, how the tattoo will age, too many details, particularly, when they are first-timers.

Help the client make wise choices by considering the following:

Lifestyle: Do they want it to be discreet? Do they want it on their foot but cannot go without shoes for the time it takes to heal? Will they be needing employment that might be affected by the tattoo showing? Are they out in the sun constantly? Will they be doing sports and sweating in the area to be tattooed? Do they love to sit in a tanning bed? Do they want knuckle tattoos but wash dishes for a living? Are they a lifeguard or swimmer constantly in water? These are the kinds of questions you can ask your client to help them decide.

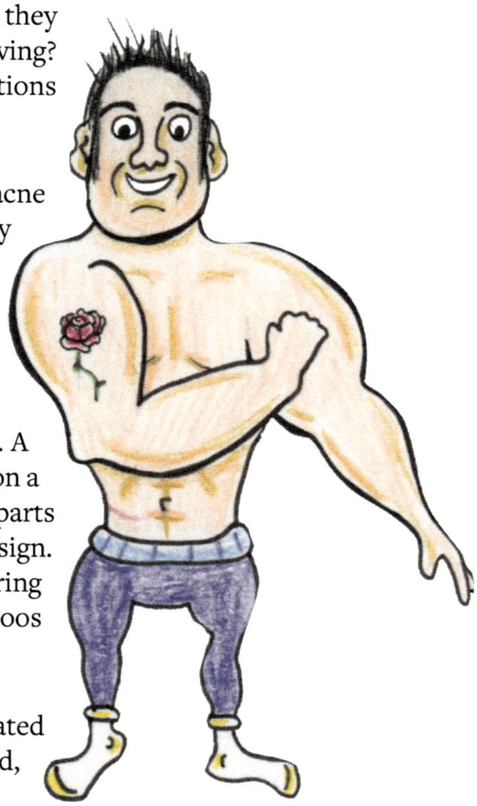

Body area: Does the client have scarring or stretch marks? Does the client have acne or raised moles? Have they recently been sunburned in the desired area? Do they have eczema or psoriasis? Some parts of the body are much more difficult to tattoo (and take longer) like stomachs, buttocks or front of the neck. Some are generally more painful like under the arm, across the sternum, near the butt crack, ankles and wrists. These areas tend to be very stingy and uncomfortable.

Size: The size of the tattoo will also help determine where a tattoo will look best. A small tattoo on a large body part will look off, for example a small tattoo centered on a large bicep. A large-scale tattoo on a small body part is also difficult to pull off, as parts of the tattoo can wrap around and be hidden, thus obscuring the focus of the design. And the smaller the tattoo, the less detail it can have due to ink spreading and blurring over time. Clients should also keep in mind whether they will be getting more tattoos and how the designs can be linked or blended together.

Shape: As the artist, you should consider shape, muscles, bones, and curvature created in body parts, as well as the flow of the tattoo. Wherever the design will be placed, consider your canvas carefully.

Consequences: It may seem obvious to you, but clients need to understand that a tattoo is permanent, and they should be certain that they are committed to having a particular design on a particular body part for life. Neck, hand and face tattoos should be considered carefully because they cannot be covered by clothes...unless you are a ninja!

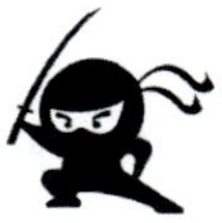

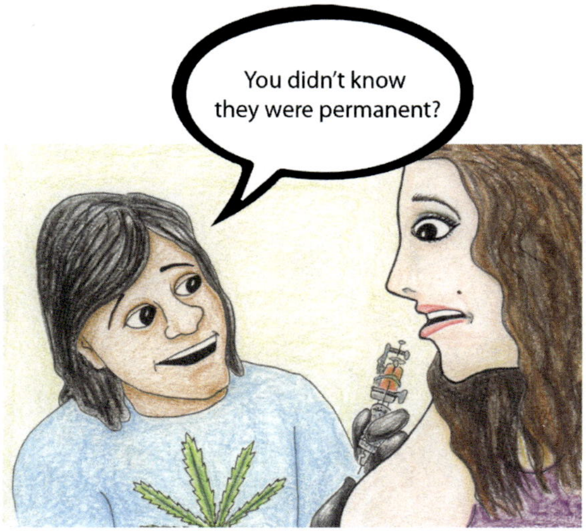

A potential client who is unsure about location and size could experiment with airbrushed or henna tattooing before they make the commitment. They could even pay you to do a fake tattoo with sharpies, so they can live with the design for a few days before taking the leap.

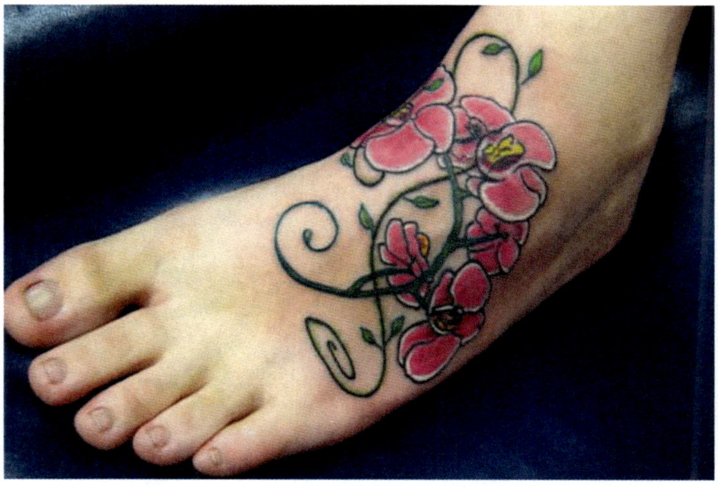

A Word on Hands and Feet:
Some artists choose not to do hand or foot tattoos and in fact some studios have a policy against it. The main issue is quality. Hands and feet are two body parts that are used daily and experience the most wear and tear. Rough work, handwashing and wearing shoes and socks make it impossible to guarantee the quality or longevity of a tattoo design in these areas. For

Shelly's Sidenote

CONSEQUENCES

Many years ago, I had a client who was about 23 and she wanted a tattoo, just above her pubic bone, of a pair of boxing gloves and the words "Hit it Like a Champ". I brought up as many good reasons why this was a bad idea as I could think of, and even enlisted her mom's help. Fortunately, she made a different tattoo choice and a few years later she profusely thanked me for talking her out of it. Now we look back and laugh!

foot tattoos to heal properly, clients would need to go without shoes and socks for several weeks; even sandal straps can rub on the healing tattoo.

Furthermore, the cells of the skin in hands and feet regenerate faster than the rest of the body, which affects the ability of ink to embed as it would elsewhere on the body. If you choose to go ahead with hand and foot tattoos, then your clients should be made aware of the challenges, to expect frequent paid touch-ups and know there is no guarantee on the quality.

A Word on Neck and Face (***excluding cosmetic tattoos***):

Tattoo artists understand the permanence of ink in the skin as well as the potential consequences of highly visible and impossible to cover tattoos. And, we have a responsibility to convey this to clients. Face and neck tattoos are a permanent decision (short of painful and expensive laser removal) and should be considered carefully, with an eye to the future and what potential consequences this decision could bring.

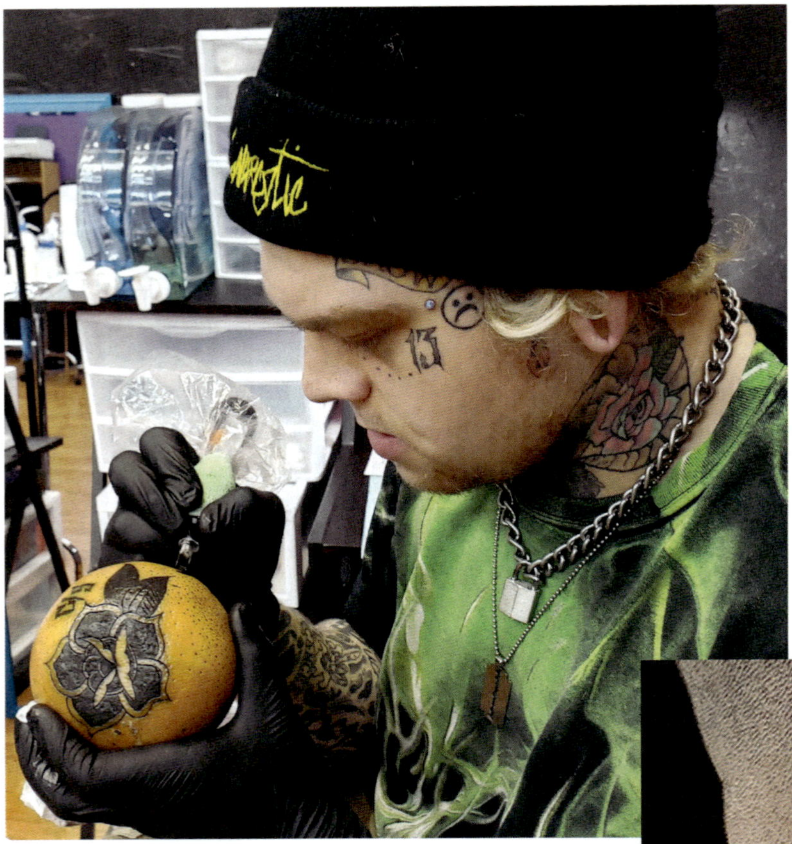

Two main issues exist with getting an artistic tattoo on the face or neck: lack of future employment opportunities (unless you become a tattooer!) and lack of acceptance, or even ridicule.

Remember, you, as an artist, are allowed, and even encouraged, to draw a line that you will not cross when it comes to doing tattoos that you are not comfortable with or feel that your client will regret.

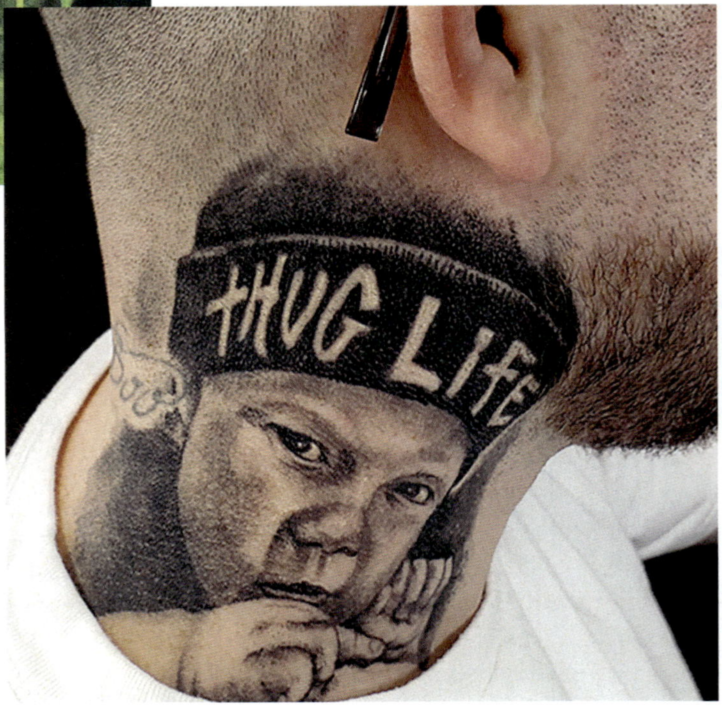

NOTE:
When tattooing over a bony spot like elbow, shin or collar bone, you can shift the skin off the bone to make it slightly more comfortable for the client as well as help prevent blow outs, which are more common in thin skin over bone.

Pain

How much will it hurt? This is one of the top questions a tattoo artist will hear. As discussed in chapter three, pain is subjective and reliant on a person's threshold, as well as tolerance, so it's impossible to answer this question accurately. Every client will react to pain differently, but there are similarities as to the sensitivity in certain areas of the body. Things that affect the likelihood of experiencing pain: tattooing closer to a bone or joint, thinness of the skin and how many nerve endings in the area. The least painful spots are typically areas with thicker skin, more fat or muscle and not over a bone.

In general, the stomach, spine, chest, ribs, lips, elbow, shin, inside of wrist, groin and armpit are considered the most painful areas to get tattooed. Conversely, the least painful areas include arms, side or back of calves, shoulder, upper back, hips, thighs and back of neck.

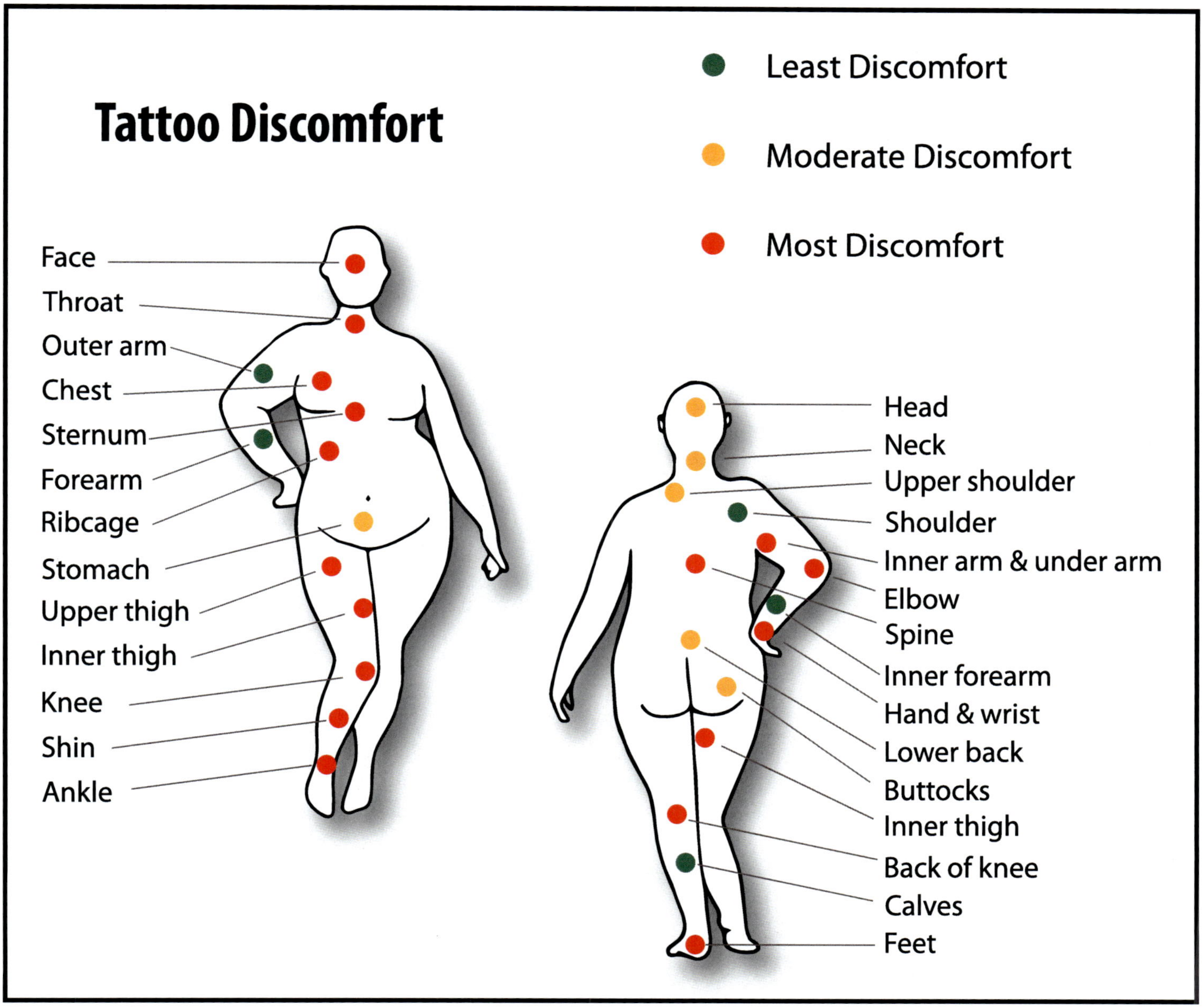

Client Intake Information

When you welcome your client to the studio, in preparation for receiving a tattoo, you will need to have them fill out an intake form, previous to starting the session.

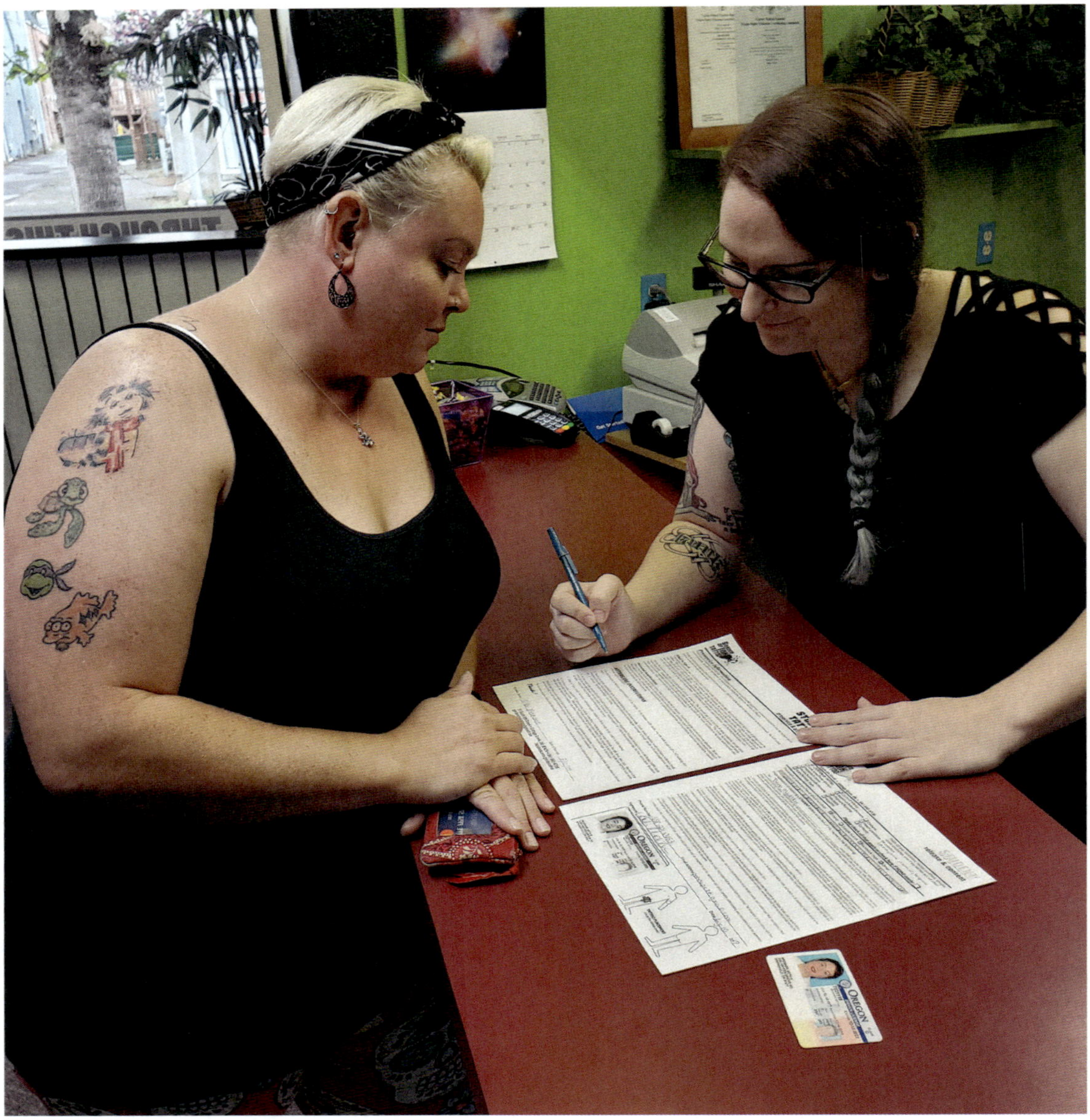

Having good client records is important to providing the best service possible as well as being informed of any potential challenges in advance. In some areas, client records are a requirement and must include specific information such as age, allergies, medications, other health issues that may affect the tattoo (such as bleeding disorders or diabetes), and medications the client is taking.

This **signed** document will serve to protect you and your studio from liability if something unforeseen should happen to the tattoo or the client blames you for something not turning out the way they wanted. (Of course we would recommend working with the client to correct any mistakes you have made, but beyond that, some people can be difficult and unreasonable in their demands.)

Most places will also require you to have a copy of the client's government-issued photo ID, such as driver's license, passport or military ID, with a clear address as well as a phone number. You can use this form to also collect email addresses which you will use to build a client email list for later marketing purposes.

And lastly, it's helpful to ask where the client heard about you and your studio so you know which of your marketing efforts are working.

Here is a copy of the intake form we use at our studio and school. We laminated the original, and then we put ID on it and make a copy. There is a generic intake form for you to use at the end of chapter twelve.

> **"Early in life I came to understand that I was the only person who could protect my own interests, and that, being alone, I must cultivate survivor skills and turn weaknesses into strengths."**
>
> *~Jill Jolliffe, Author & Activist*

Garden of Ink Tattoo

STUDENT
release & consent

AT LOCATION OF TATTOO:
- ❑ Cold sores/Fever blisters
- ❑ Psoriasis/Eczema
- ❑ Moles/Sunburn/Birthmarks
- ❑ Scars/Keloids Rash

- ❑ Coconut Allergy
- ❑ Aspirin or blood thinners
- ❑ Pregnant/Nursing
- ❑ HIV/AIDS
- ❑ Hepatitis

- ❑ Diabetic
- ❑ Heart condition
- ❑ Epilepsy

Please list your medications, medical conditions, allergies, and/or sensitivities, even if you feel they will not affect the procedure: ____________________

Please check all that apply or check here if NONE apply: ❑

Please tell us where you heard about our shop: ❑ Friend ❑ Google Search ❑ Facebook Page ❑ Other ____________

PLEASE READ AND BE CERTAIN YOU UNDERSTAND THE IMPLICATIONS OF SIGNING THIS DOCUMENT

In consideration of receiving a **STUDENT** tattoo at Garden of Ink, I agree to the following:

- That I, ______________________________ (clearly PRINT your name) have been fully informed of the inherent risks, associated with getting a tattoo. I fully understand that these risks, known and unknown, can lead to injury, including but not limited to infection, scarring, difficulties in detecting melanoma and allergic reactions to tattoo pigment, latex gloves, and/or soap. Having been informed of the potential risks associated with getting a tattoo, I still wish to proceed with the tattoo application and I freely accept and expressly assume any and all risks that may arise from tattooing.

- TO WAIVE AND RELEASE to the fullest extent permitted by law, each of the students and the tattoo studio from all liability whatsoever, for any and all claims or causes of action that I, my estate, heirs, executors or assigns may have for personal injury or otherwise, including any direct and/or consequential damages, which result or arise from the application of my tattoo, whether caused by the negligence or fault of either the student or Garden of Ink Tattoo Studio, or otherwise.

- That both the Student and the Tattoo Studio have given me the full opportunity to ask any and all questions about the application of my tattoo and all of my questions have been answered to my satisfaction. Furthermore, I acknowledge that Garden of Ink has taken every precaution possible to provide a safe and sterile environment for my service. In addition, the student has given me instructions on the care of my tattoo while it's healing, as well as possible side effects, complications and restrictions and I understand them and will follow them. I acknowledge that it is possible that the tattoo can become infected, particularly if I do not follow the instructions given to me. If any touch-up work to the tattoo is needed due to my own negligence, I agree that the work will be done at my own expense.

- I am not under the influence of alcohol or drugs, and I am voluntarily submitting to be tattooed by the student without duress or coercion.

- Neither the student nor Garden of Ink is responsible for the meaning or spelling of the symbol or text that I have provided to them or that I have chosen from the studio's flash art. Variations in color and design may exist between the tattoo art I have selected and the actual tattoo when it is applied to my body. I also understand that over time, the colors and the clarity of my tattoo will fade due to unprotected exposure to the sun and the naturally occurring dispersion of pigment under the skin.

- A tattoo is a permanent change to my appearance and can only be removed by laser or surgical means, which can be disfiguring and/or costly and which in all likelihood will not result in the restoration of my skin to its exact appearance before being tattooed.

- I release all rights to any photographs taken of my tattoo and give consent in advance to their reproduction in print or electronic form.

- I agree to reimburse each of the students and Garden of Ink for any attorneys' fees and costs incurred in any legal action I bring against either the student or the Tattoo Studio and in which either the student or the Tattoo Studio is the prevailing party. I agree that the courts of Oregon in Lane County shall have personal jurisdiction and venue over me and shall have exclusive jurisdiction for the purpose of litigating any dispute arising out of or related to this agreement.

- I acknowledge that I have been given adequate opportunity to read and understand this document, that it was not presented to me at the last minute, and I understand that I am signing a legal contract waiving certain rights to recover against the student and Garden of Ink.

- If any provision, section, subsection, clause or phrase of this release is found to be unenforceable or invalid, that portion shall be severed from this contract. The remainder of this contract will then be construed as though the unenforceable portion had never been contained in this document.

- I hereby declare that I am of legal age (and have provided valid proof of age) and am competent to sign this Agreement and I am in complete understanding and concurrence with this agreement.

Phone Number ______________________ **Email Address** ______________________

Signature ______________________________ **Date**__________ **20**_____

PLACE LICENSE HERE

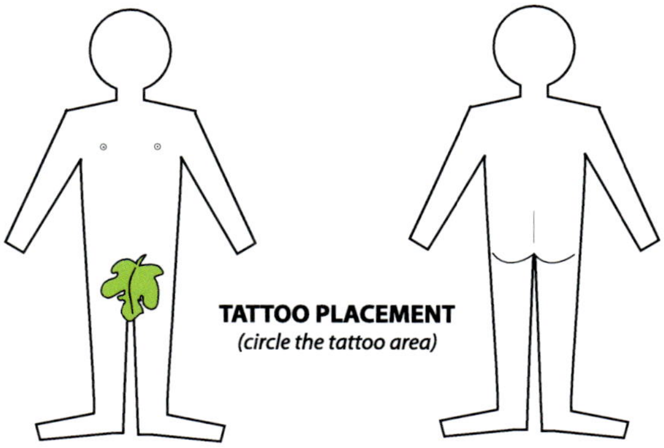

TATTOO PLACEMENT
(circle the tattoo area)

Client Preservice and Aftercare Information

> "Instead of focusing on the competition, focus on the customer."
> ~Scott Cook, American Businessman

When a new client approaches you for a tattoo, you'll need to inform them of what is involved as well as how to care for the new artwork. Aftercare of a tattoo is the subject of endless debate in the industry and this includes whether to dry heal or wet heal, cold or hot water, ointments or balms, how long to bandage, dermal or spray bandage and even plastic wrap vs. paper towel.

As we said in chapter four, the best way for you to come up with an aftercare routine that works, is to research the options, ask experienced tattooers, check local regulations and observe how your own clients heal.

The following information is what we give to clients at our studio. Feel free to adapt it to suit your needs:

Client Pre-service and Aftercare Information

PRE-SERVICE

For your peace of mind, we use professional equipment, commercial pigments and the highest sterilization standards. In addition, our artists are certified by the state as to their technical expertise.

Please be well rested and eat a good meal before your procedure! DO NOT drink alcohol or use drugs prior to being tattooed. We will refuse service to anyone who appears intoxicated.

WHAT TO EXPECT: Your tattoo will generally take two to three weeks to heal. It will be tender for the first few days, then it will develop a light crust of dry skin over the surface. This crust will gradually flake off like a sunburn. During this period, the tattoo may look uneven and/or pale in color, and some ink may flake off as well. THIS IS NORMAL. In the last stage of healing, the skin will have a tight, shiny surface. This waxy look will slowly leave, and the skin will return to its normal appearance and texture. We provide written AFTERCARE instructions below AND we will go over this with you verbally at the end of the procedure. (Remember, every person's skin is different...your healing process may vary.)

Immediately following your tattoo, there may be some seeping of blood or plasma. This is why we bandage your tattoo. Also, some people experience minor swelling or bruising depending on the location of the tattoo. In addition, as the tattoo heals, you may also experience itching. Don't scratch--pat or slap with a clean hand instead!

POTENTIAL COMPLICATIONS: Due to the time involved in healing a tattoo, there is always the risk of infection. Excellent hygiene can prevent most infections! Do not use antibiotic cream UNLESS there is infection as these products can cause allergic reactions and/or pull ink from your tattoo [we prefer witch hazel]. Although rare, allergic reaction and/or sensitivity to a particular pigment/ink can be a problem, sometimes intensified by exposure to heat or sun during the healing process.

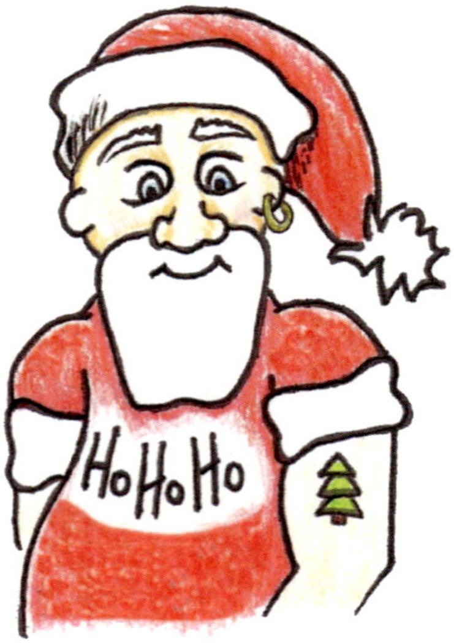

AFTERCARE INSTRUCTIONS (Please follow carefully!)

1. Leave bandage on for approximately 1.5 - 2 hours. (If the bandage really sticks, you may soak to get it off -- NO soaking after that!)

2. Wash your hands thoroughly, or be sure person helping you has clean hands. Gently remove bandage, wash your tattoo with bare hand, fragrance free soap from a dispenser

(not bar soap) and warm water--removing any ointment or blood. Pat dry with clean paper towel and air dry 15 minutes. NEVER re-bandage your tattoo.

3. At this stage some people will apply a small amount of lotion or healing ointment* VERY thinly over tattoo. Other people don't use any cream or lotion at all.

4. Repeat steps 2 & 3, one to three times per day for five to seven days. Occasionally spritz with witch hazel--helps keep infection and itch away. Crusty skin from this healing wound will contain bits of ink-THIS IS NORMAL. Allow any flakes or dried material to fall away freely—do not pick at it!

5. After five to seven days, simply moisturize your tattoo lightly whenever it feels crusty or dry, until it is fully healed.

For two weeks: absolutely NO sun-tanning, picking, scratching or soaking in any water (bathtub, hot tub, pool, lake, etc). Shower is fine but don't soak your new tattoo. Also, please wear loose clothing while tattoo heals. If you engage in activities in the sun AFTER your tattoo has healed--use sunscreen to protect your tattoo. Proper aftercare of your tattoo means you will enjoy it for years!

Please feel free to call, e-mail or message us if you have any questions or concerns. It's our pleasure to share in the creation of your personal body art and we look forward to serving you again soon! Take care of your investment!

*If irritation occurs, wash tattoo thoroughly and discontinue use of product, wait 24 hours and try a different product

NOTE: A new addition to the options in tattoo aftercare are the dermal bandages developed by burn centers. These types of bandages are similar to a piece of plastic wrap but have adhesive which seals to the skin and allows breathability--keeping the tattoo moist and protected during the critical phase of healing. There are several brands on the market including Saniderm, Second Skin, Tatu-derm and Dermalize.

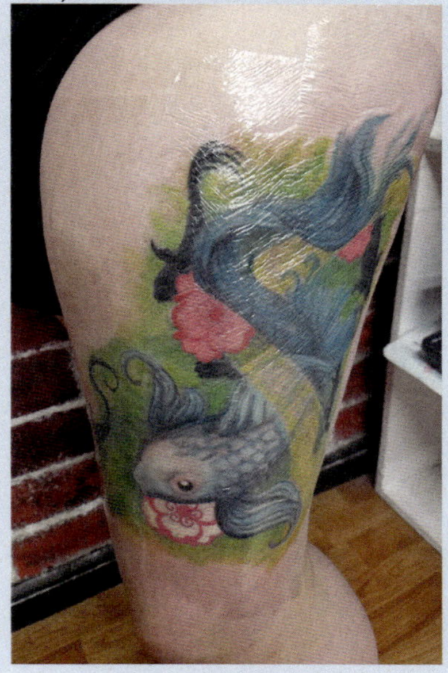

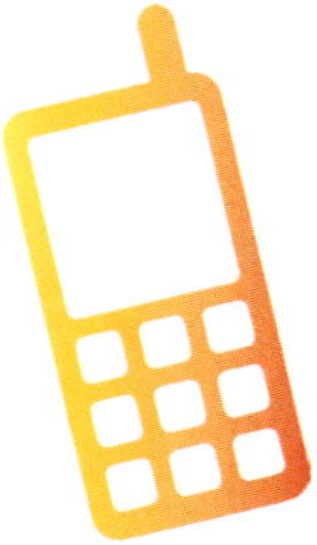

Phone and Messaging Skills

When we contact someone on the phone or through email or social messaging, we can't help but make assumptions about them. We all generalize about age, education and social status by the voice, grammar, spelling and clarity of the message conveyed. What type of impression is your phone voice making? What about your written messages? What you say and how you say it are important in making an impression on the clients you are engaging with at your studio. Use the following tips to assure that you communicate an educated message with clarity and confidence.

Phone

Clients calling you:

- Record a professional voicemail greeting. Record your message in a clear, professional voice. Be friendly, brief and to the point. Practice what you will say before you record. Leave exact instructions for the caller to follow. Remind the caller to leave their name and phone number. Have the voicemail pick up by the third ring.
- Answer your phone by the third ring. People are not inclined to wait long for an answer.
- Before you answer make sure you have a pen and paper at the ready. Write down the caller's name and use it during the conversation.
- Actively listen to the caller and take notes if necessary.

> "To effectively communicate, we must realize that we are all different in the way we perceive the world and use this understanding as a guide to our communication with others."
> -*Tony Robbins, Author & Speaker*

- Return calls promptly and, if unable to do so, explain this on your voicemail recording or offer the option of another form of contact.
- Check your messages in a timely fashion.

You calling clients:

- Speak slowly and clearly, particularly when you are leaving a message.
- Clearly state your name and business name. Spell your name as well if it is a more difficult name to pronounce.
- Slow down when leaving your number and repeat it twice.
- Clearly state your reason for calling.
- Give them a good time to return your call or ask for an alternative means of contact.

Email and Social Messaging

- Briefly introduce yourself. People may not recognize your email address or social "handle".
- Include a simple reminder of who you are in relation to the person you are contacting.
- Use a clear subject line.
- Never email or message when you are angry or highly emotional.
- Use exclamation points and capitals sparingly.
- Respond in a timely fashion or give alternate means of contact.
- Avoid one-line emails such as "ok" or "thanks". Feel free to put "no reply necessary" if you don't expect a response.
- Keep it tidy. Too many emails within emails gets tedious.
- Take time to send the message to the right people. Before you click "reply all" be sure you know who your message is going to.
- Keep your email greeting and sign-off appropriate to your audience.
- Always use a signature line, which will include your website, social links and phone number. Make it easy for people to do business with you.
- Double check grammar and spelling every time. Misspellings and incorrect grammar are the main things that make you look unprofessional!

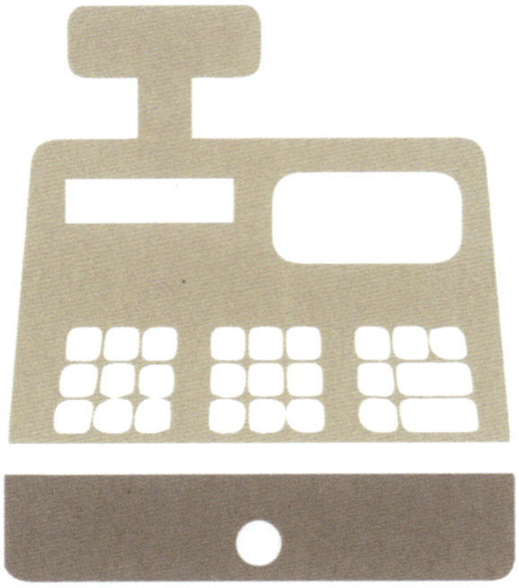

Cash Register and Merchant Services:

Current payment systems now allow businesses to track their sales and inventories with pinpoint accuracy, and give consumers more options--debit, credit, checks and even using smart phones and online payments. And yet cash is generally still the preferred method of payment for many shops and this requires a cash drawer of some kind.

Cash Handling Basics

Whether using a cash register, with buttons to represent sales and products or a tablet and swipe system, familiarize yourself with the categories represented and have a working knowledge of your studio's services and inventory.

- Enter the total amount of the sale. Say the amount out loud.
- Never leave a client's card or money lying idly on the sales counter. Any form of money should always be in motion at the register: on the way to your hand, moving to or from the cash drawer, or going back into the client's hand.
- Never leave the cash drawer sitting open.
- When retrieving client's change from a cash drawer, pull out the coins first and go up incrementally from the total sale amount, giving them the least amount of coins and bills.

- Once you have the correct change in your hand, double check amount by counting out loud as you hand the customer their change, also counting up from the sale.

Example:

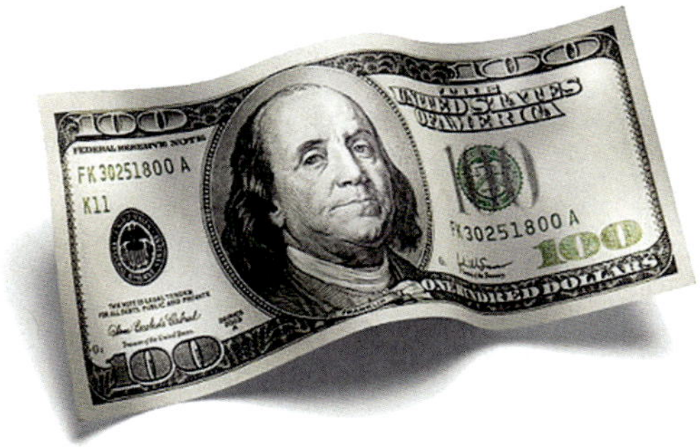

If the sale is $22.57 and customer pays with a hundred-dollar bill--the change would be $77.43. Retrieve their change from the cash drawer in the following order, counting incrementally up in your head: three pennies "$.58, $.59, $.60", one dime " $.70", one nickel "$.75", one quarter "makes $23", two dollar bills "$24, $25", one five dollar bill "$30", one ten dollar bill "$40", three twenty dollar bills "$60, $80, $100".

Now count back the change out loud to the client as you hand it over. Start by saying "$22.57 out of $100". You begin by handing them all the coins and say "that makes $23", then count out the rest this way: hand them the one dollar bills "that makes $24, $25" hand them the five dollar bill "and five is $30", hand them the ten dollar bill "$40", and then count out the twenties, "$60, $80, $100". They can clearly see that the change from their hundred-dollar bill is correct.

This may seem tedious, but it will easily help maintain the balance of the register. Accuracy is the most important aspect of working from a cash register: it ensures client satisfaction and correct bookkeeping for the studio.

When working a cash register, sometimes mistakes will happen (a jammed drawer, the wrong button or a complex refund). Stay calm and let the client know that you are taking care of the issue, and if you can't figure it out, discreetly ask a manager to show you. If a manager is unavailable, write a note explaining what happened and put it in the cash register.

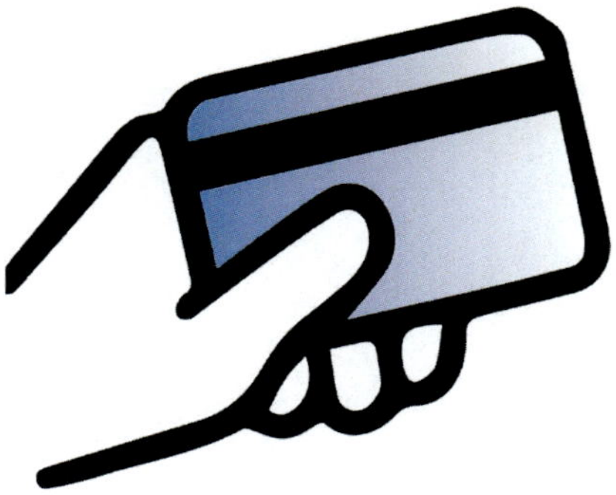

Using a **merchant service provider** allows the shop to accept card payments. Some even accept phone payments. All debit/credit card machines are different, but, in general, the card will be read using swipe or chip. Try to keep the card in the client's hand as much as possible (some merchant service providers require this) and be sure to return it immediately after the transaction, along with a copy of the receipt. Keep in mind there are even more options for accepting payment today such as: Googlepay, Cash, Square, Stripe, Venmo and Paypal.

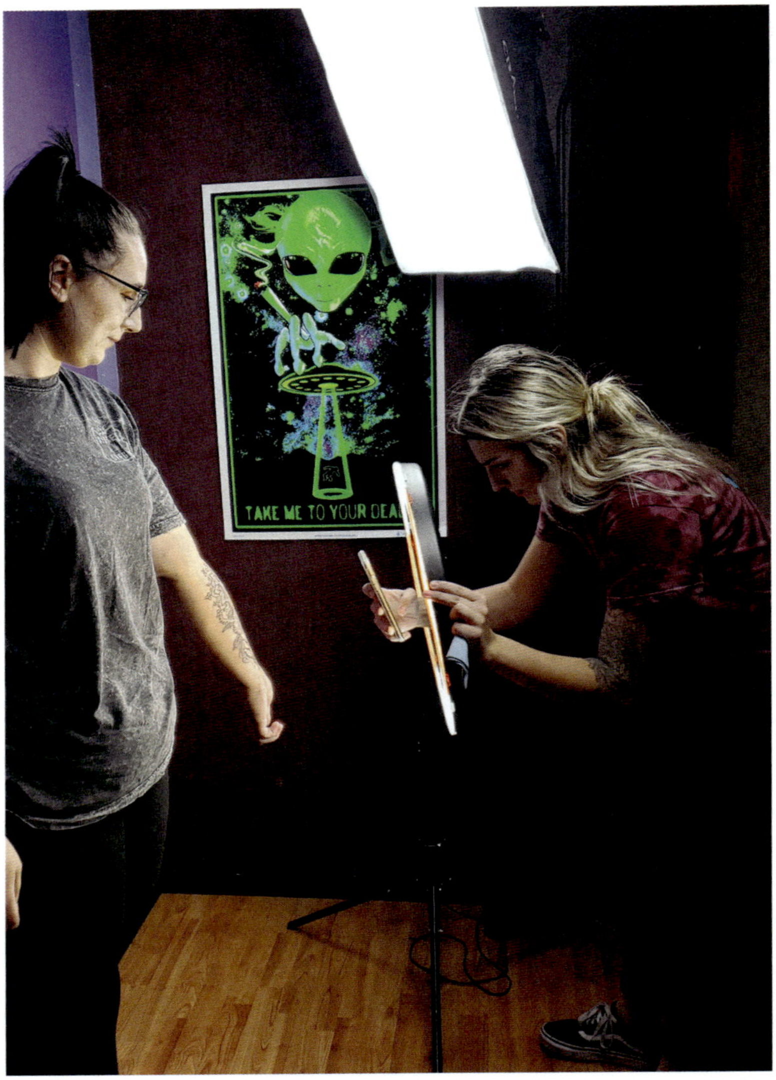

Taking Photos of Tattoos

Documenting your tattoo work by having a portfolio is essential in representing your services to the public. Taking great pictures and using a photo editing software or app to crop and fix backgrounds is straightforward.

- After the session, allow the fresh tattoo to calm down and stop seeping blood and plasma. You can help this along by having the client sit with a paper towel soaked in witch hazel or Bactine for a few minutes.
- Make sure the tattoo is clean and very dry, and any balm or ointment is wiped off. (If you are taking a picture of a healed or older tattoo, client may need to rub lotion on it to avoid the ultra-dry look.)
- Most phones come with great cameras and this can be the most convenient way to get good photos. A nice digital camera can be an option as well.
- Don't use a flash, which causes a glare, but be sure and have great lighting. Move outdoors to take advantage of natural light but avoid direct sunlight.
- Take several photos to avoid blurriness caused by shaky hands (particularly after a long tattoo session), as an artist's hands can be tired. Move around the tattoo and try different angles. Your client may need to adjust position as well.
- Generally you should stand back from the tattoo at least a couple feet. Taking the picture too close to the subject can result in blur or darkness. You can always crop away excess background later.
- Use editing app or software (such as Pixlr, Fotogenic or Photoshop) to crop, zoom, enhance or sharpen contrast. But do your best to leave the original quality intact. You can also put together frames of a tattoo image that wraps around a body part. (below)

NOTE:
For more info on photographing tattoos, check out the DVD "***Shoot it Right***", by professional photographer and tattooer Mario Rosenau.

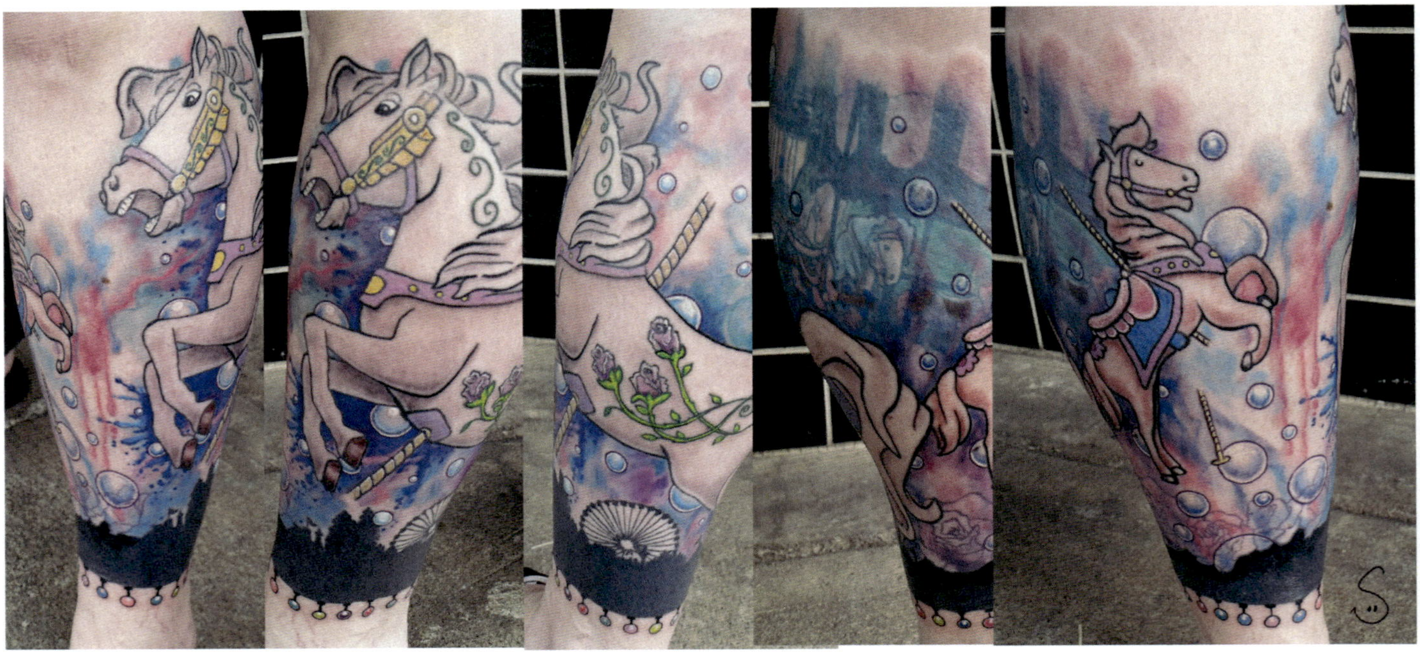

Cultivate your Client Loyalty

Finding great clients is the cornerstone of building a successful career as a tattoo artist. But keeping the clients you have is easier and less expensive than attempting to get new ones. How do you keep clients once you get them in your chair?

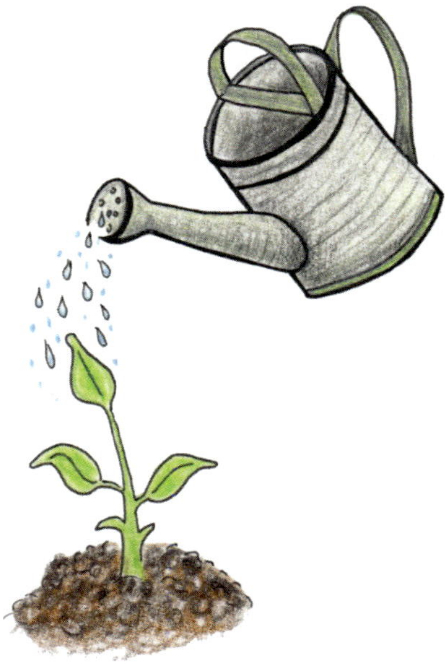

8 Keys to Client Loyalty:

1

Be curious: take an interest in your clients. Listen to their stories and inquire about their families, friends, hobbies or jobs. Remember their names. Be genuine in your conversation with them and incorporate their ideas into the artwork you create.

2

Be reliable: be punctual. Show up for your appointments early and be prepared in advance of the client arriving at your shop. Deliver what you promise and more. Call when you say you will, get that drawing done on time and keep your word. Don't forget the importance of follow-through with emails and/or phone calls. Clients like to know they can depend on you. And be honest if you do make a mistake. Take responsibility and do whatever you can to correct it.

3

Be easy to work with: most people prefer to work with someone who is cheerful and pleasant. Having a reputation that you are easy to work with will help you stand out from the general perception that tattoo artists can be arrogant, obnoxious or difficult. Putting clients at ease and helping them feel comfortable around you and in your shop will make them want to return and send friends as well. Also, if clients really like you, they begin to trust you and have an easier time accepting your artistic, and maybe even unusual, creative opinions.

4

Be attentive to details: take nothing for granted. In most cases, the client has only the most superficial knowledge of what you do. They expect you to tell them how you work, the process, the schedule, and when and what will be required of them; also, to keep them informed of all changes, and provide options when appropriate.

5

Appear busy: busy artists—the ones that are always "booked out for x number of months" are usually in high demand. Of course, you may not really be that busy at first, but you can bend the perception of your clients by talking about the many projects you are working on (they don't need to know if its painting, drawing, writing an article or actually tattooing). Also, when making appointments you can "search" your calendar for an open spot; don't show them all the empty days! People like working with the busiest businesses. It tells them you are influential and efficient and that lots of other people trust you.

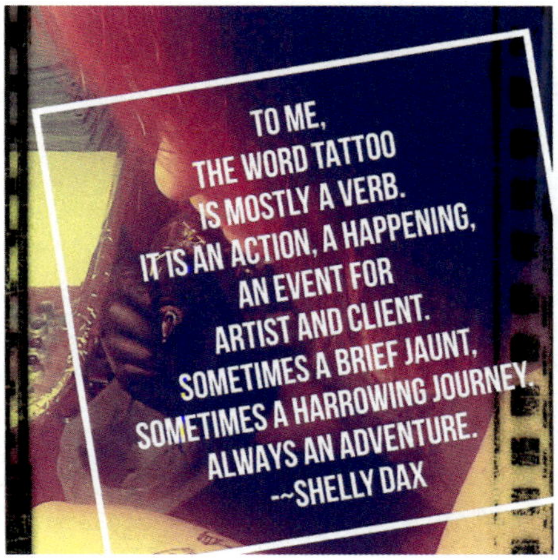

Shelly's Sidenote

ATMOSPHERE

Many people over the years have told me they were previously afraid to even walk into a tattoo shop because of a hardcore dark character in the atmosphere or uncaring perception from the staff. If the hardcore crowd is your target audience than that could be fine, but most people will return to an inviting, comfortable and respectful studio that treats the client as a partner in the creation of artwork.

Think carefully about how the public sees you and what message your attitude, demeanor and space will send.

6

Appear successful: get out into the community and promote yourself. Donate an art piece to a local charitable organization. Get a write up in the paper. Involve you and your shop in community activities. Write an article on tattooing for a local magazine. Again, you may not be very prosperous just yet, but increasing your visibility will increase the illusion of success and more success will come to you.

7

Take charge: be confidant and relaxed. Every client wants to feel taken care of and like they are in the hands of a professional artist. Appear in control and your client will trust you. Be knowledgeable so they don't doubt your skill and instructions. Reassure them their tattoo project is in capable hands.

8

Be flexible: good clients expect you to handle the design in the way you believe best. But when a client is not agreeable with something you have designed or tattooed, you should be flexible enough to make changes or corrections. Though art is subjective, and individual artists' creative processes vary enormously, the client is the one paying the bill and should leave happy and feeling like they got what they really wanted. Of course, the most successful artists will give more than expected and leave the client with a feeling of gratitude to be wearing your artwork for the rest of their lives.

Sources:
Customer Service Training 101, by Renee Evenson, ©2017
Telephone & Cell Phone Communication Skills Handbook, Patricia DeJoseph and John Damien, ©2009
Never Lose a Customer Again, Joey Coleman ©2018

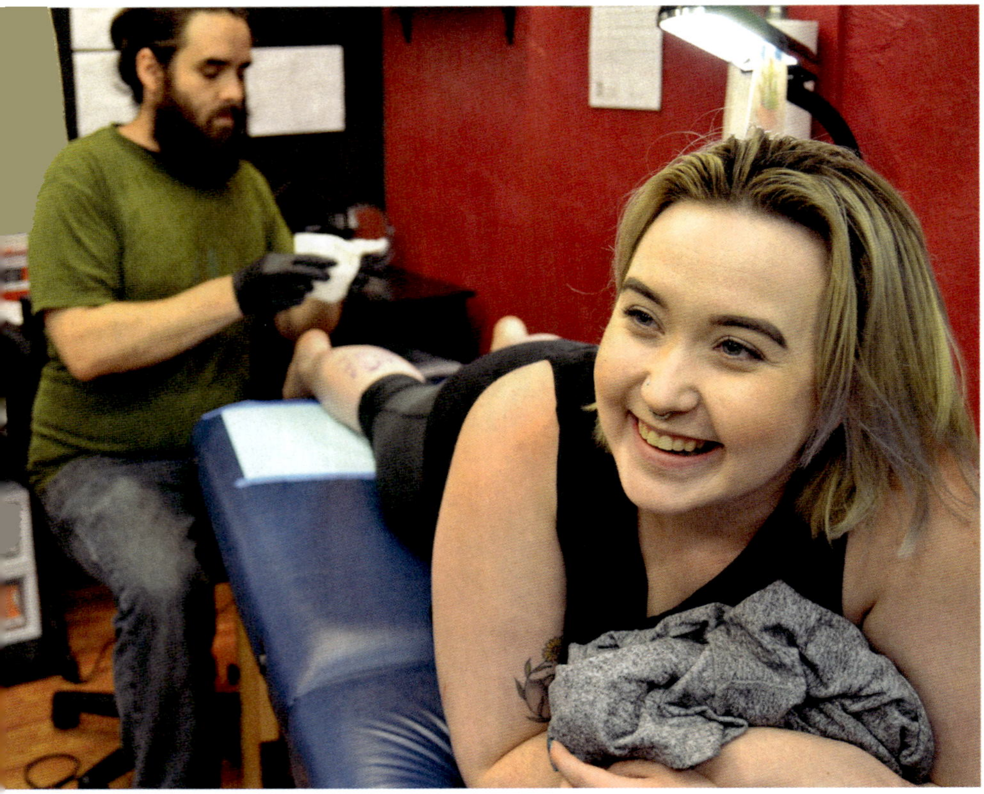

> "A customer talking about their experience with you is worth ten times that which you write or say about yourself."
>
> ~*David J. Greer, Author*

Chapter Ten Highlights

- A tattoo studio's clientele is its most vital asset.
- Always remember, in the end they pay your bills.
- The size of the tattoo will also help determine where a tattoo will look best.
- Clients need to understand that tattoos are permanent.
- Some artists choose not to do hand and foot tattoos.
- The cells of the skin in the hands and feet turn over faster than the rest of the body.
- Tattooing close to a bone or joint stings more.
- A signed client intake document will serve to protect you from liability.
- The best way to come up with an aftercare routine that works is to research the options, ask experienced tattooers, check local regulations, and observe how your own clients heal.
- Make sure your phone message makes a good impression.
- Return calls promptly.
- Keep your emails tidy and professional.
- When retrieving client's change from the cash drawer, begin with coins first.
- Make sure the tattoo is clean and dry before you take a photo.
- Don't use a flash, as it causes a glare.
- Take several photos to avoid blurriness.
- Be curious about your clients and talk with them during the procedure.
- Appear in control and your client will trust you.

Wisecracks:

Hey, my body is a temple too.

It just has stained glass windows.

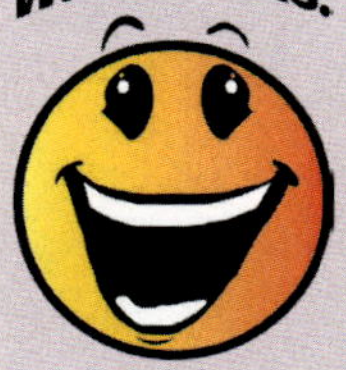

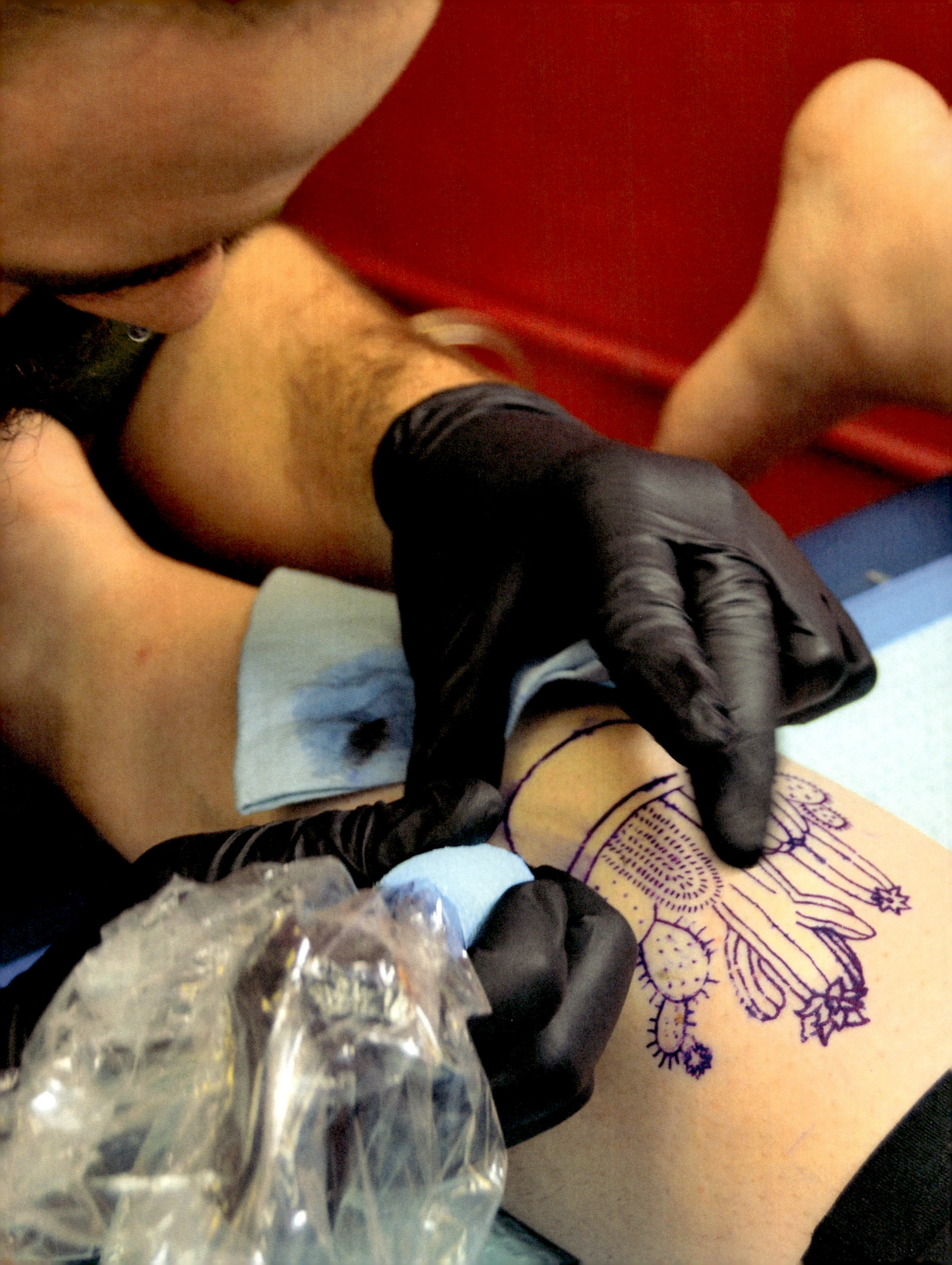

Chapter Eleven

Business & Marketing

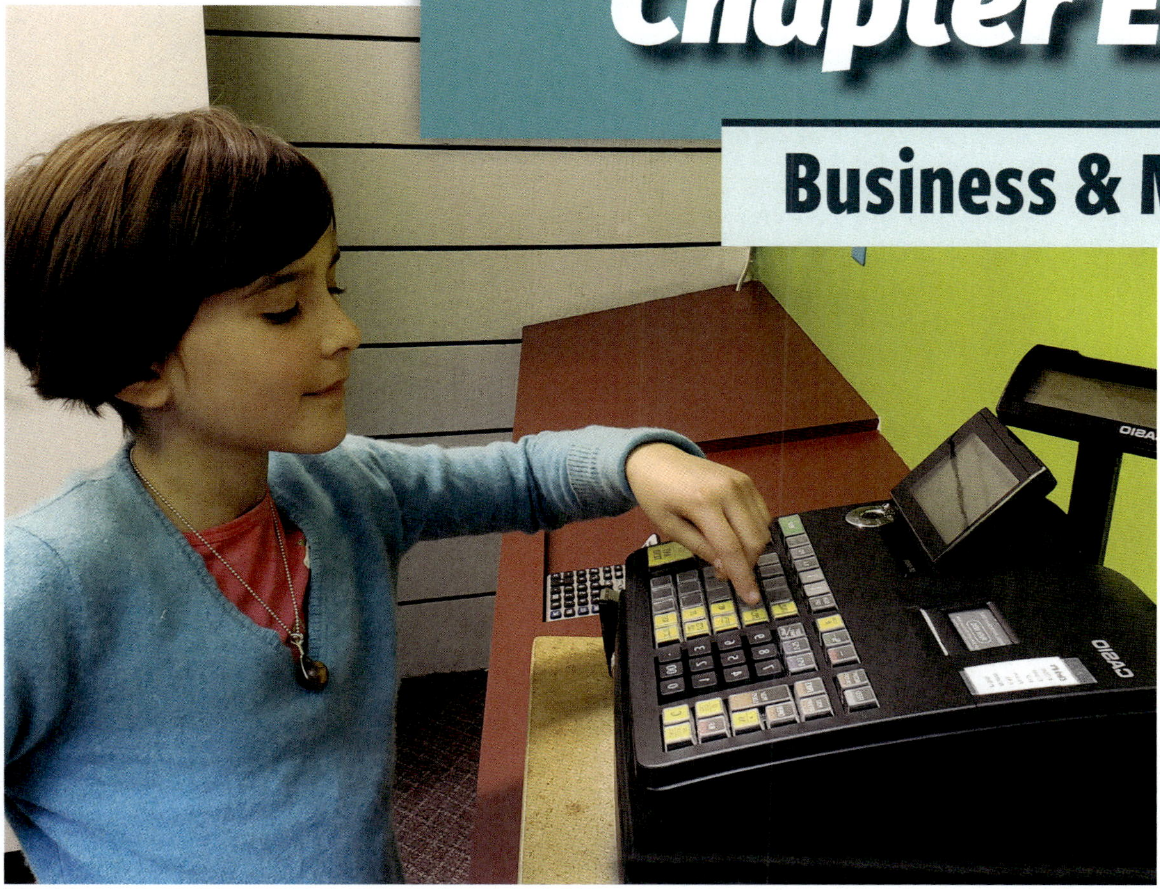

Being a tattoo artist generally means being self-employed or "in business" for yourself, even though you may not own a studio. You are typically considered an independent contractor, thus, responsible for your own bookkeeping and taxes. Even though you may work in an established studio, you are ultimately responsible for promoting yourself and developing a clientele as well. Having a basic knowledge of business and marketing skills is beneficial to becoming a success in your tattoo career.

> "The best marketing doesn't feel like marketing."
>
> *~Tom Fishburne, Cartoonist and Marketer*

Being Self-Employed

Independent Contractor

Independent contractors are in business for themselves. They earn their livelihood from their own independent work instead of relying on an employer. Sometimes artists are called freelancers or entrepreneurs as well.

> "Entrepreneurship is living a few years of your life like most people won't, so you can spend the rest of your life like most people can't."
>
> *~Unknown*

The IRS generally uses a "right of control" test to determine worker status. In other words, if the people you work for control and direct your hours, job details, you are paid by the hour, or they provide employee benefits, you would be considered an employee. But if you have flexibility and control over your own hours, furnish your own tools, can work for more than one person at a time and get paid by the job, you are considered independent.

Some Benefits of Being Self-employed

- **Increased choice**: you are your own boss and you decide whom to work for.
- **Increased freedom**: you decide when to work and how to do your job.
- **Potentially higher pay**: independent contractors are usually paid at least 20% to 40% more per hour than employees performing the same work.
- **No federal or state tax is withheld**: independent contractors normally pay estimated taxes directly to the IRS four times a year. This means you have more control over your cash flow than employees do.
- **Increased business deductions**: you can take many tax deductions for expenses related to your tattooing (e.g. supplies, advertising, printing, childcare etc). As a self-employed person, you can deduct from your income tax any necessary expenses related to your business.

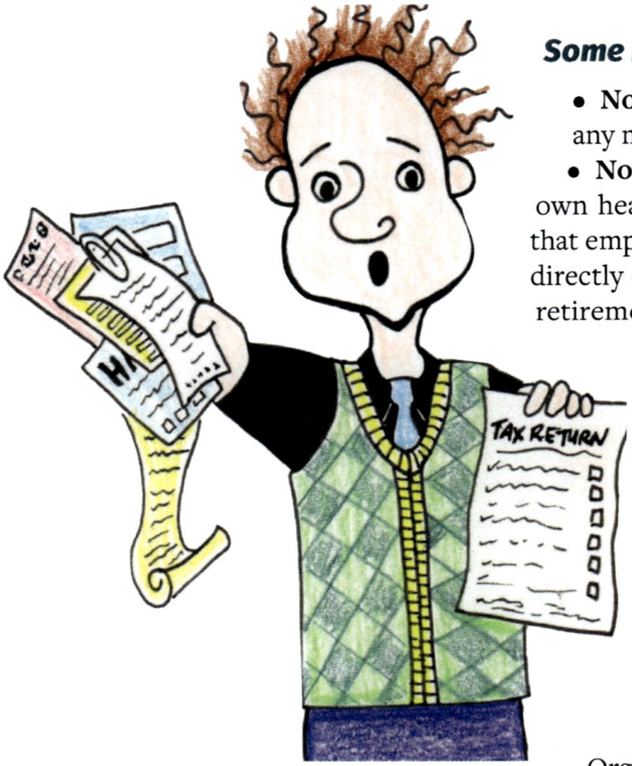

Some Drawbacks of Being Self-Employed

- **No job security**: if you don't have clients, you don't make any money.
- **No employer-provided benefits**: you must pay for your own health insurance, often at much higher rates than those that employers pay. Time lost due to vacations and illness comes directly out of your bottom line. And, you must fund your own retirement. The self-employed also don't have the safety net provided by unemployment insurance.
- **No employer-provided workers' compensation**: if a work-related injury is a self-employed person's fault, he or she has no recourse against the hiring firm.
- **You might not get paid**: you bear the risk of loss from clients who don't pay or are a no-show.
- **You must pay estimated taxes**: independent contractors must set aside enough money to make four estimated tax payments each year: April, June, September and January. Budgeting carefully is an important tool.

Organization of paperwork and planning for tax payments will help you avoid surprises on April 15th! Despite the drawbacks, most tattoo artists are delighted to experience the freedom and flexibility a career in tattooing can provide.

> **Tip**: In addition to your business checking account, from which you pay yourself and pay your expenses (operating expenses or "op ex"), open a savings account that you consistently transfer money into from your income to cover your tax payments. Find out what percentage your tax rate is and funnel that into your tax account once a week, or once a month before you spend it. For instance, if you made $500 this week, and your tax rate is 15% then immediately transfer $75 into the savings. This makes it much easier to keep that money separate and out of mind when you look at your op ex checking balance and then you can easily make your estimated tax payments quarterly.

Other Business Considerations

Tattoo Regulations

Most countries and even the various states in the U.S. are wildly different in the minimum requirements to become a tattoo artist. Some require nothing more than registering with the overseeing body and some require 1000 hours or more of apprenticeship. At least six U.S. states require attendance at a licensed tattoo school and several states ONLY require a blood borne pathogens and first aid training. You must research your own area's laws to determine what you will need to accomplish before starting to tattoo people.

We happen to be in the state of Oregon, where it is required to attend a tattoo school and the laws are strict and changing all the time. If you'd like to look at the Oregon state laws for tattooers, you can download a copy at this web address:

https://www.oregon.gov/oha/PH/HLO/Rules/EBAP-Rules-01-01-18.pdf

This will give you another perspective of what concerns are important to pay attention to, in case your area has minimal regulations.

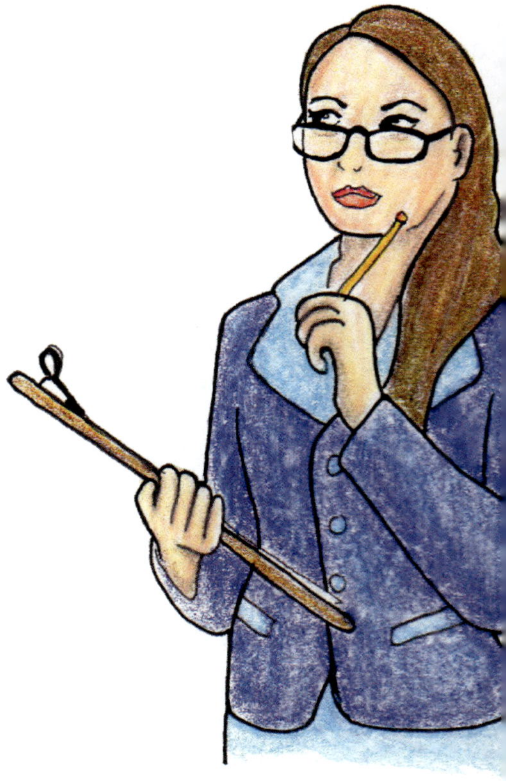

Business Expenses

As we stated earlier, you are typically considered self-employed when you are a tattoo artist, and you must consider some additional expenses that go along with starting up your own business, even if you work in someone else's shop.

In addition to quality equipment, furniture, stencil printer, lighting and work station you may need some or most of the following:

- Official apprenticeship or tattoo school-- $2500 - $12,000
- Testing or licensing--this could run several hundred dollars depending on where you live.
- First Aid and CPR class--average $75 - $150 and options include on-line classes, though some areas require attendance in person.
- Blood borne pathogens class--$15 - $60 online or in-person.
- City or state business license--varies and may not be necessary.
- Assumed business name registration--approximately $50
- Bank account--consider the minimum deposit and if you will need printed checks.
- Merchant services--usually a monthly fee + percentage of sales. May also need equipment.
- Advertising--cost depends on what you are able to afford as well as what avenues of promotion you choose. Newspaper? Business cards? Social Media? Website? Phone book? Side of a bus? Carefully consider how much promotion your studio will be offering and what avenues you'll need to explore for yourself.

Every studio is different in what they provide for their tattooers. Some may provide all disposables and charge a higher percentage, some may ask you to secure your own and charge you a lower percentage. Some shops may choose to offer a space rental fee and still others may have minimum monthly requirements on how much money you bring in.

In addition some studios may have work station, lighting, stool or furnishings available for you to use, some may not.

Average supplies needed for 2 - 3 hr. tattoo	X 6 tattoos/week	Approximate monthly inventory
1/2 roll blue shop towels (more absorbent for wiping skin) 5 sheets cheap paper towel (for wiping ink bottles, tip of needle and shaving) 8 ink cups 1 razor 1 tongue depressor 1/2 oz. Vaseline 1 oz. alcohol 6 oz. diluted green soap 2 sheets aluminum foil or plastic (to cover work area) 4 pairs gloves 1 rinse cup 4 baggies or bottle covers (for power supply, machine and bottles) 1 sheet stencil sheets 1 small garbage bag 2 needles 1 power cord cover 3 barrier film pieces (two for lamp, one for stool handle)	3 rolls blue shop towels ½ roll cheap paper towels 24 ink cups 6 razors 6 tongue depressors 3 oz. Vaseline 6 oz. alcohol 36 oz. diluted green soap 12 sheets aluminum foil or plastic wrap 24 pairs gloves 18 rinse cups 24 baggies 6 sheet stencil sheets 6 small garbage bag 12 needles 6 power cord covers 18 pieces barrier film	12 rolls blue shop towels 2 rolls cheap paper towels 192 ink cups 24 razors 24 tongue depressors 1x 13 oz. jar Vaseline 1x 32 oz bottle alcohol ¼ gallon green soap 1 roll aluminum foil or plastic wrap 96 pairs gloves 72 rinse cups 96 baggies (1 box) 24 stencil sheets 24 small garbage bags 48 needles 24 power cord covers 72 pieces barrier film

Supplies

When planning out your expenses, you will need to consider the supplies necessary for tattooing. There are many different things you could use, but the basics are covered in the table at left.

Marketing

The simplest definition of marketing is: the action of promoting and selling products or services—the key word being ACTION. To get your tattoo services noticed and grow your business, you need to attract and retain a good-sized base of satisfied clients. We can't just live on hope to get client's through the door of our studio. We need a plan.

Marketing plans are all aimed at convincing people to try out or keep using our products or services. Creating a simple marketing plan will help you strategize the action that you will take.

> "Marketing is not the art of finding clever ways to dispose of what you make. It is the art of creating genuine customer value."
>
> *~Philip Kotle, Author/Professor of Marketing*

Your Clientele

You can determine your target audience by answering questions, such as:

- Who do you want to work with? (Age group, gender, status, professions, etc.)
- What type of client will be best suited to your style of art?
- Is there an under-served geographical area you can focus on?
- Where do they get their information? How do they communicate?
- What are the advantages of your services?
- Could you offer a specialized style, perhaps not being offered in your area, such as geometric, biomechanical or portraits, or even a less conventional form of tattooing such as cosmetic or paramedical?
- Who are the competitors in your area? What do they charge? What are their strengths/weaknesses? How do they promote their services?
- Are people

Shelly's Sidenote

4 B'S

Sometimes my new tattoo students will resist the idea of promoting themselves or learning sales skills. They have an "I am an artist, not a salesperson" attitude and they simply don't want to hear the truth about what it really takes to build their clientele. They are bothered with paperwork, taxes, advertising-- "Ugh, I cannot be a slave to the mundane, I must create!"

Unfortunately, unless you have an art patron funding your career, you'll need to face the fact that budgets, banking, bills and broadcasting are a part of even the most talented artist's process.

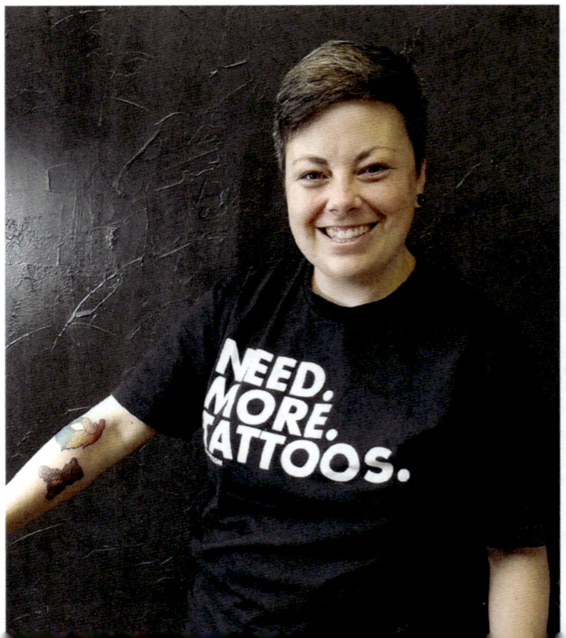

satisfied with their current artists or studios in the area? Is there a problem you could solve?

- What is your audience's primary motivation for using your service?
- What makes you, your studio or your art more exciting/interesting than others?

Remember, don't try to include everyone in your market. There is no way to offer a service that appeals to absolutely everyone. Carve out a niche and dominate!

> "Good marketing makes the company look smart. Great marketing makes the customer feel smart."
>
> ~*Joe Chernov*

Now create a list of potential clients! Even if you are just starting out, you can enlist the help of family, friends and fans of your art.

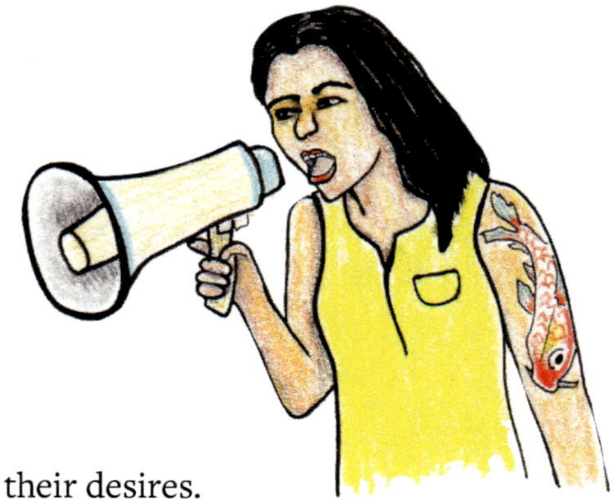

Your Marketing Message

Your compelling message tells your prospect what you do and persuades them to become your client. In your attempts to reach out to people, first focus on what benefits them. Show them that you understand their wants and needs, why you can solve their problem and offer them amazing artwork. You can include testimonials, your price and/or your guarantee.

Your message should also explain why you are the ONE who can satisfy their desires. What is it about you? What is unique, different, special, skilled or outrageous about you? Many clients will love proclaiming that YOU are their artist. Let your personality shine through your message.

Your Marketing Medium

Your marketing medium is HOW you deliver your message to your market. Choose things that make the most of your budget and deliver the message to the most people at the lowest cost. Brainstorm the best tactics to reach your target prospects.

The following is a basic list of ideas and tools you could use to get your message out:

Look Around You

- Collect competitors' ads and print materials; study them for information.
- Join an organization, association, email list or online group related to tattooing.
- Attend a workshop, convention or seminar.
- Train your clients to refer you. Make sure they have your business card and reward clients who send you business.
- Visit another city or country to observe the way tattoo studios do business in different areas.
- Stay tuned with trends in the tattoo industry. Anticipate what people may ask for.
- Ask clients why they chose you and solicit suggestions for improvement.

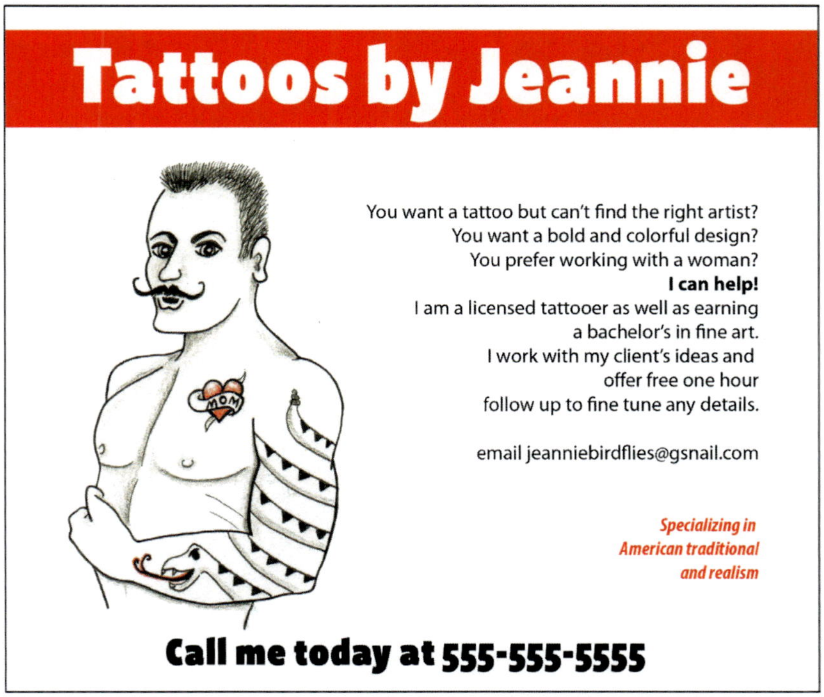

Communications

- Publish an online newsletter for clients.
- Get a website or online portfolio of your work.
- Create a postcard or calendar to give away to

Shelly's Sidenote

DOING ALL THE THINGS

While you are getting started as a tattooer, consider having multiple sources of income to support yourself, other than just tattooing, such as a part time job, selling prints of your drawings and paintings, designing posters for music shows, starting a podcast, illustrating a children's book or selling your photography. This will ensure that you can keep a roof over your head, and help you avoid the instant-noodle aisle, while you are learning the trade and building a clientele from scratch.

In addition, multiple sources of income can allow you the time to also create artwork you truly love, because you are not dependent on taking every client that walks in. Design the kind of tattoos you really enjoy creating and eventually the right folks will come along. In the meantime, you can keep the electricity on with your alternate source of income.

clients or prospects.

- Carry business cards with you at all times. You never know who you'll run into!
- Create a signature file to be used for all your email messages. It should contain contact details, including your website & social media addresses or handles.
- Include testimonials from clients in your marketing.
- Write a column for the local newspaper or a tattoo magazine (print or online).
- Start a blog.
- Have a payment method available on your phone to get that deposit "right now".

Media Relations

- Appear on a local radio show, podcast or online channel.
- Write a letter to the editor of your local newspaper.
- Consistently scan newspapers and magazines for possible PR opportunities.
- Consider putting your photo in print advertising, on your business card and on your social media. People like to see who they are connecting with.
- Submit tip articles to newsletters and blogs.
- Write an informational article for publishing or guest blog online.
- Publish a book.

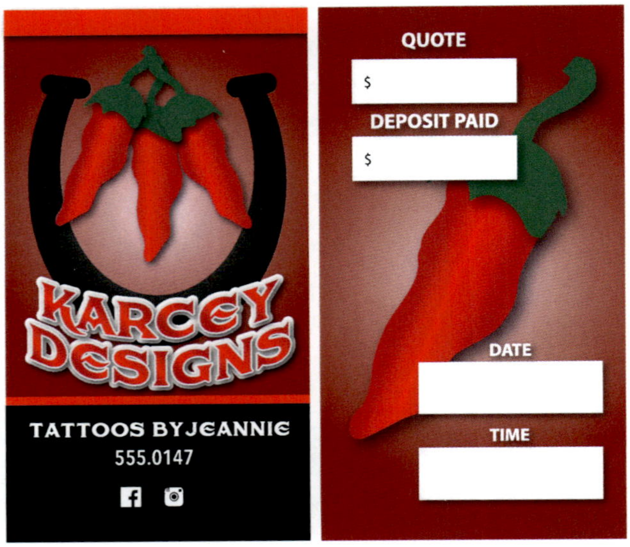

Client Relationships

- Create a pleasant space at your studio or station, where clients will be relaxed and comfortable.
- Ask your clients to come back again.
- Ask clients what you can do to help them.
- Send handwritten thank you notes.
- Send birthday cards and appropriate seasonal greetings.
- Send a book of interest or other appropriate business gift to a client with a handwritten note.

Networking and Word of Mouth

- Join your chamber of commerce or other networking organization.
- Join or organize a breakfast or lunch club with other professionals (not in your field) to discuss business and network referrals.
- Participate in an Art Walk.
- Host a holiday party.
- Hold an open house.
- Join or start a Facebook group.

"Service, in short, is not what you do, but who you are. It's a way of living that you need to bring to everything you do if you're to bring it to your customer interactions."

~Betsy Sanders, Author

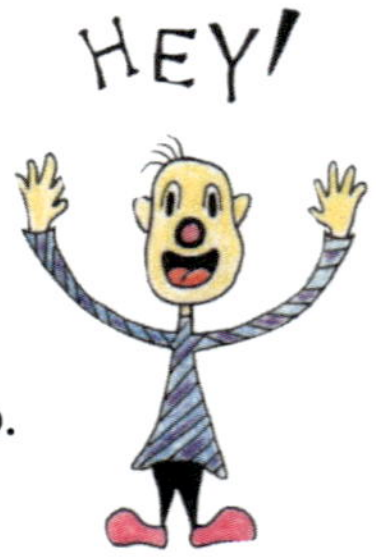

Advertising & Outreach

- Consider a hand painted or neon sign for the front of your studio.
- Teach a class.
- Create a graphic or logo that represents you and your art.
- Consider placing inexpensive ads in your local newspaper's classified section.
- Distribute merchandise with your name on them such as pens, shopping bags, or mugs.
- Consider less conventional advertising on the side of a bus, park bench or in a subway.
- Secure a booth at a tattoo convention.
- Secure a booth at a career day at a local high school.

- Sponsor and promote a contest.
- Sponsor or host a special event at your studio in cooperation with a local non-profit organization.
- Volunteer some time for a nonprofit organization.
- Hold a wine and paint party at your studio.

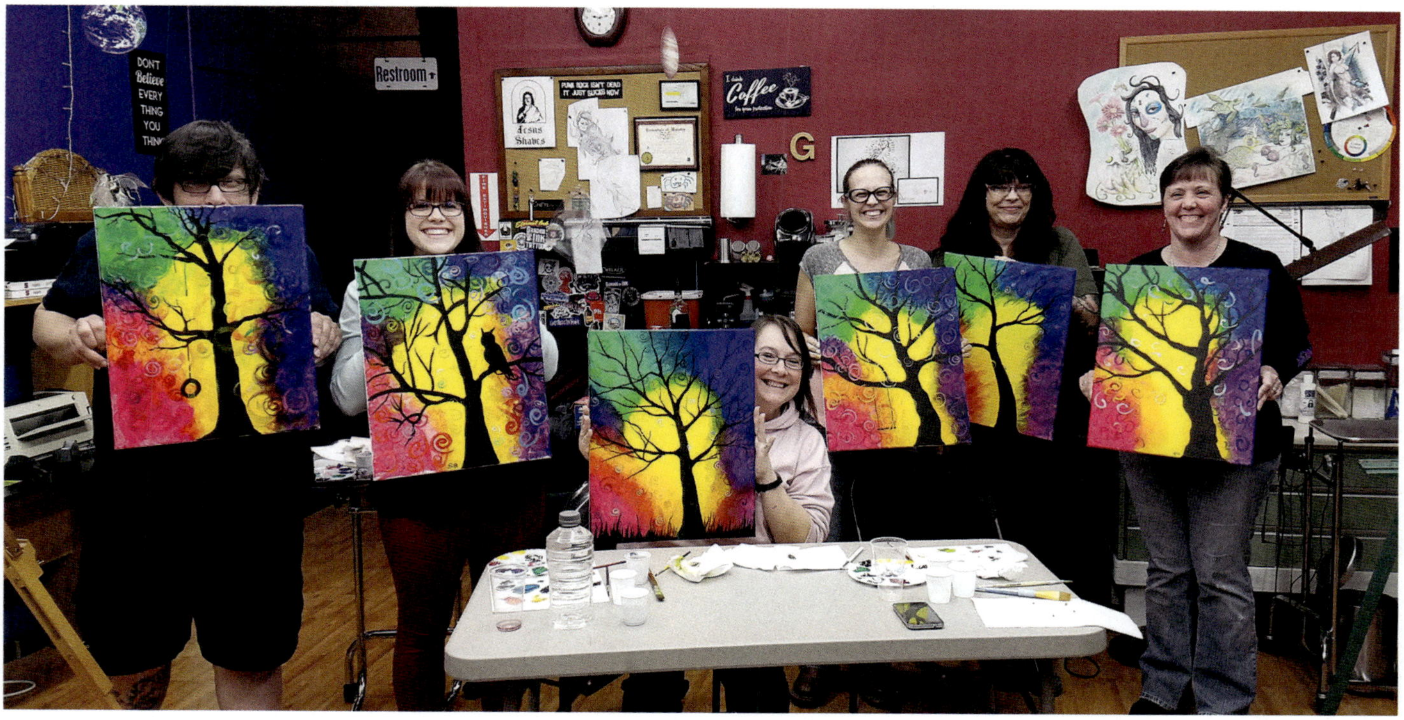

- Donate a tattoo or custom artwork to a non-profit's auction.
- Appear on a panel at a professional tattoo seminar.

Using these questions and ideas, choose your target market and choose marketing ideas that you can use to put yourself out in the public eye and get noticed. Don't get discouraged if some things don't work well. It takes time and persistence to get good at promoting yourself. Make a commitment to keep it up until you discover what works well for you.

Essential Sales Skills

Did you realize that tattoo artists must be salespeople too? Especially in the beginning of your career, you will need to develop skills to help you build your clientele. Even a naturally gifted painter's work can sit, piling up on a shelf, unseen--if they are not willing to **ask** for the sale!

- **Maintaining Self-Confidence**: if you believe in yourself and your abilities, then your clients will be inclined to believe in you as well. Even when you are first starting out, you can adopt a "fake it till you make it" attitude and practice feeling confidant. Cultivating self-assurance will help you become more assertive in expressing your artistic ideas and closing the sales. Don't give up at the hint of a "no" or the client saying, "I'll schedule later." Learn to **ask** for the sale, the deposit or the appointment.

ASK!

Shelly's Sidenote

PROMOTION CAN BE FUN

When I first started my career as a tattooer I tried numerous things to promote myself, including: joined the chamber of commerce, advertised in the phone directory, printed banners, flyers, business cards, bumper stickers and t-shirts, attended conventions, women's network breakfasts, passed out flyers at festivals, passed out my card at bars, direct mailed coupons and postcards and created a tattoo punch card. I also tried Myspace and then Facebook, put flyers under windshield wipers (oooh people hate that!), hosted artwalks, wine and paint parties, seasonal flash art days, holiday parties, holiday gift certificates, and even a poker party once where we printed our own fake money called "tattoo bucks" where the winners could exchange them for a tattoo!

But my favorite strategy was stapling a coupon to a candy bar and handing them out to kids at Halloween. The coupon said "Trick or Treat! And here's a treat for your Mom or Dad: 50% off their next tattoo!" Get creative! After all, you are an artist!

> "What makes you different or weird – that's your strength."
> ~*Meryl Streep, Actor*

- **Be a Good Listener**: take the time to ask your client questions and really listen to their answers. This shows respect and interest in their ideas. Refrain from interrupting and curb the urge to jump in too quickly while the client is talking.

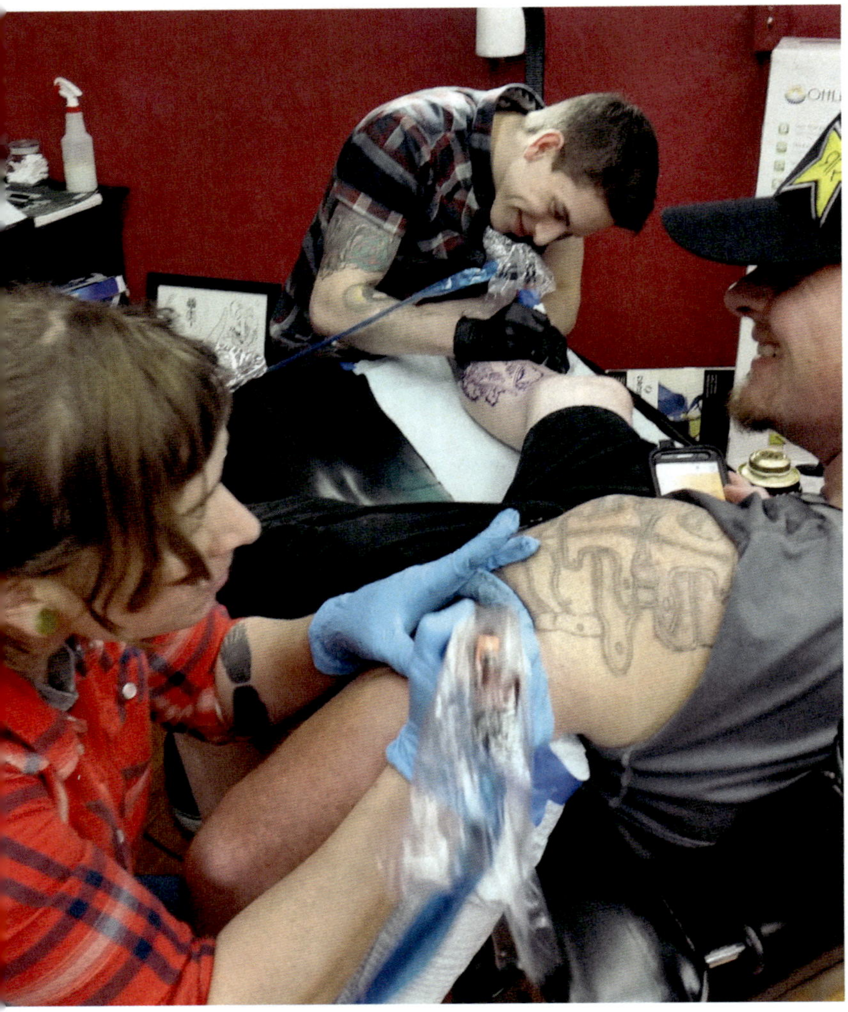

- **Persuasiveness**: the decision of a client to get a tattoo relies heavily on how they want to feel. In addition, emotions play a large role in who the client will choose to do their wearable art. Persuasiveness is the skill you need for conveying the emotional benefits to your client. If you can help your client FEEL how great it will be to get a tattoo, how expertly you will capture their ideas and how incredible they will look, then you can sell to them.

- **Building Strong Relationships**: the skill of building relationships with your client is a top priority because you spend one-on-one time with them, sometimes for many hours. Maintaining these relationships will help you develop a network in which satisfied clients will tell their friends and family about you. You will reach far more prospects through a strong network than you could manage on your own. Word of mouth is one of the most important marketing strategies and doesn't cost you anything.

- **Self-motivation**: the best artist is always a work in progress. You don't really have a boss if you are an independent contractor, thus, no one tells you what to do. You must find the motivation to continually work on your skills, learn new techniques and find ways to improve your circumstances. No one will do this for you. The drive to constantly improve will have to come from within. Fortunately, there are numerous books, workshops and online courses to assist you in your growth—even books on motivation!

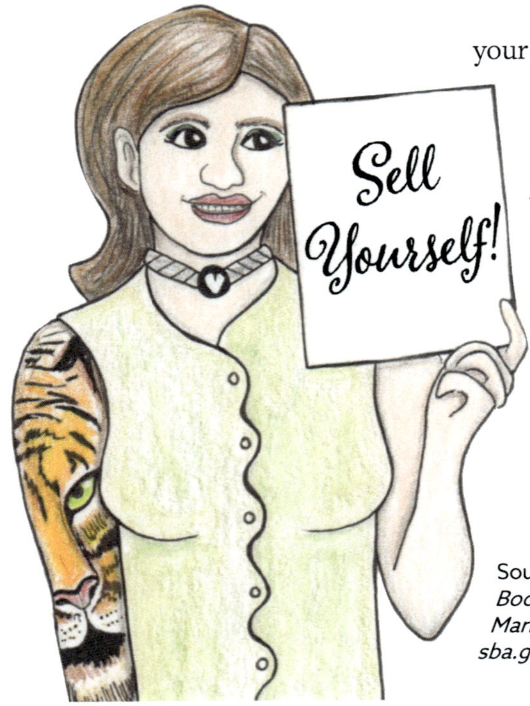

And remember, YES you are selling your art, but you are also selling YOURSELF. Learning sales skills is one aspect, but having a pleasant demeanor, concern for the client's wellbeing and showing integrity, all create clients who enthusiastically recommend you and come straight to you when they want new ink.

Sources:
Book Yourself Solid; Illustrated Guide, Michael Port, (c)2013
Marketing Strategies to Build Your Clientele, BusinessKnowledgeSource.com, (c)2018
sba.gov/course/marketing-101-guide-winning-customers, (c)2018

Chapter Eleven Highlights

- Sometimes tattoo artists are called freelancers or entrepreneurs.
- Some benefits of being self-employed include: increased choice, increased freedom, potentially higher pay, no federal or state tax withheld, and increased business deductions.
- Some drawbacks of being self-employed include: no job security, no employer provided benefits, no employer provided workers compensation, you might not get paid, and you must pay estimated taxes quarterly.
- You must research your own areas laws before starting to tattoo people.
- Marketing is the action of promoting and selling products and services.
- The key word is ACTION.
- Determine your target audience by asking yourself a series of questions, such as "Who do you want to work with" or "What makes you and your studio unique"?
- Your marketing medium is HOW you deliver the message.
- Brainstorm the best tactics to reach your target audience.
- Tattoo artists must be willing to ask people to book with them.
- Build strong relationships with your clients.

Wisecracks:

Money can't buy happiness, but it can buy tattoos.

And that's kind of the same thing.

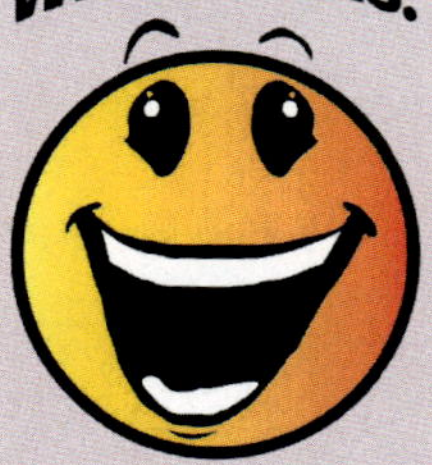

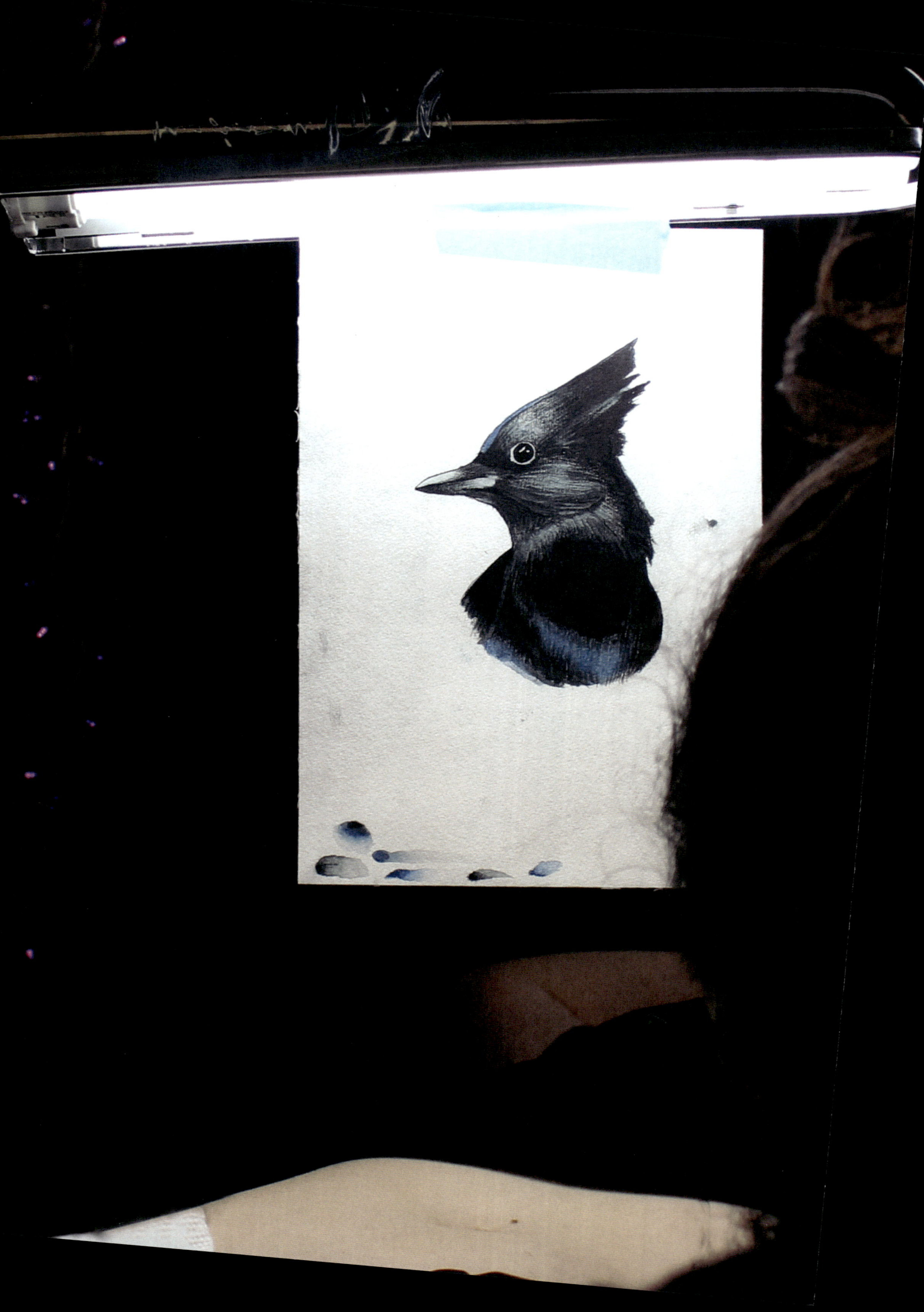

Chapter Twelve

Conclusion

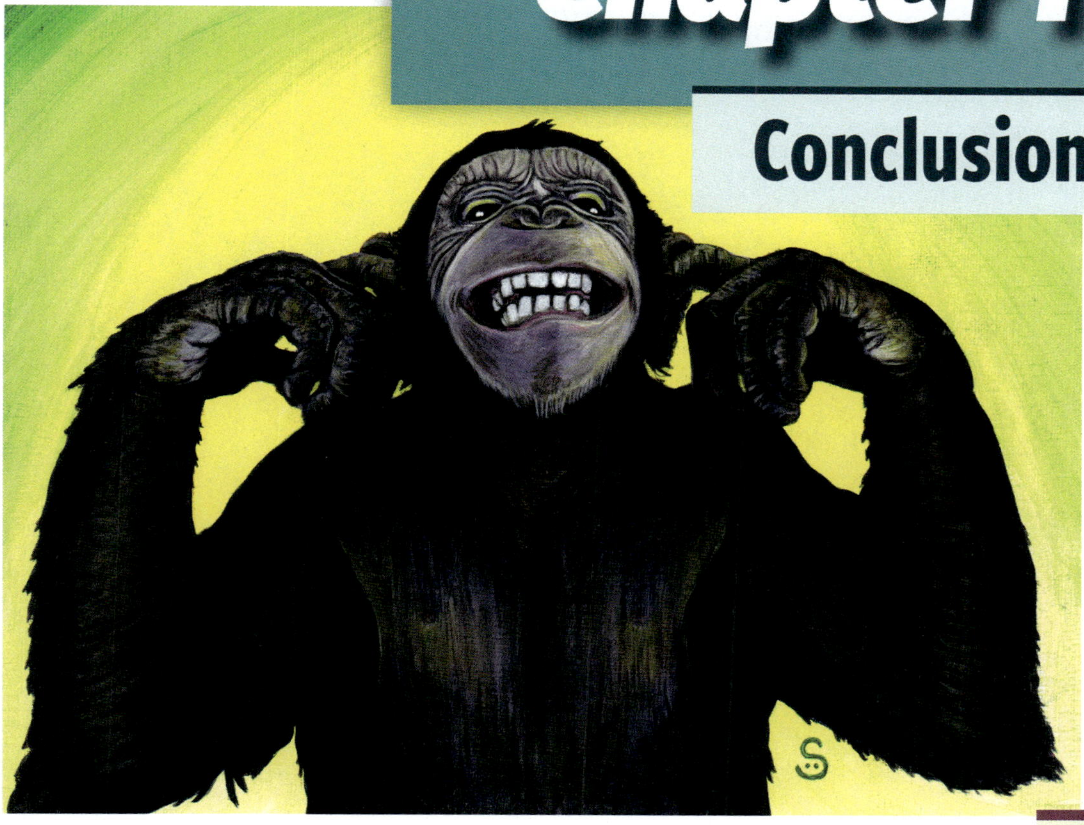

This book just scratches the surface of the vast information available out there for tattoo artists. In addition, many states require a certain number of hours of continuing education to retain your status as a licensed tattoo artist. Even if not required, it is an excellent idea to commit to a certain number of advanced training opportunities each year, whether through books, videos, online courses or seminars at tattoo conventions.

"Art is anything that's creative, passionate, and personal. And great art resonates with the viewer, not only with the creator.

What makes someone an artist? An artist is someone who uses bravery, insight, creativity, and boldness to challenge the status quo. And an artist takes it personally.

Art is a personal gift that changes the recipient. The medium doesn't matter. The intent does. Art is a personal act of courage, something one human does that creates change in another."

~Seth Godin, Author

Continuing Your Education

Here are a few of our favorite books, videos and webinars:

Technique

Reinventing the Tattoo; Technique DVD, Guy Aitchison
Coverup; A Fresh Look and *Coverup; The Next Level,* DVDs, Guy Aitchison
Tattoo Improvement Network, Jake Meeks, Youtube channel

> "In the end, people will judge you anyway. So don't live your life impressing others--live your life impressing yourself."
> ~*Eunice Camacho Infante, Author*

Method to my Madness DVD, Bob Tyrell
Get Real and *Get Real; Animal Style* DVDs, Mike Devries
Tattooing Color Portraits DVD, Nikko Hurtado
Art Core, Isolation Training for Visual Art, Jeff Gogue, WEBINAR, tattoonow.com

Building a Clientele
Book Yourself Solid; Illustrated, BOOK, Michael Port

Coil Machines
Tattoo Machine: Set up, Tuning, and Maintenance, BOOK, Joey Desormeaux
Tattoo Machines & Their Secrets (2nd edition), BOOK, Art Godoy and Steve Godoy

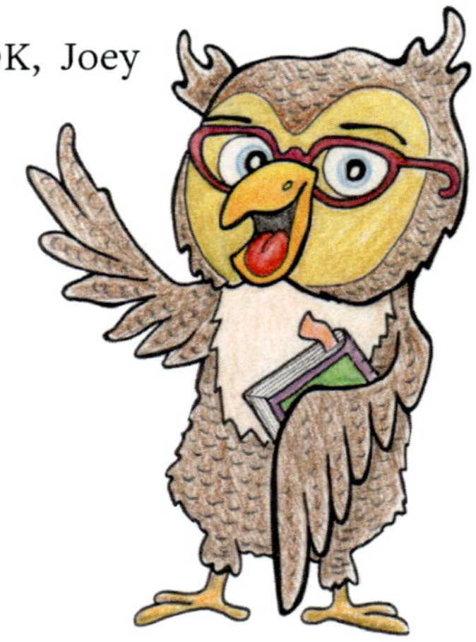

Perspective on Tattooing
Tattoo As I See It, DVD, Jeff Gogue

Coffee Table Book
Tattoo Prodigies, BOOK, Memento Publishing

Tattoo History
The Tattoo History Sourcebook, BOOK, Steve Gilbert
The History of Tattooing and its Significance, BOOK, Wilfrid Dyson Hambly

Open your Own Tattoo Studio
Building a Great Tattoo Business, WEBINAR, tattoonow.com
Start & Run a Tattoo & Body Piercing Studio, BOOK, Kurtis Mueller & Tanya Lee Howe

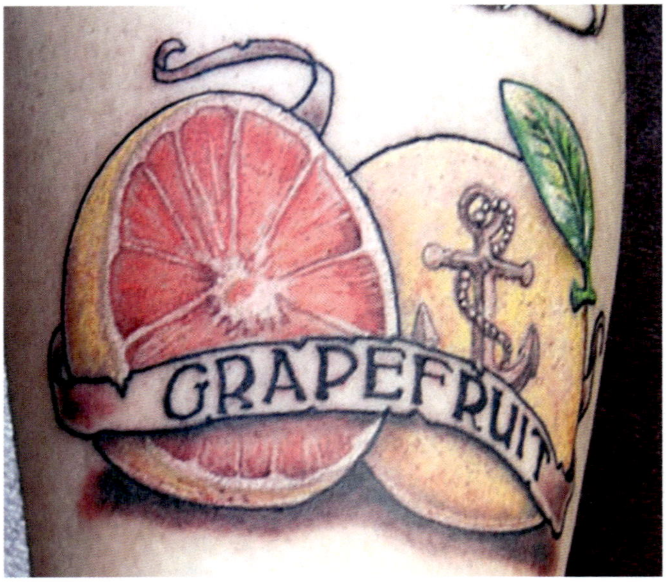

Conclusion

As we said in the beginning, we DO NOT recommend tattooing on people without some hands-on training, under an experienced tattooer. But hopefully studying this book has helped prepare you to seek out a qualified mentor, now that you have a solid understanding of what it takes to become a tattooer and you've practiced for many, many hours on grapefruits, fake skin and drawing every day! Believe it or not, a well put together portfolio of drawings and paintings, as well as skillful grapefruit & fake skin tattoos can be very impressive.

Your portfolio, together with your knowledge of the basics presented here, and a list of your prospective clients, as well as your simple marketing plan, should be more than enough to convince an experienced tattooer or tattoo instructor to take you under their wing and continue your education, either in a required formal education or an informal mentor relationship. Studio owners want to see that you are indeed educated, talented, determined and willing to do what it takes to develop your skills as well as help grow their business.

And if you'd like coaching, fun freebies and access to a positive vibe art & inspiration focused group--sign up for the *Shelly's* email list at:

www.shellydax.com

Shelly's Sidenote

YOUR CAREER

Tattoo careers come in all shapes and sizes. Why did you decide to tattoo? You may have:

- been hanging out at tattoo shops for years and wished to work your way up to an apprenticeship.
- attended art school or even have a degree in art.
- worked a full-time job, have three kids and are willing to sacrifice extras in hopes of being trained.
- desired to get in to a licensed tattoo school.
- been fascinated with tattoo history or perhaps you were a tattoo collector who has finally decided to learn for yourself.
- been drawing your whole life and people keep telling you that you should be a tattoo artist.

Despite what others may think of you, there is no one "correct" way to the path of tattooing (though ignoring safety & health issues will always be incorrect). We know there are many incredibly talented tattoo artists from around the world who each got started in a myriad of ways and have their own opinion on what makes a great tattooer.

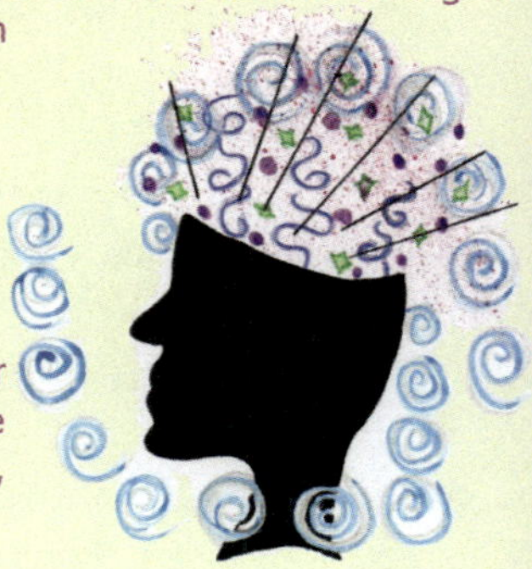

However, one major thing applies to every tattoo artist: **you should remain open to learning for a lifetime!**

Beginning from the baby steps to the end of your career you will be developing your craft. There will always be something new to learn. This is a journey...a marathon, not a sprint!

From finding your confidence, understanding the fundamentals and tackling the tools, to dealing with rejection, mistakes, cranky clients and seasonal downtime. It is sometimes a bumpy road to the success you are seeking and even becoming successful brings its own unique challenges.

Many people can be harsh and critical, and not everyone is going to like your designs. You must learn to let go of opinions that don't serve you and allow things to roll off your back. Detach from the competitive nature of the tattoo industry and hold your own vision with confidence. Only compare yourself to your previous self. And stay connected with the people who support you and enjoy your artwork.

Remember, rejection is a big part of the art world, whether tattooing, drawing or painting. But with a little humor, perseverance and determination, you will find your way. Your skills will continue to grow if you simply keep practicing, show up through the disappointing times, and remain open to new possibilities.

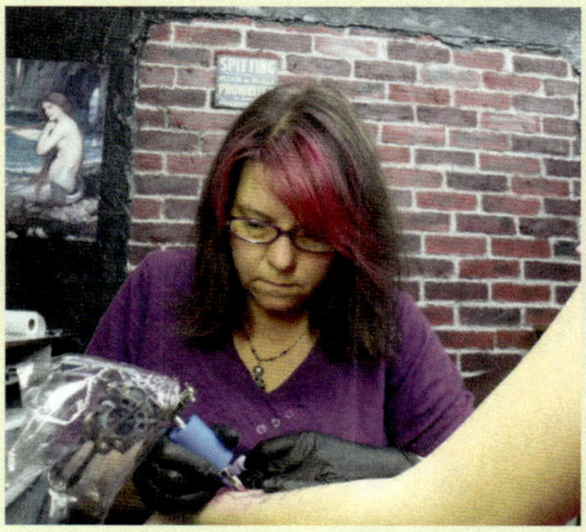

CHEERS TO THE JOURNEY!!

Shelly Dax

"Critics hang around and wait for others to make mistakes. But the real doers of the world have no time for criticizing others. They're too busy doing, making mistakes, improving and making progress."
~Dr. Wayne Dyer, Author/ speaker

★★★★★

If you LOVED **The Tattoo Textbook**, please write us a review on Amazon, Google Books, Good Reads or Kindle. We appreciate your time.

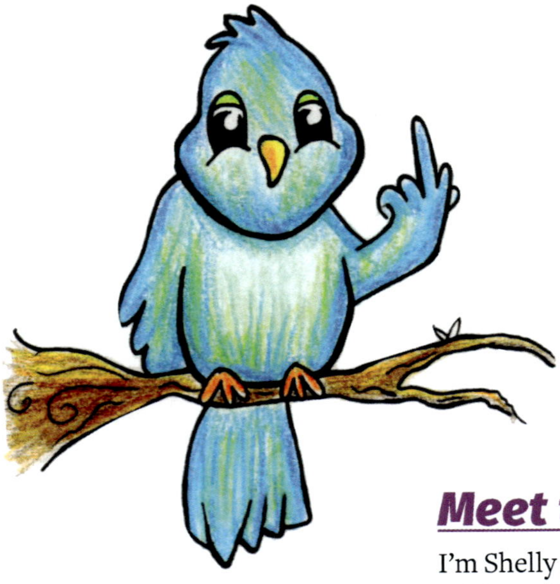

> "Recognizing that people's reactions don't belong to you is the only sane way to create. If people enjoy what you've created, terrific. If people ignore what you've created, too bad. If people misunderstand what you've created, don't sweat it. And what if people absolutely hate what you've created? What if people attack you with savage vitriol, and insult your intelligence, and malign your motives, and drag your good name through the mud? Just smile sweetly and suggest – as politely as you possibly can – that they go make their own fucking art. Then stubbornly continue making yours."
>
> ~ *Elizabeth Gilbert, Author Eat, Pray, Love and Big Magic*

Meet the Author

Fierce Pollyanna
Pol·ly·an·na
Noun
A feisty badass who is also an excessively cheerful or optimistic person.

I'm Shelly Dax--artist, writer, teacher and fierce Pollyanna! I'm a true renaissance girl–I ADORE all things artistic. Sang my first solo at age five and wrote my first story at age nine. I was bit by the artsy bug. My childhood was filled with artistic endeavors, from plays to ceramics to choir to poetry. I even learned to play piano at 16.

I also spent more than 12 years working in theatre (the old joke is-- "where all the gays, deviants and loose women hang out"); acting, directing, singing, writing and teaching, BEFORE getting licensed as a tattoo artist, and opening my tattoo studio (you know... "where all the bikers, deviants and loose women hang out!")

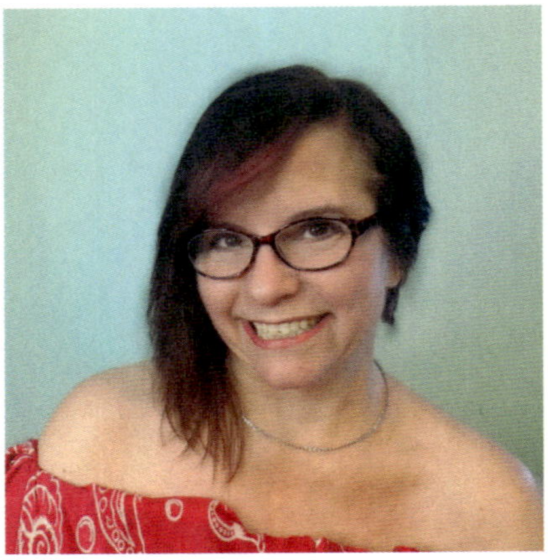

I've owned my tattoo studio since 2006 and I've been teaching tattoo school since 2011. I live in the state of Oregon, where attending tattoo school is a requirement to receive a tattoo license. I've been fortunate enough to have 60+ wonderful students over the years, who have brought their own personality, talents, skills and determination to their training. Working with some exceptional folks has pushed me to grow and search for ways to explain tattooing in the most effective terms.

Working on this book off and on for five years, and at least 30 hours a week for the last six months, has been a MUCH more tedious task than I EVER could have imagined. My partner Gil Rodello, who is also an instructor at the school, has taken on more than his share of tasks to make room for me to write. I can't thank him enough.

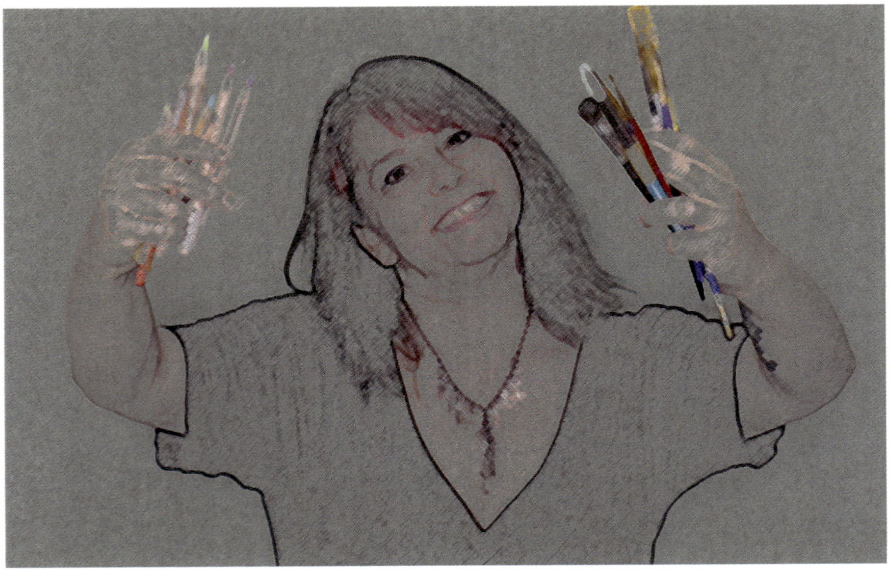

It is my fervant hope that this textbook will streamline the learning process, help eliminate the risk of unskilled tattooing, and remove some of the barriers of entry into the tattoo industry.

I personally had a very challenging beginning starting out to tattoo, and met with a lot of resistance and, to be honest, some mysogynistic assholes. It was not easy to break in, especially for women, and the atmospere back then was harsh and full of intimidation. I realize it still is in some areas. YUCK! Let's change that!

I love the idea of making it easier for others to participate in such a unique and rewarding art form and career. Tattooing is an incredible way to share creativity and connect with diverse people from all walks of life. That is one of the main reasons I wrote this book!

I am especially grateful for the tattoo students who allowed me to photograph them and their tattoo process, as well as the clients who have been so wonderfully supportive. Thanks for the testimonials and terrific reviews.

And a special thanks to Jeff Gogue; the first male tattooer I met after getting my license who was kind, helpful and for me, broke the stereotype of the typical self-important artist.

> "My friend told me I was delusional. I laughed so hard I almost fell off my unicorn!"
> *~unknown*

A Peek at My Tattoo Work

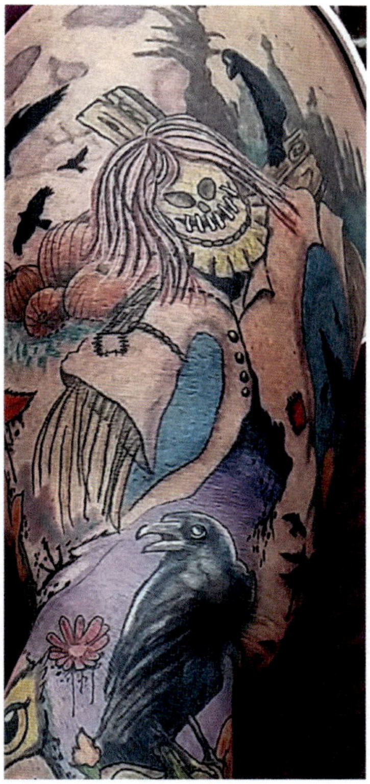

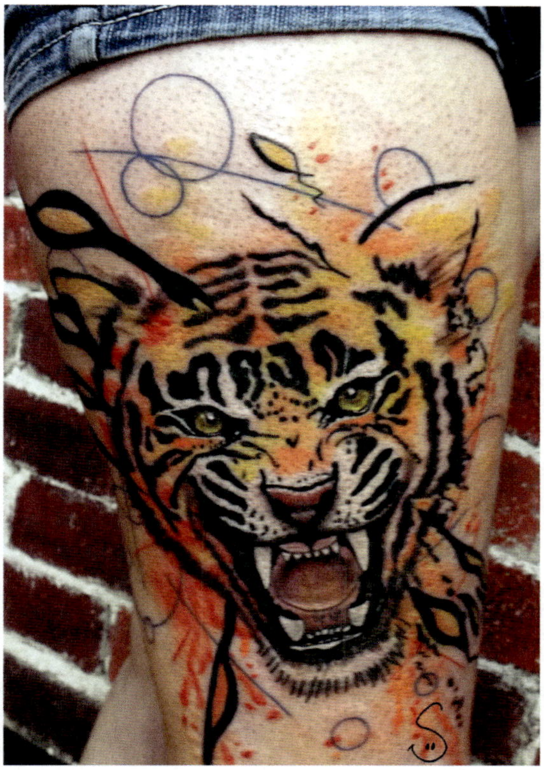

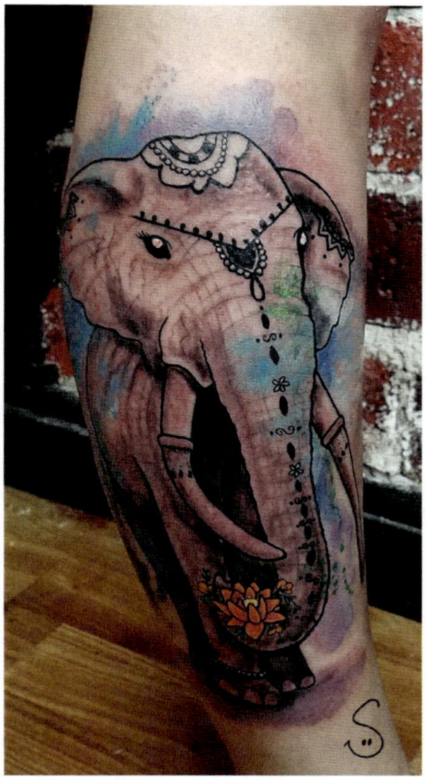

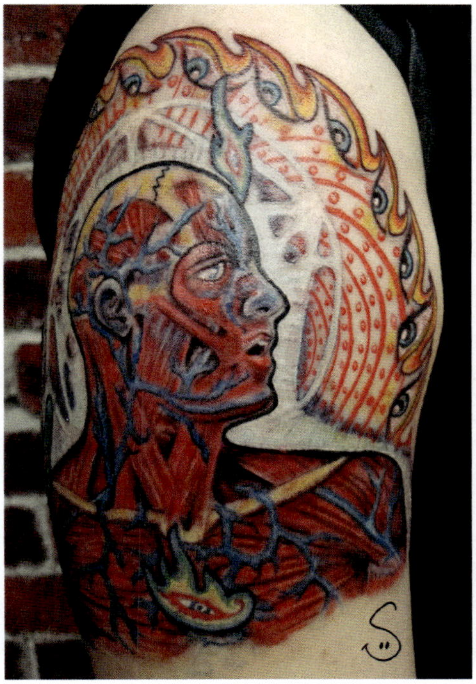

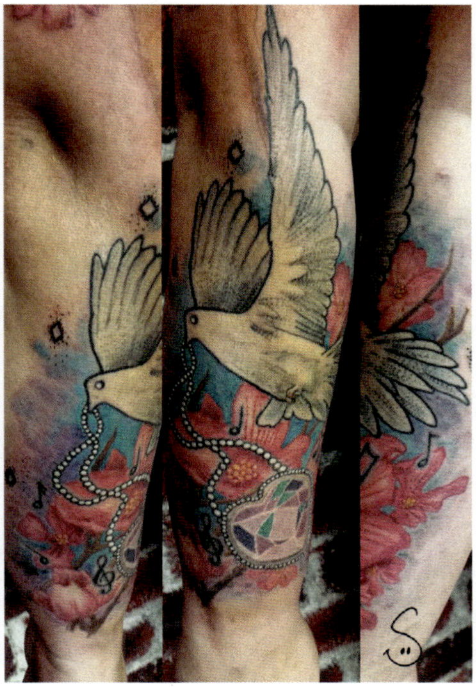

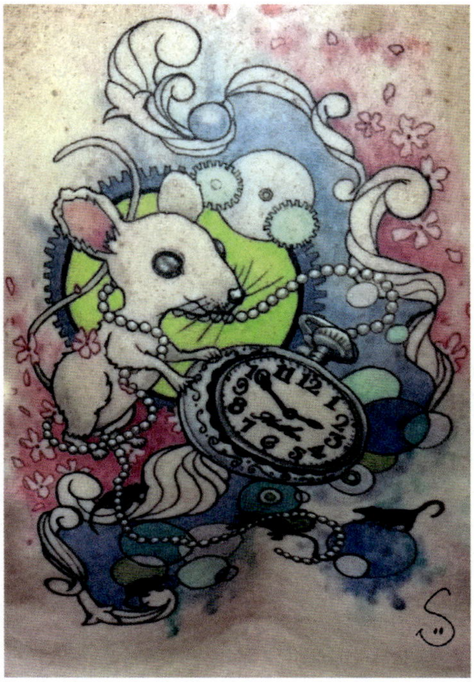

Ouside of tattooing, I enjoy painting, watercolor pencils, pebble art and sculpting clay. I also love to cook, camp, plan parties, do theatre, and laugh & play games with my family!!

I am lucky enough to be one of those fucking ANNOYING people who do what they love and love what they do. And I am extraordinarily grateful every day.

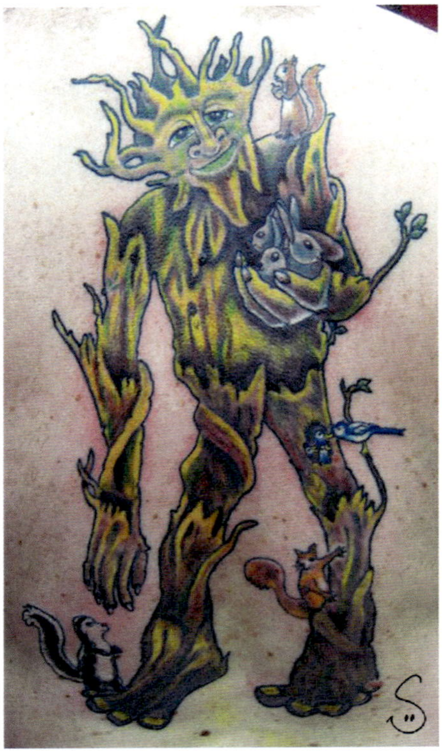

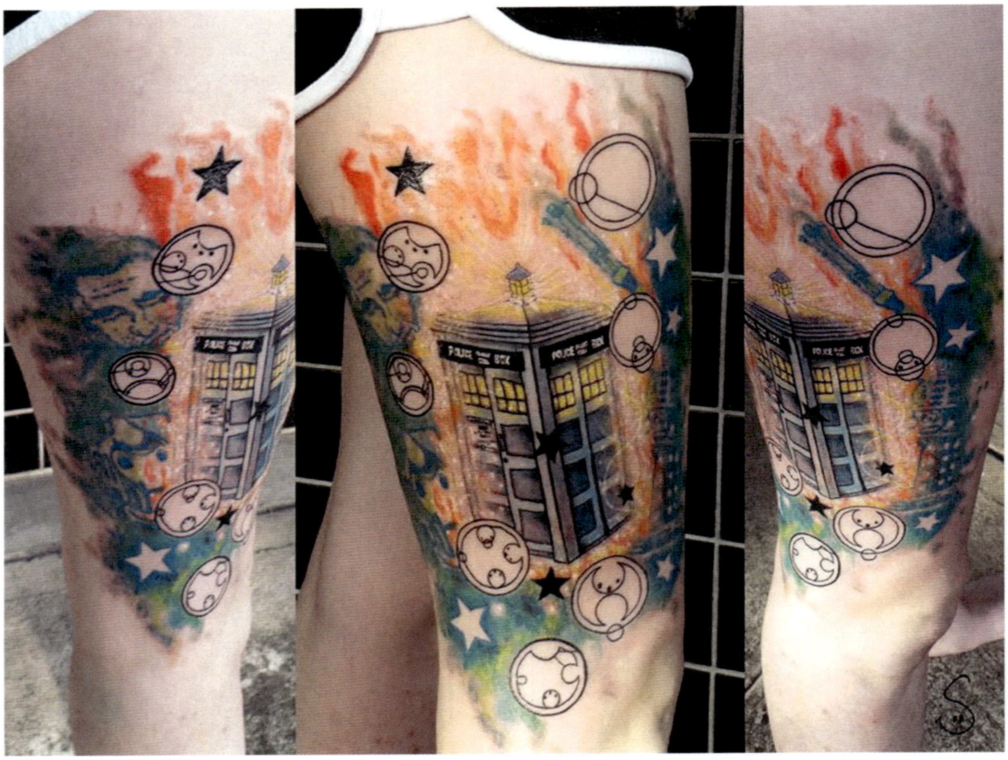

My Other Artforms

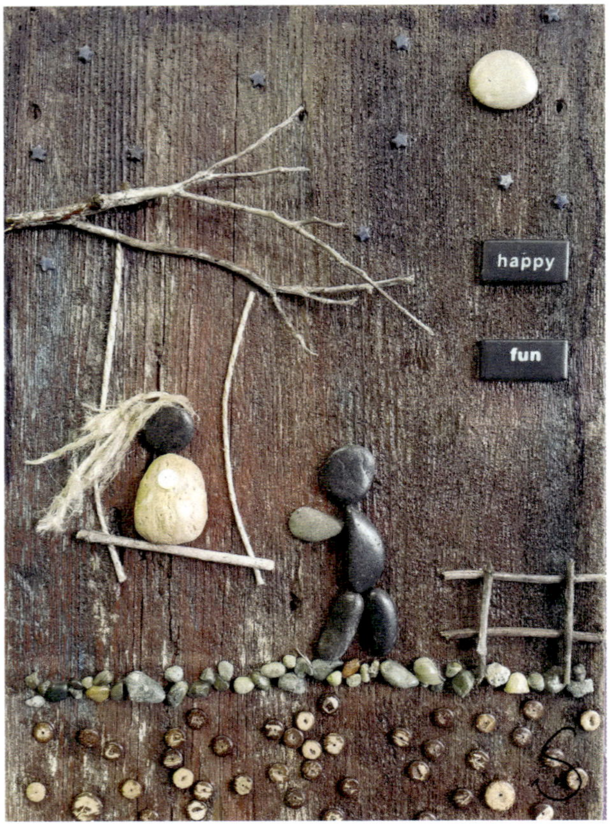

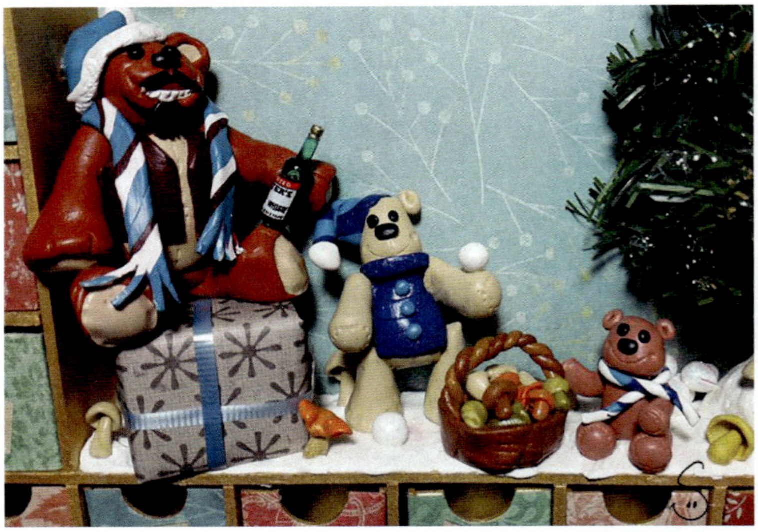

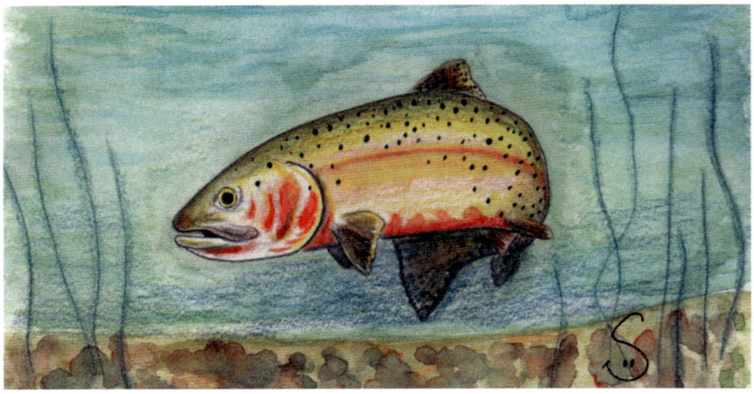

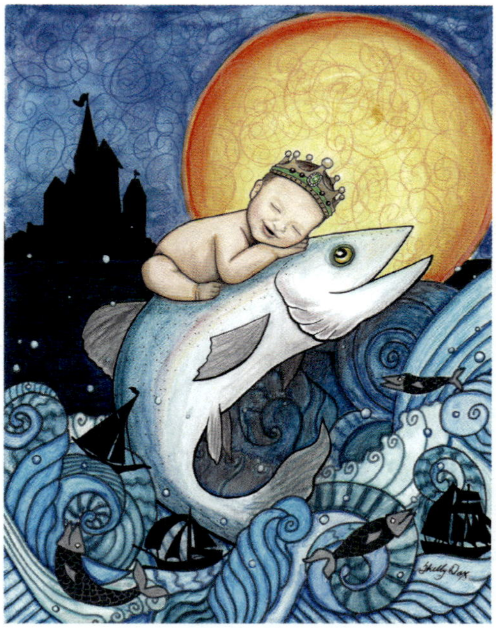
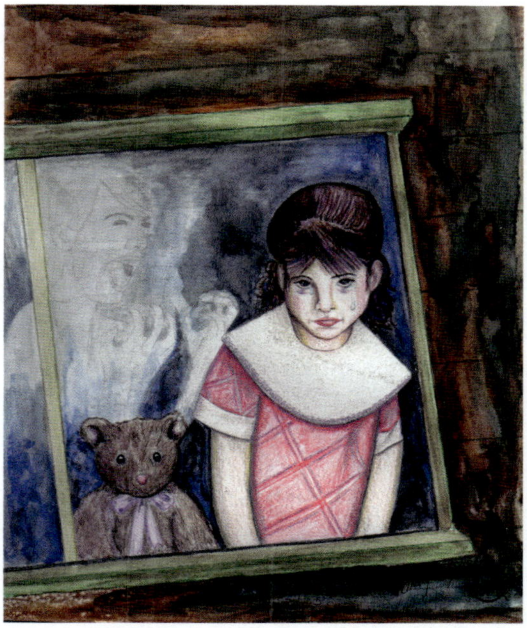
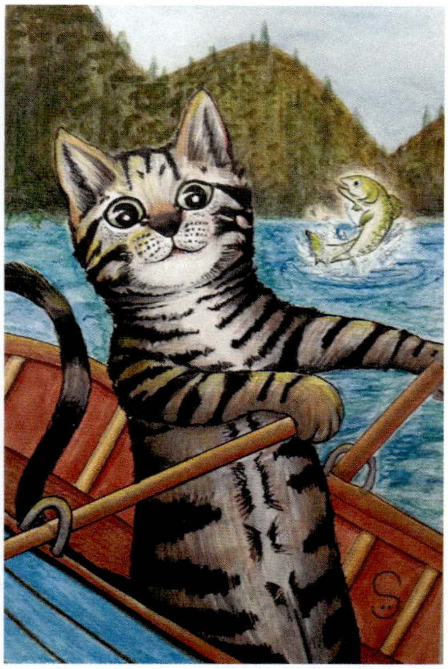
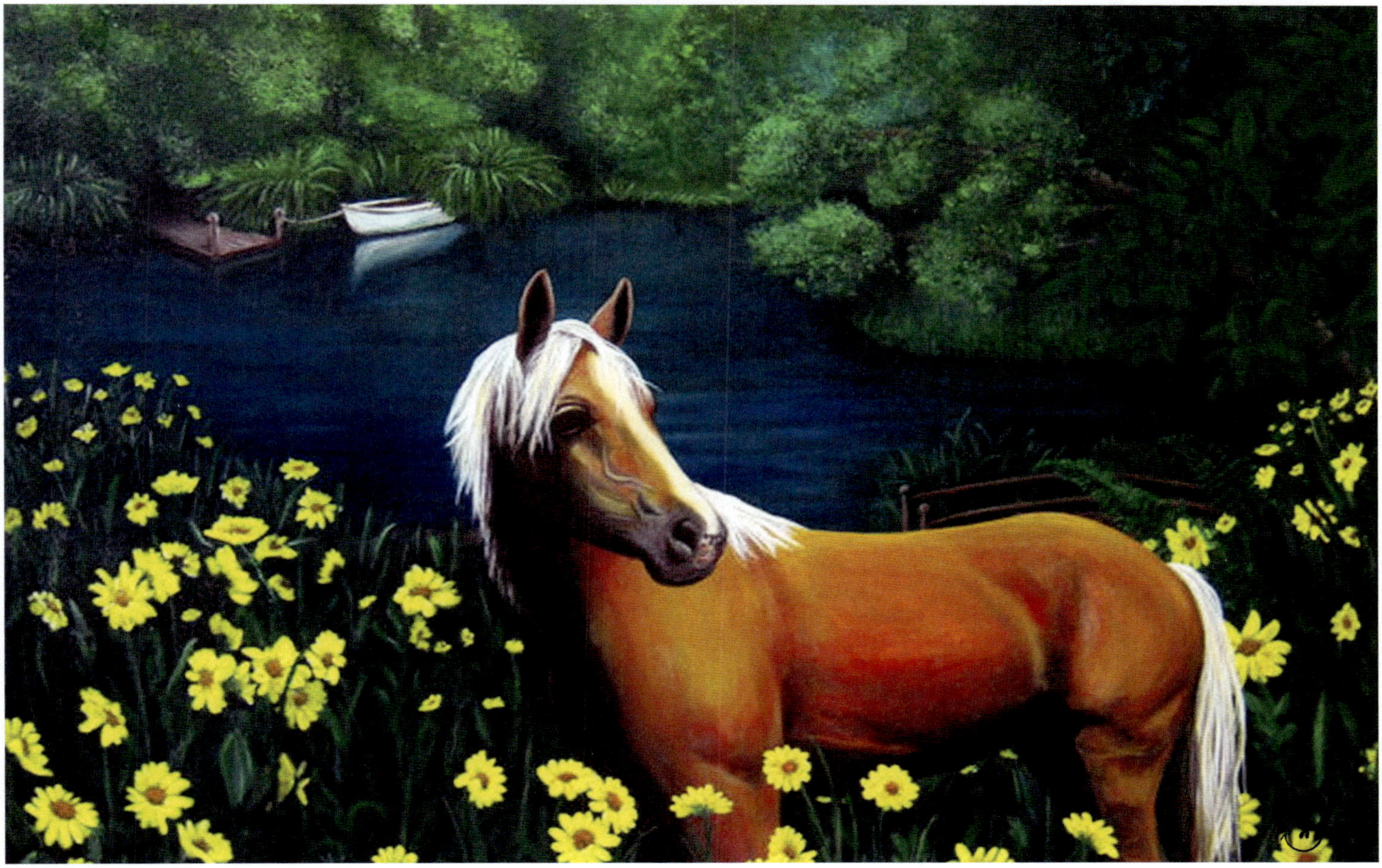

I appreciate you reading this book and plan to publish several other art, creativity and inspirational books in the future. Check out my website at: **shellydax.com**

If you have any comments or questions please let us know:
thetattootextbook@gmail.com

/shellydax **/shellydax** **/shellydax**

Shelly Dax

On the following pages you will find generic tattoo studio forms as well as tattoo flash. We give you permission to scan the forms and the flash for your own personal use or for use in your tattoo studio. Or you can simply tear the pages out and make copies. Hope you enjoy!

For more art, fun, coaching or creative inspiration, go to
shellydax.com

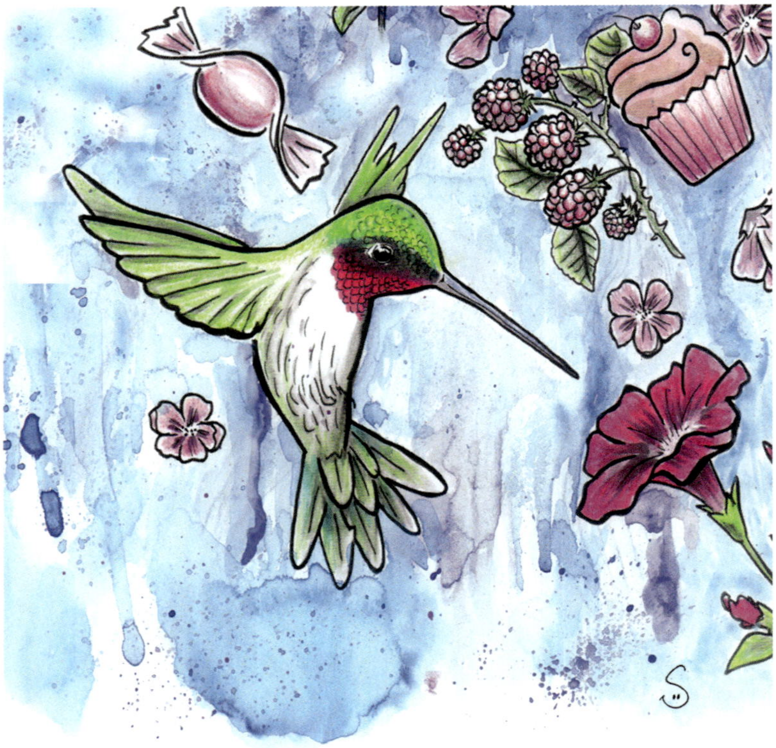

For bulk orders of 10 or more books email thetattootextbook@gmail.com

release & consent

AT LOCATION OF TATTOO:

- ❑ Cold sores/Fever blisters
- ❑ Psoriasis/Eczema
- ❑ Moles/Sunburn/Birthmarks
- ❑ Scars/Keloids Rash
- ❑ Diabetic
- ❑ Heart condition
- ❑ Coconut Allergy
- ❑ Aspirin or blood thinners
- ❑ Pregnant/Nursing
- ❑ HIV/AIDS
- ❑ Hepatitis
- ❑ Epilepsy

Please check all that apply or check here if NONE apply: ❑

Please list your medications, medical conditions, allergies, and/or sensitivities, even if you feel they will not affect the procedure:

____

____

____

____

Please tell us where you heard about our shop: ❑ Friend ❑ Google Search ❑ Facebook Page ❑ Other ____________

PLEASE READ AND BE CERTAIN YOU UNDERSTAND THE IMPLICATIONS OF SIGNING THIS DOCUMENT

In consideration of receiving a tattoo, I agree to the following:

- That I, ______________________________________ (clearly PRINT your name) have been fully informed of the inherent risks, associated with getting a tattoo. I fully understand that these risks, known and unknown, can lead to injury, including but not limited to infection, scarring, difficulties in detecting melanoma and allergic reactions to tattoo pigment, latex gloves, and/or soap. Having been informed of the potential risks associated with getting a tattoo, I still wish to proceed with the tattoo application and I freely accept and expressly assume any and all risks that may arise from tattooing.

- TO WAIVE AND RELEASE to the fullest extent permitted by law, each of the artists and the tattoo studio from all liability whatsoever, for any and all claims or causes of action that I, my estate, heirs, executors or assigns may have for personal injury or otherwise, including any direct and/or consequential damages, which result or arise from the application of my tattoo, whether caused by the negligence or fault of either the artist or our studio, or otherwise.

- That the Tattoo Studio has given me the full opportunity to ask any and all questions about the application of my tattoo and all of my questions have been answered to my satisfaction. Furthermore, I acknowledge that the Tattoo Studio has taken every precaution possible to provide a safe and sterile environment for my service. In addition, the artist has given me instructions on the care of my tattoo while it's healing, as well as possible side effects, complications and restrictions and I understand them and will follow them. I acknowledge that it is possible that the tattoo can become infected, particularly if I do not follow the instructions given to me. If any touch-up work to the tattoo is needed due to my own negligence, I agree that the work will be done at my own expense.

- I am not under the influence of alcohol or drugs, and I am voluntarily submitting to be tattooed by the artist without duress or coercion.

- Neither the artist nor Tattoo Studio is responsible for the meaning or spelling of the symbol or text that I have provided to them or that I have chosen from the studio's flash art. Variations in color and design may exist between the tattoo art I have selected and the actual tattoo when it is applied to my body. I also understand that over time, the colors and the clarity of my tattoo will fade due to unprotected exposure to the sun and the naturally occurring dispersion of pigment under the skin.

- A tattoo is a permanent change to my appearance and can only be removed by laser or surgical means, which can be disfiguring and/or costly and which in all likelihood will not result in the restoration of my skin to its exact appearance before being tattooed.

- I release all rights to any photographs taken of my tattoo and give consent in advance to their reproduction in print or electronic form.

- I acknowledge that I have been given adequate opportunity to read and understand this document, that it was not presented to me at the last minute, and I understand that I am signing a legal contract waiving certain rights to recover against the Tattoo Studio.

- If any provision, section, subsection, clause or phrase of this release is found to be unenforceable or invalid, that portion shall be severed from this contract. The remainder of this contract will then be construed as though the unenforceable portion had never been contained in this document.

- I hereby declare that I am of legal age (and have provided valid proof of age) and am competent to sign this agreement and I am in complete understanding and concurrence with this agreement.

Phone Number ____________________ Email Address ________________________

Signature ____ Date ____________

PLACE LICENSE HERE

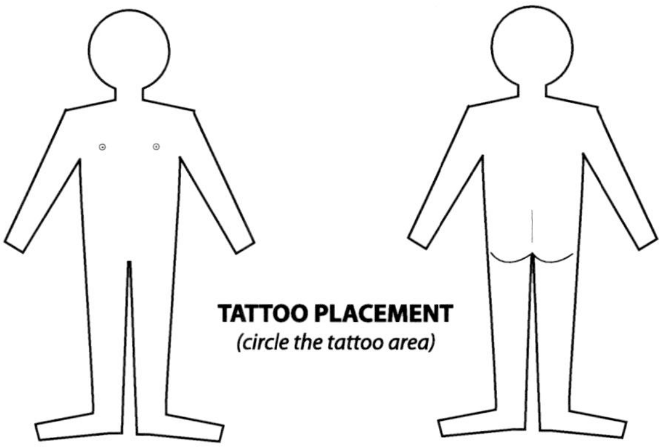

TATTOO PLACEMENT

(circle the tattoo area)

preservice & aftercare

Preservice Information

For your peace of mind we use professional equipment, commercial pigments and the highest sterilization standards.

Please be well rested and eat a good meal before your procedure! DO NOT drink alcohol or use drugs prior to being tattooed. We will refuse service to anyone who appears intoxicated.

What to Expect:

Your tattoo will generally take 10-14 days to heal. It will be tender for the first few days, then it will develop a light crust of dry skin over the surface. This crust will gradually flake off like a sunburn. During this period, the tattoo may look uneven and/or pale in color, and some ink may flake off as well. **THIS IS NORMAL**. In the last stage of healing the skin will have a tight, shiny surface. This waxy look will slowly leave and the skin will return to its normal appearance and texture. We provide written AFTERCARE instructions below AND we will go over this with you verbally at the end of the procedure. (Remember, every person's skin is different...your healing process may vary)

Immediately following your tattoo there may be some seeping of blood or plasma. This is why we bandage your tattoo. Also, some people experience minor swelling or bruising depending on the location of the tattoo. In addition, as the tattoo heals you may also experience itching. **Don't scratch**--pat or slap with a clean hand instead!

Potential Complications:

Due to the time involved in healing a tattoo, there is always the risk of infection.

Excellent hygiene can prevent most infections!

Do not use Neosporin or Bacitracin UNLESS there is infection as these products can cause reactions or pull ink from your tattoo [we prefer witch hazel]. Although extremely rare, allergic reaction and/or sensitivity to a particular pigment/ink can be a problem, sometimes intensified by exposure to heat or sun during the healing process.

AFTERCARE INSTRUCTIONS

(Please follow carefully!)

1. **Leave bandage on between approximately 1-1/2 to 2 hours.** (If the bandage really sticks, you may soak to get it off -- NO soaking after that!)

2. **Wash your hands thoroughly, or be sure person helping you has clean hands.** Gently remove bandage, wash your tattoo with bare hand, fragrance free soap from a dispenser (not bar soap) and warm water, removing any ointment or blood. Pat dry with clean paper towel and air dry 15 minutes. NEVER re-bandage your tattoo.

3. At this stage some people will apply a small amount of **healing ointment*** VERY thinly over tattoo, other people don't use any cream or lotion at all. **Repeat steps # 2 & 3, one to three times per day, for five - seven days.** Occasional spritz with witch hazel, it helps keep infection and itch away.

4. **After 5-7 days simply mosturize** your tattoo lightly whenever it feels crusty or dry, until it is fully healed.

5. For two weeks: Absolutely **NO sun-tanning, picking, scratching or soaking in any water (bathtub, hot tub, pool, lake, etc).** Shower is fine but don't soak your new tattoo. Also please wear loose clothing while tattoo heals. If you engage in activities in the sun AFTER your tattoo has healed, **use sunscreen** to protect your tattoo. Proper aftercare of your tattoo means you will enjoy it for years!

Please feel free to call, e-mail or facebook message us if you have any questions or concerns. It's our pleasure to share in the creation of your personal body art and we look forward to serving you again soon! Take care of your investment!

*If irritation occurs, wash tattoo thoroughly, discontinue use of product, wait 24 hours and try a different product.

Thanks!

Artist's Name:______________________________ Date of Service: ________________

receipt

Client: ______________________________

Phone: ______________________________

Email: ______________________________

Artist: ______________________________

DEPOSIT	QUOTE
$	$

APPOINTMENT DATE:

DATE: ______________________ TIME: __________

S M T W Th F Sa

Deposit is **non-refundable** and goes toward the cost of your tattoo
If you are late for your appointment you may be rescheduled No shows will forfeit their deposit
48 Hour notice is required to reschedule.

commission

Artist: ______________________________

Date	Client Name	Amt paid	Commission

PAID: Cash
Check #
Other ___________

TOTAL

shopping list

- ❑ Solid Black Ink Refill
- ❑ Lining Black Ink Refill
- ❑ Graywash Ink Refills
- ❑ Cord Covers
- ❑ Rinse Cups
- ❑ Petroleum Jelly
- ❑ Razors
- ❑ Sensi-wrap
- ❑ Med Tape
- ❑ Toothpicks
- ❑ Q-tips
- ❑ Tongue Depressors
- ❑ Polyacrylate
- ❑ Blue Tape
- ❑ Barrier Film
- ❑ Alcohol
- ❑ Witch Hazel
- ❑ Hand Soap
- ❑ Hand Sanitizer
- ❑ S - Glove
- ❑ M - Glove
- ❑ L - Glove
- ❑ XL - Glove
- ❑ #9 Ink Cup
- ❑ #13 Ink Cup
- ❑ #16 Ink Cup
- ❑ Surgical Masks
- ❑ Cotton Pads
- ❑ 4 Gal. Trash Bags
- ❑ Baggies
- ❑ Sandwich Bags
- ❑ Bactine

- ❑ High-level Disinfectant
- ❑ Green Soap
- ❑ Sharps Container

- ❑ Floor Cleaner
- ❑ Glass Cleaner
- ❑ Low-level Disinfectant
- ❑ 13 Gal. Trash Bags
- ❑ 39 Gal. Trash bags
- ❑ Distilled Water
- ❑ Duster Refills
- ❑ Light Bulbs
- ❑ Mop Head Refills

- ❑ Cheapy Paper Towels
- ❑ Blue Paper Towels
- ❑ Lapcloth/Bibs
- ❑ Pillow Cases
- ❑ Modesty Shield

- ❑ Toilet Paper
- ❑ Toilet Tablets
- ❑ Toilet Cleaner
- ❑ Air Freshener

- ❑ Spirit Paper
- ❑ Printer Paper
- ❑ Foil
- ❑ Plastic wrap
- ❑
- ❑
- ❑
- ❑
- ❑
- ❑
- ❑

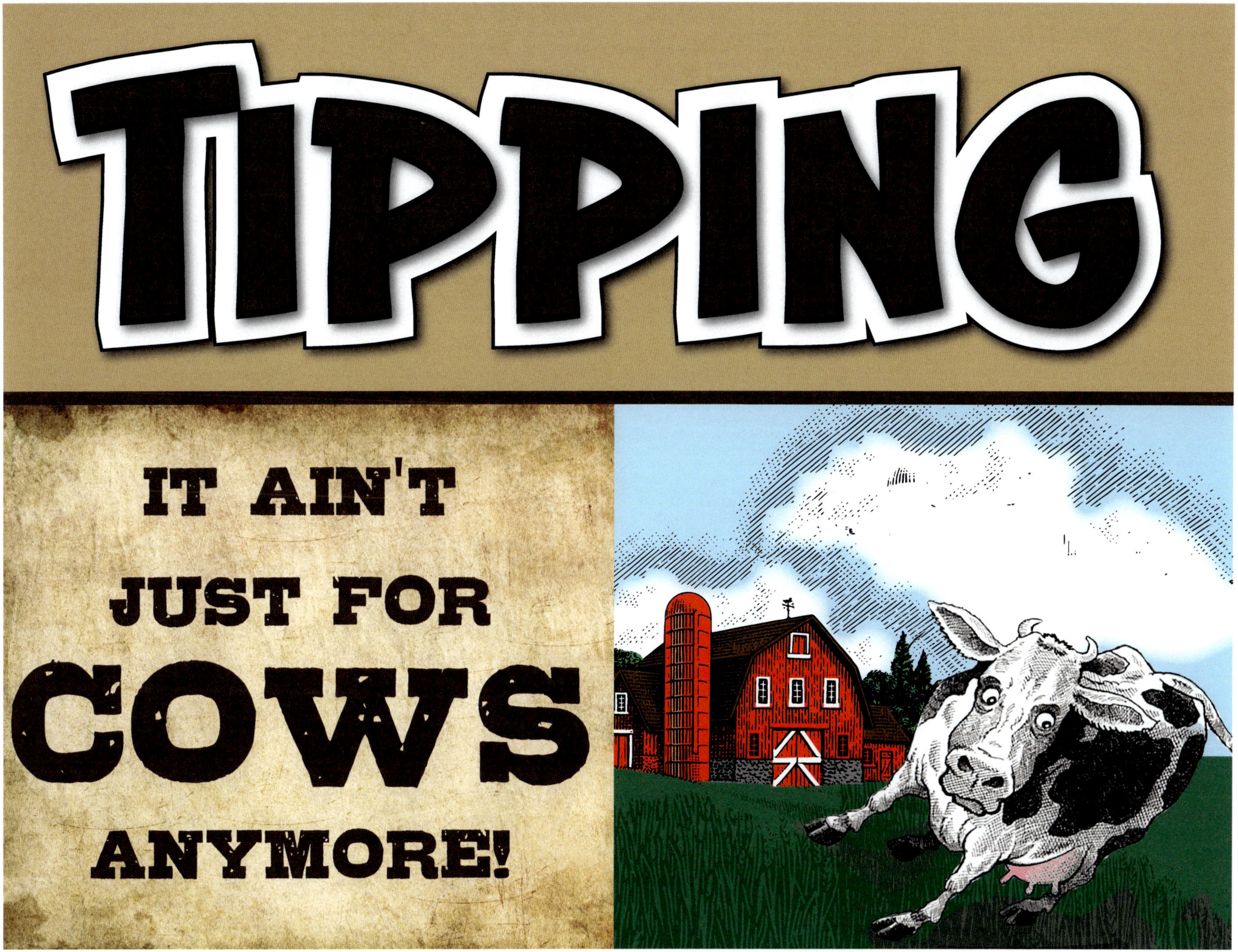
TIPPING
IT AIN'T
JUST FOR
COWS
ANYMORE!

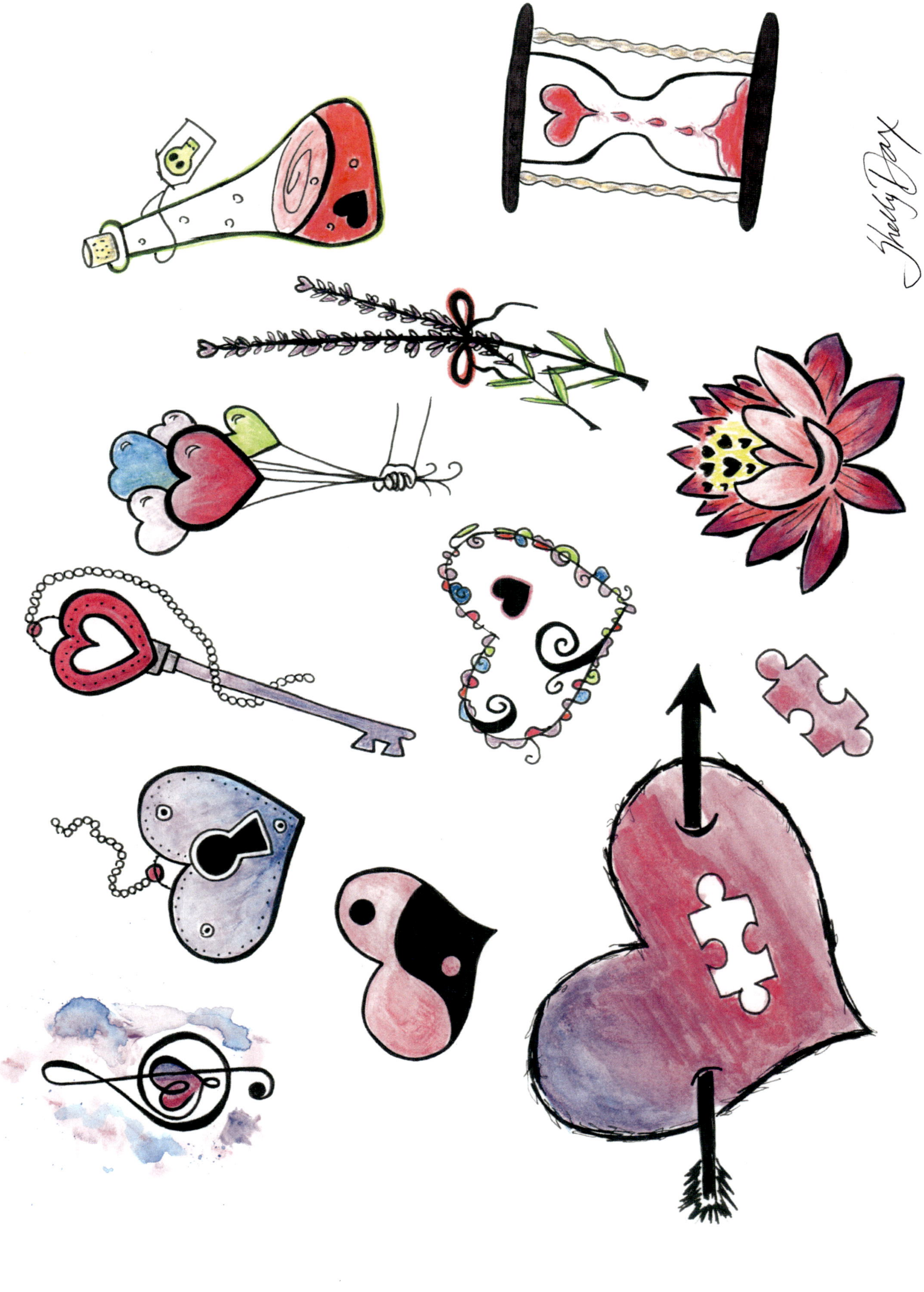

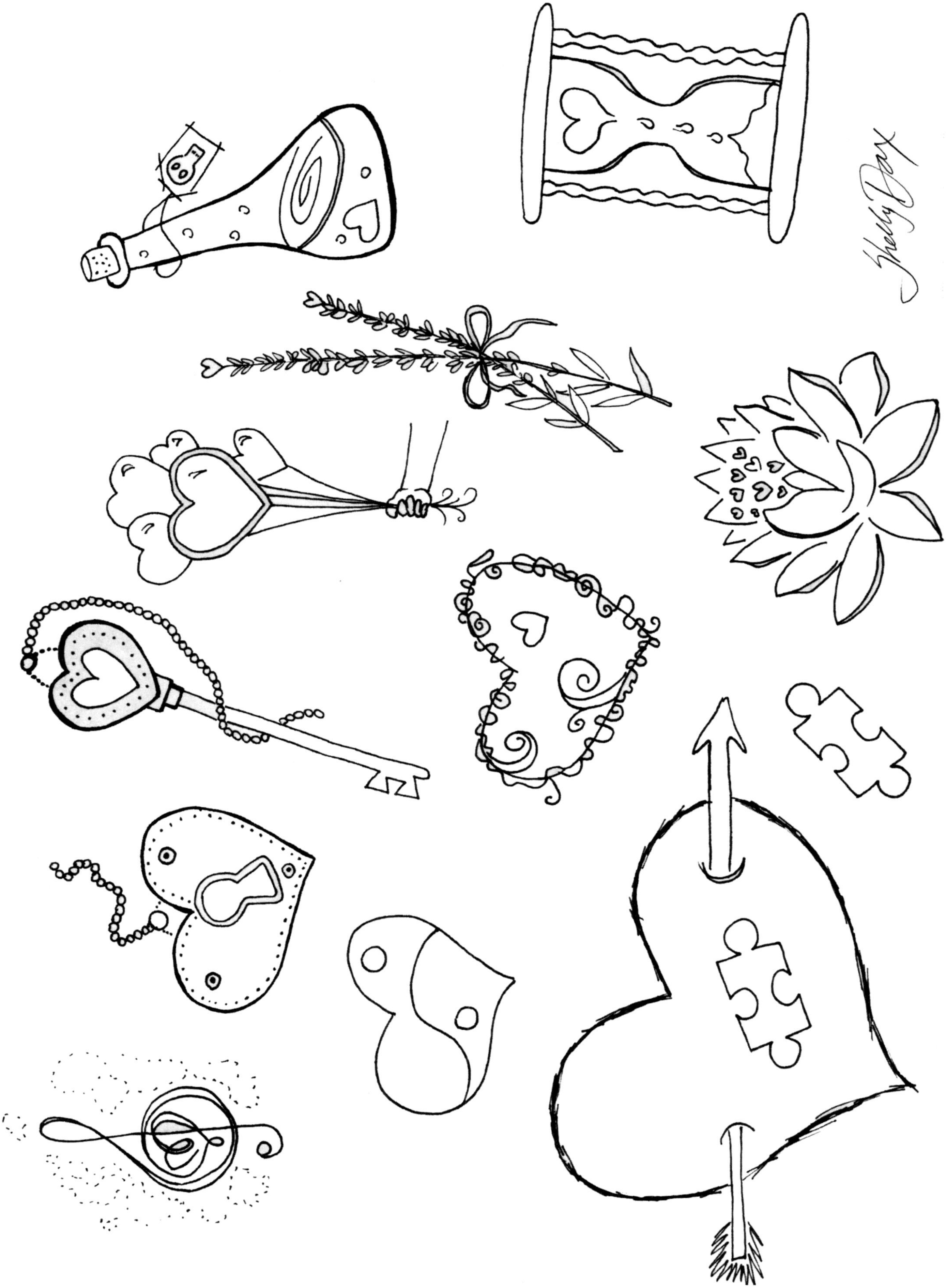
Shelly Day

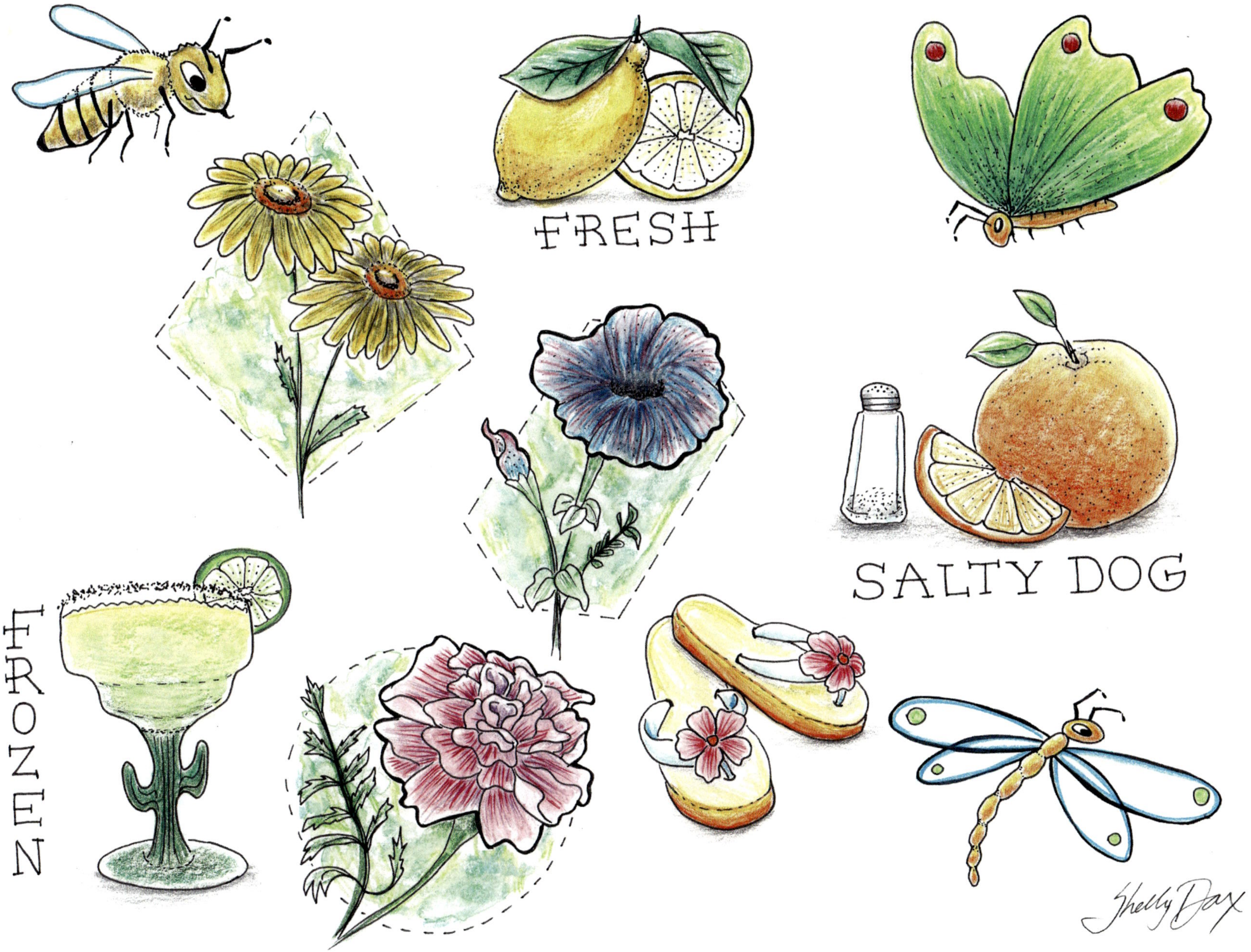
FRESH
SALTY DOG
FROZEN
Shelly Dax

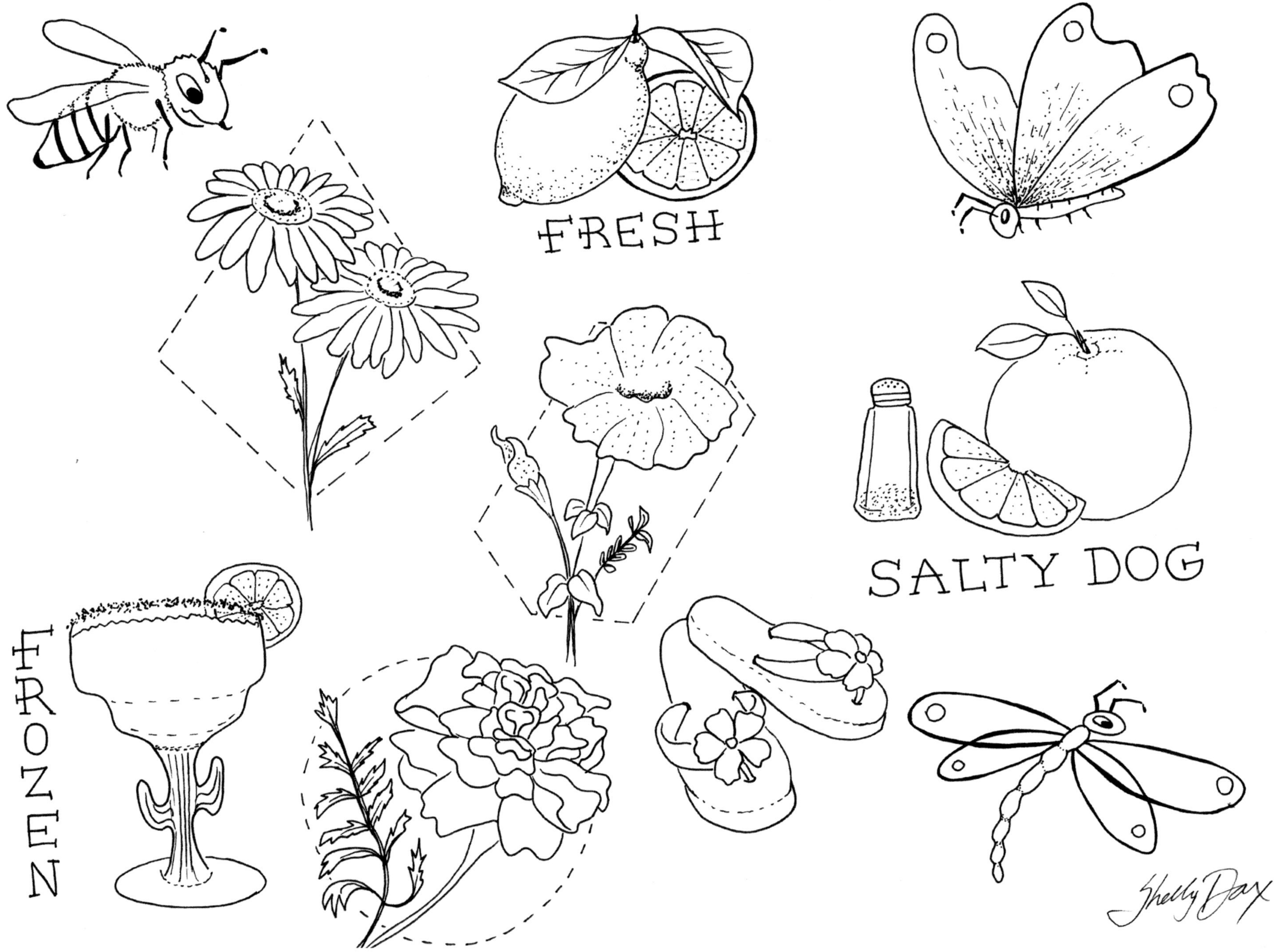
FRESH
SALTY DOG
FROZEN
Shelly Dax

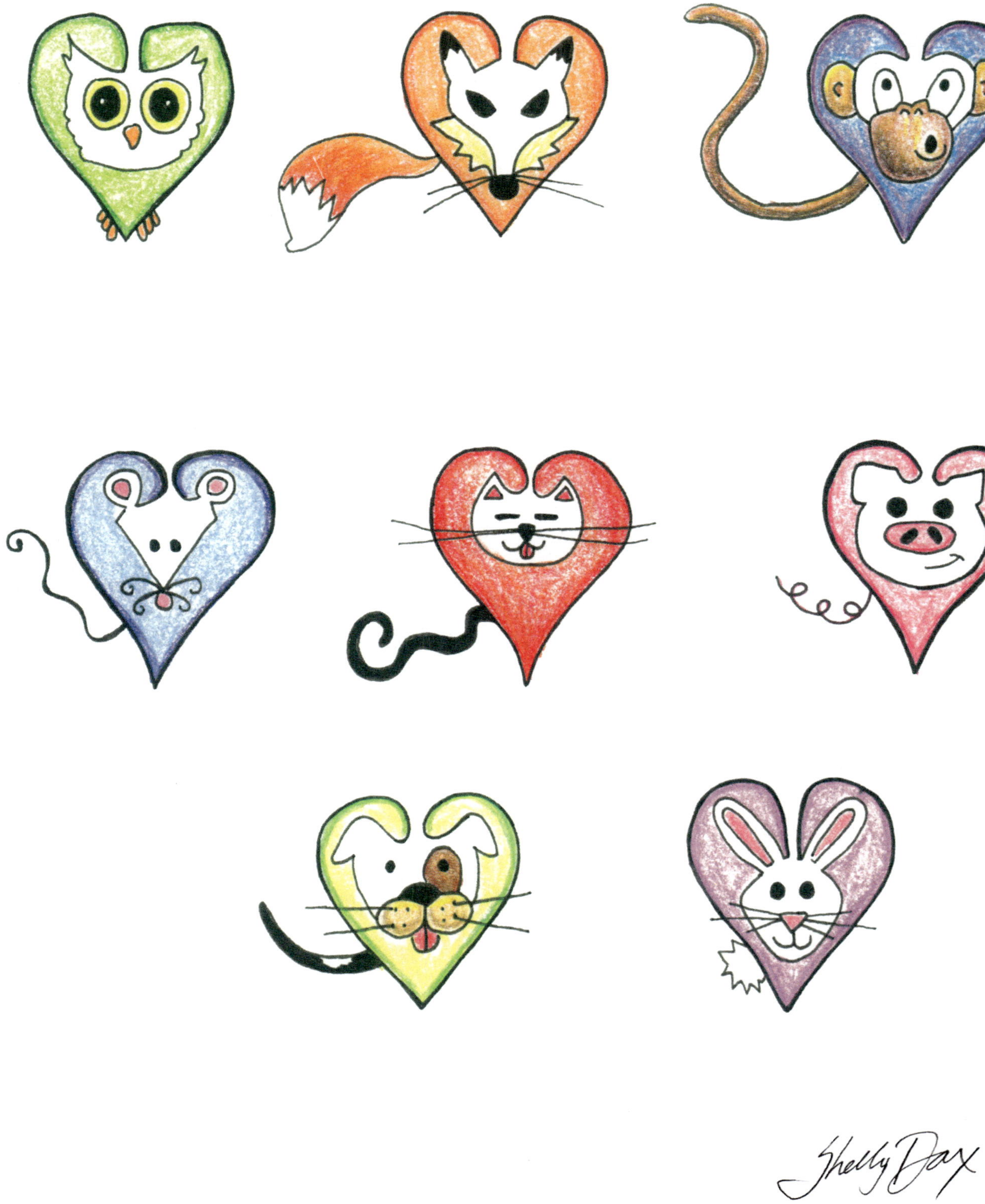
Shelly Dax

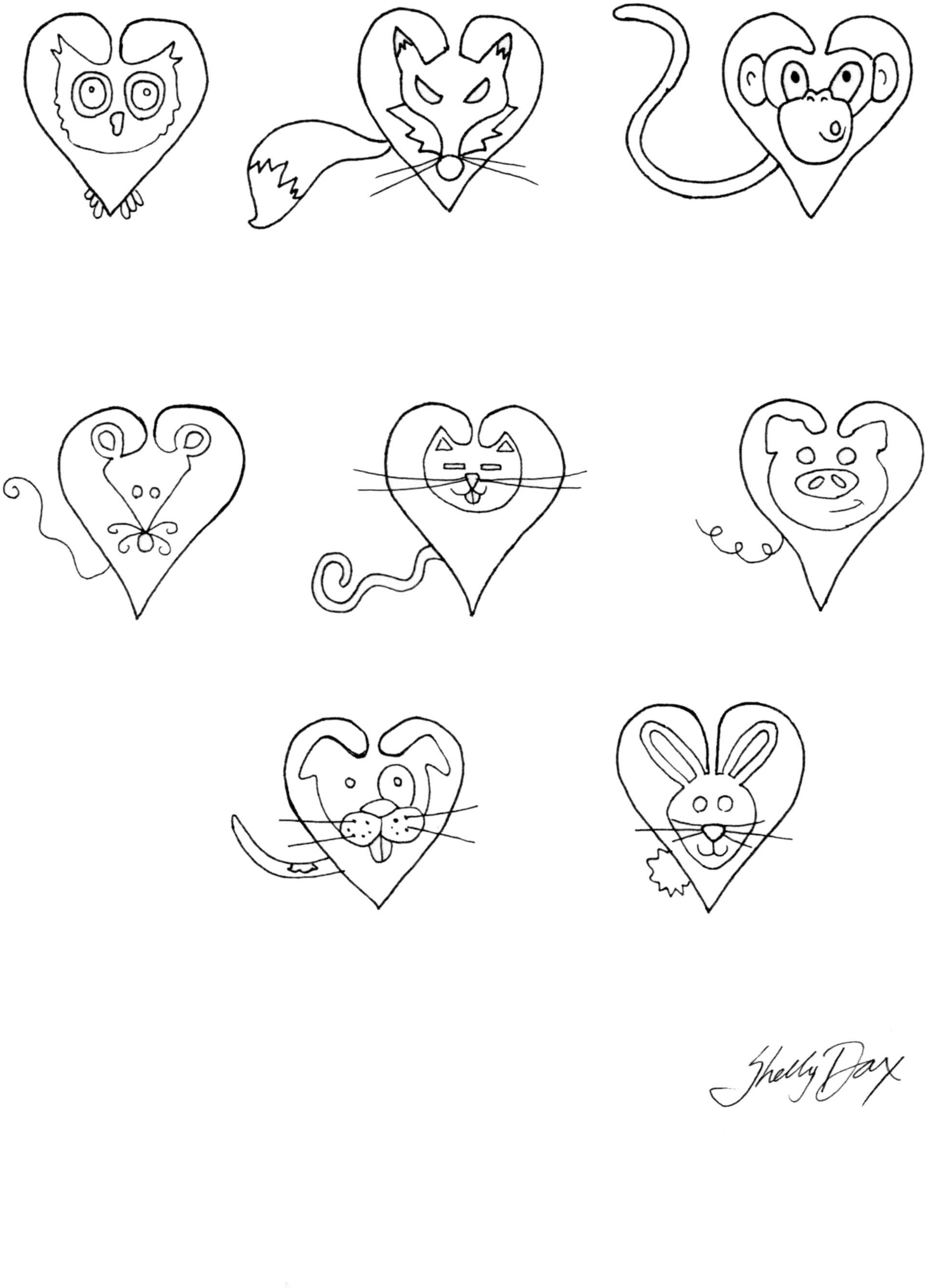
Shelly Dax

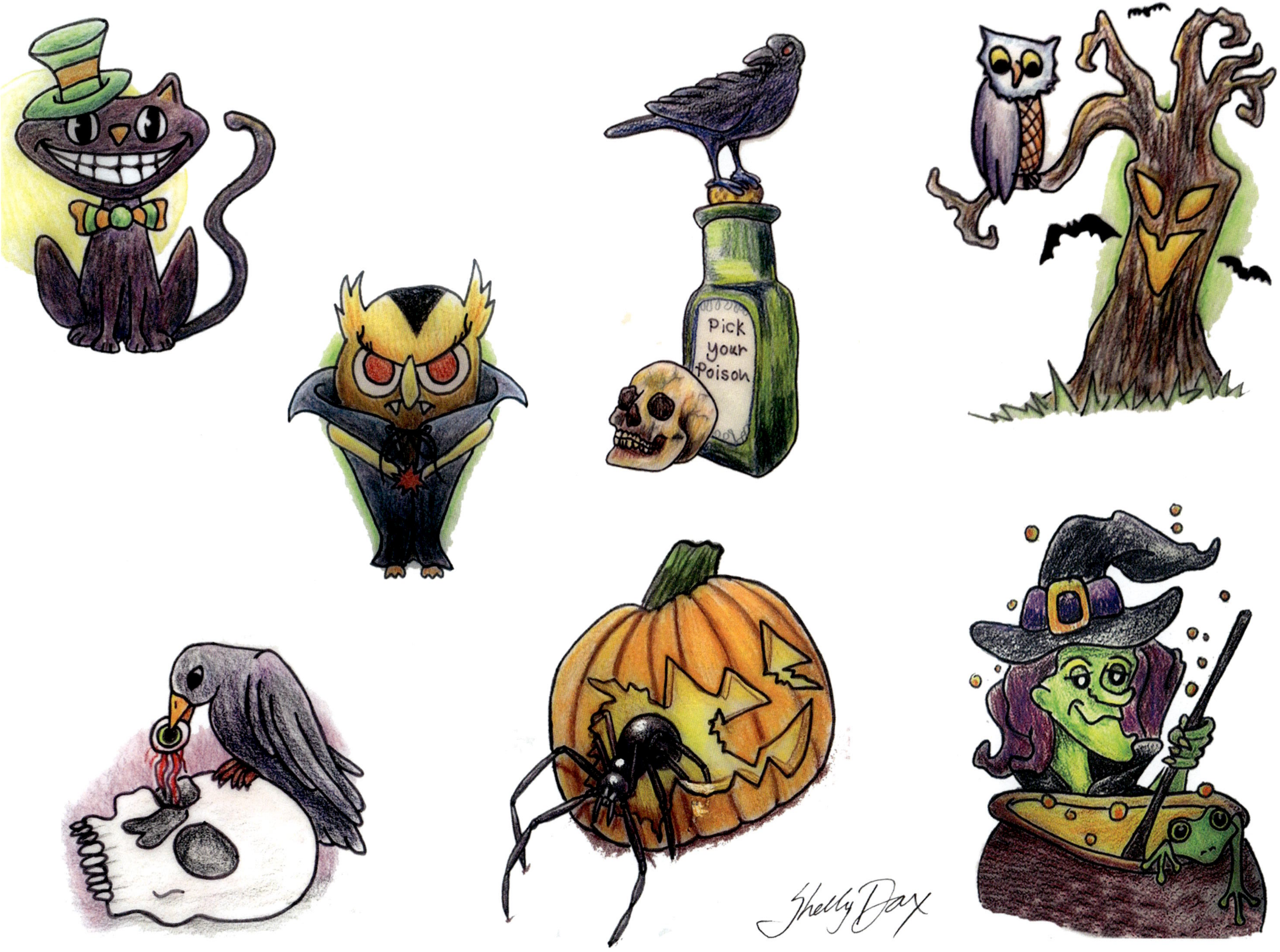
Pick
your
Poison
Shelly Dax

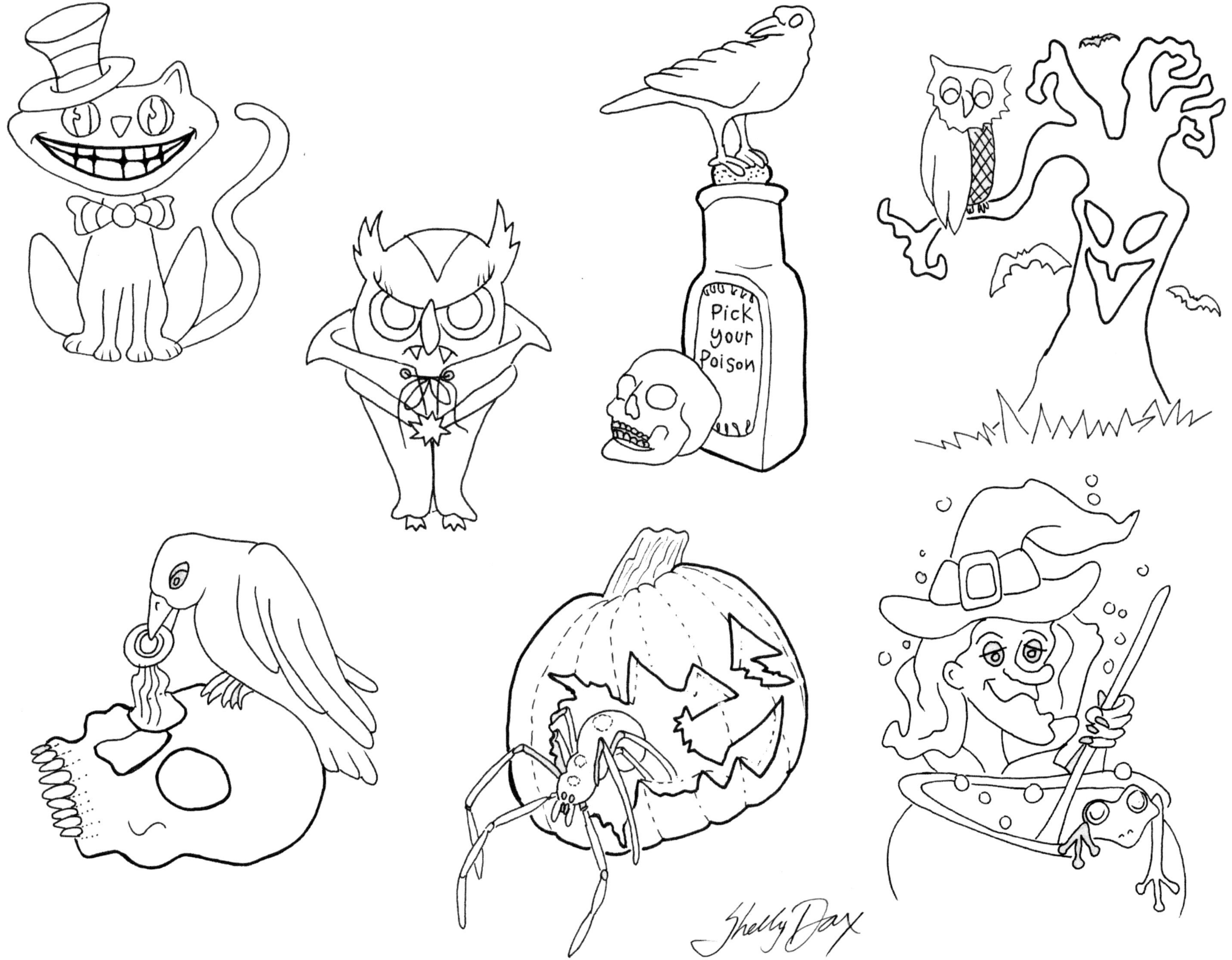
Pick your Poison
Shelly Dax

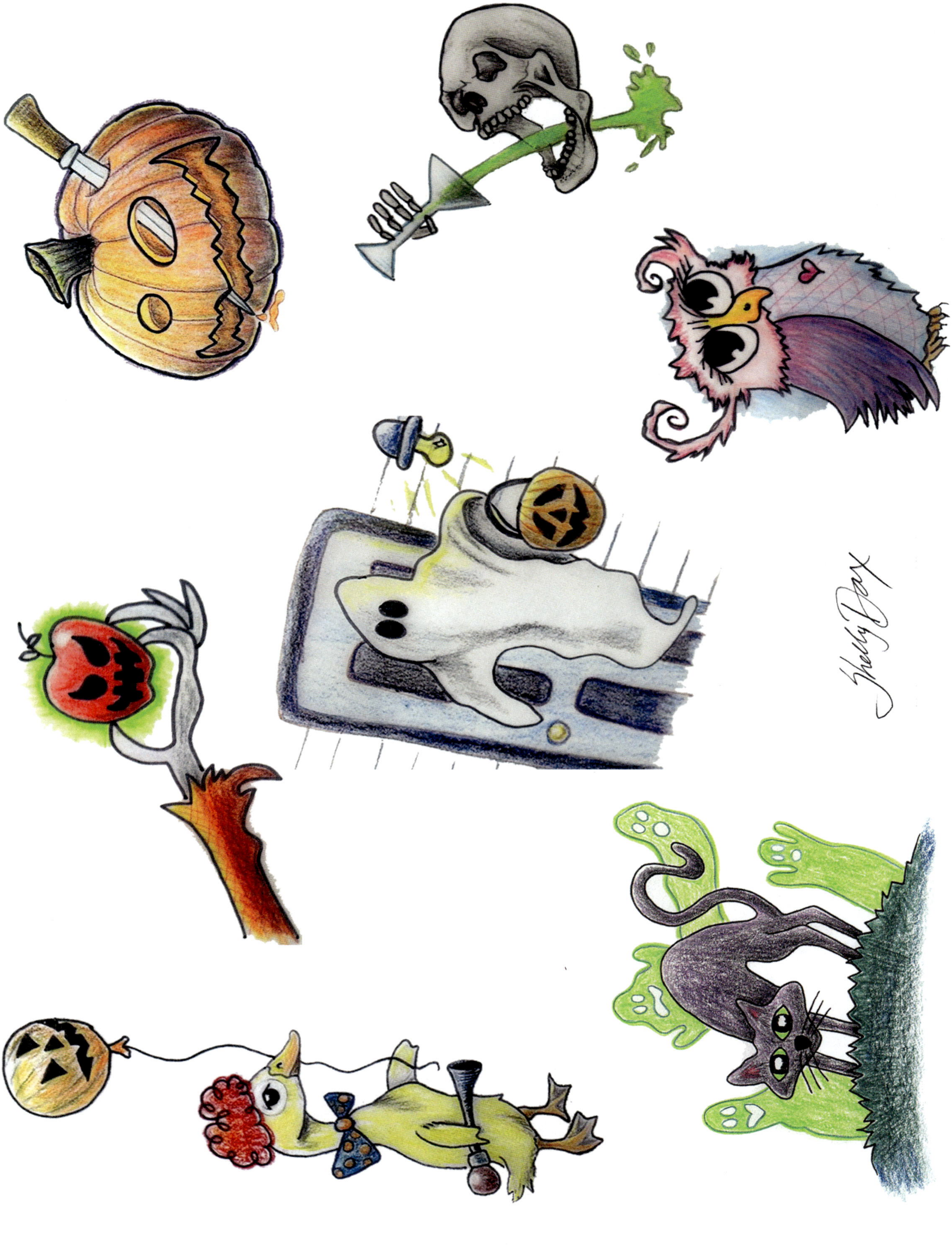

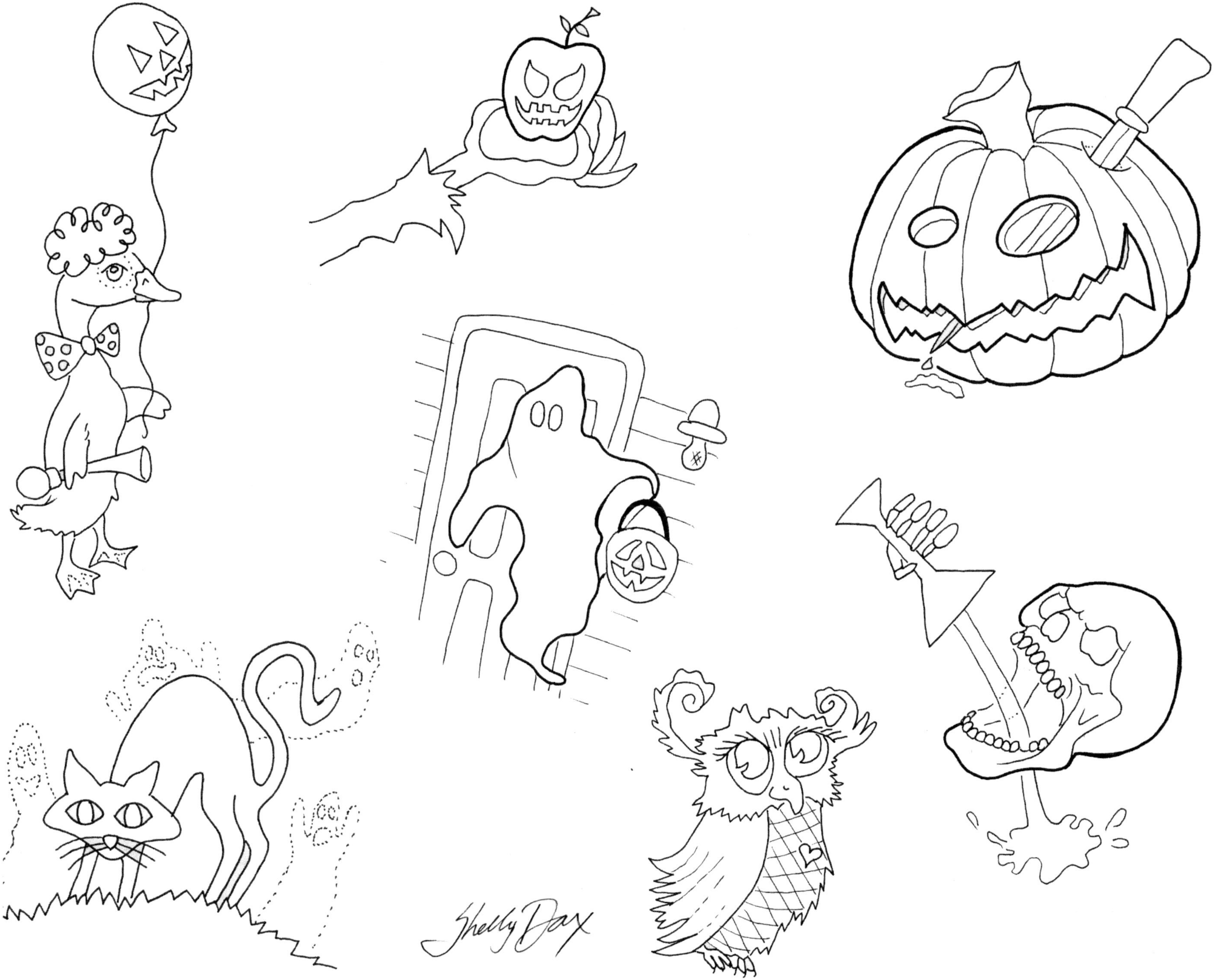
Shelly Dax

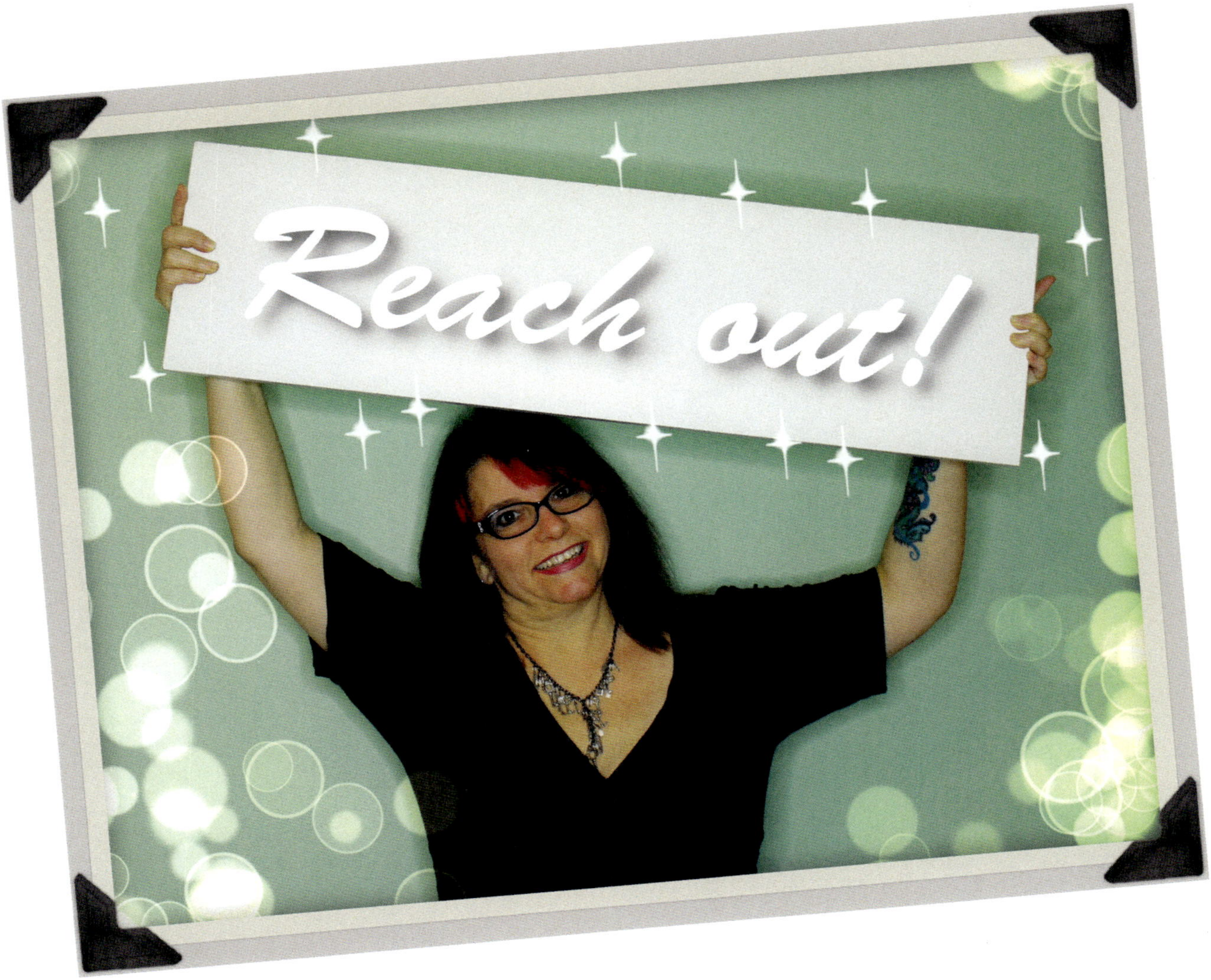

***I**f you want to be part of an inspiring and high vibe community,*
sign up for my email list at

shellydax.com

I love all things artsy, playful, uplifting and woo woo.
Join me there, if you feel the vibe!

/shellydax /shellydax /shellydax

Made in the USA
Coppell, TX
21 August 2021

60886798R00143